Encyclopedia of

AFRICAN AMERICAN HISTORY

Encyclopedia of
AFRICAN AMERICAN HISTORY

Volume 1

**Leslie M. Alexander and
Walter C. Rucker, Editors**

 ABC-CLIO

Santa Barbara, California • Denver, Colorado • Oxford, England

Copyright 2010 by ABC-CLIO, LLC

Library of Congress Cataloging-in-Publication Data

Encyclopedia of African American history / Leslie M. Alexander and Walter C. Rucker, editors.
    p. cm.
    Includes bibliographical references and index.
    ISBN 978-1-85109-769-2 (alk. paper) — ISBN 978-1-85109-774-6 (ebook)
  1. African Americans—History—Encyclopedias. 2. African Americans—Biography—Encyclopedias.
I. Alexander, Leslie M.   II. Rucker, Walter C., 1970–
    E185.E544   2010
    973'.0496073—dc22   2009051262

14 13 12 11 10   1 2 3 4 5

This book is also available on the World Wide Web as an eBook.
Visit www.abc-clio.com for details.

ABC-CLIO, LLC
130 Cremona Drive, P.O. Box 1911
Santa Barbara, California 93116–1911

This book is printed on acid-free paper ∞

Printed in the United States of America

Contents

About the Editors

Leslie M. Alexander, Ph.D., is associate professor of history at The Ohio State University, Columbus, Ohio. Her published works include *African or American?: Black Identity and Political Activism in New York City, 1784–1861.*

Walter C. Rucker, Ph.D., is associate professor of African American and African studies at The Ohio State University, Columbus, Ohio. His published works include *The River Flows On: Black Resistance, Culture, and Identity Formation in Early America.*

Contributor List

Jeffrey S. Ahlman
PhD Candidate, University of Illinois
Urbana-Champaign, Illinois

Thomas Aiello
University of Louisiana at Lafayette
Lafayette, Louisiana

Efua S. Akoma
PhD Candidate, Virginia Tech University
Blacksburg, Virginia

Jane M. Aldrich
South Carolina Historical Society
Charleston, South Carolina

Leslie M. Alexander
The Ohio State University
Columbus, Ohio

Lisa Doris Alexander
Wayne State University
Detroit, Michigan

Jeffrey Elton Anderson
University of Louisiana, Monroe
Monroe, Louisiana

Michelle E. Anderson
Loyola Marymount University
Los Angeles, California

Jessica Noelle Apuzzo
MA Candidate, Sarah Lawrence College
Bronxville, New York

Thabiti A. Asukile
University of Cincinnati
Cincinnati, Ohio

James L. Baggett
Birmingham Public Library
Birmingham, Alabama

Julius H. Bailey
University of Redlands
Redlands, California

Lori Baptista
PhD Candidate, Northwestern University
Evanston, Illinois

Renée M. Baron
The Juilliard School
New York, New York

Zawadi I. Barskile
PhD Candidate, New York University
New York, New York

Pearl Bates
Drew Theological School
Madison, New Jersey

Robert A. Bennett III
PhD Candidate, The Ohio State University
Columbus, Ohio

Ira Lee Berlet
PhD Candidate, University of Houston
Houston, Texas

Lemuel Berry Jr.
University of New England
Portland, Maine

Kenneth J. Blume
Albany College of Pharmacy
Albany, New York

Erin Boade
University of Texas
Austin, Texas

Jen Westmoreland Bouchard
Independent Scholar
Minneapolis, Minnesota

Ashley C. Bowden
MA Candidate, The Ohio State University
Columbus, Ohio

Esperanza Brizuela-Garcia
Montclair State University
Montclair, New Jersey

Alfred L. Brophy
University of North Carolina
Chapel Hill, North Carolina

William Harris Brown
North Carolina Department of Cultural Resources
Raleigh, North Carolina

Erica Ann Bruchko
PhD Candidate, Emory University
Atlanta, Georgia

David L. Brunsma
University of Missouri
Columbia, Missouri

Christopher George Buck
Independent Scholar
White Oak, Pennsylvania

Beverly A. Bunch-Lyons
Virginia Tech-National Capital Region
Falls Church, Virginia

Christina Bush
MA Candidate, The Ohio State University
Columbus, Ohio

Tamara T. Butler
MA Candidate, The Ohio State University
Columbus, Ohio

David M. Carletta
PhD Candidate, Michigan State University
East Lansing, Michigan

Valerie Caruana-Loisel
Independent Scholar
Paris, France

John A. Casey
PhD Candidate, University of Illinois at Chicago
Chicago, Illinois

JoAnn E. Castagna
University of Iowa
Iowa City, Iowa

John W. Clarke, Jr.
University of Toronto
Toronto, Ontario, Canada

Jasmine Nichole Cobb
PhD Candidate, University of Pennsylvania
Philadelphia, Pennsylvania

Rebecca L. K. Cobby
PhD Candidate, University of Nottingham
Nottingham, United Kingdom

Michael Coker
South Carolina Historical Society
Charleston, South Carolina

Ann V. Collins
McKendree University
Lebanon, Illinois

Michael A. Cooke
University of West Alabama
Livingston, Alabama

Christopher Martin Cumo
Independent Scholar
Canton, Ohio

Dawne Y. Curry
University of Nebraska
Lincoln, Nebraska

Kimberly M. Curtis
PhD Candidate, St. Louis University
St. Louis, Missouri

Jane E. Dabel
California State University, Long Beach
Long Beach, California

Rita Bernice Dandridge
Virginia State University
Petersburg, Virginia

Amanda J. Davis
University of Florida
Gainesville, Florida

Nancy J. Dawson
Historic Russellville, Inc.
Russellville, Kentucky

Nicole Joy DeCarlo
Quinnipiac University
Hamden, Connecticut

Jean-Philippe Dedieu
Institute for Research on Social Issues
Paris, France

Gregory J. Dehler
Front Range Community College
Westminster, Colorado

Lane Demas
University of California, Irvine
Irvine, California

Gerald Wayne Dowdy
Memphis Public Library
Memphis, Tennessee

John Drabble
University of Kansas
Lawrence, Kansas

Noah D. Drezner
University of Pennsylvania
Philadelphia, Pennsylvania

Stephanie Dunson
University of Rhode Island
Kingston, Rhode Island

Aghigh Ebrahimi
PhD Candidate, University of Georgia
Athens, Georgia

Jennifer Eckel
PhD Candidate, University of Texas
Austin, Texas

Gary T. Edwards
Arkansas State University
Jonesboro, Arkansas

Sean Elias
Texas A&M University
College Station, Texas

Blake A. Ellis
Baylor University
Waco, Texas

Shawntel Lyn Ensminger
PhD Candidate, Florida State University
Tallahassee, Florida

Kristen K. Epps
University of Kansas
Lawrence, Kansas

Sara K. Eskridge
PhD Candidate, Louisiana State University
Baton Rouge, Louisiana

Demetrius Eudell
Wesleyan University
Middletown, Connecticut

Theodore W. Eversole
Independent Scholar
Cincinnati, Ohio

Michael Ezra
Sonoma State University
Rohnert Park, California

David M. Fahey
Miami University
Oxford, Ohio

Mary Jo Fairchild
South Carolina Historical Society
Charleston, South Carolina

Sara Fanning
PhD Candidate, University of Texas at Austin
Austin, Texas

Jonathan Bryan Fenderson
University of Massachusetts
Amherst, Massachusetts

Jarett M. Fields
University of Wisconsin
Madison, Wisconsin

Russell Fowler
Independent Scholar
Knoxville, Tennessee

Cheryl Fury
University of New Brunswick-Fredericton
New Brunswick, Canada

Francesca Gamber
Southern Illinois University
Edwardsville, Illinois

Eric Scott Gardner
Saginaw Valley State University
University Center, Michigan

Marybeth Gasman
University of Pennsylvania
Philadelphia, Pennsylvania

Tony Gass
PhD Candidate, The Ohio State University
Columbus, Ohio

Michael Thomas Gavin
Middle Tennessee State University
Murfreesboro, Tennessee

Gene C. Gerard
Tarrant County College
Arlington, Texas

James John Gigantino
University of Georgia
Athens, Georgia

Philippe R. Girard
McNeese State University
Lake Charles, Louisiana

Amoaba Gooden
Kent State University
Kent, Ohio

Aram Goudsouzian
University of Memphis
Memphis, Tennessee

Bruce Ormond Grant
Howard University
Washington, D.C.

David M. Greenspoon
PhD Candidate, Pennsylvania State University
University Park, Pennsylvania

Robert Gudmestad
University of Memphis
Memphis, Tennessee

Denise S. Guidry
University of Florida
Gainesville, Florida

Maryalice Guilford
Fisher College
Boston, Massachusetts

Alexis Pauline Gumbs
PhD Candidate, Duke University
Durham, North Carolina

Kevin R. C. Gutzman
Western Connecticut State University
Danbury, Connecticut

LaVerne Gyant
Northern Illinois University
DeKalb, Illinois

Rebecca Hall
University of Utah College of Law
Salt Lake City, Utah

Janice D. Hamlet
Northern Illinois University
DeKalb, Illinois

Caroline M. Harper
Howard University
Washington, D.C.

Angelique Harris
California State University-Fullerton
Fullerton, California

Anita L. Harris
University of Louisville
Louisville, Kentucky

Fred J. Hay
Appalachian State University
Boone, North Carolina

Margaret Prentice Hecker
Kansas State University Libraries
Manhattan, Kansas

Paul M. Heideman
PhD Candidate, Rutgers University-Newark
Newark, New Jersey

Veronique Helenon
Florida International University
Miami, Florida

Nathan Herrod
PhD Candidate, University of Florida
Gainesville, Florida

Kevin M. Hickey
Albany College of Pharmacy and Health Sciences
Albany, New York

Lezlee J. Hinesmon-Matthews
California State University-Fullerton
Fullerton, California

Sharon Hines-Smith
Richard Stockton College
Pomona, New Jersey

Kathleen Hladky
PhD Candidate, Florida State University
Tallahassee, Florida

Bobby R. Holt
University of Tennessee, Knoxville
Knoxville, Tennessee

Alton Hornsby Jr.
Morehouse College
Atlanta, Georgia

Marilyn K. Howard
Columbus State Community College
Columbus, Ohio

Janet G. Hudson
University of South Carolina
Columbia, South Carolina

Lacey P. Hunter
Caldwell College
Caldwell, New Jersey

Nicole Jackson
PhD Candidate, The Ohio State University
Columbus, Ohio

Raymond Janifer
Shippensburg University
Shippensburg, Pennsylvania

Judson L. Jeffries
The Ohio State University
Columbus, Ohio

Brian Lamont Johnson
Gordon College
Wenham, Massachusetts

Christopher Keith Johnson
Temple University
Philadelphia, Pennsylvania

Clay M. Johnson
MA Candidate, The Ohio State University
Columbus, Ohio

Jessica A. Johnson
Columbus State Community College
Columbus, Ohio

Joan Marie Johnson
University of Cincinnati
Cincinnati, Ohio

Justin Marcus Johnston
PhD Candidate, St. Joseph's College
Standish, Maine

Kenneth S. Jolly
Saginaw Valley State University
University Center, Michigan

James Thomas Jones III
Prairie View A&M University
Prairie View, Texas

Jeannette Eileen Jones
University of Nebraska
Lincoln, Nebraska

Peter Carr Jones
MA Candidate, College of William and Mary
Williamsburg, Virginia

T. Alys Jordan
Florida A&M University
Tallahassee, Florida

Seneca Joyner
PhD Candidate, Northeastern University
Boston, Massachusetts

Nubia Kai
Howard University
Washington, D.C.

Holly M. Kent
PhD Candidate, Lehigh University
Bethlehem, Pennsylvania

Martin Kich
Wright State University-Lake Campus
Celina, Ohio

Lionel Kimble Jr.
Chicago State University
Chicago, Illinois

Shirletta J. Kinchen
PhD Candidate, University of Memphis
Memphis, Tennessee

Cynthia King
Furman University
Greenville, South Carolina

Njoki-Wa-Kinyatti
York College-The City University of New York
Jamaica, New York

Christine Knauer
PhD Candidate, University of Tübingen
Tübingen, Germany

Daniel P. Kotzin
Medaille College
Buffalo, New York

Kara M. Kvaran
PhD Candidate, Purdue University
West Lafayette, Indiana

Laurie Lahey
George Washington University
Washington, D.C.

Anthony A. Lee
University of California, Los Angeles
Los Angeles, California

Talitha L. LeFlouria
Florida Atlantic University
Boca Raton, Florida

Angela K. Lewis
University of Alabama, Birmingham
Birmingham, Alabama

Barbara Lewis
University of Massachusetts, Boston
Boston, Massachusetts

Kay Wright Lewis
PhD Candidate, Rutgers University-New Brunswick
New Brunswick, New Jersey

Thabiti Lewis
Washington State University
Pullman, Washington

Malinda A. Lindquist
University of Minnesota
Minneapolis, Minnesota

Kathryn Emily Lofton
Reed College
Portland, Oregon

Carolyn Morrow Long
National Museum of American History
Washington, D.C.

Marilyn D. Lovett
Fayetteville State University
Fayetteville, North Carolina

Dwayne A. Mack
Berea College
Berea, Kentucky

Jeffrey Othele Mahan
Texas A&M University
College Station, Texas

Sivananda Mantri
Independent Scholar
Collierville, Tennessee

Ted Downing Maris-Wolf
College of William and Mary
Williamsburg, Virginia

Clifton Marsh
Tidewater Community College
Norfolk, Virginia

Eric Martone
PhD Candidate, State University of New York at
　　Stony Brook
Stony Brook, New York

Patrick Q. Mason
American University in Cairo
Cairo, Egypt

Babacar M'Baye
Kent State University
Kent, Ohio

Nancy A. McCaslin
Independent Scholar
Elkhart, Indiana

Ryan McIlhenny
University of California, Irvine
Irvine, California

Charles Medina
University of Toledo
Toledo, Ohio

David Michel
Independent Scholar
Chicago, Illinois

Carmen De Michele
Ludwig-Maximilians University
Munich, Germany

Dawn Miles
PhD Candidate, The Ohio State University
Columbus, Ohio

Paul T. Miller
Temple University
Philadelphia, Pennsylvania

Shamika Ann Mitchell
PhD Candidate, Temple University
Philadelphia, Pennsylvania

John Morello
DeVry University
Chicago, Illinois

Jerad Mulcare
PhD Candidate, Harvard University
Cambridge, Massachusetts

Ridgeway Boyd Murphree
State Archives of Florida
Tallahassee, Florida

Steven Napier
Independent Scholar
Cincinnati, Ohio

Darrell Newton
Salisbury University
Salisbury, Maryland

Karen W. Ngonya
PhD Candidate, The Ohio State University
Columbus, Ohio

Jonathan A. Noyalas
Lord Fairfax Community College
Fairfax, Virginia

Yusuf Nuruddin
Medgar Evers College
New York, New York

Jennifer Bridges Oast
Virginia Commonwealth University
Richmond, Virginia

Jaime Ramón Olivares
Houston Community College-Central
Houston, Texas

Ted Olson
East Tennessee State University
Johnson City, Tennessee

Ajibade George Olusola
Obafemi Awolowo University
Ile-Ife, Nigeria

Fernando A. Ortiz
Alliant International University
San Diego, California

E. Bryan Cooper Owens
MA Candidate, University of California, Los Angeles
Los Angeles, California

Deirdre Benia Cooper Owens
PhD Candidate, University of California, Los Angeles
Los Angeles, California

David B. Parker
Kennesaw State University
Kennesaw, Georgia

Michael Pasquier
Florida State University
Tallahassee, Florida

Jason M. Perkins
PhD Candidate, The Ohio State University
Columbus, Ohio

Christabelle A. Peters
PhD Candidate, University of Nottingham
Nottingham, United Kingdom

Clarissa Peterson
DePauw University
Greencastle, Indiana

Otis Westbrook Pickett
MA Candidate, College of Charleston
Charleston, South Carolina

Christian Pinnen
PhD Candidate, University of Southern Mississippi
Hattiesburg, Mississippi

Lydia Plath
PhD Candidate, University of Warwick
Warwickshire, United Kingdom

Justin D. Poché
University of Notre Dame
Notre Dame, Indiana

Tiffany Pogue
PhD Candidate, Emory University
Atlanta, Georgia

Barton Edward Price
PhD Candidate, Florida State University
Tallahassee, Florida

K. Stephen Prince Jr.
Yale University
New Haven, Connecticut

Christina Proenza-Coles
Virginia State University
Petersburg, Virginia

Elizabeth Stordeur Pryor
Smith College
Northampton, Massachusetts

Dan J. Puckett
Troy University-Montgomery
Montgomery, Alabama

David Kenneth Pye
University of California, San Diego
San Diego, California

Jamal L. Ratchford
PhD Candidate, Purdue University
West Lafayette, Indiana

Monica C. Reed
PhD Candidate, Florida State University
Tallahassee, Florida

David Alan Rego
PhD Candidate, Tufts University
Medford, Massachusetts

Patricia Reid-Merritt
Richard Stockton College
Pomona, New Jersey

Michael S. Rodriguez
Richard Stockton College
Pomona, New Jersey

Jarod H. Roll
University of Sussex
Sussex, United Kingdom

Eric Rose
University of South Carolina
Columbia, South Carolina

Jill E. Rowe-Adjibogoun
Virginia Commonwealth University
Richmond, Virginia

Chishamiso Rowley
Independent Scholar
Washington, D.C.

Walter C. Rucker
The Ohio State University
Columbus, Ohio

Herbert G. Ruffin II
Syracuse University
Syracuse, New York

Ralph A. Russell
College of New Jersey
Ewing, New Jersey

Aaron D. Sachs
PhD Candidate, University of Iowa
Iowa City, Iowa

Kelly Boyer Sagert
Independent Scholar
Lorain, Ohio

Dorothy Salem
Cuyahoga Community College
Cleveland, Ohio

Rickie Sanders
Temple University
Philadelphia, Pennsylvania

Joseph C. Santora
Thomas Edison State College
Trenton, New Jersey

Anthony Santoro
PhD Candidate, University of Heidelberg
Heidelberg, Germany

Frank N. Schubert
Independent Scholar
Alexandria, Virginia

Derek Wolf Seidman
PhD Candidate, Brown University
Providence, Rhode Island

Brooke Sherrard
PhD Candidate, Florida State University
Tallahassee, Florida

Brent D. Singleton
California State University, San Bernardino
San Bernardino, California

Rose Pelone Sisson
Independent Scholar
Columbus, Indiana

Julie M. Skogsbergh
PhD Candidate, University of Massachusetts-Amherst
Amherst, Massachusetts

Jayetta Slawson
Southeastern Louisiana University
Hammond, Louisiana

Donna Smith
Northern Kentucky University
Highland Heights, Kentucky

Dorsia Smith Silva
University of Puerto Rico
Rio Piedras, Puerto Rico

Eric Ledell Smith
State Museum of Pennsylvania
Harrisburg, Pennsylvania

John Matthew Smith
Western Michigan University
Kalamazoo, Michigan

Yushau Sodiq
Texas Christian University
Fort Worth, Texas

Gary S. Sprayberry
University of Alabama
Tuscaloosa, Alabama

Kaila A. Story
University of Louisville
Louisville, Kentucky

Marva Strickland-Hill
Kentucky State University
Frankfort, Kentucky

William Mychael Sturkey
PhD Candidate, The Ohio State University
Columbus, Ohio

Lindsay Sumner
MA Candidate, The Ohio State University
Columbus, Ohio

Karen E. Sutton
Touro College
New York, New York

Moshe Terdiman
Postdoctoral Fellow, Tel-Aviv University
Tel-Aviv, Israel

David Taft Terry
Reginald F. Lewis Museum
Baltimore, Maryland

Matthew Evans Teti
Library of African Studies
Northwestern University
Evanston, Illinois

Shurita Thomas-Tate
Florida State University
Tallahassee, Florida

Michael D. Thompson
PhD Candidate, Emory University
Atlanta, Georgia

Claudette L. Tolson (Ayodele Shaihi)
Loyola University
Chicago, Illinois

Cristy Casado Tondeur
Smith College
Northampton, Massachusetts

William P. Toth
Seton Hall University
South Orange, New Jersey

Zoe Trodd
Harvard University
Cambridge, Massachusetts

David Turpie
PhD Candidate, University of Maine
Orono, Maine

Constance Porter Uzelac
Dorothy Porter Wesley Research Center
Fort Lauderdale, Florida

Sathyaraj Venkatesan
National Institute of Technology
Tiruchirappalli, India

Kirt von Daacke
Lynchburg College
Lynchburg, Virginia

Rob Walsh
Three Rivers Community College
Norwich, Connecticut

Rebecca Wanzo
The Ohio State University
Columbus, Ohio

Mindy R. Weidman
University of Connecticut
Storrs, Connecticut

Rosanne M. Welch
PhD Candidate, Claremont Graduate University
Claremont, California

Donna M. Wells
PhD Candidate, Howard University
Washington, D.C.

Simon Wendt
University of Heidelberg
Heidelberg, Germany

Samuel Paul Wheeler
Southern Illinois University
Edwardsville, Illinois

Elisa Joy White
University of Hawaii
Honolulu, Hawaii

Karsonya Wise Whitehead
Loyola College in Maryland
Baltimore, Maryland

Robert Warner Widell Jr.
PhD Candidate, Emory University
Atlanta, Georgia

Hettie V. Williams
Monmouth University
West Long Branch, New Jersey

Jamie J. Wilson
Salem State College
Salem, Massachusetts

Darius Young
PhD Candidate, University of Memphis
Memphis, Tennessee

Jason Young
State University of New York
Buffalo, New York

List of Entries

Culture, Identity, and Community: From Slavery to the Present

Gumbo
Herskovits, Melville
High John the Conqueror Root
Hoodoo
Hurston, Zora Neale
Hush Harbors
Infanticide
Jambalaya
Jas
Jazz
John the Slave Tales
Joplin, Scott
Juba Dance
Kongo Cosmogram
Kwanzaa
Laveau, Marie
Locke, Alain
Mardi Gras
Miscegenation
Mulatto
Names Debate
Negritude
Obeah
Octoroon
Parker, Charlie
Pinkster Festival
Poisonings
Prince Hall Masonry
Pryor, Richard
Quadroon
Ragtime
Ring Shout
Rogers, Joel Augustus
Root Doctors
Salt-Water Negroes
Sambo
Sanchez, Sonia
Shakur, Tupac
Shrine of the Black Madonna
Signifying
Slave Culture
Slave Religion
Soul Food
Sweetgrass Baskets
Syncretism
Tituba

Transmigration
Turner, Lorenzo Dow
Walker, Margaret
Wonder, Stevie
Work Songs
Wright, Richard

Political Activity and Resistance to Oppression: From the American Revolution to the Civil War

Abelman v. Booth
Abolition, Slave Trade
Abolition, Slavery
Adams, John Quincy
African Civilization Society
African Dorcas Association
African Free Schools
African Grove Theater
African Methodist Episcopal Church
Allen, Richard
American and Foreign Anti-Slavery Society
American Anti-Slavery Society (AASS)
American Colonization Society
American Moral Reform Society
American Revolution
Amistad
Anglo-African Magazine
Antislavery Societies
Attucks, Crispus
August First Celebrations
Ball, Charles
Banneker, Benjamin
Bell, Philip A.
Benevolent Societies
Birney, James
Boston Massacre
Boyer, Jean Pierre
Brown, John
Brown, William Wells
Brown Fellowship Society
Carpetbaggers
Cary, Mary Ann Shadd
Cinque, Joseph
Clarkson, Thomas

Political Activity, Migration, and Urbanization: Reconstruction, Civil Rights, and Modern African America

Preface

The *Encyclopedia of African American History* seeks to introduce readers to the totality of the African American experience, from beginnings in precolonial Atlantic Africa through the dawn of the 21st century. Framed by four interpretive, historical, and historiographic essays, the entire project can be summed up as an introduction to a multitude of themes, across both space and time, that allows readers to connect with the many continuities and discontinuities, tensions and agreements, tragedies and triumphs, and advances and nadirs punctuating African American history. This particular goal is best captured in the symbolism behind the visit by U.S. President Barack Hussein Obama to Ghana's Cape Coast Slave Castle in July 2009. That very moment, at which he passed through the so-called Door of No Return, represented an important point of historical convergence of themes and trends coursing through the African American experience over the past 500 years—from the commodification of black bodies in coastal factories in 15th-century Atlantic Africa to the ultimate expression of black empowerment in the form of Obama's historic election in 2008.

The four 5,000-word section essays written by project editors and members of the editorial board represent fresh interpretive and historiographic segues to the thematic and chronological areas that the editors determined were the major watersheds or pivotal moments and movements in African American history. These themes include (1) Atlantic African, American, and European Backgrounds to Contact, Commerce, and Enslavement; (2) Culture, Identity, and Community: From Slavery to the Present; (3) Political Activity and Resistance to Oppression: From the American Revolution to the Civil War; and (4) Political Activity, Migration, and Urbanization: Reconstruction, Civil Rights, and Modern African America.

Those contributing the more than 650 smaller essays, ranging in length from 300 to 4,000 words, include archivists, librarians, graduate students, and professional historians and other scholars. Each essay was closely vetted by the editors and selected for inclusion based on a handful of criteria. Above all else, the editors ensured that each entry was clear, uncomplicated, and decisive; factual, descriptive, and explanatory (while avoiding editorializing); and written for intelligent and interested nonspecialists. Given the principal audience for the *Encyclopedia of African American History*—high school students and college undergraduates—the editors solicited and selected jargon-free essays, mostly devoid of specialized and technical language, for inclusion. However, even graduate students and advanced scholars in the fields of American History, African American History, Ethnic Studies, and Black Studies will find this encyclopedia a resource for accessible and useful information. In addition, each entry includes a list of "See also" references to other essays in the encyclopedia that allows readers to easily connect together related topics and to gain more expansive understandings of particular themes.

Each entry includes a bibliography that can serve as the starting point for more advanced research. All bibliographic entries represent readily available books or articles written by professional historians and other scholars. Students, at various levels, can use the bibliographies to generate more advanced research inquiries and understandings into a vast array of topics related to African American history. In addition, more than 200 illustrations, photographs, and maps are included to further augment the essays. A keenly written introduction, along with the four lengthy section essays, provide the structural framework for the encyclopedia while a detailed subject index allows readers greater understanding of historical connections that exist across chronological and thematic divides in African American history.

A number of editorial decisions helped provide additional shape for this undertaking. Given the various controversies surrounding naming and the proper labels for African Americans, the editors decided to use three main identifiers in the encyclopedia—African American, black, and black American. Whenever possible, the editors tried to avoid using *black* as a noun as opposed to an adjective (as in, "*the black* sought to vote without intimidation"). The usage of the term—as a singular noun—is jarring and grating (and it objectifies human subjects). In the case of

groups residing in Atlantic Africa, the editors try to specify language cohorts (e.g., Akan-speakers, Ga-speakers, Igbo-speakers, etc.) and they actively resist the urge to conflate precolonial African languages with ethnic identities. Likewise, the word "tribe"—a highly problematic, loaded, and empirically unsound concept—is avoided at all costs in the encyclopedia.

Another, more difficult, editorial decision pertained to establishing chronological bookends for the encyclopedia. Though the editors did not face the same momentous task as W. E. B. Du Bois when he began writing the *Encyclopedia Africana*, the scope and scale of the current project—from precolonial Atlantic Africa to the first decade of the 21st century—meant that a few very recent events were left out of the encyclopedia. While the reader will note the entry on Barack Obama, no essays were dedicated in this project to Hurricane Katrina, the Jena 6, the deaths of John Hope Franklin and Michael Jackson, and other noteworthy events directly related to African American history. At some point, the project simply had to end. In addition, as a work of history, it is difficult to gauge the true historical relevance of certain events until several decades have passed. It may well be that some of these recent occurrences will be regarded, by future observers, as mere blips on the historical radar and that they will be greatly eclipsed by events over the next few years. The editors leave that particular assessment and judgment for future scholars to make.

Acknowledgments

It has very literally taken a community to create this project. As you might imagine, the process of identifying and compiling the information in this volume has been an overwhelming, daunting, and ultimately thrilling experience. As a result, there are many people who deserve our thanks and gratitude.

First, I would like to thank my family and loved ones who have supported me personally and professionally. I owe everything I am to their love and support: Curtis J. Austin, Sandy Alexander, Michelle Alexander, Nicole Marie Stewart, Jonathan Carter Stewart, Corinne Alexander Stewart, and Carter Stewart.

My deepest intellectual, political, and spiritual inspiration comes from the people I encountered at the Africana Studies and Research Center at Cornell University. Although many years have passed since my time as a graduate student at Cornell, I still consider the Africana Studies and Research Center my political and intellectual home. In the nurturing environment of the Africana Center, Ujamaa Residential College, and the Southside Community Center, I learned to love and appreciate the history and culture of African peoples. I have dedicated my life and career to the founding mission of Africana Studies, particularly its commitment to the rigorous study of the history, culture, intellectual development, and social organization of black people and cultures in the Americas, Africa, and the Caribbean; the need to remain grounded in the black community; and the vital importance of articulating a political agenda for black empowerment. In that spirit, I would like to thank the scholars who have personally touched my life and provided an intellectual and political model for the study of the African Diaspora: Margaret Washington, James Turner, and Sterling Stuckey.

I am also deeply grateful for the intellectual community I have developed at The Ohio State University, especially Lilia Fernandez, Stephanie Smith, Hasan Jeffries, Debra Moddelmog, Ousman Kobo, Kevin Boyle, Carol Anderson, Mytheli Sreenivas, Koritha Mitchell, Maurice Stevens, Wendy Smooth, Demetrius Eudell, Cheria Dial, Judy Wu, and John Roberts. In addition, I would like to honor the graduate student assistants who have provided invaluable service over the years, Di Luo, Dawn Miles, and Ernest Perry, along with the larger community of graduate students who have encouraged this project (some of whom have already gone on to greatness): Zawadi Barskile, Robert A. Bennett III, Ashley Bowden, Christina Bush, Tamara Butler, Jelani Favors, Tony Gass, Nicole Jackson, Gisel Jeter, Karen Ngonya, Jason Perkins, William Sturkey, Christianna Thomas, Derrick White, and Noel Voltz.

Last, but certainly not least, I would like to thank my co-editor, Walter Rucker, for sharing the trials and tribulations of this important endeavor.

—*Leslie M. Alexander*

This project would have been impossible without a long list of mentors, peers, friends, and students. As someone who benefited directly from the legacy of Carter G. Woodson—the undisputed father of African American history—I would be remiss if I did not directly thank him for first opening scholarly spaces and venues for advances in the field to be published and heard. As a student intern working for *The Journal of Negro History* during my undergraduate years at Morehouse College, I learned to appreciate all that Woodson contributed in establishing the field by initiating the Association for the Study of Negro Life and History, Negro History Week, and the *Journal*. In addition, the late John Hope Franklin carried the proverbial torch from Woodson to the newest generation of African Americanists, setting a stellar scholarly example in doing so.

More immediately, I wish to thank Alton Hornsby Jr., Marcellus Barksdale, and Barbara Tagger who first encouraged me to embrace African American history through their outstanding examples as professional historians; Jeffrey O. G. Ogbar—a fellow student at Morehouse and coworker at T. J. Maxx—who compelled me to declare a history major; and Sterling Stuckey and Ray Kea who profoundly shaped my scholarly aptitude in graduate school and beyond. I thank also a long list of colleagues and friends who provided support and encouragement along the way. Ken Goings generously supported this endeavor during his time as Chair of African American and African Studies at Ohio State. In addition, Jermaine Archer, Marcellus Barksdale, Jelani Favors, Bayo Holsey, Alton Hornsby Jr., Hasan Jeffries, Judson Jeffries, Charles Jones, Ousman Kobo, Lupenga Mphande, Nick Nelson, Ike Newsum, Venetria Patton, John Roberts, Robyn Spencer, Ronald Stephens, Akinyele Umoja, Jim Upton, Rebecca Wanzo, Derrick White, Fanon Wilkins, and Jason Young helped the project along in varying ways.

The many graduate students who did yeoman work for this endeavor have to be recognized. Ernest Perry performed invaluable service from the very inception of the project and his attention to detail and professionalism are much appreciated. Dawn Miles and Di Luo—serving as Graduate Research Assistants—completed mission critical tasks that helped the project get back on schedule. Appreciation is given for the essays contributed by the following graduate students: Jeffrey Ahlman, Zawadi Barskile, Robert A. Bennett III, Ashley Bowden, Christina Bush, Tamara Butler, Tony Gass, Nicole Jackson, Clay Johnson, Karen Ngonya, Jason Perkins, Jamal Ratchford, William Sturkey, and Lindsey Sumner.

Finally, I would like to thank my two Muses—Na'eem and Njeri—and my co-editor, Leslie Alexander, whose friendship and persistence made the completion of this project possible.

—*Walter C. Rucker*

Introduction

In 1981, Vincent Harding published his classic study entitled *There Is a River: The Black Struggle for Freedom in America*. In it, Harding described the black freedom struggle as a river, a "...a long, continuous movement...sometimes powerful, tumultuous, and roiling with life; at other times meandering and turgid, covered with the ice and snow of seemingly endless winters, all too often streaked and running with blood."[1] For Harding, the black struggle for freedom, justice, and equality was not only natural, but inevitable and undying. Thus, it was his heartfelt desire to honor and celebrate black liberation and self-determination through rigorous scholarship. As a historian, it was his responsibility, he argued, to illuminate the "mysterious, transformative dance of life that has produced the men and women, the ideas and institutions, the visions, betrayals, and heroic dreams renewed in blood that are at once the anguish and the glory of the river of our struggle in this land."[2] In Harding's view, this intellectual mission to find meaning in suffering and struggle—in triumph and tribulation—was particularly relevant to the black experience in America and was, he maintained, an essential component to fully understanding the story of our nation, our society, and our humanity. Similarly, historians such as Sterling Stuckey and Margaret Washington have also argued that black resistance and struggle were inevitable, and built upon this concept to illustrate the myriad ways in which African Americans infused their activism

with culture, spirituality, and a deep, abiding connection to their African heritage.[3]

The *Encyclopedia of African American History* embraces these notions—the historical and contemporary inevitability of black resistance, and the influence of African cultural resilience on the black liberation movement—and explores them in four sections, arranged both chronologically and thematically.

Atlantic African, American, and European Backgrounds to Contact, Commerce, and Enslavement

The opening section is dedicated to the complex, intricate, and painful story of the European/African encounter, the rise of the transatlantic trade in humans, and the early enslavement of African peoples in the Americas. In keeping with the larger theme of this study, section one interrogates the role of both European and African elites in the development and perpetuation of the trade, while simultaneously illustrating the ingenious ways in which African peoples resisted and fought against enslavement. As historian Jason Young explains in his introductory essay, interactions between Europeans and Africans were usually "uneven and coerced," yet it is also clear that Africans—enslaved and free—navigated the terrain with creativity, courage, and defiance. Thus, section one chronicles the origins of the modern

African Diaspora, and the contested nature of the early African presence in America. More specifically, it documents the political and cultural environment in which both black enslavement and the black freedom struggle were born.

Culture, Identity, and Community: From Slavery to the Present

Perhaps more than any other portion of this project, section two investigates and celebrates the power and resilience of African cultural forms in the context of American society. Spanning centuries of African American art, music, dance, spirituality, and forms of resistance—ranging from folktales, religious expression, linguistic forms, jazz music, and soul food—this section seeks to illuminate the dynamic, creative, and spirited ways in which African Americans remained connected to their African heritage despite the horrors of enslavement, segregation, and racial discrimination. As Walter Rucker reveals in his introductory essay, there has been a lively and contentious scholarly debate about the existence, form, and meaning of African cultural retentions in African American life. Yet section two demonstrates that African cultural continuities not only survived the devastating ordeal of enslavement, but served as unifying forces among Africans in America that helped create a sense of identity, racial solidarity, a spirit of resistance, a strong spiritual legacy, and a vibrant musical and literary tradition.

Political Activity and Resistance to Oppression: From the American Revolution to the Civil War

In many ways, sections three and four are in conversation with each other; they are intertwined and are essentially extensions of one another. Section three explores the nature of black political resistance in the early national and antebellum eras, giving particular attention to themes of self-determination, early Black Nationalism, abolition, and the fight for citizenship. As historian Demetrius Eudell notes in the introductory essay, the black freedom struggle during this era was heavily influenced by Revolutionary War rhetoric, which provided a common political language for the spirit of freedom among enslaved Africans and the desire for independence among white settlers. Even so, however, most American rebels were not ready to acknowledge

the ways in which the existence of slavery belied the ideal of freedom. Thus, this was a pivotal moment in African American history and American history more broadly; for while the American Revolution and the subsequent formation of the United States symbolized the triumph of democracy, it also solidified the institution of slavery and black subjugation. As this section illustrates, however, African Americans continued to draw upon their African cultural heritage to enrich and sustain their fight for freedom, justice, and equality.

Political Activity, Migration, and Urbanization: Reconstruction, Civil Rights, and Modern African America

The final section of this project begins where part three concludes—the watershed moment when African Americans were finally released from legal bondage, but were simultaneously stymied by the stubborn tenacity of American racism. As African Americans emerged from slavery, they were faced with new forms of discrimination; most notably, the rise of Jim Crow segregation. Indeed, the paradox of American society persisted; while white Americans espoused notions of democracy and freedom, African Americans languished as they suffered through disfranchisement, segregation, lynch law, and economic deprivation. This obvious contradiction became even more painfully clear during World War II when African American men were sent to fight for freedom and democracy abroad, even as their brothers and sisters faced continual persecution at home. Yet the river of freedom continued to flow. In fact, by the middle of the 20th century, the black freedom struggle became a raging torrent. The Civil Rights and Black Power movements burst onto the American political landscape, irrevocably transforming it. In the final analysis, this era was a testimony to the perseverance of the African American spirit, and the indestructible desire to attain the freedom, justice, and equality that was promised to all of America's citizens.

Conclusion

The story of African American history is clearly rooted in struggle and, ultimately, as Vincent Harding suggested, this struggle—the river of resistance—is both fundamentally human and uniquely African American. While the quest for freedom and equality certainly reflects a universal human desire, the African American battle for these ideals has been particularly fraught with tension because at the core of American society lies a crucial contradiction: the United States was founded as a country that championed liberty, justice, and equality, but the nation consistently failed to apply these values to African Americans. As one group of African American leaders in the 1850s lamented,

> A heavy and cruel hand has been laid upon us. As a people, we feel ourselves to be not only deeply injured, but grossly misunderstood. Our white countrymen do not know us. They are strangers to our character, ignorant of our capacity, oblivious to our history and progress, and are misinformed as to the principles and ideas that control and guide us, as a people. The great mass of American citizens estimate us as being a characterless and purposeless people; and hence we hold up our heads, if at all, against the withering influence of a nation's scorn and contempt.[4]

Even so, the black liberation movement persisted, transformed, thrived, and never surrendered. Thus, the story of Africans in America is, in its essence, a chronicle of a continuous, impassioned crusade to force America to live up to its founding principles: freedom, justice, and equality for all. As such, African American history is *American* history; the two are inextricably linked, and it is impossible to understand one without the other. Yet it is also a history of Africa, since the culture and values that fueled the African American freedom struggle were also deeply rooted in their African heritage. It is this complexity—the contested juxtaposition of African and American—that this volume seeks to explore.

Notes

1. Vincent Harding, *There Is a River: The Black Struggle for Freedom in America* (New York: Harcourt Brace Jovanovich, 1981), xix.

2. Ibid., xi.

3. While Sterling Stuckey and Margaret Washington are certainly not the only scholars to advance intellectual arguments of this sort, they served as mentors to the editors of this project. As such, their ideas uniquely shaped the ideology of this project and therefore their contributions are being highlighted here. Sterling Stuckey and Margaret Washington's most influential works include the following: Sterling Stuckey, *The Ideological Origins of Black Nationalism* (Boston: Beacon Press, 1972); Sterling Stuckey, *Slave Culture: Nationalist Theory and the Foundations of Black America* (New York: Oxford University Press, 1987); Sterling Stuckey, *Going through the Storm: The Influence of African American Art in History* (New York: Oxford University Press, 1994); Margaret Washington Creel, *'A Peculiar People': Slave Religion and Community-Culture among the Gullahs* (New York: New York University Press, 1988); Margaret Washington, *Sojourner Truth's America* (Urbana and Champaign: University of Illinois Press, 2009).

4. *Proceedings of the Colored National Convention, held in Rochester, July 6th, 7th, and 8th, 1853* (Rochester: Printed at the office of Frederick Douglass's Paper, 1853), 16. This quote was also reprinted in James McCune Smith, James P. Miller, and John J. Zuille, "The Suffrage Question," in *A Documentary History of the Negro People in the United States*, ed. Herbert Aptheker (New York: Citadel Press, 1951), 1:455.

Atlantic African, American, and European Backgrounds to Contact, Commerce, and Enslavement

By the turn of the 16th century, Western knowledge of Asia was based on certain theological teachings, classical tales, and phantasmagoria and was shrouded in mystery, misconception, and misunderstanding. In the fourth century BCE, legends of Alexander the Great's conquests included, among other things, tales of Cynophali, or dog-headed men, and Sciopods, or one-legged men who ran with amazing swiftness and used their massive foot as a sunshade when resting.[1] Marco Polo, who had traveled to Asia in the late 13th century, dazzled Europeans with tales of cities and civilizations whose enormity and sophistication not only matched that of Europe, but also eclipsed the West in many regards. Much like earlier legends, Marco Polo also noted the presence of some fantastic creatures including stories of Rukh, a bird of prey so enormous that it could "seize an elephant with its talons…lift it into the air, in order to drop it to the ground and in this way kill it."[2] Interestingly enough, while much of Europe's knowledge of the East tended toward fantasy, significant information regarding the topologies, societies, and cultures of Asia and India was available. In the 12th century, Muslim chronicler, Al-Idrisi, had recorded from Sicily in 1154 information on India and Southeast Asia.[3] Moreover, communities of European Jews had substantial knowledge of the East through Jewish trade and religious networks that extended from Europe into Eastern lands. In particular, Benjamin of Tudela, a Spanish Jew, traveled throughout Europe and the Middle East between 1166 and 1171, during which time he visited Italy, Greece, Palestine, Damascus, and Egypt, among other locales. Benjamin's observations, chronicled in *The Itinerary of Benjamin of Tudela*, bear the distinction of being the first work of the Middle Ages, written in Europe, to mention a possible route to China.[4] As it stands, however, the work of Al-Idrisi and other Muslim scholars went largely untranslated until the 17th century and Christian Europe generally ignored Jewish knowledge of the East.

Regarding Africa, European interest in the continent had been developing since ancient times. Herodotus and other Greek and Roman writers detailed aspects of African life and culture; but much like the chronicles of Marco Polo, these writings were infused with the fantastic and were limited and fragmented in scope. Still, some of the most outlandish stories that ancient writers recorded in reference to Africa turned out to be quite true. So Herodotus wrote in the sixth century BCE, in reference to reports of a Phoenician expedition that rounded the Cape of Good Hope, "there they said—what some may believe, though I do not—that in sailing round Libya [Africa] they had the sun on their right hand."[5] This voyage around the southern tip of Africa occurred well before the 15th-century exploits of Portuguese explorers Bartolomeu Dias, who rounded the Cape in 1488, and Vasco da Gama, who surpassed his predecessor by not only rounding the South African coast but also reaching India in 1497. Thus, the generally held notion

1

that Europeans first discovered, then navigated the western and southern coasts of Africa in the 15th century is historically inaccurate. But the perdurability of the historical "fact" of a set of European discoveries in this era (including, of course, the "discovery" of America by Christopher Columbus) invites critical attention. V. Y. Mudimbe, in considering the question, argues:

> Taken at its first meaning, this discovery [that is, this unveiling, this observation] meant and still means the primary violence signified by the word. The slave trade narrated itself accordingly, and the same movement of reduction progressively guaranteed the gradual invasion of the continent. Thus, doubtless, it was a discovery in this limited sense.... We do know what is inscribed in this discovery, the new cultural orders it allowed, and in terms of knowledge, the texts that its discourses built and whose achievement is to be found in ... the "colonial library."[6]

The historical veracity of European discoveries in Africa and in other areas of the world is secondary to a much larger project. If the notion of European discovery may not be said to tell *the Truth*, it most certainly tells *a truth*; namely that of European claims to power. As Mudimbe writes, "that discovery spells out only one viewpoint, the European."[7]

Notably, Eastern interest in and knowledge of the West was also uneven. Many people in the East, including not only Asia but also North and West Africa, regarded Europe as something of a backwater, disconnected from the centers of commodity production and commercial exchange occurring in other parts of the world. Indeed, North Africa, along with West and West-Central Africa, were key centers of global trade in the 15th and 16th centuries, being linked not only to the trans-Saharan trade, but also through the Red Sea to trading networks in South Asia.

Although European knowledge of Africa, India, and the Far East was uneven and largely inaccurate during the 15th century, many in the West desired greatly to retain access to Eastern goods, principally the spices that filtered into Europe through Constantinople, the virtual bridge between Europe and Asia. When, in 1453, Constantinople fell to Ottoman Turks, Europeans faced a veritable commercial and religious crisis. The fall of Constantinople reflected not only the fall of the Byzantine Empire, but also called into serious question Western access to Eastern goods. With Muslim political and commercial power entrenched in the Middle East, and thus in control of the lucrative spice trade,

Western Europeans sought a different route to reach the famed "spice islands."

From its propitious perch in southwestern Europe, Portugal was well suited to seek a sea route to the East. Prince Henry, son of Portugal's King João I, led a military offensive against Morocco in 1415 intended to extend the scope of Christian influence in the region. After attacking and sacking the city of Ceuta, Henry's forces looted gold, spices, oils, and other commodities. In this way, Prince Henry observed North African marketplaces and recognized first hand the wealth and riches that might be had from the Eastern trade. Upon his return to Portugal, Henry devoted himself headlong into overseas commercial expansion. In 1420, Prince Henry was appointed by Pope Martin V to govern the Military Order of Christ, an influential association of noblemen, whose mission had both religious and commercial designs. Indeed, Prince Henry came to be known as "The Navigator" due to his zealous sponsorship of Atlantic exploration. Henry became a patron of Portuguese discovery as he oversaw the development of naval arsenals and observatories and established the *Vila do Infante,* or Prince's Town, which trained geographers, navigators, and map-makers.[8] Prince Henry's expansionist designs later received papal sanction when, in 1455, Pope Nicholas V issued a bull, the *Romanus Pontifex,* which granted Christians the right:

> to invade, search out, capture, vanquish, and subdue all Saracens and pagans whatsoever ... and the kingdoms, dukedoms, principalities, dominions, possessions, and all movable and immovable goods whatsoever held and possessed by them and to reduce their persons to perpetual slavery, and to apply and appropriate to himself and his successors the kingdoms, dukedoms, counties, principalities, dominions, possessions, and goods, and to convert them to his and their use and profit.[9]

In effect, Nicholas V claimed for Catholicism all lands and persons, whether yet known or unknown, as the rightful property of the Church. Portuguese expansion, under the aegis of Prince Henry, constituted a particular form of imperialism that enjoyed the political support of the royal court, religious sanction from the highest levels of church authority, and a commercial impetus, driven by European demand for Eastern goods.

Though the early maritime exploration of the Portuguese reflected a singular national zeal and religious fervor, the varied conditions necessary for actual Atlantic expansion required technologies and expertise from a diverse group of people of various nationalities and faiths. Indeed, the Muslim presence in the Iberian Peninsula contributed much to Portuguese overseas designs. Muslims developed several devices, including the astrolabe, the compass box, and cartographic instruments that paved the way for Portuguese navigators. Moreover, the small, mobile ships capable of sailing into headwinds, known as caravels, which were so central to Portuguese expansion, were based on Arab shipbuilding technology.[10]

In 1418, Prince Henry ordered the occupation of the Madeira Islands, one of several sets of island chains that lay just to the northwest of the western African coast. He later ordered the seizure of other Atlantic islands including the Azores and Canary islands in 1424 and 1427, respectively. Initially, Portuguese forces on these islands were rather modest. They cultivated indigenous plants and introduced other crops including cereals and grapevines. In addition, Portuguese forces established raiding parties on the African continent to secure African labor to work as slaves on these islands.[11]

The rather modest agricultural production taking place on these Atlantic islands shifted drastically during the 1450s when the Portuguese began cultivating sugar on the Madeiras.[12] In great contrast to earlier Portuguese agricultural development on the island, sugar was labor intensive and required a large number of workers. Moreover, sugar production was much more complicated than the harvesting of indigenous plants and required the development of a more intricate system of production. Portuguese officials developed the plantation system on these Atlantic islands that organized and coordinated large-scale cash crop production based on forced labor captured on the African coast. The plantation system integrated large-scale colonial production and global demand, thus fostering Western European notions of mercantilism—a theory of political economy based on the establishment of foreign colonies whose principal function, generally achieved through agricultural production or mining, consists of providing the raw materials necessary for the support and encouragement of industrial production in the mother country. The plantation system was replicated on other Atlantic islands including São Tomé and the Cape Verde islands in the southern Atlantic. Increased sugar production on these islands led to a decrease in the price of the crop, which in turn, spurred demand. Indeed, the plantation system proved so profitable

that it would later be adopted by the Spanish, French, Dutch, and British in other Atlantic locales.

The Portuguese continued to establish trading posts not only along the western coast of Africa, but also in India and Indonesia. Notably, the establishment of the plantation system made clear to European powers that even without identifying an eastern route to Asia, the trade in cash crops, especially sugar, could be profitable. By the turn of the 16th century, thousands of Africans were being taken captive in order to labor on ever-expanding sugar plantations throughout the Atlantic.[13] Due to its prohibitive costs, the consumption of sugar in Europe had initially been restricted to the very wealthy, but within relatively short order, increased production caused a reduction in the price of sugar and resulted, in turn, in an explosive upsurge in demand, especially among men and women of middling status who were increasingly able to afford what had been formerly a luxury product. Increased consumption in Europe required higher production, which meant that more captives would have to be secured to labor on sugar plantations. These developments caused a significant shift in the relations between European merchants and African commercial and political agents.

Illustrative of this shift are the negotiations that occurred between Portuguese trader Diogo Gomes and Mandingo lord Nomimansa. In 1458, Prince Henry dispatched Gomes to negotiate treaties with African rulers. Henry instructed Gomes not to steal slaves or any other commodities, but rather to barter for all that he took. Gomes, however, upon arriving in West Africa saw the riches in ivory, gold, and slaves that might be taken from coastal kingdoms, and disobeyed his orders. Gomes recalled, "I took all by myself twenty-two people who were sleeping, I herded them as if they had been cattle toward the boats, and each of us did the same, and we captured that day…650 people, and we went back to Portugal…where the Prince [Henry] was and he rejoiced with us."[14] Indeed, Prince Henry likely oversaw the importation of an estimated 15,000–20,000 African captives who served in Portugal as domestic slaves.[15]

Meanwhile, rulers of rival Spain, not to be outdone by their Iberian neighbors, engaged in a program of imperial expansion. By 1492, King Ferdinand and Queen Isabella of Spain united in an effort to end the 600-year presence of North African Moors in the country. This development galvanized a new politico-religious movement bent on the extension of the power and scope of Christianity while seeking economic and commercial profit for the mother country. After having won a military victory over the Moors, Spanish authorities quickly passed legislation that called for the expulsion of Jews from the country. Spanish political and religious leaders regarded the expulsion of Muslims and Jews as one aspect of a critical religious war. But if religious conflict characterized late-15th-century Spain, the same may not be said for the entire period of Moorish rule in the Iberian Peninsula. Indeed, the remarkable religious tolerance between Christians, Jews, and Muslims that marked the period was highlighted by significant cultural and religious interaction. The period during which Abd al-Rahman III ruled in Cordoba (912–61), for example, was a time of great opulence in which intellectual circles of Muslims, Jews, and Christians contributed to a flourishing of the arts, literature, astronomy, and medicine.[16] Muslims governing in Spain did not mandate conversion to Islam and in allowing Christians and Jews to observe their faith exhibited tolerance for a people whom they regarded, based on Qur'anic readings, as "People of the Book." This is not to understate the religious and ethnic tensions that most certainly accompanied the Muslim presence in the region, especially after the 13th-century rise to power of the Almoravids. In the end, Arab architecture, language, and culture played a significant role in the region and its legacy is still evident not only in European architecture, but also in the realm of language including such commonly used words as alcohol, almanac, zero, and elixir.[17]

While the Portuguese searched for an eastward route to Asia by establishing trading posts along the coastal areas of Africa, India, and Indonesia, the Spanish gambled on a westward route. Spain sponsored the voyage of an Italian-born navigator, Christopher Columbus, who set sail in 1492 across the Atlantic in search of Asia and the lucrative spice trade. But Columbus knew full well the profits to be had from plantation-style slavery as developed by the Portuguese, and so sought not only a route to the spices of the east, but also desired access to slave labor on the order of the Portuguese example. This intense desire for labor is illustrated in the personal diary of Christopher Columbus who, upon initially coming across native Arawaks in the Bahamas in 1492, noted in his journal, "they should be good servants and intelligent...I will take at the time of my departure six natives for Your Highness." He later made similar observations: "with fifty men they can all be subjugated and made to do what is required of them...a thousand [of

them] would not stand before three of our men...they are good to be ordered about, to work and sow, and do all that may be necessary, and to build towns, and they should be taught to go about clothed and to adopt our customs."[18] In fact, Columbus did have experience with slavery and the slave trade as practiced on Africa's Atlantic islands. Columbus's final port of call before embarking on his transatlantic voyage was not in Spain, under whose flag he traveled, but the Canary Islands.[19]

Within months of Columbus's initial return, Pope Alexander VI issued a papal bull in 1493 that established the earth as the rightful property of the Church to be divided into two regions, the one half belonging to Spain and the other to Portugal. European expansion in this era constituted a particular combination of religious and political aims that is well articulated in the language of the 1493 pronouncement:

> Among other works well pleasing to the Divine Majesty and cherished of our heart, this assuredly ranks highest, that in our times especially the Catholic faith and the Christian religion be exalted and be everywhere increased and spread, that the health of souls be cared for and that barbarous nations be overthrown and brought to the faith itself.[20]

Not wavered by the papal pronouncement, European navigators, not only Spanish and Portuguese, but also Dutch, French, and English, began to develop maps and engage in their own treks across the Atlantic. Indeed, overseas expansion became crucial components of a burgeoning national zeal that swept much of Western Europe during the 15th and 16th centuries. The Atlantic Rim operated as a crucial interfaith and intercultural space where European national identities were constructed. Notably, the early development of plantation societies in the Atlantic shifted the Western European gaze away from the spices of the East toward the plantations of the Americas. As a result, the Atlantic Rim, including Europe, America, and Africa, became a complex swirl of race, commerce, and religion.[21]

Atlantic Africans played a critical role in the development of the early Atlantic, serving variously as merchants, sailors, slaves, traders, and clerics. In recent years, scholars have devoted significant attention to the lives and experiences of these Atlantic Africans, noting that during the 17th century, New World colonial societies, especially British North America, developed varied systems of forced labor, of which slavery was simply one among many. That is to say, slavery existed alongside other forms of coerced labor and did not dominate the economic, social, and cultural formations of colonial British societies as it would in subsequent generations. During this period, one notes a certain openness and fluidity with regard to racial and cultural identities that allowed for a measure of mobility that became progressively closed once the plantation societies of the Americas became more entrenched. Unlike the harshness of fully developed *slave societies* these 17th-century *societies with slaves* were less brutal and afforded for Atlantic Africans a greater measure of mobility. Indeed, during the 17th century, Atlantic Africans often served as cultural and commercial intermediaries, "employing their linguistic skills and their familiarity with the Atlantic's diverse commercial practices, cultural conventions, and diplomatic etiquette to mediate between African merchants and European sea captains."[22]

Atlantic Africans intrigue many scholars because their lives exist in stark opposition to the standard images of slavery to which many have become accustomed. Stated simply, the lives of that first generation of Atlantic Africans approximate a degree of personal freedom that would be largely unthinkable just a few decades later. Writing in *Many Thousands Gone,* Ira Berlin argues that Atlantic Africans enjoyed special knowledge and experiences along with a "genius for intercultural negotiation."[23] They were presumably more confident than other Africans and, as a result, were regularly regarded by Europeans as insolent, impertinent, and arrogant. While Berlin never makes the claim outright, the notion that Atlantic Africans exhibited sagacity and genius vis-à-vis their interactions with Europeans suggests that other Africans were less sagacious than their presumably more cosmopolitan counterparts. That Atlantic Africans led lives apart is beyond question. They traveled back and forth between the continents that comprise the Atlantic Rim and, in many cases, they had experiences that rendered their lives remarkable, often involving, among other things, piracy, military exploits, resistance, and rebellion. But this should not be read to mean that Atlantic Africans were a people apart, distinct from other Africans by talent or intellectual capability. This is an important matter because the cultural interplay indicative of the lives of Atlantic Africans is occasionally rendered so as to suggest a type of racial exceptionality. Indeed, many, though certainly not all, Atlantic Africans were the children of African women and European traders. The talent and ingenuity

that Berlin ascribes to Atlantic Africans may very well be applied to other Africans. As noted above, West and West-Central Africa had been connected through commercial, cultural, and religious networks to the Middle East, India, and Asia in the centuries preceding the Atlantic slave trade. That is, they were engaged in global systems of trade and communication and there is no reason to believe that they were not cosmopolitan in any sense of the word. We know, for example, that European traders along Africa's west coast marveled at Africans' skill with language and noted their keen ability in negotiating terms of trade.[24] As John Thornton notes, Africans were well aware of the global systems of trade and competition that marked Atlantic trade and sought, to the best of their ability, to secure beneficial terms at every point.[25]

If the 17th century offered a certain access, freedom, and mobility, a cursory look at the biographies of some Atlantic Africans encourages a qualification of the degree of mobility and movement so often attributed to blacks who lived around the Atlantic Rim during the 17th century.[26] While many argue that Atlantic Africans existed at cultural interstices, I think it important to note that this intercultural space was often uneven and coerced. That is, rather than operating in the liminal spaces between cultures, blacks around the Atlantic were ever made to approximate European culture. In the main, they adopted (or were ascribed) European names, spoke European languages, and were forced to dress and exhibit themselves in accordance with European norms of posture, composure, and attitude. Through religious conversion, the adoption of European dress, diet, and comportment, Atlantic Africans were made to mimic the cultures of the English, French, or Dutch, even if only imperfectly so. So Albert King, born Ukawsaw Gronniosaw, adopted the language and cultures of the Dutch who enslaved him in the early 18th century. Being thus "clothed in the Dutch or English manner," Gronniosaw donned not only European-styled dress, but also adopted the prejudices and predilections of his captors, coming to regard Africa as a land of devilish heathens and Europe as a space of moral and religious piety and purity.[27]

Consider, for example, the oft-cited life of Anthony Johnson, a captive African who arrived in Virginia in 1621. Johnson married, fathered four children, and eventually earned his freedom in the colony where he became a landholder in his own right. Indeed, he was among the most successful and long-lived planters in the colony. Although he was called "the ole' African" in 1654, Johnson did not die until 1670.[28] Even more than this, Johnson was confident and outspoken. He filed suit against fellow whites in his community in order to secure, protect, and recover property, including slaves, and he enjoyed some significant success in this regard. He once defended himself against allegations of slothfulness and laziness by reminding his accuser, a notable Virginia planter, "I know myne owne ground and I will worke when I please and play when I please."[29] Given his notable success in Virginia, many scholars have taken the example of Johnson's life as evidence of the greater access, mobility, and rights that blacks enjoyed in various parts of the Atlantic world during the 17th century.

Still, analysis of Johnson's presumed freedoms may be tempered by the machinations of power and patronage in colonial Virginia. Indeed, most of the advancements that Johnson made during his lifetime required the sanction of his owners, the Bennetts, who allowed him to farm independently while still a slave, marry, and baptize his children. It is perhaps this patronage that encouraged Johnson to file suit against other members of the colonial elite, though he initially proved reticent of inviting the ire of white planters. In fact, the planters against which Johnson filed suit had previously accused John Johnson, Anthony's son, of committing fornication and other enormities with a white servant, Hannah Leach. John Johnson was convicted of the crime and sentenced in 1665 to labor in the local workhouse. In the end, Anthony Johnson left Virginia at mid-century to build a life in Maryland. In 1670, some months after his death, Virginia courts failed to restore to his family lands that Johnson had owned on grounds that Johnson was "a negro and by consequence an alien," thus highlighting the growing importance of racism in colonial legislation.[30]

The generation of Atlantic Africans to which Anthony Johnson belonged quickly gave way to the rising tide of plantation slavery that swept the New World during the late 17th and early 18th centuries. The uneven, though significant, access afforded blacks in the 17th century dissipated. In addition, the various ambiguities inherent in colonial law with regard to Africans were clarified toward a greater solidification of power in the hands of the slaveholding class. In 1662, the Virginia legislature passed an act establishing that "all children borne in this country shalbe held bond or free only according to the condition of the mother, and that if any Christian shall comitt fornication with a negro man or woman, hee or shee soe offending shall pay double

the fines imposed by the former act."[31] In this single piece of legislation, colonial officials effectively took control over the sexual politics of both black and white women. That is, white women's sexuality was controlled through the institution of marriage. In line with the principle of patriarchy, a man could establish heirs through his children who, in turn, looked not to their mother for inheritance and wealth, but rather received varied privileges and rights based on paternity. Indeed, this had long been standard practice in British law. In instituting this law in 1662, colonial authorities diverged from the British practice in an attempt to control the sexual politics of black women by establishing property rights over the children born of interracial unions.

While the Virginia assembly sought to control the sexual politics of black women, so the Maryland General Assembly tackled the thorny question of freeborn white women who married blacks. After rendering synonymous blackness and slavery, thereby assigning to all members of the former category the status of the latter, the language of the act continues:

> and forasmuch as divers freeborn English women, forgetful of their free condition and to the disgrace of our nation, marry Negro slaves, by which also divers suits may arise touching the issue of such women, and a great damage befalls the master of such negroes for prevention wherof, for deterring such freeborn women from such shameful matches. Be it further enacted by the authority, advice, and consent aforesaid, that whatsoever freeborn women shall marry any slave…shall serve the master of such slave during the life of her husband.

In effect, colonial officials authorized the control of the sexual politics of freeborn women by establishing rights over them if they chose to marry men of African descent. In this way, colonial officials maintained rights over white women, be they married to a white or a black man. In other ways as well, colonial officials looked to the law to establish more firmly slavery in the Americas. Where British common law held that Christians could not lawfully be enslaved, the Virginia legislature passed an act in 1667 establishing that baptism "doth not alter the condition of the person as to his bondage or freedome." Interestingly enough, colonial authorities regarded the passage of this law as a mercy for slaves because it presumably opened the way for Christian conversion for African captives, thus ensuring the eternal salvation of their souls, even if their bodies be damned in the here and now.

While British North American colonial law paved the way for the establishment of slavery, the intensity of the slave trade that supplied the burgeoning colonies with labor increased dramatically on the western coast of Africa. European traders—no longer capable of seizing through kidnap enough Africans to satisfy colonial demand for labor—established posts along the coast of Africa and relied on African coastal traders along with royal authorities to capture and transport captives from the interior regions. In this way, African trade networks, which had previously been oriented eastward, toward the Saharan trade, became increasingly focused on the western trade, supplying European traders with African laborers. The extent to which the presence of European traders on the West Coast of Africa affected African cultures and societies has been a matter of intense historical debate for decades. These debates have been so crucial for several reasons, not the least of which results from the fact that discussions about slavery and the slave trade often occur in the midst of contemporary debates concerning racial justice, colonialism, and, perhaps most important, historical culpability.

Many of the early interpretations of the slave trade regarded it as an essential good for the societies of West and West-Central Africa, contending, among other things, that the slave trade spurred economic development for the societies involved. J. D. Fage argued, "there seems in fact to be a close correlation in West Africa between economic development…and the growth of the institution of slavery…in West Africa."[32] Early scholars implied that Africans required something like a centuries-long transatlantic slave trade before their labor and economy could be made productive. As one scholar noted, "to see enslavement as the precondition of the growth of states is étatiste and elitist in the extreme."[33]

A revision of these interpretations occurred in the midst of anticolonial movements throughout Africa and Latin America, along with the Civil Rights movement in the United States. Perhaps most influential in this scholarship was the work of Walter Rodney who argued that the Atlantic slave trade, rather than serving a positive good for the African societies involved, was actually detrimental to West and West-Central Africa. Moreover, Rodney argued that the transatlantic slave trade contributed much to the more contemporary economic, political, and social malaise affecting much of the African continent in the

postcolonial era.[34] Rodney's positions came into question in large part because, as Walter C. Rucker notes, "while it is quite true that European imperial domination of the continent indeed contorted its features and disrupted its outlines, down-streaming that specifically modern reality back to the sixteenth, seventeenth, or eighteenth centuries might be to project too much European power and control back through time."[35] In effect, though Rodney and others revised early scholarship on the slave trade, they did so at the cost of presenting Europeans as the ultimate actors and agents of historical change in Africa.

New work in the field has offered yet another revision, focusing increasingly on the active role that Africans themselves played in the development of the transatlantic slaving system. Of these John Thornton's thesis is perhaps the most controversial. Thornton, writing in *Africa and Africans in the Making of the Atlantic World,* argues that Europeans did not posses either the military nor the political power necessary to force Africans to sell slaves against their will; and further, severe competition among various European powers on the west coast of Africa meant that no one power was able to affect a monopoly over trade that would have enabled them to dictate the terms of trade. Instead, Thornton argues that Africans, as shrewdly demanding traders, were the prime negotiators of the terms of trade. As such, Thornton contends that African participation in the slave trade was voluntary.[36]

Indeed, this revisionist stance along with a downward re-estimation of the numbers of Africans enslaved during the transatlantic slavery have been read by some critics as an attempt to palliate European crimes against humanity in the past and, by implication, to minimize more recent economic and political injustices along with present-day inequalities and violence. Surely, this is not Thornton's aim, though he does seem to discount the role that European powers played in the development of the transatlantic slave trade. Perhaps more important, however, Thornton's suggestion that African participation in the slave trade was voluntary effectively reduces human action to the level of individual conscious volition. As Robin Law suggests in a review of Thornton's thesis, "although individual actions may be 'free,' the overall outcome corresponds to nobody's conscious intention, but reflects the internal logic of the economic system: in this sense rather than Europeans imposing their will upon Africans, both European purchasers and African sellers of slaves might be seen as subject to a form of economic necessity."[37] In the end, the true test of African voluntary participation lies not in the decisions of coastal slave traders and royal courts to provide Europeans with slaves, but rather hinges on the experiences of those who opted out of the trade. That is, in order to be fully voluntary, West African traders and political leaders must be shown to have been "free" not to participate in the trade. In fact, one finds that the choice to participate in the trade was not equal. The attempts made by King Afonso of Kongo are instructive here. When members of his family along with other nobility were captured and sold as slaves to Portuguese merchants, Afonso wrote to Portuguese heads of state, railing against the brutality and licentiousness of slave traders. He attempted to make the trade illegal in Kongo and expressed his conviction that as far as the Luso-Kongo trade was concerned, Kongo had need only of priests, teachers for the schools, and materials necessary for sacraments.[38] Afonso's request fell on deaf ears as the slave trade increased precipitously despite the king's desire to see it stopped. Throughout the 16th and 17th centuries, Kongo kings wrote to papal authorities and European monarchs in unsuccessful attempts to address and remedy the harmful effects of an ever-increasing trade.[39]

Perhaps Elizabeth Isichei writes it best when she argues that the trade in slaves "was essentially an exploitive alliance between a comprador class—rulers, merchants, and military aristocracy—which joined with an external exploiter to prey upon the peasant population." Indeed, Walter Rodney suggested as much years ago when he argued: "The responsibility for the slave trade, as far as Africans bear the responsibility, lies squarely upon the shoulders of the tribal rulers and elites of coastal polities. They were in alliance with the European slave merchants, and it was upon the mass of the people that they jointly preyed."[40]

Notably, recent scholarship illustrates the great lengths to which Africans at all levels of society resisted Atlantic slaving. So Sylviane Diouf argues that Africans engaged in various strategies of resistance including resettling to isolated areas, building fortresses, transforming the natural habitat, forming secret societies, and engaging in armed resistance among others.[41] By these varied methods, Diouf contends that millions of people were likely spared the horrors of the slave trade.

The entries that follow chronicle, in detail, the historical developments that resulted in the creation of an African Atlantic world between the 15th and 18th centuries. Taken together, these entries are critically important for several reasons, not the least of which stems from an intense treatment of the crucial role played by Africans in the political, social, and economic development of the Atlantic world. Notably, Africa is regarded in its specificity in this volume and thus enables a more enhanced understanding of the particular roles that specific Africans played in the development of the region during the era of slavery and the slave trade. Moreover, these entries highlight several of the key features constitutive of the modern world including the rise of burgeoning capitalist production and consumption, globalization, and industry inasmuch as the raw materials produced in colonial regions were used to support increasing factory production in Europe.[42] Because Africans on the continent along with their contemporaries and progeny held captive in the New World played a persistent role in the development of the Atlantic world, they must be regarded as critical agents of change in a burgeoning modern world, rather than as its mere victims.

Jason Young

Notes

1. John Larner, *Marco Polo and the Discovery of the World* (New Haven, CT: Yale University Press, 1999), 8, 9.
2. Manuel Komroff, *The Travels of Marco Polo* (Garden City, NY: Garden City Publishing, 1926), 313; Larner, *Marco Polo*, 80, 144–46, 60–67.
3. John Esposito, ed., *The Oxford History of Islam* (New York: Oxford University Press, 1999), 183, 329; Larner, *Marco Polo*, 12.
4. Larner, *Marco Polo*, 13; Benjamin Tudela, *The Itinerary of Benjamin of Tudela: Travels in the Middle Ages* (Malibu, CA: J. Simon, 1983).
5. Herodotus, *Herodotus*, 4 vols., trans. A. D. Godley (Cambridge, MA: Harvard University Press, 1920–25), quoted in V. Y. Mudimbe, *The Idea of Africa* (Bloomington: Indiana University Press, 1994), 18.
6. Mudimbe, *Idea*, 17.
7. Ibid.
8. Peter Russell, *Prince Henry "The Navigator": A Life* (New Haven, CT: Yale University Press, 2000), 317, 345.
9. For a fuller treatment of the *Romanus Pontifex* see Mudimbe, *Idea*, 31–37.
10. Esposito, *Islam*, 169, 180–81, 317–20.
11. Russell, *Prince Henry*, 131, 251.
12. Ibid., 90–91.
13. Ibid., 97, 131, 251.
14. Diogo Gomez, *De la Premiere Decouverte de la Guinee* (Bissau, Guinea-Bissau: Centro de Estudos da Guiné Portuguesa: Sociedade Industrial de Tipografia, 1959), 22; Hugh Thomas, *The Slave Trade: The Story of the Atlantic Slave Trade, 1440–1870* (New York: Simon and Schuster, 1997), 69.
15. Russell, *Prince Henry*, 258; Thomas, *Slave Trade*, 21–24.

16. Esposito, *Islam,* 317–18.

17. Ibid., 320.

18. Clements Markham, ed., *The Journal of Christopher Columbus* (New York: Burt Franklin Publisher, 1971 [1893]), 38, 41, 114.

19. Ibid., 17.

20. Quoted in Mudimbe, *Idea,* 30.

21. See, for example, Paul Gilroy, *The Black Atlantic: Modernity and Double-Consciousness* (Cambridge, MA: Harvard University Press, 1993); Peter Linebaugh and Marcus Rediker, *The Many Headed Hydra: Sailors, Slaves, Commoners, and the Hidden History of the Revolutionary Atlantic* (Boston: Beacon Press, 2000).

22. Ira Berlin, *Many Thousands Gone: The First Two Centuries of Slavery in North America* (Cambridge, MA: Belknap Press of Harvard University, 1998), 17.

23. Ibid., 23.

24. John Thornton, *Africa and Africans in the Making of the Atlantic World, 1400–1800,* 2nd ed. (Cambridge, UK: Cambridge University Press, 1998), 43–47, 53, 55, 57.

25. Ibid., 57–66.

26. See, for example, Berlin, *Many Thousands Gone;* Linebaugh and Rediker, *Many Headed Hydra.*

27. James Albert Ukawsaw Gronniosaw, *A Narrative of the Most Remarkable Particulars in the Life of James Albert Ukawsaw Gronniosaw, an African Prince, Related by Himself* (London: R. Groombridge, 1840 [1770]), 7–9.

28. Berlin, *Many Thousands Gone,* 41.

29. Ibid., 43.

30. Timothy Breen and Stephen Innes, *Myne Owne Ground: Race and Freedom on Virginia's Eastern Shore, 1640–1676* (New York: Oxford University Press, 1980), 43; Berlin, *Many Thousands Gone,* 90; Charles Johnson, ed., *Africans in America* (New York: Harcourt Brace, 1998), 44.

31. John Johnson's conviction for fornication with Hannah Leach would have fallen under this legislation.

32. J. D. Fage, "Slavery and the Slave Trade in the Context of West African History," *Journal of African History* 10, no. 3 (1969): 397, 400.

33. C. Wrigley, "Historicism in Africa: Slavery and State Formation," *African Affairs* 70, no. 279 (April 1971): 113–24, quoted in Elizabeth Isichei, *A History of Nigeria* (London: Longman, 1983), 107.

34. Walter Rodney, *How Europe Underdeveloped Africa* (Washington, D.C.: Howard University Press, 1974).

35. Walter Rucker, "The African and European Slave Trades," in Alton Hornsby Jr., *A Companion to African American History* (Malden, MA: Blackwell Publishing, 2005), 51.

36. Thornton, *Africa and Africans,* 125.

37. Robin Law, "Africa and Africans in the Making of the Atlantic World," *The International Journal of African Historical Studies* 26, no. 1 (1993): 192.

38. Louis Jadin and Mireille Dicorato, *Correspondance de Dom Afonso; Roi du Congo, 1506-1543* (Bruxelles: Académie Royale des Sciences d'outre-mer, 1974), 156.

39. Joseph Miller, "Central Africa during the Era of the Slave Trade, c. 1490s-1850s," in *Central Africans and Cultural Transformations in the American Diaspora,* ed. Linda Heywood (New York: Cambridge University Press, 2001), 28, 34.

40. Elizabeth Allo Isichei, *A History of Nigeria* (London: Longman, 1983), 108; Walter Rodney, *A History of the Upper Guinea Coast* (New York: Oxford University Press, 1970), 144.

41. Sylviane Diouf, ed., *Fighting the Slave Trade: West African Strategies* (Athens: Ohio University Press, 2003), xii.

42. Eric Williams, *Capitalism and Slavery* (Chapel Hill: University of North Carolina Press, 1944).

Acculturation

Acculturation describes the transformative process that occurs when two or more groups have prolonged contact. Presumably any cultural/ethnic group can experience acculturation. How this process looks in concrete terms varies as a function of the nature of the intercultural contact as well as the specific cultural elements within each group. Given the historically oppressive relationship of contact between African Americans and whites, the defining criteria of acculturation appears to be the degree to which ethnic and cultural minorities participate in the cultural beliefs, traditions, and practices of their own culture versus those of the majority group.

Though clearly acculturation was a real phenomenon experienced by Africans and their descendants throughout the Western Hemisphere, the search for cultural retentions among enslaved Africans and their descendants has received a heavy amount of the attention in recent scholarly work. Scholars across a number of disciplines have been divided into one of three major interpretive camps: the Annihilationist school, the Africanist school, and the Creolization school. Robert E. Park, a professor of sociology at the University of Chicago, was the father of the Annihilationist approach. Writing in 1919, he claimed that slavery had obliterated African culture and that nothing in the culture of African Americans living in the U.S. South could be traced back to African roots. The Annihilationist School was later championed by one of Park's former students, E. Franklin Frazier. Frazier contends, in three separate works, that slavery destroyed the black family and this reality facilitated their Americanization and the complete annihilation of African culture in the United States. As a black sociologist, he sought to de-emphasize any nonmainstream elements in African American culture in order to promote social goals like integration, black suffrage, and equal rights.

The pioneering efforts of anthropologist Melville J. Herskovits sought to counter the Annihilationists' claims. His 1941 work, *The Myth of the Negro Past,* illuminated several examples of African influences in the sacred and the secular ethos of African Americans. Herskovits not only established the foundations for the Africanist School, he also challenged several prevailing myths about African American life in the United States. By demonstrating tangible cultural links between Africa and its diasporic communities—that is, communities of Africans dispersed outside of Africa—Herskovits took full aim at several misconceptions, including the notion that Africans came from extremely diverse cultures and were randomly distributed in the Americas in a concerted attempt to undermine their ability to fashion a collective identity. The Africanist School, therefore, actively searches for evidence of "Africanisms" in areas such as religion, language, family, and socialization among other areas.

The third school of thought, serving as an interpretive middle ground between the Annihilationists and the Africanists, is the Creolization School. This approach is epitomized by the work of anthropologists Sidney Mintz and Richard Price. In 1976 they published *The Birth of African-American Culture* with the intent to critique and revise Herskovits's earlier findings. They claimed that Africans transported across the Atlantic to become slaves in the Americas developed and created a culture that cannot be characterized simply as African. According to their research, the nature of the slave trade and enslavement in the Americas made the continuity of African culture nearly impossible. Mintz and Price contend that, while African culture was an important element of African American culture, it was by no means central and not independent of European influences or new cultural developments in the Americas arising out of the slave experience. In this regard, acculturation (or creolization) was something that began in the holds of slave ships and continued through the experiences of enslaved Africans on Western Hemisphere plantations. African American culture, therefore, is a product of cultural fusion and was as connected or disconnected to Africa as it was to Europe and the unique social and cultural milieus of the Americas.

Acculturation will continue to exist as a concept and lived experience for centuries to come. As globalization broadens economic and political ideas, it also increases contact among a diverse group of people. The end result of such sustained contact is the creation of cultural polyglots, which, themselves, are the result of acculturation. For African Americans the process may be encapsulated best by conceptualizations like W. E. B. Du Bois's "Double Consciousness," Paul Guilroy's "Black Atlantic," or Ira Berlin's "Atlantic Creoles."

See also: Amalgamation; Atlantic Creoles; Double Consciousness; Salt-Water Negroes

Michelle E. Anderson
and Walter C. Rucker

Bibliography

Gomez, Michael. *Exchanging Our Country Marks: The Transformation of African Identities in the Colonial and Antebellum South.* Chapel Hill: University of North Carolina Press, 1998.

Herskovits, Melville J. *The Myth of the Negro Past.* New York: Harper, 1941.

Mintz, Sidney, and Richard Price. *The Birth of African-American Culture: An Anthropological Perspective.* Boston: Beacon Press, 1976.

Patterson, H. O. L. "Slavery, Acculturation and Social Change: The Jamaican Case." *The British Journal of Sociology* 17 (1966):151–64.

Teske, Raymond H. C., and Bardin H. Nelson. "Acculturation and Assimilation: A Clarification." *American Ethnologist* 1 (1974):351–67.

Van Der Berghe, Pierre L. "The African Diaspora in Mexico, Brazil and the United States." *Social Forces* 54 (1976):530–45.

Walker, Sheila, ed. *African Roots/American Cultures: Africa in the Creation of the Americas.* New York: Rowman and Littlefield, 2001.

Watson, R. L. "American Scholars and the Continuity of African Culture in the United States." *The Journal of Negro History* 63 (1978):375–86.

Yelvington, Kevin A. "The Anthropology of Afro-Latin America and the Caribbean: Diasporic Dimensions." *Annual Review of Anthropology* 30 (2001):227–60.

African Burial Ground, New York City

The New York African Burial Ground—the oldest and largest cemetery for enslaved Africans in the United States—was unearthed in 1989 as construction workers prepared to install a 34-story federal office building in lower Manhattan. Following the discovery that the building site was situated above an 18th-century "Negroes Burying Ground," a crew of archaeologists was employed to conduct an archaeological excavation. In 1991, the construction of the federal office building ensued alongside an extensive archaeological dig that uncovered the skeletons of more than 400 enslaved Africans buried at the cemetery during the early to late 18th century. The excavation and construction project was suspended in 1992 following a congressional mandate issued largely in response to a public demand. The African American New York community pressured the federal government to ensure that the skeletal remains of their African ancestors be appropriately studied and ultimately reinterred.

In 1992, a team of researchers from Howard University's department of sociology and anthropology began studying the skeletal remains found at the African Burial Ground site. The New York African Burial Ground—formerly referred to as the Negroes Burying Ground—was established in 1712 and used until 1794 as the final resting place for "people of African descent, paupers (poor people), and British and American prisoners of war during the American Revolution" (Hansen and McGowan, 2). The enslaved populations interred at the burial site were believed to have originated from West Africa, West-Central Africa, and the Caribbean, exported to the North American mainland through the Atlantic slave trade.

By 1644 when the British acquired New Amsterdam, subsequently renaming the territory New York in reverence of the Duke of York, increasing numbers of enslaved Africans were channeled into the colony to labor for British colonists. As a consequence of the English acquisition of New Amsterdam, black New Yorkers—enslaved and free— were subject to more restrictive laws that suppressed New York Africans' ability to participate in the social and religious institutions that existed in colonial New York. With the strict governance of the social, religious, and political welfare of enslaved New Yorkers came orders that regulated the activities of enslaved blacks during nonlaboring hours. Due to the special edicts designed for persons of African descent residing in New York City during the colonial period, New York Africans were forced to bury their deceased outside of the New York City limits.

With the suppression of the social and human liberties of enslaved Africans in New York City, enslaved blacks fashioned the African Burial Ground as one of the initial social institutions established by enslaved Africans in the colony. The institution of slavery and its practitioners consistently challenged the humanity of the enslaved who were routinely forced to relinquish their identities through arbitrary "renaming" practices, separated from kin—blood born and fictive, prohibited from the exercise of religious expression, and defrauded the ability to communicate through the use of indigenous African languages. The assault on the African identity, culture, physical and social mobility, and overall humanity, coupled with the legal mandates that prohibited enslaved blacks from sharing burial space with whites, made necessary the African Burial Ground among other Negroes Burying Grounds interspersed throughout the African Diaspora.

West African culture remained a consistent influence on enslaved Africans in the Americas during the colonial and postcolonial periods. The effect of West African culture on enslaved blacks in New York was articulated through the retention of various West African traditions and beliefs, especially as it related to funerary customs. The use of burial shrouds, the ritual adornment of bodies and coffins, and even the physical orientation of the bodies demonstrate links to West African spiritual practices alive in colonial

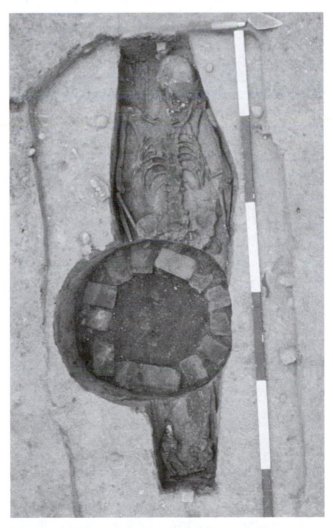

Photograph of Burial 213 at New York's African Burial Ground shows a brick drain constructed during the 19th century extending down through the grave. (National Park Service)

New York City. Researchers involved in the African Burial Ground Project recognized almost immediately the African continuities that existed, reflected in the various ornaments, engravings, jewelry, beads, coins, coffins, and other artifacts uncovered at the site.

The skeletal remains of enslaved Africans discovered at the African Burial Ground site provide important cultural evidences, but also points to the brutality that the enslaved were forced to endure in New York. The skeletal remains of a young adult woman, burial #25, discovered October 16, 1991, signified the frequent inhumane and brutal physical treatment regularly enacted upon the enslaved. The musket ball resting in her rib cage furnished a horrific example of the abuse that many enslaved men, women, and children encountered in New York. The African Burial Ground provides a constant reminder of the strength and resiliency of African peoples during the colonial era, and inspires a greater interest in further exploring the contributions and impact of enslaved populations on American society.

See also: Africanisms; Grave Decorations

Talitha L. LeFlouria

Bibliography

Blakey, Michael L., and Lesley M. Rankin Hill, eds. *The New York African Burial Ground: Skeletal Biology Final Report, Volume I.* Washington, D.C.: The African Burial Ground Project, Howard University, for U.S. General Services Administration, 2004.

Hansen, Joyce, and Gary McGowan. *Breaking Ground, Breaking Silence: The Story of New York's African Burial Ground.* New York: Henry Holt, 1998.

Medford, Edna Greene, ed. *The New York African Burial Ground History Final Report.* Washington, D.C.: The African Burial Ground Project, Howard University, for U.S. General Services Administration, 2004.

Wilder, Craig Steven. *In the Company of Black Men: The African Influence on African American Culture in New York City.* New York: New York University Press, 2001.

African Diaspora

Over the span of nearly four centuries, more than 4 million Africans were taken from their homelands and brought to North America, South America, and the Caribbean Islands. Africans were taken from various regions of Africa, but mostly from coastal areas. The Guinean coast is home to the Bantu and the Mande cultures. By virtue of their geographical placement, many of these populations ended up working on plantations or as domestic servants in the United States.

This phenomenon is typically referred to as the Atlantic slave trade. It also marks the beginning of the African Diaspora in the Americas. These people, who were separated from everything they knew (in terms of family members, linguistic groups, and cultural norms), managed to preserve their traditions in their new and unknown environments. This is how the African Diaspora was formed. Members of the Diaspora kept alive the religions, languages, and stories that served as portals to their existence in Africa. Gradually, many of these African practices would inform the cultural elements (culinary, musical, and otherwise) that comprise Creole and African American cultures.

When discussing the African Diaspora, the term "cultures" must be used in the plural form. Due to the diversity of peoples coming from Africa as well as the regional specificities of the areas in which they ended up in the New World, myriad cultures developed. Each possessed a unique combination of religious, linguistic, and social elements. In addition, each had a different economic and political relationship to slavery as an institution. Slavery practices also influenced where the most members of the African Diaspora were placed. Regions that were known for plantation farming, such as the Deep South, typically had more slave communities than certain Northern states. Therefore, there was greater diversity among the African populations in the South (due to the greater number of imported slave labor) than in the North (where the same or similar cultural populations tended to procreate, thus passing on cultural traditions from one generation to another).

Even though each diasporic culture had its specific norms, one similarity to be found throughout many is the way in which Christianity was used to preserve certain African religions. As counterintuitive as this may sound, members of the Diaspora used Christianity as a disguise for their own beliefs. Throughout the slave trade, many slaves were evangelized and forced to be baptized by their owners. This was done primarily as a means of controlling them. As a result, these baptized members of the Diaspora commingled their African beliefs with the tenets of Christianity and created their own theologies and belief systems. Members of the Diaspora especially identified with the more mystical (or even magical) parts of Christianity. Thus, they found Christianity to be conducive to their African belief systems and practiced a combination of these religions. Claiming to be having "Christian" gatherings (so as not to be punished by their owners for practicing African religions), slaves would engage in these hybrid religious practices as a way of preserving some aspects of their spiritual traditions.

These populations, cultures, and themes are currently studied under the field of Diaspora Studies. This field was created in the late 20th century and addresses a variety of displaced or dispersed ethnic populations as well as the cultures born of these geographical shifts. As myriad Diaspora studies scholars have indicated, the term "Diaspora" has the connotation of forced movement due to exile, national conflict, slavery, or racism. Preeminent scholars of African Diaspora Studies include Paul Gilroy, Kwame Anthony Appiah, Robin D. G. Kelley, Carole Boyce Davies, and Henry Louis Gates.

The African Diaspora in the United States continues to grow and become more diverse thanks to recent histories of immigration to the United States from certain parts of Africa, specifically Congo, Ethiopia, Somalia, Guinea, Rwanda, and Burundi. Thus, the African Diaspora in America is a constantly shifting and growing cultural phenomenon. It changes with each wave of immigrants and set of cultures that enter the country and evolves when these cultures meet and intermingle with the preexisting cultures in a certain geographical area.

See also: Atlantic Slave Trade; Black Atlantic; Pan-Africanism; Trans-Saharan Slave Trade

Jen Westmoreland Bouchard

Bibliography
Davies, Carole Boyce, Ali A. Mazrui, and Isidore Okpewho, eds. *The African Diaspora: African Origins and New World Identities.* Bloomington: Indiana University Press, 2001.
Gilroy, Paul. *The Black Atlantic: Modernity and Double Consciousness.* Cambridge, MA: Harvard University Press, 1993.
Gomez, Michael Angelo. *Reversing Sail: A History of the African Diaspora.* Cambridge, UK: Cambridge University Press, 2005.
Hamilton, Ruth Simms. *Routes of Passage: Rethinking the African Diaspora.* East Lansing: Michigan State University Press, 2007.

Africanisms

For most of the 20th century, historians have explored the continuity of African culture in the United States. Studies such as Melville J. Herskovits's *Myth of the Negro Past* (1941), Lorenzo D. Turner's *Africanisms in the Gullah Dialect* (1949), and Lawrence Levine's *Black Culture and Black Consciousness* (1978) studied the African cultural elements in the music, language, folklore, sculpture, textiles, and religion of African Americans. In their works, the scholars developed many theories that demonstrate substantial retention of African culture in the United States.

According to Christopher L. Miller, the term "Africanism" refers to the study of the retaining African speech patterns, styles, or performance. In a similar tone, V. Y. Mudimbe associates the word "Africanism" with the approach that early scholars such as Maurice Delafosse, Melville J. Herskovits, and Claude Levi-Strauss developed in the 1950s and 1960s in order to analyze African legends, fables, and oral traditions and develop data that could contribute to understandings of people of African descent. Yet the study of Africanisms in the Americas is traceable to the debate on the genesis of African American culture which, according to Lawrence Levine, began in the 1860s when white American folklorists such as Lucy McKim, D. K. Wilgus, and William Francis Allen attempted to study the structure and origin of slave religious music. This work, which was the genesis of the White-to-Black school of acculturation, maintained that religious music among African Americans imitated European compositions with slight variations.

By the 1920s, James Weldon Johnson and Alain LeRoy Locke, two major scholars of the Harlem Renaissance, challenged the White-to-Black thesis. In *The Book of American Negro Spirituals* (1925), Johnson notes that black spirituals were derived solely by people of African descent under the conditions of living in alien environments. Like Johnson, Alain Locke believes that the early African slaves in the United States created the spirituals. Yet Locke views these songs as part of an African American tradition that is also the heritage of all Americans. Locke's theory of the diverse origins of the spirituals is apparent in his 1925 essay "The Negro Spirituals" where he argues that the songs are both African American and American. Unlike most early scholars, Locke stresses the resilience, humanity, and universality of the spirituals.

Despite Locke's thesis that the spirituals are American and universal at the same time, the debate on African retentions has remained centered on whether the elements in African American culture are of European or African origins. In the first half of the 20th century, some black scholars denied outright that any remnant of Africanisms survived in African American culture. In *The Negro Family in the United States* (1968), E. Franklin Frazier contends that African Americans, in the process of adapting to life in the Americas, created cultural modes and forms that had little to do with Africa. Frazier's thesis was inconsistent with the new directions that anthropologists had taken since the 1930s with regard to the question of retention of African culture in the New World.

By the late 1930s, the idea that African elements were not retained in the United States had become scientifically untenable. In *The Myth of the Negro Past,* Melville J. Herskovits championed the cause of African cultural retentions in African American culture. Specifically, he argues not only that African elements might have been retained in African American worldviews, rituals, and folklore but also that such retentions might have influenced Euro-American culture as well.

Like Herskovits, Lorenzo D. Turner argues in *Africanisms in the Gullah Dialect* (1949) that African Americans preserved their African culture and traditions and mixed them with European American patterns to contribute to the formation of the New World cultures. Turner discovered many African elements in the syntax, word formation, and intonation of African Americans. In this book, he found in the United States, especially in the South, words of African origin such as *guba* (peanut) (Kimbudu, Angola), *gombo* (okra) (Tshiluba, Belgian Congo), and *tot* (carry) (Vai, Liberia and Sierra Leone). In *Africanisms in the Gullah Dialect,* Turner also identified hundreds of Gullah names that derive from African words.

In a similar vein, the 1970s saw a new upsurge of works seeking to connect African American culture to Africa. John W. Blassingame's *The Slave Community: Plantation Life in the Antebellum South* (1979) is a major example of this scholarship, since it argued that the antebellum slaves were deeply rooted in their African worldviews and folk rituals of courtship, wedding, drumming, and worshipping. In his comparison of the courtship rituals of the Ewe people of Africa with those of slaves in antebellum America, Blassingame found a similar use of riddles and memorization of poems that black men recited to the women they wanted to court.

By the mid-1970s, great emphasis was placed on the importance of slave folklore. Lawrence Levine's *Black Culture and Black Consciousness* (1977) found that African folk practices such as Voodoo, spiritual cure of sickness, and folktales permeated antebellum slave culture. Following Levine, other scholars stressed the importance of Voodoo and other African folk practices in the Americas. In *Flash of the Spirit: African and Afro-American Art and Philosophy* (1984), Thompson found in the United States, Brazil, and Cuba the influence of Kongo herbalist healing and divination lore in the presence of "conjurors" and "root doctors." Thompson also found the influence of African religion in the presence of charms, ritual dances, and Voodoo crossroad signs in New World black religions.

Known as Voodoo, Hoodoo, and conjure in the United States, Voudoun in Haiti, Shango in Trinidad, Candomblé and Macumba in Brazil, Santeria in Cuba, Cumina or Obeah in Jamaica, Vodun is the West African belief in supernatural phenomena manifested in the acts of healing, divination, the casting of spells, and the use of curative herbs, roots, rituals, amulets, charms, and oral and transcribed incantation. As a religion that permeates the African Diaspora, Voodoo is generally defined as a synthesis of religions of Dahomey, Yorubaland, and Kongo with an infusion of Roman Catholicism. Yet, the sacrificial rituals, conjuring, and magic of the religion can also be traced to coastal West Africa where the beliefs that parallel those of Voodoo had stronger presence in Dahomey, Kongo, and Nigeria than in Senegal, Mali, and Guinea. The West African traditions of Vodoo creolized in Haiti where many African-derived terms are used to describe the ritual.

Like Thompson, William D. Piersen found elements of African religions in black American culture. In *Black Yankees: The Development of an Afro-American Subculture* (1988), Piersen argues that 18th-century African Americans believed, like Africans, that their soul would return home [to Africa] when they died. Piersen tells the story of Jin, a mid-18th-century Congo slave woman in Deerfield, Massachusetts, who collected pierced coins, colored beads, and stones as objects, believing that she would carry them with herself to Africa when she died. In a similar tone, Sterling Stuckey's *Slave Culture: Nationalist Theory and the Foundation of Black America* (1991) identifies many African elements in African American folktales, ring shouts, counterclockwise dances, and ancestral worships. In *Going through the Storm: The Influence of African American Art in History* (1994), Stuckey argues that songs, like folktales, were forms of oral tradition that slaves used to develop a context that placed them closer to Africa than the Western Hemisphere.

The discussion above shows that Africanisms are traceable to slave culture and to the various aspects of New World black cultures such as names, courtship rituals, Voodoo religion, and literature. By revisiting the scholarly debates on the pervasiveness or absence of African elements in the New World, one can gauge the strength of these survivals. Evidently, the cultural and demographic diversity of Africa requires a broader definition of the African influence and a fuller account of how it is perceptible in 20th-century African American culture.

See also: Black Folk Culture; Slave Culture; Slave Religion

Babacar M'Baye

Bibliography

Blassingame, John W. *The Slave Community Plantation Life in the Antebellum South.* New York: Oxford University Press, 1979.

Frazer, E. Franklin. *The Negro Family in the United States.* Chicago and London: University of Chicago Press, 1968.

Herskovits, Melville J. *The Myth of the Negro Past.* New York and London: Harper and Brothers, 1941.

Johnson, James Weldon, and J. Rosamond Johnson. *The Book of American Negro Spirituals.* New York: Viking Press, 1925.

Levine, Lawrence. *Black Culture and Black Consciousness: African-American Folk Thought from Slavery to Freedom.* New York and London: Oxford University Press, 1977.

Mbiti, John S. *African Religions and Philosophy.* New York: Anchor, 1970.

Miller, Christopher C. *Blank Darkness: Africanist Discourse in French.* Chicago: University of Chicago Press, 1985.

Piersen, William D. *Black Yankees: The Development of an Afro-American Subculture in Eighteenth-Century New England.* Amherst: University of Massachusetts Press, 1988.

Stuckey, Sterling. *Going through the Storm: The Influence of African-American Art in History.* New York: Oxford University Press, 1994.

Stuckey, Sterling. *Slave Culture: National Theory and the Foundation of Black America.* New York: Oxford University Press, 1991.

Thompson, Robert Farris. *Flash of the Spirit: African and Afro-American Art and Philosophy.* New York: Vintage, 1984.

Thompson, Robert Farris. *The Four Moments of The Sun: Kongo Arts in Two Worlds.* Washington, D.C.: National Gallery of Arts, 1981.

Turner, Lorenzo D. *Africanisms in the Gullah Dialect.* Chicago: University of Chicago Press, 1949.

Asiento

The asiento was a contract awarded by the Spanish Crown that bestowed rights to import African slaves to Spain's colonies in the New World. In 1494 the Spanish Crown officially renounced claims to Africa by the Treaty of Tordesillas, but the development of plantation agriculture in Spanish America required large-scale importation of African slaves. Subsequently, beginning in the early 1500s, various European merchants and companies began purchasing monopoly privileges to import a certain number of slaves at a fixed price and in a specified time to Spanish America.

The union of the Spanish and Portuguese crowns, from 1580 to 1640, stimulated the more regularized slave import system known as the asiento, whereby an agreement was made between a private contractor and the Spanish government in which the entrepreneur or company purchased a monopoly over the importation of a certain number of slaves, at a set price and in a specified time, to Spanish America. In 1595, the Crown concluded the first asiento with a Spaniard, but the Portuguese quickly dominated the system. The standard of importation was a pieza de Indias, or Indies piece, a young adult male in good physical condition. Women, children, and older males counted as fractions of a pieza de Indias.

The asiento was a prized possession and a major issue in a number of wars. Not only were profits to be made in the slave trade, but the asiento provided cover for importing contraband goods to Spanish America with the cooperation of corrupt Crown officials. Holders of the asiento often resold their licenses to subcontractors. The Dutch dominated the asiento system in the second half of the 17th century. After a French Bourbon assumed the Spanish Crown in 1700, French merchants were awarded the asiento. In 1713, after defeat in the War of the Spanish Succession, Spain awarded the asiento to Britain. The English Crown then designated the South Seas Company to fulfill the contract. By the 1750s, reformist Bourbon officials had started attacking the institution along with other anachronistic government monopoly controls on trade that were often circumvented by colonists. In 1789, the asiento system was abolished as the Spanish Empire was officially opened to all foreign traders.

See also: Atlantic Slave Trade; Dutch West India Company; Hispaniola

David M. Carletta

Bibliography

Palmer, Colin. *Human Cargoes: The British Slave Trade to Spanish America, 1700–1739.* Urbana: University of Illinois Press, 1981.

Rawley, James A. *The Transatlantic Slave Trade: A History.* New York: W. W. Norton, 1981.

Atlantic Creoles

The term "Atlantic Creoles" generally refers to people born in regions of the Atlantic World (the four continents that surround the Atlantic Ocean) whose origins lie outside the areas in which they were born. The term "Creole" may also be associated with a specific language and/or culture. Atlantic Creoles developed various Creole languages, which draw on the vocabulary of modern European languages, but with a grammatical structure atypical of those languages. For example, a Portuguese Creole language developed among the settlers of the Atlantic islands such as Cape Verde and São Tomé, off the West African coast, as early as the 16th century. The growth and development of American Creole languages relied heavily on Creole-speaking slaves who could teach other slaves. Africans probably never spoke the Creoles as native languages, but soon Americans, the children of the first generation of slaves, did. As Africans from different regions interacted with each other and Europeans, their New World language gradually emerged as the first, or "creolized" language of American-born blacks.

The term "Creole" takes on various meanings across time and regions of the Atlantic World. In Sierra Leone, Creoles are the descendants of slaves who were repatriated between 1787 and 1870, from all over the West African coast, and settled with help from philanthropists, missionaries, and the British government. Cut off from their own traditions, the Creoles acquired the cultural ideals of the British and, aided by missions, gained substantial educational and professional advantages over the peoples of the interior and indeed over most West Africans. In the 19th century, they became clerks, parsons, teachers, lawyers, and doctors and played an important role in the administrative and educational development of the whole of English-speaking West Africa. The Creoles' consciousness of their own superiority and disrespect for the indigenous peoples' cultures, however, created hostility and deep mistrust between the Creoles and other Sierra Leoneans. These Creoles were the elite of African society in Sierra Leone.

In 16th-century-colonial Latin America, Creoles were individuals of pure Spanish or Portuguese descent born in America. The social hierarchy in the early Spanish empire distinguished between Creoles and a higher status group called *Peninsulares*. Both the Creoles and the *Peninsulares* were considered pure Spanish, with one differentiation—the

Peninsulares were born on the Iberian Peninsula. Today in Brazil the term "Creole" refers to blacks. In Nicaragua, Creoles are native-born blacks and inhabit the east coast of the country along with Indian and Hispanic groups. The Nicaraguan Creoles originated as shipwrecked or escaped slaves, or slave laborers used by the British in the 17th century to work in the lumber camps and plantations. Some of them feel a stronger alliance to the British than to fellow Nicaraguans on the west coast, who tend to regard them as foreigners. The Nicaraguan Creoles speak English. In the Latin American country of Belize, the identity of Creoles takes on a racial meaning with a negative attitude among light-skinned Creoles toward blacks. Both groups, however, are considered "Creole."

In North America, when Africans first arrived in the Chesapeake during the early 17th century, they interacted culturally and physically with white indentured servants and American Indians. Interracial sexual contacts (miscegenation) produced people of mixed race. In New Orleans, Louisiana, "Creoles" were people of any race or mixture, descended from settlers in Louisiana before it became part of the United States in 1803 after the Louisiana Purchase. The term also refers to a broader culture. Although people with African lineage may not have been included in this definition, a broader use of the term was common by the late 18th century with references to "free Creoles of color" and to slaves of pure African descent born in Louisiana as "Creole slaves." Contemporary usage of the term in New Orleans encompasses a broad cultural group of people of all races who share a French or Spanish background.

Creoles in the 18th-century British Empire (those born and reared within colonial society) were distinguished from newly arrived Africans. The continuing large-scale importation of Africans created a constant dynamic within slave communities everywhere—a dynamic that changed as the population balance shifted from African to Creole predominance. A growing number of mulattos—offspring of sexual unions between white and black parents—produced further complications. Where Africans formed the majority population, as they did in the Caribbean for much of the 18th century and in the Carolina Lowcountry for many years, Creoles often experienced ridicule and exclusion from community life. As Creoles became the majority, they often looked down on the Africans. By 1740, most colonial slaves were no longer considered Africans. They had become Creoles, also the contemporary term for American-born blacks.

By 1750, the number of African slaves comprised about 40 percent of Virginia and Maryland's total population, and four-fifths of them were Creoles. Eventually, strong bonds developed between new arrivals and Creole slaves.

One Creole population that absorbed European values lived among whites in Charleston and Savannah. These Creoles were often mixed-race relatives of their masters and enjoyed social and economic privileges. Cultural exchanges became an essential part of the process of creolization that led African parents to produce African American children. Miscegenation and creolization often occurred together, producing physical and cultural change. At the same time, in British colonial North America, mixed-race people were defined as black. Although biracial slaves—those of mixed African and European ancestry—enjoyed some advantages, as a group their legal status remained as slaves. Creolization and miscegenation transformed the descendants of the Africans who arrived in North America into African Americans.

In the Caribbean region the term "Creole" refers to anyone, regardless of race or ethnicity, who was born and raised in the region. It also reflects the blending of the various cultures (African, French, British, and Spanish among others) that influenced the area. This is also referred to as the creolization of a society. On Jamaica and other Caribbean islands, planters divided slaves into three categories: Creoles (slaves born in the Americas), old Africans (those who had lived in the Americas for some time), and new Africans (those who had just survived the middle passage). For resale, Creole slaves were worth three times the value of those considered to be "unseasoned" new Africans. These new Africans were called "salt-water Negroes" or "Guinea-birds" by planters and Creole slaves. Seasoning was the beginning of the process of making new Africans more like Creoles.

See also: Acculturation; Black Atlantic

Maryalice Guilford

Bibliography

Adams, Francis D., and Barry Sanders. *Alienable Rights: The Exclusion of African Americans in a White Man's Land, 1619–2000.* New York: HarperCollins, 2003.

Andrien, Kenneth J., ed. *The Human Tradition in Colonial Latin America.* Wilmington, DE: Scholarly Resources, 2002.

Bohannan, Paul, and Philip Curtin. *Africa and Africans.* New York: The Natural History Press, 1971.

Breen, T. H., and Timothy Hall. *Colonial America in an Atlantic World.* New York: Longman, 2004.

Goodwin Jr., Paul B. *Global Studies: Latin America.* Guilford, CT: McGraw-Hill, 1998.

Harris, Joseph E. *Africans and Their History.* New York: Penguin, 1987.

Harvey, Robert. *Liberators: Latin America's Struggle for Independence.* Woodstock, NY: Overlook Press, 2000.

Haynes, Keen. *A History of Latin America.* Boston: Houghton Mifflin, 2000.

Hine, Darlene Clark, et al. *The African-American Odyssey.* Upper Saddle River, NJ: Prentice Hall, 2005.

Olaniyan, Richard, ed. *African History and Culture.* Essex, UK: Longman, 1982.

Thornton, John. *Africa and Africans in the Making of the Atlantic World, 1400–1680.* New York: Cambridge University Press, 1992.

Trotter Jr., Joe William. *The African American Experience.* Boston: Houghton Mifflin, 2001.

Atlantic Islands

European expansion, African plantation slavery, and the development of the Atlantic World began in the Atlantic islands off the coast of northwest Africa: the Canary Islands, Madeira, the Azores, Cape Verde, and São Tomé. In the 14th century, West African watercraft was specialized for coastal, riverine, and interior travel along the Gambia, Senegal, and Niger rivers, which connected with overland routes across the Sahara. With exceptions, West Africans did not pursue seafaring in the open Atlantic nor did they settle several of the islands along the Atlantic coast. The navigational difficulties presented by the eastern Atlantic's Canary Current prevented Mediterranean and Arabic sailors from successfully navigating the Atlantic coast of Africa as well. Grain trade connecting Europe's large inland seas—the Mediterranean, Baltic, and North seas—stimulated innovation in Iberian shipbuilding as well as accidental voyages of discovery. Ultimately, the prospect of a sea route to West Africa's goldfields prompted a collaboration of Iberian, Italian, French, and English people, vessels, and capital in the pursuit of short-range maritime exploration along the West African coast.

The rediscovery of the Canary Islands by Malocello in 1312 signaled the start of European exploitation of the Atlantic islands as sources of profit and expansion. The Canaries were filled with natural products for commodification: timber, honey, hides, and dyestuffs. The Canaries were inhabited, and the Portuguese and Spanish raided the islands for cattle and people whom they sold as slaves in

Mediterranean markets. Iberian endeavors to build trading factories and slave-raiding forts in the Canary Islands made them the first site of European trading and raiding in the Atlantic. In 1402 Castile sponsored the first permanent colonization of the Canaries with Norman colonists. In the following century the Canary Islands produced sugar, wine, and sheep and cattle products. Because the Canary Islands were a source of profit for Europeans, much attention was devoted to their navigation, shipping south of the Straights of Gibraltar increased, and raiding and commercial activity expanded farther south. The Canaries served as a crucial base for the development of additional European raiding and trading operations along the African coast as well as for the colonization of uninhabited Atlantic islands to the west.

In the 15th century, Portuguese colonized the uninhabited islands of Madeira, the Azores, Cape Verde, and São Tomé and exported their wild products: honey, wax, and wood. Madeira and the Canaries soon began to export large quantities of wheat, cultivated by Canarians pressed into service, as well as dependent laborers from Europe, to consumers in Portugal, North Africa, and West Africa. Madeira also produced and profitably exported wine; however, the cultivation of sugar, particularly in Madeira and, later, São Tomé, had the largest economic impact for the Atlantic islands, and, ultimately, the Atlantic World. Preceding production in the New World, Portuguese and northern Italians developed a sugar plantation complex in the Atlantic islands where a nonreproducing slave labor force produced massive quantities of sugar for export.

The cultivation of sugarcane had originated in Southwest Asia during the ancient period and gradually spread westward to Persia. In the 12th and 13th centuries, Arabs brought sugar cultivation to the Mediterranean where the first plantation system emerged. Mediterranean shippers imported bond laborers from southern Russia (Slavs from whom the word *slave* derives), the eastern Mediterranean, and North Africa to produce sugar for a European market. By the 14th century, Cyprus produced large quantities of sugar with the labor of Syrian and Arab slaves, and the plantation system, based on coerced labor, large land units, and long-range commerce, moved still west, to Sicily. The Sicilian sugar plantation served as a model for the Portuguese and Spanish colonies in the Atlantic islands where climate and soil were favorable and nearby African sources provided coerced workers. In 1420 Portugal's Prince Henry

sent to Sicily for cane plantings and sugar technicians. The desire for cane field labor fundamentally altered the nature of Portuguese slavery from domestic servitude to plantation labor. In the 15th and 16th centuries almost all of the Atlantic islands experienced sugar booms. By the 1460s, Madeira was the largest producer of sugar in the Western world.

The Atlantic islands provided a model and a launching ground for New World sugar cultivation based on African slavery and the plantation system; their successful exploitation prompted European explorers to seek additional islands further west in the Atlantic Ocean. The prospect of finding new Atlantic islands and the aspiration of reaching India inspired Christopher Columbus's voyage of 1492. Trained in the Madeira sugar trade as a young man, Columbus brought his experience to the New World on his second voyage of 1493 when he introduced sugar cane plantings to the Caribbean. In the following century, the immense profits of sugar plantation in the Americas prompted the expansion of the Atlantic slave trade. The Atlantic islands not only established the pattern of European colonization and plantation for the New World, but also served as crucial way stations for Atlantic slavers.

See also: Atlantic Slave Trade; Sugar Plantations

Christina Proenza-Coles

Bibliography

Curtin, Philip D. *The Rise and Fall of the Plantation Complex: Essays in Atlantic History.* New York: Cambridge University Press, 1989.

Eltis, David. *The Rise of African Slavery in the Americas.* New York: Cambridge University Press, 2000.

Mintz, Sidney. *Sweetness and Power: The Place of Sugar in Modern History.* New York: Penguin Books, 1986.

Thornton, John. *Africa and Africans in the Making of the Atlantic World, 1400–1800.* New York: Cambridge University Press, 1998.

Wright, Donald. *African Americans in the Colonial Era.* Arlington Heights, IL: Harlan Davidson, 1990.

Atlantic Slave Trade

In the 15th century, Europeans—beginning with the Portuguese—engaged in trade relations with Africans along the Atlantic coast which, over time, would lead to the one of the most tragic chapters in human history. In search of commercial opportunities and allies against the Islamic conquest of

Iberia, Portuguese navigators encountered a series of kingdoms and smaller polities in West and West-Central Africa. This contact with Atlantic Africans, beginning in the period after 1444, culminated in the erection of Elmina Castle by the Portuguese on the aptly named Gold Coast. Given the names the Portuguese chose for their castle and for the region they established it in, it should be no surprise that gold and gold-mining became the central elements of commercial activity for the first century after contact. Even before this historical moment, a number of economic and political forces converged to explain the eventual rise of the Atlantic slave trade. First, the Portuguese and the Spanish colonized a number of Atlantic islands, beginning in the 14th century. Second, sugar and sugar-cultivation techniques were rapidly spreading eastward from West Asia and Arabia. Third, since at least the 12th century CE, the trade in enslaved West African women to serve primarily as domestic servants in North Africa and Arabia produced a lucrative stream of commerce. It was this convergence of Iberian colonization from the north, Asian sugar from the east, and African slavery from the south that allowed for the enormous trade in enslaved Africans and their transportation across the Atlantic for more than three centuries.

It is important to note, however, that though slavery existed in Africa before European contact, it could often be quite different from chattel bondage in the Americas. While it is always difficult to evaluate whether a system of slavery was "benign" or "mild," quite a few qualitative differences are evident: slaves in Atlantic Africa were often manumitted; slavery did not transcend generation, it was not an inheritable status and, thus, race or nativity were never employed as signifiers of caste; slaves could, at times, achieve high social rank, status, and wealth; and the relationships between slaves and their African owners were not always mediated by the use or threat of force. With this said, it is also quite true that a continuum of slave experiences existed in Atlantic Africa from brutal chattel slavery to relatively milder forms of clientage and debt servitude. Perhaps the most important difference between African and European/American variants of slavery was that women were the most significant group of enslaved Africans in Atlantic Africa and, in the Atlantic slave trade, men were strongly preferred by European slave buyers.

Qualitative differences between African and European/American variants of slavery were given voice in a number of ex-slave narratives. Perhaps the most written about and

analyzed ex-slave memoir is Olaudah Equiano's *Interesting Narrative*. In many ways, his life opens an instructive window into the internal workings of the slave trade as well as the critiques and fears of European traders as voiced by enslaved Africans. Despite recent commentary to the contrary, Equiano's account includes verifiable information and perhaps epitomizes an "authentic" Igbo account of enslavement and the Middle Passage. Kidnapped in 1756 from the Igbo village of Essaka—a minor eastern tributary of the Kingdom of Benin—Equiano was held as a slave by various African merchants for six months before finally arriving at the coast of Calabar. He apparently embarked on a ship in the Bight of Biafra with other Igbo-speakers, for it was among some of his own language cohort that young Equiano found some degree of comfort.

The brutality of the European crew and the intolerable conditions on this ship confirmed Equiano's belief that he had indeed been handed over to evil spirits and demons who intended to eat his flesh. This apparently was a ubiquitous belief among captives from the Bight of Biafra who witnessed the various horrors and inhumane abuses made famous by the European traffickers of enslaved Africans. It was in this horrid context that two of his countrymen committed suicide by jumping into the ocean. Equiano himself noted an intense interest in following the path of his comrades. At least according to this particular account, the alleged Igbo propensity for suicide was directly related to the savage treatment they received at the hands of European shippers. In this particular regard, then, enslaved Africans voiced their collective opposition to abuse at the hands of Europeans through the most drastic means. This perhaps solidifies the point that Africans perceived qualitative differences in their status as slaves once they were handed over to Europeans.

Slavery, in its variety of forms, was widespread in Atlantic Africa primarily because enslaved Africans were the principal form of private, income-producing property throughout the region. In an area with an overabundance of land, gaining access to—and control over—additional labor became a primary motivator for Atlantic African kingdoms and city-states. In this regard, the concept of private land ownership never fully developed in Atlantic Africa and, when kingdoms or city-states expanded militarily, the goal was typically to gain control over more people by capturing smaller polities or villages and forcing them to pay tribute. In sum, the Atlantic African ruling classes keenly understood the labor theory of value, which contends that human effort is the principal means to derive value or revenue from natural resources and raw goods Indeed, in a sense, owning land amounts to owning dirt and land only really becomes valuable when human labor is applied to it. So the principal thrust of military conquest in Atlantic Africa focused on acquiring additional tributaries and labor, not territory.

Slavery, pawnship, clientage, indentured and debt servitude, and other forms of forced labor were means to guarantee agricultural surplus and steady flows of revenues for powerful states in Atlantic Africa. This private ownership or control over labor does not mean that forced labor was central to Atlantic African economies. It does mean that the idea of humans becoming commodities predated the arrival of Europeans in Atlantic Africa and set the stage for the Atlantic slave trade.

The preexistence of slavery and other forms of forced labor was augmented by a long-standing trans-Saharan slave trade, which was the first step in the formation of an Atlantic African Diaspora. The trans-Saharan slave trade, beginning sometime near the 12th century, was used by the Portuguese after 1448, decades before they established castles and fortresses along the Atlantic African coast. With European interests in acquiring slaves increasing exponentially after the establishment of colonies in the Atlantic islands and the Western Hemisphere, the former trans-Saharan slave trade shifted from North Africa to the Atlantic coast by the late 1490s to early 1500s. Thus, the indigenous African forms of slavery and slave trading facilitated the role that Europeans would begin to play in Atlantic World affairs.

In addition to the existence of indigenous forms of slavery and slave trading in Africa, several key factors contributed to the decisions made by Europeans to rely so heavily on enslaved African labor in the Western Hemisphere. Due to their exposure to a tropical disease ecology, Atlantic Africans had developed natural resistances to malaria—a disease that wiped out large numbers of Native Americans and Europeans. Thus, the rice swamps of the Carolinas or the tobacco fields of the Chesapeake were not as deadly for enslaved Africans, making them an ideal labor pool. Another important determinant was the fact that the vast majority of enslaved Africans came from agricultural surplus-producing societies. This meant that Atlantic Africa was densely populated and thus a prime location to use as a foundation for a substantial labor force. It also meant that, unlike the subsistence to small surplus-producing Native Americans encountered in the Caribbean, coastal Brazil, or North America, enslaved Africans were more likely to be used to the intensive labor required for cash crop cultivation. This was especially true in the case of rice cultivation in the Carolinas and Georgia. In both colonies, enslaved Africans from Sierra Leone and Senegambia had a particularly useful expertise in rice cultivation, which generated enormous profits in the Southern colonies. In this regard, both African brawn and brains made them an attractive group of dependent laborers for European plantations throughout the Americas.

Finally, because men and women tended crops in Atlantic Africa, both groups could be enslaved by Europeans, ensuring a self-reproducing labor force. This circumstance proved advantageous to European planters on a number of different levels. First, early attempts to enslave Algonkians in the Chesapeake had utterly failed, mainly because of the unique gender division of labor among this native

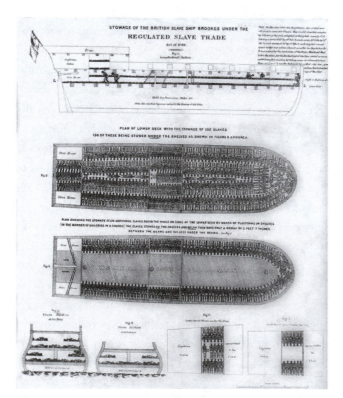

This plan of a British slave ship, included with the Regulated Slave Trade Act of 1788, depicts, in horrifying detail, the inhumane conditions used by the slavers. The plan notes the ability to transport over 400 slaves on the lower deck, with many of the human cargo cramped into spaces underneath closely packed shelves. (Library of Congress)

group. In most Algonkian societies, women tended crops and men hunted. Thus, when British colonists attempted to enslave the men for tobacco cultivation, this enterprise was doomed to failure. While all European powers tended to concentrate on importing enslaved African men, even if they managed to bring over large numbers of enslaved women, both groups were fully equipped and socialized to engage in agricultural labor. Second, by importing men and women together, the natural outcome would be enslaved children and a new generation of labor. This was deemed advantageous over using white indentured servants, in the Chesapeake especially. Not only did the service of indentured workers terminate after a set number of years, but their children were always legally free and owed no labor obligation to their parents' master. By enslaving the womb of African women, planters throughout the Americas could guarantee a steady supply of labor that transcended generations.

When the Portuguese first arrived on the Atlantic coast of Africa in the 15th century, they witnessed commerce on a scale Europeans had not seen since Roman times. West Africa, far from being the backwater many scholars have envisioned it as, was one of the key centers of trade in the early modern world. Linked to East and North Africa via the trans-Saharan trade and, as a result, indirectly connected to Arabia, India, and Indonesia, goods were flowing into Atlantic Africa that originated thousands of miles away. Ultimately, the Portuguese search for the mythical Prester John—combined with their commercial interests—led to the establishment of trading posts, factories, and fortresses along the West and East African coasts beginning in the early to mid-16th century. By effectively replacing East African Swahili merchants in the Indian Ocean trade network, the Portuguese positioned themselves as a global power with economic interests in Africa, Arabia, India, and Indonesia.

In the birth of the Atlantic World, one of the most important events that led to the Atlantic slave trade was the colonization of the numerous inhabited and uninhabited Atlantic islands by Iberians. By the 1450s, the Portuguese had colonized the previously uninhabited Azores, Madeira, the Cape Verde Islands, and São Tomé and, within a few decades, had transformed each territory into a profitable sugar plantation colony. This pattern was repeated by the Spanish in the Canary Islands with one slight difference—the Canaries were already inhabited by the Guanches. This group,

of likely Native American origin, became a slave labor force throughout the Atlantic islands, and both Spain and Portugal quickly became experts in acquiring additional dependent labor. By the early 1500s, all of the Atlantic islands were using a mixture of Guanche, Moor, and Atlantic African slave labor, establishing a pattern that would be replicated on a much a larger scale in the Americas.

Beginning with Christopher Columbus's 1492 expedition through to the establishment of Hispaniola and Brazil as sites of Iberian colonization in the Americas, the patterns that began in the Atlantic islands became a foundation for a variety of activities engaged in by the Spanish and Portuguese. The depopulation of the Taino in the Spanish Caribbean and the Tupi-Guarani in Portuguese Brazil created a massive demand for labor in these burgeoning sugar plantation colonies. The solution to this demand for labor was offered first by Bartolomé de Las Casas, a Spanish friar who supported the mass importation of African slaves as a means of protecting Native Americans living in the Caribbean and elsewhere. The flood gates were opened soon after, beginning with the massive importation of enslaved Africans into Portuguese Brazil. In the early 1570s, Portugal conquered Angola and established peaceful commercial relations with the nearby Kongo Kingdom. West-Central Africa therefore would be an early source of labor for the Portuguese colony of Brazil and the rest of the Americas, accounting for about 45 percent of all enslaved Africans brought to the Western Hemisphere between 1519 and 1867.

Entering the fray by the late 1580s were the English, who began to establish a series of settlements in North America. The first permanent English colony, Jamestown, was founded in 1607. Though they struggled mightily for the first four years, by 1611 the colonists of Jamestown had discovered a means to create enormous profits—tobacco cultivation. After a brief and failed experiment with Native American slavery, the tobacco planters of the region began to rely heavily on white indentured servants. This solution was only a stop-gap and became completely unfeasible after 1640. Indentured servants, including the 300 Africans imported into the Chesapeake between 1619 and 1640, represented a significant set of problems to tobacco planters: they only worked a set number of years before they were freed; once freed, they received "freedom dues" including seed, land, farming tools, and guns; as land-owning tobacco farmers, ex-servants represented a source of competition for the tobacco-planting elite; and the increased production of tobacco caused by the ever-increasing number of tobacco planters drove down the price of the once lucrative crop.

The problems inherent in the indentured servant system were magnified in the 1640s when, for no clear reason, a higher percentage of white servants survived their terms of indenture to accept their freedom dues. This required immediate reaction by the Tidewater elite who moved to eliminate land as a portion of the freedom dues, purchased most of the arable land, and extended the term of indenture with the hope that more servants would die before becoming free. While they successfully stunted the creation of more competition, the Tidewater planting elite also managed to destroy their most reliable source of labor. While the notion of land ownership had appealed to the English poor, compelling many thousands to come to the Chesapeake to labor in the tobacco fields, this incentive was gone and other North American colonies offered better economic opportunities and higher living standards. Beginning in 1640, a slow but decided shift toward racialized slavery occurred in the Chesapeake colonies, which culminated in the legalization of slavery by the late 1660s and the increasing importation of enslaved Africans. The intense rivalry between several European powers—Spain, Portugal, the Netherlands, France, and England—convulsed both sides of the Atlantic in a series of imperial conflicts. A number of colonies changed hands in the Americas and a number of trading posts and fortresses were captured and recaptured by a long line of European interests. Between the 1590s and the 1670s, Portugal was integrated into the Spanish Crown; northern European pirates were attacking Iberian possessions throughout the Atlantic; the Dutch waged long-standing wars against the Spanish, the Portuguese, and the English; the French gained a sizable foothold in the Americas with their colonization of the western half of Santo Domingo; and the English founded several North American and Caribbean colonies in direct opposition to Spanish territorial claims. In the decade between 1637 and 1647 alone, the Dutch West India Company claimed the Portuguese possessions of Elmina, Príncipe, Angola, and São Tomé through military conquest. Even though the Dutch could manage to control Angola only from 1641 to 1648, they had effectively replaced the Portuguese as the dominant European power in Africa by the mid-1640s. This complex web of interconnections within the Atlantic World, fostered by trade, international rivalry, and war,

became an essential component in the development of a number of Euro-American societies.

While European nations were vying for power in the Atlantic, a number of expansionist kingdoms emerged in Atlantic Africa during the 15th and 16th centuries, which played fundamental roles in the slave trade. While the "intertribal" warfare model was once the dominant theory in explaining the rapid expansion of slave-trading activities in Atlantic Africa, there was perhaps more conflict between European powers than between African kingdoms and city-states. Nevertheless, the very nature of military expansion and the tributary system in Atlantic Africa meant the creation of a large number of slaves for purchase by European buyers. Principally, the kingdoms of Asante, Dahomey, Benin, Kongo, and Futa Jallon—among many others—expanded significantly, creating political and social ripples that displaced hundreds of thousands of people. At the same time, European traders were importing guns and horses, which further contributed to military expansion and displacement.

At least during the early years of this trade relationship between European merchants and African traders, there existed a partnership based on equality and balance. European slave raiding undoubtedly occurred, but it was not the primary way by which enslaved Africans were acquired. Instead, Europeans typically followed African protocol and obeyed African laws, paid rent for their use of coastal slave fortresses, and even paid tribute to coastal kingdoms. In certain cases, European merchants had their goods confiscated and lost trade privileges if they violated protocols established by coastal polities. In other cases, Europeans lost their lives in retaliation for raiding for African slaves. In this regard, one of the many locations of power of the slave trade resided in Atlantic Africa among African kingdoms. Thus, they played a much larger role in the creation of the Atlantic World and the formation of the Atlantic slave trade than previously understood.

One pattern that shaped African-European relations was the significant amount of resistance to the continuation of the slave trade mounted by certain Atlantic African polities and even enslaved Africans themselves. This is one level of agency that is often understated or ignored by scholars of the Atlantic slave trade. Resistance to the slave trade occurred on a number of different levels: the 400 or more instances of shipboard revolts; the thousands of suicides during the Middle Passage; the formation of escaped slave communities in Atlantic Africa; the numerous mass revolts organized by slaves or peasants; the involvement of a handful of religious opposition movements, inspired by Islam, Christianity, or African religion; and active attempts by states or their leaders to suppress the trade. Indeed, it may even be possible to discuss the African roots of abolitionism given the fact that, as early as 1614, an Islamic scholar named Ahmad Baba al-Timbucti wrote a detailed legal treatise that critiqued and undermined the various justifications for enslavement.

In terms of the demography of the slave trade the Du Bois Institute CD-ROM compiled by David Eltis, Stephen Behrendt, David Richardson, and Herbert Klein, which provides the best and most reliable set of estimates, shows that some 11 to 12 million were exported from Africa, about 10 million were imported alive into the Americas, and roughly 1.5 million died on ships during the Middle Passage. While the estimates regarding the mortality rates onboard slave ships have raised a great deal of commentary, students of this topic should be cognizant of the fact that the 1.5 million estimate does not include the untold millions who died in forced marches from inland markets to coastal markets, those who perished in the squalid conditions of slave dungeons, and those who did not survive seasoning in the Americas or who died within their first three to five years as slaves. While reliable estimates for mortality rates will never be fully achieved, some 14 to 26 million Africans died during the slave trade, and the millions of survivors—on both sides of the Atlantic—bore the psychological scars of their collective trauma for centuries thereafter.

See also: African Diaspora; Asiento; Equiano, Olaudah; Cugoano, Quobna Ottobah

Walter C. Rucker

Bibliography

Austen, Ralph. "The Slave Trade as History and Memory: Confrontations of Slaving Voyage Documents and Communal Traditions." *William and Mary Quarterly*, 3rd ser. 58 (2001):229–51.

Curtin, Philip. *The Atlantic Slave Trade: A Census.* Madison: University of Wisconsin Press, 1969.

Davidson, Basil. *The African Slave Trade: Precolonial History, 1450–1850.* Boston: Little, Brown, 1961.

Davies, K. G. *The Royal African Company.* London: Longmans Green, 1970.

Eltis, David. *The Rise of African Slavery in the Americas.* Cambridge, UK: Cambridge University Press, 2000.

Eltis, David, Stephen Behrendt, David Richardson, and Herbert Klein, eds. *The Trans-Atlantic Slave Trade: A Database on CD-ROM.* Cambridge, UK: Cambridge University Press, 1999.

Handler, Jerome S. "Survivors of the Middle Passage: Life Histories of Enslaved Africans in British America." *Slavery and Abolition* 23 (2002):25–56.

Inikori, Joseph, and Stanley Engerman, eds. *Forced Migration: The Impact of the Export Slave Trade on African Societies.* London: Hutchinson, 1981.

Miller, Joseph C. *Way of Death: Merchant Capitalism and the Angolan Slave Trade, 1730–1830.* Madison: University of Wisconsin Press, 1988.

Taylor, Eric Robert. *If We Must Die: Shipboard Insurrections in the Era of the Atlantic Slave Trade.* Baton Rouge: Louisiana State University Press, 2006.

Thornton, John. *Africa and Africans in the Making of the Atlantic World, 1400–1800.* New York: Cambridge University Press, 1998.

Bacon's Rebellion

Bacon's Rebellion was the first rebellion in the American colonies. In 1676 Nathaniel Bacon, a Virginia planter, led a rebellion against the government of Sir William Berkeley. Bacon's Rebellion was one of the first collaborations between whites and blacks in colonial America. The white and black settlers of Virginia united against their common enemy—the Virginia ruling class. This partnership escalated fears within the ruling class as to what would protect them and their power from the united poor masses. It was out of this fear that the institution of racial slavery was born. While slavery and indentured servitude had been present in the colonies prior to Bacon's Rebellion, the rebellion turned slavery into a predominantly racial institution. The large majority of slaves from the rebellion onward would be solely of African descent.

Bacon lived on the frontier. He, like many of his fellow frontier planters, felt that Governor Berkeley was not adequately protecting the planters from the Native Americans. Consequently, Bacon and his fellow frontier planters united to defend themselves against the Native Americans. Bacon petitioned Berkeley for a commission to allow himself and his followers to move forcefully against the Native Americans. Berkeley, as the head of the government, and thus the head of the militia, refused Bacon's request. Berkeley felt Bacon was not trying to defend himself against the Native Americans, but rather was trying to stir up trouble among the settlers who were already unhappy with the colony's government. The Virginia settlers were becoming increasingly dissatisfied with both Berkeley and his government. High taxes and special privileges awarded to those close to the governor were two of the settlers' biggest complaints. Bacon, therefore, received a lot of support from the Virginia masses.

Despite Berkeley's refusal, the planters regarded the Native Americans as a larger threat than the Governor. Consequently they moved on the offensive and attacked the nearby Native Americans. When Berkeley heard of the planters' actions he declared Bacon guilty of treason. The colonial legislature then met in June to resolve the issue. The legislature granted Bacon a commission to fight the Native Americans and also implemented laws to lower taxes and reform the abuses of power within the government. Despite the legislature's ruling, Berkeley refused Bacon the commission. Bacon, along with more than 500 supporters, then marched into Jamestown.

The conflict between Berkeley and Bacon had escalated. Both men strove to garner all the support they could. Bacon even promised to give land to any servant who rose up against his master. Many of the Virginia settlers had long been unhappy with the government of Berkeley, and therefore allied themselves with Bacon. In September 1676 the Governor and his supporters were driven out of Jamestown to a refuge on the eastern shore. To discourage their return, Bacon and his followers burned down the town of Jamestown. A month later, Bacon unexpectedly died. Without its charismatic leader, Bacon's Rebellion quickly fizzled out. Berkeley and his followers returned to the colony and reasserted their authority. Berkeley hanged more than 20 of the rebellion leaders and let his men loose to plunder Bacon's supporters.

While Indian policy seemed to have been the deciding factor that brought on rebellion, there were many other issues involved. High taxes, low prices for tobacco, and indentured servitude were all protested by the settlers. In 1676, when Bacon and his followers began the rebellion, many of the Virginia settlers—white and black—united to use the rebellion as a means to protest Berkeley and his government. The end result was twofold. First, the rebellion brought both white and black settlers together to fight for one cause. Second, the rebellion demanded and successfully brought reform to the colony of Virginia. Many of the reforms that the Virginia settlers sought were conceded by the Virginia government. In London, the Crown authorities saw Bacon's Rebellion as the result of bad government

in the colonies. King Charles II's primary concern was the cultivation of tobacco. Rebellions, in his opinion, took the colonists' attention away from cultivation. Consequently, after Bacon's Rebellion, King Charles II dispatched an army to restore order in Virginia. King Charles also demanded the removal of Governor Berkeley. The king believed that if Berkeley was not liked by the settlers more rebellions would be imminent. More rebellions would take more attention away from the cultivation of tobacco and thus reduce the profits of the Crown. In 1677 Berkeley was ordered back to England, where he died within the year.

See also: Chesapeake Colonies; Indentured Servitude; Racialized Slavery

Mindy R. Weidman

Bibliography

Steele, Ian K. *Warpaths: Invasions of North America.* New York: Oxford University Press, 1994.

Washburn, Wilcomb E. *The Governor and the Rebel: A History of Bacon's Rebellion in Virginia.* Chapel Hill: University of North Carolina Press, 1967.

Wiseman, Samuel, and Michael Leroy Oberg, eds. *Samuel Wiseman's Book of Record: The Official Account of Bacon's Rebellion in Virginia.* Lanham, MD: Lexington Books, 2005.

Barracoons

Surfacing in the late 15th century with the emergence of the Atlantic slave trade, barracoons are identified as small pens or shelters that held captured Africans, as slaves for sale, prior to their departure for the New World. Located along the coast of Africa, barracoons ranged in size and form; they varied from small, makeshift confinements without protection from natural elements to larger, more developed and protected structures. In any case, regardless of the simplicity or sophistication of the structure, a captive's stay at a barracoon was not pleasant. Rather, it was marked by sickness, hunger, disease, and death; in fact, countless men, women, and children died while awaiting embarkation.

Upon arriving at a barracoon, the men were separated from the women, at which time their heads were shaved, and bodies stripped of any and all clothing. Furthermore, the imprisoned individuals were inspected by European doctors to determine their health. The purpose of these inspections was to identify and separate able-bodied individuals

Slave barracoon in the Gallinas, on the coast of Africa, about 1850. (Rischgitz/Getty Images)

from the poor and sickly, and to ensure that the strong and healthy would survive the transatlantic voyage. Although men and women were separated and apprehended in different confinements, captured individuals were not separated according to ethnic origins or their place of extraction. All were treated with the same harshness, regardless of their place of origin, sex, or age.

Confinement in a barracoon would last anywhere from a couple of weeks to months. Time spent in a barracoon was contingent on two factors: the slaver's ability to accommodate additional and preferred slaves on their ships, and the health of the enslaved—whether or not it was believed that he or shoe would have survived the Middle Passage.

Barracoons also marked sites where captured Africans were introduced to Christianity. Oftentimes, upon boarding the ships that would transport slaves to the New World, slaves were baptized and branded with a cross or the trading company's coat of arms. The baptismal, from the point of view of the European slaver, represented a religious conversion where the slave was expected to discard African religions. In addition, the branding signified a change in the captured status from an individual to a commodity, or property.

See also: Atlantic Slave Trade

Ashley C. Bowden

Bibliography

Gomez, Michael A. *Exchanging Our Country Marks: The Transformation of African Identities in the Colonial and Antebellum South.* Chapel Hill: University of North Carolina Press, 1998.

Lovejoy, Paul E. *Transformations in Slavery: A History of Slavery in Africa.* 2nd ed. Cambridge, UK: Cambridge University Press, 2000.

Bight of Benin

The "Bight of Benin," a term used by Europeans in the Atlantic slave trade era, refers to the West African coastal region between the Volta and Benin rivers and the body of water within the open bay. East of the Volta River was called the "Slave Coast" and constituted regions that faced the Bight of Benin. This area includes present-day Togo, Benin (formerly Dahomey), and western Nigeria. The Bight of Benin region was a consistent supplier of slaves from the 17th through the early 19th centuries, and the site of two powerful ancient African kingdoms—the forest state of Dahomey and Benin.

The kingdom of Dahomey (present-day Benin), located to the north of the rainforest region, was established around 1625. One element of early Dahomean culture was human sacrifice, practiced in annual rituals and ceremonies.

Dahomeans also believed in witchcraft, which at times they considered as the source of a king's illness. Religion revolved around an established priesthood, and the king served as the nation's high priest. Priests professed their view on the nature of man and divinity, and the establishment of the social and divine order.

Dahomey was organized along military lines and governed by a highly centralized authority with a king (*oba*) who was granted total power by his people. He appointed local rulers, army officers, and administrators. Dahomean women were appointed along with men in government offices and in various roles as advisors to men and replacements during wars. The women's military corps was a functioning unit. Europeans referred to these women as "Amazons." These military women included female commanders who fought alongside men. They engaged in rigorous training and combat and were regarded as equals of men. With unwavering loyalty and service from all citizens and appointed officials, the king became one of the most powerful monarchs along the West African coast, even though the kingdom was small and poor. Dahomey enjoyed uniqueness as one of the few absolute monarchies in the region.

Early Dahomey's power and prestige depended on profits from the slave trade to a greater extent than that of almost any other West African state.

The Dahomey coast trade was second to the Gold Coast in importance as a trade network moving goods from Togo, Dahomey, the eastern part of Upper Volta, the western part of Nigeria, and northwest Nigeria down the Sudanic belt, into several key trading towns. The Portuguese established a successful and profitable trading station in Dahomey. Beginning in the early 1600s, Dahomey took advantage of the demand for slaves to expand its military power and used the profits from the slave trade to invest in firearms. Access to new weapons expanded Dahomey's regional power and allowed the *obas* to centralize their authority. In 1725, Dahomey was strong enough to extend its borders. The powers in central Dahomey controlled most of the coast and the European slave trade. The Atlantic slave trade increasingly grew to be the basis of Dahomey's economy. Different trading towns along the Bight of Benin from modern Benin to Cameroon continued to participate in the Atlantic slave trade until 1850–1860 when the British launched a major antislave trade offensive. Dahomey, however, continued to thrive from the slave trade in the second half of

the 19th century. After the abolition of slavery and suppression of the slave trade, Dahomey's prosperity declined. The French occupied the area, defeating and disbanding the famous brigade of women—the Amazons—who were the best of Dahomey's soldiers. The French declared Dahomey a French Protectorate in 1892. They challenged a historically powerful system of African nobility, and it took them more than 50 years of treaty-making to establish Dahomey as one of their colonies.

The original Benin kingdom, located in western Nigeria, was also part of the Bight of Benin. According to tradition, the Benin dynasty was founded by immigrants from Ife three centuries before the arrival of the Portuguese in the 15th century. It was one of the earliest African states to come into contact with Europeans. Most of Benin's history lies in the Coastal Contact Period (1475–1850), but the genesis of its state dates back to an earlier period. Benin City was fairly large by the 15th century. By the time the Portuguese arrived on the Guinea coast, Benin was already firmly established with a royal court, and its founding dynasty was in its 10th reign. The Portuguese found a rich and civilized kingdom. Visitors in the 16th and 17th centuries described Benin as a great city, and one that could be fairly compared to European cities of the time. What started out as a city and mini-state progressed over a long period of time to a kingdom type of government.

Significant for its development in size and level of political structure as a forest state, Benin rose to political eminence and ultimately became the main state of the Edo-speaking peoples. Between the 15th and 18th centuries, its empire stretched across the southern tier of Yoruba states to Lagos and Badagry, near the western edge of modern Nigeria. The kings of Benin initially refused to take part in the Atlantic slave trade, but they did participate later. In 1516, the Benin king restricted the export of male slaves. Benin exported an estimated 10,000–12,000 slaves in 1763. In the early 19th century, Benin dropped out of the slave trade entirely but thrived and survived as a major state until close to the end of the 19th century when it was conquered by the British in 1897. As a militarily powerful early state, Benin exercised considerable political and cultural influence over extensive areas becoming best known for its early works of remarkable bronze art.

According to 19th century oral tradition, Benin learned the art of brass-casting from Ife in the 13th century. Benin artists and craftsmen were producing magnificent bronze castings as early as the 14th century. Bronze sculptures from Benin reflect great art and a technical proficiency in metallurgy suggesting that the forest people were just as advanced as those of the savanna region. The Benin kingdom is better known for its brass sculptures than any other brass-casting center in West Africa. Benin is also known for its ivory, and ivory sculpture continues to be produced in some areas today.

See also: Atlantic Slave Trade; Kingdom of Benin; Kingdom of Dahomey

Maryalice Guilford

Bibliography

Ajayi, J. F., Ade Crowder, and Michael Crowder. *History of West Africa.* Vol. 1. New York: Columbia University Press, 1976.

Bohannan, Paul, and Philip Curtin. *Africa and Africans.* Garden City, NY: Natural History Press, 1971.

Curtin, Philip D., et al. *African History.* Boston: Little, Brown, 1978.

Edge, Wayne. *Africa: Global Studies.* Dubuque, IA: McGraw-Hill, 2006.

Gilbert, Erik, and Jonathan T. Reynolds. *Africa in World History: From Prehistory to the Present.* Upper Saddle River, NJ: Prentice Hall, 2004.

Harris, Joseph E. *Africans and Their History.* New York: Penguin Books, 1987.

Lewis, L. A., and L. Berry. *African Environments and Resources.* Boston: Unwin Hyman, 1988.

Mair, Lucy. *African Kingdoms.* New York: Oxford University Press, 1977.

Mannix, Daniel P., and Malcolm Cowley. *Black Cargoes: A History of the Atlantic Slave Trade 1518–1865.* New York: Penguin Books, 1962.

Pakenham, Thomas. *The Scramble for Africa.* New York: Avon Books, 1991.

Reader, John. *Africa: A Biography of the Continent.* New York: Vintage Books, 1999.

Bight of Biafra

As a bay in the Gulf of Guinea, the Bight of Biafra was once known for its exportation of African slaves. Located along the West African coast, and extending northerly from the Niger River delta to Gabon's Cape Lopez, the Bight of Biafra encompasses 371 square miles. Nigeria, Cameroon, Equatorial Guinea, São Tomé, Principe, and Gabon are all countries that are located along the Bight of Biafra. The Bight of Biafra was based mainly on the ports of Bonny, Brass, Opobo, and Calabar (formerly Old and New Calabar). The term "Biafra" has European roots. As a name given to the

area by European travelers, and reinforced with maps, Biafra essentially encompasses the entire region east of the Niger, where it further extends to Mount Cameroon and also to parts of Senegambia. The Bight of Biafra changed the way that Africans participated in the slave economy. African intermediaries traded slaves to Europeans who had established castles along the coast to house Africans before being shipped across the Atlantic Ocean. With their ships packed tightly and loosely, European slavers prepared their chattel for redistribution in the Americas. Most of the time, slaves stayed belowdecks in cramped quarters where Europeans parceled out food, in spoons, to them, which they ate with their bare hands. The Bight of Biafra played a leading role in the slave trade.

From the 1740s on, the Bight of Biafra along with Benin dominated the transatlantic slave trade, accounting for 47 percent of the slaves exported. Figures revealed that from that time period on, the trade in slaves expanded from about 1,000 slaves per year to 17,000 per year in the 1790s. Most of the slaves ended up in the Chesapeake Bay region of Maryland and Virginia, where they adapted to performing grueling manual labor. With no centralized pattern of enslavement, each polity controlled its spheres of influence. Aboh and Idah dominated the interior trade, and private cartels participated freely in the commercial process. Not only were slaves exported, but inhabitants also maintained their own slave institution and culture. Based on the system of clientage, and debt peonage (whereby pawns performed service for a specified amount of time), Africans had their own form of slavery long before the arrival of Europeans and their chattel economy. Europeans commercialized slavery whereas Africans wanted to settle debts or obtained slaves through raids or wars. As a result of European presence and the appearance of Africans as intermediaries who brought Africans from the interior to the coast for sale, the commercialization that erupted during then transatlantic slave trade altered the way that Africans participated in the slave economy. No longer did Africans trade among themselves. Other inducements that Europeans offered compelled African merchants to sell other Africans to European traders for a variety of goods.

Biafra earned historical distinction for another reason. Along its bight developed a city of its namesake, the Republic of Biafra (ROB), located in southern Nigeria. The Republic seceded from Nigeria for three years from March 30, 1967, to January 15, 1970. During its short stint of independence, the countries of Gabon, Haiti, Côte d'Ivoire, Zambia, and Tanzania recognized the Republic as an independent state. Other countries such as France, the former Rhodesia, and South Africa provided covert military aid. In 1972, following the secessionist Biafran War, the ruling leader obliterated everything with the name Biafra, thereby anointing the area with the new name of the Bight of Bonny. This attempt to eradicate Biafra's historical value was unsuccessful as the bight continues to garner academic and lay attention.

See also: Atlantic Slave Trade; Chesapeake Colonies; Equiano, Olaudah; Igbo

Dawne Y. Curry

Bibliography

Brown, Carolyn A. *Repercussions of the Atlantic Slave Trade: The Interior of the Bight of Biafra and the African Diaspora.* Trenton, NJ: Africa World Press, 2005.

Hall, Gwendolyn Midlo. *Slavery and African Ethnicities in the Americas: Restoring the Links.* Chapel Hill: University of North Carolina Press, 2005.

Lovejoy, Paul. *Transformations in Slavery.* Cambridge, UK: Cambridge University Press, 1983.

Bosman, Willem

Willem Bosman (1672–?) was born in Utrecht, Holland. He set out for West Africa at the age of 16 and spent 14 years in the service of the Dutch West India Company on the Guinea coast. The establishment of the company was a reflection of Dutch commercial designs on Spanish and Portuguese possessions in Africa and the Americas. The company sought to monopolize the Guinea coast portion of the Atlantic slave trade that supplied captive labor to New World plantations. In 1637, the Dutch succeeded in ousting the Portuguese from São Jorge de Mina, also known as Elmina, the largest and oldest European fort on the coast. Bosman became the second most important Dutch official on the coast of Guinea after being appointed to the Dutch West India Company's Elmina factory, where African coastal merchants sold slaves they obtained from the interior.

Besides Elmina, other Dutch West India Company forts lined the Guinea coast, serving as ship repair stations, as well as emporiums for ship supplies, trade goods, and above all, slaves. Africans allowed the Europeans to construct forts on their land in return for rent and were willing to ally with Europeans because agreements protected their position as middlemen in the trade. Having consented to restrict their trading to a particular European nation, the African coastal merchants would expect that nation's military support during disputes with their neighbors. The notes, as these commercial papers were called, seldom remained long in the hands of the same Africans, and the forts themselves rarely could be held for any great length of time by the same European nation. The construction of forts was not always the result of reciprocal contacts between Africans and Europeans. Often, forts were built against the will of the local inhabitants, leading to war.

Bosman's account of his experience in Africa, *A New and Accurate Description of the Coast of Guinea,* was written during the waning years of the Dutch West India Company's power on the Guinea coast. The interior beyond Elmina was highly unstable, as Africans raided their weaker neighbors and sold them as slaves to Europeans, or fought each other in an effort to control the trade routes leading to the European coastal forts. Other Europeans, notably the English, French, and Portuguese, presented considerable challenges to the Dutch. Perhaps the most serious setback to the strength of the Dutch West India Company, indeed a major cause of its final demise, were the intrusions of interlopers who profited by ignoring the commercial prerogatives of the company. Bosman complained that many interlopers were financially supported by noncompany merchants in Holland.

See also: Atlantic Slave Trade; Dutch West India Company; Elmina; Factor; Gold Coast; Gulf of Guinea

David M. Carletta

Bibliography

Bosman, Willem. *A New and Accurate Description of the Coast of Guinea; Divided into the Gold, the Slave, and the Ivory Coasts. A New Edition with an Introduction by John Ralph Willis and Notes by J. D. Fage and R. E. Bradbury.* New York: Barnes and Noble, 1967.

Bosman, Willem. "Trading on the Slave Coast, 1700." In *The Atlantic Slave Trade,* edited by David Northrup, 71–74. Lexington, MA: D. C. Heath, 1994.

Bunce Island

Bunce Island (or *Bance*), once the largest British slave castle on the Rice Coast of West Africa, is a tiny island approximately 20 miles up the Sierra Leone River from the Atlantic Ocean, in the largest natural harbor on the African continent.

Established about 1670 (the year Charles Towne was founded in the Carolina Colony), the island operated as a slave castle until shut down by the British government in 1807—after tens of thousands of kidnapped Africans from that region were shipped through the facility and on to the Caribbean Islands and the colonies of South Carolina and Georgia. Africans of this region (the Rice Coast) had grown numerous varieties of rice for hundreds of years and could command a premium price as enslaved workers for the rice plantations in the Lowcountry region of those colonies. During its time as a slave castle, several London-based companies operated the facility, including the Gambia Adventurers, the Royal African Company of England—which had official recognition from the British Crown, plus Grant, Oswald and Company and John and Alexander Anderson, both private firms.

Richard Oswald, one of the wealthiest merchants in London, was the principal owner of Bunce Island by the 1750s. Oswald established a lucrative business arrangement with Charleston merchant and rice planter Henry Laurens, who brokered the sale of cargoes from Bunce Island for Oswald in Charleston. Laurens received ships from ports around the Atlantic that had stopped at Bunce Island to load a cargo of Africans from Oswald's operations, then would advertise the arrival of those vessels with their expected contents, and sell the cargo on commission. Laurens also sent his own slaving vessels to Bunce Island to return to Charleston, advertising their human cargo as possessing the skills and knowledge necessary for rice production.

See also: Carolinas; Gullah; Laurens, Henry; Rice Cultivation; Royal African Company; Sierra Leone

Jane M. Aldrich

Bibliography

Opala, Joseph. *Bunce Island: Historical Summary.* New Haven, CT: Gilder Lehrman Center for the Study of Slavery, Resistance, and Abolition at Yale University, 2004 [published in part online at http://www.visitsierraleone.org/bunce-island.asp (accessed August 1, 2008)].

Sellers, Leila. *Charleston on the Eve of the American Revolution.* Chapel Hill: University of North Carolina Press, 1934.

Cape Coast Castle

Standing at 23,000 square feet, and located a couple of miles from Elmina Castle along the west coast of modern Ghana, Cape Coast Castle is a slave dungeon that held captured Africans as slaves for sale in the transatlantic slave trade. First established by the Swedish as a trading fort for the exchange of materials and goods in 1653, Cape Coast Castle soon became a dungeon for holding enslaved Africans for sale and transport across the Atlantic. Because of its strategic location, European powers constantly fought for control over possession of the slave castle; since its inception, the Swedish, Dutch, Portuguese, and British actively contested each other for dominion over the castle and, as a result, it changed hands several times. Finally, in 1664 the British gained control over the castle; from 1664 until the abolition of the Atlantic slave trade in 1807, Cape Coast Castle served as the headquarters for the British for the duration of their involvement in the slave trade.

Similarly to other slave dungeons, upon arriving at Cape Coast Castle, men and women were separated, horded into segregated dungeons, and then chained together. Regardless of sex or point of origin, all slaves were harshly treated, poorly fed, and subjected to physical abuse and psychological trauma. In contrast to other slave dungeons along the former Gold Coast, Cape Coast Castle is particularly unique because, unlike other slave warehouses such as Elmina and Christianborg castles, and other makeshift dungeons, slaves at Cape Coast Castle were confined underground until embarkation for the New World. Slaves were held below the ground by slavers to prevent the possibility of potential uprisings. The underground dungeon was exposed to the earth; the floor was covered with feces, blood, mucus, and other bodily excretions. Furthermore, the close confinement and overcrowding, in addition to unsanitary living conditions, contributed to the spread of diseases such as dysentery, diarrhea, malaria, and smallpox. Many untold thousands died at Cape Coast and, very likely, far more enslaved Africans died in the various slave dungeons dotting the Atlantic African coastline than on slave ships.

What is even more unique about Cape Coast Castle is its strategic positioning along the coast of Ghana. Specific to Cape Coast Castle is its natural barrier of jagged and once-impermeable rocks that nearly prevented penetration to the coast. Because of its location, slave traders had to travel from their ships to the coast in smaller boats. Given the rough waters, the trek from the Atlantic to the littoral was frequently marked by numerous deaths via drowning as a result of capsized boats.

Today, Cape Coast Castle stands as a World Heritage Site, as identified by the United Nations Educational, Scientific and Cultural Organization (UNESCO). Cape Coast

Cape Coast Castle along the west coast of Ghana. (Julius Cruickshank)

Castle also serves as a point of destination where many people, especially persons of African descent, travel to visit yearly. Recently, a placard has been placed on the other side of the so-called Door of No Return that reads "Door of Return." This Door of Return welcomes the descendants of enslaved Africans dispersed throughout the Western Hemisphere as a result of the transatlantic slave trade and is, perhaps, a lasting testament to their collective victory over the tragic historical circumstances that occurred at Cape Coast Castle.

See also: Atlantic Slave Trade; Elmina

Ashley C. Bowden
and Walter C. Rucker

Bibliography
Hartman, Saidiya. *Lose Your Mother: A Journey along the Atlantic Slave Route.* New York: Farrar, Straus and Giroux, 2007.
Reed, Ann Marie. "Sankofa Site: Cape Coast Castle and Its Museum as Markers of Memory." *Museum Anthropology* 27, nos. 1–2 (2004):13–23.
St. Clair, William. *The Door of No Return: The History of Cape Coast Castle and the Atlantic Slave Trade.* New York: Blue-Bridge, 2007.

Carolinas

Carolina colonies depended upon the economic success of four major agricultural items, sugar, rice, indigo, and cotton, and the transatlantic slave trade. From the 1600s to the 1740s, planters demanded a labor supply from the Windward (Sierra Leone and Liberia) and Gold (Ghana, Togo, and Benin) coasts for rice production. Between the 1750s and 1787, an influx of slaves from Senegambia (Senegal and Gambia) facilitated indigo cultivation. By the early 19th century, cotton production demanded slaves from the Kongo-Angola region.

In 1670s, British sugar planters and enslaved Africans from the island of Barbados arrived in the port of Charles Town, South Carolina. Although the first set of enslaved Africans in the Carolinas originated from the Gold Coast, three major shifts contributed to the change in African regional preference: competition with Caribbean colonies, introduction of rice, and the prevalence of slave resistance.

During the early 17th century, British and French colonies in the Caribbean dominated sugar production and the transatlantic slave trade. Since Gold Coast slaves were favored by owners of British Caribbean sugar plantations, planters in the Carolinas circumvented the competition by expanding their slave market to include peoples from Kongo-Angola, Senegambia, and the Windward regions.

A second factor contributing to the shift from Gold Coast slaves was an increase in slave resistance in the Caribbean and the Carolinas. Enslaved Africans from the Gold Coast were linked to and accused of instigating slave insurrections in Antigua and Jamaica. As a result, several legislative acts curbed the importation of slaves not directly from the African continent. In 1717, Carolina government enforced a head tax on slaves from other American or Caribbean colonies. In response to the Stono Rebellion of 1739, which occurred near Charleston, South Carolina, fewer West-Central Africans were imported beginning in 1740 since colonial authorities blamed "Angolans" for the uprising. From the 1740s through the end of the slave trade, South Carolina would import larger numbers of Africans from Senegambia and Sierra Leone.

The third factor contributing to the shift in African labor preference was the introduction of rice into the Carolinas. In 1680, Captain John Thurber brought gold seed rice from the island of Madagascar, located off the east African coast, and dispersed to fellow colleagues in South Carolina. Once the seed proved to be an agricultural and economic success, the plantation system became a major source of rice cultivation. The influx of slave labor from the African continent increased to maintain the region's growing number of rice plantations.

In the 1750s, planters relocated rice fields from the inland to tidal and river swamps, where the plant was more susceptible to flooding by freshwater. The land required to successfully grow rice was located in humid areas plagued by tropical diseases. European laborers and landowners often contracted and died from tropical diseases such as malaria, carried by mosquitoes, and cholera. Under such conditions, plantation laborers shifted from European indentured servants to enslaved Africans. Peoples of the Windward Coast were found to be ideal for rice cultivation for two reasons: rice was a staple crop along the Windward Coast and the people of the region were immune to malaria. Malaria-resistance was later linked to the group's production of sickle-shaped blood cells, which prevented the pathogen's survival and transmission. Since European planters were unable to survive in the tropical environment of the rice plantations,

the properties were maintained under the system of absenteeism. Plantation owners assigned a person to manage the daily concerns of the property while they traveled to Europe or islands in the Caribbean, or resided further inland.

By the mid-18th century, indigo became an important article for export and source of wealth among Southern colonial planters. Since the crop required dry, light soil, indigo, like rice, was also cultivated in the South Carolina Sea Islands. The production of indigo became tedious and time-consuming as months of cultivating, drying, monitoring, and steeping were necessary in order to produce the most valued form of the commodity—a blue-violet dye. As the process became a health concern, as steam and chemicals from steeping were often lethal, cotton emerged as the new staple in the Carolinas. By the 1790s, the need for similar agricultural environment and demands of the English market allowed cotton to replace indigo as the dominant crop in the Carolina colonies.

Plantation slavery in the Carolina colonies differed from the systems found in the Caribbean and other American colonies and contributed to the development of African American cultures in the Carolinas. Rice cultivation gave rise to the task system and absenteeism, which played major roles in the cultural development of South Carolina Sea Islands' Gullah communities. In the task system, a slave was assigned one acre of land requiring weeding, hoeing, tilling, or harvesting. Once the "task" is completed, slaves could tend to their own gardens, known as "Negro" or "slave" fields, or travel to the markets to sell any crops or goods they produced. Without the presence of European influence, absenteeism allowed the plantation to become a space for enslaved Africans to develop their own language and culture.

See also: Angolan/Kongolese; Atlantic Slave Trade; Bunce Island; Gold Coast; Gullah; Juba Dance; Malaria; Rice Cultivation; Senegambia; Sierra Leone; Stono Rebellion; Task System; Turner, Lorenzo Dow; West-Central Africa

Tamara T. Butler

Bibliography

Creel, Margaret Washington. *"A Peculiar People": Slave Religion and Community-Culture among the Gullahs.* New York: New York University Press, 1988.

Johnson, Guion Griffis. *A Social History of the Sea Islands.* Chapel Hill: University of North Carolina Press, 1930.

Montgomery, Michael, ed. *The Crucible of Carolina: Essays in the Development of Gullah Language and Culture.* Athens: University of Georgia Press, 1994.

Turner, Lorenzo Dow. *Africanisms in the Gullah Dialect*. Ann Arbor: University of Michigan Press, 1973.

Young, Jason R. *Rituals of Resistance: African Atlantic Religion in Kongo and the Lowcountry South in the Era of Slavery*. Baton Rouge: Louisiana State University Press, 2007.

Chesapeake Colonies

The first African slaves of the Chesapeake colonies arrived in Jamestown, Virginia, on a Dutch trading ship. The Virginians bought the slaves, but they treated them as indentured servants. Indentured servants served a contractual term, whereas slaves were bound for life. Africans were able to join the white indentured servants, once their contract expired, and they established farms and families themselves. Unfortunately, the Chesapeake colonies quickly ran out of labor, because indentured servitude was not sufficient to satisfy the increasing demand of the main staple crop, tobacco. As a result of the labor shortage, the Chesapeake colonies began to import African slaves, once the survival rate of new arrivals reached a satisfactory percentage. By the mid 1600s, roughly 1,700 Africans lived in the colonies, about one-fifth of them free.

The role of slaves quickly changed with the advent of the plantation society in the Chesapeake colonies. Whereas slaves were formerly part of the society, baptized, and even allowed to travel, the plantation regime now heavily restricted the slaves' rights. Based on the color of their skin, slaves were easy to identify and to ostracize. The settlers of the Chesapeake quickly followed the model of British Caribbean islands, where slavery and plantations had been in place since the early 1600s. Colonial judges singled out African indentured servants and levied harsher penalties for equal crimes committed by whites. Virginia recognized slavery by law in 1661, and in 1662 a second law stipulated that the child would follow the status of the mother, free or enslaved.

In 1676, Bacon's Rebellion further encouraged the planters to establish tighter control over slaves. Nathaniel Bacon led a rebellion against the ruler of the colony. Bacon's rebels consisted of white indentured servants, as well as 10 percent of Virginia's black males. Planters concluded that slaves were the more dependable workforce, since they could be legally subjected to bondage for life. In addition, their black skin made it easier for planters to detect fugitive slaves and thus simplified the control of the labor force. Tobacco planters especially preferred slaves to indentured servants, and when Indian slaves were no longer available at the end of the 17th century, planters began the mass importation of African slaves. From 1695 until 1700, more African slaves were imported than in the previous 20 years. With increasing numbers of African slaves, Virginia passed its first slave code in 1680.

In the first decade of the 18th century, 8,000 new slaves were imported into the Chesapeake. These slaves were predominantly male and the standard of living of these slaves steadily decreased, as planters became more interested in making a quick profit. Planters followed the Caribbean model of "seasoning" slaves: they stripped the new arrivals from all ties to their homeland. This became necessary because the Chesapeake colonies started to import slaves directly from Africa, rather than from the British Caribbean colonies. One of the first ties removed was their African name, but planters failed to completely erase the slaves' African identity. A second slave code in 1705 limited the rights of free blacks, regulated the right of black people to bear arms, and discouraged planters from freeing their slaves by attaching numerous provisions designed to stop the planter from acting. Slaves that were manumitted had to leave the colony within six months, or they would receive severe corporal punishment from the colonial legislature.

As long as tobacco prices remained stable and high in Great Britain, planters in the Chesapeake continued to import slaves in large numbers. However, after 1750, the soil of the Chesapeake was exhausted and the demand in Great Britain dwindled. The tobacco boom turned into a tobacco crisis, and planters cut their acreage and switched to wheat cultivation. Wheat required less slave labor than tobacco, which also led to a decrease in the slave imports after 1750. Nevertheless, slaves constituted one-third of the population in Maryland and two-fifths of the population in Virginia on the eve of the American Revolution. Slaves were not evenly distributed across the Chesapeake colonies; slave numbers were significantly larger in the coastal regions. Subsistence farmers, whose demand for slave labor was low, primarily settled the backcountry of Virginia and Maryland. However, about 61 percent of American slaves lived in the Chesapeake colonies in 1750.

The Chesapeake colonies differed from their British sister colonies in the Caribbean. Slaves never constituted the majority of the population, and nonslaveholders outnumbered slaveholders. In the Chesapeake colonies, unlike in the Caribbean, the birth rate of slaves exceeded the death rate, which led to an ever-growing Creole (American-born) population of slaves. The Creole slaves developed slave communities in the Chesapeake colonies that mixed traits of their African heritage such as burial rites, music, and dance with traits of American colonists such as religion, clothing, and names. Slaves constantly forced their owners to rethink the master-slave relationship, often in favor of the slaves. This mixture formed a unique kind of slavery that was challenged, but not overthrown, by the American Revolution and developed continuously through negotiations between master and slave.

The British tried to incite slave flight during the Revolution and Lord Dunmore's Proclamation in 1775 to slaves to fight for the British incited widespread panic among white planters. During the Southern Campaign of the British Army, slaves fled plantations in large numbers. The British settled a small number of these slaves in Nova Scotia, but many slaves either died of diseases in military camps, were given to British officers as slaves, or were left behind to be recaptured by their former masters. The American Revolution changed the life of slaves just as much as the life of all Americans.

See also: Atlantic Slave Trade; Bacon's Rebellion; Freedom Dues; Headright System; Indentured Servitude; Jamestown, Virginia; Jefferson, Thomas; Lord Dunmore; Rolfe, John; Tobacco

Christian Pinnen

Bibliography

Berlin, Ira. *Generation of Captivity: A History of African-American Slaves.* Cambridge, MA: Belknap Press, 2003.

Breen, T. H., and Stephen Innes. *"Myne Owne Ground": Race and Freedom on Virginia's Eastern Shore, 1640–1676.* New York: Oxford University Press, 1980.

Kolchin, Peter. *American Slavery: 1619–1877.* New York: Hill and Wang, 1993.

Cugoano, Quobna Ottobah

Quobna Ottobah Cugoano (1757–?) was an abolitionist and writer who advocated for the repatriation of former enslaved Africans in Sierra Leone. Born in a Gold Coast Fante city-state named Agimaque (or Ajumako) near Assini, Cugoano's very name denotes his Gold Coast, Akan-speaking heritage. Quobna, an Akan-day name for a male born on a Tuesday, was a name he probably received seven days after his birth. His father was a companion of the king of Agimaque (or Agimaquehene) and Cugoano was a frequent visitor in the Agimaquehene's court, even befriending a number of his children. While staying with an uncle, Cugoano was kidnapped by slave raiders at age 13 with about 20 other children and transported to a coastal trade factory. After a three-day stay, he was transported by ship to the infamous Cape Coast Castle. Once the ship had received a full cargo of enslaved Africans, it disembarked to Grenada and Cugoano later reflected on the human misery he witnessed on this slaver—including the frequent rape of African women and an attempted revolt that was discovered and brutally crushed by the ship's crew.

After about 10 months of working on a sugar plantation in Grenada and another year living in various locales throughout the Caribbean, Cugoano was purchased by Alexander Campbell and arrived in England just months after the Mansfield decision in the *Somerset* case of June 22, 1722, which ended slavery in England. After his arrival, Cugoano was baptized as "John Stuart" at St. James's Church in 1773 and, by 1784, he was employed by Richard and Maria Cosway—two artists who eventually connected Cugoano to prominent figures like William Blake. On July 28, 1786, Cugoano enlisted the aid of Granville Sharpe to help save Harry Demane—an enslaved man who was literally tied to the mast of a ship headed to the British Caribbean. After this successful intervention, Cugoano would write a letter to the Prince of Wales in order to encourage his support in abolishing the slave trade and slavery.

Cugoano, along with Olaudah Equiano and 24 other black men, became actively involved in the Sons of Africa—a group that sought rights for the black community in England and the abolition of slavery. This was the context in which he wrote a 1787 treatise entitled *Thoughts and Sentiments on the Evil and Wicked Traffic of the Slavery and Commerce of the Human Species.* This work was a sustained diatribe against the slave trade and slavery and was the first of its kind published by a former enslaved African in the Anglophone world—preceding Equiano's narrative by two years. According to Vincent Carretta, Cugoano's *Thought and Sentiments* is also the first historical work on slavery and the slave trade written by an Anglophone African, and he may have been the first African to criticize European colonization in the Americas.

By 1791, Cugoano had ended his long-standing employment with the Cosways and was apparently working with the Sierra Leone Company as an active proponent of emigration and repatriation. In his last known set of writings, a letter to Granville Sharp and a shorter version of *Thoughts and Sentiments* written in 1791, Cugoano states that he was planning to sail to New Brunswick, Nova Scotia, and, from there, he was to join Nova Scotia ships to Sierra Leone where he hoped to open a school for repatriated Africans. No records exist detailing Cugoano's later life as he completely disappears from the historical record after 1791.

See also: Abolition, Slave Trade; Atlantic Slave Trade

Walter C. Rucker

Bibliography

Adams, Francis D., Barry Sanders, Ignatius Sancho, Ottobah Cugoano, and Olaudah Equiano. *Three Black Writers in Eighteenth Century England.* Belmont, CA: Wadsworth Publishing, 1971.

Carretta, Vincent, and Philip Gould. *Genius in Bondage: Literature of the Early Black Atlantic.* Lexington: University Press of Kentucky, 2001.

Cugoano, Quobna Ottobah. *Thoughts and Sentiments on the Evils of Slavery and Other Writings.* New York: Penguin Books, 1999.

M'Baye, Babacar. *The Trickster Comes West: Pan-African Influence in Early Black Diasporan Narratives.* Jackson: University Press of Mississippi, 2009.

Potkay, Adam, and Sandra Burr, eds. *Black Atlantic Writers of the 18th Century: Living the Exodus in England and the Americas.* New York: St. Martin's Press, 1995.

Woodard, Helena. *African-British Writings in the Eighteenth Century: The Politics of Race and Reason.* Westport, CT: Greenwood Press, 1999.

de Las Casas, Bartolomé

Bartolomé de las Casas (1471?–1566) was a Spanish Dominican priest who spent much of his long life fighting against the cruelty and subjugation of the indigenous people and African slaves in the Spanish colonies in the New World. Ironically, his empathy regarding the plight of the Taino and other indigenous people led Las Casas to be one of the first to support the large-scale importation of African slaves into the Spanish Americas.

Las Casas's father was a struggling merchant; he and several family members were involved in Christopher Columbus's voyages to the New World. Bartolomé also joined these enterprises, sailing for Hispaniola in the West Indies with its governor in 1502. His service there was rewarded with a royal land grant, an *encomienda*, which included forced labor. Las Casas served as a catechism teacher (*doctrinero*) to the aboriginal peoples. Although some historians believe he was ordained to the priesthood before he left Spain, others claim he was not ordained until 1512 or 1513. He may have been the first person to receive holy orders in the Americas.

These early years in the New World provided many illustrations of the brutality and corruption of royal officials toward those forced to labor for the Spanish overlords. Through his experiences in the New World, his study of scripture, and the guidance of a Dominican confessor, Las Casas came to a new appreciation of the plight of these subject races.

In 1514 Las Casas gave a sermon announcing he was giving his serfs back to the governor. He returned to Spain in 1515, knowing that he had to pursue his campaign for improved conditions for the native people in the heart of the Spanish government. Las Casas found a powerful ally in the archbishop of Toledo, Francisco Jiménez de Cisneros. Together they designed the *Plan para la reformación de las Indias,* which named Las Casas priest-procurator of the Indies. Las Casas was also to take part in a commission investigating the condition of the subject people.

Much of Las Casas's life was spent honing his moral and legal arguments against colonial oppression while trying to gain access to the Spanish ruler, Charles I (Emperor Charles V), and his influential courtiers. Las Casas's impassioned arguments before the Spanish Parliament in 1519 were instrumental in convincing the king to endorse a colony of free Indians. Only Spaniards committed to peaceful coexistence with the natives were allowed within the prescribed zone (the coast of Paria). Lack of Spanish support, open hostility from the defenders of the encomienda system, and an aboriginal uprising took their toll on the community. By 1522 it was evident the project had failed.

Seeking solace in his religious vocation, Las Casas joined the Dominican order in Santo Domingo shortly thereafter (1523). It was during this phase of his life that he began to write one of his major works, the *Apologética historia summaria de las gentes Indias,* and his magnum opus, the *Historia de las Indias.* The *Historia* was a catalogue of aboriginal suffering but it is also a morality tale. Las Casas predicted that God would not suffer the subjugation and cruel treatment of the aboriginal peoples and would ultimately bring down His judgment upon the European conquerors.

During the 1530s, Las Casas continued revising his manuscripts as well as writing letters to Spain railing against the encomienda system in the Spanish colonies. He wrote *De único vocationis modo* (1537), in which he articulated why peaceful evangelization of non-Europeans would yield the best spiritual results. Las Casas's arguments were bolstered by the *Bulla Sublimis Deus,* in which the pope proclaimed the Indians' equality, rationality, and the necessity of their receiving Christian instruction.

Las Casas's advocacy of the Indians and condemnation of colonial exploitation won both important allies and enemies. He hoped his efforts had reached fruition when Charles passed the *Leyes Nuevas.* These "new laws" placed restrictions on the encomienda system and named Las Casas bishop of Chiapas in Guatemala to oversee their implementation (1544). Las Casas went so far as to deny absolution to those who used the encomienda system to oppress the Indians. This brought about a firestorm of opposition and he left for Spain in 1547.

Las Casas carried on his fight in the Old World. He used his influence at court and on the Council of the Indies as a platform for advocating the protection and education of aboriginals. This brought him into direct conflict with Juan Ginés de Sepúlveda, who argued that the Indians were childlike and needed to be under Spanish subjugation for their own welfare. The learned Sepúlveda based his arguments on Aristotelian principles and proved himself a match for Las Casas. Sepúlveda also had the added weight of defending a well-established system of aboriginal servitude that was extremely popular and profitable for New World colonists. Their debate (1550–1551) has attracted much contemporary and subsequent attention. Las Casas is generally regarded as the victor.

Las Casas carried on his mission until his death in 1566, acting as an advisor to the King and the Council of the Indies as well as producing more written works focusing on oppression in the New World. Though Las Casas was among the first to suggest the importation of African slaves, he would later regret this after witnessing their harsh and brutal treatment.

Bartolomé de Las Casas, a 16th-century Spanish historian and Dominican priest, worked diligently to highlight the plight of the Taino and other indigenous peoples living in the Caribbean. (Library of Congress)

He lived into his 90s at a time when such longevity was truly remarkable. While Las Casas was, in many ways, a "voice crying in the wilderness" of his own age and, in the centuries that followed, his works have found a new resonance in the modern era. While modern secular readers may reject his profoundly Christian worldview, his tireless efforts to fight colonial domination in the New World are much more in step with our own day than his own.

See also: Atlantic Slave Trade; Encomienda; Hispaniola

Cheryl Fury

Bibliography

Castro, Daniel. *Another Face of Empire: Bartolomé de Las Casas, Indigenous Rights, and Ecclesiastical Imperialism.* Durham, NC: Duke University Press, 2007.

Friede, Juan, and Benjamin Keen, eds. *Bartolomé de Las Casas in History: Toward an Understanding of the Man and His Work.* DeKalb: Northern Illinois University Press, 1971.

Wagner, Henry Raup, and Helen Rand Parish. *The Life and Writings of Bartolomé de Las Casas.* Albuquerque: University of New Mexico Press, 1967.

Destination, Florida

With the founding of the colony of Carolina in 1670, the Spanish presence in Florida served as a facilitating space for escaped African slaves. The very existence of Spanish St. Augustine, established in 1565, drew enslaved Africans from British plantations and, between March and November 1739, runaways from Carolina helped to establish the semiautonomous black town of Gracia Real de Santa Teresa de Mose—two miles north of St. Augustine. The initial draw to Florida might have been due to the prior experience of many enslaved Africans brought to Carolina with both Catholicism and an Iberian language (Portuguese).

Beginning in 1491, the Kingdom of Kongo in West-Central Africa voluntarily converted to Catholicism due to the influence of Portuguese-speaking Capuchin missionaries and the baptism of the king of Kingo Nzinga a Nkuwu. In addition to this, nearby regions in West-Central Africa witnessed the spreading influence of Catholicism and a uniquely Africanized version of Christianity with the Portuguese founding of a permanent presence in Luanda beginning in 1575. In urban centers and rural hamlets alike, Africanized Christianity may have spread to the degree that the majority of enslaved Africans shipped from West-Central Africa were self-avowed Christians or had significant prior exposure to Christianity. In addition, the exposure to and mastery over Portuguese by these Atlantic Creoles likely facilitated communication with the Spanish in Florida.

Even before Gracia Real de Santa Teresa de Mose (Fort Mose) was founded, the Spanish Crown had issued a series of edicts in the period between 1693 and 1733. Thousands of Carolina slaves, understanding the unique geopolitical circumstances, exploited the imperial rivalry between the English and Spanish in order to secure their freedom. Indeed, it is very likely that the 1739 Stono Rebellion in South Carolina was ultimately a movement initiated by enslaved Africans from West-Central Africa seeking asylum in Spanish Florida.

While thousands left Carolina and Georgia (established in 1732) for Florida, not all of them ended up in St. Augustine or Fort Mose. Some formed maroon societies while others joined with the Seminoles, creating unique biracial enclaves in which aspects of South Carolina and Georgia Gullah culture (e.g., rice cultivation) became embedded. In the course of the First, Second, and Third Seminole Wars,

the so-called Black Seminoles fought to protect both their freedom and their Seminole Indian allies. Ultimately, many Black Seminoles were removed from Florida and like other members of the "Five Civilized Nations," they were relocated to the Oklahoma Indian Territory.

Between the 18th and 19th centuries, escaped slaves and their progeny lived in 15 black or biracial settlements or villages, including Fort Mose (1738–1740 and 1752–1763), the Fort at Prospect Bluff (1812–1816), Bowlegs Town I (1780s–1812), Bowlegs Town II (1813–1818), Mulatto Girl's Town (1818–1820s), Payne's Town (1790s–1813), King Heijah's Town (1818–1823), Big Swamp (1800s–1840s), Okahumpka (1818–1820s), Powell's Town (1818–1840s), Pilaklikaha (1803–1840s), Chocahatti (1767–1830s), Bukra Woman's Town (1818–1823), Boggy Island (1814–1840s), and Sarasota (1750s–1840s). When Florida was ceded to the United States in 1821, it no longer effectively served as a frontier or haven for escaped slaves. Even in that case, free black and biracial forts, villages, and towns continued to exist into the 1840s and served as the lasting manifestations of black agency, the unique geopolitical circumstances evident in Florida, and mutually beneficial alliances with Seminoles and Spaniards.

See also: Atlantic Creoles; Black Seminoles; Fugitive Slaves; Gullah; Kongo Kingdom; Seminole Wars; Stono Rebellion; West-Central Africa

Walter C. Rucker

Bibliography

Colburn, David, and Jane Landers, eds. *The African American Heritage of Florida.* Gainesville: University Press of Florida, 1995.

Landers, Jane. *Black Society in Spanish Florida.* Urbana: University of Illinois Press, 1999.

Landers, Jane. "Gracia Real de Santa Teresa de Mose: A Free Black Town in Colonial Florida." *American Historical Review* 95 (February 1990):9–30.

Porter, Kenneth, ed. *The Black Seminoles: History of a Freedom-Seeking People.* Gainesville: University Press of Florida, 1996.

Twyman, Bruce Edward. *The Black Seminole Legacy and North American Politics, 1693–1845.* Washington, D.C.: Howard University Press, 2000.

Du Sable, Jean Baptiste Point

Jean Baptiste Point Du Sable (1745?–1818) was an entrepreneur who is acknowledged as the first known settler in the area now known as Chicago. The son of a French sea captain and an African-born former slave, Du Sable was born around 1745, in Saint-Marc, Sainte Dominique (present-day Haiti). Not very much is known about Du Sable's early life except that his mother may have been killed by the Spanish when he was 10, and he probably escaped death by swimming out to his father's ship. His father sent him to France to be educated, and he learned to speak English and Spanish in addition to his mother tongue. When he returned from France, he went to work on his father's ships. When Du Sable was about 20, he undertook a voyage to New Orleans. The vessel sank and Du Sable was injured. When he arrived in New Orleans without his identification papers, he discovered the port had been taken over by the Spanish government. He was in danger of being captured and sold as a slave, but was rescued by French Jesuit priests who protected him until he was well enough to travel again.

Du Sable traveled up the Mississippi River to the St. Louis area, and then settled in a frontier area near what is now Peoria, Illinois. He was accepted by the local Potawatomi Indians and took a Potawatomi woman, named Kittahawa, but whom he called Catherine, as his wife. In order to be given permission to marry her, the 25-year-old Du Sable had to become a member of her nation. The Potawatomi called him "Black Chief," and he became a high-ranking member of the nation. They had a son, Jean, and a daughter, Susanne, together. They prospered financially and eventually owned more than 80 acres of land in the Peoria area.

Before it became a city, Chicago was a trading center, and, as its first permanent resident, Du Sable operated the first elaborate fur-trading post during the first two decades before 1800. In the late 1770s Du Sable headed north to explore the region near the shores of the Great Lakes. He saw potential in a swampy area that had been passed over by previous European explorers. The Indians called this land *Eschikagou* (Chicago), the place of bad smells due to the odor of the swampland. Whites in the area had been fearful of attacks from hostile Native Americas. Du Sable, however, got along well with various Indian groups, and he knew several of their languages. He stayed and built a five-room house, the first permanent structure in the area. It stood in what is now downtown Chicago. In 1782 Du Sable established a trading post that grew successfully, becoming well known all around the Great Lakes region. The trading post became the main supply source for fur trappers, traders, and Indians in the area. After a few years, Du Sable's trading post also supplied staple food items to trading posts in Canada and Detroit. It had a mill, bakery, dairy, smokehouse, poultry house, and workshops, barns, and stables. Du Sable's business thrived, and he owned much livestock. Du Sable became well known for trading goods throughout the Midwest. As a result, he became very wealthy. In 1784, he brought his wife and children to live with him in Chicago. Du Sable's granddaughter, Eulalie, was born in 1796. She was the first non-Indian baby born in Chicago.

After the death of his wife and son, Du Sable sold his property in Chicago for $1,200 and moved to St. Louis, Missouri, to live with his daughter, her husband, and granddaughter. When his daughter and her husband moved to Canada, Du Sable bought a house on a farm in St. Charles, Missouri, that he deeded to his grandchildren on the condition that granddaughter Eulalie care for him until his death and then bury him with Catholic rites in a Catholic cemetery. For the next few years, Du Sable lived on his St. Charles farm. Jean Baptist Point Du Sable died on August 29, 1818, at the age of 73.

In 1968, Du Sable was officially recognized by the state of Illinois and the city of Chicago as "the Founder of Chicago." In recognition of his pioneering role, the U.S. Postal Service, on February 20, 1987, issued a Black Heritage Series 22-cent stamp in honor of Du Sable. The Du Sable Museum of African American History, on Chicago's South Side, is named in his honor in addition to his homesite, a high school, a park, and a harbor in downtown Chicago. The Chicago Du Sable League is dedicated to the preservation and dissemination of Jean Baptiste Point Du Sable's life and history and in maintaining his respectful place in American, African American, and Chicago history.

See also: American Revolution

Janice D. Hamlet

Bibliography

Du Bois, Shirley Graham. *Jean Baptiste Pointe Du Sable: Founder of Chicago.* Englewood Cliffs, NJ: Responsive Environments Corp, 1953.

Meehan, Thomas A. "Jean Baptiste Point Du Sable, the First Chicagoan." *Journal of the Illinois State Historical Society* 56 (1963):439–53.

Simon, Elizabeth Matlock, and Hubert V. Simon. *Chicago's First Citizen, Jean Baptiste Pointe Du Sable: A Historical Sketch of a Distinguished Pioneer.* Chicago: E. Matlock-Simon and H. V. Simon, 1933.

Dutch New Netherland

The history of forced labor in New Netherland began in 1625 with the arrival of a Dutch warship that unloaded a cargo of Africans plundered from a Portuguese vessel on the Atlantic. The status of the first Africans brought to Dutch North America was not clearly defined initially and there existed a number of avenues forced laborers could use to obtain freedom that were open for at least a few decades. The idea of permanent and racialized slavery did not develop in the region until the mid-1660s. Like their counterparts in the Chesapeake, the first Africans arriving in New Netherland inhabited a nebulous social space between indentured servitude and slavery. Initially it seemed that they would have the same opportunities as their European counterparts and would, perhaps, share the fruits and rewards the New World offered. To borrow the words of Peter Wood, the "terrible transformation" that led to the eventual development and proliferation of race-defined slavery during the second half of the 17th century helped determine the poisonous race relations that have manifested throughout much of North American history.

Established primarily as a fur-trading post by the Dutch West India Company, New Netherland and its Dutch settlers struggled during the early years of the colony's history to find sufficient sources of revenue and labor. Concentrating most of their efforts on major territorial claims in West Africa and the Caribbean—Gorée and Curaçao, respectively—the directors of the company had little interest in investing the significant amount of capital necessary to make New Netherland a successful settler colony. As a result, the Dutch West India Company proposed two separate plans to solve the economic problems faced by its North American colony. The first solution was the establishment of patroonships or landed estates granted to the wealthy. Patroonships, much like the headrights bestowed by the Virginia Company in the Chesapeake, were incentives meant to encourage immigration to America. Wealthy Dutch settlers receiving landed estates under this system had the responsibility of attracting and paying the necessary transportation costs for up to 50 new settlers each. This plan met with only limited success with the establishment of only one patroonship during the entire period of Dutch rule in New Netherland. The company's second and most successful plan was the importation of Africans to be used

primarily as agricultural laborers and as workers in the construction of public buildings and military fortifications.

The names of some of the first Africans imported into New Netherland—Paul d'Angola, Simon Congo, and Anthony Portuguese—clearly denote their origin in West-Central Africa. In the early 1570s, Portugal conquered Angola and established peaceful commercial relations with the nearby Kongo Kingdom. West-Central Africa therefore would be an early source of labor for the Portuguese colony of Brazil and, due to the actions of Dutch warships and privateers on the Atlantic, both British Virginia and Dutch New Netherland would import a number of Africans from this region as well. When the Dutch West India Company was first chartered in 1621, it began an aggressive campaign against Portuguese claims in Atlantic Africa and the Americas in an attempt to undermine the Portuguese trade monopoly and to acquire Africans by more direct means. The company captured portions of Brazil by 1637 and moved to wrest control of a number of possessions in Africa away from its Portuguese rivals.

In an attempt to fulfill its public promise to provide the colonists with as many enslaved African laborers as possible, the company sought to become the primary conduit of Africans entering Dutch American colonies. In the decade between 1637 and 1647 alone, the Dutch West India Company claimed the Portuguese possessions of Elmina, Príncipe, Angola, and São Tomé through military conquest. Even though the Dutch could only manage to control Angola from 1641 to 1648, they had effectively replaced the Portuguese as the dominant European power in Atlantic Africa by the mid-1640s. This complex web of interconnections within the Atlantic World, fostered by trade, international rivalry, and war, became an essential component in the development of a number of Euro-American societies.

By 1627, a total of 14 Africans had arrived in Dutch New Netherland and this initially slow trickle became a torrent over the course of the next half century. The absence of cash crops such as sugar, tobacco, or rice did not slow the need for African labor in Dutch North America. In fact, the importation of Africans became the principal focus for the company with the arrival of the first slave ship in 1635. In addition, as a result of its direct control over large portions of Brazil between 1637 and 1654, the company was able to create a unique trade relationship between New Netherland and Brazil. In a trade arrangement drafted in 1648, the colonists in New Netherland agreed to ship fish, flour, and produce to Brazil in exchange for as many African laborers as they required. Within four years of the establishment of the Brazil–New Netherland commercial agreement, direct trade with West Africa for slaves was opened and a slight reorientation of the slave trade began. In prior decades, the Dutch were satisfied with plundering Portuguese slave ships or establishing direct trade relations with Brazil or Spanish America to procure African laborers. As a result, the majority of Africans entering New Netherland were from Loango and other West-Central African regions. Enslaved "Angolans" or West-Central Africans would prove essential to the economic viability of the colony during its early years.

By allowing Africans to be directly imported into North America via Dutch West India Company–owned or commissioned ships, New Netherland soon began to receive a number of Gold Coast Akan-speakers exported from Dutch-controlled trading factories in West Africa to supplement the West-Central African imports. After capturing Elmina Castle from the Portuguese in August 1637, the Dutch would control the most important slave-trading factory along West Africa's Gold Coast. The immediate result of the capture of Elmina was the importation of Gold Coast Africans into Dutch American colonies. This new source of African laborers became even more important after 1648 when the Portuguese managed to recapture their Angolan possessions from the Dutch, which effectively cut off a major source of West-Central African imports. Also, with the Portuguese recapture of Brazil, the unique commercial arrangement between New Netherland and Brazil was brought to an abrupt halt.

The dominant position in Africa and the Americas enjoyed by the Dutch came to an end in 1664. The Second Anglo-Dutch War of 1664–1667 helped create a major power shift throughout the Atlantic World. During the course of the war, the English seized most of the Dutch claims along the Gold Coast with the notable exception of Elmina Castle. Equally important, the English managed to capture New Netherland. Angered over repeated violations of the Navigation Acts of 1651 and 1660, the English Crown decided that New Netherland was a significant obstacle to its economic interests in the Americas. By claiming this region as theirs, the English grabbed control of the contiguous territory from the Chesapeake to the New England colonies. Having already proven the military vulnerabilities of Dutch colonies during the First Anglo-Dutch War of 1652–1654, the English were able to peacefully capture New Netherland

after a brief naval blockade. Peter Stuyvesant—Director General of the Dutch West India Company and Governor of New Netherland—capitulated on September 8, 1664, effectively ending four decades of control by the company over what would soon become New York.

See also: Atlantic Slave Trade; Dutch West India Company; Gold Coast; Patroonship

Walter C. Rucker

Bibliography
Boxer, Charles R. *The Dutch Seaborne Empire, 1600–1800.* New York: Oxford University Press, 1965.
Goodfriend, Joyce. *Before the Melting Pot: Society and Culture in Colonial New York City, 1664–1730.* Princeton, NJ: Princeton University Press, 1992.
Jameson, J. Franklin, ed. *Narratives of New Netherland, 1609–1664.* New York: Charles Scribner's Sons, 1909.
Korbin, David. *The Black Minority in Early New York.* Albany: University Press of the State of New York, 1971.
McManus, Edgar. *A History of Negro Slavery in New York.* Syracuse, NY: Syracuse University Press, 1966.

Dutch West India Company

The Dutch West India Company was a private joint-stock company that received its first charter in 1621 from the States General of the United Provinces of the Netherlands, the Dutch national assembly, for commerce and colonization in the Western Hemisphere and Africa. The company's board of directors represented investors in the various Dutch republics, and the company was awarded a monopoly on Dutch trade with Africa, the Atlantic islands, the Caribbean, and the American mainland. Granted extensive powers by the Dutch government, the company made treaties with foreigners, administered justice, and maintained armed forces. With military and economic support from the public funds of the States General, Dutch West India Company ships began traveling to the west coast of Africa and across the Atlantic as interlopers in areas of the world claimed for colonization by Spain and Portugal in the Treaty of Tordesillas.

The Dutch West India Company played a major role in the 17th-century Atlantic slave trade, though the total Dutch portion of the trade from the 16th through the 19th centuries was never more than 5 percent. Portugal's profitable sugarcane plantations in northeastern Brazil attracted

Dutch attention and led to the Dutch West India Company's seizure of the captaincy of Pernambuco in 1630. Seeking to provide more slaves for its Brazilian colony, the company attacked several Portuguese forts in Africa. In 1636, a West India Company force captured the Portuguese fort at São Jorge da Mina (Elmina), the main Portuguese outpost in West Africa. For a short time in the mid-17th century, the company also controlled Central Africa's main slave port, São Paulo de Luanda in Angola. The company held 7 of the 14 captaincies of Brazil before being driven out by the local populace in 1654. The Dutch invasion of Portuguese Brazil and the war to oust them allowed many slaves the opportunity to escape to maroon societies. During the era of Dutch colonization in northeastern Brazil, more than 30,000 slaves were imported to work for the area's predominantly Portuguese sugar plantation owners.

In the second half of the 17th century, the company supplied slaves mainly to Spain's American and Caribbean colonies through both legal and illegal trade, often operating as a subcontractor for assorted merchants and companies that held an official asiento with the Spanish Crown. In the Caribbean, the Dutch West India Company controlled Aruba, Curaçao, and Bonaire, three small islands off the coast of Venezuela. Farther north, the company held the islands of Saba and St. Eustatius, and part of the island of St. Maarten. Curaçao became the hub for Dutch West Indian trade and the main slave distribution center to Spanish America. Slaves were transferred on a lesser scale from St. Eustatius to the French Caribbean. The Dutch exploited the Caribbean, as well as the Guiana region of South America, for sugar cultivation. By 1700, the colony of Dutch Guiana, present-day Suriname, contained some 50,000 slaves. After 1700, Dutch Guiana received the majority of slaves transported by the company.

In North America, the Dutch West India Company was primarily interested in the lucrative fur trade. The company oversaw the colony of New Netherland, which included North America's first permanent Dutch settlement at Fort Orange in what is today Albany, New York, as well as New Amsterdam, now New York City. The majority of New Netherland's slaves arrived via Curaçao. Slaves numbered around 450 and made up 5 percent of the total population of the colony, estimated at 9,000 in 1667 when the Dutch ceded New Netherland to the English. Large deficits and free trade policies caused the company to be dissolved in 1791.

See also: Atlantic Slave Trade; Dutch New Netherland; Elmina; Gold Coast

David M. Carletta

Bibliography
Goslinga, Cornelis C. *The Dutch in the Caribbean and in the Guianas, 1680–1791*. Dover, NH: Van Gorcum, 1985.
Goslinga, Cornelis C. *The Dutch in the Caribbean and on the Wild Coast, 1580–1680*. Gainesville: University of Florida Press, 1971.
Postma, Johannes Menne. *The Dutch in the Atlantic Slave Trade, 1600–1815*. Cambridge, UK: Cambridge University Press, 1990.
Shorto, Russell. *The Island at the Center of the World: The Epic Story of Dutch Manhattan and the Forgotten Colony That Shaped America*. New York: Doubleday, 2004.

Elmina

Constructed by the Portuguese in 1482 on the Gold Coast (modern Ghana) of West Africa, the Castelo São Jorge da Mina, Elmina, was the first significant European fortification in sub-Saharan Africa. The castle fortress, erected under the direction of Commander Diogo de Azambuja, solidified a Portuguese monopoly on Gold Coast trading for more than a century. The fortress represented a permanent foothold in tropical Africa, and as a result, rival European naval powers, such as the British and Dutch, felt compelled to construct similar fortifications across the West African coast. Dozens of structures dotted the region in the succeeding centuries, changing forever the relationship between Europeans and both the coastal African populations as well those in the interior regions.

Elmina was built near an existing African settlement of Akan-speaking people who welcomed the construction of the fort, both sides seeing its existence as advantageous to their trading prospects. The local Africans gained a stable supply of goods and some measure of protection from warfare, while the Portuguese were able to reduce the vulnerability of shipboard trading from hostile European navies and gained larger storage and administrative spaces. Commerce initially consisted of gold and some natural products from the interior such as ivory and wood. In later centuries the slave trade would define the castle's major export; however, during the first several decades African slaves were imported into Elmina from other coastal regions outside of the Gold Coast. This was due to a prohibition established by the Portuguese against enslaving local people on the Gold Coast, fearing that slave raiding would interfere with the profitable gold trade.

Elmina was built a decade before Christopher Columbus set sail for the New World, but by the 17th century, the mining of large gold deposits in the Americas lowered the value of, and European dependence on, African gold. At the same time, the Dutch were ascending as a naval power and wrested control of Elmina from the Portuguese in 1637. Gold remained a major trade good for the Dutch, yet there was also an increased demand for labor in the New World, and Elmina's traders turned to trafficking in enslaved human beings at unprecedented numbers. Most of the slaves were brought from the interior to be traded on the coast and were often held for several months in the castle's slave dungeons while awaiting purchase. Elmina was a comparatively small-volume slave trading port, with undersized slave quarters compared to other coastal castles on the Gold Coast. Nonetheless, having been the forerunner of European trade centers in Africa, its name remains synonymous with the horrors of the transatlantic slave trade.

The Dutch held the fort for 235 years, until the British took possession of Elmina by treaty in 1872. The slave trade had long ended, and the Dutch were eager to tap other sources of wealth in other parts of Africa and particularly in Asia. Many of the town's inhabitants refused to acknowledge the authority of the new power; the British responded by razing most of the surrounding town. After nearly 400 years, the British had become the sole European power on the Gold Coast.

See also: Atlantic Slave Trade; Cape Coast Castle; Gold Coast

Brent D. Singleton

Bibliography

DeCorse, Christopher R. *An Archaeology of Elmina: Africans and Europeans on the Gold Coast, 1400–1900.* Washington, D.C.: Smithsonian Institution Press, 2001.

Feinberg, Harvey M. *Africans and Europeans in West Africa: Elminans and Dutchmen on the Gold Coast during the Eighteenth Century.* Philadelphia: American Philosophical Society, 1989.

Hartman, Saidiya V. *Lose Your Mother: A Journey along the Atlantic Slave Route.* New York: Farrar, Straus and Giroux, 2007.

Holsey, Bayo. *Routes of Remembrance: Refashioning the Slave Trade in Ghana.* Chicago: University of Chicago Press, 2008.

Encomienda

Encomienda was a system of labor employed by the country of Spain within its own borders, and abroad in its possessions in the New World, during the late 15th to late 18th centuries. The encomienda is rooted in the tradition of medieval feudalism and is marked with two very distinct forms. The first version of the encomienda was practiced by the Christian rulers in Castile. Loyal citizens called *encomenderos* were temporarily granted by the sovereign the right to govern parcels of territory, which included population centers. Such areas were formerly under Muslim rule and had been reabsorbed into the Christian kingdoms during the period of the Reconquista. The encomenderos were permitted to collect a stipulated portion of the revenue from the reclaimed territory and were due the same services normally expected by the Crown.

The encomienda evolved as the Spanish empire seized control of territory from native populations in the New World. The American version of the encomienda began in the late 15th century with Christopher Columbus in Hispaniola. In an effort to feed the Spanish settlers and maximize tribute from the Native Americans under their sway, Columbus assigned a set number of Native Americans to labor for select citizens. This arrangement came to be known as *repartimiento*. Although Queen Isabella questioned the legal and ethical issues regarding the Native Americans who were placed in outright slavery or under the repartimiento, both systems continued. To get the unwilling Native Americans working to provide for the incoming Spanish settlers, who often were unable to fend for themselves the first few years, and set them to the grueling work in the mines, the governor of Hispaniola, Nicolas de Ovando, formalized the repartimiento in 1502.

Ovando altered it into a system similar to the encomienda found in Castile, but adapted to their current situation. Control was given over specified numbers of Native Americans rather than a geographic region. Some of the provisions developed by Ovando were that the property rights of the natives were to be honored, no physical harm was to come to them, and any of the Spaniards who had taken wives or daughters against their will as their own had to return them to their families, and further had to seek consent to marry.

Perhaps the most pivotal provision involved the spiritual welfare of the Native Americans. Properly indoctrinating the "savages" into the Christian church was the cornerstone of the encomienda system in the New World. Native Americans were to promptly abandon their ancient worship, attend services in the Catholic Church on a regular basis, and be properly baptized. This lent the encomienda a moral imperative to salve over the frequent abuses and excesses.

The Native Americans were to be considered free subjects, but it was necessary to employ their labor for farming or mining for the good of the commonwealth. Any returns for their labor was at the discretion of the Spanish. Measures to quell the inevitable dissent included a provision that no native was allowed to bear arms and another that prevented "Moors"—a term used to describe Berber Muslims, Jews, heretics, or *reconciliados* (people reconciled to the church)—from coming into the Indies.

A royal missive from Queen Isabella formalized much of Ovando's earlier instructions, stating that the Indian inhabitants were "free and not servile," that their spiritual education was paramount, and they were to work the fields and toil in the mines on behalf of the Spanish in exchange for wages determined by the local government. The result was a brutal system that was slavery in all but name and which decimated the native population.

Dominican missionaries, moved by the suffering of the natives, pleaded with Ferdinand for better treatment of his subjects. A council made up partly of theologians comprised the first codes of Native American law in 1512–1513, the Laws of Burgos. These 35 articles were to provide a more humane and Christian life for the natives. Their plight was later taken up by a Dominican convert named Bartolomé de Las Casas. Las Casas submitted a proposal that advocated freedom for the natives and the abolishment of the encomienda.

Under pressure to revise the system for humanitarian concerns, but mainly to reign in the power of the encomenderos, Charles I in 1520 ruled that the institution was to be phased out of the imperial arsenal; existing encomiendas were allowed to continue but if vacated they were not to be reassigned. Despite these changes Charles was compelled to revise the Laws of Burgos in 1542. Ultimately, any efforts at serious reform of this troubled system was hindered by the revenue generated.

The success of the encomienda paved the way for other exploitative labor systems such as debt peonage and the hacienda system. The encomienda, or one of its derivative offshoots, accompanied future Spanish colonization

in the Americas. Such systems were practiced in Puerto Rico, in Mexico after Cortes conquest of the Aztecs, in Peru after Pizarro's conquest of the Incan Empire, and in New Mexico. The encomienda system did not cross over into Florida, as it had fallen out of favor with the Crown by that point of settlement.

The encomienda gradually lost effectiveness due to the greatly reduced Native American population and change of focus from mining commodities to sustained agriculture. The encomienda was nonhereditary and as the number of encomenderos decreased, the population was reclaimed by the Crown. Pockets of this transitional labor system survived in the Platine region and in Paraguay until the late 1700s.

See also: de Las Casas, Bartolomé; Hispaniola; Reconquista

Michael Coker

Bibliography

Elliott, J. H. *Imperial Spain 1469–1716.* London: Penguin Books, 1963.

Gibson, Charles. *Spain in America.* New York: Harper Torchbooks, 1966.

Keith, Robert. *Encomienda, Hacienda and Corregimiento in Spanish America: A Structural Analysis.* Durham, NC: Duke University Press, 1971.

Simpson, Lesley Byrd. *The Encomienda in New Spain.* Berkeley: University of California Press, 1950.

Weber, David. *The Spanish Frontier in North America.* New Haven, CT: Yale University Press, 1992.

Estévan

Estévan (ca. 1500–1539), also referred to as Esteban, Esteban the Arab, Estevanillo, Estevanico, or Estevanico de Dorante, appears to have been born in the city of Azamor in Morocco. While accounts vary as to whether he was a willing participant or enslaved by a Spaniard on the expedition, Estévan joined the expedition of Narvaez when he was 28 to 30 years old, sailing from San Lucas de Barrameda, Spain, in 1527. The expedition began with 506 participants who landed on the coast of Florida. After a period of aimless wandering and skirmishes with the local native peoples, the Spaniards dwindled to 240 people.

Along with the remaining explorers, Estévan set sail across the Gulf of Mexico where the group was beset with more catastrophes and only four survived the journey—three Spaniards and Estévan. (Some sources identify all four survivors as Africans.) With no support, the four men struggled for eight years as they wandered across the unknown landscape, periodically battling and/or enslaved by the local groups. Eventually, the men became skilled in the native methods of medicine and were revered for their skills. All were elevated in stature to that of "Medicine Men" within the native communities.

Estévan, especially, developed skill using the Indian dialects and at understanding the characteristics of the individual groups. When the chance arose for the four gentlemen to return to Spain, the three other men accepted the opportunity while Estévan chose to remain in Mexico. He was greatly valued for his experience by the newly arrived Spanish who were interested in expanding Spain's influence in the region. Again, accounts vary as to Estévan's reasons for remaining in Mexico as one theory suggests that his language skills and social power as a Medicine Man allowed him substantial freedom and wealth within the native society, demanding gems and women from the local groups.

In 1539 Estévan was sent as a scout with two friars in search of the Seven Cities of Gold. Reportedly, as they traveled throughout the Southwest, the Spanish friars realized that Estévan was more easily accepted by the northern groups than they were and sent him on ahead to negotiate with groups as they approached new areas. The friars sent Estévan ahead into the Suni pueblo of Cibola where he was killed by the Zuni Indians—some say because they would not tolerate his demands for riches and women.

The role of Estévan in the exploration and discovery of new areas of Mexico and the American Southwest continues to be debated. The pejorative and continued use of "Estevanillo" and "Estevanico" as his name concerns scholars who argue that, as an enslaved African, he is assigned inappropriate and unattractive characteristics that are intended to rob him of his accomplishments. Many do agree that in his trip to Cibola he was the first non-native person to enter the territory that is now New Mexico, although Spaniards generally are given that credit.

See also: Atlantic Creoles; Hispaniola

Jane M. Aldrich

Bibliography

Schneider, Dorothy, and Carl J. Schneider. *An Eyewitness History of Slavery in America: From Colonial Times to the Civil War.* New York: Checkmark Books, 2001.

Wright, Richard R. "Negro Companions of the Spanish Explorers." *Phylon (1940–1956)* 2, no. 4 (1941):325–33.

Factor

Factors were agents of European commercial enterprises operating along the African coast beginning in the late 15th century. The term referred to European merchants who resided in the trading facilities, called factories. Many factors took African wives. Their offspring often became factors themselves, and were called *lancados* or creoles.

Factors functioned primarily as intermediaries between European/American merchants and African merchants. To ensure high quality of trade goods, factors inspected each shipment of goods from Europe and America, which included textiles, guns, and liquor. From Africans, factors traded a variety of commodities, which included gold, ivory, and dyes. These items were warehoused in storage facilities within the factory so as to make them quickly available for sale to European ship captains. Factors also conducted a lucrative slave trade with African merchants from the interior of the continent. Once obtained, slaves awaiting sale were kept in a special enclosed area of the factory known as a barracoon.

The *lancados* and creoles had a significant impact on African society. By the 18th century, there were more than 100 in the Elmina factory along the Gold Coast of West Africa, and they were just as numerous elsewhere along the west coast of Africa. European in dress and manners, knowledgeable about local practices, and multilingual, they were able to function easily in both societies. Rarely accepted by either society, however, they created their own separate societies. As cultural and economic brokers, they took advantage of the increasing competition among European and African traders. Without a specific European or African identity, however, they were placed in a very vulnerable position. Sometimes they were enslaved themselves. By the 19th century, as the slave trade declined, so did the importance of the factors.

See also: Atlantic Slave Trade; Bosman, Willem; Dutch West India Company; Elmina; Gold Coast; Royal African Company

Daniel P. Kotzin

Bibliography

Northrup, David, ed. *The Atlantic Slave Trade.* Boston: Houghton Mifflin, 2002.

Thornton, John. *Africa and Africans in the Making of the Atlantic World, 1400–1680.* New York: Cambridge University Press, 1992.

Freedom Dues

Freedom dues refer to the payment given to indentured servants by their masters, upon completion of their term of service. Most often these dues came in the form of clothing, land, seeds to plant crops such as tobacco, and sometimes livestock. Indentured servitude, as was carried out by settlers in the Virginia colony, was the solution proffered around 1620, to the crisis of labor shortage in the colonies. In exchange for a term of indenture, sometimes previously specified and at other times negotiated upon arrival, European immigrants had their passage from Europe to the colony paid. Initially, indentured servants were exclusively from England but later came from various places in Europe, including Scotland, Ireland, and Germany. These immigrants were overwhelmingly men of lower socioeconomic status in their home countries, who despite high mortality rates, came from Europe to Virginia in hopes of establishing themselves through the acquisition of wealth and gaining the social ascent that came with it.

For planters, initially, indentured servitude proved to be an effective system, as the numbers of newly freed servants who, using their freedom dues, established their own small tobacco farms, were minimal and therefore were not deemed a serious threat to the profits of their previous owners. After the middle of the 17th century, however, as death rates began to fall and life spans increased, the numbers, and indeed the profits, of the emerging planter class began to jeopardize those of the master class.

Several solutions were proposed to combat the adverse economic effects of the emerging planter class. One such measure used to address depressed tobacco prices and subsequent loss of profits was to extend servants' terms of indenture. Servants who engaged in behaviors that were deemed transgressive or disruptive, including but not limited to absconding, stealing, sexual liaisons resulting in childbirth, could be penalized though the lengthening of the term, among other more brutal forms of punishment.

However, the increasing emergence of the planter class was only one factor of an array including weather, war, and cessation that worked in concert to depress profits and rouse frustration and disillusionment among planters in Virginia. Eventually, it became apparent that economic effectiveness of indentured servitude had run its course, and some other, more permanent, less expensive, measure would have to be implemented if Virginias were to quell rebellious undercurrents and once again see the profits they enjoyed in the earlier part of the 17th century. Although slaves were present in the colonies in small numbers from approximately 1619, roughly the same time indentured servitude began to take hold, slavery as opposed to indentured servitude proved to be no more economically advantageous, but rather more costly, as the price of slaves compared to that of white immigrants, coupled with high death rates, was simply not as cost-effective as indentured servitude. By the 1660s, however, slavery would prove to be the answer to the problem of indentured servitude and become, arguably, the single most important factor, whose tenure and legacy would be essential in coloring the economic, social, and political landscape of what would become the United States.

See also: Chesapeake Colonies; Headright System; Indentured Servitude; Jamestown, Virginia

Christina Bush

Bibliography

Galenson, David W. "The Rise and Fall of Indentured Servitude in the Americas: An Economic Analysis." *The Journal of Economic History* 44 (1984):1–26.

Morgan, Edmund S. *American Slavery, American Freedom: The Ordeal of Colonial Virginia.* New York: W. W. Norton, 1975.

Shade, William G., and William R. Scott, ed. *Upon These Shores: Themes in the African American Experience 1600 to the Present.* New York: Routledge, 2000.

Futa Jallon

The history of the whole area from the Gambia to Sierra Leone was dominated from the beginning of the 18th century on by the development of the great Fulbe state of Futa Jallon. Thanks to it, long-distance trade carrying Sudanic influences found its way to the coast and there linked up with the Europeans. The Fulbe founded the Muslim state of Futa Jallon only after 1727.

Futa Jallon used to raid for slaves and imported a large number from the hinterland or took them from the coastal minority peoples. Some were then made available for export.

Futa Jallon developed as a center of Islamic learning. During the 18th century, Futa Jallon developed as an important intellectual center of Islam. Students were sent from great distances to study at the Islamic schools that had been established throughout the Futa Jallon region.

But, above all else, it was through trade that the Fulbe extended their influence throughout the region. The slave trade continued to be of paramount importance to the state of Futa Jallon long after its formal abolition by the British in 1807. Many slaves taken by the Fulbe were war captives, victims of various campaigns that had taken place between Futa Jallon and its neighboring rivals.

See also: Senegambia; Sierra Leone

Moshe Terdiman

Bibliography
Ade Ajayi, J. F., ed. *General History of Africa VI: Africa in the Nineteenth Century until the 1880s.* Oxford, UK: Heinemann International, 1989.
Gray, Richard, ed. *The Cambridge History of Africa.* Vol. 4, *From c. 1600 to c. 1790.* Cambridge, UK: Cambridge University Press, 1975.

Ghana

Founded by Soninke-speaking peoples, the Sudanic empire of Wagadu (Ghana) was the first of its kind in the region. Wagadu is also known more popularly as Ghana, a name derived from the Soninke word for "king," which Arab and North African merchants applied to the entire kingdom beginning in the eighth century CE. While the precise origins of Wagadu are unclear, in a text entitled *Tarikh as-Sudan* written in Timbuktu in 1650 the author claimed that there were at least 22 kings of Wagadu before CE 622. If true, this would place the origins of the kingdom at about CE 300. By CE 800, Wagadu had emerged as a powerful trading kingdom with an advantageous geographic locale in the region known as the Sahel. This transitory zone between the northern desert and the southern forests proved a fortuitous region for Wagadu as its rulers had the ability to collect tax revenues from the lucrative gold–salt trade. In addition to these revenues, the kingdom managed to subjugate an increasing number of smaller polities that were forced to pay tribute in the form of agricultural surplus, gold, and other commodities.

Wagadu's capital city, Kumbi Saleh, was the epitome of the wealth of the growing empire. Housing 15,000 to 20,000 people, Kumbi Saleh was the largest city in West Africa before CE 1300. Its stone houses and tombs, the elaborate royal court, and several magnificent mosques were important features of the capital. In Kumbi Saleh and coursing through trade centers throughout Wagadu were commodities originating from hundreds, if not thousands, of miles away, including horses, dates, silk, cowrie shells, and ivory. Wagadu's commercial power was more than matched by its military might. With the ability to field up to 60,000 conscripted and regular soldiers, the empire was the dominant military force in the western Sudan. In addition, iron smelting and the importation of horses combined to create significant military advantages that would be shared by subsequent Sudanic empires. Iron weapons—particularly swords, lances, javelins, and arrow tips—and the use of fast-moving cavalries allowed Wagadu to crush all local states. This uncontested domination came to an end in 1076 when the Almorvids, a kingdom of Islamic North Africans, defeated Wagadu's military and conquered the empire. The Almorvids had been Wagadu's principal rival for control over trans-Saharan trade routes. With Wagadu's defeat, its former tributary states would vie for power for more than 150 years before the emergence of Mali as the next great Sudanic empire.

See also: Mali; Sahel; Senegambia; Songhai; Sudanic Empires; Timbuktu; Tribute

Walter C. Rucker

Bibliography
Conrad, David C. *Empires of Medieval West Africa: Ghana, Mali, and Songhay.* New York: Facts on File, 2005.
Davidson, Basil. *West Africa before the Colonial Era.* London: Longman, 1998.
Quigley, Mary. *Ancient West African Kingdoms: Ghana, Mali, and Songhai.* Chicago: Heinemann Library, 2002.

Gold Coast

Derived from the Portuguese in the late 15th century and later adopted by the British, Gold Coast is the colonial name of the region located on the coast of West Africa, neighboring present-day Togo to the east, Côte d'Ivoire to the west, and Burkina Faso to the north. The region comprises primarily the Akan, Ewe, Ga, and Moshi-Dagomba peoples. Gold, as the name suggests, was plentiful in this region, attracting both African and European traders. In the early

18th century with the emergence of European interests in the New World, humans replaced gold as the main export from this region. Captives from the Gold Coast were highly valued in parts of North America such as Jamaica and South Carolina.

The Akan controlled the gold trade by the 14th century, exchanging cloth, kola nuts, and salt with Muslim traders from the north. The focus of the northern gold trade changed with the arrival of the Portuguese in 1471. Attracted to the large quantity of gold in this region, the Portuguese labeled the area "Costa d'Mina." They traded firearms and captives from other parts of Africa for gold. In 1482, the Portuguese established their first trading post, São Jorge. Soon after, other European nations such as France, the Netherlands, and Great Britain built their own posts along the coast.

The increasing demand from European nations with New World colonies shifted the trade from gold to human captives. The firearms supplied by Europeans aided the growth of the slave trade by provoking wars of conquest and, consequently, more captives.

During the 17th and 18th centuries, European traders identified Africans exported from this region as "Kromantine." The term, also seen as "Coromantin" and "Caramantee," refers to an English trading post and a commercial village located on the coast. The English as well as the Dutch preferred captives from the Gold Coast because they were considered good farmers and domestic servants. The Dutch enslaved large numbers of captives from this region in Suriname, while the English shipped their prisoners to the West Indies and South Carolina.

The structure of the trade and politics on the Gold Coast changed again in the early 19th century after European nations abolished the slave trade. European nations resumed their interest in gold, while the Asante and Fante (subgroups of the Akan) nations fought wars for territorial control. The British gradually dominated the region by creating a protectorate over the Fante states in 1844, battling the Asante in a series of wars, and declaring the Gold Coast a Crown colony in 1874. The Asante refused to acknowledge the British treaty of protection and in 1896, the British exiled the Asante king, Prempeh I, and formally annexed the Asante nation and northern territories. After a British attempt to obtain the Golden Stool, an Asante symbol of authority, Yaa Asantewaa led the nation in a final uprising that resulted in Asante defeat. In 1901 the British had colonial rule over the Asante and Fante nations. After World War I, the British colonial government obtained its final territory from parts of German Togoland, which brought all of present-day Ghana under colonial rule.

On March 6, 1957, under the leadership of Kwame Nkrumah, people in the Gold Coast gained their independence. Nkrumah renamed the region Ghana after the western Sudanic kingdom.

See also: Atlantic Slave Trade; Coromantee; Elmina; Kingdom of Asante; Nkrumah, Kwame

Zawadi I. Barskile

Bibliography

Gomez, Michael. *Exchanging Our Country Marks: The Transformation of African Identities in the Colonial and Antebellum South.* Chapel Hill: University of North Carolina Press, 1998.

Hartman, Saidiya V. *Lose Your Mother: A Journey along the Atlantic Slave Route.* New York: Farrar, Straus and Giroux, 2007.

Kea, Ray A. *Settlements, Trade, and Polities in the Seventeenth-Century Gold Coast.* Baltimore, MD: Johns Hopkins University Press, 1982.

Ward, W. E. F. *A History of the Gold Coast.* London: G. Allen and Unwin, 1948.

Gorée Island

Gorée is a 45-acre island off the west coast of the African nation of Senegal. As a result of its convenient location (at the entrance to the Middle Passage), Gorée became the center of the European slave trade from 16th century to the 19th century. Throughout this time, it was ruled in succession by the Portuguese, Dutch, English, and French. Gorée Island was used as a holding ground for slaves before they were sold. Millions of Africans were captured and brought to Gorée before being shipped across the Atlantic to landowners in South America, North America, and the Caribbean. Given what we now know about the immensity of the slave trade, millions of Africans went to the House of Slaves, the main holding area, and passed through the Door of No Return before being sent across the Middle Passage.

The main structure on Gorée, the House of Slaves, was built by the Dutch in 1777. In the House of Slaves, up to 30 men would be shackled and forced into an eight-square-foot room to sit for days until they were sold. Children were separated from their mothers and piled into cells specifically

Room in the House of Slaves on Gorée Island off the coast of Senegal. (Shutterstock)

for them. The mothers were kept across the courtyard from their families, as to inhibit conversation between them. Slaves were fed once a day. They were naked, save a small piece of fabric around their waists, and forced to defecate in their cells. Above these holding areas there were more luxurious accommodations for the dealers and European officials who hosted parties and dinners on a regular basis. In 1848, the French abolished slavery and freed the slaves who were left on Gorée. At this time, there were 6,000 inhabitants on Gorée, 5,000 of them former slaves.

The island was named a United Nations Education, Scientific, Cultural Organization (UNESCO) World Heritage Site and is now one of Senegal's major tourist attractions. The island has been visited by myriad foreign dignitaries and international figures, including the pope, Nelson Mandela, President Bill Clinton, and President George Bush. The principal sites on the island include the Maison des Esclaves (The House of Slaves), The IFAN Museum (dedicated to the history of Senegal), Le Musée de la Femme (The Women's Museum, which discusses the role of women in West African societies), and Le Musée Maritime (The Maritime Museum).

See also: Atlantic Slave Trade; Signares

Jen Westmoreland Bouchard

Bibliography

Barboza, Steven. *Door of No Return: The Legend of Gorée Island.* New York: Cobblehill Books, 1994.

Harrison, Richard. *Gorée Island: The Island of No Return: Saga of the Signares.* Mt. Clemens, MI: Gold Leaf Press, 1996.

Griot

A griot is a member of a hereditary caste of praise singers, poets, genealogists, storytellers, musicians, and oral historians in West African society. The griot are present among the many peoples of West Africa such as the Mandinka, Malinke, Fulani, Hausa, Tukulor, Wolof, and live in many parts of West Africa today, including Mali, Gambia, Guinea, and Senegal. The role of the griot in African history and society is multifaceted. Africa as a continent with 54 countries and over 1,000 major ethno-linguistic groups coupled with multiple communal dialects (some with no relationship to the major language groups of the continent) has a long oral tradition of which the profession of the griot is integral. "Griot" is a French transliteration of the word *guirot* and in English understood as griot and griottes for females. The Portuguese pronounced the term as *criado* for servant. In West African dialects, the word *jeliya* ("transmission by blood," indicating the hereditary nature of the title), which comes from the root word *jeli* or *djeli* ("blood"), is used for "griot" by Africans residing in areas that formerly constituted the Mali Empire (1235–1645). The Mali Empire was founded by Sundiata (1235–1260) and at its height encompassed the geographic area from Chad and Nigeria in central Africa to Mali and Senegal in West Africa today. The first professional griot, Balla Fasseke, appeared during the Mali Empire and founded the Kouyate line of griots as mentioned in "The Epic of Sundiata."

Griots both performed and preserved traditions through story and song. They were responsible for learning both the quantity and content of a song, melodies, and rhythms, thereby preserving the story, genealogy, and history of a warrior king or village. Griots have been said to possess the ability to sing of one's "fortune or doom" because the words they espouse as "keepers of the word" are considered sacred and powerful. Each village, clan, and royal warrior family had a griot that maintained an oral record and told stories of births, marriages, battles, and other significant historical events. Griots have been known to memorize the entire genealogy or family history of everyone in an entire village going back for centuries. The African American author of *Roots: The Saga of an American Family* (1976) Alex Haley claimed to have heard the stories of his long-lost relative Kunta Kinte from the stories of West African griots. According to Haley, through his encounter with a West African griot in 1966, he was able to hear the story of Kunta Kinte's capture and enslavement. The history of West Africa has been largely preserved through the stories of the griot.

Aspects of the griot's craft in terms of poetics, music, and the centrality of orality survive in African and African American contemporary culture. These characteristics include call-and-response, repetition, contrapuntal rhythms, and the use of symbolism and metaphor to represent events or people in time. Elements such as these are present in blues, jazz, and hip-hop music today. The griot has not disappeared from African history. Although griots were customarily provided with gifts for their services, many griots today have talent agents, record compact discs, and receive fees for their professional services. The Cheick Oumor Sissoko film *Guimba the Tyrant* features a griot character, and the writer Ahmadou Kourouma incorporated important griot characters into his novels *Waiting for the Wild Beasts* and *Allah Is Not Obliged*. An estimated 90 percent of Senegalese musical performers today claim the status of griot.

See also: Mali; Occupational Castes; Oral Culture; Senegambia; Songhai; Sundiata: The Epic of Old Mali

Hettie V. Williams

Bibliography
Ebron, Paula A. *Performing Africa*. Princeton, NJ: Princeton University Press, 2002.
Hale, Thomas. *Griot and Griottes: Masters of Words and Music*. Bloomington: Indiana University Press, 1999.
Hoffman, Barbara G. *Griots at War: Conflict, Conciliation and Caste in Mande*. Bloomington: Indiana University Press, 2001.
Wright, Donald R. *Oral Traditions from the Gambia: Mandinka Griots*. Athens: Ohio University Press, 1979.

Gulf of Guinea

The Portuguese explorer Nuno Tristo sailed around the coast of West Africa, reaching the Guinea area in about 1450, searching for the source of gold and other valuable commodities, notably slaves. With the help of local groups in about 1600, the Portuguese, and numerous other European powers, including France, Britain, and Sweden, set up a thriving slave trade along the West African coast. It will never be known exactly how many human lives were bought and sold in the slave markets along the Guinea coast, but it is today approximated at 10 million.

Dahomey fell within that area of West Africa that received the toponym of the Slave Coast. Throughout the 17th century, the Dutch had obtained some slaves from Allada, especially after 1635 when their Brazilian possessions required African labor. The period of notoriety began when the Dutch were joined by other Europeans in the scramble for slaves from 1670 onward. The French started trading at Allada in 1670. They built the first European factory at Whydah in the following year and English slave traders

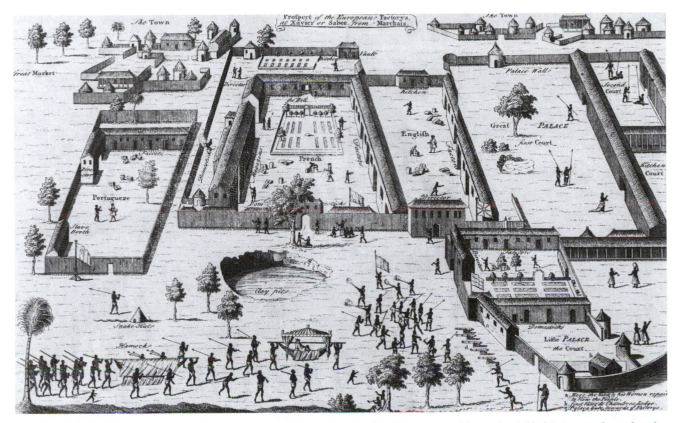

An 18th-century engraving of a slave compound maintained by traders from four European nations on the Gulf of Guinea in the mid-18th century. (Library of Congress)

established a factory in Allada in 1674. Up to about 1671, an estimated annual average of about 3,000 captives were exported from Aja ports. Within a decade, the figure was probably doubled at Allada, and Whydah went to the forefront. Thus, coastal societies were fully exposed to the damaging impact of the European slave trade.

See also: Atlantic Slave Trade; Bight of Benin; Bight of Biafra; Bosman, Willem; Gold Coast; Kingdom of Dahomey; Sierra Leone

Moshe Terdiman

Bibliography

Gray, Richard, ed. *The Cambridge History of Africa.* Vol. 4, *From c. 1600 to c. 1790.* Cambridge, UK: Cambridge University Press, 1975.

Headright System

When the first permanent English colony in North America, Jamestown, was founded in 1607 it was immediately beset by a series of problems. In addition to the colonists being ill prepared to create sufficient amounts of food, they struggled with the Powhatan Confederacy and a sheer inability to locate easily exploitable resources. The combination of famine and wars with local Native Americans meant that Jamestown would struggle to maintain the population needed to make the colony a success. By 1611 the colonists of Jamestown had discovered a means to create enormous profits in the form of tobacco cultivation. However, with high mortality rates came a severe lack of labor in order to make this new cash crop reach its profit potential. In an attempt to solve the labor crisis, the Virginia Company of London granted headrights to settlers in Jamestown as a means of recruiting more people, growing the population, and meeting the labor demand in the tobacco fields.

Beginning in 1618, headrights were legal grants to land offered to settlers in Jamestown and could range from 50 to 100 acres of land for those willing and able to make the Atlantic crossing to Virginia. Moreover, headrights were granted as bounties to tobacco planters who were willing to finance the transportation costs of anyone willing to serve a five- to seven-year term of indenture and to be employed, principally, growing tobacco. In this way, the already established tobacco planters received two critical and highly profitable benefits through headrights—more land and a steady supply of labor.

The headrights in the Chesapeake were similar to patroonships granted to Dutch settlers in New Netherland. In fact, the use of headrights spread to other English colonies including Maryland, South Carolina, and North Carolina. Despite the initial success of this system, indentured servants, including the 300 Africans imported into the Chesapeake between 1619 and 1640, represented a significant set of new problems for tobacco planters: they only worked a set number of years before they were freed; once freed, they received "freedom dues" including seed, land, farming tools, and guns; as land-owning tobacco farmers, ex-servants represented a source of competition for the tobacco-planting elite; and the increased production of tobacco caused by the ever-increasing number of tobacco planters drove down the price of the once-lucrative crop.

See also: Chesapeake Colonies; Freedom Dues; Indentured Servitude; Jamestown, Virginia; Patroonship; Tobacco

Walter C. Rucker

Bibliography
Morgan, Edmund S. *American Slavery, American Freedom: The Ordeal of Colonial Virginia.* New York: W. W. Norton, 1975.
Wood, Peter H. *Strange New Land: Africans in Colonial America.* New York: Oxford University Press, 1996.

Hispaniola

The island of *Hispaniola,* today's Haiti and the Dominican Republic, weaves together the stories of the indigenous inhabitants of the island, the *Tainos,* the slaves, and the French and Spanish colonial powers. Sent by the government of Spain, Christopher Columbus first arrived on the island in 1492, and soon after his arrival, Spaniards began arriving in mass numbers in order to establish farms, ranches, and mines, drawing from the vast amounts of resources the new land had to offer. Many of the native inhabitants began to die at alarming rates, resulting from harsh treatment and/or from the plethora of diseases brought by the colonists. In response to this loss, and in need of a labor force to support the growing economy, the colonists began importing African slaves to work the land. In 1494, on his second voyage to America, Columbus settled on the north coast of the island, and officially established the colony known as Santo Domingo.

The western third of the island, colonial Saint Domingue, which is known today as Haiti, had been given to the French by the Spanish in 1697. By 1791, nearly 100 years after the transfer of colonial power, it is estimated that more than 864,000 African slaves had been imported by the French, thus allowing the colony to become one of the main economic centers in the New World. In fact, the plantation-based economy, with about 8,000 plantations that produced crops for export, led in sugar and coffee production, producing nearly half of that consumed in Europe and the Americas. In addition, Saint Domingue produced large quantities of molasses, rum, indigo, and cotton, also for export.

Population totals in 1790 estimated more than half-a-million people living in Saint Domingue. Of the three social divisions of people, the whites, or *grands blancs,* were at the top of the social hierarchy, totaling about 40,000. The slaves, the majority of whom were African-born, were at the bottom of social hierarchy, and totaled about 450,000 in number. In between these two groups were the "freed people," or *affranchis,* who were also referred to as mulattos, and they totaled about 28,000 in number. The *affranchis* were particularly significant because many members of this group had a dual social role in that they had particular economic interests and legal rights similar to those of whites, but many, unless they could pass for white, suffered discrimination based on their color, thus allowing them to also identify with the slaves. They also had a stronghold on a vast percentage of the economic resources, which was a source of tension with the whites, but became a moot point when the slaves revolted.

Born a slave in 1743, Pierre-Dominique Toussaint Louverture became a key figure in the slave-led revolt. The revolt coincided with the French Revolution in Paris, and given Saint Domingue's economic wealth, both England and Spain were interested in the land. The revolt in essence had become a "three-way racial war" among the whites, mulattos, and the slaves over access to economic resources. Toussaint joined the revolt in 1791, providing the structured and organized leadership needed at the time. He initially joined forces with the Spanish against the French, then defeated both the Spanish and English, and re-aligned with the French given that, in 1793, they had officially abolished slavery in Saint Domingue with civil rights given to

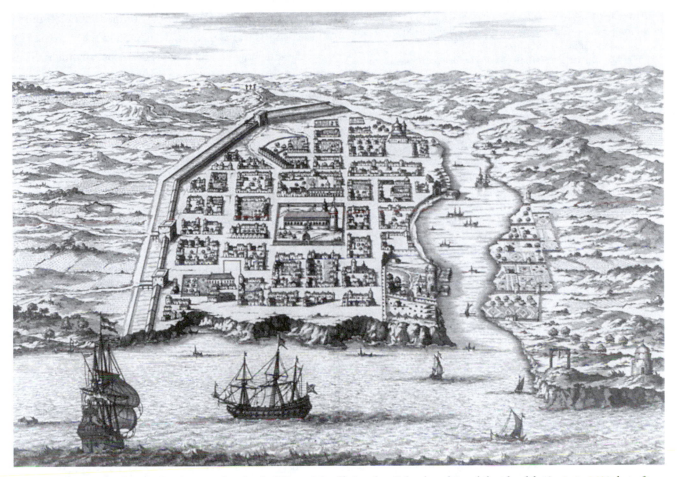

Engraving from 1671 of Santo Domingo on the island of Hispaniola. Christopher Columbus claimed the island for Spain in 1492, but after 50 years of exploiting its resources and bringing disease to its inhabitants, Spain found Santo Domingo to be an unprofitable colony. The destruction of the native population of Hispaniola prompted Bartolomé de las Casas to suggest the use of enslaved Africans as a replacement labor force in the Spanish Americas. (Library of Congress)

all regardless of color. Late in 1800, Toussaint then marched into Santo Domingo with his armies and overtook it. Soon after entering, he announced the emancipation of all slaves on the island and incorporated the former Spanish colony into his own state, which was still a French colony. Toussaint continued to lead until 1802, but was tricked by the French that same year and imprisoned. He died in 1803, the same year that Jean-Jacques Dessalines, one of Toussaint's army commanders, was finally able to defeat the remaining French insurgency. Dessalines became the first president of the republic of Haiti, declaring its independence on January 1, 1804.

Political struggles over land in the colony of Santo Domingo ensued over the next 44 years, with political rule changing hands between the Spanish and the French at various times, with Haiti ruling the colony from 1822 to 1844. Finally, on February 27, 1844, the colony of Santo Domingo

was able to proclaim its independence after Jean-Pierre Boyer, the Haitian ruler who had occupied Santo Domingo for the last 22 years, was overthrown. Juan Pablo Duarte, the leader of *la Trinitaria*, a secret nationalist organization, along with Ramón Mella and Francisco del Rosario Sánchez, were responsible for overthrowing Boyer. It was at this time they established a constitution and declared themselves to be a new nation, the Dominican Republic. Unfortunately, this was only the beginning of a long and tumultuous relationship between Haiti and the Dominican Republic, and a series of political struggles between the two nations has ensued.

See also: Asiento; Boyer, Jean Pierre; de Las Casas, Bartolomé; Encomienda; Haitian Revolution; Las Siete Partidas; Louverture, Toussaint

Julie M. Skogsbergh

Bibliography

Fagg, John Edwin. *Cuba, Haiti, and the Dominican Republic.* Englewood Cliffs, NJ: Prentice-Hall, 1965.

Geggus, David Patrick. *Haitian Revolutionary Studies.* Bloomington: Indiana University Press, 2002.

Geracimos, A. "A Mystery in Miniature: An Enigmatic Button Once Decorated the Uniform of Haitian Liberator Toussaint Louverture." *Smithsonian Magazine* 30 (2000):20–21.

Mintz, S. W. "Can Haiti Change?" *Foreign Affairs* 74 (1995):73–87.

Moya Pons, Frank. *The Dominican Republic: A National History.* Princeton, NJ: Markus Wiener, 1998.

Nicholls, David. *Haiti in Caribbean Context: Ethnicity, Economy and Revolt.* New York: St. Martin's Press, 1985.

Igbo

Igbo-speakers from the Bight of Biafra—the inland region of modern Nigeria—had a significant influence on what became African American culture. Known variably as Ebo(e), Ibo(e), and Eboan, Igbo-speakers represent loosely connected language cohorts and not a single or unified ethnic group or people. The Bight of Biafra itself was a region of vast cultural diversity and included a variety of language cohorts—Igbo, Ibibio, Igala, Efik, and Ijo, among others. Despite this diversity, three-quarters of all enslaved Africans embarked on European ships in Biafra and Calabar were of likely Igbo- and Ibibio-speaking backgrounds. During the course of the Atlantic slave trade, it became standard practice to lump together most if not all Africans exported from the Bight of Biafra under the "Igbo" linguistic and cultural banner.

Kwa language groups including Igbo-speakers originated, historically, near the confluence of the Niger and Benue rivers and these groups eventually migrated to their present-day homeland near the Niger and Cross rivers in modern Nigeria. Igbo-speakers and others are credited with the rise of Nok culture—an iron-based society in existence between 500 BCE to CE 200. By the 9th century CE, Igbo speakers founded the Nri and Igbo-Ukwu—the latter known for the production of bronze figurines and statuettes using the lost wax technique. Igbo-speaking expertise in metalsmithing and metallurgy served as a basis for the development of the famous Benin and Ife bronzes created beginning in the 10th century CE. These earlier Igbo-speaking societies were also notable for their high population densities, political decentralization, and agrarian economies—patterns that would persist into the 17th and 18th centuries.

By the beginning of the 17th century, Igbo-speaking groups had largely settled into the areas they currently occupy, but the development of a unified identity among these peoples was something facilitated in the Americas by slavery and in the Biafran interior by European imperialism. In this way, speaking Igbo and being Igbo were not the same thing (just as speaking English and being English are not). Typically, identity in the precolonial Biafran interior—and for that matter, other parts of the African continent—was based on local or provisional concerns. Thus, across the various Igbo-speaking cities and villages, despite similarities in language and culture, the people would have understood themselves to be distinct based on a range of factors, including political affiliation with a particular polity. The "Igbo" did not exist as a distinct ethnicity in Atlantic Africa until they were created in the 20th century as a direct consequence of British colonial policy and the need for solidarity in the presence of a new and foreign enemy. Like a number of ethnonyms used by Europeans during the slave trade era, Calabar, Moko, and Igbo were imprecise and, at times, overlapping identities that Africans in this region did not create or embrace. However, "Igbo" was a term Igbo-speaking people embraced abroad and the best example of this comes from the most famous Igbo-speaker to be enslaved in the Americas—Olaudah Equiano.

In the Americas, the Igbo were generally reviled as enslaved imports due to their alleged propensity to commit suicide. In general, European preferences for certain African ethnic groups in the Americas were due to a range of factors—the cost of importing enslaved Africans from certain regions, limited access to certain slave markets on the Atlantic African coast, or the demand for Africans from specific regions with expertise in the cultivation of certain crops and other skills. In the case of the Igbo, the various stereotypes associated with them—their propensity for suicide, their slight stature, and physical endurance—relegated them to backwater slave colonies and, in some cases, relegated them to domestic service. Regarding their concentration in backwater colonies, the Du Bois Institute database bears out this conclusion. The Du Bois database, for example, demonstrates that of 101,925 enslaved Africans from identifiable locations sent to Virginia, 44.8 percent came from the Bight of Biafra. In South Carolina—a more central colony in terms of the slave trade—enslaved Africans from the Bight of Biafra accounted for just 9.89 percent of identifiable imports; in British North America/the United States as a whole, Bight of Biafra exports were 18.6 percent of those imported. So it is possible to discuss, as historians Lorena Walsh, James Sidbury, and Douglas Chambers have, a Bight of Biafra (Igbo) enclave in Virginia as a phenomenon unique in North America.

The Igbo-speaking imports into the Chesapeake played a significant factor in the rise of Afro-Virginian culture. One implication of the presence of so many Igbo-speakers was the proliferation of Igbo terms and concepts—*okra, buckra, obia*—or discrete Igbo cultural practices (e.g., the Jonkonu celebration, funerary customs, and spiritual beliefs) in Jamaica, Virginia, and other regions of the Anglophone Americas that imported significant numbers of Africans from the Bight of Biafra. Another implication was the possibility that Gabriel Prosser—leader of the failed Richmond, Virginia, slave revolt in 1800—was accorded a great deal of respect and veneration because of his blacksmithing skills and the spiritual powers associated with this trade among the peoples living in the Biafran interior. In fact, three separate blacksmiths were claimed to have been part of the leadership core of this attempt to capture and raze the capital of Virginia.

See also: Buckra; Coromantee; Ebo Landing; Transmigration

Walter C. Rucker

Bibliography

Byrd, Alexander X. "Eboe, Country, Nation, and Gustavus Vassa's Interesting Narrative." *William and Mary Quarterly* 63 (2006):123–48.

Chambers, Douglas B. "'My Own Nation': Igbo Exiles in the Diaspora." *Slavery and Abolition* 18 (1997):72–97.

Chambers, Douglas B. "The Significance of Igbo in the Bight of Biafra Slave-Trade: A Rejoinder to Northrup's 'Myth Igbo.'" *Slavery and Abolition* 23 (2002):101–20.

Gomez, Michael. *Exchanging Our Country Marks: The Transformation of African Identities in the Colonial and Antebellum South.* Chapel Hill: University of North Carolina Press, 1998.

Northup, David. "Igbo and Myth Igbo: Culture and Ethnicity in the Atlantic World, 1600–1850." *Slavery and Abolition* 21 (2000):1–20.

Sidbury, James. *Ploughshares into Swords: Race, Rebellion, and Identity in Gabriel's Virginia, 1730–1810.* New York: Cambridge University Press, 1997.

Walsh, Lorena S. *From Calabar to Carter's Grove: The History of a Virginia Slave Community.* Charlottesville: University of Virginia Press, 1997.

Indentured Servitude

Before the introduction of African slaves to the North American colonies in 1619 and as a result of the inability to enslave the native Indian population, most un-free labor in the American colonies, prior to 1700, came in the form of white indentured servitude. Many Native Americans groups residing in what became British North America were not a successful labor source due to the fact that many died from Old World diseases or were unaccustomed to the skills required for surplus agricultural production. In some cases, particularly among Algonquian-speaking groups, a unique gender divide of labor in which women performed agricultural work and men hunted would have made their successful enslavement difficult given the English proclivity for enslaving men in the production of cash crops. Additionally, settlers could expect reprisals if they enslaved the local native peoples.

Thus, voluntary indentured servants accounted for nearly half the white settlers in all the colonies outside of New England. The term derived from the indenture, or contract, signed by poor persons, who promised to work for a fixed number of years in return for the cost of their transatlantic voyage. Generally, the term of service lasted five to seven years and once their service ended, indentured servants hoped to become landowners themselves. During the 17th century the desire for land drew to the North American colonies a significant number of English, Irish, and German men and women willing to serve as un-free laborers.

Most of those who chose to become indentured servants came from British cities infested with poverty, pollution, and disease. The hard work and loss of personal freedom was seen as a small price to pay for the opportunity to start over in the New World. Nevertheless, not all servants went voluntarily. Some criminals escaped prison or death through a sentence that relocated them to the colonies. Still others in the poverty-ridden urban centers were "kidnapped" and sold into servitude.

Most indentured servants immigrated to the Chesapeake region (the Virginia and Maryland colonies) throughout the 17th and early 18th centuries. Of the English emigrants to the region during that period, nearly 60 percent came under indenture. These servants would live in their master's household, where they were given room and board but no other wages or compensation during their term of service. The contract could be sold or transferred from one master to another without consent from the servant. The vast majority of servants were single people who were not allowed to marry until they were independent. By law, at the end of the contracted period, most servants were granted "freedom dues," goods, and sometimes land, to support themselves as independent settlers.

Although the system of indenture was more formalized than most labor arrangements in England during this period, the practice was similar to that of a trade apprenticeship that most Englishmen were familiar with. An apprenticeship was a dependent position that usually lasted for seven years; the apprentice would live and eat in the master's house. In turn the master would train the young apprentice in a useful craft. Often this process was a step in becoming part of a guild or led to the status of a master craftsman. Some historians see the indentured servants as an extension of the apprenticeship of servants in the art of husbandry (farming).

The system of indentured servitude and the labor that it brought to the Chesapeake colonies was in demand due to the agricultural needs of the settlers. Free settlers needed laborers to clear land for agricultural production and to tend the tobacco fields. Paid wage labor was too expensive and there was little natural population growth within the free white community. Due to the hot, humid climate and harsh terrain of swamps and dense forests, many settlers died in the first years. This high mortality rate meant that early in the settlement process, population growth could only be achieved by bringing in people from outside the North American colonies. After they had become accustomed to the climate and fought off diseases like malaria, a process called at the time "seasoning," the population began to naturally increase. Once tobacco was grown widely in the Tidewater regions of the Chesapeake, a readily accessible and cheap workforce was essential to make profits. Indentured servitude fit the bill and the population of the Chesapeake swelled based on the influx of servants. In the mid-1620s the population of Virginia was recorded at 1,200. By 1660 the population had risen to nearly 21,000.

Based on the cost of their transport to the New World, compared to that of daily or weekly wage laborers, indentured servants were at the time the most cost-effective labor force. For this reason they remained in high demand for most of the 17th century and due to the type of work required of the servants, the white population in Virginia and Maryland was drastically distorted. Most indentured laborers were young adult males, thus an unbalanced sex ratio developed. By the mid-17th century, men outnumbered women six to one among emigrants to the Chesapeake region. This situation, along with the disease environment of Virginia and Maryland, slowed the formation of stable family units. It was not until the 18th century that a more balanced gender ratio developed in the Chesapeake region. In New England family migrations from the Old World were the norm and a more temperate climate resulted in high fertility rates along with low death rates. In the initial settlement of New England, around one-third of the settlers were indentured servants. After the Great Migration of the 1630s, few indentured servants were imported to New England.

Treatment of indentured servants, just as it did for slaves, differed greatly from one master to another. According to legal statutes slaves, servants, and any other dependents could be beaten for insubordination. Punishment for servants who ran away was severe. Initially, running way could be punished by death. Later Virginia and other colonies moved away from capital punishment and substituted extra service time to the servant's term of indenture. According to local and colonial law, the extra time ranged from 10 days for each day a servant was away to thousands of days of additional service. Additionally, a master could sell the reminder of the servant's service and prohibit his right to marry.

However, local courts in the Chesapeake provided protection for servant's rights, which gave servants more protection than slaves. By law masters were required to provide appropriate lodging and food for their servants; they could not make a second indenture with servants who had completed their term; also, they were not allowed to overwork or mistreat servants beyond the statutory limitations for corporal punishment. Servants fared better than slaves in other respects; they had access to the courts and were entitled to own land.

Servants who believed they had been mistreated could bring their masters to court through a petition. Unlike slaves or servants in Britain, they had full testimonial capacity. Court records indicate that they often succeeded in their claims regarding poor treatment over food, shelter, or clothing. Yet, when witnesses were required to substantiate the claims, the servant filing the complaint ran a risk of failure, since more often than not the witness was another servant. These servant witnesses were not always reliable because they feared reprisals from the master. A significant number of cases indicate that masters often abused their servants. This abuse could take the form of beatings or overwork, which included requiring a servant to work at night. Masters who were found guilty of the charges against them received "punishments" ranging from directions from the court to stop the offending acts to minimal fines.

The social status of indentured servants was another way in which their plight fared better than slaves. Historians have found that prior to entering into their indenture, servants' occupations ranged from husbandmen and yeoman farmers to artisans, tradesmen, and laborers. There were also unskilled workers, unemployed persons (debtors), and criminals. Whatever their status upon entering into indentured servitude, there was no stigma for them when they became freemen.

From the early to mid-1600s, there are a number of cases of former indentured servants experiencing successful lives in the New World after they finished their contracts. Most married shortly after they were freed, some became successful landowners, and a few rose to positions of power. In 1629 seven members of the Virginia legislature were formerly indentured servants. However, at the end of the 17th century and early 18th century, many indentured servants were not given land. Some became artisans or skilled craftsmen and worked as laborers in an ever-increasing competitive market. Nearly 80 percent, however, either died as servants, returned to England, or became part of the lowest segment of colonial free society, poor white workers. This growing population of landless, disgruntled former servants led to an increased desire for slaves and to Bacon's Rebellion, which signaled an eventual end to indentured servitude.

In 1676, Nathaniel Bacon, a rich English squire's son who had been in Virginia for only two years, led a band of mostly former indentured servants and small farmers in attacks on both frontier Indians and the Virginia governor, Lord Berkeley. They desired more land and wanted the colonial government to help push the Native Americans off the land. Bacon's men eventually burned Jamestown, but failed in their attempt to take control of the government. Bacon fell ill and died near the end of the conflict. Governor Berkeley gained control and executed 23 of the rebels. The king considered Berkeley's actions too harsh and recalled him to England. In the end, Virginia's planters began to consider indentured servants a possible risk.

In addition to Bacon's Rebellion, several other factors contributed to the end of indentured servitude in colonial North America. First, the economic situation in Britain improved to a point where many of the urban poor could find employment at home and thus indentured service was not as enticing. Next, mortality rates in the Chesapeake region improved, birth rates increased, and the free white population experienced a natural population growth. Finally, most planters and small farmers found it more economical to purchase African slaves who would not be freed after five to seven years. African slavery as the mode of labor was what colonists in the Chesapeake and throughout the other colonies turned to in the late 17th and 18th centuries.

See also: Bacon's Rebellion; Chesapeake Colonies; Freedom Dues; Headright System; Jamestown, Virginia; Johnson, Anthony; Malaria; Tobacco

Ira Lee Berlet

Bibliography
Berlin, Ira. *Many Thousands Gone: The First Two Centuries of Slavery in North America.* Cambridge, MA: Belknap Press of Harvard University, 1998.
Breen, T. H., and Stephen Innes. *"Myne Owne Ground": Race and Freedom on Virginia's Eastern Shore, 1640–1676.* New York: Oxford University Press, 1980.
Cooper Jr., William J., and Thomas E. Terrill. *The American South: A History.* Vol. 1. New York: McGraw-Hill, 1991.
Kolchin, Peter. *American Slavery 1619–1877.* New York: Hill and Wang, 1993.
Morgan, Kenneth. *Slavery and Servitude in Colonial North America: A Short History.* New York: New York University Press, 2001.

Jamestown, Virginia

Jamestown was the capital of Virginia from the English colony's founding in 1609 until it was replaced by nearby Williamsburg 90 years later. Almost as soon as the colonists in Jamestown discovered the potential of tobacco as a cash crop, they began to import African slaves to help them grow it. Seventeenth-century Afro-Virginians' experiences with slavery were quite different from what their descendants would face in the 18th and 19th centuries. During most of the 17th century, only a small number of blacks lived in Virginia, and they were often treated as well (or as badly) as the English indentured servants who lived and worked alongside them. Seventeenth-century Afro-Virginians lived in a society in which racial distinctions were not yet seen by most whites as reasons for discrimination; some blacks were never enslaved, and there was even a chance for fortunate slaves to obtain their freedom and prosper as respectable small planters. But economic, demographic, and political changes in the last quarter of the century—particularly after Bacon's Rebellion in 1676—eroded the opportunities that blacks had taken advantage of earlier in the settlement's history. By 1699, when Jamestown lost its position as the colony's capital, Virginia blacks had likewise lost most of the potential for freedom and economic independence that they had briefly enjoyed.

The first record of Africans in Virginia is the purchase planter John Rolfe (widower of Pocahontas) made of 20 blacks from a Dutch ship in 1619. Recent research throws into question whether the slaves were newly arrived from Africa or transplanted slaves from the sugar-producing islands of the Caribbean, or if the ship was really Dutch. Another unanswered question is whether the score of blacks purchased by Rolfe were treated as slaves for life, or as indentured servants, serving for a term of years before earning their freedom. Rolfe's purchase of African labor in 1619 was one way of satiating Virginia's new demand for tobacco laborers. Five years earlier, Rolfe had discovered that sweet West Indian tobacco would grow well in the Virginia soil. The addictive crop was so profitable that soon the settlers were growing tobacco in the streets of Jamestown. Men were eager to expand their tobacco production by acquiring workers, but in a place with so few colonists, and so much land, it was almost impossible to hire a free person to work for wages. It was just too easy for free individuals to acquire their own land and grow tobacco themselves. Wealthy Virginians first met this challenge by importing white indentured servants from England. In exchange for passage to Virginia and the basic necessities of life, an indentured laborer worked for his master or mistress between three to seven years. Thus, some of the first blacks brought to Virginia were freed after serving a term of years similar to that of white indentured servants because their English masters were either uncomfortable with or unsure about the legality of chattel slavery. Other masters immediately accepted the idea of permanent slavery and held their African bondsmen for life.

During the first several decades of the colony's history, the number of blacks in Virginia grew very slowly. In 1650, there were only about 300 blacks, and that number had only increased to about 2,000 by 1676. Until the last decade of the 17th century, blacks never made up more than a small fraction of the total population of Virginia. The first black Virginians were mostly Creoles, individuals born into slavery in other parts of the Americas, such as Brazil or the Caribbean islands. Because the Virginia planters could not yet absorb shiploads of slaves directly from Africa, they acquired slaves a few at a time from trading ships that had already stopped at Spanish, Portuguese, or Dutch colonies that had been importing Africans for a century before the founding of Jamestown. Prior to their arrival in Virginia, these Creole slaves had already become familiar with many aspects of European culture, such as their languages, styles of dress and manners, legal systems, and Christian religion. Thus, the first blacks in Virginia seemed less foreign, less "savage," than would later arrivals coming directly from Africa.

Because slaves were both few in number and often acculturated to European ways, 17th-century black Virginians faced less discrimination than slaves would a century later. Some mastered English society so thoroughly that historians have dubbed them "black Englishmen." One example of a black who thrived in the racially fluid 17th century was Anthony Johnson. When Johnson arrived in Virginia in 1621, he was known simply as "Antonio a Negro." By 1635, he and his wife, Mary, had obtained their freedom and moved to the eastern shore of Virginia. Johnson and his family eventually acquired land and slaves of their own. When Johnson's slave, Casor, ran away and sought shelter with Johnson's white neighbors, Johnson successfully sued in court for the return of his slave. Johnson's life illustrates much about slavery and race relations in 17th-century Virginia. First, he moved from slavery to freedom. Laws had not yet been passed that limited an owner's ability to manumit his or her slaves, and many owners chose to do so. Before 1680, 20 percent of blacks were free in some Virginia counties. Second, Johnson was able to purchase land and prosper as a small farmer. Just as white indentured servants were sometimes able to become successful landowners at the end of their indentures, Johnson's status as a freedman and a black man did not limit his opportunities. Third, Johnson became a slave owner in his own right. As a tobacco planter, he had the same need for labor as white planters did. There is no evidence that Johnson's neighbors were troubled by a black slave owner, or that Johnson himself was troubled with a sense of hypocrisy. Finally, Johnson was able to win a court case against his white neighbors for the return of his slave. His race did not limit his legal rights; his ownership of land and labor gave him status in his community. Property was more important than race in marking a person's worth in 17th-century Virginia. Further, the court found in his

A Dutch man-of-war brought the first African captives to Jamestown in 1619. (Library of Congress)

favor—another sign that Johnson's white peers did not hold his race against him.

Even blacks who were destined to remain slaves experienced greater opportunity and less racial discrimination than would blacks in the 18th and 19th centuries. Slaves usually lived and worked alongside whites, including indentured servants and their owners, who were rarely wealthy enough to leave the fields. Likewise, owners rarely spent the effort to build a separate slave "quarter" for one or two slaves. Thus, slaves often partook of the same food, shelter, and working conditions as the whites around them. The only thing that differentiated them from other servants was the length of their servitude. Living in close proximity with one another, blacks often formed friendships and romantic attachments with whites, especially indentured servants. Race was less important to white indentured servants than their shared situation as poorly treated laborers. Slaves and indentured servants sometimes ran away together, indicating a degree of camaraderie and trust in one another. Interracial sexual unions were common, and interracial marriage was

not unknown. In just one example, Elizabeth Kay, a mulatto woman from Northumberland County, successfully sued for her freedom in 1656 because her father had been white. Afterward, Kay married William Greensted, the white attorney who had assisted her in the court case. Slaves sometimes also created close bonds with their owners. In the 1660s, a white York County man freed his slave in his will, then designated the newly freed man both the inheritor of his estate and the guardian of a young white girl in his care.

What, then, caused this transformation from the racially open society of the 17th century to the virulently racist one that developed in the 18th? Political, economic, and demographic changes in Virginia from about 1660–1700 laid the foundation for this change. First, Virginia planters continued to use laborers to work in their tobacco fields, but by the 1660s, the number of English people willing to become indentured servants in Virginia had dropped considerably. This occurred because the birth rate in England had dropped, thereby raising the wages the poor could receive at home. Also, those Englishmen who still desired to travel to America had other more appealing choices by end of the century, such as Pennsylvania and South Carolina. By 1700, almost no one willingly came to Virginia as a servant. Planters coped with their labor needs by buying slaves instead. Planters were already familiar with the idea of slavery because of the small number of slaves who had been in the colony for decades. Although slaves were considerably more expensive than indentured servants, the rising life expectancies that benefited all Virginians in the second half of the 17th century also made slave ownership more affordable. If a slave cost twice as much as a servant with a seven-year term, but they both were likely to live only five years, the lower-priced servant was the obvious choice. But if, with the rise in life expectancy, each person was likely to live another 10 or 15 years, the purchase of a slave made more sense, and eventually became the better bargain. This proved especially true when slave women bore children, who replenished their master's labor supply at little additional cost.

These factors explain why slaves replaced indentured servants, but not the reasons for the growing racial discrimination among whites in Virginia. One reason is related to demography; as the demand for slaves grew, ships began carrying cargoes of slaves directly from Africa to Virginia for the first time beginning in the 1680s. These Africans were often newly enslaved, and unfamiliar with

English customs, language, laws, and religion. They were much less assimilated than the Creoles who had made up the majority of slaves before 1680, and to white Virginians they seemed strange and less human than the earlier Afro-Virginians had. In addition, there were greater numbers of blacks in Virginia than ever before. The large numbers of unassimilated slaves seemed threatening, and white Virginians began to discriminate against them in ways that had never before seemed necessary. This was especially true in the wake of Bacon's Rebellion in 1676, the largest social upheaval in Virginia history before the Revolution. During Nathaniel Bacon's revolt against Virginia's leadership in Jamestown, indentured servants, poor landless white free men, and slaves banded together to the fight the emerging Virginia gentry. After the rebellion was over, the dangers of a combined underclass of poor whites and black slaves was not lost on the wealthy white planters. They began to actively promote discrimination against blacks in order to drive a wedge of racial difference between poor whites and slaves. They accomplished this in part by passing laws that punished blacks more harshly than whites for identical crimes, forbade marriage between whites and blacks, and limited blacks' ability to use the courts to defend themselves against white depredations. Gradually, poor whites began to associate themselves more with upper-class whites than with black slaves who shared their economic condition.

By the end of the 17th century, as the Jamestown era ended, blacks in Virginia were much worse off than they had been when the colony was new. The foundation for a society that despised and mistreated African Americans had been laid by an elite that both feared black Virginians and hoped to profit by them.

See also: Bacon's Rebellion; Chesapeake Colonies; Freedom Dues; Headright System; Indentured Servitude; Racialized Slavery; Rolfe, John

Jennifer Bridges Oast

Bibliography

Berlin, Ira. *Many Thousands Gone: The First Two Centuries of Slavery in North America.* Cambridge, MA: Belknap Press of Harvard University, 1998.
Breen, T. H., and Stephen Innes. *"Myne Owne Ground:" Race and Freedom on Virginia's Eastern Shore, 1640–1676.* New York: Oxford University Press, 1980.
Kulikoff, Allan. *Tobacco and Slaves: The Development of Southern Cultures in the Chesapeake, 1680–1800.* Chapel Hill: University of North Carolina Press, 1986.

Morgan, Edmund S. *American Slavery, American Freedom: The Ordeal of Colonial Virginia.* New York: W. W. Norton, 1975.
Parent Jr., Anthony S. *Foul Means: The Formation of a Slave Society in Virginia, 1660–1740.* Chapel Hill: University of North Carolina Press, 2003.

John, Prester

Prester John, and his kingdom, refers to what Europeans on expeditions of conquest and imperialism into various regions of the world, specifically Africa, recognized as a potential Christian ally against an expansive Muslim enemy. Prester John's Kingdom was believed to be located in what would be modern-day Ethiopia. Despite various points of contention regarding Prester John's origin and whether he was merely an allegorical figure or an actual historical personage, Prester John no less represents larger ideas about European exploration and exploitation from the 12th century on, and can be understood as a catalyzing figure for imperial conquest. Though there was a degree of haze surrounding his existence, there does exist some confirmed information regarding Prester John.

A letter ostensibly written and sent by him in 1165 to Byzantine Emperor Manuel Comeneus who later forwarded it to Fredrick Barbarossa, Holy Roman Emperor, was a significant document in positioning Prester John favorably into the minds of Europeans. The letter is supposedly marked by a tone of condescension as Prester John goes on to promulgate the enormity of his wealth and power and vastness of his diverse Christian sovereignty and the various natural wonders that his kingdom possesses, while simultaneously professing his humility, which he states should be apparent through the adoption of the name Prester as opposed to a more grand appellation. Prester John and his kingdom are of particular importance to Iberian ideas of conquest, and he represents an important lens through which to understand much of the complexity and motivation behind European conquest, specifically in regard to geopolitical and economic interests.

In terms of geopolitics and economics, European colonizing expeditions are conceived of in terms of two types of goals—long term and short term. During the 1500s in Iberia there existed a Christian minority within a larger Muslim majority. For this minority the idea of an established Christian kingdom already in Africa coupled with imperialist aims was important, as Prester John's Kingdom could be potentially invaluable in the success of ousting Muslims from the Iberian Peninsula. The idea that the motivation for African exploration was born from the desire to transcend the expansive Muslim hegemony and gain control of the eastern trade routes into Arabia and through parts of Asia such as India and Indonesia constitutes a long-term goal.

Short-range goals, on the other hand, were less concerned with sweeping objectives such as becoming free from Muslim dominion or controlling expansive trade routes, but instead focused on the step-by-step process of expeditions that was more in alignment with the financial constraints of expeditions. Despite the differences that existed between long-term and short-range goals of European expansion, both were marked by an element of economic gain.

Under the realm of economics European expansion and conquest took on two distinct trajectories. The first type of European expansion in Africa sought to finance small expeditions along the coast through the acquirement of certain mainland goods such as gold and slaves. During these types of short voyages, there was the expectation that along the route either trading or raiding would take place. The other type of European expansion was concerned with exploitable land. For Europeans, the purpose of acquiring this land, which may or may not have been previously inhabited, was the acquisition of valuable raw goods. The colonization of these lands underwent a general process by which they were prepared for cultivation and subsequent profit production. After the removal of existing profit-producing materials, such as timber or honey, was carried out, the colonized land would be prepared for its primarily profit-producing function as crops such as sugar or wheat were introduced.

In the 1500s, upon their arrival on the western coast of Africa, the Portuguese were privy to an expansive commercial network and trade. Goods originating from places as far east as Indonesia were being funneled into Africa via the trans-Saharan trade. The Portuguese quest for Prester John also led to substantive effects of exploration. Although the search for Prester John is primarily associated with the Portuguese, the modes and motivations for exploration in Africa would be adopted later by other European powers in the 17th and 18th centuries. The aftermath of the search for Prester John worked in concert with Portuguese commercial aspirations, prompting the erection of various fortresses

as well as trading posts on both the coasts of East and West Africa. These entrepôts would eventually equip the Portuguese with a strategic global location through which they could carry out trade throughout Africa as well as in Arabia, India, and Indonesia. The early establishment of a colonial presence throughout Africa by the Portuguese was merely an example of the colonization efforts that would be carried out by numerous European powers, including England, France, Germany, Italy, and others. Eventually Europe's imperialist presence and objectives would diffuse throughout Africa and would leave an indelible mark not only on Africa, Europe, and various parts of the Atlantic World, but on the entire globe as well.

See also: Reconquista

Christina Bush

Bibliography

Alvares, Francisco, Henry Edward John Stanley, C. F. Beckingham, and George Wynn Brereton Huntingford. *The Prester John of the Indies; A True Relation of the Lands of the Prester John, Being the Narrative of the Portuguese Embassy to Ethiopia in 1520.* Cambridge, UK: Published for the Hakluyt Society at the University Press, 1961.

Nowell, Charles E. "The Historical Prester John." *Speculum: A Journal of Medieval Studies* 22 (1958):435–45.

Slessarev, Vsevolod. *Prester John; The Letter and the Legend.* Minneapolis: University of Minnesota Press, 1959.

Thornton, John. *Africa and Africans in the Making of the Atlantic World, 1400–1800.* Cambridge, UK: Cambridge University Press, 1992.

Johnson, Anthony

Anthony Johnson (ca. 1600–1670), sold to the English at Jamestown of the Virginia Colony in 1621, is referred to in early documents as "Antonio a Negro." He was sold for his labor in some form of servitude similar to enslavement. Records refer to him as "servant" as opposed to "slave" and, at that early date in Virginia, both European and African immigrants entered the colony in a form of indentured servitude. Not much is known about his early years in Virginia. Antonio worked on the Bennett family's plantation and was one of five individuals (out of 56 people) to survive an attack by the local Native Americans in 1622. The census of 1625 listed him as "servant." He married an African woman ("Mary, a Negro") from the same plantation. Antonio apparently was not only a strong worker, but also won the personal approval of the Bennett family as they became his benefactor. Under their sponsorship, Antonio was allowed to farm some acreage independently while still enslaved. He and Mary were able to work their way out of indentured servitude by purchasing the balance of their contract. Together they had children, whom they had baptized. Once freed, Antonio anglicized his name to Anthony Johnson.

By 1650, the man now known as Anthony Johnson had acquired not only his freedom, but also a 250-acre estate, where he probably grew tobacco and corn while tending a herd of cattle. Further, his son John received a patent for 550 acres and Anthony's son Richard owned a 100-acre estate. Johnson and his sons were clearly men of substance in early Virginia and, along with holding property and farming independently, they were slaveholders who accumulated sizable estates for their heirs. Indeed, Anthony Johnson may have held contracts on indentured servants of both African and European origin. The Johnson family, and other free black families of early Virginia, enjoyed the same rights as their white counterparts in their community and could employ the law to protect themselves and their interests.

The experience of Anthony Johnson and his family illustrates the fluidity of the community for Africans in mid-17th-century Virginia as well as somewhat of a balance of power and rights between races—albeit racial discrimination did exist—that would not survive much beyond Johnson's lifetime. In 1653 the Johnson family suffered a heavy financial loss due to fire and successfully petitioned the court for relief on their tax debt. Next, in 1655, Johnson sought legal action against a white man, Robert Parker, for detaining a slave owned by Johnson. Again, Johnson sought legal action and successfully regained custody of John Casor, a black man who was now legally determined to be Johnson's slave.

By the early 1660s, as racial tensions grew in Virginia, slave laws began to clearly state that indentured servitude was an appropriate form of service only for individuals arriving from Christian homelands, or Europeans. Individuals brought to the colony from Africa, a non-Christian region, would be subject to a lifetime of enslavement. Johnson and his family, concerned by the tightening of the race laws within their community and the increasing racial discrimination they experienced, moved to the Somerset area of Maryland where they once again prospered.

Anthony Johnson died in Somerset, Maryland, in 1670. That same year, courts back in Virginia determined that, as

Negroes, he and his family were technically aliens. Therefore, they had no rights to land ownership in the colony. The court confiscated all lands previously owned by the Johnson family on behalf of the Crown.

See also: Chesapeake Colonies; Freedom Dues; Indentured Servitude; Jamestown, Virginia; Tobacco

Jane M. Aldrich

Bibliography

Berlin, Ira. *Many Thousands Gone: The First Two Centuries of Slavery in North America.* Cambridge, MA: Belknap Press of Harvard University, 1998.

Breen, T. H., and Stephen Innes. *"Myne Owne Ground": Race and Freedom on Virginia's Eastern Shore, 1640–1676.* New York: Oxford University Press, 1980.

Wright, Donald R. *African Americans in the Colonial Era: From African Origins through the American Revolution.* 2nd ed. Wheeling, IL: Harlan Davidson, 2000.

Kingdom of Asante

Of the many Akan-speaking states in the Gold Coast region of West Africa emerged a powerful and centralized kingdom known as Asante. Before the rise of Asante, two sizable Akan states—Denkyira and Akwamu—competed for power and access to lucrative trade routes during the early 17th century. Indeed Denkyira, which had a number of smaller tributary states within its dominion, practically monopolized the gold and kola trade in the Pra-Ofin river basin. By the 1670s, Osei Tutu, a member of the Oyoko clan and a vassal in the court of Denkyira who rose in the ranks to become a general in the Denkyira military, established control over a trading center named Kumasi. In defecting from Denkyira, Osei Tutu began to group local clan leaders and regional kings of tributary states under the collective domination of Denkyira into loose military and political alliance.

In 1695, this loose alliance of clans and city-states was formally brought together into a military pact with the intent to overthrow the Denkyirahene—the king of Denkyira. With his close adviser and friend, *Okomfo* Anokye, Osei Tutu gathered together local rulers to witness a miracle that catapulted him to the role of king of a new and powerful nation. According to legend, *Okomfo* Anokye, declaring that he was on a mission from the Akan supreme god—Onyame—called down a Golden Stool from the very heavens to rest on the knees of Osei Tutu in full view of the assembled royalty. *Okomfo* Anokye announced that the Golden Stool contained the soul of the Asante people. In addition, he marked the spot where the stool descended with a sword and noted that if the sword was ever pulled from the ground, the newly founded Asante kingdom would come to an end. With these important and transcendent cultural symbols, the Asante kingdom rose and began a steady march to complete military and political consolidation in the region.

Asantehene Nana Osei Tutu, king of the confederation of Akan-speaking states, made Kumasi the capital of the kingdom and organized a massive army equipped with guns imported from Dutch and Danish traders along the coastline. By 1700, Asante defeated Denkyira and by 1715, Osei Tutu led his armies to victories against Twifu, Wassa, and Aowin. These victories allowed Asante direct access to Elmina and other European-controlled coastal factories. From this point forward, the Kingdom of Asante would be a major player in the Atlantic slave trade and in the dispersal of enslaved Africans from the Gold Coast. After a century of expansion and political domination, Asante controlled most of the country of modern Ghana, some of the inland region of Côte-d'Ivoire, and portions of modern Togo. Their dominion would not be threatened until the advent of British imperial incursion in the period between 1873 and 1900.

See also: Atlantic Slave Trade; Elmina; Gold Coast

Walter C. Rucker

Bibliography
McCaskie, T. C. *State and Society in Pre-Colonial Asante.* Cambridge, UK: Cambridge University Press, 1995.

Wilks, Ivor. *Forests of Gold: Essays on the Akan and the Kingdom of Asante.* Athens: Ohio University Press, 1993.

Yarak, Larry W. *Asante and the Dutch, 1744–1873.* Oxford, UK: Clarendon Press, 1990.

Kingdom of Benin

Benin was an influential city-state in northwest Africa from the 15th to the 17th century. It was founded by the Edo or Bini people in the 13th century, and by the early 14th century a royal court was in place. It was always ruled by a powerful king who was usually a former war leader. The king, however, later became a more religious figure. The kingdom extended throughout what is presently southern Nigeria.

One of its most successful kings was Ozoula. During his reign, from about 1480 to 1504, Benin established many commercial and diplomatic relations with Portugal. In 1481 emissaries from the king of Portugal visited the court of the king of Benin. Portuguese soldiers aided Benin in its wars. Gwatto, the port of Benin, became the depot to handle the peppers, ivory, and increasing numbers of slaves offered by the king of Benin in exchange for coral beads, textile imports from India, and European-manufactured articles, including tools and weapons.

Benin profited from its close ties with the Portuguese and exploited the firearms bought from them to tighten its hold on the lower Niger area. Two factors checked the spread of Portuguese influence and the continued expansion of Benin. First, Portugal stopped buying pepper because of the availability of other spices in the Indian Ocean region. Second, Benin placed an embargo on the export of slaves, thereby isolating itself from the growth of what was to become the major export from the Nigerian coast for 300 years. Benin continued to capture slaves and to employ them in its domestic economy, but it remained unique among Nigerian polities in refusing to participate in the transatlantic trade. Gradually, the power of the kingdom decreased and eventually, in 1897, the area was annexed to British Nigeria.

See also: African Imperialism; Atlantic Slave Trade; Bight of Benin; Gulf of Guinea

Moshe Terdiman

Bibliography
McClelland, Elizabeth M. *The Kingdom of Benin in the Sixteenth Century.* London: Oxford University Press, 1971.

Millar, Heather. *The Kingdom of Benin in West Africa.* Tarrytown, NY: Benchmark Books, 1997.

Kingdom of Dahomey

Dahomey was an African kingdom situated in what is now Benin. The kingdom was founded in the 17th century and survived until the late 19th century, when it was conquered by French troops from Senegal and incorporated into France's West African colonies.

The origins of Dahomey can be traced back to a group of Aja from the coastal kingdom of Allada who moved northward and settled among the Fon people of the interior. By about 1650, the Aja managed to dominate the Fon, and Wegbaja declared himself king of their joint territory. Based in his capital of Agbome, Wegbaja and his successors succeeded in establishing a highly centralized state, in which all land was owned directly by the king, who collected taxes from all crops that were produced.

Economically, however, Wegbaja and his successors profited mainly from the slave trade and relations with slavers along the coast. Dahomey's kings embarked on wars to expand their territory and began using rifles and other firearms traded with Europeans for captives, who were sold into slavery in the Americas. Most of the slaves were acquired either by trade into the interior or by raids to the north and west into Nigeria. Under King Agadja (ruled 1708–1732), the kingdom conquered Allada, where the ruling family originated, thereby gaining direct contact with European slave traders on the coast. Europeans began arriving in the area in the 18th century. Trading posts were established in Porto Novo, Ouidah, and Cotonou. This relationship continued into the mid-19th century.

Dahomey was very reluctant to give up the slave trade in the 19th century and continued to carry on a clandestine trade past the mid-19th century. However, without the slave trade, Dahomey could no longer maintain the same level of military superiority over other kingdoms. Thus, King Guezo signed a treaty establishing French protectorates in Cotonou and Ouidah. Dahomey was finally conquered by France in 1892–1894. Most of the troops that fought against Dahomey were native African.

See also: African Imperialism; Atlantic Slave Trade; Bight of Benin; Gulf of Guinea

Moshe Terdiman

Bibliography

Argyle, William John. *The Fon of Dahomey: A History and Ethnography of the Old Kingdom.* Oxford, UK: Clarendon Press, 1966.

Bay, Edna G. *Wives of the Leopard: Gender, Politics, and Culture in the Kingdom of Dahomey.* Charlottesville: University of Virginia Press, 1998.

Kongo Kingdom

The Kingdom of Kongo was founded in the 14th century. In the 15th century, the kingdom stretched from the Congo River in the north to the Loje River in the south and from the Atlantic Ocean in the west to beyond the Kwango River in the east. Several smaller autonomous states to the south and east paid tribute to it.

The Kingdom of Kongo came into contact with Portugal in 1483. In the early 16th century, the king and most of the kingdom adopted Christianity and welcomed numerous European missionaries, traders, and craftsmen. The kingdom reached the height of its political power in the 16th century during the reign of Afonso I (1505–1543) and its alliance with the Portuguese, but the establishment of the Portuguese port of Luanda and the colony of Angola as well as the interests of the Portuguese residents there in increasing their private fortunes, especially through capturing Africans and selling them into slavery, undermined this relationship.

After the death of King Afonso I, Kongo declined rapidly and suffered devastating civil wars from the late 17th through the early 18th centuries, when many of its people were enslaved and sent to the Americas. Thus, the slave trade, which undermined the social structure of Kongo, continued to weaken the authority of its king.

In 1641, King Garcia II allied himself with the Dutch in an attempt to control Portuguese slave traders, but in 1665, a Portuguese force decisively defeated the army of Kongo and from that time onward the kingdom disintegrated into a number of small states, all controlled to varying degrees by the Portuguese. The area of Kongo was incorporated mostly into Angola and partly into the Independent State of the Congo in the late 19th century.

See also: Kongo Cosmogram; Mbebma, Nzinga (Afonso I); Vita, Dona Beatriz Kimpa; West-Central Africa

Moshe Terdiman

Bibliography

Davidson, Basil. *The African Slave Trade: Precolonial History, 1450–1850.* Boston: Atlantic Monthly Press Books, 1961.

Hilton, Anne. *The Kingdom of Kongo.* Oxford, UK: Clarendon Press, 1987.

Thornton, John Kelly. *The Kingdom of Kongo: Civil War and Transition, 1641–1718.* Madison: University of Wisconsin Press, 1983.

Young, Jason R. *Rituals of Resistance: African Atlantic Religion in Kongo and the Lowcountry South in the Era of Slavery.* Baton Rouge: Louisiana State University Press, 2007.

Las Siete Partidas

Las Siete Partidas, the Seven-Part Code, was a set of laws codified in medieval Spain, some of which were crucial to the legal foundation of modern slavery in the New World. The code, possibly the most consequential and comprehensive set of laws of the medieval period, was compiled in Castile between 1251 and 1265 under Alfonso X the Wise. The laws went into effect around 1348 and became the foundation for all Spanish jurisprudence. Beginning with Spanish expansion in the 16th century, the code spread to Spain's New World possessions in the Americas, Asia, and Africa, giving the code the widest territorial influence of any single legal code.

In Iberia the institution of slavery relied on the legal precepts of the ancient Visigoths and Romans as well as the Byzantine Justinian Code that combined Roman and Church law in the early medieval period. Traditionally slavery was justified by the rules of war; slaves were furnished by the vanquished and prisoners of battle. In the early medieval period, as a result of the Islamic conquest of southern Spain (711–1492) and the Crusades spanning the 11th to the 13th centuries, religion became a significant component of the justification of war and enslavement. The *Siete Partidas* built on these legal and ethical traditions.

The Castilian code permitted individuals as well as municipal and religious organizations to own slaves and codified the criteria that had justified enslavement. Prisoners of just wars, particularly non-Christians, as well as condemned persons, children of enslaved mothers, and those who voluntarily sold themselves into slavery for debt relief or other economic reasons were regarded as legitimate slaves. The *Siete Partidas* appended the traditional conditions with two additional categories of persons eligible for slavery: children of priests were required to serve as slaves in their father's churches and Christians who provided war material to Moors could be legally enslaved. Muslims, Jews, and others considered infidels could not legally own Christian slaves.

The *Siete Partidas* protected certain rights for enslaved individuals and provided a number of legal channels for manumission. Christian slaves were entitled to marry one another with the masters' permission, and masters were legally bound to grant permission unless they could prove that the union posed a serious danger to their interests. Masters were prohibited from exhibiting cruel treatment, including separating families, excessive physical punishment, starving slaves, or exploiting them sexually. Masters who did not abide by these laws could be taken to court, and, if proven guilty, their slaves would be sold to another master or, in certain cases, manumitted. Slaves who displayed exceptional service to a master or the state were eligible for manumission. Slaves were legally permitted to ply a trade and to own property; they had the legal right to earn, borrow, and lend money and to purchase their freedom or that of another. Slaves were permitted to bring legal suits, testify in court, and organize religious brotherhoods.

The laws of the *Siete Partidas* addressing the rights of masters and slaves in medieval Spain reflected a system of slavery that was largely domestic, urban, and temporary and affected an enslaved population of various nationalities. Sub-Saharan and North African soldiers and slaves accompanied the occupying Muslim armies, and those captured in battle were considered Spanish property, while other Africans arrived in Spain via slave markets or as free persons. Sardinians, Greeks, Russians, Spaniards, Canary Islanders, Turks, Egyptians, and Moors were among the various peoples who served as slaves in medieval and early modern Spain. While the laws of the *Siete Partidas* were closely aligned with the Catholic Church and favored Christians, slaves in medieval Spain might be Christian as well as Jewish or Muslim. The slave laws of the *Siete Partidas* did not refer to nationality or race. Because the *Partidas* reflected the Spanish cultural and religious belief that enslavement was an unfortunate and accidental status rather than a natural state, the burden of proof of a person's enslaved status fell on the owner; without positive evidence, an alleged slave would be freed.

After 1500, the *Siete Partidas* spread to Spain's overseas possessions, including Cuba, Puerto Rico, Mexico, Peru, the Philippines, Florida, and Louisiana. While Spain developed colonial policy in subsequent centuries to regulate the transatlantic slave trade and the growth of plantation slavery, both of which were on a scale unparalleled in the ancient and medieval worlds, Spanish legislators continued to rely on several elements of the *Siete Partidas*. The influence of the *Partidas* made for greater legal rights, protections, and channels to freedom for slaves in the Spanish Americas relative to British North America. How much these rights were observed in practice is a matter of scholarly debate. Nonetheless, numerous slaves in Spanish-influenced regions such as Cuba and Louisiana petitioned courts to uphold their rights and either won or purchased their own freedom based on the legal precedents of the *Partidas*.

Elements of the *Siete Partidas* remained in force in Florida, Louisiana, and Texas even after these territories went from Spanish to American possession. The *Partidas* continue to undergird basic law in Spanish America and the Philippines.

See also: Atlantic Slave Trade; Hispaniola

Christina Proenza-Coles

Bibliography

Blackburn, Robin. *The Making of New World Slavery.* New York: Verso, 1997.

Burns, Robert I., ed. *Las Siete Partidas.* Translated by Samuel Parsons Scott. Philadelphia: University of Pennsylvania Press, 2001.

Landers, Jane. *Black Society in Spanish Florida.* Chicago: University of Illinois Press, 1999.

Tannenbaum, Frank. *Slave and Citizen: The Negro and the Americas.* New York: Vintage Books, 1946. Reprint, Boston: Beacon Press, 1992.

Laurens, Henry

Henry Laurens (1724–1792), who rose from the son of an immigrant Huguenot to one of the wealthiest men of the elite planter class in the Carolina Lowcountry, is remembered as a merchant, a statesman active in the colonial assembly, a militia leader during the Cherokee Expositions in the 1760s, a patriot and president of the Continental Congress during the American Revolution, and a diplomat at the Treaty of Paris. Laurens should also be remembered as one of the most successful brokers of enslaved Africans in the Carolina Colony.

Forming a commercial partnership with George Austin in 1747 (Austin and Laurens) and adding George Appleby to the firm in 1759 (Austin, Laurens, and Appleby), the firm handled the traditional goods shipped in the region: exporting rice, indigo, deerskins, and naval stores and importing wine, textiles, rum, sugar, and Africans. By 1760 Laurens had acquired enough wealth to establish himself as a planter of rice and indigo, holding four plantations in South Carolina, including Mepkin, Wambaw, Wrights Savannah, and Mount Tacitus; and two in Georgia, Broughton Island and New Hope—as well as multiple lots of land in the cities of Charleston and Savannah. In 1762 he dissolved his shipping partnerships and continued trading on his own.

Laurens brokered the sale of Africans in Charleston in arrangement with Richard Oswald, one of the wealthiest merchants in London. Oswald was the principal owner of Bunce (*Bance*) Island, the largest British slave castle on the Rice Coast of West Africa in what is now Sierra Leone, a region where rice has been grown for hundreds of years. Laurens received ships from ports around the Atlantic that had stopped at Bunce Island to load a cargo of Africans from Oswald's operations and would advertise the arrival of those vessels with their expected contents, selling the cargo on commission. Often the ships would be loaded with rice and local goods for payment due the vessels' owner. Laurens also sent his own slaving vessels to Bunce Island to return to Charleston, advertising their human cargo as possessing the skills and knowledge necessary for rice production. In 1764, Henry Laurens boasted that he had sold the cargo of his ships for higher prices than anyone else in the colony. This joint venture made both Oswald and Laurens extremely wealthy men.

By 1769 Laurens ended his participation in the business of importing Africans as an involuntary workforce for the rice plantations of the Lowcountry. His explanation was that he no longer had a business partner for the operation. However, in 1776, he wrote to his son regarding his ambivalence about slavery and reportedly began to make plans to manumit his slaves. Many historians argue that Laurens wrote this letter after receiving his copy of the Declaration of Independence and used this statement to his son as evidence that Laurens was expressing opposition to slavery—and was one of the only men of the lower South to express such an opinion. While a few members of Laurens enslaved populations may have received their freedom, he still was in possession of almost 300 slaves as late as 1790.

See also: American Revolution; Bunce Island; Carolinas; Jay, John; Rice Cultivation; Sierra Leone

Jane M. Aldrich

Bibliography

Hamer, Philip M., et al., eds. *The Papers of Henry Laurens.* 16 vols. Columbia: University of South Carolina Press, 1968–2003.

McDonough, Daniel J. *Christopher Gadsden and Henry Laurens: The Parallel Lives of Two American Patriots.* Selinsgrove, PA: Susquehanna University Press, 2000.

Mercantini, Jonathan. *Who Shall Rule at Home?: The Evolution of South Carolina Political Culture, 1748–1776.* Columbia: University of South Carolina Press, 2007.

Sellers, Leila. *Charleston on the Eve of the American Revolution.* Chapel Hill: University of North Carolina Press, 1934.

Loose Pack

One of the more intriguing historical issues connected to the Atlantic slave trade is whether loose pack or tight pack materially increased or decreased mortality during the course of Middle Passage. Since the 1960s a debate has ensued based upon contemporary accounts, and scholars have positioned themselves pro or con. Revisionist scholars have assessed the loose pack versus tight pack issue in a manner less cut and dry than the initial arguments.

Historian Daniel P. Mannix in his book titled *Black Cargoes,* published in 1965, presented the position of both advocates of tight pack and loose pack. Slave traders who favored loose pack believed that maximizing space onboard slave vessels, providing better nutrition, and allowing some latitude for slaves to exercise during their forced confinement would effectively reduce Middle Passage mortality. Consequently, advocates of loose pack believed that they received a better price for surviving slaves. Decades after Mannix wrote his seminal work on the Middle Passage, some scholars continue to expound on the philosophy of slave traders who practiced loose pack.

Contemporaries during Middle Passage likewise took sides on the debate. Loose pack had its share of supporters. For instance, Thomas Weaver, a slave trade agent, wrote officials of the Royal African Company that the spatial allotments on slave vessels were insufficient and that overcrowding contributed to unnecessary mortality during Middle Passage. On several occasions, Weaver sent letters of complaint about overcrowding. While there is no direct evidence that the Royal African Company agreed or took any substantive steps to address Weaver's concerns about sanitation aboard the company's slave vessels, the company did theoretically respond to other similar inquires.

About the same time period that Weaver expressed concerns about the sanitation onboard slave vessels, Sir Dalby Thomas, a prominent English politician, thought the tight pack philosophy would illicit negative critiques based on moral concerns. He wrote officials of the Royal African Company to instruct their agents not to overcrowd slave vessels. However, agents being employed on a commission basis had a vested interest to maximize slave cargo. Therefore, the company had to find another means to get compliance with its wishes. Thus, company officials contacted factors, white men who bartered directly with African slave traders. Factors were freelance businessmen of a sort. The Royal African Company issued instructions to factors to not overcrowd slave vessels. How responsive factors were to these sets of instructions remains an unanswered question. *See also:* Abolition, Slave Trade; Atlantic Slave Trade; Factor; Royal African Company; Tight Pack

Michael A. Cooke

Bibliography

Feelings, Tom. *The Middle Passage: White Ships/Black Cargo.* With Introduction by John Henrik Clarke. New York: Dial Books, 1995.

Mannix, Daniel P. *Black Cargoes: A History of the Atlantic Slave Trade, 1518–1865.* In collaboration with Malcolm Cowley. New York: Viking Press, 1965.

Palmer, Colin A. *Human Cargoes: The British Slave Trade to Spanish America, 1700–1739.* Urbana: University of Illinois Press, 1981.

Malaria

Malaria derives its name from the Italian *mal-aria,* meaning "bad air." Yet it is actually a Protozoan disease that is spread by the Anolpheles mosquito. Centuries ago it was common in the marshy areas around Rome, hence the Italian origins of the name, and because of this connection, malaria was also called Roman Fever.

The minuscule Protozoa that causes the disease is of a parasitic variety known as Plasmodium and alternatively affects both human and insect hosts. The developmental age of the disease is unknown, but it is very ancient and is believed to have originated in Africa and spread over the centuries with human migration to the Mediterranean, India, and Southeast Asia. There are four types of malaria: *plasmodium vivax, plasmodium.ovale, plasmodium malariae,* and *plasmodium falciparum.*

Malaria has a worldwide impact and is now endemic in Africa, South America, Southeast Asia, and India. It is currently estimated that some 500 million people in these areas are exposed to malaria. One estimate of the human cost is 2.5 million deaths a year with approximately 1 million children succumbing to the illness. The destruction of the Anolpheles and their breeding grounds by pesticides remains the best control technique. Some critics challenge environmental policies that have limited pesticide use and specifically, DDT, which was an effective and cheap disease control agent.

Although generally seen as a tropical disease common to second and third world developing countries, malaria is sometimes found in developed and Northern Hemisphere countries. This migration of the disease labeled "airport malaria" is a cause for increased concern. In these instances infected mosquitoes are transported in airplanes from endemic areas such as Africa and then escape to infect the airport public, causing disease in those who have never traveled to malaria-infected areas. There is also some speculation that with global warming and globalization malaria might become more common in areas previously thought immune from the disease.

The Anopheles mosquito has been known for many years as the transmission agent for the disease, but it was only in 1948 that the full stages of the life cycle were uncovered. The female mosquito requires blood to mature her eggs and it is with the female that the parasite develops. Humans provide this blood supply. After biting its victim but before actually feeding, the mosquito injects her saliva, which contains malaria parasites called sporozoites. The sporozoites enter the bloodstream and come to reside in the human liver where they penetrate and grow rapidly. The liver cells rupture and parasites known as merozoites enter the red blood cells. Once in the red blood cells, the parasites develop into two cycle forms, sexual and asexual.

The sexual cycle produces male and female gametocytes that circulate in the blood and then enter the female mosquito when it takes a blood meal from its victim. The male and female gametocytes combine to form oocysts in the wall of the mosquito's stomach. These oocysts develop over a few days and contain large numbers of sporozoites that take root in the mosquito's saliva and are thus placed to repeat the cycle of infection.

In the asexual cycle the parasites form schizonts in the red blood cells that contain many merozoites. After a cell ruptures the merozoites are released to attack new red blood cells.

In order to combat all types of malaria there are various drug therapies currently in use. The best known was Quinine, which was used for centuries and until the 1930s, the only reliable treatment for the disease. Today drugs such as Malarone, Halofantrin (Halfan), and Metfloquine (Larium), among others, are in common use.

A particular evolutionary offshoot of malaria that affects the African American population is sickle cell disease. This inherited disease gained its name because the normally disc-shaped red blood cells become crescent or sickle-shaped. The result is poor cell function and anemia caused by an abnormal type of hemoglobin referred to as hemoglobin S. This genetically aberrant hemoglobin evolved in Africa as a protective device against malaria outbreaks and is known as the sickle cell trait. The condition produces blood clots that cause recurrent pain known as sickle cell pain crises. Sickle cell disease can be a serious danger over time when frequent crises damage many bodily systems.

At present only bone marrow transplants offer a cure for sickle cell anemia. However, transplants are difficult. Drugs such as hydroxyurea, introduced in the 1990s, offer better management and can prevent complications.

Approximately 1 out of 12 African Americans has the sickle cell trait, a trait also found in other ethnic groups exposed over time to malarial conditions. A further 1 out of 500 African Americans are affected by actual sickle cell disease. The first description of sickle cell disease was by Dr. James B. Herrick of Chicago in 1910, following his treatment of a West Indian patient whose anemia was characterized by unusual red cells.

See also: Atlantic Slave Trade; Chesapeake Colonies; Gulf of Guinea; Hispaniola

Theodore W. Eversole

Bibliography
Bloom, Miriam. *Understanding Sickle Cell Disease.* Jackson: University Press of Mississippi, 1995.
Boland, Peter B., et al. *Malaria Control during Mass Population Movements and Natural Disasters.* Washington, D.C.: National Academies Press, 2002.
Desowitz, Robert S. *The Malaria Capers: More Tales of Parasites, People-Research and Reality.* New York: W. W. Norton, 1993.
Honigsbaum, Mark. *The Fever Trail: Malaria, the Mosquito and the Quest for Quinine.* New York: Macmillan Press, 2001.
Serjeant, Graham R., and Serjeant, Beryl E., eds. *Sickle Cell Disease.* Oxford, UK: Oxford University Press, 2001.

Mali

The second great Sahelian kingdom was that of Mali. The Sahel is the savannah region south of the Sahara, which, after 750, became the center of culturally and politically dynamic cities and kingdoms because of the strategic importance of the Sahel for trade across north Africa.

The first great Sahelian kingdom was Ghana, but the Islamic revolution of the Almoravids, a Berber people living north of Ghana, splintered that kingdom. The Almoravids did not succeed in building their own Islamic kingdom in the region. The Almoravid revolution, however, led to energetic Islamic proselytizing all throughout the Sahel. Many of the ruling families converted to Islam.

One of these ruling families, the Keita, forged the successor to the Ghanaian Kingdom, the Kingdom of Mali. As with Ghana, Mali was built off of the monopolization of the trade routes from western and southern Africa to eastern and northern Africa. The most lucrative of these monopolies was the gold trade. Mali was located farther south than Ghana; the Malians lived in an agriculturally fertile land. Mali was also located along the upper Niger River, while Ghana had been located to the west. The bulk of the gold trade proceeded up the Niger River, so this gave Mali a firmer grip on this lucrative monopoly. Furthermore, controlling the Niger River and the cities that lie on its banks were important for trade and travel. The Niger was a central artery of commerce for both west and north African trade routes. Mali's control of the Niger River helped it to grow and prosper.

Mali was not a true empire, but rather the center of a sphere of influence. The territory controlled by Mali comprised three distinct regions: the Senegal region with people speaking Niger-Kongo languages, the central Mande states occupied by Soninke and Mandinke, and the region of Gao occupied by people who spoke Songhay.

The historical founder of Mali was the magician Sundjata Keita, or Sundiata, one of the most legendary figures in African history. Sundjata, who ruled Mali between the years 1230–1255, began as a royal slave and magician among the Soso peoples who then ruled the Ghanaian empire. According to African oral histories, the small state of Kangaba, led by Sundjata, defeated the nearby kingdom of Soso at the Battle of Kirina in 1235. The clans of the heartland unified under Sundjata, beginning a period of expansion. The rulers of Mali nominally converted to Islam, but held strong ties with Mande religions.

Under Sundjata and his immediate successors, Mali expanded rapidly west to the Atlantic Ocean, south deep into the forest, east beyond the Niger River, and north to the salt and copper mines of the Sahara. The city of Niani

Djinguereber Mosque in Timbuktu was built in the 14th century during Mansa Musa's reign as emperor of Mali. (Emilio Labrador)

may have been the capital. At its height, Mali was a confederation of three independent, freely allied states (Mali, Mema, and Wagadou) and 12 garrisoned provinces.

The most significant of the Mali kings was Mansa Musa (1312–1337), who expanded Mali influence over the large Niger city-states of Timbuktu, Gao, and Djenne. Mansa Musa was a devout Muslim who built magnificent mosques all throughout the Mali sphere of influence. His gold-laden pilgrimage to Mecca made him an historical figure even in European history writing.

It was under Mansa Musa that Timbuktu became one of the major cultural centers not only of Africa, but of the entire world. Under Mansa Musa's patronage, vast libraries were built and *madrasas* (Islamic universities) were endowed. Timbuktu became a meeting place of the finest poets, scholars, and artists of Africa and the Middle East. Even after the power of Mali declined, Timbuktu remained the major Islamic center of sub-Saharan Africa.

After the death of Mansa Musa, the power of Mali began to decline. Mali had never been an empire proper, and subject states began to break off from the Mali sphere of influence. In 1430, the Tuareg Berbers in the north seized much of Mali's territory, including the city of Timbuktu, and the Mossi Kingdom to the south a decade later seized much of Mali's southern territories. Finally, the kingdom of Gao, which had been subjugated to Mali under Mansa Musa, gave rise to a Songhai Kingdom that finally eclipsed the power of Mali.

See also: Ghana; Musa, Mansa; Sahel; Senegambia; Songhai; Sudanic Empires; Sundiata: The Epic of Old Mali

Moshe Terdiman

Bibliography

Fage, J. D. *A History of Africa.* London: Hutchinson, 1978.

Levtzion, Nehemia. *Ancient Ghana and Mali.* London: Methuen, 1973.

Niane, Djibril Tamsir. *Sundiata: An Epic of Old Mali.* Harlow, UK: Pearson Longman, 2006.

Thobhani, Akbarali. *Mansa Musa: The Golden King of Ancient Mali.* Dubuque, IA: Kendall/Hunt, 1998.

Matrilineal Societies

Matrilineal societies are groups where descent is traced through mothers' rather than fathers' bloodlines. Distinguished from the concept of matriarchy that refers to female power and control, matrilinity focuses on female relatedness, descent, and lineage. In matrilineal societies political titles, exchanges of wealth, goods, and services are passed down from mothers to daughters and/or men to their sisters' sons rather than their own biological sons. Daughter-based investment of family wealth, defined as exchanges between grandparents/parents and granddaughters/daughters, are also typically found in matrilineal societies. Anthropological studies report strong connections between societies in "horticultural" or farming stages of evolutionary development with low levels of paternal confidence and the occurrence of matrilineal culturally supported patterns. Although matrilineal societies occur less frequently than patrilineal ones (where descent is traced through fathers' bloodline), they are recurrent and found in all regions of the world, including Africa (e.g., Akan in Ghana, Toka in Zambia, and Chewa in Malawi).

Cultural experiences with matrilineal societies were undoubtedly part of the sociocultural experience of many enslaved African Americans. Contemporary scholars such as Nobles and Sudarkasa identified many similarities between African and African American cultural patterns in marriage, family and kinship structure and functioning. However, others like E. Franklin Frazier, maintained the vicissitudes of slavery, emancipation, and urbanization virtually destroyed any African cultural retentions. Further, whether due to cultural values and beliefs or large-scale social structural forces, characteristics of matrilineal societies are evident within African American life today.

African American mothers and daughters hold pivotal roles within families and kin networks that are fluid and often diverse. Exchanges of wealth, money, resources, emotional support, child care services, physical care, and so forth occur frequently over the life cycle between mothers, daughters, sisters, and other female kin. Even among African American elderly, adult daughters and elderly mothers have been found to exchange emotional, financial, and physical support to help maintain themselves and/or their households reflective of lifelong patterns of reciprocity over their life course. Generally, networks of African American women constitute the foundation or relatedness and stability within many families and kinship systems. These female interpersonal relationships of connectivity also appear to coexist with forms of social organization more patrilineal or patriarchal in nature.

Societies with mixed matrilineal and patrilineal characteristics are not uncommon when examining forms of social organization globally. Although some scholars and policy makers have suggested that matrilineal and matriarchal patterns contribute to family dysfunction and welfare dependency, others note their contributions to enhanced social functioning. Few quantitative studies have examined low levels of paternal confidence comparatively between patrilineal and matrilineal societies and any association this may have with family dysfunction and dependency.

Considering the persistence of current sociodemographic trends in modern times, specifically the economic disenfranchisement of African American males, high rates of never married, divorced, widowed, and separated African American females, high mortality and incarceration rates for African American males, and the historic higher demand for the labor of African American females, it is highly likely matrilineal social organizational patterns will endure in black life and culture.

See also: Coromantee; Gold Coast; Kingdom of Asante

Sharon Hines-Smith

Bibliography
Allison, Robert. "The Origins of African American Culture." *Journal of Interdisciplinary History* 30 (1999):475–81.
Dixon, Patricia. *African American Relationships, Marriages, and Families.* New York: Routledge Taylor and Francis, 2007.
Holden, C., R. Sear, and R. Mace. "Matriliny as Daughter-Biased Investment." *Evolution and Human Behavior* 24 (2003): 99–112.
Smith, Sharon. *African American Daughters and Elderly Mothers: Examining Experiences of Grief, Loss, and Bereavement.* New York: Garland, 1998.
Sudarkasa, N. "African American Families and Family Values." In *Black Families,* edited by H. P. McAdoo, 9–40. Thousand Oaks, CA: Sage, 1997.

Mbebma, Nzinga (Afonso I)

Born the son of King Nkuwu Nzinga, Mbemba (1460–1543), commonly referred to as Afonso I, ruled the Kingdom of the Kongo for 24 years from 1509 to 1543. His reign, during the first half of the 16th century, highlighted peaceful interactions with the kingdom and Prince Henry the Navigator's Portugal. Initially, relations were so amicable that he instituted Portuguese as the language of stately business.

Portuguese influence also existed with the legal system, feudal titles, and court procedures. Besides incorporating Portuguese culture and systems, Mbemba ruled his territory, which extended from present-day Angola to the Democratic Republic of the Congo, with an iron gauntlet. As a ruler over the northern province of Nsundi, Mbemba extended the kingdom's borders north of the Congo River's natural boundary. Territorial expansion was a major feat, which gave the kingdom jurisdiction over another area plus allowed Mbemba to incorporate new inhabitants. Guiding his political leadership was his acceptance and adoption of Christianity.

As a devout Christian, Mbemba differed from his father, who renounced the religion, and grew quite skeptical of his son. For his convictions, Mbemba lost control over his province, and had to regain his father's trust, which he succeeded in doing. His allegiance to Christianity was not just an individual pledge, as he tried to convert his kingdom's people to his newfound faith and to marry Christianity with his indigenous religions. All Europeans with the exceptions of teachers and missionaries forcibly left the kingdom as he expulsed them. Mbemba not only established the Catholic Church in the Kongo, he also provided for its financing. Subjects paid taxes. Schools also marked this religious transition and cultural infusion that occurred. All provinces had schools, however, only for persons of nobility; commoners received no educational training. He even enhanced his own education by studying theological books, and according to the Portuguese Royal Captain Rui d'Aguiar, Mbemba was so committed to learning that he fell asleep while reading the works. His insatiable appetite for education expanded to his brethren and subjects, whom he sent to study in Europe. His son Henrique Kinu a Mbemba, for example, earned the title of bishop of Utica, in North Africa; however, although the Vatican conferred him this position, he actually served the Kongo region from the early 1520s to his death in 1531.

Mbemba also became embroiled in international matters. Chief among them was the role of the Portuguese and the slave trade. He disapproved of the practice even though slavery predated the Europeans' arrival. Several letters penned, beginning in 1526, documented his complaints and accusations that the Portuguese illegally purchased slaves. Mbemba also mentioned visible signs of property ownership, manner of capture, and inference of travel from the interior to the coast. In providing a description of Portuguese method of slave acquisition, Mbemba distinguishes between illegitimate and legitimate trade.

Amid his letter-writing campaign and slavery's documentation, Mbemba issued a threat. In no uncertain terms, he told the Portuguese that he would close the slave trade altogether, an idea that he later aborted for the establishment of an examination committee. The newly constituted examination committee had this charge: to determine the legality of all enslaved persons. Mbemba wanted to control the exchange of human chattel for Portuguese merchandise by mandating that any European wishing to purchase goods had to inform three Kongo noblemen and officials of the Kongo court. Failure to comply with the terms meant a loss of goods acquired by the Portuguese. Mbemba negotiated an agreement, which comprised two physicians, two apothecaries, and one surgeon, all medically qualified to treat the diseases that plagued the kingdom. Kongo inhabitants also received European firearms, horses, cattle, and goods from the Americas. For these inducements, Mbemba allowed slavery to continue. In fact, Mbemba retained his own supply of slaves.

Noted principally for his promotion of Christianity as the state religion, Mbemba left an impressionable legacy. His stance on slavery was admirable, although he contradicted his public convictions when he held his own slaves. The fact that he served as a barrier to Portuguese capitalism and mercenary goals was a testament to his character. His "reward" for this stalwartness was an unsuccessful assassination attempt. On Easter Day in 1540, eight Portuguese tried to shoot him. When he died, Mbemba was at least 80 years old in 1542 or 1543. His death, which was marred by a disintegrated state, in large part due to the Portuguese presence, sparked a succession battle. Grandchildren and heirs desiring his coveted position fought among themselves. One son Pedro emerged from the familial fray to succeed his father, but his term was short-lived. Mbemba's grandson Diogo overthrew Pedro in 1545, forcing him to seek refuge in a church. All other future leaders had Mbemba's blood, as descent flowed linearly. Three of his daughters, for example, gave birth to future kings. Mbemba reaped success as a leader, parent, politician, and pragmatist. His ideologies showcased his resolve and belief in the Christian faith.

See also: Kongo Kingdom; West-Central Africa

Dawne Y. Curry

Bibliography

Diouf, Sylviane A. *Kings and Queens of Central Africa.* New York: F. Watts, 2000.

Gray, Richard. "A Kongo Princess, the Kongo Ambassadors and the Papacy." *Journal of Religion in Africa* 29, no. 2 (1999): 140–53.

Jadin, Louis. *Correspondence de Dom Afonso, Roi du Congo, 1506–1543.* Brussels: Koninklijke Academie voor Overzeese Wetenschappen, 1974.

Thornton, John Kelly. *The Kingdom of Kongo: Civil War and Transition, 1641–1718.* Madison: University of Wisconsin Press, 1983.

Young, Jason R. *Rituals of Resistance: African Atlantic Religion in Kongo and the Lowcountry South in the Era of Slavery.* Baton Rouge: Louisiana State University Press, 2007.

Middle Colonies

The middle colonies of Pennsylvania, New York, and New Jersey are bordered on their north by New England and on the south by the Chesapeake states of Maryland, Delaware, and Virginia. Their geographic location allowed for the diffusion of ideas, customs, and economics from both north and south to collide to form a distinct colonial identity. The African American experience in the middle colonies began with slavery and eventually transformed to wage labor through emancipation programs that developed along with Enlightenment ideas during the American Revolution. However, even after Emancipation, African Americans experienced discrimination and restrictions on their movements, professions, and living arrangements.

The first African Americans in the middle colonies arrived from the West Indies in bondage. In 1626, members of the Dutch West India Company diverted a shipment of slaves from their colonial interests in the Caribbean to the new colony of New Netherland. The city of New Amsterdam (New York) desired these slaves because the colony was suffering a labor shortage. Low colonial migration as well as small numbers of indentured servants caused the Dutch to look toward slavery to provide them with the labor necessary for the colony to expand and survive. In New Netherland, slaves were used to build roads and forts for defense, as well as clear land for agriculture, providing the Dutch settlers with a constant supply of food and defenses against British and Indian incursions.

The presence of slaves in New Amsterdam soon spread across the Hudson River into New Jersey. Dutch settlers used slaves for agriculture in the fertile fields of northeast New Jersey and established a slave-dominated East Jersey labor system that would endure until the beginning of the 19th century. In addition, Dutch traders soon began trading slaves to Dutch farmers who settled along both sides of the Delaware River as well as the colony of New Sweden. Slavery eventually moved into the Philadelphia area in the late 1600s when Quaker settlers arrived with William Penn to establish their "holy experiment."

The experience of the early colonists in Pennsylvania, New York, and New Jersey was repeated until Emancipation. Primarily, slavery in the middle colonies grew because of the lack of substantial white populations, the availability of cheap land, and the desire of white settlers to own and farm land. The combination of these factors made wage labor on larger farms or for the public good extremely unpopular. The dearth of wage labor in the middle colonies soon made slavery a popular and acceptable substitute measure. Therefore, to farm even the most modest of fields, slavery became a necessity.

Those colonists who could afford a large capital expenditure typically bought slaves after they arrived from the West Indies (very rarely were there direct shipments from Africa because it was felt that Africans not familiar with slavery were too dangerous). Those with larger farms or resources purchased slaves primarily for agricultural labor. However, slaves expanded their presence in colonial society by becoming coopers, blacksmiths, shoemakers, carpenters, and other types of artisans. Slaves also worked in the iron industry along the New York–New Jersey border.

After the acceptance of slaves outside of their traditional agricultural roles, slave owners began to hire out slaves for wages. Owners received a constant income from their investment while simultaneously retaining access to the slave during harvest season. Hiring out slaves allowed farmers to recoup the losses they had previously been victim to when their slaves sat idle during off-peak growing times. This dilemma was especially felt in the middle colonies as compared to the South, since the crops slaves helped grow (wheat, millet, barley, flax, corn, vegetables, and apples) were not as valuable economically as the rice, cotton, or tobacco of the South. In addition, since a typical New York slave grew wheat on a medium-sized farm, his economic output was substantially smaller than slaves in the South, thus slave owners had to find a way for slaves to increase their income potential, therefore, the hiring-out system became popular.

Slavery, then, did not become associated with any one occupation and continued as a substitute system of wage labor. Since slavery never became associated with cash crop production, the slave population in the middle colonies never matched that of the South; however, the middle colonies possessed more slaves than New England during the same time period. In 1770, New York contained the most number of slaves with approximately 20,000 or about 12 percent of its total population. New Jersey had approximately 8,500 slaves or 7.0 percent of its total population classified as slave, while Pennsylvania had about 5,500 slaves or 2.3 percent of its total population.

Although the economic roles and numbers of slaves in the middle colonies were vastly different from Southern society, their treatment did not differ. State legislatures passed Black Codes that prescribed the legal basis of slavery and regulated that system. New Jersey became the first in 1704, while New York followed in 1706. Both of these codes mandated severe punishments for criminal offenses, legally defined who qualified as a slave under the law, and restricted black liberties and freedoms. Castration and burning at the stake were only two of the punishments that New Jersey courts used to punish slaves convicted of rape and murder, respectively. Additionally, the treatment at the level of master and slave mirrored the South. Whippings, separation of families, or increased work were frequently used mechanisms masters employed against disobedient slaves. However, it is important to recognize that the treatment of slaves differed widely based on individual masters, as it did in the South.

Maltreatment caused slaves to rebel through a variety of means: work stoppages, running away, or open revolt. Northern farmers noted that without constant supervision, slaves would not complete farm work while newspaper ads routinely advertised for the return of fugitive slaves. In regard to open revolt, organizing any structured rebellion was difficult in the North, since the average slave owner only owned one or two slaves. Large holdings that created an independent slave culture were largely nonexistent in the North. Therefore, the creation of culture and organizing a revolt usually occurred in an urban environment. Two rebellions of note occurred in New York City in 1712 and 1741. On April 1, 1712, slaves burned a house and shot the whites who were inside when they attempted to escape the fire. Eight whites died and twelve were wounded. Special courts prosecuted the slaves, and they were executed later that year. The Conspiracy of 1741 revolved around blacks setting fire to various buildings in New York City, including Fort George. Several blacks were convicted and burned at the stake for allegedly setting fire to the city. In each case, the rebellions caused New York and its neighbors in New Jersey to reevaluate their slave codes and attempt to enforce tighter control on their slave populations.

The American Revolution dramatically changed the shape of slavery in the Northern colonies. The outbreak of war fueled abolitionist sentiment that had been present since the mid-1700s. Rhetoric touting that the relationship between slavery and freedom was the same as between the American Colonies and Great Britain soon galvanized a share of the population to question the suitability of fighting for freedom while at the same time enslaving another race. The largest group of antislavery supporters still remained the Quakers. Although the Quakers who originally settled in Pennsylvania had used slave labor, by 1761, Quakers in New Jersey and Pennsylvania had outlawed slaveholding among their own members and determined that they should help rid the United States of the evil institution. Quaker activism helped to introduce numerous bills into the colonial legislatures and began the attack on slavery. Quakers initially lobbied for better treatment for slaves, ending the importation of Africans into the colonies, and the end of stringent requirements for manumitting slaves, which in most colonies required a slave owner to post a bond as high as 200 pounds as well as pay a yearly supplement in order to free a slave, leading many slave owners to choose to keep their slaves instead of manumitting them.

Pennsylvania vied with Massachusetts as the leader in Northern abolition. Philadelphia, the largest center of Quaker activism in the United States, pressured Pennsylvania to support abolition. Coupled with the rhetoric of freedom stemming from the Revolution, the Pennsylvania legislature passed a gradual emancipation bill in 1780 that granted freedom to children born to slaves after they reached the age of 28 years old. Emancipation in Pennsylvania resulted from the support of Quakers and the Enlightenment idea of freedom, but also from an examination of the economic situation in the state. Since Pennsylvania possessed a large enough population of wage laborers, the abolition of slavery did not extremely hurt the state economically. However, those farmers along the Delaware River, coupled with racist tendencies of the population at large, led to the failure of achieving complete abolition by the state legislature in 1800. However, slavery met a quick death in Pennsylvania, since by 1820, only 211 slaves remained in the state, and by 1840, slavery completely disappeared within Pennsylvania's borders.

Abolition did not come as easily to New York and New Jersey as it did in Pennsylvania. The year 1784 saw the defeat of a New York abolition bill based primarily on economic grounds by Dutch planters in the lower Hudson Valley. After that defeat, New York Quakers allied with the newly formed New York Manumission Society to introduce another abolition bill in 1785. After another intense lobbying campaign, New York passed a gradual emancipation law that took effect on July 4, 1799. Any child born to a slave after that date would be free after 28 years of indenture for men and 25 for women. Key to the passage of the emancipation bill was a compensated abolition program that allowed slaveholders to abandon their slaves' newborn children to the care of the state. After the abolition of slavery across the North, New York emancipated all slaves born before July 4, 1799, as of July 4, 1827. On July 4, 1827, slavery in New York finally died.

New Jersey, the last Northern state to enact a gradual emancipation program, had, along with New York, the longest relationship with slaves. New Jersey passed a gradual emancipation law that took effect on July 4, 1804. The bill essentially provided the same provisions as the New York plan; however, New Jersey never passed a complete abolition program as New York did. Slavery existed in New Jersey until the passage of the Thirteenth Amendment (which New Jersey initially rejected) in 1865, thus ending the slave experience in the North.

After Emancipation, free blacks took on many of the same jobs as they had when they were slaves. They competed for jobs as wage laborers in New York and Philadelphia or worked on farms across central New Jersey. Although they were free, blacks were refused the right to vote and suffered racism throughout the 19th century. After Emancipation, many whites who supported abolition turned to the colonization movement to help alleviate the large number of free blacks in the cities and towns of the middle colonies. Thus, the rhetoric of freedom that emanated from the Revolution neither freed all blacks from bondage nor eliminated racism.

See also: African Burial Ground, New York City; African Methodist Episcopal Church; Dutch New Netherland; Dutch West India Company; Gradual Emancipation; New England

Colonies; New York Conspiracy of 1741; New York Revolt of 1712; Northern Slavery; Patroonship; Pinkster Festival

James John Gigantino

Bibliography

Alexander, Leslie M. *African or American?: Black Identity and Political Activism in New York City, 1784–1861*. Urbana: University of Illinois Press, 2008.

Hodges, Graham. *Root and Branch: African Americans in New York and East Jersey, 1613–1863*. Chapel Hill: University of North Carolina Press, 1999.

Lepore, Jill. *New York Burning: Liberty, Slavery, and Conspiracy in Eighteenth-Century Manhattan*. New York: Random House, 2005.

McManus, Edgar. *Black Bondage in the North*. Syracuse, NY: Syracuse University Press, 1973.

Nash, Gary. *Quakers and Politics*. Princeton, NJ: Princeton University Press, 1968.

Nash, Gary, and Jean Soderlund. *Freedom by Degrees: Emancipation in Pennsylvania and Its Aftermath*. New York: Oxford University Press, 1991.

White, Shane. *Somewhat More Independent: The End of Slavery in New York City, 1770–1810*. Athens: University of Georgia Press, 1991.

Musa, Mansa

Mansa Musa (?–1337) is the best known of the emperors of Mali, largely because of his pilgrimage to Mecca in 1325 and the widespread fame of his visit to Cairo. The pilgrimage had important consequences for the subsequent history of the western Sudan, a region that haunted men's minds thereafter. Egypt, the Maghrib, Portugal, and the merchant cities of Italy took an increasing interest in Mali.

Once on the throne, Mansa Musa set about consolidating the achievements of his predecessors and making the central authority be obeyed. He was assisted by an eminent general, Saran Mandian, who strengthened the emperor's authority not only in the valley of the Niger as far as Gao and beyond, but also throughout the Sahel, winning the submission of the Saharan nomads, who were often robbers and rebels.

Mansa Musa made elaborate preparations for his pilgrimage. In accordance with tradition, he levied special contributions from every trading town and every province. Although the figures given by the Arab writers are probably exaggerated, they give some idea of the power of the Mali emperor. There were said to be 60,000 porters and 500 servants decked in gold, each carrying a golden staff. Mansa Musa was received in Cairo with the honors due to the great sultan he was, and created a great impression by his bearing and his generosity. The important thing is that he established sound economic and cultural relations with the countries he traveled through.

Some of this wealth and power directly relates to the unique position of his empire along the Niger River basin and the crossroads of many major trans-Saharan trade routes. Two of these traded commodities were salt and gold. These were so important that in the 14th century they were used as currency. Salt trade originated from the north of Mali in the mines of Taghaza. The gold mines of Bambuk, on the other hand, lay within Mali territory. This gold was the source of half of the world's supply and greatly contributed to Mansa Musa's wealth. During his life, Mansa Musa also gained control of Timbuktu, which stood at the crossroads of the Niger, an important means of transport, and the Saharan desert trade routes. This was the city where the Saharan salt merchants and the gold-laden caravans converged. This provided Mansa Musa control of these two major commodities, and with this control, his wealth increased.

Mansa Musa returned home from his pilgrimage with a famous architect, Isāk al-Tuedjin, who built the great mosque at Gao. In Timbuktu the architect built another great mosque and a royal palace. Mansa Musa attracted many men of letters to his court and was himself skilled in Arabic. After his pilgrimage, the Marinids of Fez and the merchant cities of the Maghrib began to take a lively interest in Mali, and the rulers exchanged gifts and ambassadors. Musa set up Koranic schools and had bought many books in Cairo and the holy places.

As a builder, Mansa Musa left an enduring mark on all the cities of the Sudan, with their characteristic buildings of beaten earth strengthened with wood. The mosques of Jenne and Timbuktu were the prototypes of what is called the Sudanic style. As a patron and friend of literature, Musa helped lay the foundations of the Arabic literature of blacks, which was to bear its finest fruit in the cities of Djenne and Timbuktu in the 14th and 15th centuries. Under his rule Timbuktu rose not only to become an important city in the trans-Saharan trade route but also the center of Islamic scholarship. Muslims came from distant countries to receive an education at Sankore University that he built in Timbuktu. Thus, these centers attracted Muslims from all over the world, including some of the greatest poets, scholars, and artists of Africa and the Middle East. This greatly increased the fame of Mali.

Mali achieved the apex of its territorial expansion under Mansa Musa. The Mali Empire extended from the Atlantic coast in the west to Songhai far down the Niger bend to the east, from the salt mines of Taghaza in the north to the legendary gold mines of Wangara in the south. Mansa Musa died in 1337. He had brought stability and good government to Mali, spreading its name abroad.

In the long run, partly due to Musa's conspicuous flaunting of wealth, when ships of Portugal's Prince Henry captured Cueta in 1415, Moorish prisoners told more details of the gold trade. Henry sent his explorers down the African coast to find a route across sub-Saharan Africa in order to contain Islam.

See also: Mali; Sudanic Empires; Timbuktu

Moshe Terdiman

Bibliography

Bell, Nawal Morcos. "The Age of Mansa Musa of Mali: Problems in Succession and Chronology." *The International Journal of African Historical Studies* 5, no. 2 (1972):221–34.

Fage, J. D. *A History of Africa*. London: Hutchinson, 1978.

Levtzion, Nehemia. *Ancient Ghana and Mali*. London: Methuen, 1973.

Pancella, Peggy. *Mansa Musa: Ruler of Ancient Mali*. Chicago: Heinemann Library, 2004.

New England Colonies

Slavery in New England, more urban than rural, despite the presence of several large plantations, especially in Rhode Island and Connecticut, began as a colony-building measure before the middle of the 17th century. Slaves were called on to do whatever was needed, thus developing extensive expertise. Even though the slave population in New England was never huge, the colonialists took enormous profits from the trade, in ship-building; in brokering loans; in providing root vegetables, meat, and fish to feed slaves across a far-flung network; and by supplying wood and building materials for homes and other structures in the South and West Indies. In little more than a century, thanks to many streams of income, slavery spelled immense prosperity for New England. Thus, the region developed an enviable

standard of living and established itself as a political, educational, and cultural capital. It is worth considering if the financial significance that New England developed, which allowed it to launch a campaign for independence, could have happened minus the profit slavery consistently afforded.

In 1641, Massachusetts, which initially included Maine, was the first New England colony to legalize slavery. This occurred in the midst of declining immigration from England and Europe. Slaves, African and Native American, took up the slack, providing free labor from an early period. The exact date when the first African came to New England is shrouded, but a shipment carrying cotton, tobacco, salt, and slaves arrived in Salem in 1638. William Bradford, governor of the Bay Colony, so noted in his journal and also indicated that the ship had sailed from the Caribbean. Not long before, the same ship had taken to the islands some Pequot slaves, mostly men and boys, who were war captives. The February arrival that Bradford recorded was the return voyage for the *Desire*, which had been built in Salem expressly for the slave trade.

Some Africans came to New England with special aptitudes and knowledge. In 1721, Onesimus, who had a reputation for being a clever slave, convinced his master, Cotton Mather, that the only way to stop the spread of smallpox in Boston was to prick the skin and add a bit of infection to the body. Back home in Africa, he said, few ever died of the disease because it was understood that introducing it to the system in small amounts dulled its effect. Mather persuaded Zabdiel Boylston, a doctor, to test the remedy, which significantly cut the number of casualties. Three decades later, another exceptional slave arrived on the Boston wharf. A sickly girl, in time, she quickly grew stronger, and her intellect was undeniable and unmistakable. Phillis Wheatley mastered Latin and Greek and English in short order, becoming a published poet with a volume of verse to her credit while she was in her twenties.

Because some slaves fared better than others and since the concentration of slaves in colonial New England was less than in the agrarian South, never reaching more than 5 percent overall, which happened just prior to the American Revolution, it is assumed that slavery weighed lightly there. But slavery, the loss of ownership in the self, is never inconsequential. The colonists understood this because they argued that the British had enslaved them, robbing them of personhood, and this was the basis on which they went to war. A number of slaves understood the irony, and used it to advantage, pushing for freedom. One such former slave was Prince Hall, who organized a chapter of black masons in Boston, with a mission of amassing political and social capital. Hall was contemporary with Crispus Attucks, a runaway slave of African and Native American background, who was the first to shed blood for liberty and independence in the incipient nation.

When the American Revolution began, more than 15,000 slaves lived in New England, with the highest percentage in Rhode Island and the greatest number in Massachusetts. In Boston, Africans constituted a 10th, but in Connecticut and in Massachusetts generally, they represented roughly 4 percent, some of whom were free, even though they did not necessarily fare better in freedom. After purchasing himself in 1760, Venture Smith continued to save, eventually buying liberty for his sons, daughters, and wife. Several decades before Smith documented his experience in a narrative, there emerged among the slave populations in Rhode Island, Connecticut, Massachusetts, and New Hampshire a common cultural life expressed in Black Election Day festivities.

This social holiday brought blacks from far and wide to commune together with music, games, and spirits, assembling for the purpose of choosing a leader, either a black governor or king, who took on a governance role in the community, sitting in judgment over disputes. Africans saw themselves and were seen as a separate people, and they rallied to create their own institutions, drawing sustenance from the camaraderie of togetherness while they displayed their cultural stamp and sense of communal standing in their own eyes and in those of others.

See also: Attucks, Crispus; Election Day; Northern Slavery; Tituba; Wheatley, Phillis

Barbara Lewis

Bibliography
Farrow, Anne, Joel Lang, and Jennifer Frank. *Complicity: How the North Promoted, Prolonged, and Profited from Slavery.* New York: Ballantine Books, 2005.
Greene, Lorenzo Johnston. *The Negro in Colonial New England, 1620–1776.* New York: Columbia University Press, 1942.
Piersen, William D. *Black Yankees: The Development of an Afro-American Subculture in 18th Century New England.* Amherst: University of Massachusetts Press, 1988.
Temin, Peter, ed. *Engines of Enterprise: An Economic History of New England.* Cambridge, MA: Harvard University Press, 2000.

New York Conspiracy of 1741

The New York Conspiracy of 1741, also called the Great Negro Plot, refers to the alleged plot by slaves, free blacks, and poor whites to rebel and burn colonial New York City. In a series of show trials and confessions, the New York Supreme Court elicited the details of the plot, with the final outcome being the execution of 34 people and the deportation of more than 70 others.

In the months before the string of fires broke out, the alleged conspirators, black and white, often met in Manhattan's waterfront taverns, like the one owned by John Hughson. Three frequent patrons of Hughson's tavern were the slaves Caesar, Prince, and Cuffee, collectively called the "Geneva Club." Caesar, Prince, Cuffee, and others regularly stole goods and exchanged them for money or alcohol at Hughson's. The Irish prostitute Margaret Kerry had a room at Hughson's paid for by Caesar, who was the father of the child Kerry was carrying. Mary Burton, also of Irish descent, was the 16-year-old indentured servant of John Hughson, who would become a critical witness in the later trials.

On March 2, 1741, more than two weeks before the first fires broke out and a conspiracy was suspected, the slaves Caesar and Prince were arrested for burglary. Shortly thereafter, on March 4, the servant Mary Burton was questioned by the undersheriff and confirmed that Caesar and Prince had stolen items and stored them at Hughson's. She also began to reveal details about the supposed plot by those who frequented Hughson's to rise up and destroy the city.

On March 18, 1741, several buildings within New York's Fort George were engulfed in flames. One of these buildings was the mansion of Lieutenant Governor George Clarke. From there the fire moved to the chapel and barracks within the fort. The fire eventually jumped the walls of Fort George, burning the adjacent Secretary's Office, where many important city documents were held. The documents were saved; the building was not.

The Fort George fires were the most destructive, but several other fires occurred in the following weeks. On March 25, Captain Peter Warren's house was ignited (but saved with little damage). April 4 and April 6 saw six more fires between them. In total, there were at least 13 fires of varying destructiveness between March 18 and April 6, 1741.

Between April 11 and April 17, government officials came to the conclusion that the fires were the result of arson

A slave plot in New York City results in the burning of two slaves at the stake in 1741. In all, 31 slaves were executed after the conspiracy. (Mary Evans Picture Library/The Image Works)

and were part of a larger conspiratorial plot by the city's slaves. Throughout April and May, they arrested several slaves they believed to be connected to the arsons, including Geneva Club member Cuffee and another slave named Quack. A series of trials in the New York Supreme Court commenced on April 21 and continued through August 31, 1741. City recorder and judge Daniel Horsmanden oversaw the trials and recorded the proceedings, later publishing a report.

On May 1, 1741, Caesar and Prince were tried and convicted of burglary. A week later, on May 8, they were sentenced to death. On May 11, both were publicly hanged, and Caesar's corpse was gibbeted and publicly displayed. Between Caesar and Prince's trial and their sentencing, on May 6, John Hughson and his wife, Sarah, along with Margaret Kerry, were tried and convicted of feloniously receiving stolen goods. All three were found guilty on June 8 and were publicly hanged on June 12, 1741.

As the months progressed, the accusations became more frequent and more widespread. On May 29, 1741, Cuffee and Quack were tried for arson, found guilty, and sentenced to death. They were burned at the stake the next day. The executions of the alleged ringleaders in the spring were followed by a number of trials in the summer that resulted in the execution and banishment of many other slaves. Some were hanged, some were burned at the stake, and others were transported out of the colony. In total, 13 black men were burned at the stake, 17 were hanged along with 4 whites, and more than 70 were sentenced to transport out of New York.

The reactions of white New Yorkers, particularly those of the Supreme Court judges and jury, were the product of a broader paranoia about slave rebellion. The New York Slave Revolt of 1712 and the Stono Rebellion of 1739 in South Carolina, among other acts of rebellion, remained in the memories of both free and enslaved New Yorkers. This memory provided a source of suspicion and antagonism toward slaves and slave gatherings (like the alleged gathering and plotting at Hughson's tavern).

There is considerable scholarly debate about who was actually responsible for the fires. Given the unfair nature of the trials and the seemingly coerced nature of many of the confessions, it is unclear who was telling the truth during the trial. Much like the Salem Witch Trials of 1692, paranoid accusations and coerced confessions served as adequate evidence of a broad conspiracy.

See also: New York Revolt of 1712; Northern Slavery; Slave Resistance

Jerad Mulcare

Bibliography

Davis, Thomas J. *A Rumor of Revolt: The "Great Negro Plot" in Colonial New York.* New York: The Free Press, 1985.

Hoffer, Peter Charles. *The Great New York Conspiracy of 1741: Slavery, Crime, and Colonial Law.* Lawrence: University Press of Kansas, 2003.

Lepore, Jill. *New York Burning: Liberty, Slavery, and Conspiracy in Eighteenth-Century Manhattan.* New York: Alfred A. Knopf, 2005.

New York Revolt of 1712

One of the largest early revolts in North America occurred in New York City in 1712. On the first of January of that year, a number of enslaved men and women met and performed a blood oath in preparation for a planned revolt to take place early in April. On April 7, 1712, at about two in the morning, more than two dozen enslaved men and women gathered in an orchard behind the house of a local cooper in New York City's east ward (near Wall Street on the east side of the city). They came armed—having stolen knives, guns, axes, and whatever weapons they could get their hands on. The slaves set fire to one of the cooper's outbuildings. When whites approached to put the fire out, the slaves killed nine men and wounded five or six others. Using this fire as a distraction to cover their escape from the city, the slaves fled the scene, running north through the woods toward freedom. Robert Hunter, the colonial governor of New York, immediately called out the militia to "drive the island" and through this method and through strict house-to-house searches in the town, 27 men and women were arrested. The militia found the bodies of six additional slaves who had killed themselves before they could be captured. The prisoners were quickly tried and convicted, and 21 of these men and women were immediately executed. One of the convicted women was pregnant, and her execution was stayed until after she gave birth. The punishment was brutal: some were burned at the stake, while others were broken on the wheel. One slave was suspended from chains until he died.

At the time of this revolt, New York City was a thriving British colony, its economy based in the booming slave trade and slave plantation system. Transatlantic slave traders ran their business from the city, and merchants became wealthy providing England's monocultural sugar-growing islands in the Caribbean with staple crops grown by settlers and their slaves in the fertile Hudson Valley. In addition to agricultural work in the city and in outlying farms, enslaved Africans worked the docks, served in homes, worked in a variety of skilled trades, and supplied provisions to local markets throughout the city. Many slaves were "rented" to work on city construction projects. The wounded skeletons of slaves found in New York City's African Burial Ground provided mute testimony to how hard they were worked. For example, several women buried there were found with skull collapse from being forced to carry huge burdens on their heads.

The institution of slavery preexisted English rule, beginning in 1626 shortly after the Dutch occupation and settlement of what was then called New Amsterdam. At the time of the English takeover, in 1664, there were four times the number of slaves in New York as there were in the Virginia colony. The population of slaves continued to increase, and by the turn of the 18th century, slaves made up more than 30 percent of the total population of the city. The slave population included captives from western Africa, "seasoned" slaves born in the West Indies, and descendants of these born in New York. The slaves involved in the 1712 revolt were identified as "Coromantee," from Akan-speaking nations of present-day Ghana, and "Paw Paw," a term used for the Fon of Dahomey in present-day Togo. The names of those executed included Anglo-American names such as Sarah and Abigail, as well as Akan day-names such as Quaco and Quashi.

See also: African Burial Ground, New York City; Coromantee; New York Conspiracy of 1741; Northern Slavery; Slave Resistance; Society for the Propagation of the Gospel in Foreign Parts

Rebecca Hall

Bibliography
Aptheker, Herbert. *American Negro Slave Revolts.* New York: International Publishers, 1987.
Foote, Thelma. *Black and White Manhattan: The History of Racial Formation in Colonial New York City.* New York: Oxford University Press, 2004.
Rucker, Walter. *"The River Flows On": Black Resistance, Culture, and Identity Formation in Early America.* Baton Rouge: Louisiana State University Press, 2005.

Newton, John

John Newton (1725–1807), slave trader, hymn writer, Church of England divine, was born in London on July 24, 1725. He was the only son of a captain in the merchant marine who traded in the Mediterranean, and was later appointed governor of York Fort in Hudson's Bay, British North America, where he died in 1750. Newton's mother was a devout Nonconformist. By his own account, after the death of his beloved mother, and his father's remarriage, Newton was emotionally and intellectually neglected both at home and the boarding school he attended at Stratford in Essex. When he turned 11 years of age, he made the first of five voyages on his father's ship to the Mediterranean. Later in life he reflected upon this time, writing that his propensities for sin were increasing. Before the age of 16, despite a number of attempts at moral self-reform (the first time as a result of a serious riding accident, another time due to the drowning of a friend on a British man-of-war on which Newton was also supposed to have sailed), he fell into further moral decay.

During the next few years, Newton vacillated between nominal attempts at religious observance and licentious behavior. In 1743, after returning from a voyage in the Mediterranean, Newton's father was able, through connections, to procure for his son a promotion to midshipman aboard a naval vessel that was assigned to patrol the English coast just before the outbreak of hostilities between France and Britain during the War of the Austrian Succession. Newton deserted before HMS *Harwick* was to sail on a return voyage to the West Indies, but was captured by the military, returned to his vessel, and stripped of all vestiges of rank and privilege.

It was after arriving in Madeira that Newton first inadvertently entered the slave trade when he managed to talk his way into joining a slave-trading ship bound for Sierra Leone. His continued profligacy onboard led to a falling out with the captain, and instead of continuing on the second part of the voyage to the West Indies, he remained on the African coast, becoming a servant to a prosperous slave trader who lived with an African woman. Newton claimed that he suffered tremendous abuse and countless indignities at the hands of both the woman and the slave trader. Within a year, however, the master consented to release him from his employment, and Newton went to work for another slave trader under far better conditions. In later life, after Newton became an active leader in the fight for the abolition of African slavery throughout the British Empire, he looked back upon the 18 months that he spent in wretched servitude as an important firsthand experience of the tremendous physical and emotional dislocation and barbarity that resulted from his embrace of his role as a slave trader.

Soon after Newton's reversal of fortune, though, his father, upon hearing that his son was not well, sent a ship to the African coast with orders to find Newton and return him to England. After almost perishing in a violent storm on the return voyage to England aboard the *Greyhound,* Newton underwent his first conversion experience. He underwent a second conversion experience when, after marrying and then commanding a slave ship to the African coast, he fell violently ill, but recovered. Newton returned to England in 1752, but then over the next few years made two more voyages to Africa as a participant in the slave trade. During the years from 1750–1754, Newton kept a detailed journal of his day-to-day participation in the slave trade, which consisted of purchasing slaves all along the west coast of Africa, then trafficking the human cargo to the West Indies or North America for sale. Throughout his journal Newton documented in extensive detail just how systemic, lucrative, and competitive as a commercial enterprise the African slave trade was. Despite the potential financial rewards involved, however, his entries reveal that the buying and selling of slaves was fraught with danger as well as disease, poor weather, and the constant threat of insurrection by both the ship's crew and African captives.

In 1754, due to a deterioration in health, Newton quit the slave trade and maritime work in general. After settling in Liverpool in 1755 to take up a civil service appointment as a tide surveyor, a post he held until 1760, he applied to become a clergyman in the Church of England, but was at first unsuccessful. After serving for a brief period as a Nonconformist minister, in 1763, he befriended the evangelical aristocrat Lord Dartmouth, who used his influence to enable Newton to be ordained as an Anglican clergyman. Over the course of his professional life as a minister, Newton served congregations in both Olney, Buckinghamshire, and later in London. More important, for the beginning of what later became the Anglo-American abolition movement, Newton's recollections of his years as a slave trader, published as *An Authentic Narrative* (1764), and *Thoughts upon the African Slave Trade* (1788), played a crucial role in convincing influential late-18th-century members of the British establishment, like William Wilberforce, Charles Simeon, and Hannah More, of their moral and religious obligations to convince the British public of the urgent need to support the passing of legislation that would make it a crime to participate in the international slave trade. In addition, Newton wrote the lyrics to "Amazing Grace" in 1772. The hymn became an anthem, of sorts, for advocates of human rights and justice even as late as the 21st century.

John Newton spent his final years serving his congregation at St. Mary Woolnoth in London, and died on December 21, 1807.

See also: Abolition, Slave Trade; Atlantic Slave Trade

John W. Clarke, Jr.

Bibliography

Martin, Bernard, and Mark Spurrell, eds. *The Journal of a Slave Trader (John Newton), 1750–1754.* London: Epworth, 1962.

Newton, John. *The Works of the Reverend John Newton, with a Life of the Author by R. Cecil.* London: Henry G. Bohn, 1854.

Occupational Castes

Occupational castes are specialized groups of skilled artists and artisans found within the hierarchal social structure of several West African ethnic groups. Originating in the empire of Ghana/Wagadu among the Soninke people, occupational castes emerged when individuals with specialized skills, who, in attempting to safeguard and perpetuate those skills among family members, formed endogamous marriage relationships with people of the same occupation. Not to be confused with the caste system in India that designates hundreds of castes from the highest to the lowest outcaste in accordance with their lineages, the occupational castes of Africa comprise one distinct group of usually four or five skilled occupations. While draconian rules and proscriptions often limit the freedom and human rights of the lower castes within the religious-based Hindu caste system, the occupational castes of Africa are totally free and have the same rights as other citizens.

There are, however, certain restrictive taboos associated with occupational castes: they are not allowed to marry outside of their caste, and in some cases there are specially prescribed funeral rites held only for caste groups. For example, in the past, the griot (historian/musician) caste could only be buried inside the trunks of trees, and although they may exert a tremendous influence on the political authorities, they are never permitted to be heads of state.

The Soninke social hierarchy is divided into three major branches:

1. *Horro/Horon* (Nobles)
2. *Nyaxamalo* (Occupational Castes)
   a. *gesere* (historians/musicians/singers)
   b. *tage* (blacksmiths)
   c. *garanke* (leatherworkers)
   d. *sake* (woodcarvers)
3. *Komo* (Slaves)

The *Nyaxamalo* became known as the *Nyamakala* among the Mandenka or Mandingo whose social divisions are:

1. *Horon* (Nobles)
2. *Nyamakala* (Occupational Castes)
   a. *jeli/jeliyu* (historians/musicians/singers)
   b. *numu* (blacksmiths/woodcarvers)
   c. *garanke* (leatherworkers/weavers)
   d. *fune/finah* (Islamic praise singers)
3. *Djon* (Slaves)

Also known as "the people of talent," the *nyaxamalo* and *nyamakala* represent the occupational castes and were once highly respected for the indispensable skills and knowledge they contributed to the building and functioning of the society. Their eminent status gradually deteriorated, first, during the Age of Violence, the Islamic jihads of the late 18th and 19th centuries, and definitively with the compounding of European colonialism that subverted the preexisting political economy and modes of production. The slave class was eliminated under colonialism, but the occupational castes no longer enjoyed the prestige and esteem they were formerly accorded; they were relegated instead to a lowly status in the eyes of the nobles, though they were still feared for their extraordinary powers of *nyama*.

Nyama in Mandenka signifies "vital force," a spiritual energy that has the power to exact uncontrollable vengeance on a victim. *Kala* means "handle" or "antidote." People of talent are believed to be the possessors of an abundance of *nyama* who also have the ability to manipulate and control the *nyama*, thus they are called *nyamakala*.

The griots, masters of the *nyama* in the word, can honor or disgrace a person with their eloquent manipulation of speech. They were advisors to the king, mediators in national and international disputes, ambassadors, officiators of rites of passage ceremonies, historians, social and cultural anthropologists, philosophers, musicians, composers, singers. Blacksmiths and woodcarvers mastered the *nyama* of fire, metal, and wood; the leatherworkers controlled the *nyama* of animal hide, and so forth.

Occupational castes spread throughout West Africa with the migrations and political and cultural influence of the Mandenka and Soninke peoples. The nomadic Fula/Fulani and the Tukulor who initially had no occupational castes adopted the Mandenka caste system as late as the 17th century. Ethnic groups who branched from the Soninke and

Mandenka, such as the Serere, Wolof, Songhai, Khassonke, Dyula, and Wangara, among others, inherited the occupational caste system from their predecessors.

See also: Ghana; Senegambia; Sudanic Empires

Nubia Kai

Bibliography

Conrad, David C., and Barbara E. Frank. *Status and Identity in West Africa: Nyamakalaw of Mande.* Bloomington: Indiana University Press, 1995.

Hale, Thomas A. *Griots and Griottes.* Bloomington: Indiana University Press, 1998.

N'Diaye, Bokar. *Les Castes du Mali.* Paris: Présence Africaine, 1995.

Oral Culture

Ancient writing traditions do exist on the African continent, but most Africans today, as in the past, are primarily oral peoples, and their art forms are oral rather than literary. In contrast to written literature, "orature" is orally composed and transmitted, and African oral arts are verbally and communally performed as an integral part of their popular culture. The Oral Arts of Africa are rich and varied, developing with the beginnings of African cultures, and they remain living traditions that continue to evolve and flourish today.

The oral literatures, like the cultures that produce them, constantly develop and change across time, culture, place and regional style, performer, and audience for a variety of reasons. Everyone in most African societies participates in formal and informal storytelling as interactive oral performance—such participation is an essential part of African communal life. Basic training in a particular culture's oral arts and skills is an essential part of children's indigenous education on their way to initiation into full humanness. In many instances, ethical and educational values are taught to the children through oral literature at different stages of their lives to ensure that they grow with these values in order to enhance their contribution to the development of the society. African societies have developed high aesthetic and ethical standards for participating in and judging accomplished oral artistic expressions or performances—and audience members often feel free to interrupt less talented or respected secular performers to suggest improvements or voice criticisms. Critiquing oral performance takes place

at three different but connected stages—pre-performance, intra-performance, and post-performance—with a view to achieve genuine rendition and representation of the cultural values of the people.

African orature is a communal participatory experience where everyone in the society participates in both formal and informal oral performance that is an essential part of African social life. The orature of the people speaks in the communal voice of the collective wisdom and knowledge and carries demure social and ethical values. Various cultural ideas of the people are conserved memorably by employing various stylistic devices for easy recapitulation and rendition. In many instances, oral expressions deviate from the syntactic norms of the literate culture, and the language is lively and cryptic in nature. This attribute of oral culture enhances speaker-listener's relationship in communication scenery. Although the oral artists in oral culture have rights to demonstrate dexterousness and adroitness in their performances, still they are culturally constrained and bound to ensure that their creativity fits into the ways of doing it in the society. For example, among the Yoruba of southwestern Nigeria, it is the practice of the oral artists to pay homage to their masters and those artists who had performed in a similar genre prior to their own time of performances. This is usually encapsulated in the saying, "*Orin mi náà kó, orin ògá mi ni,*" meaning, "It is not my song but my master's song." The underlying factor in the above statement is that the oral artists must present their orature as fitting the traditions of the ancestors or the society that owns the lore.

Long after the incursion of writing culture in oral culture society, indispensable information on how to perform society's social institutions was left unwritten, especially in the religious rites and ritual performances. When they are written, the "livingness" trait has been distorted as it is void of sound and inflection. Not only this, but the pragmatic essence that has to do with the context of performance is lost. This is because much of the poetry associated with the African deities is contextually performed; they cannot be performed in other contexts.

In preliterate societies and cultures, spoken words were highly revered and mastered by the people, as it used to be the community's repertoire of collective wisdom, knowledge, and experiences; they could be likened to "human libraries," "archives," or walking sacred texts, capable of astonishing feats of remembering for the benefit and survival of the people and their culture. Oral narratives are practical, flexible, and spiritual; these living "texts" have no particular definitive version, and they vary, acclimatize, and change with the performer, audience, time, place, space, and utility. But the magical, spiritual powers of the spoken word, and its skillful verbal performance, are devalued by the literate culture. One of the major features of oral culture is that literal translation cannot give us a full sense of what is being said due to the poetic nature of most orature because it involves a lot of foregrounding of standard language.

Specifically, the Yoruba people, like their African counterparts, believe that there are "Special Forces" that are released by the spoken or sung word in oral performances. This is sometimes regarded as the magical and spiritual powers of the spoken word. The belief about the powers embedded in the spoken word is a common phenomenon in Africa, even in the literate communities.

Due to the flexibility trait it has, the oral literature of the people lends itself to various changes in the society, especially in this era of globalization where there is a tendency for acculturation and interculturation. Oral literatures are thus performed in diverse ways to accommodate contemporary happenings. Aside from this, the phenomenon of global migration also has a serious effect on the oral culture of the people in time's perspective. The oral culture is lending itself to various Internet facilities in this global era as well.

See also: Griot; Sundiata: The Epic of Old Mali

Ajibade George Olusola

Bibliography

Gleason, Judith, ed. *Leaf and Bone: African Praise-Poems.* New York: Penguin, 1994.

Mpanje, Jack, and White Landeg. *Oral Poetry from Africa: An Anthology.* New York: Longman, 1983.

Ong, J. Walter. *Orality and Literacy: The Technologizing of the Word.* London and New York: Routledge, 2002.

Patroonship

A patroonship was a private farming community on a vast estate in New Netherland that was granted to investors. The investors, contracting with the Dutch West India Company (WIC), promised to stimulate the population growth in the area and expand trade. The investor was expected to import, at his own expense, at least 50 European colonists within four years of being granted the land and supply the land with agricultural animals and tools needed for the private farming community. In return for their passage to the New World, colonists agreed to bind themselves to serve the patroon for a period of 10 years, cultivate his land, pay him rent, grind grain at his mill, and offer him the option of purchasing their agricultural produce.

Patroonships were similar to Europe's feudal kingdoms. The patroon furnished a pastor and schoolmaster, administered justice, established courts, collected rent from tenants, and was given approximately 10 percent of all the grain, fruit, and other products his tenants produced on the land. The system was not successful, partly because land in the colonies was free to those who wanted to settle it. Five patroonships along the Hudson River and Delaware Valley were originally registered with the WIC. Four of the five were not successful. The one moderately successful patroonship, Rensselaerswijck, was owned by a Dutch diamond merchant and director of the WIC and lay near the confluence of the Mohawk and Hudson rivers in the area of present-day Albany, New York. Its limited success can be attributed to the patroon's successful negotiations with the WIC, which permitted him to keep fur pelts in return for a small payment to the company, participate in the fishing trade, and trade with other colonies. The Tin Horn rebellion in 1844 extinguished the patroonship system.

See also: Dutch New Netherland; Dutch West India Company; Headright System; Middle Colonies

Nancy A. McCaslin

Bibliography

Bachman, Van Cleaf. *Peltries or Plantations; The Economic Policies of the Dutch West India Company in New Netherland, 1623–1639.* Baltimore, MD: Johns Hopkins Press, 1969.

Goodfriend, Joyce D. *Before the Melting Pot: Society and Culture in Colonial New York City, 1664–1730.* Princeton, NJ: Princeton University Press, 1992.

Harris, Leslie M. *In the Shadow of Slavery: African Americans in New York City, 1626–1863.* Chicago: University of Chicago Press, 2003.

Shorto, Russell. *The Island at the Center of the World: The Epic Story of Dutch Manhattan and the Forgotten Colony That Shaped America.* New York: Doubleday, 2004.

Vanema, Janny. *Beverwijck: A Dutch Village on the American Frontier, 1652–64.* Albany: State University of New York Press, 2000.

Punch, John

John Punch (dates unknown) was at the center of a series of events, which, in many ways, led the colony of Virginia down the road to racialized slavery. In 1640, three indentured servants ran away together to Maryland from Virginia. They had the same owner, John Gwynn, a planter on the Chesapeake Bay. By name and ethnic origin, they were James Gregory, a Scotsman; Victor (no last name), a Dutchman; and John Punch, an African. Officials captured all three, returned them to Virginia, and placed them on trial. On July 9, 1640, members of the Virginia General Court handed down a landmark decision. They sentenced Gregory and Victor to receive 30 lashes each, and to complete their contracted time and an additional year with their master. Then Gregory and Victor were to serve the entire colony for another year. However, the court sentenced John Punch, the African, to serve Gwynn for the rest of his life. Thus, John Punch became the first African to be a slave for life, by law, in Virginia.

Before this, Africans were indentured servants, similar to whites. Both toiled in the fields equally oppressed. The crop in those fields was tobacco. Growing tobacco was very labor-intensive. Moreover, just like today's businesses, 17th-century planters wanted the greatest profit at the least expense.

Labor was the largest expense for tobacco planters in the Chesapeake. A captive labor force was the most cost-effective way to get the job done. Initially white planters had all white indentured servants. However, the less fortunate Europeans were ill suited to the climate and work, and servitude carried with it a time limit, an obligation to pay freedom dues or money and tools to compete against them. Next, the planters turned to Algonquians and other Native Americans in the region to cultivate cash crops. Native Americans were accustomed to the climate, and that contract carried no obligation of freedom. However, the Native Americans were at home, and in their culture, fieldwork was women's work. Men were hunters and anglers. Therefore, when white planters attempted to force Native American men to work the fields, they refused to do what they perceived to be women's work and many of them absconded. Finally, the planters turned to Africans to supply their labor force. Africans were, for a variety of reasons, seen as a more than suitable labor force. Both men and women were accustomed to surplus agricultural production, they had built-in resistances to malaria and other tropical diseases that had been transplanted to the Chesapeake, and they had little knowledge of the lay of the land, which made escaping a bit more difficult—though Punch's case proved that they did seek to abscond quite often.

For all these reasons, the Virginia General Court set a precedent with John Punch. By making him a servant for life, they paved the way for lifetime and intergenerational servitude for all African Africans to furnish the colony with a permanent labor supply

See also: Chesapeake Colonies; Freedom Dues; Indentured Servitude; Racialized Slavery

Karen E. Sutton

Bibliography

Catterall, Helen Tunnicliff. *Judicial Cases Concerning American Slavery and the Negro.* 5 vols. Washington, D.C.: Carnegie institution of Washington, 1926–1937. Reprint, New York: Negro Universities Press, 1968.

McIlwaine, H. R., ed. *Minutes of the Council and General Court of Colonial Virginia, 1622–1632, 1670–1676, with Notes and Excerpts from Original Council and General Court Records, into 1683, Now Lost* (Richmond, VA: The Colonial Press, Everett Waddy, 1924).

Morgan, Edmund S. *American Slavery, American Freedom: The Ordeal of Colonial Virginia.* New York: Norton, 1975.

Queen Nzinga (Njinga Mbande)

Queen Nzinga, also known as Njinga Mbande or Dona Anna de Souza (1583–1663), was an African queen, diplomat, and warrior from Angola who challenged Portuguese control of her country in the 1600s through warfare and diplomacy. Queen Nzinga was born among the Mbundu of Ndongo of royal birth and seized power during the rise of European expansion and trade into Africa, also known as the time period of the Atlantic slave trade, roughly 1415 to 1807. Challenges from the Portuguese and other European powers such as the English and Dutch prompted a series of reactions from the Kingdom of Ndongo. The Portuguese arrived in the region ca. 1483 and managed to secure a coastal colony at Luanda by 1575. The Portuguese in particular exerted tremendous pressure on the Kingdom of Ndongo through the person of Portuguese official Bento Cardoso, who devised a system in 1608 that demanded the delivery of slaves to the Portuguese through a Ndongo notable; in the event that the notable failed to deliver said slaves, the notable was in turn enslaved.

After 1608, dozens of notables were henceforth enslaved by the Portuguese. After 1611, Portuguese influence increased through contact with neighboring Africans. The Portuguese used the assistance of Imbangala warriors, a neighboring people to the Ndongo from central Africa, from 1612–1622 against the Ndongo, bringing the kingdom to the verge of collapse. Conflicts between Africans and the Portuguese intensified significantly in the 17th century. Nzinga came to power in dangerous times. The Mbundu people embraced strict constraints on female political power and generally resisted attempts to organize into larger confederations. It was in this climate that Queen Nzinga arose to power.

Nzinga was born to *ngola a kiluanje* Kia Samba and Guenguela Cakombe ca. 1583. The Portuguese mistakenly referred to Ndongo as Angola based on the term "ngola," a word used to refer to the king or ruler. Ndongo emerged as a regional kingdom as a result of direct trade with the Portuguese, but as the Portuguese established contacts with neighboring African societies (such as the Imbangala), the pressure to colonize Ndongo accelerated. This was a time of increased hostilities between the Portuguese and the kingdom they termed "Angola." Queen Nzinga's brother *ngola* Mbandi came to power in the 1620s and reportedly had Nzinga's child murdered. Nzinga fled but returned to negotiate a treaty with the Portuguese at Luanda in 1622, claiming to represent the Kingdom of Ndongo. When the Portuguese diplomat at Luanda refused Nzinga a chair, she sat on the back of a kneeling servant as depicted in a drawing of the meeting by a Dutch artist. Before securing an audience with the Portuguese, Nzinga accepted the Catholic baptism. This was an act of political expediency that helped to establish Nzinga as the legitimate leader of Ndongo as supported

Queen Nzinga's (Njinga) relations with the Portuguese were marked by conflict. When she went to Luanda, headquarters of the Portuguese in Angola, to negotiate with the governor he refused her a chair, a courtesy due one of equal rank. She is said to have sat down, as shown in this engraving from the 1620s. (Art Resource)

by the Portuguese. Her brother died under suspicious circumstances in 1623, and by 1624, Nzinga subsequently seized power in Ndongo ruling from 1624–1663.

Nzinga was a skillful diplomat, warrior, and politician in that she secured the support of major European powers by converting to Catholicism as well as the support of escaped slave communities to consolidate her power base in the region. Nzinga was surrounded by African rivals and European challengers to Portuguese power in the region while leader of Ndongo. She was able to find middle ground through a series of alliances with both her African rivals, such as the Imbangala, and European challengers, such as the Dutch. She offered escaped slaves their freedom in exchange for their loyalty and made an alliance with the Dutch to circumvent Portuguese demands. Confederations between Ndongo and neighboring African groups were created to gain control of slave routes. Nzinga also organized a guerrilla army and appointed her sisters as war leaders. She led troops into battle, dressed as a man, took the title of *ngola* or king, and kept male concubines.

Nzinga's quest for control of Ndongo was a constant struggle for legitimacy within Mbundu politics and against the Portuguese, along with other European powers. The Mbundu associated political power with males and held prohibitions against females holding positions of leadership amid an intricate network of local kinship and lineage factions. Customarily, the Mbundu *ngola* was drawn from one of many lineage groups. Therefore, Nzinga's seizure of power in Ndongo has been viewed as a *coup d'état,* as she had been forced to search beyond the Mbundu for political legitimacy, which she found through support of the Portuguese. When the Portuguese rescinded their support after 1624, Nzinga forged an alliance with the Imbangala and escaped slaves from Portuguese territories until she was forced to flee Ndongo for Matamba, located on the northeastern border of her former Ndongo Kingdom in 1629. At Matamba, Nzinga created an entirely new government. Women held stature as rulers in Matamba lineage systems prior to the 17th century. Through the 1630s, Nzinga used her armies to block Portuguese influence in the region and by the 1640s, had forged an alliance with the Dutch. This enabled Nzinga to build up her base of power in Matamba and dominate areas previously controlled by the Portuguese. With the Dutch departure in 1648, Nzinga was eventually forced to subsequently make a series of concessions with the Portuguese until her death in 1663.

Queen Nzinga is one of the most documented rulers in colonial African history. She was unique in that, during a time of great crisis in African affairs, she was able to serve as warrior, diplomat, and politician. Her quest for power and legitimacy is unprecedented in history.

See also: Angolan/Kongolese; West-Central Africa

Hettie V. Williams

Bibliography
Miller, Joseph C. "Nzinga of Matamba in a New Perspective." *Journal of African History* 16, no. 2 (1975):201–16.
Orchardson-Mazrui, Elizabeth. *Nzinga, the Warrior Queen.* New York: The Jomo Kenyatta Foundation, 2006.
Schwarz-Bart, Simone. *In Praise of Black Women: Ancient African Queens.* Madison: University of Wisconsin Press, 2001.
Thornton, John K. *The Kingdom of Kongo: Civil War and Transition, 1641–1718.* Madison: University of Wisconsin Press, 1983.
Thornton, John K. "Legitimacy and Political Power: Queen Njinga, 1624–1663." *Journal of African History* 32, no. 1 (1991):25–40.

Racialized Slavery

Slavery, or the state of bondage in which one person is chattel to another for the purpose of extracting labor, has existed since the beginning of recorded human history. Racialized slavery, or slavery based on a person's perceived racial identity, emerged alongside the development of the concept of race. Historians have long been confounded by questions of race in the early modern world: how did early modern Europeans think about bodily difference? How did they employ visible physical and cultural differences to build the Atlantic system of race-based slavery? In conjunction with the expansion of trade and, specifically, the development of the Atlantic slave trade, race as a concept developed in the Western world between the 11th and 18th centuries. Racialized slavery, a system of permanent servitude based solely on color, became a legalized practice in the early 18th century.

When the first 20 Africans arrived in the Jamestown colony in 1619, it is evident that their status as servant or slave was anything but clear. There is some reason to believe that the colonists viewed them as indentured servants to be held for a term of years and then freed. For a time the use of African labor remained limited. Planters continued using

European indentured servants, even when Africans began to steadily arrive in the colonies. However, by 1670, slave traders began to directly import African slaves to North America. The movement of slaves remained small for a time as the Royal African Company of England dominated the trade.

In 1697, the Royal African Company's monopoly on the slave trade to North America ended. From that point forward, the black population in North American began to rise as the cost of slaves declined due to increased competition. By 1700, the slave population had reached 25,000 in British North America, with most living in the Southern colonies. Within 60 years the slave population had exploded to approximately 250,000, and generally African slaves had replaced the use of white indentured servants.

Early in the 17th century the legal status of African slaves remained fluid. In some areas white indentured servants and black slaves worked together on comparatively equal terms. As the 17th century came to an end, a firm distinction appeared between blacks and whites. Increasingly a situation developed in which blacks would remain in bondage permanently and their children would also be slaves. The system was reinforced by the ever-increasing belief by whites regarding the inferiority of the black race.

At the start of the 18th century colonial assemblies began to pass what were known as "slave codes." These codes granted masters nearly absolute authority over their slaves. The only factor that determined who was subject to the slave codes was color. Unlike the Spanish colonial governments where people of mixed race were granted a higher status than those of pure African ancestry, Anglo-America failed to recognize such distinctions.

These slave codes continued to evolve as the American colonies became the United States. Most Southern states had various forms of slave codes, which regulated most aspects of slave life. Slaves were forbidden from holding property and could not leave their master's property without permission. Nor could slaves be out after dark, and the law forbade them from congregating with other slaves except for church. Additionally, slave codes prohibited slaves from defending themselves against white aggression. Whites were not supposed to teach slaves to read or write and slaves could not testify in court. With regard to the slave family, the slave codes failed to recognize that they existed. Slaves could not marry or divorce, and had no legal right

to keep their children from being sold to another master. On the subject of race, the codes were also clear and very rigid. They followed the one-drop rule: If an individual had one drop of black blood or African ancestry, he or she was considered black. Often this could simply be the product of rumor, as there were cases of slaves appearing to be white who it was said had a single black great-grandparent. Whatever the case, by the antebellum period slavery in the southern United States was legally codified and fully based on a person's perceived race.

Any review of recent scientific literature on race will confirm that scientists conclude that race is not an actual category of human biology, but rather a social construct whose meanings and uses have changed over time. Nevertheless, few people believe these findings and even fewer act as if race does not exist. Therefore one must look to the social sciences (history, philosophy, theology, etc.) for an explanation of how this concept developed and how it was tied to slavery.

According to some scholars, the roots of modern, Western racism are based firmly in the Iberian Peninsula. They find the concept of race sprouting in the 11th century and developing throughout the Enlightenment; this ideology came to fruition in the 15th century. Modern racism has tried to develop justification for the superiority of one group over another, and to base this superiority on biological, psychological, and spiritual factors that may be permanent. Early "racial" views, such as those of the ancient Hebrews, the early Christians, and the Greeks, either proposed a way for overcoming alleged inferiority by conversion to the superior group, as the Jews and Christians did, or by allowing for a process of assimilation, as the Greeks did for those they called "barbarians."

The Muslims who dominated Iberia from the 8th to the 15th century shaped Spanish and Portuguese ideas of race. Muslims, Jews, and Christians of Iberian origin refined and sharpened language that suggested black inferiority. As these peoples traveled, traded, and enslaved those in sub-Saharan Africa, this concept of racial inferiority took shape. By the 15th century it was fully developed and accepted by many in the Muslim and Christian worlds. As the Spanish Christians began to regain control of the peninsula during the 1400s, racial thought began to include Jews. Large numbers of Jews had been forced to convert to Catholicism and two groups emerged: Old Christians and New Christians. Anyone who had a Jewish ancestor in the previous five generations was still a New Christian and faced restrictions that barred that person from going to college, joining some religious orders, and holding government jobs. The Inquisition was established in part to control the situation and keep Jews apart, regardless of what they believed. In its new form, modern racism developed two new and important characteristics. First, modern racism differed from Ancient racism in that minority or conquered groups had no way to leave the discriminated group. No longer were religious conversions allowed or any legal means available to become part of the dominant group. The second change comes about as a result of the Enlightenment, through what David Hume referred to as the application of the experimental method to moral subjects, and produced the basic justification for modern racist theories with regard to people of color. This theory sees those non-European, dark peoples as inherently inferior. The theories offered first by the Spanish and Portuguese in the 16th century, mainly about Indians, and those offered in the 17th and 18th centuries, mainly by the English, English Americans, and the French about Africans, provide the basic structures of racist thought for the next centuries.

Scholars have also determined that religion played a key role in Western Europeans' ideas on race. Both Americans and Europeans saw notions of racial division in the Bible, debating whether Jesus was white or black, whether Moses provided a precedent for miscegenation by marrying an Ethiopian woman, whether Adam was white, black, or red, and other such topics. Initial encounters among early modern Europeans, Africans, and the inhabitants of the New World served to reinforce the biblical notion of common human descent among European Christians. European commentators almost universally accepted the notion of monogenesis, the idea that all human beings descended from Adam. Despite this firm attachment to the principle of the unity of mankind, some biblical interpretations pointed to a definite hierarchy among men. Of particular note was the supposed "Curse of Ham" or "Curse of Canaan," a remarkable reading of a passage of Genesis in which Noah supposedly cursed the descendants of his son Ham to be the servants of his son Japheth. By and large, Southern white Protestants claimed biblical sanction for slavery. They wanted to have their Bible and their slaves so they turned to the Curse of Ham/Canaan, Noah's utterance that the children of Ham/Canaan (blacks) would serve the children of Japheth (whites).

When investigating white attitudes about race during the centuries of American slavery, scholars have frequently written of change over time, but the suggested chronologies have shown a good deal of variety. For some, due to their reading of English cultural prejudices, American racism dated from the arrival of the first black people in the English colonies in the 17th century. For others, slavery only became consciously based on "racial" ideology in the era of the American Revolution. Still others, making connections between intensive abolitionist pressure against slavery from the 1830s onward and apparent increase in defensive slaveholder references to black biological inferiority, see explicit racialized slavery as a phenomenon of the antebellum period.

Numerous theoretical and ideological approaches have been used by scholars who have sought to date the racialization of American slavery. From studies using psychology, sociology, economics, and cultural history to those based on Marxist or Weberian ideologies, scholars provide varied explanations about the origins of "race" in America. Some scholars have used multiple disciplines together to further their research. A leading scholar of American attitudes about race, Winthrop Jordan, took what might be called a psycho-cultural approach in his research. He argued that English culture had for centuries been predisposed to weight "blackness" with negative associations (dirty, evil, sinister, fearful, deadly), and he felt that this cultural tradition, together with the "shock" of contact with Africans, led English colonists to see black people as natural slaves. Thus, from the beginning, American slavery was based on the idea of race.

Another historian, Edmund S. Morgan, took a broad socioeconomic approach. He saw the development of slavery as an institution based on race taking place as a planned class reaction by the Virginia elite following Bacon's Rebellion. The rebellion had uncovered perilous divisions between the elite landowners and white laborers. In turn, the landowners embraced a policy of emphasizing the privileges of freedom for the white laboring class, while fixing enslaved black people at the bottom of the property-based social structure.

Also taking a socioeconomic approach, Ira Berlin tackles slavery from the perspective of a labor historian. Berlin sees race as being more than just socially constructed; for him it is also "historically constructed," and reconstructed in the varying circumstances of labor struggle during centuries of slavery. For Berlin, the cotton revolution of the late 18th and 19th centuries represented a major period in the increasing pressure on slaves. He suggests that Southern whites solidified their image of blacks in these years. According to Berlin, slaveholders had in some earlier periods accepted a common humanity with African slaves, yet during the 19th century race was more rigidly defined, thus confining blacks to a place of perpetual inferiority.

Historian Barbara J. Fields, a Marxist scholar, has much in common with the broad socioeconomic approach but, because of her explicit interest in theorizing class and the interconnections between race and class, her work has been important in bringing about more theoretical accuracy in writing about race and slavery. Fields suggests that psycho-cultural writers incorrectly see racism, not as a social construction, but rather as an ancient, wide-ranging force that is inherent in all societies. She argues that racism arises out of class interests, is a historical product, and has a debatable beginning. Fields maintains race is an ideology that develops to legitimize patterns of class interests and grew out of a unique bourgeoisie relationship and interests that unfolded during the American Revolution.

George M. Fredrickson has reservations with Marxist determinism and about a singular class analysis. He asserts that class alone cannot continuously explain racism. Rather, following the ideas of sociologist Max Weber, he combines class with the concept of a sense of "ethnic status," representing group traditions and identities, which, although produced by particular historical experiences, do not necessarily reflect current economic class interests.

Fredrickson suggests that, in investigating the links between American slavery and racism, we should distinguish between "societal" or implicit racism and explicit/rationalized or biological racism. He does not suggest that, in the first years of the colonial era, whites immediately responded to blacks with ideas of inbuilt racism. Rather, he contends that while societal racism developed from the late 17th century, it was only from the 1830s that explicit biological racism emerged. This resulted from the unique circumstances of the abolitionist attack on slavery and with pseudoscientific researches into race, along with class-conscious elite initiatives. Slaveholders consciously exploited new biological ideas in order to appeal to white tribalism. In Frederickson's view, this new racism formed the basis for a highly aggressive white worldview, with planter interests promoting the notion of the "master race." Black slavery served the interests of all whites by shielding them from drudgery and servitude. Supposedly, slavery then joined all whites together in a sense of being members of a "herrenvolk democracy" (democracy for the "master race").

Researchers have been attentive to questions concerning the development of biological racism and the nature of racialized slavery. Some historians imply a basic continuity in biological racism, while others see various discontinuities. Critics of psycho-cultural historians suggest a delay in the onset of biological racism, since they generally see racism as arising through a period of exploitation. Nonetheless, it may be that what actually happened did not fit with either the idea of an ancient racism or with the notion of delayed racism. It could be that for socio-economic rather than for psycho-cultural reasons, there was a continuous pattern of biological racism among white Americans. Also it could be that there was, from the beginning, a pattern of whites seeing black people in a range of differing ways. Whatever the cause, by the 19th century American slavery had become racialized slavery in the minds of the people and the legal codes that governed the practice.

See also: Bacon's Rebellion; Chesapeake Colonies; Punch, John

Ira Lee Berlet

Bibliography

Berlin, Ira. *Many Thousands Gone: The First Two Centuries of Slavery in North America.* Cambridge, MA: Belknap Press of Harvard University, 1998.

Boxer, C. R. *Race Relations in the Portuguese Colonial Experience, 1415–1825.* Oxford, UK: Oxford University Press, 1963.

Fields, Barbara J. *Slavery and Freedom on the Middle Ground: Maryland during the Nineteenth Century.* New Haven, CT: Yale University Press, 1985.

Fredrickson, George M. *The Black Image in the White Mind: The Debate on Afro-American Character and Destiny, 1817–1914.* Hanover, NH: Wesleyan University Press, 1971.

Gossett, Thomas F. *Race: The History of an Idea in America.* Dallas, TX: Southern Methodist University Press, 1963.

Jordan, Winthrop D. *White over Black: American Attitudes towards the Negro, 1550–1812.* Chapel Hill: University of North Carolina Press, 1968.

Kidd, Colin. *The Forging of the Races: Race and Scripture in the Protestant Atlantic World, 1600–2000.* New York: Cambridge University Press, 2006.

Morgan, Edmund S. *American Slavery, American Freedom: The Ordeal of Colonial Virginia.* New York: W. W. Norton, 1975.

Patterson, Orlando. *Slavery and Social Death: A Comparative Study.* Cambridge, MA: Harvard University Press, 1982.

Reconquista

"Reconquista" is a term that is traditionally used to describe the centuries-long struggle of Christian forces, beginning roughly 718 and ending in 1492, to reclaim land under Muslim domination in Spain. In 711, Muslim forces crossed the Straits of Gibraltar from Morocco in North Africa into the territory now identified as Spain. This expeditionary army defeated the Visigoths, the Germanic rulers of Spain, at the decisive Battle of Guadalete. The capital of Toledo fell to the invaders before the end of 711. Within a decade the Muslims dominated most of the Iberian Peninsula. These conquerors would come to be identified in later literature as Moors, an inexact term that loosely described the Arab and North African invaders, as well as their later descendants.

With these new sovereigns came many changes. There was the introduction of a new state sponsored religion (Islam), new systems of government (the Emir, Caliphate, and Taifa kingdoms), a new capital (Córdoba), and a new title for the occupied land, al-Anadlus. This new designation was possibly a reference to the earlier Vandal inhabitants of Spain, or perhaps a reference to the Atlantic region.

Al Walid I of the Umayyad Caliphate Dynasty, which ruled the Muslim world, oversaw governing the occupied land. The Umayyad Caliphate suffered from internal and external dissent, and was unable to successfully expand the Muslim reach into Spain's northern provinces. In 718 the standard of rebellion was raised under Pelagius or Pelayo, a Visigoth noble. Pelayo's forces clashed with their Muslim adversaries multiple times over the years, culminating at the Battle of Covadonga, ca. 718–725. Although the Muslim forces were defeated, this defeat and the continued existence of Pelayo's rebels was seen as of little significance to the reigning Caliph. Christian chroniclers, however, especially in the later centuries, placed great importance on the battle, and it is often marked as the beginning of the Christian reconquest, or *Reconquista*. Pelayo was crowned king in the independent kingdom of Asturias.

Approximately 20 governors were placed at the helm of Spain, in just 40 years after the initial conquest. This series of brief rules, some lasting just months, destabilized the region further. This internal strife limited expansion. Raids were conducted across the boundaries of Spain by 717, and into neighboring Frankish territory. These conflicts led to the Battle of Poitiers, also called the Battle of Tours in 732.

Muslim forces were defeated, and again it was treated as a skirmish, while Christian commentators invested great significance to the Frankish victory over the "infidels." Although there is no clear consensus from modern historians, many argue that this battle is responsible for checking the Muslim advance across Europe.

In 740 Alfonso I, who followed Pelayo and was possibly his son-in-law, solidified the kingdom of Asturias. Berber troops revolted against the Caliph, abandoning the northern expanses of Spain. Alfonso incorporated some of these vacated lands into Austria. Unable to hold all of the abandoned area, he ordered the Duero River valley to the south devastated, turned into a barren region that separated Asturias and the rest of Spain.

In 750 the Abbasids, a rival Muslim dynasty, overthrew the Umayyads in a bloody revolt. One of the Umayyad royal family, Abd-ar-Rahman I, escaped and by exploiting existing dissent was able to reclaim power for his family in 756. In a political decision he appointed himself emir of the Emirate of Córdoba—although this was a lesser title, for all purposes ar-Rahman ruled Spain.

Disaffected Muslim nobles invited Charlemagne in 778 of the neighboring Frankish kingdom to take part of an expedition against ar-Rahman in exchange for fealty. This agreement quickly disintegrated with the factions fighting against each other, and Charlemagne's forces retreated, the rearguard of his army destroyed at the action of the Battle of Roncesvalles Pass, an event that produced the famous epic *The Song of Roland*.

The separate Christian kingdoms did not always enjoy harmonious relationships with each other. There was substantial in-fighting, which led to interfaith alliances. One such example is the confrontation between Ramiro I, King of Aragon, a Christian king, against al-Muktadir, the king of Zaragoza. Another Christian kingdom, Castile, allied with al-Muktadir and took part in the battle. One of the Castilian participants was Rodrigo Diaz de Vivar, better known to history as El Cid. Cid's later exploits on behalf of the Reconquista cause would give the world another famous epic.

For the next several centuries the struggle between Christian rebels and Muslims continued. The Christian realms grew and multiplied. From the period of 970–1035, Sancho III the Great, King of Navarre, unified most of Christian Spain. The balance of power shifted sharply back toward the Muslim occupiers in the latter half of the 10th century. Recognizing that they were still not strong enough to shake off Muslim rule entirely or continue costly multifront wars, with Islam and each other, the Christian kings of Spain pledged homage and paid tribute to the caliph at Córdoba.

The Caliph al-Mansur was especially aggressive, actively raiding the Christian lands for slaves and plunder. In 997, he sacked the venerated shrine of Santiago de Compostela. Al-Mansur died ca.1002–1008; without his forceful leadership, the power shifted again from Córdoba.

In 1031, the Umayyad Dynasty, long beset with internal strife, came to an end. This centralized authority was replaced with a series of Tafia kingdoms, smaller regions ruled by individual Muslim emirs. Reunification of the fractured Muslim kingdoms was attempted by a successor of al-Mansur. The gains made by al-Mansur and the Almohad Dynasty were reversed after the Battle of Las Navas de Tolosa in 1212. This decisive victory paved the way for the capture of Córdoba in 1236. By 1248, only Granada remained as a Muslim outpost.

In 1469, Queen Isabella and King Ferdinand were married. This union brought together the splintered Christian kingdoms, including Aragon and Castile. These rulers were dubbed "The Catholic Monarchs" for their devotion to the faith. In 1492, they successfully captured Granada, thus ending the Reconquista of Spain. Later that year, under their patronage, Christopher Columbus sailed to the New World.

The nearly eight centuries of Reconquista had a profound effect on the identity of the Iberian Peninsula, effects that rippled outward to impact Europe and even crossed the Atlantic to the New World. One of the first major effects was the rise of militarism. Numerous military orders, such as the Order of Santiago and the Order of Calatrava, sprung up in this time period. Orders such as these were often composed of knights from noble families, whose mission was mingled with religious ideals. The struggle of the Spanish Christians against Muslims was taken up by the rest of Christian Europe. During the medieval period several popes called for Crusaders to challenge the Muslims in Spain, and offered special indulgences to those who answered the call. The Muslim world viewed its cause as just and religious in nature as well. Many thousands of volunteers from Spain, North Africa, and farther abroad joined their crusade to protect and spread in Spain.

Extended exposure to differing religious ideologies had mixed effects. There were prolonged periods of peace and tolerance between the differing faiths, Islam, Christian, and Judaism. In the Muslim kingdoms non-Muslims were permitted to worship in peace as long as certain conditions were met. These included such concessions as openly acknowledging the superiority of Islam, not proselytizing to Muslims, and paying special tributes or taxes. In an effort to assimilate, some Christians learned Arabic, adopted Muslim dress and names. This group was referred to as Mozarabs. Non-Muslims and even those who converted may have been tolerated, but were placed at the bottom rungs of the societal hierarchy.

The later Muslim dynasties were more fundamentalist in nature, and treatment of Jews and other Christians took on a harsher slant. Persecution was not just practiced by one faith. In 1478, the Catholic Monarchs Ferdinand and Isabella were granted permission to enact the Inquisition in Spain. With the Christian kingdoms coalescing into a unified whole, it was thought necessary to ferret out heretics and monitor the activities of the Jews who had converted to Christianity. In the early 16th century the Moriscos, Muslims who had converted to Christianity, were especially suspect, and eventually this resulted in a mass expulsion from Spain of all those who had ever been followers of Islam.

Growth and development did take place in the arts and sciences. The city of Córdoba became a cultural epicenter. Population estimates are as high as half-a-million inhabitants for this single city at a time when a Western Christian city had closer to 10,000. European libraries could boast a few hundred books, but the library at Córdova reportedly contained several hundred thousand during the height of Muslim rule. The city contained numerous schools and universities. Muslim scholars actively translated and studied Greek works of philosophy, transmitting those ideas to Western Europe.

The arts flourished during periods of the Muslim rule. Ibn-Rushd, also known as Averroes, was one of the most famous scholars produced by Muslim Spain. Averroes was an accomplished doctor and astronomer who wrote a series of famous commentaries on the works of Aristotle. Ali Ibn Arabi, a religious scholar who also wrote works of influential poetry and prose, was educated in al-Anadlus. Ibn al-Arab, a philosopher, was also a product of Muslim Spain.

In the field of medicine, the surgeon Abulcasis wrote a multivolume medical encyclopedia called *Al-Tasrif*, which was translated into Latin and disseminated across Europe. The pioneering chemistry work of Jabir Ibn Haiyan was made possible through an education in Córdoba. The botanist Ibn al-Baitar and his groundbreaking pharmaceutical works was also a product of Muslim Spain.

The field of architecture within Spain during the Reconquista period was greatly influenced by Muslim thought. Grand enduring works were constructed throughout occupied Spain. The Great Mosque of Córdoba, an impressive example of Islamic architecture, was erected in the late eighth century and still stands as a Christian church. In Granada the massive Alhambra was built to house the Muslim rulers in the 14th century. It too still stands today, as a popular tourist attraction. Certain signature elements of "Moorish" architecture, such as intersecting and multifoil arches, remain part of the Spanish tradition today.

Muslim occupation and the resulting population surge transformed whole areas of Spain from rural into high-population urban centers. This brought many different merchants and industries into Spain, including high-demand manufacturing such as paper making and textile production, which created a complex trading network with the rest of Europe. When all of these considerations are factored in, the term "Reconquista" takes on a much broader meaning; one that encompasses not just the centuries-long warfare between Muslims and Christians and the struggle for the possession of land and the hearts of the people, but one that also means a period of great change and growth in the civilization of Western Europe.

See also: John, Prester

Michael Coker

Bibliography
Elliott, John Huxtable. *Imperial Spain 1469–1716*. London: Penguin, 2002.
Fletcher, Richard. *Moorish Spain*. Berkeley: University of California Press, 1993.
O'Callaghan, Joseph F. *A History of Medieval Spain*. Ithaca, NY: Cornell University Press, 1975.
Pierson, Peter. *The History of Spain*. London: Greenwood Press, 1999.
Watt, Montgomery W. *A History of Islamic Spain*. Edinburgh, UK: Edinburgh University Press, 1965.

Rice Cultivation

A pamphlet of 1609 is the earliest evidence that farmers thought of introducing rice into North America. The pamphlet suggested Virginia rather than the Carolinas as ideal for rice, and in 1648, Virginia governor William Berkeley grew 15 bushels of the grain. From Virginia, colonists may have brought rice to South Carolina. Alternatively, it may have reached South Carolina by ship sometime before 1680. Colonists struggled with the crop until they imported a variety from Madagascar, an island to the east of Africa, sometime between 1685 and 1696. This variety had a more recent Asian origin than the varieties grown in West Africa. Once in South Carolina, this variety hybridized, either naturally or by human aid, with other rice plants to produce a type of rice suitable for cultivation in the colony.

From the outset Africans were the prime movers of rice culture. The growth in their number paralleled the increase in rice production. By 1708, blacks edged out whites in South Carolina 4,100 to 3,500. By 1720, the planters of South Carolina were importing 600 slaves per year and by 1725, 1,000. By 1730, blacks outnumbered whites two to one. Between 1771 and 1775, slave owners imported nearly 20,000 Africans. Coincident with this growth, rice exports from South Carolina rose from 10,000 pounds in 1698 to 394,000 in 1700 to 81,476,325 in 1773. The planters intertwined labor and production by seeking slaves who knew how to grow rice. As early as 1700, ships from South Carolina rounded up Africans from Gambia, an area where they had grown rice for centuries. In the 18th century, 43 percent of slaves imported into South Carolina had lived in the rice-growing regions of West Africa or Madagascar.

These Africans brought to the New World the methods for cultivating rice. Because rice is a semiaquatic plant, much of its cultivation centers on the amassing and transporting of water to the fields upon which rice is sown. Rice is a variable plant, and although some varieties may be grown on land that receives periodic rain but is otherwise not saturated, most varieties must be grown on land inundated with water. This requirement necessitates the cultivation of rice on soil impervious to the percolation of water through it. Clay or a loam with clay subsoil is best. Once he had chosen suitable land, the farmer relied until roughly 1720 on rainfall to supply water, a practice that produced low yields. In this system the farmer broadcast seed on dry land and hoped for enough rain to nourish his crop. As they had for centuries, the African workers sought to augment rain with whatever freshwater (rice will not grow in saline soils) was close at hand. By situating farmland below the elevation of a pond or swamp and by digging trenches along the banks of these pools, laborers enabled gravity to bring water to a field. To hold water on the land, they girdled it with an embankment of earth, creating an artificial pond. By placing a wooden gate at the point of lowest elevation along an embankment, laborers could release water in increments until they had a depth of two to eight inches, varying the depth of water with the height of rice plants. As a rule, laborers kept water at a depth just below the joint at the lowest panicle of rice. At harvest laborers drained the land to permit easy access to the crop. Rice cultivation in this manner was effective but limited by topography. Only land near an elevated pond lent itself to this system.

Around 1750, South Carolina planter Makewn Johnstone harnessed the tide to expand rice culture to land that had no topographical advantage. He understood that as the tide rises, it pushes freshwater up the rivers that snake through South Carolina. By enclosing a rectangle of land along a river with an embankment on all four sides, a planter could create a kind of freshwater reservoir. To control the flow of water, workers built a gate in the side of an embankment along a river such that it opened to admit water as the tide rose and closed as it receded to trap water in the reservoir. By abutting farms on the remaining three sides of the embankment and putting a gate in each side, workers could release water from the reservoir to land on which they had sown rice. A variant of this system was to enclose all land of the same elevation in a single embankment no matter its size. Depending on the slope of the land, laborers might divide a field into a series of enclosed rectangles, each of uniform elevation and each differing from an adjoining field by as little as a few inches. Each enclosed rectangle formed a paddy. The effect was akin to terracing the land and required much labor to level sections of ground so each held a uniform layer of water. Canals brought water from rivers to inland fields as well as connected fields that were not contiguous. The size of a field varied not only with the contour of the land but with the number of slaves. A planter enclosed only as much land as his slaves could hoe and plant in a week.

In 1747, South Carolina planter William Butler calculated that 22 slaves could hoe and plant 6 acres of land per day or roughly 40 acres per week. Of these, Butler assigned 8 to dig a trench for seed. Rather than broadcast seed, 2 sowers would plant seed in a trench at four- to five-inch intervals. Butler assigned the remaining 12 the task of covering a trench with earth. In a variant of this practice, a sower encased each seed in a ball of mud to prevent it from rising out of the soil once inundated with water. Another variant, one common in the Sudan, was the planting of two or three seeds in a hole with holes in a row and at two- to five-inch intervals. In an address before the Carolina Plantation Society, Theodore D. Ravenel, who grew rice along the Cooper, Edisto, and Combahee rivers, recommended planting rice between March 10 and April 15.

As on the Caribbean sugar plantations, the hoe was the tool of cultivation on the paddy. Gangs of slaves hoed the ground at planting, after which the land was inundated for two to four days to saturate the seed. After this initial inundation, laborers drained the land to permit the seed to germinate. Workers allowed plants to grow several weeks, hoed a second time, then inundated the soil for the next four to six weeks, raising the water as the plants grew. The water not only nourished the plants but also formed a barrier against the germination of weeds after the second hoeing. Alternatively David Doar, owner of Harrietta Plantation in South Carolina, recommended weeding soon after rice germinated and 12 days thereafter to minimize the number of weeds prior to inundation. He recommended inundation when rice had grown to 1-1/2 inches. If weeds persisted, the laborers either drained the field so they could weed by hand or cut weeds just below the water surface so the weeds suffocated, a practice common in West Africa. Butler urged frequent drainage and inundation of a field for fear that stagnant water spread diseases.

Slaves cleared land after the harvest in autumn rather than waiting until spring, though the method of clearance varied by its African antecedent. The Bamana and Marka from the Macina were accustomed to clearing the land with great care, turning the soil to expose all roots and rhizomes, which they removed by hand. Other Africans from this region turned the soil to uproot weeds after harvest but did not remove weeds by the root with the result that some germinated in spring. The Africans from the region east of Timbuktu cleared land in a superficial way, simply by scraping the soil with a hoe, a practice that allowed still more weeds to germinate in spring. Ravenel recommended that workers burn crop residue after clearing the land of it. He cautioned against plowing under crop residue rather than burning it for fear that insects would overwinter in it. The practice of plowing under crop residue was more common upland than in the lowlands, according to Ravenel.

In the 19th century, the onus of cultivation began to shift from human to machine. Planters along the Mississippi

Slaves unloading rice barges in South Carolina. (North Wind Picture Archive)

River in the 1850s used the steam engine to pump water from the river to their fields. Rice cultivation, long the province of the Carolina coast, had swept west. In 1892, agricultural scientist Seaman A. Knapp emphasized that farmers could cultivate rice with the same machinery they used on wheat. That year Knapp estimated that mechanization had made rice farmers 300 percent more efficient than they had been only five years earlier. In 1894, engineers A. D. Mc-Farlain and C. L. Shaw formed the first irrigation and canal company in Louisiana to bring water to rice farmers. By 1898, the McFarlain Irrigation Company and its competitors had dug 150 miles of canals that served 55,000 acres of paddy in Acadia Parish, Louisiana. By 1900, 25 canal companies operated in Louisiana. From Louisiana, rice spread to Arkansas and Texas. In 1903, the Arkansas Agricultural Experiment Station began to compare different methods of irrigating rice. By then scientists had begun to experiment with vacuum pumps to draw water from the surface or from an underground well.

During the 20th century, machines and chemicals pervaded all aspects of rice culture. Tractors equipped with disks and lasers can level soil at a slope of 2 vertical feet for every 1,000 feet of horizontal surface. Levee plows build embankments. Twenty-four-row planters drill seed into the soil. Herbicides keep weeds at bay. Technology supplanted the drudgery that made rice cultivation onerous for centuries.

See also: Bunce Island; Carolinas; Gullah; Sierra Leone; Sweetgrass Baskets; Task System

Christopher Martin Cumo

Bibliography

Dethloff, Henry C. *A History of the American Rice Industry, 1685–1985.* College Station: Texas A&M University Press, 1988.

Doar, David. *Rice and Rice Planting in the South Carolina Low Country.* Charleston, SC: Charleston Museum, 1936.

Heyward, Duncan Clinch. *Seed from Madagascar.* Chapel Hill: University of North Carolina Press, 1937.

Lawson, Dennis T. *No Heir to Take Its Place: The Story of Rice in Georgetown County, South Carolina.* Georgetown, SC: The Rice Museum, 1972.

Littlefield, Daniel C. *Rice and Slaves: Ethnicity and the Slave Trade in Colonial South Carolina.* Baton Rouge: Louisiana State University Press, 1981.

Nuttonson, M. Y. *Rice Culture and Rice-Climate Relationships with Special Reference to the United States Rice Areas and Their Latitudinal and Thermal Analogues in Other Countries.* Washington, D.C.: American Institute of Crop Ecology, 1965.

Salley Jr., Alexander S. *The Introduction of Rice Culture into South Carolina.* Columbia: South Carolina Historical Commission, 1919.

Smith, C., Wayne, and Robert H. Dilday, eds. *Rice: Origin, History, Technology, and Production.* New York: John Wiley and Sons, 2003.

Wood, Peter. *Black Majority: Negroes in Colonial South Carolina from 1670 through the Stono Rebellion.* New York: Alfred A. Knopf, 1974.

Yoshida, Shouichi. *Fundamentals of Rice Crop Science.* Manila, Philippines: The International Rice Research Institute, 1981.

Rolfe, John

John Rolfe (1585–1622) was born in Heacham, Norfolk, England, in 1585. Little is known about his early life, but it is known that he and his wife, in 1609, boarded the *Sea Adventure (or Venture)* to sail with approximately 100 other settlers to Jamestown, Virginia, the colony the Virginia Company had founded two years earlier. A hurricane off the coast of the Bermudas wrecked the ship on which the Rolfes were sailing, but the passengers reached shore safely and began constructing two smaller ships that would take them to Jamestown. The colonists were stranded on the island several months but they found the island's people hospitable and the food supply adequate.

During the time they were in Bermuda, Mrs. Rolfe gave birth to a daughter, but the baby girl died before the colonists left the island. In May 1610, the colonists left Bermuda and began a 10-day voyage to Virginia. Mrs. Rolfe died shortly after their arrival in Jamestown.

Jamestown had been financed and sponsored by the Virginia Company because the English government wanted a permanent colony in North America to eliminate possible Spanish colonization of the area. The Virginia Company expected the Jamestown colonists to find valuable resources and initiate commercial endeavors that would return profits to the company and to England.

Tobacco was an indigenous plant in Virginia but the Virginia Company was not interested commercially in the native crop because of the tobacco's harsh taste. Rolfe began to plant the native tobacco seeds with some he had obtained from a Caribbean island, and he developed a plant with leaves that had a less harsh taste than the native crop. In addition to the tobacco leaves producing a more pleasing taste, the tobacco plants also grew well in the low marshy lands near Jamestown. When Rolfe shipped his first tobacco crop to England, tobacco became the colony's first marketable product and provided the English with an alternative to the sweeter tobacco known as "Spanish leaf," which was grown from West Indies plants by the Spaniards. The American tobacco was less expensive than the Spanish product, and in England, Sir Walter Raleigh promoted its use as a medicine and a recreational drug.

In 1614, the widower Rolfe wrote to Sir Thomas Dale, governor of Virginia, to ask the governor's approval of his marriage to a young Indian woman, Pocahontas. Pocahontas, 20 years younger than Rolfe and the daughter of the Powhatan federation leader, Chief Powhatan, had been kidnapped a year earlier by English colonists and had been brought to Jamestown to be exchanged for weapons and English prisoners her father held. Before any exchange took place, Pocahontas had learned English, had converted to Christianity, and had been baptized and christened with the name Rebecca. In his letter to the governor, Rolfe explained that he was a devoutly religious person, that he loved Pocahontas, that he believed his marriage to Pocahontas would be for the betterment of the colony, and that the marriage would not compromise his standing in the church or in his community. Rolfe also asked Powhatan's permission to marry Pocahontas. Permission was granted and Rolfe married Pocahontas in the spring of 1614.

Rolfe's marriage to Pocahontas upset England's King James, who believed that Rolfe might want to become king of Virginia because he had married an Indian princess. However, the English settlers favored the marriage and expressed hopes that the marriage would promote and facilitate the transfer of Indian lands to the settlers. In 1616, the Rolfes left Jamestown with their infant son and several Powhatan Indians to travel to England to express support for the Virginia Company and to encourage further settlement in the colony. During their visit, the Rolfes traveled extensively, met important people, and raised money and attracted settlers for the Virginia colony, and were introduced at the court of King James I and Queen Anne.

As the Rolfes were preparing to return to Virginia in 1617, Rebecca and their son, Thomas, became ill. It is not clear whether Rebecca died of smallpox, tuberculosis, or pneumonia, but she died before the ship left England and was buried in Gravesend. Rolfe returned to Virginia but made provisions for his infant son to remain in England until his health would permit a return to Jamestown. Thomas remained in England to complete his education and returned to Jamestown after his father's death.

When Rolfe returned to Jamestown, he became actively involved in the colony's government, serving as secretary and recorder of the colony for five years and then being appointed to the Council of State and serving in the House of Burgesses. He continued planting and farming tobacco on his plantation, and he married the daughter of an English colonist. To this marriage was born a daughter.

Powhatan died eight years after his daughter had married Rolfe. During that time relations between Powhatan's federation and the settlers remained peaceful and the Jamestown community expanded into a permanent settlement. After Powhatan's death, tensions increased between the settlers and the Powhatans and relations between the two groups deteriorated. In 1622, Rolfe died unexpectedly and suddenly. It is not clear whether his death was the result of an illness or of an Indian attack led by Pocahontas's uncle, Opechancanough.

See also: Chesapeake Colonies; Jamestown, Virginia; Tobacco

Nancy A. McCaslin

Bibliography

Grizzard, Frank E., and D. Boyd Smith. *Jamestown Colony: A Political, Social, and Cultural History.* Santa Barbara, CA: ABC-CLIO, 2007.

Horn, James P. P., ed. *Writings: With Other Narratives of Roanoke, Jamestown, and the First English Settlement of America.* New York: Library of America, 2007.

Royal African Company

The Royal African Company, a slave-trading organization originally called "The Company of Royal Adventurers Trading to Africa," was chartered in Great Britain in 1662. The Company has been attributed with providing for an increasing demand for laborers and expanding the number and trafficking of slaves to unprecedented levels. The market for sugar as well as other raw products and materials began to rise in Europe in the late 16th and early 17th centuries. Labor became increasingly more difficult to supply to the growing and developing colonies. Individuals with a vested self-interest lobbied the British government for an exclusive charter that would grant them a virtual monopoly on the slave trade to North America. Prior to the creation of The Company of Royal Adventurers Trading to Africa, there were three other commercial entities companies in operation. All three companies had exclusive Royal Charters that had been granted by the British Crown entitling them to a monopoly on the African markets. Those companies

operated under charters that had not been officially enacted by the British Parliament. Prior to the establishment of the Company, slavery scarcely existed in the colonies. As a result of the establishment of the Company, the British are credited with exporting millions of Africans to the colonies against their will. The Company was headed by the Duke of York, James II (the person whom New York is named for and who later became King of England). Ironically, the most famous of all its investors was the English philosopher John Locke. The king of Britain at the time was Charles II, who personally advocated and promoted slavery.

Even before Christopher Columbus landed in the Caribbean, occasionally sailors and pirates had profited from slave trafficking, but it was never that prevalent. It was regarded as a "dirty" business in those days. What might be considered as a "great English paradox" is that the society and culture of England in the early 1600s saw slavery as very immoral and unethical. In order to supply labor, the Royal African Company was established mostly through corrupt bargaining and by the British Crown under King Charles II, who encouraged slave trade. With no official policy as to its purpose, the original Royal charter granted by the king was to the Company of Royal Adventurers Trading to Africa, which would later become the Royal African Company. In the official charter granted in 1660, exclusive privileges were given to the Company for African trading. In 1662, slave trading privileges were granted to the Company.

The London merchants now had a monopoly over the trade, which, even in 1660, brought complaints of others who wanted access to the African trade. The first few years of the Company were unprofitable. The Company was restructured in 1663 and thereafter became very profitable. After 1663, the Company of Royal Adventurers Trading to Africa focused almost entirely on the slave trade. From 1663–1670, the Company's average profits were 100,000 British pounds annually. After 1670, the Company began to struggle with the emergence of other private traders who began to reduce the Company's profits. Adding to the Company's problems were the Second Anglo-Dutch War (1664–1667) and the Third Anglo-Dutch War (1672–1674). In 1667, the Company was in financial ruin, and the British Crown provided the financial resources to keep it functioning. Trading and commercial activity was also restricted in the period between the two wars from 1667 through 1672. For a brief period in 1672, it was forced to stop trading entirely.

In 1672, the Crown, along with additional resources, took the Company of Royal Adventurers Trading to Africa and formed the Royal African Company. Operating with the same basic policies, goals, resources, and monopoly that the previous organization had, the Royal African Company was basically the same organization with a different name. It was after 1672 and the next few decades that followed when most Africans were enslaved and brought to the colonies as a labor supply. The Company built walled structures on coastal Africa to hold Africans until they could be loaded and shipped. In effect, the resulting monopoly of the Company included all goods, slaves, ships, and plantation production involving Africans and ensured that they were controlled by the Royal African Company. After 1672, the quantity and the cost of slaves rose dramatically.

From 1680 and 1686, the Royal African Company enslaved and sold an average of more than 5,000 slaves per year and had sponsored more than 250 slave expeditions by 1688. By 1689, more than 100,000 Africans had been forcibly brought to the colonies. Most of the Company's stock was owned by businessmen who also had holdings in North America. The Company's outstanding debts rose gradually with every year it was in operation, and by 1690, it was indebted for more than 160,000 British pounds. As time went by, controversy surrounding the company arose from other English commercial entities and the plantation owners in the colonies. Both complained of inflation that had exacerbated since 1672. Other merchants wanted to get involved in the slave trade. Plantation owners complained that they needed more slaves and many of the ones they had received suffered from disease, starvation, and were weakened from being transported from Africa in inadequate ships. Commercial interests seized the opportunity by capitalizing on the interests of the plantation owners by insisting that opening up the markets to all traders would more adequately supply the needs of the plantations and would increase productivity in Britain by supplying more products. In addition, many argued that any benefits that the government derived from being able to regulate the trade were eliminated due to having only a select few that profited from trading. In July 1698, the British expelled King James II in the Glorious Revolution and halted the Company's exclusive African trading privileges.

As a result, the Company's profits were significantly reduced with competition. Any other merchant who now wished to become involved in the African trade had to pay the Company a 10 percent tax on all goods and slaves shipped. The purpose of the tax was to maintain the Company's ports and facilities. Even with the revenue derived from the tax, the Company was struggling. Company officials still maintained for several years that the other merchants involved in the trade were intruders on their territory and attempted to persecute those individuals. The Company's stock value and profits continued to decline and the British government repealed the tax, but it was unable to win back exclusive privileges.

After the year 1700, the total average of slaves transported by British vessels annually grew to more than 20,000. The British, by far, now led the world in the slave trade. In addition, America had changed over the course of the rise of the Royal African Company from labor based upon indentured servants who could work in the Americas to pay off debt and to be relieved of criminal sentences to a labor force that was based on the enslavement of Africans. At its height, the Royal African Company had shipped in excess of 150,000 Africans, against their will, from freedom in Africa to slavery in the colonies. Politically, the Crown's efforts to regulate and control slave trafficking was never popular in England and was never really efficient. Some scholars challenge that slave trade overall was never really profitable. In the long run, most of the Company's profits were almost completely eliminated with the construction and maintenance of the ports and facilities needed to continue the trade. During the period that the Company maintained its monopoly of the slave trade, it shipped most of the healthier and more vibrant Africans to the Spanish colonies while at the same time transported the weaker and older slaves to the British colonies. The plantations in America were also charged the greatest prices for the slaves they imported.

After the turn of the 18th century, merchants involved in the slave trade increased dramatically. Before the year 1710, there were more than three times the number of non-Company vessels to Company vessels involved in slave trafficking. Also the market prices that plantation owners were paying for Africans had skyrocketed. Before the year 1700, the average price that plantation owners were paying for Africans amounted to approximately 3 British pounds in trade goods. By 1710, the price had increased to more than 12 British pounds. From 1700 to 1710, the major British merchant in Bristol, England, transported more than 160,000 Africans to the West Indies alone. The involvement of the Royal African Company in the slave trade had a tremendous effect upon Britain's economy. Once the trading began in large numbers after 1660, both Bristol and Liverpool flourished and increased dramatically in population and in economic activity. Throughout its existence, although based in London, the ships of the Royal African Company sailed primarily out of the harbors of Bristol and Liverpool. Throughout the 17th and 18th centuries, around one-and-a-half million Africans were captured and transported to the colonies by the British. The Royal African Company was responsible for half that number. It is the Royal African Company who most historians and scholars attribute with transforming the colonies from a system of indentured servitude to a system of racial slavery.

Historians are able to discover much about the slave trade through records that were maintained by the Royal African Company. Its records contain detailed listings of trade and commerce of everything from humans to sugar. The firearm industry in Britain was primarily maintained through the slave trade. An average of 150,000 firearms were exchanged annually by the Royal African Company for humans. By 1712, though, the debts of the Royal African Company led it to lobby the British Parliament for additional funding or for debt relief. The British government did pass legislation that allowed for the Company to secure payment on some outstanding balances and to gain additional time to pay off some of its debts. By 1713, Britain had gained the exclusive privilege of transporting slaves to the Spanish Americas under the conditions of the Treaty of Utrecht. The treaty ended the fighting between Spain and the other countries of Europe after the death of the last Spanish Habsburg.

By 1730, the Royal African Company was suffering from so many financial difficulties that it had insufficient funds to keep up the maintenance on the ports and facilities needed to continue the trade. As a result, the British government allocated 10,000 pounds annually from that point on as upkeep on those constructions. The Royal African Company, after losing money for decades in the slave trade, finally discontinued slave trafficking in 1732. The Company sold the Africans it held in its facilities waiting to be shipped on the African coast to other companies. After 1732, the Company was only indirectly involved in slave trafficking. Most of its efforts were for African exploration, in which Africans were involved in moving inland in the search of special raw materials and gold. The Company's new adventures were even less successful in raising revenue

than before; it continued to lose money and went bankrupt in 1750. In 1750, the British Parliament dissolved the Company and its ports and facilities were donated to the merchants trading to Africa. The American Colonies by this time were heading toward the American Revolution. There were conflicting interests pushing for the abolishment of slave trafficking, but the British were more involved than ever overall with slave trading. In retrospect, the Royal African Company brought about increased regulation of the trade, but by doing so, it also brought about a tremendous increase in the number of Africans that were sold into slavery.

See also: Atlantic Slave Trade; Cape Coast Castle; Factor; Gold Coast; Sierra Leone

Steven Napier

Bibliography

Davies, Kenneth Gordon. *The Royal African Company.* New York: Atheneum, 1970.

Klein, Herbert S. *The Atlantic Slave Trade.* Cambridge, UK: Cambridge University Press, 1999.

Law, Robin. *The English in West Africa, 1691–1699.* The Local Correspondence of the Royal African Company of England, 1681–1699, pt. 3. Oxford, UK: Oxford University Press for The British Academy, 2006.

Thomas, Hugh. *The Slave Trade: The Story of the Atlantic Slave Trade, 1440–1870.* New York: Simon and Schuster, 1997.

Walvin, James. *Black Ivory: A History of British Slavery.* Washington, D.C.: Howard University Press, 1994.

Sahel

"Sahel," an Arabic word for seashore, is used to describe a belt of land that expands from the west coast to the east coast across the continent of Africa. This land belt is directly below the desert region and directly above the forest region. Specifically, the Sahel is the area where the Sahara desert meets the grasslands and the savannah regions of Africa. This area is known as the "coastline" of the Sahara desert. The east and west borders of this region are the Atlantic Ocean to the west and the Red Sea to the east. The modern-day countries that this land belt extends through are Burkina Faso, Chad, Eritrea, Mali, Mauritania, Niger, Nigeria, Senegal, and Sudan. It is to be noted that although the belt may extend through these countries, the entire countries do no lie within the belt, only a portion. The area below the Sahel is also known as the Bilad-al Sudan, or the "Land of the Blacks" in Arabic.

The Sahel had many trading posts that connected the salt trade from the north to the gold trade of western Africa. Therefore, the Sahel became the "coastline" that emerged after traversing the expansive, yet symbolic, sea of sand (the desert). This trade system existed during the time period when the ancient kingdoms of West Africa were forming and flourishing. The salt mines in the north were generally controlled by Berbers, who brought salt to trade from the mines such as those in Taghaza and Taoudenni to be traded for gold from the kingdoms of Takrur, Ghana, and Kanem, to name a few. This trade was essential to rise of the West African kingdoms. The Sahel itself included such places as Timbuktu, Djenne, and Gao.

The passage across the Sahara desert and into the Sahel was a journey that could take up to two months. The passage was grueling and many dangers were encountered along the way, some stemming from the lack of water available and others related to poisonous or pesky animals such as scorpions and sand lice. The Berbers of northern Africa navigated the desert well, and eventually with the help of the camel, formed caravans that facilitated the trade for those involved. After surviving the dangers of the desert, one would reach the Sahel or the grasslands where some trade occurred and then continue to the forest region where additional trading posts were located.

During the trade of salt and gold, the religion Islam began to be spread through the Sahel and into the kingdoms of West Africa. The influx of Islam was directly related to trade, as many times the traders from the north were Muslim and would require that those they traded with would convert to Islam, thus facilitating the spread of Islam. With the spread of Islam came the erection of Islamic schools and learning centers, one of which, Sankore University of Timbuktu, is located within the Sahel (in modern-day Mali). These trans-Saharan trade routes brought along with them the Islamic slave trade, in which slave raids that occurred in West Africa would supply enslaved persons to be traded to northern Africa and the Mediterranean. In the Islamic slave

Sahel region near Timbuktu, Mali, in West Africa. An important feature of the western Sudan, the sahelian region was the site of intense commercial activity which led to the rise of Ghana, Mali, and Songhai. (Ian Nellist)

trade, enslaved males were typically used as eunuchs and enslaved females were generally placed in harems. Many times, those persons traded were traded for horses brought down from the north.

Some of the people that inhabit the area known as the Sahel live nomadic lives as pastoralists. Many raise livestock, including sheep and goats. The livelihood of these people depends heavily on rainfall, as there have been many droughts over the years that have created devastating famines. The land area that the Sahel covers is vast, but the climate of that land area is fairly consistent. This consistency means that when one area is suffering from drought, all of the areas are normally suffering the same. During times of drought, some move father south toward the forest region, where water may be in more abundance.

There is food cultivation in some areas of the Sahel. Rice is grown around the western coastline of the region, and sorghum along with other grains that require little moisture are grown throughout the Sahel. The soil throughout most of the Sahel is not conducive for agriculture, as it is very sandy and lacks the nutrients necessary for many large-scale crops. Weather conditions and rainfall affect the aspirations for productivity, and the Sahel has fallen victim to drought many times in the 20th century. These droughts created detrimental conditions for those who live in this region, and, unfortunately, during those times, many perished because of malnutrition and disease. Major droughts affected the Sahel in 1914, from 1968 to 1974, from 1982 to 1983, and again from 1984 to 1985.

See also: Ghana; Mali; Rice Cultivation; Senegambia; Songhai; Sudanic Empires; Timbuktu; Trans-Saharan Slave Trade

Dawn Miles

Bibliography

Cross, Nigel, and Rhiannon Barker. *At the Desert's Edge: Oral Histories from the Sahel.* London: Panos Publications, 1991.

Fyle, C. Magbaily. *Introduction to the History of African Civilization.* Vol. 1, *Precolonial Africa.* Lanham, MD: University Press of America, 1999.

Harris, Jessica. "Same Boat, Different Stops: An African Atlantic Culinary Journey." In *African Roots/American Cultures: Africa in the Creation of the Americas,* edited by Sheila Walker, 169–82. Lanham, MD: Rowman and Littlefield Publishers, 2001.

July, Robert W. *A History of the African People.* 5th ed. Prospect Heights, IL: Waveland Press, 1998.

Shillington, Kevin. *History of Africa.* Rev. ed. New York: St. Martin's Press, 1995.

Seasoning

As part of the process of the Atlantic slave trade, seasoning would follow the sale of captives to owners in the Western Hemisphere. Throughout the Caribbean and coastal Brazil, owners normally separated slaves into two categories: Creoles and "Bozales" or salt-water Negroes. Creoles were slaves born in the Americas and were much more highly valued than newly enslaved and imported Africans due to their knowledge of a European language and the development of a useful skill set; they were, in this regard, "seasoned" slaves. Bozales, also referred to as salt-water Negroes, New Negroes, or Guinea-birds, were newly imported, had difficulties communicating with Creoles and white owners, and had to be "broken-in" in order to become effective and efficient laborers. Thus, seasoning was a process by which Bozales became more like Creoles.

In the process of seasoning, new Africans would serve as "apprentices" for Creoles in learning the work regimes and social norms of the plantation. In addition to the apprenticeship, seasoning also implied a process by which new Africans acclimated to the new disease environment and plantation discipline. Many, as a result, died during seasoning. In Brazil, 15 percent of all new Africans died during the first year of seasoning. On Caribbean sugar plantations, about half of all new arrivals died within the first three years of their arrival. Roughly, one in four of all slaves arriving in 18th-century Virginia died within their first year. Likewise, 33 percent died within a year in Carolina. Since seasoning sought to "create" a slave, it was intended as a mechanism of behavior modification. In some cases, new Africans would be worked until exhaustion and beaten with the intent of forcibly making them more pliable and less resistant. More typically, seasoning meant the creation of new names, the introduction to European languages and Christianity, and an attempt at complete creolization (or acculturation).

Despite overt attempts to force cultural changes through seasoning, new Africans did not completely forget their cultures of origin. Cultural mixing certainly occurred, both between African groups and between Africans and their new European host culture. However, new Africans viewed new cultural formulations through the lens of their cultural backgrounds. When they spoke European languages, they transformed and Africanized them, creating a number of Creole dialects that had distinctive African linguistic features in grammar, vocabulary, and phonetics. Jamaican Patois, Papiamento in Curacao, and Gullah in South Carolina are just a small handful of examples of this. In addition, when new Africans became familiar with the tenants of Euro-American Christianity, they Africanized that too—inserting spirit possession, music, expressive dance, and the belief of transmigration in the creation of new religious forms. Finally, the unique foodways, folklore, and healing traditions of new Africans found new and transformed expressions throughout the Western Hemisphere.

See also: Acculturation; Atlantic Slave Trade; Gullah; Salt-Water Negroes

Walter C. Rucker

Bibliography

Curtin, Philip. *The Atlantic Slave Trade: A Census.* Madison: University of Wisconsin Press, 1969.

Davidson, Basil. *The African Slave Trade: Precolonial History, 1450–1850.* Boston: Little, Brown, 1961.

Handler, Jerome S. "Survivors of the Middle Passage: Life Histories of Enslaved Africans in British America." *Slavery and Abolition* 23 (2002):25–56.

Thomas, Hugh. *The Slave Trade: The Story of the Atlantic Slave Trade, 1440–1870.* New York: Simon and Schuster, 1997.

Senegambia

Senegambia is the West African region that comprises portions of the Futa Jallon Plateau and the Senegal and Gambia river basins, corresponding to all or part of modern-day Gambia, Guinea Bissau, and Senegal, as well as portions of Guinea, Mali, and Mauritania. Due to its relative geographical proximity to both Europe and the Americas, Portuguese, Dutch, British, and French trading outfits fought for domination and the establishment of trade centers in the region. The Europeans developed coastal centers such as Gorée Island and Saint-Louis, both of which were used extensively to engage in the slave trade. As a consequence, Senegambia became a predominant source of slaves sent to the New World during the 15th and 16th centuries, supplying up to 40 percent of all slaves during some periods. By the early 17th century, Senegambia became less reliant on the slave trade by diversifying its exports to agriculture, animal products, and other natural resources, from then on supplying only 10 percent or less of total slaves.

Senegambia had long been in contact with and was influenced by surrounding Muslim peoples, and many Senegambian traders and social elite were Muslim. The greater population generally subscribed at least superficially to Islam. During various eras in the region's history, Islamic revival movements sprang forth, particularly during the 19th century. The jihad of Umar Tal (1797–1864) in the mid-19th century resulted in the establishment of the Tukulor Empire, which encompassed the eastern portions of Senegambia. Tukulor and all of Senegambia were eventually folded into the colony of French West Africa in 1895.

See also: Atlantic Slave Trade; Futa Jallon; Ghana; Gorée Island; Mali; Rice Cultivation; Sahel; Sierra Leone; Songhai

Brent D. Singleton

Bibliography

Barry, Boubacar. *Senegambia and the Atlantic Slave Trade.* New York: Cambridge University Press, 1998.

Curtin, Philip D. *Economic Change in Precolonial Africa: Senegambia in the Era of the Slave Trade.* Madison: University of Wisconsin Press, 1975.

Signares

The signares were a group of primarily mixed-race women who lived on the islands of Saint-Louis and Gorée in Senegal, West Africa, during the 17th and 18th centuries. Saint-Louis is located in the Senegal River. Gorée is approximately one-half-mile long and only a few hundred yards wide and is located by the Cape Verde Peninsula. These islands had European settlements established by the French, Portuguese, and Dutch beginning in the mid-1600s. The signares were able to obtain great wealth and esteemed social status and became icons of beauty and fashion through the 18th century.

The European men who settled on these islands were typically sailors and soldiers from France. These men married the local women, who often were mixed-race women. The women who entered into these marriages were active in trade, as women tended to dominate the marketplaces of West Africa. The houses that the signares lived in were known for their beauty. Many of the houses were at least two stories; the first floor would contain the kitchen, storerooms, and holding cells for slaves that were for sale. The signares would occupy the uppermost floor in the house, which had large rooms with windows that allowed for temperature control. The houses were typically surrounded by beautifully constructed walls. There were also smaller buildings surrounding the house for the signares' artisans to work, as they may employ carpenters, tailors, and blacksmiths, among others.

It was typical for the signares to marry more than once, such as in cases where her husband had to leave the island and would not be able to return, or if she became a widow, she was permitted to marry again while keeping all of her acquired goods and wealth. If it was the signare's first marriage, she was expected to be a virgin, and to ensure this when her marriage was consummated, it was done so on a white sheet that would be collected the next day and raised on a flagpole as evidence of her purity. This was not done for the following marriages.

The signares were able to acquire gold and gems by trading hogsheads filled with salt to the sailors who would

Signare from St. Louis Island accompanied by her servant, from Encyclopedie des Voyages, *by Jacques Grasset de Saint-Sauveur, 1796. (Bibliotheque des Arts Decoratifs, Paris, France/Archives Charmet/The Bridgeman Art Library)*

come to the islands. They would have the gold that they received melted and formed into lavish necklaces and bracelets that they would wear on a regular basis. The signares were also known for their dress, more significantly, the scarves that they wore on their heads that were decorated with bright colors. When going out, they would wear gold earrings, skirts and bodices made of taffeta, red Moroccan slippers, gold or silver anklets, and additional jewelry, depending on the occasion.

The signares also became well known for their dances, known as "folgares" that would last from night into the morning. The dances were meant for the signares to interact with the French men so that those who were single could mingle, and the younger women would attend to study how the signares interacted with the men so that they would be prepared when they became of age. There would be palm wine to drink and also imported wine from France. There was also a beer available for drink called *pitot*. Griots, or professional storytellers, were at the dances and would entertain by singing and dancing. The men at the parties would bring handkerchiefs that they would throw at the signares while they were dancing. Whoever had a handkerchief land on her would hand deliver it back to the owner and thank him with an exaggerated bow.

Signares, upon their arrival to the islands, would learn intricate sewing techniques and would quickly become fluent in French. Being trilingual, typically fluent in French, Wolof, and Crioula, these women were an asset to the French men as they were able to translate and negotiate trade deals with the people who only spoke Wolof. The French men who became the husbands of these women would provide the women with many servants and slaves. It was typical for a signare to have a European servant who worked as her chambermaid. The signare would also have a large number of slaves of African descent who assisted with domestic duties, trade, and artisanal work.

Signares had significant societal roles in the societies of Gorée Island and Saint-Louis, and they became the women that European men and local people wanted to be associated with. They were able to acquire great wealth, through marriages and through their participation in trade of goods to the French sailors who would frequent the islands. The children who were the products of these marriages were also able to gain recognition, and many were granted official government positions when they came of age. Signares were responsible for the social atmosphere of the islands and set fashion trends that transcended the islands they inhabited.

See also: Atlantic Slave Trade; Gorée Island; Senegambia

Dawn Miles

Bibliography

Brooks, George E. "The *Signares* of Saint-Louis and Gorée: Women Entrepreneurs in Eighteenth Century Senegal." In *Women in Africa: Studies in Social and Economic Change,* edited by Nancy J. Hafkin and Edna G. Bay, 19–44. Stanford, CA: Stanford University Press, 1976.

Hargraves, John D. "Assimilation in Eighteenth-Century Senegal." *The Journal of African History* 6 (1965):177–84.

Searing, James F. *West African Slavery and Atlantic Commerce: The Senegal River Valley, 1700–1860.* Cambridge, UK: Cambridge University Press, 1993.

Society for the Propagation of the Gospel in Foreign Parts

King William III established the Society for the Propagation of the Gospel in Foreign Parts (SPG) in response to concerns from his advisors over the religious welfare of colonists living in America. The 1701 SPG charter called on teachers and priests to enter the mission field and tend to the health of the Anglican church in America. Months later the mission was expanded to include Africans and Native Americans. For this, the SPG stands out as one of the first major Christian institutions that dedicated its efforts and resources to evangelizing enslaved Africans.

In 18th-century North America, SPG policies toward Africans were controversial; many whites believed Christian education and baptism would disrupt slavery. Those who objected to the Christianization of slaves were concerned about the threat of literacy, the development of slave religious institutions, and the possibility that Christianity might endorse liberty. It was the position of the SPG that Christianization did not undermine the system of slavery, but helped to create obedient slaves who understood that the reward for hard work and deference came in the afterlife. Although the policies of the SPG were not intended to liberate slaves or advocate abolition, missionaries generally encouraged masters to treat slaves with paternalistic kindness.

In 1703, the SPG appointed Elias Neau to missionize among the Native Americans in New York. Believing he could be more successful converting African slaves, Neau requested that the church assign him to serve the black population. The first SPG missionary to specifically reach out to enslaved Africans, Neau spent much of this time convincing white masters to release their slaves for weekly Christian education. In classes Neau read from the Bible, taught slaves to read, led prayers, encouraged the memorization of creeds and psalms, and prepared individuals for baptism. Prompted by resistance and concern from slave masters that baptism would endanger slavery, Neau sponsored a 1706 New York law asserting that baptism did not change the civil status of slaves. A slave revolt in 1712 and continuing suspicion from slave masters complicated Neau's efforts at reaching blacks in New York, though he was consistently impressed by the willing, studious, and pious attitudes of his black students above all others.

Hearing about Neau's efforts, dozens of SPG missionaries began to seek out Africans for conversion. In the South, particularly South Carolina, missionaries met with limited success. Though dedicated to converting Africans, many SPG missionaries were still hesitant to baptize blacks or teach them to read and struggled fiercely with slave masters who were cruel and refused to send their slaves to classes. Throughout the colonies, missionaries overwhelmingly described antagonisms with slaveholders as the major impediment to wholesale conversion since they found slaves to be most amenable to instruction. To remedy this problem, the SPG supported legislation to make the Christianization and baptism of slaves compulsory. Despite obstacles, by 1717, South Carolina missionary Dr. Le Jau reported weekly meetings with 30 to 40 slaves and boasted that large numbers of whites were convinced that Christianity encouraged obedience and submission among their slaves.

By 1730, SPG funds had become limited and mission work was largely relegated to individual parish priests who continued to convert blacks on a much smaller scale. Neau's center in New York remained the Society's primary vehicle for black education and expanded its operations in 1743 to include a day school. The school educated about 40 children a year and offered night classes for adults. Society efforts waned throughout the second half of the 18th century and came to an end during the Revolutionary War when SPG missionaries, British loyalists, were driven out of the country and targeted because of their affiliations with the Church of England.

See also: Evangelism; Middle Colonies; New York Revolt of 1712

Kathleen Hladky

Bibliography
Comminey, Shawn. "The Society for the Propagation of the Gospel in Foreign Parts and Black Education in South Carolina, 1702–1764." *The Journal of Negro History* 84, no. 4 (1999):360–69.
O'Connor, Daniel. *Three Centuries of Mission: The United Society for the Propagation of the Gospel, 1701–2000.* London: Continuum, 2000.
Vilbert, Faith. "The Society for the Propagation of the Gospel in Foreign Parts: Its Work for the Negroes in North America before 1783." *The Journal of Negro History* 18, no. 2 (1933):171–212.

Songhai

Songhai, or Songhay, is the largest of the former empires in the western Sudan region of North Africa. The state was founded in ca. 700 by Berbers on the Middle Niger, in what is now central Mali. The rulers accepted Islam ca. 1000. Its power was much increased by Sunni Ali (1464–1492), who occupied Timbuktu in 1468. Songhai reached its greatest extent under Askia Muhammad I (ca. 1493–1528).

The Songhai originated in the Dendi region of northwestern Nigeria and ended up in western Sudan, centered on the Big Bend of the Niger River. There are two capitals in Songhai. The first capital is Kukiya, which is located north of the Falls of Labezanga (the present frontier between the republics of Mali and Niger). The second capital, Gao, developed north of Kukiya at the terminus of the Saharan tracks.

The Songhai Empire, regarded by scholars and laypersons alike as one of Africa's greatest empires, rose to prominence in the late 1400s during the rule of Sunni Ali. During his reign, most of what was formerly the Ghanaian and Mali empires was incorporated into the Songhai Empire.

Sunni Ali marched on Timbuktu and captured it along with its great University of Sankore, which had thousands of students from many parts of the world. During the waging of a seven-year war, Sunni Ali captured the city of Jenne; he then married the queen of Jenne, Queen Dara, and they reigned together. Sunni Ali eventually gained control over the entire middle Niger region.

Sunni Ali, in addition to restoring order to the Sudan (the Arabic expression for West Africa), was also a brilliant administrator. He divided the Songhai Empire into separate provinces and placed each province under the control of its own governor. Sunni Ali developed new methods of farming and created for Songhai a professional navy. Sunni Ali embraced and respected the Islamic faith of his trading partners, which accounted for much of his success as a ruler. By the time of his death in 1492 the Songhai Empire surpassed the greatness of the other West African empires that preceded it.

Following the death of Sunni Ali, his son, Sunni Baru, ascended to the throne for a short time before he was overthrown by Askia Muhammad Toure. Askia Muhammad Toure had been a general under Sunni Ali and was successful as a ruler largely as a result of his acceptance of Islam. He appointed Muslim leaders to the larger districts of his empire and applied Islamic law in place of Songhai's original code of laws.

Askia Muhammad Toure greatly improved the learning centers of the Songhai by encouraging scholars to come from other parts of Africa as well as Europe and Asia to settle in Timbuktu and Jenne, and built as many as 180 Koranic schools in Timbuktu alone. The Sankore University in Timbuktu developed a reputation for scholarship in rhetoric, logic, Islamic law, grammar, astronomy, history, and geography.

During his reign, the Songhai Empire was characterized by order, stability, and prosperity. He opened up the ranks of government service. Previously, the status of the leaders of the empire was determined upon the basis of birth. Under Askia Muhammad Toure, however, men could achieve high office based upon their scholarship and intellect regardless of their social position. Askia Muhammad Toure also organized and established a permanent professional army that enabled him to expand the territory of Songhai and turn the Songhai Empire into the largest empire in western and central Sudan.

He was deposed by his son, and in the subsequent conflicts among his successors, the empire slowly began to decline. The break-up of the state was accelerated by a Moroccan invasion in 1591. The end of the Songhai Empire also meant the end of the region's history as a trading center.

See also: Ghana; Mali; Sudanic Empires; Timbuktu; Toure, Askia Muhammad

Moshe Terdiman

Bibliography

Fage, J. D. *A History of Africa.* London: Hutchinson, 1978.

Gomez, Michael. "Timbuktu under Imperial Songhay: A Reconsideration of Autonomy." *Journal of African History* 31 (1990):5–24.

Levtzion, Nehemia. *Ancient Ghana and Mali.* London: Methuen, 1973.

Stono Rebellion

As early as 1687, slaves in South Carolina were fleeing toward Spanish territory in Florida. They were responding to the King of Spain's decree, which said that any runaway slave of the British colonies was to be received at St. Augustine and given freedom and protection from the British. In 1733, the decree was repeated and Spanish emissaries were sent to try and incite a large slave rebellion within South Carolina. The trek from South Carolina through Georgia to St. Augustine was not easy. For this reason, slaves who planned their escape killed their masters, then took horses, food, and other items for the journey. These slaves usually ran away as individuals or in very small groups but no large groups had attempted the journey—until the Stono Rebellion.

On September 9, 1739, the brewing of conspiracy erupted in the Stono Rebellion when a group of 20 "Angolan" slaves carried out the largest and bloodiest insurrection of the 18th century. After gathering near South Carolina's Stono River, the rebels decided to first secure weapons and ammunition by robbing a storehouse. The rebels confronted and killed the storekeepers, severed their heads, then placed them on the stairs before leaving. Now armed, the rebels moved toward Mr. Godfrey's house and killed him, his daughter and son, then burned his house. By this time, more rebels joined the original group. They marched southward along the "Pons Pons" road shouting for liberty with flags displayed to the sound of two drums. They passed Wallace's Tavern toward daybreak but left without hurting him because he was a good man and kind to his slaves. However, when they came to Mr. Lemy's house, they plundered it and killed him, his wife, and his child. They continued on to Mr. Rose's and resolved to kill him but he was saved by a man who hid him.

While heading north, Lieutenant Governor Bull saw the rebels. He rushed toward the Willtown Presbyterian Church to raise a militia. Already armed, according to the law, the men of the church formed a militia. At the same time Gov. Bull was raising the militia, the rebels continued southward. They burned Colonel Hext's house, killed his overseer and his wife. Consecutively, they burned Mr. Sprye's house, Mr. Sacheverell's, and Mr. Nash's house, also killing the whites found in them. Mr. Bullock escaped but his house was also burned.

After traveling between 10 and 15 miles, the rebels, now numbering almost 100, stopped in an open field and began celebrating, dancing, singing, and beating drums to draw more Negroes to them. While in the open field, the militia came on the warriors and a fight ensued. The rebels fired two shots with no results. The militia's return fire brought down 14 of the rebels. During the exchange, some rebels ran back to their respective plantations while others stayed and fought. One of the rebels came within point-blank range of his master, confronted him, then misfired; in return, his master shot him through the head. Many Negroes were shot on the spot while some were taken, questioned, then shot. Some rebels who tried to escape were captured by the planters who cut their heads off and placed them on every mile post they came to.

About 30 escaped from the initial confrontation and continued southward. Mounted on horseback, the planters caught up to this group and another battle took place in which the rebels fought boldly but again were taken by the planters and killed on the spot; some were hanged and others were gibbeted. While there is no record of any of the rebels reaching St. Augustine, a few of the remnants eluded capture for nearly a year. In all, approximately 40 blacks and 20 whites were killed.

For many of South Carolina's colonists, the Stono Rebellion was a nightmare come true. By 1730, South Carolina's economy had become so dependent on African slaves the ratio of blacks to whites was 2 to 1. Attempts were made to entice more whites to settle there; however, the response was slow. Planters and colonists were aware of the growing danger of importing too many African slaves; however, rice had become a cash crop and required intense labor. With the number of slaves increasing and Spanish conspiracy on the rise, the time for rebellion had come. The Stono rebels struck with a force unknown to South Carolinians. As a result, many rural colonists left the area.

The Stono rebels were previously warriors in Africa. They knew how to use guns and designed their rebellion appropriately. Their experience as warriors gave them the courage and willingness to take on a colony. This was not flight—it was open defiance that expressed a collective yearning for freedom. Although their strike for freedom was quelled before it could come to fruition, it sent a message to South Carolinians that their slaves were not to be underestimated.

The legal response to the Stono Rebellion was swift and damaging. Among the most important changes to the law was the status of the slaves. Whereas previously considered freehold property (slaves of an estate), slaves were now relegated to "chattel" (the personal property of their owners). In addition to a change in status, slaves were prohibited from gathering in groups, and in direct response to specific actions taken during the Stono Rebellion, taking part in rebellion, coercing others to rebel, and acts of arson were considered felonies punishable by death; drums and horns were also prohibited. After the Stono Rebellion, the slaves in South Carolina were rendered nearly immobile; however, their flights toward freedom continued.

See also: Angolan/Kongolese; Carolinas; Destination, Florida; Slave Resistance

Jarett M. Fields

Bibliography

Littlefield, Daniel. *Rice and Slaves: Ethnicity and the Slave Trade in Colonial South Carolina.* Baton Rouge: Louisiana State University Press, 1981.

Smith, Mark, ed. *Stono: Documenting and Interpreting a Southern Slave Revolt.* Columbia: University of South Carolina Press, 2005.

Wood, Peter. *Black Majority: Negroes in Colonial South Carolina from 1670 through the Stono Rebellion.* New York: W. W. Norton, 1974.

Sudanic Empires

The Sudanic empires is the name given by Western historians to the West African empires of Ghana, Mali, and Songhai that spanned the period from the first century CE to the end of the 16th century in a politically hegemonic continuum. The earliest, the Empire of Ghana, was the imperial model for the succeeding empires of Mali and Songhai, inheriting similar social hierarchies, political and economic organization, cultural and religious practices, and ethnic groups.

Ghana, or as it was called by its inhabitants, Wagadu/Wagadou, was founded around CE 100 by the Soninke, who according to their tradition, migrated from the city of Sonin/Aswan in upper Egypt to the region of southeastern Mauritania. Fleeing the domination and racial discrimination of their Greco-Roman colonizers, these Nubians heard of a Bilad-al Sudan or "Land of the Blacks" where they could settle comfortably among their own, and because of their advanced knowledge and military skills, become a powerful nation in the West. True to the prophecy of the Bida, the serpent-djinn who became the guardian spirit of Wagadu, the empire did become great, expanding its territorial authority according to oral history, from the Atlantic coast all the way to Lake Chad.

Mama Dinga, the legendary founder and hero of Wagadu, was a general of a massive army in southern Egypt (Nubia) who migrated with his army to the Western Sahel where he established political hegemony. Mama Dinga, however, did not remain in Wagadu; he left his empire to his son Djabe Cisse and returned to Nubia. The *Tarikh Al-Fettash,* one of the few surviving texts of the Songhay Empire, states that 22 kings had ruled Wagadu before the birth of the Prophet Muhammad, which places the inception of the empire around CE 100. A land rich in gold, copper, iron, and diamonds, Wagadu was a center of trade entering North and West Africa through bridges of caravans traversing the Sahara. The tran-Saharan trade was a lucrative market economy whose network spread across the Mediterranean into Europe and eastward across North Africa into Asia. The gold of ancient Ghana was inexhaustibly plentiful and well known in the international trade world.

Arab historian Al-Bakri, who wrote a detailed ethnography of Ghana during the mid-11th century, describes the capital of Ghana, Kumbi Saleh, as a densely populated city with a vibrant commercial center and houses made of stone and acacia wood. Excavations carried out by archaeologists since 1904 confirm the existence of a populous commercial city with an international trade network. Wealth that was based at that time on the gold standard put Ghana in the echelon of one of the wealthiest nations in the world.

By the late 11th century, the Sahara-dwelling Sanhaja, Lamtuna, and Massufa groups coming under the unifying military influence of Umar Ibn Yasin merged into the imperial army of the Almoravids and attacked the Soninke rulers of Ghana in 1076. This was the first blow of a series of disasters that led to the demise of a great empire. Though the Soninke recaptured the lands taken by the Almoravids 12 years later, the government was weakened politically and financially. The definitive disaster told in the Soninke legend of Wagadu was a seven-year drought that destroyed all the cultivable lands and dried up the rich gold reserves produced from the gold-bearing rains. These phenomenal rains were the special gift of Wagadu's protective deity, the Bida of Wagadu, who demanded in exchange the annual sacrifice of the most beautiful virgin of the empire. When the Bida was killed by Mamadou Sahko Dekote, the outraged fiancé of a chosen sacrificial virgin, the empire was cursed with drought for seven years, seven months and seven days. The famine that ensued decimated the population and forced millions to seek greener pastures in other parts of West Africa. The people scattered north, south, east, and west, leaving a once-great populous empire to the anonymity of the encroaching sands.

Many of the Soninke and Kakolo groups migrated and settled southeast of Kumbi-Saleh along the Niger Bend, renamed their country Mande, and called themselves the *Mandenka* ("People of Mande"). *Malinke,* which is the Fula's term for "People of Mali," has a slightly different nuance in that it includes not only the Mandenka but Soninke, Fula, and Songhai lineages that were incorporated into Malian society under Sundiata. Malinke is used here as the postimperial name, while Mande refers to the small warring kingdoms that existed prior to the rise of Sundiata. Such was the status of Mande before Sumanguru/Soumaoro Kante, king of the Mande kingdom of Sosso/Susu, waged war against the other Mande states and brought them under his dominion.

Sundiata Keita, son of Nare Maghan Kon Fatta Konate, the king of Niani, was a child of a miraculous birth and a disadvantaged childhood who overcame his physical and social limitations to become an exceptional warrior and king. Diviners had predicted even before the marriage of his parents that Sundiata would be the successor to his father, but Sassouma Berete, the first wife of Maghan Kon Fatta, conspired to put her son, Dankaran Touman, on the throne by first attempting to kill Sundiata and then sending him and his mother, Sogolon Conde, into exile. It was during Sundiata's exile that Sumanguru Kante attacked Niani, plundering and subjugating its peoples and launching a reign of terror against any who opposed him.

Determined to take back his country from the Sosso, Sundiata formed a formidable army along with other kings vanquished by Sumanguru and defeated the Sosso. He then restored the sovereignty of the conquered kingdoms and reorganized them into the empire of Mali. Niani became the capital of the empire and a great political and commercial center. Al-Umari and Ibn Khaldun, who wrote about Mali during the 14th century, reported that Niani was highly populated, well watered, and financially stabilized with an affluent market where caravans from the Magrib, Ifriqiya, and Egypt frequently exchanged goods brought from every country. The nations that were part of the empire were guaranteed their autonomy as well as the protection and support of the empire so long as they paid tribute and adhered to the principles of the constitution.

Sundiata's military conquests were extended under the leadership of his brilliant generals Tira Maghan Tarawele (Traore), Fran Camara, and Fakoli Koroma, who conquered all the lands that had been under the control of Ghana, then moved westward, conquering the kingdom of Jaloff and establishing several kingdoms in Senegambia, Guinea, and Guinea Bissau, the largest of which was Kaabu.

Sundiata's son and successor, Mansa Wulin, and his general succeeded in capturing Gao and Tekrur. Stretching from the Atlantic coast to Gao, the empire inherited the flexible federation structure of the empire of Ghana. Each country retained its institutions and authorities that ruled alongside the *farin* or governor representing the imperial authority of Mali. Only the Malinke military maintained garrisons throughout the regions to ensure the security of the territory against invaders and brigands.

There were four major structural changes in the Malinke government that distinguished it from the government of Ghana. One was a 44-article constitution defining social and political relationships, hierarchies, customs, terms of succession, and the fundamental human rights of women, men, and children. Sundiata proclaimed an end to the institution of slavery and all the nations of Mali took an oath to abolish slavery and the slave trade in their territories. A law requiring all able-bodied men and women to cultivate the land regardless of their occupation greatly expanded Mali's agricultural output, and a law granting ownership to those who cleared the land initiated a national incentive for collective work, production, and distribution of goods and services. Far from the feudal system generally designated to a medieval Sudanese economy, the government of early Mali spawned an economic structure that resembled an African communal economy; every citizen of Mali was given access to tools, cultivable land and its production.

Lastly, Sundiata codified the 33 clans of the Malinke, designating their relationships (*sana-khu*), and sworn alliances that served as an internal fortress of solidarity. Furthermore, he elevated and formalized the art of the griot (historian) when he declared that the griot represents "the head, the eyes, ears, mouth, and soul of Mali." Art, music, architecture, religion, metaphysics, science, trade, history, every minute and indispensable element of culture was augmented by ennobling, first, the individual human being, and by extension, all the knowledge and practices that foster human development. An empathetic humanism anchored Sundiata's enormous span of ideas that ushered in a new epoch of artistic innovation and sociopolitical probity.

The *mansas* who succeeded Sundiata, though never historically capable of matching the legendary role of founder/culture hero, were nevertheless exceptional leaders in their own right. Mansa Wulin, the son and first successor to Sundiata, was a great king who followed in his father's footsteps, expanding Mali's territories and enforcing the laws Sundiata had instituted. His brother, Wati, who succeeded him, was less successful. Khalifa, another brother of Wulin and Wati, was mentally disturbed and would kill Malinke people for sport. Sundiata's grandson succeeded Khalifa but was usurped by Sakura, a powerful slave of the royal court, whose political and cultural expansion of the empire impacted North and West Africa. After Sakura died, the kingship reverted to the traditional Keita lineage of Sundiata. Mansu Ku, the son of Mansa Wulin, succeeded Sakura and Mansa Muhammad succeeded his father.

The royal lineages that followed were legitimate Keita heirs descending from Sundiata's younger brother, Manding Bori. Fraternal inheritance of the throne was customary in Mali's system of succession, and the dynasty of Manding Bori reinvented the empire in its own image of exploration and magnificence. Manding Bori/Bokari, known in written Arabic texts as Abubakr Muhammad II, ascended the throne in 1311 but shortly afterward abdicated his position and led a mass expedition of about 2,000 ships into the Atlantic. Kanku Musa, the younger brother of Manding Bokari, became the emperor of Mali in 1312 after Manding Bokari did not return to Mali. During his reign, Mali reached the height of its political power, prosperity, intellectual development, and trade relations, and Mansa Kanku Musa's famous pilgrimage to Mecca in 1325 placed Mali on

the world map as a great empire rich in gold, ivory, copper, iron, and other resources exchanged in an international market. Mansa Musa distributed so much gold to countries he passed on his way to Mecca that the gold standard in Egypt suffered from severe deflation for years afterward.

It was during Mansa Musa's pilgrimage that his generals annexed Gao, the seat of Songhai power and influence, extending the imperial territory to the farthest eastern region. The son of Mansa Musa, Maghan II, reigned for a short time after Mansa Musa's death, then the legitimate heir according to Mande tradition, the brother of Musa, Mansa Sulayman (1336–1358), took the throne.

During the reigns of Mansa Musa and Mansa Sulayman, Mali's territorial domain comprised the entire Sahel-Sudan region, thus bringing many diverse peoples and cultures under the same imperial authority. The confederated political organization remained the archetypal model for the empire's new acquisitions; each country's autonomy was maintained and protected.

The biggest threat to Mali's continuous hegemony came from the eastern provinces of Gao and Timbuktu that had originally belonged to Songhai but was annexed by the Mandenka under Mansu Kanku Musa's rule. Having a different ethnicity, a civilization that predated Mali by several centuries, an ancient oral and written tradition, and a long history of autonomy, material wealth, and military power, the proud, independent people of Songhai were never comfortable under foreign rule. The Songhai rebellion began in the very womb of Mali at the Niani royal court of Mansu Musa where Ali Kolon, the founder of the Dia (Shi/So) dynasty and grandfather of Sunni Ali Ber, was raised and educated. Ali Kolon and his younger brother, Sulayman Nare, were kidnapped when they were boys after Mansa Musa's generals conquered Gao, and though they were accorded the same royal treatment of Mande princes, they never renounced their loyalty to Songhai and fled Niani after Musa's death determined to recapture Gao and Timbuktu. By the end of the 14th century, Ali Kolon's armies ousted the Mandenka from Gao and reclaimed their independence, setting off a series of military offenses that gradually supplanted Mali's imperial power.

The greatest of the Dia (Shi/So) emperors was Sunni Ali Ber who led his armies on a mission of expansion, conquering Djenne and recapturing Timbuktu in 1468, only two years after his enthronement. As a ruler Sunni Ali Ber was charismatic, clever, ambitious, militarily adept, extending the territorial horizon and building the economy through his construction of towns, schools, dykes, canals, markets, and trading centers. He forced the Tuaregs back to the northern Sahel and led attacks against the Mossi, Dogon, and Bariba. At the time of his ill-fated death in 1492, Sunni Ali had gained control of the vast empire of Songhai that extended from Dendi to Macina along the Niger Bend and surpassed Mali in territorial acquisitions, economic affluence, and political authority. Mali persisted alongside Songhai until the end of the 16th century, mainly because the western Mandenka's profitable trade with the Europeans financed the empire's operations, but it was no longer the dominant power of the Sahel.

Completing the imperial concatenation of the three great West Sudanic empires, Songhai's Dia dynasty developed in the royal court of Mali in the same way the Mande had developed in the womb of Ghana, and within this contextual space they unravel like a historical trilogy. Sunni Ali Ber organized the empire on the Ghana-Mande model, establishing new provinces called *koi* that were the equivalent of the Mandenka *farin* and appointing *qadis* (judges, nobility) to the predominately Muslim towns, but instead of adopting the loose-knit Mande federational system, Songhai centralized the imperial political structure, making each *koi* directly responsible to the monarchal authorities at Gao. Songhai's political economy with its complex hierarchal structure and absolute central authority had a modern appearance and represented a break with the confederated states of the former Sudanic empires.

From the 11th century onward when Islam significantly penetrated the region, the Songhai dynasties were persuaded to construct their government on the legal structure of an Islamic theocracy. When a king or emperor was inaugurated, he was given a signet ring, a sword, and a copy of the Qur'an, symbolizing the spiritual ethical constitution on which the laws of the empire are allegedly based. Songhai had a distinctly Sahelian Islamic flavor and officially required that every head of state must profess the Muslim religion. Sunni Ali inherited the faith of his foreparents but had little loyalty to the orthodoxy and narrow interpretation of the Muslim clerics, openly practicing the esoteric tradition and mystical sciences for which the Shi/So were famous.

Ali's insistence on practicing the occult traditions brought him into deep ideological conflict with the Muslim intelligentsia and jurists of Timbuktu. Refusing to be a pawn of the Muslim jurists, Sunni Ali declared himself the premier and absolute priest of the land who believed his metaphysical knowledge far excelled the pedagogical knowledge of Muslim scholars. He had many of the Muslim clerics killed, and upon his death, civil war broke out between the Dia dynasty and the Muslims.

Muhammad Toure, who was Sunni Ali's close confidante, protégé, and lieutenant of the Hombori region, revered the emperor like a father but was disturbed by his persecution of the Muslim scholars and eventually broke ties with him. Upon Sunni Ali's death, Muhammad Toure seized power and started a new dynasty of *Askias* that lasted 100 years. A devout Muslim, brilliant militarist and politician, Askia Muhammad was an enlightened emperor who carefully supervised the administration of the empire in an effort to root out corruption; he introduced an accurate system of weights and measurements, increased market inspectors, and encouraged fair trade that brought great wealth to the empire. Extending Sunni Ali's territorial acquisitions on all frontiers, he annexed Macina, Zara, and Agades, controlled the Sahara as far north as the salt mines of Teghazza, and conquered the prosperous Hausa towns of Kano, Katsina, and Zaria. The national council and judiciary system were reorganized and government officials were replaced with Askia Muhammad's supporters, but he continued to build Songhai around the centralized, bureaucratic system instituted by Sunni Ali. Songhai reached a peak of intellectual and religious activity under the Askia dynasty and came to an abrupt end with the sacking of Songhai by the Moroccans in 1591.

See also: Ghana; Mali; Sahel; Senegambia; Songhai; Trans-Saharan Slave Trade

Nubia Kai

Bibliography

Charry, Eric. *Mande Music.* Chicago: University of Chicago Press, 2000.

Gomez, Michael Angelo. *Reversing Sail: A History of the African Diaspora.* Cambridge, UK: Cambridge University Press, 2005.

Levtzion, Nehemiah. *Ancient Ghana and Mali.* London: Methuen, 1973.

Levtzion, Nehemiah, and J. F. P. Hopkins, eds. *Corpus of Early Arabic Sources for West African History.* Translated by J. F. P. Hopkins. Cambridge, UK: Cambridge University Press, 1981.

Niane, Djibril Tamsir, ed. *General History of Africa IV: Africa from the Twelfth to the Sixteenth Century.* London: UNESCO-Heinemann; Berkeley: University of California Press, 1984.

Niane, Djibril Tamsir. *Sundiata: An Epic of Old Mali.* Translated by G. D. Pickett. London: Longman Group, 1965.

Sertima, Ivan Van. *They Came before Columbus.* New York: Random House, 1976.

Sugar Plantations

Sugar was the basis of the first plantations in the New World. The Portuguese, who had established sugar plantations on Madeira Island in the mid-15th century, began growing sugar in Brazil in 1516 with exports to Europe no later than 1519. At first, the Portuguese enslaved the Tupi-Guarani—the major Native American group residing in coastal Brazil—to labor in the cane fields. As late as 1560, few Africans supplemented this labor. By the 1580s, plantations in Pernambuco had 2,000 African slaves, roughly one-third the labor force. One plantation in Bahia tallied 38 African slaves of its 103 laborers in 1591, but all its slaves were African by 1638, mirroring the transition to African labor throughout Brazil in the early 17th century. Biology and culture shaped this transition. The Native Americans, separate from the people of Eurasia and Africa for millennia, had no immunity to the diseases of these regions and so died of smallpox and other Old World diseases once in contact with Europeans. Africans, on the other hand, lived in the same disease environment as Europeans and had greater immunity than did the Amerindians. An African slave who survived his first year in Brazil, the period of seasoning, was likely to survive longer than a Native American field hand. Moreover, agriculture had sunk deeper roots in Atlantic Africa, the point of origin of many slaves, than in pre-Columbian Brazil. The Portuguese could more easily superimpose the grind of the plantation on Africans than on the Amerindians. With labor secure and the demand for sugar high in Europe, Brazilian production rose from 10,150 metric tons of sugar in 1614 to nearly 19,000 metric tons in 1710. By 1737, however, production slipped to 13,600 metric tons, underscoring that the industry had fallen on hard times. Between 1650 and 1710, Brazilian sugar lost 40 percent of its share of the European market. By 1690, Brazilian sugar totaled only 10 percent of the market.

The Caribbean planters had risen to challenge the early supremacy of Brazil. As early as 1493, Christopher Columbus had introduced sugar into the Caribbean. In the scramble to control the islands, the British, by the early 17th century, claimed Barbados, Jamaica, and the Leeward Islands. In 1663, Parliament granted a monopoly to the Company of Royal Adventurers Trading to Africa, and in 1672, to its successor, the Royal African Company, to provision the planters with slaves. Between 1640 and 1700, the sugar barons of Barbados imported 134,500 slaves, of Jamaica 85,000, and of the Leeward Islands 44,100. From 8,176 tons in 1663, sugar exports from the British Caribbean rose to 50,000 tons by 1750, and 75,000 tons by 1775.

From the Caribbean, sugar spread to Louisiana. In 1795, Frenchman Jean Etienne de Bore exported the colony's first sugar crop. Planters flocked to the region after the Louisiana Purchase of 1803, and in 1812, Louisiana entered the union as a slave state. Between 1810 and 1860, the number of slaves in the cane fields grew from fewer than 10,000 to 88,439. The planters concentrated production south of Baton Rouge. By the mid-1830s, production reached 55,000 tons of sugar, by 1849 137,000 tons, and by 1861 253,000 tons. Sugar concentrated wealth in a few hands. In 1860, 525 planters, 12.5 percent of Louisiana's slave owners, owned two-thirds of the slaves. These planters owned on average 110 slaves, 730 acres of land and equipment worth $14,500, and produced 77 percent of Louisiana's sugar crop. The richest planter, John Burnside, owned 940 slaves and $2.6 million in assets. By the Civil War, sugar cultivation had spread to Texas, South Carolina, Georgia, Alabama, and Mississippi.

The Civil War replaced slavery with wage labor. In 1862, Union General Benjamin Butler decreed that planters pay male laborers $7 a month plus a $3 allowance for clothing. Butler did not specify a wage for female laborers, though one may suppose that planters paid women less than men. If this system was not slavery, it was akin to serfdom, for Butler dispatched army patrols to keep workers on the same plantation. Intent on preserving planters' access to labor, Butler nonetheless limited their authority by forbidding corporal punishment. The sugar crop was a casualty of war. The 1862 harvest totaled only 47,850 tons. Planters blamed the Union Army and the indolence of workers for their woes. At issue was the pace of work. Sugar must be milled within 48 hours of harvest to avoid spoilage. This narrow window of opportunity required coordination between field and mill and 24-hour operation of the mill. Laborers unhappy with their white overseers slackened pace during harvest and refused to work the mill at night. Labor sought an advantage by bargaining with planters for better wages, a practice the Union Army condoned in 1864. Planters reacted by colluding to keep wages low and by pledging not to hire workers from another plantation. The most effective tactic was the withholding of half wages until the end of harvest.

The tussle between worker and planter persisted after the Civil War. Sure of the planter's vulnerability during harvest, workers struck then for higher wages and full payment the first Saturday of each month. Some planters relented, whereas others sought to reduce wages by increasing the supply of labor. They hired agents to recruit workers from other states. In the 1870s, planters experimented with Chinese, Scandinavian, Italian, Dutch, Irish, Spanish, and Portuguese labor, all without restoring the subservient workforce of the antebellum era.

Planters fretted over more than labor. In 1898, an epidemic of sugarcane mosaic virus swept the cane fields and only the introduction of virus-resistant sugar varieties saved the plantations. The use of a mechanical harvester after 1935 diminished the need for labor. Since World War II, plantations have concentrated in a few hands. Between 1957 and 1995, the number of plantations in Louisiana declined from 10,260 to 690. These plantations encompass 364,000 acres along the Mississippi River and the bayous. In 1996, Louisiana produced a record crop of 1,058,000 tons. That year Louisiana produced 30 percent of the U.S. sugar crop. Florida, which produced its first crop in 1931, had by 1996 surpassed Louisiana, growing 40 percent of the country's sugar. In Florida, the plantations lie south of Lake Okeechobee. The soft soil confines mechanical harvest to one-quarter of the land. Men from the Caribbean cut the rest by hand as they have in the Caribbean for nearly four centuries.

See also: Hispaniola; Royal African Company

Christopher Martin Cumo

Bibliography

Dunn, Richard S. *Sugar and Slaves: The Rise of the Planter Class in the English West Indies, 1624–1713.* Chapel Hill: University of North Carolina Press, 1972.

Follett, Richard. *The Sugar Masters: Planters and Slaves in Louisiana's Cane World, 1820–1860.* Baton Rouge: Louisiana State University Press, 2005.

Rehder, John B. *Delta Sugar: Louisiana's Vanishing Plantation Landscape.* Baltimore, MD: Johns Hopkins University Press, 1999.

Rodrigue, John C. *Reconstruction in the Cane Fields: From Slavery to Free Labor in Louisiana's Sugar Parishes, 1862–1880.* Baton Rouge: Louisiana State University Press, 2001.

Schwartz, Stuart B. *Sugar Plantations in the Formation of Brazilian Society: Bahia, 1550–1835.* New York: Cambridge University Press, 1985.

Wilkinson, Alec. *Big Sugar: Seasons in the Cane Fields of Florida.* New York: Alfred A. Knopf, 1989.

Sundiata: The Epic of Old Mali

"The Epic of Sundiata" is the tale of Sundiata Keita (literally "lion king"), the 13th-century exiled West African prince who, called by his people to return and lead them, liberated the Mande people from the oppressive rule of the Susu King Sumanguru Kante and became *Mansa* or king. This victory against the Susu marked the beginning of the great Mali Empire, which occupied much of present-day Mali and Guinea. The Mali Empire existed, although in a declining state at the end, until 1546 when it fell to Songhai forces. The epic is a celebration of Sundiata's victory and serves as a foundational narrative for the many people—such as the Malinke, Mandingo, and Dyula—who claim Mande ancestry.

Because of its widespread dissemination throughout many regions of West Africa, Sundiata is also known as Soundiata, Sunjata, and Sunjara. Likewise, the Sundiata epic itself has many variations. The core of the story nonetheless remains the same: Sundiata's birth to an ugly woman; his frailty as a child; his mastery of his physical frailty; his exile, return, defeat of Sumanguru Kante using his superior knowledge of sorcery; and Sundiata's ascendancy as king.

The epic, a privileged form within Mande culture, is transmitted orally and told by a griot or *jeli,* a master oral performer who occupies a unique position in the world of the Mande. Despite his inherited position in the *nyamakala* or artisan class, he also inherits membership into a highly specialized group of men who are the sole disseminators of the Sundiata epic. Apprenticed by a father or relative, the griot is well versed in the history, genealogies, and cultural traditions of the Mande. He plays the balafon and kora; he knows verbal and nonverbal communicative traditions of the culture. The griot serves as a reference and advisor to leaders. In addition to commemorating and reifying Sundiata, his job is to use each performance of Sundiata to moralize, teach, and reinforce cultural values. In this way, the griot renders "The Epic of Sundiata" into a living text; each telling is different and situational. Also, the griot's role in the epic is self-reflexive insofar as the griot usually plays a significant role in the exploits of Sundiata. In the Niane version, for example, Sumanguru Kante kidnaps Balla Fasséké, Sundiata's griot, so that Sundiata's motivation is, in large part, an attempt to get his griot and by extension, his legacy, back.

"The Epic of Sundiata" has become standard academic reading in the United States, particularly in college courses where it has become a seminal tenet of humanities curricula. Specifically, the Niane version has become somewhat canonized as the most popular version, owing in part to its literary form. The inclusion of "The Epic of Sundiata" in American university courses has done much to revise Eurocentric notions about epic traditions in particular and African primitivism more generally.

See also: Mali; Oral Culture; Sudanic Empires

Renée M. Baron

Bibliography
Austen, Ralph, ed. *In Search of Sunjata: The Mande Oral Epic as History, Literature, and Performance.* Indianapolis: Indiana University Press, 1999.
Niane, D. T. *Sundiata: An Epic of Old Mali.* Translated by G. D. Pickett. London: Longman Group, 1965.
Suso, Bamba, and Banna Kanute. *Sunjata.* Translated by Gordon Innes with the assistance of Bakari Sidibe. London: Penguin Books, 1999.

Task System

The task system was one of the two distinct types of labor that were practiced during the era of slavery in British North America. In this system, slaves would be assigned a particular amount of work that came to be called a task to be completed in a particular day, and then once they were through with it, they were free to do anything with their time. The task system was primarily practiced in Lowcountry South Carolina and Georgia. It evolved between the late 17th century and the early 18th century. The task system coexisted with the gang system where slaves would wake up at the crack of dawn and toil together in a group until sunset.

Several explanations have been provided to explain the emergence of the task system. First, the absenteeism of the slave owners may have necessitated the creation of a system that required less white supervision. For slave owners in the Lowcountry South, the prevalence of malaria made it necessary for them to be absent from their plantations at certain times of the year. However, this argument by itself is not completely convincing since it does not explain why the planters in the Caribbean did not fully adopt the system despite the fact that absenteeism started relatively earlier in that region. A more satisfactory explanation stems from considering the staple crop requirements. Unlike in areas where crops like tobacco required meticulous and year-round care, rice growing in the Lowcountry provided different circumstances. Rice growing did not require direct supervision but rather a few straightforward steps to ensure successful growth.

What exactly constituted a task came to be redefined over time and also varied according to the locations and the work at hand. For example, between 1750 and 1860, in turning up land the task size was one-quarter of an acre, for second hoeing the task varied from half an acre to three-quarters of an acre over the years. When it came to ginning cotton, a task consisted of ginning 90–100 pounds of cotton. If slaves completed their daily assigned tasks, they would be allowed to plant crops on the pieces of land that their masters gave them. They planted corn, rice, beans, and kept animals as a means of subsistence.

The use of the task system definitely elicited mixed reactions from the various players. There are some who considered it dangerous as it gave too much free time to the slaves. This was considered dangerous because slaves could then have time to plot rebellions. Those who felt it was not appropriate to use the task system had several issues in mind. One issue was that since the slaves now had time to plant their own crops and sell them, they proved to be competition for white farmers.

Soon the white slave owners started using legislation to curb the spread and strength of slaves' entrepreneurship. One of the earliest pieces of legislation was passed in 1684, which forbade exchange of any goods between slaves or between slaves and free men unless their masters consented to it. In essence, slaves were allowed to sell their products to their masters only. However, subsequent laws passed showed that earlier ones had proved ineffective. By 1714, another law that prohibited slaves from planting any corn or peas or rice was passed. But in 1734, having realized the ineffectiveness of the former act, slave owners passed another act stipulating that slaves could not sell any produce to anyone but their masters.

For many adherents of the task system, there was a shared belief that if a slave owned property, he was less likely to run away. Therefore, since the task system allowed for time to accumulate wealth, they felt it was the best system to use. For others, it was advantageous because they believed it gave slaves the morale to work extra hard on their masters' plantation knowing they could work at their own plots of land.

Some scholars have felt that it was a system that was more benevolent to the slave as opposed to the gang system. While it is true that once slaves completed their task, they could do whatever they pleased, sometimes the plantation owners deliberately increased the task size so that slaves would not have any time of their own. This turned out to be a major source of exploitation for many slaves.

See also: Carolinas; Gang System; Gullah; Rice Cultivation

Karen W. Ngonya

Bibliography

Littlefield, Daniel C. *Rice and Slaves: Ethnicity and the Slave Trade in Colonial South Carolina.* Baton Rouge: Louisiana State University Press, 1981.

Morgan, Philip D. "Task and Gang Systems: The Organization of Labor on New World Plantations." In *Work and Labor in Early America,* edited by Stephen Innes, 189–220. Chapel Hill: University of North Carolina Press, 1988.

Morgan, Philip D. "Work and Culture: The Task System and the World of Low Country Blacks, 1700 to 1800." *William and Mary Quarterly* 39 (October 1982):564–99.

Philips, Ulrich Bonnell. *American Negro Slavery: A Survey of the Supply, Employment and Control of Negro Labor as Determined by the Plantation Regime.* Baton Rouge: Louisiana State University Press, 1966.

Tight Pack

Throughout the Atlantic slave trade a debate raged over the merits of loose pack and tight pack in storing African slaves aboard slave vessels during Middle Passage. Advocates of tight pack argued that wholesale loss of life was inevitable. Therefore, storing as many Africans on vessels as possible paid a better profit than loose pack. Supporters of tight pack were not convinced that better nutrition, sanitation, and space for slaves guaranteed a greater return of profit. Contemporaries of the Atlantic slave trade and scholars who studied the era concluded that after 1750, the overwhelming majority of captains of slave vessels were practitioners of tight pack. Some captains even devised charts for their vessels to maximize the slaves they stored. Without question, practitioners of tight pack operated a macabre business.

Slaves held on tight pack slave vessels typically found themselves in the bottom of the hold with hundreds of other captives. Conditions in the holds of slave vessels were appalling. The crew of slave vessels forced the captives to lay prone in a space about the size of a coffin. In fact, for many captives, this space came to be their final "resting" place on this earth.

On many vessels, owners of the ships built an additional shelf to cram even more slave cargo onboard. A few European societies grew increasingly uncomfortable with the slave trade. Great Britain attempted to limit the extent of slaves by regulating so many captives per tonnage of vessels. These regulations did not deter enterprising slave traffickers from illegally maximizing the captives destined for Middle Passage.

The evident human cruelty led John Newton, a slave ship captain, to resign from participation in the Atlantic slave trade and become a minister. Newton wrote the famous hymn "Amazing Grace." African slaves destined for the New World via slave vessels suffered the highest mortality rate of any group, civilian or military, traveling the Atlantic Ocean. During the course of the Atlantic slave trade, well in excess of 10 percent of human beings shackled in the holds of slave ships did not survive Middle Passage.

The grotesque aspects of the Atlantic slave trade influenced the English Parliament to enact laws to regulate English slave vessels. Members of the Parliament argued that overcrowding contributed to excessive mortality of African captives. Parliament in the late 18th century passed two acts in an effort to improve living conditions during Middle Passage. Nevertheless, the English Parliament expressed no interest in abolishing English participation in the Atlantic slave trade. Parliament primarily acted out of concern for public relations rather than human compassion.

The Dolben Act of 1788 championed by Sir William Dolben was the first of two Parliamentary measures designed to give the appearance of improving conditions during Middle Passage aboard English-flag vessels. The Dolben Act restricted the number of slaves-per-ton in the expectation that mortality rates of slave and crew would be substantially reduced during Middle Passage. Parliament in 1799 enacted a law that decreased the legal limits of slave cargo by measuring permissible space belowdecks. Parliament sought to abandon the use of mere ship tonnage and concentrated instead on usable space. The net effect of these two reforms did decrease the slaves-per-ton ratio from 2.6 to 1 slave per ton.

Notwithstanding efforts to legislate loose pack on slave companies and white entrepreneurs bent on practicing tight pack, recent historical studies indicate that there is no statistical correlation between ships with less slave captives and those with more. Mortality statistics support this interesting hypothesis. Regardless what European slave trade is studied, the findings are consistent. Revisionist historians have concluded that other variables affected mortality in a more profound way than loose or tight pack. Inoculation of captives, faster-sailing vessels, and shorter sailing times somewhat negated the effect of crowding aboard slave vessels.

See also: Atlantic Slave Trade; Loose Pack; Newton, John

Michael A. Cooke

Bibliography

Feelings, Tom. *The Middle Passage: White Ships/Black Cargo.* New York: Dial Books, 1995.

Klein, Herbert S. *The Atlantic Slave Trade.* New York: Cambridge University Press, 1999.

Klein, Herbert S., Stanley L. Engerman, Robin Haines, and Ralph Shlomowitz. "Transoceanic Mortality: The Slave Trade in Comparative Perspective." *William and Mary Quarterly* 58 (2001):93–117.

Mannix, Daniel P. *Black Cargoes: A History of the Atlantic Slave Trade, 1518–1865.* New York: Viking Press, 1965.

Palmer, Colin A. *Human Cargoes: The British Slave Trade to Spanish America, 1700–1739.* Urbana: University of Illinois Press, 1981.

Timbuktu

Timbuktu, the city of knowledge and the capital of Islamic Mali, was established by Tureq nomads in the early 12th century as a camp for traders. Timbuktu earns its name from a well, owned by a woman, Bouctou. The well, salt, and gold attracted many travelers to the area. Timbuktu, located in southern Sahara adjacent to the Niger River, is part of the Republic of Mali. As Timbuktu grew in population and importance, it became the subject of occupation by neighboring West Africans, Portuguese, and French. The invasion was to control sub-Saharan trade—the salt and gold industry as well as the slave trade. Timbuktu became part of the Mali Empire in CE 1330. Before that, it enjoyed a great reputation during the reign of King Mansa Musa. West Africans perceived Timbuktu as the economic and cultural capital

equal to Rome, Fez, and Mecca. As a center of learning and scholarship, it drew visitors, merchants, traders, students, and great scholars from the Muslim world.

Timbuktu became prosperous when its inhabitants became Muslims and established trade with Muslims from Morocco. Even though Timbuktu was famous for its Islamic heritage, education in Timbuktu was not limited to Islamic studies; it included natural sciences, geography, and medicine as attested to by the manuscripts written by Timbuktu scholars. In 2003, the Library of Congress displayed Arabic manuscripts from Timbuktu, among which are books on medicine. Timbuktu reached its peak of intellectual reputation during the reign of Mandingo Askia's Empire (1493–1591).

In the 16th century and before the arrival of the Portuguese, Timbuktu had more than 100,000 inhabitants with great schools, colleges, universities, and well-funded public and private libraries. Timbuktu had three great mosques that were centers of learning—Djingareyber, Sankore, and Sidi Yahia—whose designs and buildings represent African Islamic architecture. Timbuktu also became prosperous with thriving trade in gold, salt, and ivory. This shows the high level of civilization attained in Timbuktu in the Middle Ages. The glory and fame of Timbuktu declined in 1591 when the Moroccans invaded and destroyed it. Later, the Portuguese came and established trade with West African coasts and thus limited Timbuktu's trade with its neighbors. This cut-off inflicted a devastating blow to Timbuktu's advancement in trade and learning. Merchants and scholars moved out of Timbuktu gradually due to this decline.

In 1893, the French occupied Mali and took Timbuktu. Hence, Timbuktu lost its remaining strategic trade routes and wealth. The French occupiers despised Islamic institutions. The study of Arabic and Islamic sciences lost their prime positions as the French language was introduced. Timbuktu's valuable and classic Islamic books were kept in private libraries, which limited their usage by the public. Timbuktu became a lost city; its population dropped drastically. It was abandoned politically and commercially. Neither modern roads nor trains were built by the French to connect Timbuktu with big cities or with the capital. Boats and camels remain the common means of transportation today to reach Timbuktu.

At present, 33,000 to 40,000 people live in Timbuktu, which reflects ancient mud-building as if it had never witnessed any civilization. Foreign tourists visit Timbuktu

Sankore Mosque housed an Islamic madrassa which was at the center of the great Islamic scholarly community at Timbuktu during the 15th century. (David Kerkhoff)

occasionally on camels and boats; more awareness has been raised about the city's Islamic past. The Mali government has appealed to the international community and UNESCO to assist it to restore Timbuktu's ancient mosques and its Islamic libraries. Most people remember Mali today because of Timbuktu and its legendary king, Mansa Musa. Timbuktu, the "Pearl" of medieval Mali, one of the most radiant seats of culture and civilization in West Africa, has now become a city of sand and dust.

See also: Mali; Musa, Mansa; Songhai; Sudanic Empires; Toure, Askia Muhammad

Yushau Sodiq

Bibliography

Hunwick, John O. *Timbuktu: Its Origin and Development after Islam Entered Africa.* Princeton, NJ: M. Wiener, 2007.

Saad, Elias N. *Social History of Timbuktu: The Role of Muslim Scholars and Notables, 1400–1900.* Cambridge, UK: Cambridge University Press, 1983.

Sattin, Anthony. *The Gates of Africa: Death, Discovery, and the Search for Timbuktu.* New York: St. Martin's Press, 2005.

Tobacco

Tobacco is native to Virginia. Native Americans grew it as part of their religious traditions. They believed that in smoking tobacco, they inhaled the smoke into their very souls. Once exhaled, the smoke carried their prayers up to the gods. The European settlers of Jamestown, Virginia, adopted the habit of smoking tobacco, though it was devoid of any religious contexts. In 1612, Englishman John Rolfe planted a variety of tobacco from the Caribbean island of Trinidad that yielded a leaf superior in aroma to the indigenous varieties of Virginia and, beginning in the 1620s, tobacco was the leading export of the colony. In 1627, Virginia exported to England 500,000 pounds of tobacco, in 1635 1 million pounds, and in 1670 15 million pounds. Exports followed demand, which increased in Europe 20 times between 1617 and 1640 and 100 times by 1780.

The craving for tobacco drove both production and the demand for labor. Unlike sugar, tobacco is not inherently a plantation crop and did not benefit from an economy of scale. Small farmers relied on their families and hired labor, but free labor in colonial Virginia was too scarce to meet the needs of the large planters. Instead they imported indentured servants from England. Demographic and economic conditions in England created surplus labor for tobacco growers in the colonies. Until roughly 1650, the birthrate in England outpaced the growth in the number of jobs. Wages fell, driving the urban poor to indenture themselves in exchange for passage to America and the promise of freedom at the end of their term. After roughly 1650, the birthrate stabilized and the pool of indentured servants began to shrink in the 1680s. By then the sugar barons of the Caribbean had demonstrated the profitability of slave labor and the planters of the Chesapeake switched from indentured servant to African slave. In 1660, Virginia and Maryland totaled 1,700 slaves and in 1680, 4,000. Between 1695 and 1700, the planters imported 3,000 new slaves, as many as they had bought the previous two decades. Setting aside hired help, by 1690, four-fifths of labor in York County, Virginia, was slave and only one-fifth indentured. Tobacco was the first crop in North America to use slave labor, establishing the labor system that the rice plantations of the Carolinas, the sugar plantations of Louisiana, and the cotton plantations of the Lower South would replicate.

Tobacco depleted the soil of minerals. Plentiful land led farmers to cultivate new land on the margin of the frontier rather than to restore fertility to depleted soils. They converted old tobacco fields to grain and pasture, and the cultivation of new land spread tobacco to North Carolina after 1670 and as far north as the Ohio River by 1800. Into the 20th century, farmers in southern Ohio grew tobacco for cigars. There, tobacco farms used free labor. In the South, slavery persisted until 1865. As was true of cotton, many postbellum tobacco farms were a mix of tenant and sharecropper. As in the colonial period, small farms relied on hired labor. In the second half of the 19th century, scientists urged tobacco farmers to restore soil fertility by adding fertilizers to their soil and the U.S. Department of Agriculture established a program to breed new varieties of tobacco. After World War II, soybeans rivaled tobacco on the clay soils of the South, bringing diversity to lands that otherwise depended on tobacco monoculture. Since the 1960s, physicians and scientists have publicized the hazards of tobacco. Conversely, popular culture makes tobacco seductive to youth.

See also: Chesapeake Colonies; Indentured Servitude; Jamestown, Virginia; Johnson, Anthony

Christopher Martin Cumo

Bibliography
Kulikoff, Allan. *Tobacco and Slaves: The Development of Southern Cultures in the Chesapeake, 1680–1800.* Chapel Hill: University of North Carolina Press, 1986.
Menard, Russell R. "The Tobacco Industry in the Chesapeake Colonies, 1617–1730: An Interpretation." *Research in Economic History* 5 (1980):123–61.
Wetherell, Charles. "'Boom and Bust' in the Colonial Chesapeake Economy." *Journal of Interdisciplinary History* 15 (1984):185–210.

Toure, Askia Muhammad

Askia Muhamamd Toure (1442–1538), variously known as Askia al-hajj Muhammad b. Abi Bakr and Askia Muhammad the Great, ruled the Songhai Empire from 1493 to 1529 and is considered one of the great West African rulers. Under his rule, the borders of the empire expanded to encompass nearly 500,000 square miles of the West African Sahel (arid strip of land south of the Sahara) and savannah regions, including much of modern-day Mali and Niger, as well as the northern portions of Burkina Faso and Nigeria. After serving as a general to two of his predecessors, Askia Muhammad came to power in a coup, deposing Abu Bakr b. Ali, the son of Sunni Ali Ber (r. 1464–1492), after two decisive military battles. He ruled the empire from the ancient city of Gao along the Niger River, but also had control of Timbuktu, the semiautonomous scholarly center of medieval West Africa. His dynasty lasted for a century, overseeing the golden age of Timbuktu and Songhai.

Askia Muhammad was from the Soninke ethnic group and was a devout adherent to Islam, making a pilgrimage to Mecca in 1497–1498. In Cairo, he received the authority to act as a deputy of the Caliph, the overall leader of Muslims, which gave him legitimacy in the eyes of local Islamic scholars who looked upon him as a pious patron. Askia Muhammad's affable relationship with the scholarly elite in both Gao and Timbuktu helped secure his place in the documented history of the region. This was in contrast to his predecessor, Sunni Ali, who was lukewarm to Islamic practices at best and often hostile toward the Islamic scholars.

Tomb of Askia Muhammad Toure, ruler of the Songhai Empire from 1493 to 1528, at Gao in present-day Mali. (Werner Forman/Art Resource, NY)

As a result, the two most important historical chronicles of Timbuktu, Tarikh al-Fattah and Tarikh al-Sudan, portray Sunni Ali as a ruthless tyrant and show nothing but adoration for the enlightened Askia Muhammad. The support of religious leadership further solidified the legitimacy of both

his rule and plans for expanding the empire to surrounding non-Muslim regions.

Through a series of wars with Songhai's neighbors, Askia Muhammad was able to conquer territory and create tributary relationships as far away as the Saharan city

Taghaza to the north, Aïr in the east, the edge of Borgu in the south, and the Senegal River in the west. His superior tactics and troop numbers often secured victory, but he was thwarted in Borgu and the Mossi States, and had limited success in Hausaland. As a consequence of the warfare, Songhai captured many prisoners and enslaved them under the auspices of the Songhai state or sold them to North African traders. Large numbers of slaves were taken during many of the campaigns; some accounts reveal that large parts of cities had to be set aside to house the captives. Only non-Muslims could be enslaved according to religious law; however, Muslim states could be and were forced into a tributary relation with Songhai. Ironically, most of the soldiers of Songhai were themselves more or less servile to the state.

Askia Muhammad inherited a strong central government from Sunni Ali, but Muhammad strengthened it even further, adding new positions and functions to oversee the governance of the enlarged territory. He also consulted with prominent Muslim scholars on how to rule his empire, men such as Egyptian Jalal al-Din al-Suyuti, Muhammad ibn Abd al-Karim al-Maghili of Tlemcen (in modern Algeria), and local scholars from Timbuktu. The advice ranged from the mundane to the permissibility of forcing leaderless local Muslim peoples under his authority and deposing tyrannical Muslim rulers for the greater good of Muslims. Although al-Maghili's advice had contemporaneous impact, his work would also be cited and acted upon more than three centuries later by 19th-century jihadists such as Umar Tal and Shaykh Usuman dan Fodio. The latter's military campaigns, legitimized largely by al-Maghili's rulings, led to enslaved captives on all sides of the conflict being sold into slavery and sent to the Americas.

Askia Muhammad's son Musa deposed him in 1529. He was banished for a period and then returned to live the rest of his life restricted to the royal palace before dying in 1538. The succeeding 50 years would bring internal struggles and revolts as Askia Muhammad's descendents vied for power, all of which allowed for the Moroccan invasion in 1591 and an end to the Songhai Empire, Askia dynasty rule, and the fortunes of Timbuktu as a scholarly center.

See also: Songhai; Sudanic Empires; Timbuktu

Brent D. Singleton

Bibliography

Blum, Charlotte, and Humphrey Fisher. "Love for Three Oranges; or, The Askiya's Dilemma: The Askiya, Al-Maghili and Timbuktu, c. 1500 A.D." *Journal of African History* 34 (1993):65–91.

Bovill, Edward W. *The Golden Trade of the Moors: West African Kingdoms in the Fourteenth Century.* Princeton, NJ: Markus Wiener, 1995.

Gomez, Michael Angelo. *Reversing Sail: A History of the African Diaspora.* Cambridge, UK: Cambridge University Press, 2005.

Hunwick, John O., ed. *Sharia in Songhay: The Replies of Al-Maghili to the Questions of Askia Al-Hajj Muhammad.* Oxford, UK: Oxford University Press, 1985.

Hunwick, John O., ed. *Timbuktu and the Songhai Empire: Al-Sadi's Tarikh al-Sudan down to 1613 and Other Contemporary Documents.* Leiden, the Netherlands: Brill, 1999.

Trans-Saharan Slave Trade

Trans-Saharan slave trade refers to the capture, enslavement, and transport of human beings, originating mostly from south of the Sahara Desert in North Africa, to areas both within the desert and points north and east. While it was at its peak between the 8th and 19th centuries of the common era, the trade spanned much of the first millennium CE. Despite its longevity, only relatively modest academic attention has been paid to the trans-Saharan slave trade and the African Diaspora it spawned in the Mediterranean region as well as in West and South Asia.

Long-distance trade networks across the Sahara Desert existed as early as 800 BCE. The camel was introduced to North Africa in the first century CE and was in widespread use among Berbers, nomads inhabiting North Africa, by CE 400. Its relative hardiness and ability to travel long distances with little water expanded desert trade capacity significantly. Although salt mined in the desert was the primary commodity and driver of the trade, slavery was indeed an early part of the trans-Saharan trade. As the trade developed, slavery and salt were quite related to one another in the Saharan context, as captives were sometimes put to work in the desert salt mines. Much later, by the mid-1800s, merchants often found it impossible to purchase salt unless they had slaves to trade in return.

While slavery was a element of the early trade across the Sahara, slave trading in the region grew most rapidly after CE 600–700, with the emergence of an Islamic empire spanning much of what is now West Asia, parts of Europe, and North and West Africa. The spread of Islam created a greater demand for slaves. Initially, many slaves in Muslim societies were obtained as a result of conquest under the expanding Islamic empire. However, as many of the conquered peoples converted to Islam, Muslims began to seek out other populations for the purposes of enslavement.

Most of the people who were captured, enslaved, and transported during the trans-Saharan trade originated in the Sahel region south of the Sahara, stretching from the area that is now Chad and Sudan, west to what is now Senegal and Gambia. Most slaves were transported north, across the Sahara desert to Muslim-controlled areas along the Mediterranean coast, both in North Africa and in southern Europe and points east. Slaves transported during the trade were usually obtained via raids or kidnapping, often by the Tuareg, a nomadic Saharan people. Slaves transported along these routes endured excruciatingly long journeys with little water, in one of the earth's most extreme climates. The mortality rate among enslaved persons during these journeys was high, and the physical and emotional consequences experienced by slaves as a result of their forced departure from home, their strenuous voyage across a vast desert, and their introduction to a strange new world would have been intensely painful.

The people transported north across the desert and into slavery during the trans-Saharan slave trade were largely women. Women were highly valued in the slave trade because of the relatively wider range of roles they were able to fulfill when compared to men. Many of them were employed in domestic labor positions, and as concubines and sex workers when they arrived at their destination. Thus, sexual exploitation was a salient feature of the trans-Saharan slave trade.

In Islamic societies, slaves were not necessarily enslaved for life, though many certainly were, but sometimes had the possibility of freedom if manumitted by their masters. Enslaved women who gave birth to children fathered by their masters were sometimes freed, and children born under such circumstances were free. However, children fathered by an enslaved man and born to enslaved women generally inherited the condition of slavery. Other means of manumission included the purchase of one's own freedom, and in a few cases, conversion to Islam.

Trade in slaves, salt, and gold continued to flourish in the Saharan for centuries, expanding trading networks in multiple directions, many of which eventually linked the Saharan slave trade to Atlantic ports where European demand for slaves developed beginning in the 15th century and growing significantly in the years that followed. Although the Atlantic slave trade officially ended in the early 19th century, the trans-Saharan slave trade persisted for nearly another century afterward.

Despite the large number of Sahelian African people—possibly millions—transported across the Saharan desert during the first millennium CE, there does not exist today an African Diaspora in the Mediterranean region or in West Asia that rivals the size and visibility of that created in the Americas and the Caribbean by the transatlantic slave trade. Scholars speculate that the relatively lower number of men transported out of Africa during the Saharan slave trade, the isolation of African slaves from one another, high rates of disease and mortality among Africans enslaved in the Muslim world, and a history of social and marital integration is what has prevented the proliferation of African diasporic communities in Mediterranean regions. However, the apparent absence of a visible African Diaspora, particularly in the Mediterranean world, is a question that historians continue to pursue.

See also: Atlantic Slave Trade; Sahel

Lindsay Sumner

Bibliography

Cordell, Dennis. *Dar al-Kuti and the Last Years of the Trans-Saharan Slave Trade.* Madison: University of Wisconsin Press, 1985.

Savage, Elizabeth, ed. *The Human Commodity: Perspectives on the Trans-Saharan Slave Trade.* London: Frank Cass, 1992.

Shillington, Kevin. *History of Africa.* New York: Palgrave Macmillan, 2005.

Tribute

Tribute was the practice among Atlantic African kingdoms and city-states of demanding payment in form of labor or produce from the kingdoms, city-states, or rural villages and other territories or polities they conquered or extended their political and economic influence. This payment of tribute—whether in kind of specie—has come to be closely associated with the Atlantic slave trade as surplus urban labor—derived in part from individuals forced to pay off tribute obligations owed by their polity—was siphoned off and sold to Europeans. It was also a principal means by which kingdoms and smaller polities generated their wealth since it meant owning or controlling one of the few truly valuable commodities in Atlantic Africa—human labor.

The concept of tribute may have evolved from the need to create wealth from the land. For most agricultural-based polities, wealth lay not in the abundance of land, but rather in the ability of people to make that land productive. Thus the acquisition of labor became the most primary objective in the expansion of many African states and kingdoms. By conquering a particular territory, the conquering polity was in essence earning control over a source of labor as surplus agricultural products would be sent as a portion of tribute payments to politically and militarily dominate states. In addition to agricultural surplus (or tribute in kind), tribute payments could also include currency in the form of cowrie shells or gold dust (specie) or slaves. These slaves would be put to work in the land owned by the king and other ruling elite.

Sometimes the territories offering tribute were not necessarily conquered people but rather those who decided to submit themselves under a particular kingdom to gain its protection from other enemies. One way in which these kingdoms would show their submission would be through the payment of tribute, by giving a number of slaves to work in the king's land or to serve in the army. In return, the more powerful king would offer protection to the submitting kings against other invaders.

In terms of wealth production, the only legally recognized way of producing wealth was the ownership of slaves who provided labor. This was because, unlike the plantations in the New World owned by private hands, in Atlantic Africa the concept of private land ownership was never fully developed. Therefore, unlike in Europe where land taxation was more generally employed, in Atlantic Africa tribute payments were determined by population size of the tribute-paying state (also referred to as a tributary). Tribute systems were also used in conjunction with labor conscription for the construction of state projects or the creation of mass armies during times of war. Again, the size of the tributary would determine the number of conscripts to be sent in service of the state.

Ownership of slaves and land was not restricted to the king only. There were those considered "nobles" who were mainly of the ruling class. They too owned land that was cultivated by slave labor. Their land ownership was mainly sanctioned by the king, since they were given this land while holding a particular office under the domain of a particular king. On conquering a particular territory, the king would appoint several people to rule over these territories in his behalf. Such appointments came with benefits like having land and slaves at their disposal. These benefits were considered as payment of tribute to the conquering king.

It is important to note, however, that although the slave system existed in Africa, it cannot be wholly compared to what came to be known as the transatlantic slave trade. In the case of the transatlantic slave trade where plantation owners had nothing in their minds but profit, slaves were overworked, mistreated, and degraded in order to maximize profit. But in transatlantic Africa, slaves were more or less treated like peasant cultivators. Since land was available to whoever wanted to cultivate it, slaves in Africa had an opportunity to own wealth that could be produced from cultivating the land. Slaves also had an opportunity to own wealth, rise through ranks, even becoming kings, as was the case of King Osei Tutu who founded the Ashanti Empire, and be integrated into the community they were enslaved in.

Regarding the use of the term "slavery," it is true that because of what it came to mean thanks to the transatlantic slave trade, it is not possible to remove the negative connotation it carries. However, as shown above, the form of slavery practiced in Atlantic Africa was not similar in terms of its motives. In Atlantic Africa, slavery as an institution was a system placed by law as a means of wealth production as land could not be owned. Furthermore, the development of commerce and of social mobility even in trade relied heavily on slavery, since porters and agricultural work required labor. This labor was readily supplied in the form of slaves.

It was therefore not surprising that when Europeans came in to look for slaves, they were able to succeed since slavery was not a foreign concept. Atlantic Africa, just like any society that has ever existed, was not egalitarian, and this meant the existence of the elite who exploited the common people. The ruling class, who from the start had access to slaves who worked on their land, began selling them off to Europeans, who in turn sent them to the New World. In time, when a certain kingdom conquered another, there was a capturing of prisoners of war who would be sold off as slaves to Europeans, unlike earlier times when they would work for the conquering kings. Such was the case in the West-Central African Kingdom of Kongo and the various kingdoms in the Angola region. In essence, the presence of the tribute system fed significantly into the transatlantic slave trade.

See also: Atlantic Slave Trade

Karen W. Ngonya

Bibliography

Kea, Ray A. *Settlements, Trade, and Polities in the Seventeenth-Century Gold Coast.* Baltimore, MD: Johns Hopkins University Press, 1982.

Rucker, Walter. "The African and European Slave Trades." In *The Blackwell Companion to African American History,* edited by Alton Hornsby Jr., 48–66. Malden, MA: Blackwell Publishers, 2005.

Thornton, John K. *Africa and Africans in the Making of the Atlantic World, 1400–1800,* 2nd ed. Cambridge, UK: Cambridge University Press, 1998.

Vita, Dona Beatriz Kimpa

Kimpa Vita (1684–1706) was baptized as Beatriz and was therefore also known under her Christian name, Dona Beatriz. She was a Congolese prophet and the founder of a Christian movement that became known as Antonianism. Her teaching was rooted in the traditions of the Roman Catholic Church in Kongo. Her movement recognized the papal primate but was hostile against the European missionaries in Congo. Due to the great number of documents found in the archives of Italian Capuchin missionaries, the years of Kimpa Vita's life are some of the best documented in Kongo's history. The missionaries in the eastern part of Congo produced detailed diaries about their lives in Africa in general and about Donna Beatriz.

She was born around 1684 in a small provincial town near Mount Kibangu at the banks of the Mbidizi River in the eastern end of the Kingdom of Kongo (today part of Angola). As all Kongolese, who had been Catholics for nearly two centuries, she was baptized as soon as a priest passed her town. She was given the Christian name Beatriz by her parents, and as a local feature the Portuguese title "Dona" was given to every female. Her name in Kikongo was Kimpa (her given name) Vita (her father's name). Dona Beatriz's family were members of the highest group of Kongolese nobility, the Mwana Kongo or "Child of Kongo." This circumstance was a source of pride but it implied neither wealth nor political power. The Mwana Kongo clans were those who claim a king of Kongo somewhere in their past.

At the time of Kimpa Vita's birth, the Kingdom of Kongo was torn by armed turbulences. A period of civil war followed the death of King Antonio I at the battle of Mbwila (1665). As a result, the former capital of São Salvador (today Mbanza Kongo) was abandoned in 1678, and

the country was divided into major factions ruled by rival pretenders to the throne. The Capuchin missionary Fra Bernardo da Gallo reports that Dona Beatriz had her first vision when she was about eight years old. In her vision, two *nkitas* (white children from the Other World) played with her and gave her a beautiful glass rosary. She started to get a strong inclination toward religion.

As Kimpa Vita grew older, her interest in the spiritual side of life increased, and it became obvious that she was specially gifted. She was trained to become a *nganga* (meaning "knowledge" or "skill" in Kikongo), a person said to be able to communicate with the Other World. Dona Beatriz became a particular kind of medium called *nganga marinda,* whose special ability was to address social problems as well as individual ones. This very respected office involved helping people who had problems originating from the Other World. As a miranda nganga, she was also linked to the so-called Kimpasi society (*kimpasi* means "suffering" in Kikongo). Young initiates were chosen from the community, like in the case of Kimpa Vita, and put inside a secret and isolated enclosure. They were taught new languages as well as occult knowledge and had to swear an oath of secrecy. The Capuchin missionaries considered the Kimpasi societies as devils incarnate and declared all initiates excommunicated. Around 1699, Dona Beatriz concluded that her practice as nganga marinda was too close to evil *kindoki* (meaning "religious power"). She renounced her office and focused more on the beliefs of the Catholic Church.

After leaving her life as nganga behind, Dona Beatriz got married, but she could not adjust to married life. It was hard for someone who had lived the life of spiritual freedom and independence to adapt to a husband. Her first marriage did not last long, to be followed by a second one that did not survive the initial phase of living together. Both times, she moved back to her parents' house and refunded the bride wealth.

In 1703, Dona Beatriz and her neighbors left the Mbidizi Valley and joined the new colonists dedicated to restoring the former capital, São Salvador. King Pedro IV, one of the rival rulers of Kongo, encouraged the restoration of the abandoned city, together with his vows about the restoration of Saint James's Day and the involvement of the Capuchins in the peace process. The colonists were tired of the endless civil wars in the country and were full of religious fervor. Many had become followers of an old woman, Apollonia Mafuta, who had visions of the Virgin Mary. The

Virgin told Mafuta that Jesus was particularly angry with the people of Kibangu for not coming down to restore the old city of São Salvador and God would punish the Kongolese for their wickedness. Jesus's anger, so learned Mafuta in her visions, was specially directed toward King Pedro IV.

In August 1704, as Apollonia Mafuta's ministry went on, Dona Beatriz fell ill with a mysterious sickness. She later reported to Fra Bernardo da Gallo that she died and that she was reborn as Saint Anthony. The Saint had entered her dead body, and she received the divine commandment to go and preach. She followed the example of the Capuchins and distributed her personal property. She set off to preach to the king in Kibangu, but Pedro IV refused to see her. She argued that neither the king nor the Capuchin priest Fra Bernardo were determined enough to restore the kingdom and therefore she would do it herself. Apollonia Mafuta supported her, claiming that she was the real voice of God. Both women preached against greed and jealousy and the misuse of kindoki.

Dona Beatriz claimed that she died each Friday and spent two days in Heaven talking to God, just to return to earth on Mondays. While in this state, she learned that Kongo must reunite under a new king. The civil war that had plagued Kongo since the battle of Mbwila in 1665 had angered Christ. God ordered her to build a specific Kongolese Catholicism and to unite the country under one king. She destroyed the Kongolese *nkisi* (charms inhabited by spiritual entities), as well as Christian paraphernalia.

Much of Dona Beatriz's teaching is known from her prayer, "Salve Antoniana," that converted the Catholic prayer "Salve Regina" into an anthem of her movement. It taught that God was only concerned with believers' intentions and not with actual sacraments or good works. She continued her teaching through several sermons. These sermons focused on three important issues. First, that Saint Anthony, the patron of Portugal, was the most important saint of all, in fact, a "second God." Together with Saint James Major, he was also the patron of Kongo. She demanded to her followers that they should only pray to him. Specially, infertile women should devote themselves to him, since he can relieve them from sterility. Second, she reconfirmed Mafuta's vision, saying that Jesus was angry with the Kongolese people and they have to expect severe punishment. She urged that her followers should pray and ask for mercy. Third, she told the Kongolese to be happy. Saint Anthony would protect them and good things would

happen to his devotees. She convinced them that her arrival meant that the Kongolese could have saints of their own, just as the Europeans did. So far, the Capuchines insisted that the Catholic Church had its origins outside Kongo and that the most important saints of the country, Saint Anthony of Padua and Saint Francis, were Italians, just like them. Therefore, black Kongolese saints do not exist.

In Dona Beatriz's visions, God revealed to her the real church history that the Capuchin missionaries were hiding from the Kongolese. Jesus had been born in São Salvador. He had been baptized in Nazareth, but this was only a fake name for his real place of baptism, which was located in the northern Kongolese province of Nsundi. Also, Mary was Kongolese and her mother, Anna, was a slave of the Marquis Nzimba Mpangi. Saint Francis was also of Kongolese origin and Saint Anthony was now present within her body.

Father Bernardo da Gallo witnessed one of Dona Beatriz's possessions by Saint Anthony. Although Kongolese regarded possession as an acceptable form of revelation, the Catholic priest considered the practice as diabolic. Furthermore, the European Christian tradition does not accept that a divine revelation comes from a possession. Only the devil can possess the human body and a rite of exorcism is the remedy. So Dona Beatriz was most likely possessed by the devil or a demon, not by Saint Anthony.

Since Pedro IV refused to see her in Kibangu, she decided to visit his rival King João II at Bula (near the Kongo River close to Matadi) in October 1704. But João II chased Dona Beatriz and her followers away. Her experiences in Bula and Kibangu showed her that the Kongolese nobility was not interested in her vision of restoring and reuniting the country, while the common people were eager to support her. They saw in her the ideal ruler, a social revolutionary and a peacemaker. She would use her kindoki to fight against the greed and violence of the ruling kings.

In 1705, Dona Beatriz and thousands of her mostly peasant followers returned to São Salvador. She was now the undisputed mistress of the royal capital and determined to fulfill her mission of restoration. Rumors of her powers had spread throughout the country. She built herself a small house behind the ruins of the cathedral and started preaching from there. To help her with her work, she began to commission her "Little Anthonys," who were to become Saint Anthony's missionaries all over the country. Each of the Little Anthonys would be as much possessed by the saint as Dona Beatriz herself, but keeping a lower status.

After 1705, they mostly traveled in pairs to the provinces. They were expelled out of the coastal province of Soyo, but they were much more successful in the dissident southern part of Soyo and Mbamba Lovata. There, they won many converts, especially among partisans of the old queen Suzana de Nóbrega. Their preaching was linked to Dona Beatriz's, but it soon took local patterns that altered her message. While the Kongolese nobility rejected the Little Anthonys, they were able to win over masses of common people. In one case, two Little Anthonys had persuaded a whole district to stop baptizing their children. Dona Beatriz said in her famous preaching Salve Antoniana that baptism was not necessary, as God would know the intention in their hearts.

Dona Beatriz started to preach a new era of wealth in her sermons and her noble followers started to see her movement as a potential to gain political power. The Antonian movement was becoming involved in the politics of the kingdom and the political authorities were no longer able to control the forces that had been unleashed by her preaching.

In 1704, Dona Beatriz started a close relationship with a man named João Barro, who became her Guardian Angel, also known as Saint John. She became pregnant twice, but aborted with herbal medicine. In 1705, she became pregnant a third time and the medicine failed to work. Since she preached that her followers and the Little Anthonys should lead a life in chastity, her pregnancy became a problem and she began to doubt her mission. To keep her pregnancy secret, she left São Salvador until she gave birth to a boy called Antonio.

In 1706, shortly after she gave birth, Dona Beatriz together with Apollonia Mafuta, João Barro, and their newborn son were captured and brought to the temporary capital of Evululu. There they were condemned as heretic to death by burning. She was tried under Kongolese law (not the law of the Church) by a council of the Capuchin friars Bernardo da Gallo, Lorenzo da Lucca, and Manuel da Cruz Barbosa. The execution took place on July 2, 1706. The life of Antonio, her child, was spared.

The Antonians had a strong local organization and could outlive Dona Beatriz. Many of her followers believed that she was still alive. It was only in 1709 when the military forces of Pedro IV took São Salvador that the political force of her movement vanished. Most of her noble followers returned to the beliefs of the Catholic Church.

In 1739, some of her followers who were sold as slaves to America carried out a revolt known as the Stono Rebellion in South Carolina. More recently, some see present-day Kimbanguism as a successor to Dona Beatriz's teaching. Its followers claim that she came back in September 12, 1887, in the body of Simon Kimbangu. Traditions circulating in Mbanza Kongo today also place great significance in the role of Dona Beatriz's mother as a source of inspiration for her and also as a key figure in the continuation of the movement, but contemporary sources make no mention of this. Even though some see her as an "African Joan of Arc," Pope Paul VI had rejected a request of her rehabilitation in 1966.

See also: Kongo Kingdom; Stono Rebellion; West-Central Africa

Carmen De Michele

Bibliography
Thornton. John. *The Kongolese Saint Anthony: Donna Beatriz Kimpa Vita and the Antonian Movement, 1684–1706.* Cambridge, UK: Cambridge University Press, 1998.

West-Central Africa

The region referred to as West-Central Africa is at times discussed as a lower, coastal extension of West Africa. The region comprises the countries of Angola, Benin, Cameroon, the Democratic Republic of Congo, Congo, and Nigeria. From the tropical rainforests of Equatorial Guinea to the Congo River basin and the desert landscapes of the Sudan, the region is geographically diverse.

The region was colonized during the 16th through 19th centuries by various European powers, including France, Belgium, Portugal, and Britain. European languages still used for commerce and education in these areas include French, Portuguese, and English. Major exports of the region include coffee, cocoa, rubber, and timber. In addition, this west-central region of Africa contains some of Africa's richest areas for unlicensed oil (petroleum) and mineral exploration (namely iron ore).

Many slaves who ended up in the United States were from West-Central Africa. Others came from Mozambique and Madagascar (formerly French and Portuguese colonies). Slaves were captured from certain areas more than others. Nearly one-third of all slaves were taken from the Congo region. Another third came from the area that is now known as Benin and Nigeria.

Over the last two decades, many countries in the west-central region have experienced political difficulties resulting in major armed conflict and the displacement of thousands of people. As a result, even the countries with the most functional governments are burdened by poverty, lack of education, and high external debt.

See also: Angolan/Kongolese; Kongo Cosmogram; Kongo Kingdom

Jen Westmoreland Bouchard

Bibliography

Vansina, Jan. *How Societies Are Born: Governance in West Central Africa before 1600.* Charlottesville: University of Virginia Press, 2004.

Vansina, Jan. *Paths in the Rainforests: Toward a History of Political Tradition in Equatorial Africa.* Madison: University of Wisconsin Press, 1990.

Wheatley, Phillis

Phillis Wheatley (1754–1783) was the first African American to publish a book and the second published female poet in what would become the United States. Thought to have been born in Gambia in West Africa and enslaved and transported to Massachusetts in bondage, Phillis Wheatley is known as the first African American published poet. However, Wheatley's significance in the African American literary tradition has been contested for almost 100 years.

During the Harlem Renaissance, literary historian Arthur Schomburg, while praising Wheatley, noted that her poetry cannot be considered great. James Weldon Johnson complained that Wheatley's poetry never spoke out against slavery and that she showed "smug" contentment regarding her escape from Africa. This criticism of Wheatley's so-called color blindness continued during the Black Arts Movement associated with the reclamation of black poets in the 1960s. In 1962, Rosey Poole lamented Wheatley's lack of strength and explained that rather than being an important literary figure, she was a "literary curio." In 1964, Vernon Loggins called her a mere imitator. By 1972, R. Lynn Mason argued that while Wheatley's poetry may not establish her as a "Soul Sister," she must at least be considered as an important part of the African American literary canon. It was June Jordan, in an essay entitled "The Difficult Miracle of Black Poetry in America: Or Something like a Sonnet for Phillis Wheatley" in 1985, who fully reclaimed Wheatley as an important literary figure and pointed out the revolutionary potential of her poems.

Phillis Wheatley was purchased as an enslaved maidservant by John and Susanna Wheatley on July 11, 1761, when she was seven or eight years old. In the Wheatley household, where unlike many enslaved children, she was allowed to read, Wheatley demonstrated her prodigious intellect. By the age of 12, she had published her first poem, "On Messrs Hussey and Coffin" in the *Newport Mercury* in 1767. And Selena Hastings, Countess of Huffington and a friend of the Wheatleys, helped Phillis Wheatley to publish her collection *Poems on Various Subjects Religious and Moral* in 1773. Wheatley's publication of a book on religious and moral subjects directly contradicted the prevailing racist logic of the time, which insisted that enslaved people, particularly enslaved women, were morally corrupt, and thus required the controlling framework of slavery. The publication of *Poems* was met with a variety of reactions. Many critics, including Thomas Jefferson, claimed that she could not have written the poems (despite the prefatory "attestation" of 17 men of the Boston elite that she had) and dismissed it as a simple act of imitation. However, Phillis Wheatley toured the American Colonies and Britain with her poems, and it was her acclaim as a poet that eventually won her freedom from slavery on October 18, 1773.

After the death of Mary Wheatley, the daughter of the people who had purchased Phillis Wheatley, Phillis Wheatley married John Peters, a free black grocer. Peters and Wheatley had three children but two of them died during the marriage. Peters left Wheatley, who returned to work as a servant and died at the age of 31 during childbirth in a boarding house and her third child died as well. Wheatley had written a second manuscript of poems during this part of her life, but it has never been found. June Jordan points out the poems of a "free black woman" would not have been marketable in those times and reminds critical readers of her work that what she was able to publish with white support in the 18th century may not have reflected her desires or opinions, but rather the limits of her enslaved situation.

Wheatley wrote poems about the importance of Christianity, elegies for prominent members of Boston Society, a poem in praise of King George when he repealed the Stamp

Phillis Wheatley, born in West Africa and brought to colonial Massachusetts as a slave, became an accomplished poet in Boston and traveled to London to publish her work. (Library of Congress)

Africans are children of God and therefore equally likely to become angelic as their white counterparts.

Despite or due to the many opinions on the significance of Wheatley's poetic work, her publication succeeds in bringing the discussion of the African American women's literary production in America into the 18th century. *See also:* American Revolution; Hammon, Jupiter; Senegambia

Alexis Pauline Gumbs

Bibliography

Caretta, Vincent. *Phillis Wheatley: The Complete Writings.* New York: Penguin Classics, 2001.

Hayden, Robert. *Kaleidoscope: Poems by American Negro Poets.* New York: Harcourt and Brace, 1967.

Hunter, Jane Edna, 1882–1950. *Phillis Wheatley: Life and Works.* Cleveland: National Phillis Wheatley Foundation, 1948.

Johnson, James Weldon. *The Book of American Negro Poetry.* New York: Harcourt and Brace, 1922.

Loggins, Vernon. *The Negro Author.* Port Washington, NY: Kennikat Press, 1964.

Matons, R. Lynn. "Phillis Wheatley—Soul Sister?" *Phylon* 33, no. 3 (1972):222–30.

Act, and poems in support of the freedom of the colonists. In 1776, she wrote a poem "To His Excellency George Washington" in celebration of the American Revolution. R. Lynn Matson points out that in Wheatley's many elegies, she represents death as a journey across water, a metaphor also found in many spirituals developed and sung by enslaved people.

June Jordan points out that in her poem "To the University of Cambridge," Wheatley attributes her writing to an "intrinsic ardor," not to the generosity or tutoring of the Wheatley family, and applauds Wheatley for creating herself as a poet in an incredibly unlikely circumstance. Wheatley's most relevant and remembered poem within African American studies is her poem "On Being Brought from Africa to America," which is thought to deal most explicitly with the situation of slavery from which the poet wrote at the time. Many critics complain that Wheatley depicts her enslavement as a good thing when she writes that mercy was what brought her from a "pagan land," but others celebrate the fact that Wheatley used her tenuous position as prodigy poet to argue against racism. Wheatley states that

Woolman, John

John Woolman (1720–1772) was born October 19, 1720, into a rural Quaker community in Burlington County, West Jersey. Abandoning lucrative business opportunities in favor of a more balanced life, he became an influential itinerant Quaker minister, and was instrumental in that church's adoption of a strong antislavery position. Although abolitionism was not new in Woolman's era, his persistence, genuine commitment to the Quaker doctrine of universal love for both slaves and slaveholders, and persuasive writing is often credited as a driving force behind the Quaker Church's commitment to abolitionism.

John Woolman, son of Samuel Woolman and Elizabeth Burr Woolman, grew up on his father's farm on the Rancocas Creek, six miles south of its juncture with the Delaware River. He attended the local Quaker school. At 21 Woolman went to work for a local merchant in the nearby town of Mount Holly. During his apprenticeship, in the winter of 1742, his employer asked Woolman to draw up a bill of sale for a female slave. Although Woolman completed the task, the uneasiness he felt crystallized his belief that keeping slaves was inconsistent with the teachings of his faith. In 1749, Woolman married Sarah Ellis. The couple had two children, but only their daughter Mary survived infancy.

At the age of 23, John Woolman was recorded as a minister by his local meeting, or Quaker congregation. Although the Quakers had no paid clergy, those people recognized by their peers as ministers were recorded in the minutes and issued a certificate that recognized their gift and facilitated missionary work, which was a priority for Woolman. In 1746, a trip through Maryland, North Carolina, and Virginia increased his commitment to his antislavery ideals. This experience, and another in 1757, led him to write his most notable antislavery treatises. The first, *Some Considerations on the Keeping of Negroes, Part I,* published in 1754, focused primarily on slaveholders rather than slaves, and claimed that the institution constituted a denial of God's commandment to love all people equally. In *Part II,* published in 1762 by Benjamin Franklin's press, Woolman looked more deeply into the harm done to slaves. Additionally, using examples from history and the law, Woolman pointed to flaws in many arguments used to justify slavery and demonstrated that the practice perpetrated a grievous wrong against innocent people. In time, Woolman's thoughtful arguments became important abolitionist texts.

At the 1758 Quaker meeting in Philadelphia, Woolman galvanized those in attendance and helped establish a committee to expand his work of ministering to slaveholding Quakers. Although he made attempts to affect public policy, Woolman worked for change primarily on a personal level, successfully convincing Quaker slaveholders to free their slaves through gentle persuasion and with a message of universal love. Woolman's message did not reach the many slaveholders outside the Quaker community.

Woolman's *Journal* is a classic of American literature, often considered on par with Benjamin Franklin's *Autobiography.* Woolman's spiritual and social theories were admired by Transcendentalists like Ralph Waldo Emerson, influential British intellectuals such as Samuel Taylor Coleridge and Charles Lamb, and later by John Greenleaf Whittier, who produced an edition of the journal in 1871.

In the 20th century, Woolman's views on wealth and poverty inspired muckraking author Theodore Dreiser. Woolman's published work combines Quaker spirituality and mysticism with an interest in social justice dedicated to antipoverty, pacifism, and justice for Native Americans, as well as abolition.

At the heart of Woolman's critique was the belief that God ordered the universe, and provided every person on earth with a living to which they were entitled. Most clearly in his essay titled, "A Plea for the Poor; or, A Word of Remembrance and Caution for the Rich," Woolman argued that greed for wealth or status drove some to neglect their families and spiritual lives in favor of profitable labor, or, more problematically, to exploit the labor of others. The world would retain God's felicitous design if people moderated their desires, pursuing only their true needs. Breaking with many theorists of his time, Woolman traced the cause of society's evils, including slavery, war, and poverty, to greed and concentration of wealth. Throughout his life he did his best to avoid participating in the oppression of others. Woolman avoided products produced by any form of exploitative labor. He wore undyed clothes in consideration of the slave labor used to manufacture dyes. During his travels he paid slaves in silver for any work done on his behalf. Woolman lived according to his ideals to the last. In 1772, he journeyed to England, and although he was not in good health, traveled in steerage in empathy for the sailors who worked on the ship. He died of smallpox in York on October 7, 1772.

See also: Abolition, Slavery; Quakers (Society of Friends)

Jennifer Eckel

Bibliography

Cady, Edwin. *John Woolman: The Mind of a Quaker Saint.* New York: Washington Square Press, 1965.

Heller, Mike, ed. *The Tendering Presence: Essays on John Woolman.* Wallingford, PA: Pendle Hill Publications, 2003.

Moulton, Phillip P., ed. *The Journal and Major Essays of John Woolman.* New York: Oxford University Press, 1971.

Rosenblatt, Paul. *John Woolman.* New York: Twayne Publishers, 1969.

Whitney, Janet. *John Woolman, American Quaker.* Boston: Little, Brown, 1942.

Culture, Identity, and Community: From Slavery to the Present

From the early 17th century to the mid-19th century, more than a half-million Africans were enslaved and brought to the shores of North America to primarily engage in cash crop cultivation. Scholars, activists, and others have written extensively about the implications of the process by which human beings were intentionally taken from their homes, separated from family and friends, raped and tortured, and forced into a permanent and servile status. One of the most remarkable and tragic eras in human history, the Atlantic Slave trade—despite its destructive and dislocating tendencies—did not have the power to completely obliterate the lives of enslaved Africans. Instead the resiliency of their collective spirit allowed them to continue or create new cultures, identities, and communities in the Western Hemisphere. Indeed, this story is far from a narrative of destruction, defeat, and death; it is ultimately a chronicle of human triumph against seemingly impossible odds.

Feeding the growing labor demands of rice, sugar, tobacco, and cotton plantations during the era of slavery, enslaved Africans and their Creole or American-born descendants forged distinctive communities out of a complex set of Atlantic African cultural, political, and social pasts. In many instances, they even adopted or assumed group identities in the Western Hemisphere such as "Coromantee," "Amina," "Eboe," "Chamba," "Canga," or "Lucumí," which harkened back to their African past. Although these enslaved communities were also shaped by European and Native American values—as well as the socially limiting institution of plantation slavery—the foundations of these cultures, identities, and communities were and continue to be solidly African. The result of this mixture of Atlantic African social and cultural mores shaped the creation of such uniquely African American forms and traditions as jazz, blues, gospel, and rap music; John Henry, High John the Conqueror, and Brer Rabbit folk tales; the Charleston, the ring shout, and break dancing; Gullah, Geechee, and other Africanized variants of English; and even the preparation and use of certain foods (e.g., collard greens, rice, black-eyed peas, okra, and gumbo). Clearly then, African cultural practices not only influenced African American culture, but also were a shaping feature of American culture.

The notion that enslaved Africans and their descendants successfully managed to maintain active cultural links to their African past has been debated for decades. Scholars, from a wide range of disciplines, have contributed their perspectives on multiple sides of this issue. As a result of such attention, four schools of thought have emerged during the course of the 20th and 21st centuries—the Annihilationist, the Africanist, the Creolization, and the Diasporic schools. Sociologist Robert E. Park, the father of the Annihilationist school, wrote in 1919 that American slavery destroyed all vestiges of African culture and that nothing in the culture of African Americans living in the U.S. South was from their African backgrounds. This approach was later championed by E. Franklin Frazier—a former student of Park and a fellow sociologist. As one of the first black scholars to contribute to this debate, Frazier contended in the 1930s that slavery obliterated the black family and that this facilitated the Americanization of slaves and the utter annihilation of African culture in the United States. Given the context in which his works were written, Frazier was seeking to de-emphasize any African elements in African American culture in order to promote such goals as integration, social equality, and voting rights. If it could be proven that African American culture was influenced by the African past, this would potentially support the claims of white supremacists, who argued that African Americans were inherently different or inferior and should be separated from whites as a result.

More recently, historian Jon Butler has made a contribution to the Annihilationist school in his 1990 work titled *Awash in a Sea of Faith: Christianizing the American People.* In a chapter titled "The African Spiritual Holocaust," Butler contends that African religious systems were completely destroyed in North America and that this facilitated the conversion of enslaved Africans to Christianity. Butler does allow for certain African cultural continuities, particularly in burial practices and conjuration. However, his focus is on the destruction of African religious systems as opposed to disjointed ritual acts and beliefs. Butler's argument, in part, rests on the fact that very few contemporary whites wrote about the practice of African religion among slaves. This invisibility of the practice of slave religion may have been a result of purposeful acts on the part of the enslaved community, which had good reason to prevent whites from knowing the inner workings of their spiritual worldview. Butler does not account for this possibility, and his interpretation has added additional fuel to an already heated debate.

The pioneering efforts of anthropologist Melville J. Herskovits effectively addressed the claims of the Annihilationist school. In the 1940s, Herskovits published *The Myth of the Negro Past,* which focused attention on the topic of African cultural transmissions and continuities in the Americas. He was among the first in the Africanist school, and his work sought to counter a number of myths about Africa and the Africans residing throughout the Western Hemisphere, in an attempt to undermine racial prejudice in the United States. By demonstrating tangible cultural links between Africa and diasporic communities,

Herskovits took full aim at the myth that African Americans essentially have no history. In addition, he addressed the misconception that Africans were brought to America from diverse cultures and were distributed in a manner that destroyed their cultures. Another myth Herskovits sought to dispel was the notion that African cultures were so savage that European customs were actively preferred by enslaved Africans. The lasting importance of his research is in highlighting numerous examples of Africanisms—or African cultural retentions—in both the secular and sacred dimensions of African American culture. Herskovits's argument was not that African Americans were Africans culturally, but that they maintained key aspects of their African heritage. This research helped put to rest various racist myths and misperceptions while forwarding the notion that African American culture was something worthy of serious scholarly consideration.

The middle ground between the Annihilationist and the Africanist schools, what has been referred to as the Creolization school, is epitomized in the work of anthropologists Sidney Mintz and Richard Price. When Mintz and Price published *The Birth of African-American Culture,* it was intended to critique Herskovits's earlier findings regarding the presence of Africanisms in African American culture. They argued that enslaved Africans shipped to the Americas developed and created cultures and societies that could not be characterized simply as "African." Essentially, the nature of the slave trade and enslavement made the direct continuity of African culture impossible. Although African culture may have been crucial in the creation of African American culture, Mintz and Price contend that it was neither central nor independent of European influences or new cultural developments in the Americas.

Mintz and Price opposed several aspects of Herskovits's interpretations, from his claim of West African cultural homogeneity to his argument that specific African cultural groupings formed in the Americas. Mintz and Price contend that West African culture was not monolithic and that purposeful ethnic "randomization" actively was engaged in by slave traders, ship captains, and plantation owners in the Americas. Many of their conclusions are based on the premise that Atlantic Africa had vastly numerous and diverse cultures. Although there is little doubt that cultural differences existed in Atlantic Africa, what has been contested by a number of scholars is the degree of this diversity. On one end of the debate, the works of Herskovits and Joseph

Holloway support ideas of cultural homogeneity. Holloway asserts that because most North American slaves originated from West-Central Africa, the idea of a monolithic Bantu cultural heritage and its links to the birth of African American cultures would be quite applicable. Although there are clearly flaws in this sort of approach, the idea of a monolithic Bantu culture or its significant contribution to African American culture finds support in the works of a number of scholars. On the other end of the spectrum, Mintz and Price likely exaggerate the amount of diversity using African languages as a tool of measurement. The truth lies between the two extremes, and ample evidence for this conclusion can be found in recent scholarship.

The fourth school, known as the Diasporic approach, combines the best elements of the Africanist and Creolization schools. Championed principally by Atlantic African historians, this school traces cultural continuities and discontinuities by tracing specific groups in their journeys across the Atlantic through the establishment of African American communities. By starting the historical analysis in Africa, these scholars have attempted to track coherent groups of people in order to see the many ways that they either maintained their cultural identities or adopted new ones. This has been the focus, for example, of the scholars working on the Nigerian Hinterland Project and has been part of the interpretive approaches of a number of recent historians, including John Thornton, Michael Gomez, and Douglas Chambers among many others.

More than anything else, the Diasporic school focuses specific attention on Atlantic African history as a means of correcting many of the interpretive mistakes made by advocates of the Africanist and Creolization schools. For example, John Thornton in *Africa and Africans in the Making of the Atlantic World* demonstrates that researchers have tended to overestimate the amount of cultural diversity in Atlantic Africa because they ascribe ethnic identities to every distinct language and regional dialectic. The problem is that Atlantic Africans were multilingual, and certain languages and regional dialects were so related that they could be mutually understood. Thornton further concludes that Atlantic Africa was not nearly as diverse as other scholars have assumed and that, in fact, the region can be divided into just three distinct cultural zones and seven subzones: Upper Guinea, which included the Mande language family and two variants of the West Atlantic language family; Lower Guinea, which included two variants of the Kwa language family; and the Angola zone, which included two variants of the western Bantu language family. Because Atlantic Africans were multilingual and were not as culturally diverse as previously claimed, then it is entirely possible that the cultures, identities, and communities they forged in the Americas had a great deal of structure and order.

Another issue of importance in Thornton's assessment is the claim that European traders, slave ship captains, and plantation owners engaged in active and conscious efforts to ethnically randomize enslaved Africans. If practiced, this measure could effectively undermine the ability of enslaved Africans to foment rebellion on slave ships or plantations in the Americas because they would not have an effective means of communication. It would also hinder the creation of a more unified culture and identity among enslaved Africans. According to Thornton, however, cultural randomization was not a significant aspect of the slave trade. In sociological terminology, he contends that the enslaved Africans on a typical slave ship were groups as opposed to crowds. In other words, they had some significant links to each other before they were brought onboard ships and were not just randomly and haphazardly selected. This, in addition to other points raised by Thornton, has obvious implications for the maintenance of particular Atlantic African cultural practices and for the development of African American identity.

Michael Gomez, in *Exchanging Our Country Marks,* expands on Thornton's conclusions by showing that significant African cultural enclaves developed in the Americas as a result of a number of factors. One of these factors, he argues, was the lack of cultural diversity in Atlantic Africa. Whereas Thornton contends that Atlantic Africa could be divided into three culturally distinct zones, Gomez demonstrates that there were six cultural zones in this region: Senegambia, Sierra Leone, the Gold Coast, the Bight of Benin, the Bight of Biafra, and West-Central Africa. In addition, Africans from certain regions shared cultural affinities that facilitated the process of hybridization or mixing between African groups. In discussing the ways in which Africans borrowed from each other, Gomez, like others in the Diasporic school, can demonstrate and even explain cultural discontinuities. Unlike scholars in the Creolization school, who mainly focus on the African adoption of European culture, advocates of the Diasporic approach are much more interested in explaining how African ethnic groups borrowed from each other.

While still clinging to their ethnic identities, enslaved Africans shaped a new set of cultures in the Americas. As shown by advocates of the Diasporic school, these new cultures were not simply a combination of European and African cultures. Instead, Gomez and others in this school make convincing claims that the first step toward the birth of an African American culture was intra-African cultural mixing. In other words, in the process of becoming African American, Igbos, Mandes, Akans, Angolans, and others borrowed from each other and, over time, became one people. In this way, scholars in the Diasporic school can demonstrate a significant amount of cultural discontinuity. Because various enslaved African groups borrowed from each other's cultures, then clearly these cultures changed over time and represent a discontinuity and disconnection with the African past. However, the Diasporic school also explains cultural continuity and connection, but in ways slightly different from advocates of the Africanist school.

For example, one significant trend among scholars in the Diasporic school has been to move away from generalizations about "African" cultural continuities, to emphasizing instead the contributions that specific African ethnic groups (e.g., Igbo, Yoruba, Fon, Mande, Akan) made to development of African American culture.

Exported from the factories and slave castles along the Atlantic coast of Africa, enslaved Africans boarded ships and suffered through the so-called Middle Passage—one of the most horrifying experiences in human history. In the midst of this tragic story, historian Sterling Stuckey contends that the slave ships crossing the Middle Passage were melting pots that forged a single people out of numerous African ethnicities. Even if ethnic randomization occurred, the horrors of the Middle Passage and enslavement helped forge a cultural, social, and political unity among enslaved Africans. This was an ongoing process, beginning with the enslavement experience in Atlantic Africa and continuing in certain regions of the Americas well into the 19th century. Both Gomez and Douglas Chambers demonstrate that, throughout the Americas, enslaved Africans created ethnic enclave communities and saw themselves as members of African-derived named groups. They readily identified themselves as members of separate "nations" initially until a more unified identity was created as a result of the circumstances and conditions of enslavement.

This initial sense of national identity was a direct result of import patterns in the Atlantic slave trade. As Daniel Littlefield notes, European planters developed a number of ethnic preferences based on perceptions of traits that certain enslaved African groups supposedly had. Thus, Europeans created shifting and alternating hierarchies of ethnic and regional preferences that were employed and gave some shape to import patterns in locales throughout the Americas. In colonies such as Jamaica, Barbados, and South Carolina, Gold Coast Akan-speakers were coveted by some planters for their alleged propensity for loyalty and hard work; in other colonies, or even among other planters in colonies that seemingly coveted Gold Coast Africans, these slaves were considered unruly and rebellious. Igbos and others from Calabar or the Bight of Biafra were reviled because of an alleged propensity for suicide. Angolans were supposedly paradoxically prone to docility and flight.

European preferences for certain African ethnic groups were likely due to a range of factors—the cost of importing enslaved Africans from certain regions; limited access to certain slave markets on the Atlantic African coast; or the demand for Africans from regions with expertise in the cultivation of certain crops and other skills. Certainly among slave traders and plantation owners, there was no clear consensus on the behavioral characteristics of any African group. This reflects what seems obvious from the vantage point of hindsight; the reason African groups do not fit into generalized behavioral categories is that, like the rest of humanity, Africans can and will display a broad spectrum of behavior. Whether real or imagined, these perceptions of African behavioral characteristics did contribute to the formation of ethnic enclave communities in North America as well as elsewhere.

Harvard University's Du Bois Institute slave trade database bears out this conclusion. This important and exhaustive project provides an accurate picture of the Atlantic slave trade and includes information for roughly 60 percent of all slave-trading voyages. The Du Bois database demonstrates that of the 101,925 enslaved Africans from identifiable locations sent to Virginia, 45 percent came from the Bight of Biafra. In South Carolina, enslaved Africans from the Bight of Biafra accounted for just 10 percent of identifiable imports; in the United States as a whole, Bight of Biafra exports were 19 percent of the 317,748 enslaved Africans recorded in the Du Bois database. So we can discuss a Bight of Biafra or Igbo enclave in Virginia as a circumstance unique in North America. Not only does this database corroborate many of the findings of Stuckey, Gomez, Margaret Washington, Douglas Chambers, and others, but it also opens new possibilities in the study of the formation of African American culture.

Although the nature of African ethnic enclaves varied over time, it is now possible to pinpoint the nature of these concentrations and track specific cultural influences. Between 1701 and 1800, 26 percent of enslaved Africans from identifiable regions and embarking on ships to the Carolinas came from West-Central Africa. The 1739 Stono Revolt, initiated principally by enslaved Angolans from West-Central Africa, forced the proprietors and slave owners of South Carolina to reduce their reliance on Africans from this region. Also, because of the emphasis on rice cultivation in the South Carolina Lowcountry and sea islands, Africans from rice-producing regions of Upper Guinea—Senegambia (25 percent) and Sierra Leone (9 percent)—became important demographic factors and largely replaced the earlier West-Central African import stream. These three cultural contingents played active roles in the formation Gullah and Geechee culture. Elements of the West-Central African, Senegambian, and Biafran (11 percent) contingents of South Carolina's slave population apparently created an alliance in 1822, under the leadership of Denmark Vesey, in an attempt to foment a rebellion. Although the details of this conspiracy are currently in dispute, it is clear that separate bands of Gullahs, Igbos, Mande-speakers, French-speaking Saint-Dominguans, and American-born slaves had formed and found between them areas of commonality. In some ways, this could have been an early expression of Pan-Africanism.

Many dance forms in the United States were influenced by West-Central Africans, particularly in regions in which they were heavily concentrated. The Charleston—formerly known as the Juba—was a dance that in form and timing had analogues in the martial dance styles of the Kongo Kingdom. Charleston, South Carolina, the final destination of thousands of West-Central Africans, was so associated with this dance that the Juba became known as the "Charleston" by the early 20th century. Even the word "Juba" has a West-Central African origin, meaning "to beat time in a rhythmic pattern." In a typical performance, older black men would rhythmically "pat juba" by slapping their hands on their thighs—in imitation of the drum—while others would perform the dance. Both the patters and the dancers would sing as an integral part of the Juba dance.

By combining "drumming," singing, and elaborate and competitive dances, the Juba/Charleston resembled West-Central African military dances and derivative martial arts. The Juba/Charleston was also characteristic of the various dance styles—inspired by West-Central African cultural elements—performed at the aptly named "Congo Square" in New Orleans during the early 19th century. Interestingly, many of the Congolese from West-Central Africa arriving in Louisiana after 1800 were transported there from South Carolina, which demonstrates the remarkable amount of interconnection in the African Diaspora. In addition to the Juba/Charleston, West-Central Africans were important in the development of baton-twirling, jazz music, and break dancing—an art likely derived from a West-Central African–inspired Brazil martial dance known as *capoeira*.

Between 1701 and 1800, 45 percent of Africans entering Virginia from identifiable regions were embarked on ships leaving ports in the Bight of Biafra. Thus, Virginia imported a disproportionately large number of Igbo-speakers and others from Calabar and surrounding regions. As Lorena Walsh, James Sidbury, and Douglas Chambers contend, this emphasis on Igbo imports played a significant factor in the rise of Afro-Virginian culture. One cultural implication of the presence of so many Igbo-speakers was the proliferation of Igbo terms and concepts—*okra, buckra, obia*—or discrete Igbo cultural practices (e.g., the Jonkonu celebration, funerary customs, and spiritual beliefs) in Jamaica, Virginia, and other regions of the Anglophone Americas that imported significant numbers of Africans from the Bight of Biafra. Another implication, discussed by Sidbury, was the possibility that Gabriel Prosser—leader of a failed Richmond slave revolt in 1800—was accorded a great deal of respect and veneration because of his blacksmithing skills and the spiritual powers associated with this trade among the peoples living near the Niger River delta and Senegambia. In fact, three separate blacksmiths were claimed to have been part of the leadership core of this attempt to capture and raze the capital of Virginia.

Information regarding imports into areas such as North Carolina, Georgia, Maryland, the Middle Colonies (with the exception of New York), and the New England colonies is scanty at best, and scholars can detail the slave trade in these regions only through inference and suggestive evidence. As the principal port of entry for enslaved Africans,

Charleston satisfied most of the demand for forced labor in North Carolina and Georgia. The result of this commercial connection meant that both colonies/states likely had demographic patterns and ethnic enclaves similar to those found in South Carolina. Maryland imported a large number of Africans from Senegambia (49%) and did not mirror the reliance on imports from the Bight of Biafra found in its Chesapeake neighbor, Virginia. For the remainder of the slaveholding regions of North America, Gomez contends that Virginia, Maryland, South Carolina, and Georgia supplied enslaved Africans to places such as Kentucky, Mississippi, Alabama, and Tennessee.

Although there has been a major problem in tracking African imports into certain regions, the Du Bois Institute database and other sources reveal much about imports in colonial New York and Louisiana. The Dutch colony of New Netherland—later to become New York—witnessed two different waves of African immigrants. The first, lasting for the initial few decades of Dutch rule, was dominated by the importation of West-Central Africans. The second wave focused on Africans from the Gold Coast. Combined, both of these contingents may have contributed to such cultural formations as the Pinkster festivals, the "Congo" dances in Albany, and specific funerary practices associated with the African Burial Ground in New York City (e.g., carved symbols on coffins, the use of burial shrouds, and internment with earthenware, beads, and other objects). A definite Gold Coast presence is noted in both the 1712 New York City revolt and the alleged conspiracy of 1741; in both instances, enslaved Africans with Akan names predominated among the leadership core.

Though Louisiana shifted from French to Spanish and finally to American control after 1803, the demographics of the slave trade are relatively easy to trace. The principal import groups into Louisiana were Africans from Senegambia, the Bight of Benin, and West-Central Africa. As the most numerically significant African group in Louisiana, the Congolese and other West-Central Africans contributed to expressive culture (e.g., dance contests in New Orleans' Congo Square and baton twirling), cuisine (e.g., gumbo and jambalaya), and even body gestures (e.g., standing with arms akimbo) in Louisiana. The significant African contingent from the Bight of Benin, as well as enslaved Santo Dominguans arriving in New Orleans in the wake of the 1791 revolution, brought with them spiritual beliefs that became Voodoo and Hoodoo in Louisiana. The Voodoo/ Hoodoo complex is a syncretic blend of Fon, Yoruba, and West-Central African metaphysical and religious concepts, and in Louisiana, it likely incorporated Catholic icons and elements from West-Central African and Senegambian belief systems.

During her reign as "Voodoo queen" in New Orleans from 1830 to 1869, Marie Laveau routinely evoked the names of Fon and Yoruba deities—Legba and Damballa—in her ritual ceremonies. In addition, Gwendolyn Midlo Hall shows that spiritual beliefs, the knowledge of "herblore," the production of poisons and curatives, and the creation of charms in Louisiana were brought to the region with the earliest slave imports. The Bambara from Senegambia played an important role in these areas. Although the term "Bambara" has a number of meanings and ethnic connotations, in the context of Louisiana, it referred specifically to non-Muslim Africans from Senegambia who were captured in jihads and sold to European merchants. However defined, this group significantly influenced the nature of slave culture in Louisiana. For example, *zinzin*—the word for an amulet of power in Louisiana Creole—has the same meaning and name in Bambara. *Gris-gris* and *wanga* were other Bambara or Mande words for charms referred to in colonial and antebellum Louisiana. Even the Arabic-derived Mande word for spiritual advisor or teacher—*marabout*—appears in the records of colonial Louisiana.

Based on the reality of ethnic enclaves and the information regarding the pattern and structure of the Atlantic slave trade revealed by the Du Bois Institute database, we can conclude that ethnic mixing was never achieved by European shippers and slaveholders. The fact is that randomization was not feasible on either side of the Atlantic, and patterns of ethnic concentration that emerged in the Caribbean and South America also emerged in North American colonies/states. In spite of this mounting evidence, however, a number of scholars remain skeptical about the close cultural connections between Africa and the Americas. Among the many critics of the notion of cultural continuities is Philip D. Morgan. In seeming agreement with the interpretations of Sidney Mintz and Richard Price, he forwards the notion of ethnic randomization on both sides of the Atlantic, which, in turn, served as a facilitating factor for creolization and acculturation. Using the preliminary results of the Du Bois Institute database, Morgan claims that unlike Brazil and certain portions of the Caribbean, North America received a much more heterogeneous

African population than previously assumed. The difference between Morgan's conclusion and those forwarded by Gomez, Chambers, and others might be due to the geographic scale on which they focus. By looking at the slave trade on a continental scale (e.g., all of North America), Morgan sees a very mixed group of African imports; however, by focusing on smaller regional units, such as states or colonies, other scholars have seen much more pattern to the slave trade and much less ethnic randomization.

These regional patterns and concentrations meant that full-fledged language communities of specific African ethnic groups probably emerged throughout North America. These language communities contributed to the rise of Africanized regional dialects in the United States and even the infusion of a number of African words. The Gullah and Geechee of the South Carolina and Georgia coastline are the most studied example of this phenomenon. As anthropologist Sheila Walker and ethnolinguist David Dalby illustrate, African American speech—even in the late 20th century—continues to bear the marks of this level of linguistic connection to Africa. Such common words and expressions as "hip" (as something "in" or "cool"), "cat" (as a hip or cool person), "dig" (as in "do you understand?"), "jive," "wow," "jazz," "OK," and "tote" have roots among the Wolof, the Bantu, and the Gola of Atlantic Africa. Likewise, even some common grammatical constructions, such as double negatives or the expression "he been gone," have strong analogues in the languages of Atlantic African peoples.

It was, perhaps, from these early African language communities that other African-derived forms and practices emerged. For example, the African American notion of eating black-eyed peas for luck on New Year's Eve has direct analogues throughout the African Diaspora, including similar beliefs and practices in the Danish Virgin Islands, Senegal, Brazil, and Martinique. Spirit possession, as an intrinsic element of African diasporic ritual practice, can be found in any number of black religions and religious institutions, including African American Christianity (in the guise of "catching the ghost"), Haitian Vodun, Cuban Santeria, Brazilian Candomblé, and a large number of Atlantic African systems. In addition to these ritual beliefs, African Americans continue to employ other African-derived practices and expressive modes, including musical improvisation (e.g., rap freestyles and jazz music), call and response, blue notes, and vocal instrumentation (e.g., the beat box

and the jazz scat). Combined, these examples point to a rich and ever-evolving culture with tangible and continuing links to Africa and its Diaspora.

Walter C. Rucker

Bibliography

Blassingame, John. *The Slave Community: Plantation Life in the Antebellum South.* New York: Oxford University Press, 1972.

Butler, Jon. *Awash in a Sea of Faith: Christianizing the American People.* Cambridge, MA: Harvard University Press, 1990.

Chambers, Douglass. "Ethnicity in the Diaspora: The Slave-Trade and the Creation of African 'Nations' in the Americas." *Slavery & Abolition* 22 (2001):25–39.

Chambers, Douglass. *Murder at Montpelier: Igbo Africans in Virginia.* Jackson: University Press of Mississippi, 2005.

Creel, Margaret Washington. *"A Peculiar People": Slave Religion and Community-Culture among the Gullahs.* New York: New York University Press, 1988.

Dalby, David. "The African Element in Black American English," in Thomas Kochman, ed., *Rappin' and Stylin' Out,* 170–86. Urbana: University of Illinois Press, 1972.

Eltis, David, Behrendt, Stephen, Richardson, David, and Klein, Herbert, eds. *The Trans-Atlantic Slave Trade: A Database on CD-ROM.* Cambridge, UK: Cambridge University Press, 1999.

Frazier, E. Franklin. *The Negro Family in the United States.* Chicago: University of Chicago Press, 1939.

Gomez, Michael. *Exchanging Our Country Marks: The Transformation of African Identities in the Colonial and Antebellum South.* Chapel Hill: University of North Carolina Press, 1998.

Hall, Gwendolyn Midlo. *Africans in Colonial Louisiana: The Development of Afro-Creole Culture in the Eighteenth Century.* Baton Rouge: Louisiana State University Press, 1992.

Herskovits, Melville. *The Myth of the Negro Past.* Boston: Beacon Press, 1941.

Heywood, Linda. M., ed. *Central Africans and Cultural Transformations in the American Diaspora.* Cambridge, UK: Cambridge University Press, 2002.

Holloway, Joseph, ed. *Africanisms in American Culture.* Bloomington: Indiana University Press, 1991.

Jones, LeRoi. *Blues People: The Negro Experience in White America and the Music That Developed from It.* New York: William Morrow, 1963.

Levine, Lawrence. *Black Culture and Black Consciousness: Afro-American Folk Thought from Slavery to Freedom.* New York: Oxford University Press, 1977.

Littlefield, Daniel. *Rice and Slaves: Ethnicity and the Slave Trade in Colonial South Carolina.* Baton Rouge: Louisiana State University, 1981.

Mintz, Sidney, and Richard Price. *The Birth of African-American Culture: An Anthropological Perspective.* Boston: Beacon Press, 1976.

Morgan, Philip. *Slave Counterpoint: Black Culture in the Eighteenth-Century Chesapeake & Low Country.* Chapel Hill: University of North Carolina Press, 1998.

Mullin, Michael. *Africa in America: Slave Acculturation and Resistance in the American South and the British Caribbean, 1736–1831.* Chicago: University of Illinois Press, 1994.

Park, Robert, E. "Racial Assimilation in Secondary Groups with Particular Reference to Negro." *American Journal of Sociology* 19 (1914):606–23.

Rucker, Walter. *The River Flows On: Black Resistance, Culture, and Identity Formation in Early America.* Baton Rouge: Louisiana State University Press, 2005.

Sidbury, James. *Ploughshares into Swords: Race, Rebellion, and Identity in Gabriel's Virginia, 1730–1810.* New York: Cambridge University Press, 1997.

Sobel, Mechal. *The World They Made Together: Black and White Values in Eighteenth-Century Virginia.* Princeton, NJ: Princeton University Press, 1987.

Stuckey, Sterling. *Slave Culture: Nationalist Theory & the Foundation of Black America.* New York: Oxford University Press, 1987.

Thompson, Robert Farris. *Flash of the Spirit.* New York: Vintage Books, 1983.

Thornton, John. *Africa and Africans in the Making of the Atlantic World, 1400–1680.* New York: Cambridge University Press, 1992.

Walker, Sheila, ed. *African Roots/American Cultures: Africa in the Creation of the Americas.* New York: Rowman & Littlefield Publishers, 2001.

Walsh, Lorena S. *From Calabar to Carter's Grove: The History of a Virginia Slave Community.* Charlottesville: University of Virginia Press, 1997.

Watson, R. L. "American Scholars and the Continuity of African Culture in the United States." *The Journal of Negro History* 63 (1978):375–86.

Amalgamation

"Amalgamation" was the first term used to describe interracial sexual contact. Early colonists believed that sexual relations between people of different races was disgraceful behavior that shamed not only the English man or woman but also the Christian Church. This was especially true with respect to white–black sexual unions, which would obscure cultural differences and undermine ideas of racial superiority.

To be sure, laws enacted to prohibit amalgamation were less concerned about white male offenses against black women than they were about black men cohabitating with white women. Although all acts of illicit sexual behavior out of wedlock were severely punished before 1662, the Virginia legislature made heritable bondage certain and illicit sexual behavior race-based when they ruled that the child of a black woman would always follow the status of its mother. Because mixed-race people became black in the colonial era, economic advantage was given to the master class, enabling the sexual promiscuity of white males and the sexual oppression of black women while normalizing the ownership of black women's reproductive labor.

In 1691, Virginia banned interracial sexual contact of any kind, yet interracial sex between blacks and whites and blacks and Native Americans was commonplace in the 17th and 18th centuries. The Native American population had drastically declined by the time Africans were imported in any significant number, and over time interracial relationships with them would decline also. There is extensive evidence, however, of mixed-race children of Native American and African descent in the 18th century, with many of the early plantation estates established near or on well-worked Indian lands. And much to the concern of the European community, African Americans and Native Americans did form alliances across racial boundaries, given that many Native Americans were also enslaved. During and after the 18th century, laws concerning the enslavement of Native Americans changed several times. Many states adopted laws forbidding the enslavement of Native Americans, which led many African Americans with Native American forbearers to file freedom suits in court in the hopes of achieving their liberation.

After the American Revolution, racial prejudice against blacks began to harden. The universal rejection of black emancipation by Thomas Jefferson, for example, was sustained by the belief that if blacks were freed, an unacceptable blurring of racial definitions would occur in a society of superior and inferior people. In 1787, Jefferson wrote in his *Notes on the State of Virginia* that these differences were a complete obstacle to the black slave's emancipation unless they were "removed beyond the reach of mixture" so as not to pollute the purity of the Anglo-Saxon origins of the American people. Additionally, Americans in the North and the South believed that if blacks were emancipated, a race war would occur that would lead to the extermination of the inferior race.

Proslavery advocates used fears of racial mixing to justify keeping slaves in bondage. By the 1830s they used the word "amalgamation" extensively against abolitionists, calling them "amalgamationists"; they claimed that abolitionists encouraged the mixing of the races by promoting social equality and freedom for the enslaved. They used print culture extensively, delineating extreme caricatures of African American physical features and dress to influence white rejection of abolitionism and to heighten anti-black sentiment in the North and the South.

American fascination with aggressive Anglo-Saxonism and the racial nationalism that the Revolutionary generation transmitted to future generations would lead to the negrophobia and intensive racial theories that emerged in the 19th century. The rise of scientific racialism in Europe in the 1830s spread to the United States by the 1840s and 1850s. American race scientists such as Samuel George Morton, Josiah Mott, and Louis Agassiz produced studies that were concerned with proving that apparent differences in people were biological and that African Americans were actually a different species. The quasi-scientific assessments in these publications would play a large part in the growing belief over the 19th century that differences in color meant black intellectual and physical inferiority and that these differences were fixed in nature. Thus, by the Civil War, racial purity became a moral imperative because amalgamation would ultimately lead to the extinction of the white race. Egypt and Carthage were cited as examples of how mongrelization had ruined past great civilizations.

David Goodman Croly coined the word "miscegenation" in 1863 to describe the intermarrying of blacks and whites in a pamphlet he anonymously wrote titled *Miscegenation: The Theory of the Blending of the Races, Applied to the American White Man and Negro* to exacerbate the already existing racial fears of white Americans and to hopefully derail Abraham Lincoln's second run for presidency.
See also: Acculturation; Miscegenation

Kay Wright Lewis

Bibliography
Berlin, Ira. *Many Thousands Gone: The First Two Centuries of Slavery in North America.* Cambridge, MA: Harvard University Press, 1998.
Burns, Kathryn. *Colonial Habits: Convents and the Spiritual Economy of Cuzco, Peru.* Durham, NC: Duke University Press, 1999.
Higginbotham, A. Leon, Jr. *In the Matter of Color: Race and the American Legal Process, the Colonial Period.* New York: Oxford University Press, 1978.
Horowitz, Helen Lefkowitz. *Rereading Sex: Battles over Sexual Knowledge and Suppression in Nineteenth-Century America.* New York: Random, 2002.
Horsman, Reginald. *Race and Manifest Destiny: The Origins of American Racial Anglo-Saxonism.* Cambridge, MA: Harvard University Press, 1981.
Jordon, Winthrop. *White over Black: American Attitudes toward the Negro, 1550–1812.* Chapel Hill: University of North Carolina Press, 1968.
Morgan, Jennifer L. *Laboring Women: Gender and Reproduction in New World Slavery.* Philadelphia: University of Pennsylvania Press, 2004.

Anansi the Spider

Anansi the Spider is a folk hero, originating among the Ashanti people of West Africa. Enslaved Africans brought Anansi the Spider stories to the plantations in the Caribbean and the Americas and narrated the Anansi tales as a reminder of their African heritage. A trickster with human qualities, Anansi tries to outwit his rivals, sometimes winning and other times not. Anansi is usually a likable character who gets into troubled or funny situations. Some tales depict Anansi as a bad character. Either way, the Anansi tales provide the listening audience with an important moral, or life lesson, at the end of each story.

Anansi's tales vary by region, including through variations in the spider's name (such as Ananse and Nanci) or through the spider being replaced by a rabbit or another animal figure in a local tale. A popular children's tale in North America is Gerald McDermott's *Anansi the Spider: A Tale from the Ashanti*, first published in 1972. A lovable spider with whom children can sympathize, Anansi leaves home for a journey but gets into trouble. Anansi's sons quickly mobilize to save their father. Sky God decides the Sun should remain in the Sky and not be given to Anansi as a reward for one of his sons. The telling of this tale allows children to learn about the Ashanti folk hero, West African colors and designs, and the Ashanti language rhythms.
See also: Africanisms; Black Folk Culture; Gold Coast

Margaret Prentice Hecker

Bibliography
Arkhurst, Joyce Cooper. *The Adventures of Spider: West African Folktales.* Boston: Little, Brown, 1964.
Bowen, Dorothy. "Spiders in African Children's Stories." *School Library Media Activities Monthly* 20, no. 10 (June 2004):39–40.

Lefever, Harry G. "Unraveling the Web of Anansi the Spider: The Trickster in the West African Diaspora." *Journal of Caribbean Studies* 9, no. 3 (Winter 1993/Spring 1994):247–65.

McDermott, Gerald. *Anansi the Spider: A Tale from the Ashanti.* New York: Henry Holt, 1986.

Ancestral Spirits

The belief in ancestors, or the "living dead," is deeply rooted in many African religions and spiritual philosophies. In most cases, the central belief is that death is not final, but merely a transformation from one world to another. Although the concept is often misunderstood by academics and those in various religious communities, the omnipresence of the ancestor cannot be disputed among those who believe.

Whether an African is an Akan, a Yoruba, a Wolof, or a member of some other ethnic group, the ancestors, although deceased, are linked to their living descendants and communicate consistently with the living to guide and instruct them throughout their lives. Furthermore, the ancestors, by virtue of their status in the spiritual world, guide the living with a certain moral authority. When people are obedient and respectful of the ancestors, they are rewarded. In contrast, when the ancestors are forgotten or treated with disdain, the living are punished. This principle reflects the fundamental belief that to forget the ancestors is to disregard self; an ancestor is merely an extension of self because the living are descendants of the ancestors.

Respect for the ancestors can be expressed in admiration for tradition; consequently, the living celebrate the memories of their ancestors through rituals including offerings of food and drinks and prayers. It is a rule within most African religious systems that not every ancestor is revered; instead, only those ancestors who lived an exemplary life are celebrated.

The Akan refer to the ancestors as *nsamanfo,* whereas the Yoruba people annually celebrate *Egungun* (the spirit of the ancestors materialized) in a festival usually marking the beginning of the new yam season. The Yoruba believed that the ancestors who farmed the land for many years should share in the fruits of the harvest.

When the enslaved Africans were brought to the Americas, they brought their culture with them, which manifested in several different religions: for example, Santeria in Cuba and Puerto Rico, Vodoun in Haiti, Candomble in Brazil, and Voodoo in New Orleans and other parts of Louisiana. In most instances, Christian slave owners demonized African religious beliefs; therefore, the enslaved had to disguise their practices, and that included their connection with their ancestors. Quickly, the enslaved Africans learned to adapt their African religious rituals. Many of the enslaved believed that upon death they would return to Africa or that when the ancestors were properly remembered, they would return as children newly born into the family.

During the Black Power movement in the United States, there was a resurgence of African cultural practices, and many African Americans began to practice African religions. One such example would be the Oyotunji African Village in Sheldon, South Carolina, which was founded in 1970 by Oba Efuntola Oseijeman Adelabu Adefunmi I. The village is dedicated to preserving Yoruba culture and religion, and special celebrations in memory of the ancestors are held in the village annually.

Even today, some European and American scholars believe that practitioners of African religion do not relate to a Supreme Being; furthermore, these academicians relegate all African religion to mere ancestor worship, failing to realize that the ancestors—being closest to one's family—serve as intermediaries to the Supreme Being.

See also: Africanisms; Black Folk Culture; Slave Religion; Transmigration

Nancy J. Dawson

Bibliography

Awolalu, Omosade. *Yoruba Beliefs and Sacrificial Rites.* London: Longman, 1979.

Gyekye, Kwame. *African Cultural Values: An Introduction.* Accra, Ghana: Sankofa Press, 1998.

Mbiti, John S. *African Religions and Philosophy.* 2nd ed. Heinemann: Oxford, 1999.

Raboteau, Albert J. *Slave Religion: The Invisible Institution in the Antebellum South.* New York: Oxford University Press.

Anderson, Marian

Marian Anderson (1897–1993), internationally acclaimed operatic contralto, was born in the "Negro Quarter" of South Philadelphia and was recognized at an early age for her musical talents. By the age of six she was singing at her family church—the Union Baptist Church on Fitzwater and Martin

Streets—and her earliest musical education and voice lessons, as a teenager, were provided through the generosity of her church and members of her community. Studying first under local contraltos, by 1920 Anderson began to study under Giuseppe Boghetti, benefiting from a fundraising concert sponsored by the Union Baptist Church.

In the 1920s, Anderson established her career singing in African American communities around the United States, making her first recording of spirituals in 1924, winning a contest to sing with the New York Philharmonic in 1925, and performing at Carnegie Hall in 1928. By the late 1920s and throughout the 1930s, she performed at concert halls and with opera companies across Europe and Asia. Anderson, like her mentor Roland Hayes, valued the legacy of African American music and established a repertoire in excess of 100 African American spirituals from which she would choose closing numbers for her recitals. This element, which became a signature of her concert performances, has become a tradition continued since by many well-versed African American classical singers, including Jessye Norman, William Warfield, and Kathleen Battle.

Anderson returned from performing and studying around the globe with a newfound fame and recognition of her talent. In 1938, she made an intensive tour of the Southern states, with over 70 concert dates and was awarded an honorary doctorate of music from Howard University. In 1939, her manager booked Anderson to perform in concert at Constitution Hall in Washington, D.C. When the management of Constitution Hall reported that the original concert date was previously booked and that the hall was unable to make another booking for Ms. Anderson, it became publicly known that the owner of the concert hall, the Daughters of the American Revolution (D.A.R.), held a policy that did not allow African American artists to perform on its stage. The D.A.R.'s public discrimination against the world-renowned singer drew widespread criticism. The public resignation of First Lady Eleanor Roosevelt from the D.A.R. and her comments about the group's policy in her weekly newspaper column elevated awareness of the slight against Anderson to an international level. Through the secretary of the interior, the Roosevelt administration invited Anderson to give a concert on the steps of the Lincoln Memorial. On April 9, 1939, Easter Sunday, Anderson performed live from the Lincoln Memorial for 75,000 people, with an audience of 1 million plus watching the live televised broadcast. Anderson was a recipient of the Spingarn Medal that same year.

Marian Anderson, internationally celebrated opera singer, performed at the Lincoln Memorial in 1939; an event viewed as symbolic in the Civil Rights movement. (Library of Congress)

For the balance of her career, Anderson was a prominent figure performing around the world and representing the United States as a sort of "good will" ambassador. That role became official in 1958 when Anderson was officially designated as a delegate to the United Nations. Throughout the Cold War, though, Anderson's strong beliefs and work as a civil rights and peace activist sometimes put her at odds with the U.S. government and African American community leaders. Signing the World Peace Appeal (Stockholm Appeal) of 1950, an antinuclear movement from the Eastern Bloc countries, was highly suspect during the Cold War. Even while carrying out her UN duties or speaking on U.S. policy, Anderson made her personal views known as well. For example, after delivering a policy statement in 1955 on her delegation's position to the General Assembly concerning the U.S. position on the newly formed Nigeria's claim on the Cameroons, Anderson did not hesitate to publicize her opposition to that policy. She also broke ranks by speaking publicly about race relations in America while on a concert tour in Asia.

Anderson broke many race barriers in the United States. She became the first African American to sing at the Metropolitan Opera in New York in 1955. In 1961, Anderson once again sang in Washington, D.C., when she performed the National Anthem at the inauguration of President John F. Kennedy. In 1963, President Kennedy presented her with the Presidential Medal of Freedom. She began her farewell tour the next year—with her starting venue at Constitution Hall—and retired from singing in 1965. In 1972, she received a Peace Prize from the United Nations. Marian Anderson passed away in 1993 at the age of 96 and is buried in Eden Cemetery in Philadelphia.

See also: Cold War and Civil Rights; National Association for the Advancement of Colored People; Roosevelt, Eleanor

Jane M. Aldrich

Bibliography
Anderson, Marian. *My Lord, What a Morning: An Autobiography (Music in American Life)*. New York: Viking Press, 1956.
Arsenault, Raymond. *The Sound of Freedom: Marian Anderson, the Lincoln Memorial, and the Concert That Awakened America*. New York: Bloomsbury Press, 2009.
Dudziak, Mary L. *Cold War, Civil Rights: Race and the Image of American Democracy*. Princeton, NJ: Princeton University Press, 2000.
Keiler, Allan. *Marian Anderson: A Singer's Journey*. Urbana: University of Illinois Press, 2002.
Plummer, Brenda Gayle. *Rising Wind: Black Americans and U.S. Foreign Affairs, 1935–1960*. Chapel Hill: University of North Carolina Press, 1996.

Angolan/Kongolese

Angolan and Kongolese are often used in reference to persons belonging to the ancient kingdom of the Kongo, whose influence stretched well beyond its modern boundaries. Spelling Kongo with a "K" distinguishes inhabitants of the old Kongo kingdom from the modern-day "Congo." The Kongo kingdom stretched from present-day Gabon, in the north, eastward to the Kwango River and southward to northern Angola. The sovereignty of the Kongo kingdom lasted from the early 15th century to the late 18th century. One of its major chieftainships was in modern-day Angola. As a result, Angolans and Kongolese shared many cultural traits. Both Angola and the Kongo receive their names from the Portuguese.

As the Portuguese gradually took control of the Atlantic coastal strip throughout the 16th century by a series of treaties and wars, they eventually formed the colony of Angola. Slave traders during the 1500s first used the name "Kongo" in reference to the BaKongo people. As the Atlantic slave trade increased, the term was used to describe any person brought from the Atlantic coast of Central Africa to the Americas. The meaning of "Angola" also broadened with the intensification of the Atlantic slave trade. "Ngola" referred specifically to the ruler of the Ndongo part of modern-day northern Angola, but by the mid-18th century, it was used almost interchangeably with Kongolese.

When Angolans were enslaved and brought to the New World, they were known for their warrior skills and their conjuring powers. These attributes played an important part of group resistance to slavery in the Americas; not only were Angolans leaders in the Stono rebellion of South Carolina, but it was also "Gullah" Jack, a conjurer, who provided the conspirators in the Denmark Vesey plot with special powers. The descriptors "Gulla," "Gullah," and "Gola" usually referred to Africans in the Americas who were from Angola. The "Gullah" islands off the coast of South Carolina and Georgia have a language and culture that is a product of their Angolan origins and American residency.

Angolan and Kongolese presence can be found in many places of the Atlantic world. In the Maroon communities of Brazil, Angolan presence was noted by observers, and symbols, such as the Kongo cosmogram, suggest an equally influential presence of Kongolese. In both Puerto Rico and Cuba, Kongo priests still practice the rituals of their African ancestors.

See also: Gullah; Kongo Cosmogram; Stono Rebellion

Jarett M. Fields

Bibliography
Thompson, Robert F. *Flash of the Spirit: African and Afro-American Art and Philosophy*. New York: Vintage Books, 1984.
Thornton, John K. *Africa and Africans in the Making of the Atlantic World, 1400–1680*. New York: Cambridge University Press, 1992.
Washington, Margaret C. *A Peculiar People: Slave Religion and Community Culture among the Gullah*. New York: New York University Press, 1988.

Animal Trickster Stories

"Trickster" literally means cheater, or joker. It evokes a buffoon-like image but also involves a mythical dimension.

The very notion of the trickster comes from ancestral beliefs, manifested within African American folklore. The trickster is an archetypal representation gifted with magical powers and personified by a tripartite entity, partly divine, partly human, and partly animal. Plus, this protean figure embodies a transitional status and has the power to cross boundaries; for instance, a trickster such as Esu (in the Fon mythology) is talented with the knowledge of all languages and therefore stands as the ubiquitous figure of mediation.

The theme of trickster stories puts forward a double topic. First, it brings out the notions of African mythology and of oral transmission of a folkloric heritage. Trickster stories convey riddles and morals but have also provided the tools for survival. Tales are intended to soothe the mind of an uprooted people through the transmission of these pieces of folkloric legacy. Historically, animal trickster stories symbolize the projection of the dominating/dominant relationship that existed between masters and slaves—hence, both the allegorical meaning of the possibility of extirpating oneself out of traps thanks to clever tricks and the recurring theme of revenge in folktales. What is more, the trickster tale partakes of a contrapuntal answer addressed to the dominating culture.

Second, it hints at the rhetorical device that consists of concealing meaning and misleading the trickster's target, a concept named the "signifying monkey" by Henry Louis Gates Jr. This transposition of an underlying meaning through symbolic protagonists echoes the linguistic process of codification that characterizes African American Vernacular English.

Traditionally, animal trickster tales feature at least two protagonists, the prankster and his stooge. The former stands in a position ahead of the latter insofar as he retains knowledge that he aims to deliver to the gullible, but in an indirect way and not without making fun of him first. The trickster deploys crafty actions in order to achieve his trick or to overcome the hindrance. Thus, a range of winding paths unfold before him, such as the exploitation of superstitious creeds, the use of flattery, the invention of pretexts, the blurring of his target's perspective and vision, the transformation of his own appearance, and the power to become invisible. Despite the multiplicity of subterfuges available to him, the trickster never veers from his original purpose, and his strategy is somehow equivalent to the device of irony.

The animal trickster tale is the most famous type of folk tale. In the African American tradition, the trickster may be embodied by a rabbit, a fox, a hare, a bear, a wolf, a coyote, a whale, a hyena, and a monkey. "The False Message, Take My Place" and "Some are Going, and Some are Coming" constitute illustrations of the misleading message and the blurred vision, respectively. The former tale includes the Rabbit and the Wolf, the first of whom was trapped by a man and is hanging in a sack at the end of a tree branch, waiting to be slain. The Rabbit offers the Wolf the chance to go to heaven, and the Wolf credulously accepts without understanding that the Rabbit intends for them to exchange places. In "Some Are Going, and Some Are Coming," the Rabbit traps the Fox by passing on to the Fox the blurring vision by which the Rabbit himself was just trapped. After jumping into a bucket in order to reach a piece of cheese at the bottom of a well, he invites the Fox to jump into the other bucket to share the food with him, and thanks to the Fox's weight and naiveté, the Rabbit is able to come back to the surface; the cheese was actually a reflection of the moon. It is interesting to notice that in these two tales, the Rabbit was not clever enough to avoid being trapped himself but was cunning enough to bounce back by himself and at another's expense.

To sum up, the general function of a trickster tale is similar to that of a fable, during which a character may suffer temporarily, but ultimately acquires a new awareness. However, the purpose of the trickster's maneuver is not to produce a scapegoat. The deceiving and upsetting phases that the "temporary victim" undergoes as a result of the trickster's antics are necessary steps for the former's spiritual improvement toward knowledge and awareness. The outcome of the stories usually involves the victim discovering that he has been duped. The trickster tale consists of the depiction of an initiation, a rite of passage, undergone by the trickster's victim, a binary pattern that reminds us of the meta-diegetic level of the writer–reader relationship.

See also: Africanisms; Anansi the Spider; Black Folk Culture; Brer Rabbit

Valerie Caruana-Loisel

Bibliography

Courlander, Harold. *A Treasury of Afro-American Folklore.* 1976. Reprint, New York: Marlowe, 1996.

Cumberdance, Daryl. *400 Years of African American Folktale from My People.* New York: Norton, 2002.

Gates, Henry Louis, Jr., and Nellie Y. McKay. *The Norton Anthology of African American Literature*. New York: Norton, 1996.

Levine, Lawrence W. *Black Culture and Black Consciousness*. London: Oxford University Press, 1978.

Armstrong, Louis

Louis Armstrong (1901–1971), more than any other single figure, took jazz, the music of his New Orleans childhood, and made it into an internationally recognized art form, in part by pioneering the improvisational solo. A cornet player who later switched to trumpet, Armstrong also influenced generations of singers with his gravelly voice and early use of scat singing. His style exemplified the 1920s, known as the "Jazz Age," when many jazz critics thought he peaked. He went by colorful nicknames—Dippermouth, Gatemouth, Pops, Satchelmouth (shortened to Satchmo by a British journalist)—and invented or popularized jazz terms such as "jive," "chops," and "mellow."

The New Orleans of Armstrong's youth was a place saturated with cultural influences—French, Spanish, Canadian, British, Caribbean, and African—and the innovative styles of music springing from that interaction. Before the Civil War, black musicians were already combining European and African traditions in the music they played for dancers at Congo Square (now Louis Armstrong Park). At the turn of the century, band leaders competed for predominance in nightclubs, and early jazz pianists such as Jelly Roll Morton honed their skills providing musical entertainment in New Orleans' Storyville, the vice district.

Into this milieu, Armstrong was born to Mayann Albert, a 15- or 16-year-old girl who had come to the city from rural Louisiana seeking opportunity, and Willie Armstrong, whom she had met there. Armstrong always maintained his birthday was July 4, 1900, a patriotic coincidence for a man who also liked to say he and jazz grew up together. After his death, the discovery of a Catholic baptismal record showed he was born August 4, 1901. Willie left soon after his son's birth, though he later reunited with Mayann, who then gave birth to Louis's sister Beatrice, known as Mama Lucy. Mayann left the two children with their grandmother until Louis was five. He later strongly hinted that his mother probably turned to prostitution at this time, though she carefully hid such work from her children.

After a few years with his grandmother, a time that he remembered as idyllic, Louis went to live with his mother, sister, and a succession of "stepfathers" in Back O' Town, New Orleans' poorest neighborhood. At age seven, Louis began working for the Karnofskys, Jewish immigrants who had emerged from poverty and worked their way up in the world buying and selling junk. Louis relished eating dinner with them and listening to their Russian lullabies. For much of his life, Armstrong let people think the Colored Waifs' Home gave him his start playing cornet. But in his private writings, he wrote extensively about the Karnofskys and the way they had helped him buy a used cornet as an upgrade from the tin horn he blew driving their rag wagon. He began singing and playing the cornet with a quartet on street corners for spare change.

On January 1, 1913, celebrating the New Year, Louis fired a gun and was arrested and sent to the Colored Waifs' Home. There he received his first formal musical training, from Peter Davis, who ran the school's brass band. Louis became the student leader of the band. Unbeknownst to him, his biological father took a keen interest in getting him released from the home, even though Louis wanted to stay. When he left at age 13, at least a hundred establishments in the city featured jazz. Louis chose to hang around the one featuring Joe "King" Oliver. He played with Oliver, whom he credited with most of his musical education, until the older man's move to Chicago. Also during this period, Louis informally adopted his cousin's son, Clarence, after her death. Clarence, mildly retarded from an accident, remained Armstrong's only child.

At 17, Armstrong entered into the first of four marriages, with a prostitute named Daisy Parker. For most of the six-year marriage, Armstrong was playing jazz elsewhere. For two years, he played with Fate Marable's orchestra on a riverboat. At a stop in Davenport, Iowa, he met and influenced Bix Beiderbecke, an aspiring white musician who also became a 1920s jazz standout.

After his riverboat stint, Armstrong received a summons to join King Oliver's band in Chicago. There he married the pianist Lil Hardin. Lil had studied music at Fisk University and led Armstrong to believe she had been valedictorian. Actually, she had dropped out after a year because of frustration over her lack of proper training. Though Armstrong was later less than complimentary about Lil's playing, she became a sensation in Chicago when she took a job playing piano for a music store and was picked up by the New Orleans Creole Jazz Band, which through personnel changes became Oliver's outfit.

Armstrong recorded 37 performances, including "Chimes Blues," with King Oliver. The records are in the polyphonic New Orleans style, which still did not accommodate solo work by individual standouts. Over time, Lil became convinced that Oliver was holding her husband back. She surprised Oliver by persuading Armstrong to quit and take work with Fletcher Henderson's band in New York City while she stayed with the band. When Armstrong returned from his stint in New York, Lil arranged for him to play under the billing "World's Greatest Trumpet Player," embarrassing him greatly. She left the Oliver band to lead a band featuring Armstrong. During the late 1920s, Armstrong solidified his reputation as history's most influential jazz musician with his recordings with the Hot 5 and Hot 7—bands put together for the sole purpose of recording in studios—including "Heebie Jeebies," in which he sang scat. Legend had it that this was the first recorded scat singing and that it had come about when Armstrong dropped the music. However, it is not the first recorded scat singing and seems too purposeful to have been caused by dropped music. These sessions also yielded "West End Blues," which opened with a nine-measure Armstrong cadenza that is possibly the most famous solo in jazz.

In 1931, Armstrong made a triumphant return to New Orleans. Eight jazz bands and a large crowd greeted him at the train station. He visited the Waifs' Home, sponsored a baseball team, and had an honorary cigar named for him. When a racially charged misunderstanding led to the cancellation of a free concert for blacks, Armstrong vowed to come back to give a secret concert for blacks only, which he did in 1935.

For years, while still married to Lil, Armstrong lived with a girlfriend, Alpha Smith. He finally obtained a divorce from Lil in 1938, just in time to marry Alpha as their relationship began to disintegrate. Shortly afterward, he met a dancer named Lucille Wilson, known as "Brown Sugar," at the reconstituted Cotton Club in New York. In contrast to Alpha, who Armstrong later complained had an insatiable thirst for fine things he could barely afford, Lucille was a grounding influence. She bought them a home in Corona, Queens, creating the kind of home base Armstrong had done without for years. They remained married for the rest of his life.

Many jazz critics saw Armstrong's 1930s swing period as inferior. In the 1940s, Armstrong criticized the innovative

harmonies and purposeful elitism of bop musicians, who in turn denounced his stage show and movie appearances as "Uncle Tomming." In the same decade, Armstrong benefited from a "purist" revival of interest in 1920s jazz. Impatient, though, with such purists' efforts to categorize music, Armstrong continued to record and perform any type of music that appealed to him. His rendition of "What Did I Do to Be So Black and Blue," originally a song about a dark-skinned woman losing a lover to a lighter rival, became for Armstrong a commentary on race; Ralph Ellison's main character in *Invisible Man* goes into a reverie listening to Armstrong's recording. As a trumpet player, and especially as one formerly known for such superhuman feats as playing two hundred high Cs in a row, Armstrong struggled at times to keep his lip in shape for performances, and for weeks or months, he would rely more on singing than on trumpet playing. In the 1950s, he recorded three landmark albums of duets with Ella Fitzgerald. For decades his concert repertoire remained steady, characterized by the inclusion of "When It's Sleepy Time Down South," "Indiana," and a selection of Armstrong's biggest hits.

Armstrong developed a lifelong love of writing from the time he moved to Chicago and acquired a typewriter. He wrote hundreds of chatty letters to friends, tossed off autobiographical sketches, and contributed occasional pieces to magazines, such as "Why I Like Dark Women" (1954) for *Ebony*. A ghostwritten autobiography appeared, but unhappy with it because it used unbelievable dialect and ignored material Armstrong had provided, he wrote the widely read *Satchmo: My Life in New Orleans* in 1955. He planned a second volume named *Gage,* a slang term for the marijuana he smoked almost every day, but manager Joe Glaser intervened.

Armstrong made another memorable appearance in his hometown in 1949 when he served as King of the Zulus for his New Orleans burial society, the Zulu Social Aid and Pleasure Club. Armstrong was deeply honored to serve in the position, though many not familiar with Mardi Gras traditions were shocked to see Armstrong, who had denounced blackface, wearing wildly exaggerated blackface for the role. Many African Americans were embarrassed by Armstrong's antics, not only as King of the Zulus but also in his onstage act and in occasionally questionable movie roles. But scat, praised as an art form, had origins in minstrel shows, and entertainment was a part of jazz back in New Orleans. When Armstrong toured Britain in 1932, crowds who had fallen in love with his records grew

Louis Armstrong was one of the 20th century's most important jazz innovators and performers. (Library of Congress)

horrified when they saw the comedic aspects of his stage show. The British music press called him barbaric and gorilla-like, and night after night, audience members walked out in disgust. For his part, Armstrong pointed to the legacy of Bill "Bojangles" Robinson, perhaps mainly remembered for two movie roles as a jolly tap-dancing servant to Shirley Temple. Armstrong considered Robinson a deeply talented artist in his stage performances.

The ambivalence many younger blacks saw in Armstrong made his mid-1950s stances against the racial status quo all the more shocking. In 1957, not long after someone threw a stick of dynamite at a theater where he was playing to a mixed Southern crowd, Armstrong saw television coverage of the school desegregation situation in Little Rock, Arkansas. Incensed at the sight of whites heckling black schoolchildren, Armstrong called President Dwight

Eisenhower "two-faced," with "no guts," and proclaimed that the government would go to hell for its treatment of African Americans. The comments were just enough ahead of their time that Armstrong was denounced publicly by Sammy Davis Jr. and Adam Clayton Powell, not to mention banned from many radio stations. Soon after, Armstrong decided not to perform in Louisiana, which had instituted a ban on integrated bands—including Armstrong's All Stars—even though the practice was ruled unconstitutional.

Armstrong made musical history in 1964 when he knocked the Beatles off the top of the charts with a recording of "Hello, Dolly!" to promote the new musical of the same name. Among his 1967 recordings was "What a Wonderful World," a ballad that sold well in England but not the United States. The song subsequently charted in the 1980s when released as a single from the movie *Good Morning,*

Vietnam. Perhaps one of his most incongruous later recordings was the 1968 album *Disney Songs the Satchmo Way,* with performances of "When You Wish Upon a Star" and "Chim Chim Cher-ee."

Armstrong slowed down in his final three years, often under doctor's orders not to play trumpet. Celebrating his birthday on July 4, 1971, he told reporters he would soon resume performing. He died in his sleep two days later. *See also:* Black Folk Culture; Jazz

Brooke Sherrard

Bibliography

Armstrong, Louis. *Satchmo: My Life in New Orleans.* London: Peter Davies, 1955.

Bergreen, Laurence. *Louis Armstrong: An Extravagant Life.* New York: Broadway Books, 1997.

Giddens, Gary. *Satchmo: The Genius of Louis Armstrong.* Cambridge, MA: Da Capo Press, 2001.

Miller, Marc H., ed. *Louis Armstrong: A Cultural Legacy.* Seattle: University of Washington Press, 1994.

Bailey, Pearl

Pearl Bailey (1918–1990) was a well-respected 20th-century singer, actress, comedienne, and author. She is most famous for her screen roles in *Carmen Jones* (1954) and *Porgy and Bess* (1959), as well as a 1975 stage production of *Hello, Dolly,* all of which featured predominantly African American casts.

Bailey was born in Southampton County, Virginia, on March 29, 1918, and raised in Newport News, Virginia, by her parents, Joseph and Ella Bailey. She was the youngest of four children. Joseph Bailey served as a pastor at the local House of Prayer, and by the age of three, Pearl was singing and dancing in her father's church. In 1922, the Baileys moved to Washington, D.C., and the parents divorced soon after. Bailey moved with her mother to Philadelphia, where, at the age of 15, she sang in public for the first time, winning an amateur talent contest at the Pearl Theater, where her older brother Bill was a featured performer. The theater gave her a five-dollar prize and an offer of two weeks of work. The theater had promised to pay her 30 dollars for each week, but she never received pay for her work because the theater closed before the end of her run. Bailey left school and went on to win an amateur contest at the Apollo

Theatre in New York and continued to secure singing and dancing parts in productions around the Philadelphia area, before touring as a club singer in coal-mining towns across Pennsylvania during the Great Depression. While touring, Bailey had a short-lived marriage to a fellow performer that lasted only 18 months.

Bailey gradually worked her way into larger and more prestigious clubs, eventually performing at the Savoy in Washington, D.C., and the Blue Angel in New York City. During World War II, she traveled with the USO, entertaining troops with her singing and dancing. Her work with the USO, combined with her increasing following as a club performer, led her to work with some of the biggest jazz musicians and big band leaders of the era, including Count Basie, Huddie Ledbetter, and Cab Calloway. Bailey's popularity as a club act led to other opportunities on the stage and screen. In 1946, she was cast in *St. Louis Woman,* her first role on Broadway. In 1948, Bailey married for a second time, to John Randolph Pinkett. The marriage lasted until 1952, when she divorced Pinkett and married jazz drummer Louie Bellson, with whom she remained until her death.

Although Bailey was featured in a number of films in the late 1940s and early 1950s, she received her first chance at movie stardom when she was cast in *Carmen Jones* (1954). Her performance was a hit and opened up many more acting opportunities for her. Bailey took roles that allowed her to work with some of the biggest names in acting at that time, including Sammy Davis Jr. and Bob Hope. In 1959, she was cast in the film adaptation of the George Gershwin musical *Porgy and Bess,* costarring Sidney Poitier and Dorothy Dandridge. Bailey performed in a number of plays and movies and consistently received good reviews but never achieved movie star status. In 1967, she starred in a production of *Hello, Dolly* that featured an all African American cast. In the early 1970s, she had her own television show and later starred in a series of Duncan Hines commercials, in addition to voicing characters for animated feature films such as *The Fox and the Hound.*

Bailey was an avid Republican and a favorite of President Richard Nixon, who often asked her to perform at the White House. In 1970, Nixon appointed her America's "Ambassador of Love." In 1975, Nixon's successor, Gerald Ford, appointed Bailey as a special representative to the United Nations, and she attended several meetings. Bailey also appeared in a number of advertisements endorsing Ford's 1976 election campaign.

In the late 1960s, Bailey turned her attention toward writing. She published two autobiographical books, *The Raw Pearl* (1968) and *Talking to Myself* (1971). She also wrote *Pearl's Kitchen* (1973), *Hurry Up America, and Spit* (1989), and *Between You and Me* (1990). Later in life, Bailey decided to complete the education she had given up in order to become a performer. She finished her high school degree and enrolled in Georgetown University and, in 1985, earned a BA degree in theology.

Bailey won a Presidential Medal of Freedom in 1988 for her contributions to American cultural life. She died less than two years later on August 17, 1990, in Philadelphia, of heart disease at the age of 72. Pearl Bailey is buried in Rolling Green Memorial Park in Westchester, Pennsylvania.
See also: Black Folk Culture; Poitier, Sidney

Sara K. Eskridge

Bibliography
Atkins, Cholly, and Jacqui Malone. *Class Act: The Jazz Life of Choreographer Cholly Atkins.* New York: Columbia University Press, 2001.
Bailey, Pearl. *Pearl's Kitchen: An Extraordinary Cookbook.* New York: Harcourt Brace Jovanovich, 1973.
Isaacs, Edith. *The Negro in the American Theatre.* New York: Theatre Arts, 1947.
Wetterau, Bruce. *The Presidential Medal of Freedom: Winners and Their Achievements.* Charlottesville: University of Virginia, 1996.

Basie, Count

William "Count" Basie (1904–1984) was born in Red Bank, New Jersey, to Harvey and Lilly Ann Basie. During his formative years, Basie expressed a deep interest in music and began studying the organ and piano. He was particularly influenced by stride piano, a virtuosic genre that is characterized by intricate melodic embellishments and complex syncopation. In the mid-1920s, Basie traveled to New York to take organ lessons from Fat Waller, an important exponent of stride. Waller, who had an engagement at Harlem's Lincoln Theater, occasionally invited his young student to play the organ.

Kansas City, however, became the pivotal place where Basie would realize his aspirations of becoming a professional musician. He became the organist for singer Gonzelle White and played regularly for silent films at the Eblon Theater. Basie gained further experience when he moved to Oklahoma to play with the Blue Devils, led by bassist Walter Page. The Blue Devils, with their incomparable style of blues, left a profound impression on Basie. In 1929, Basie returned to Kansas City to join one of the most popular bands in the area, the Bennie Moten Orchestra. Although Moten was the band's pianist, he gradually brought Basie into the band as a substitute and staff arranger. Basie eventually became the band's pianist and worked diligently to perfect his musical skills.

After the unexpected death of Moten in 1935, Basie formed his own ensemble that included former members of the Moten band. He accepted an extended engagement at the Reno Club in Kansas City, an important decision that would affect his career both musically and professionally. In addition to performing weekly at the Reno Club, the band was broadcast to several parts of the nation, including Chicago and New York. It was during the nightly broadcasts that musicians, promoters, and the public became aware of this remarkable band out of Kansas City. New York promoter and entrepreneur John Hammond, while in Chicago, heard Basie's band and subsequently traveled to Kansas City. Other music executives visited Basie, and consequently, he signed with Decca Records and became the headliner at New York's Roseland Ballroom.

Count Basie's rise in jazz continued during the swing era of the 1930s and 1940s. Jazz became a national phenomenon because of the emergence of big bands, outstanding soloists, big-band arrangements, improvisation, and popular icons. Basie's ensemble epitomized the very essence of swing with their blend of blues, improvisation, and sophisticated arrangements. Exceptional musicianship, especially the musicians' imaginative improvisational skills, accounted for the band's classic and distinct style. Most notable among the group were trumpeters Buck Clayton and Harry "Sweets" Edison and saxophonists Hershel Evans and Lester Young. Undoubtedly, Basie's most enduring accomplishment was the assemblage of his incomparable rhythm section, featuring guitarist Freddie Green, bassist Walter Page, and drummer Jo Jones. As a tightly knit section, these musicians established a steady tempo through the use of walking bass patterns, a seamless flow of chord changes, and recurring ride rhythms. "One O'Clock Jump," "9:20 Special," and "Jumping at the Woodside" are typical examples of the kinds of complex and sparse arrangements and recurring riffs that defined the orchestra's unmatched style. Basie's unique pianistic style would also characterize the band's approach to jazz performance and composition. Basie's style exhibited simplicity in thematic material and improvisation and the influences of blues and boogie-woogie. This approach is exemplified in his solos, which are unified through the use of simple melodic ideas, the spontaneous use of space, and the restatement of the main theme. By the early 1940s, the Count Basie Orchestra had received numerous accolades from the public, executives, and musicians and was lauded as one of the best bands of the Swing Era.

After the decline of swing in the mid-1940s, Basie continued to perform with his orchestra and sextets. In the 1950s, the Count Basie Orchestra embarked on its first of several international tours. With new musicians and arrangers Frank Foster, Frank Wess, Thad Jones, and Neal Hefti, the orchestra took a diverse repertory of music to Copenhagen, Amsterdam, Paris, and Munich. The orchestra's style had evolved to produce a rich library of compositions that were modern but that did not replace the fundamental Basie style. Hefti's composition *Li'l Darlin'* retained the sparseness that characterized the early Basie style, whereas Foster's *Shiny Stockings* represented a more modern sound.

In addition to concerts, Basie recorded with countless premier vocalists and musicians, including Ella Fitzgerald and Frank Sinatra. *Ella and Basie* and *Sinatra-Basie* are two representative recordings that received auspicious reviews for their popular songs, well-crafted arrangements, and remarkable musicianship.

In the 1970s, Basie continued to perform at colleges, high schools, jazz festivals, and other important venues, despite being slowed by a heart attack and other physical problems. Count Basie was undoubtedly one of America's most eminent bandleaders. He was partly responsible for developing and evolving the jazz idiom and for making it a substantial part of American popular culture. Count Basie died of pancreatic cancer on April 26, 1984.

See also: Black Folk Culture; Jazz

Ralph A. Russell

Bibliography

Basie, Count. *Good Morning Blues: The Autobiography of Count Basie, as Told by Albert Murray.* Cambridge, MA: Da Capo Press, 2002.

Gioia, Ted. *The History of Jazz.* New York: Oxford University Press, 1997.

Shipton, Alyn. *A New History of Jazz.* London: Continuum, 2001.

Bebop

Developed primarily by black musicians working in New York City in the late 1930s and early 1940s, bebop is the basis for most modern jazz. Unlike swing, bebop is not dance-oriented; it is a passionate but cerebral form of jazz played primarily by small groups. Its practitioners often see it more as an art form than as a type of entertainment.

Bebop did not develop in a vacuum. It grew out of existing jazz forms, particularly swing, which had become popular in the 1930s. Swing was big band–oriented and was often performed in large ballrooms where patrons danced the jitterbug to the music. During this swing era, jazz musicians such as Art Tatum, Coleman Hawkins, and Duke Ellington began to experiment with bebop-style chord progressions. There were also alterations in the way instruments kept time; for instance, drummer Jo Jones began to develop the new jazz style of drum playing.

Then, in the early 1940s, some of the younger jazz musicians working in New York City began to extend these experiments with the elements of rhythm and harmony during jam sessions in Harlem and on 52nd Street. Their creative experimentation led to a radically new sound. Unfortunately, there were a series of music industry strikes between 1942 and 1944. This kept them from recording this new music, and it was not until 1945 that the wider public, via recordings, was introduced to bebop.

Key to the development of bebop was Minton's Playhouse in Harlem and Monroe's Uptown House on 52nd Street in Manhattan and, to a lesser extent, a number of other clubs on 52nd Street. Here, in after-hours jam sessions, such musicians as Kenny Clarke and Max Roach on drums, Dizzy Gillespie on trumpet, Charlie Christian on electric guitar, Charlie Parker on alto sax, Thelonious Monk and Bud Powell on piano, and Oscar Pettiford on double bass would play into the morning hours, developing the new bebop sound.

Minton's Playhouse was a tiny club at 118th Street and St. Nicholas Avenue in Harlem. It had originally been part of the kitchen area of the Cecil Hotel when clarinetist

Henry Minton opened it as a jazz club. He put former big band leader Teddy Hill in charge of running it. It provided an amiable place—with plenty of down-home Southern cooking—for musicians to stretch out musically after performing at other clubs in the New York area.

The house band at Minton's included Nick Fenton on bass, Joe Guy on trumpet, Thelonious Monk on piano, and Kenny Clarke on drums. After a few sets by the house band, musicians would take turns sitting in, improvising and experimenting. Two of these house band members are considered founding fathers of bebop. Thelonious Monk, born in Rocky Mount, North Carolina, in 1917 (but raised in Manhattan), became famous for his radical piano playing and for his great jazz compositions, such as "Round Midnight." He was a musical prodigy and dropped out of high school after his sophomore year to go on the road as a professional musician. Kenny Clarke, born in 1914 in Pittsburgh, Pennsylvania, extended the drum-playing innovations of Jo Jones by moving the timekeeping to the ride cymbal. He used the snare drum and the bass drum for "dropping bombs"—rhythmic comments on the melody.

Another of the prime developers of bebop and frequent guests at Minton's was trumpeter, arranger, and composer Dizzy Gillespie. Born in 1917 in Cheraw, South Carolina, he attended high school in North Carolina at the private, all-black Laurinburg Institute, where he studied music theory. Musical historians have tagged him as the "teacher." Aside from his inventive, brilliant playing, he would often explain the workings of bebop to younger or less experienced musicians, thus helping to disseminate bebop theory. Unlike most of the beboppers, he enjoyed the entertainment side of performing, and his trademark beret, goatee, and horn-rimmed glasses became the public image of the hip bebop musician. Many of his compositions, such as "A Night in Tunisia" and "Salt Peanuts," have become jazz standards.

Finally, alto saxophonist Charlie Parker, nicknamed "Bird," jammed at Minton's and is also considered one of the founding fathers of bebop. Born in Kansas City, Kansas, in 1920, he was a brilliant soloist who demonstrated with his unsurpassed technical skill the beauty and possibilities of bebop. A tragic figure, he fought most of his life against alcohol and drug addiction and died at the age of 34.

This new bebop sound was in stark contrast to the sound of big band and swing. The size of the band was part of the difference, given that most of the bebop bands had between four and six players. This facilitated one of other aspects of bebop: everyone in the band did improvisational solos. The music used unexpected chord changes, often relying on a chromatic scale. The speed of the playing demanded great technical skill and often used difficult eighth-note runs. As has already been mentioned, the role of the drum and the piano changed with bebop. Pianists were more likely to "comp" than to use a stride style of playing. Instead of using his left hand to keep time by alternating between the bass notes and the chords (the stride style), the bebop pianist used the left hand to play chords at intermittent and irregular times to comment on the soloist ("comping"). The drummer, in addition to keeping time with the ride cymbal instead of the bass drum and "dropping" bombs, played the drum as if were an instrument rather than just a time keeper. The bass players became increasingly important for keeping the beat.

Bebop was commercially popular between 1945 and 1949. During the 1950s, variations on bebop, known as West Coast cool jazz (a smoother, softer version of bebop) and hard bop (which added soul and gospel music), became popular. The bebop influence and its innovations continue today.

See also: Black Folk Culture; Ellington, Duke; Jazz; Parker, Charlie

William P. Toth

Bibliography

Joyner, David. "Jazz from 1930 to 1966." In *The Cambridge History of American Music.* Ed. David Nicholls. New York: Cambridge University Press, 1998.

Maggin, Donald L. *Dizzy: The Life and Times of John Birks Gillespie.* New York: Harper Entertainment, 2005.

Owens, Thomas. *Bebop—The Music and the Players.* New York: Oxford University Press, 1995.

Yanow, Scott. *Bebop.* San Francisco: Miller Freeman Books, 2000.

Black Atlantic

The term "Black Atlantic" was first penned by black British/African Caribbean sociologist Paul Gilroy. A major premise of this concept is that black culture is global, multifaceted, and international, particularly from a diasporic perspective. This presence of black people (due in part to the slave trade) has created an intercultural space that allows participants to connect the historical connections between

Africa, western Europe, and America. Simultaneously, the Black Atlantic describes the development of black identity as an ongoing process that is stimulated by travel and the exchange of artistic endeavor. These same identities have been compared to the histories of Europe and their places within modern history. Furthermore, black people are, like those in European cultures, firmly connected to notions of modernity. The notion of the Black Atlantic also examines how the abduction of blacks from Africa and subsequent notions of racism and oppression have inspired various artists to develop expressions that help express ideologies of freedom. Although some early expressions of self were forbidden for slaves, music was often allowed as a means of expression, thereby influencing other forms of art and expression. Visual culture also helped to push the limits of black expression, forming a subcultural or countercultural presence within the Western world.

The premise also argues that it is important to move beyond the confines of nationality and ethnicity. Each is considered too constraining to the endless possibilities of self-definition. Although many black cultures from around the Atlantic Ocean in Europe, the Caribbean, and America have been constructed as a part of national cultures, creating such identities as African American, Gilroy posits the notion that black intellectuals have examined the Western world on a more transnational basis, considering their countries of origin as unimportant by comparison. Understanding the impact of slavery on the West is essential to understanding Gilroy's notions of double consciousness, first discussed by W. E. B. Du Bois. Many of this same black intelligentsia have not only defended aspects of the West; they have also been its harshest critics. Gilroy argues that modernity must not only acknowledge the subjugation of slavery, but also understand how this phenomenon creates the need for a double consciousness, a consciousness that was characteristic of those black intellectuals seeking to explore the Diaspora. Gilroy also argues that the development of black culture has depended on music as a binding mechanism for black people everywhere. Gospel, rock and roll, rap, and hip-hop all expose how multiple cultures of blackness draw artistic and intrinsic value from each other, making the notion of blackness all the more complex and engaging. However, Gilroy would argue that these notions of diasporic identity are never static or "pure"; instead there are hybrid and fluid, always reforming. He also argues that the very notion of diasporic thinking was adopted into Pan-African political discourse by way of Jewish notions of identity. Ultimately, he maintains that discussions and exchanges of ideas between both groups must be cherished and upheld.

See also: African Diaspora; Atlantic Creoles; Atlantic Slave Trade

Darrell Newton

Bibliography

Amin, Samir. *Eurocentrism.* New York: Monthly Review Press, 1989.

Bhabha, Homi. *The Location of Culture.* London: Routledge, 1994.

Gilroy, Paul. *The Black Atlantic-Modernity and Double Consciousness.* Cambridge, MA: Harvard University Press, 1993.

Hall, Stuart. "The Whites of their Eyes: Racist Ideologies and the Media." *The Media Reader.* London: BFI, 1990.

Black Churches

The expression "black churches," also referred to as "the black church," has been used to refer to four groups of organizations: denominations founded by, formed of, and led by blacks; black congregations that belong to white denominations; independent congregations; and loose fellowships of black churches. This entry makes reference only to the major black denominations: Methodist, Baptist, Holiness, and Pentecostal.

During enslavement, Africans were forced to worship with their masters. Blacks were segregated within the white churches and were not free to worship God according to their culture. In time, however, enslaved people began worshipping in secret prayer meetings, escaping the supervision of their masters.

Between 1773 and 1775, Southern slaves founded the first black (Baptist) church in Silver Bluff, South Carolina. Similarly, in 1794, Absalom Jones and Richard Allen, in opposition to mistreatment at St. George's Methodist Episcopal Church, organized St. Thomas African Episcopal Church and Bethel African Methodist Episcopal Church in Philadelphia, Pennsylvania. Twenty-two years later, Allen organized other Methodist congregations into the African Methodist Episcopal Church (AME), the first black denomination in America. Black Methodists in New York also became weary of prejudice; Peter Williams Sr. and James Varick, among others, organized the African Methodist

Episcopal Zion Church (AMEZ), a new denomination, in New York City in 1796. In the South, blacks remained in the white Methodist fold until 1870, when they left to form the Colored Methodist Episcopal Church (CME). In 1954, the word "colored" was removed, and the CME became the Christian Methodist Episcopal Church.

From the very beginning, black churches reflected black political thought. For example, Bethel AME, pastored by Richard Allen, was a center of black emigration to Haiti. Denmark Vesey, Rev. Morris Brown, and Nat Turner all used religion in planning armed slave revolts. The abolitionist movement was also deeply connected to the black church; it was in the basement of a black church that the New England Antislavery Society, the first such society, was organized in Boston in 1832. In 1843, black Ohio Baptists organized the Union Antislavery Baptist Society, the first black abolitionist society. Harriet Tubman and Sojourner Truth, two Christian women among others, also participated in the abolitionist movement.

During and after Reconstruction (1866–1877), blacks founded many schools to help freed people get a higher level of literacy and education. American blacks also developed a sense of responsibility toward foreign missions in Africa. In 1897, the Lott Carey Foreign Mission Convention was founded as an independent organization whose aim was to focus on missions in Africa. Black missionaries built numerous churches, schools, and orphanages in Africa with African American donations. Concern for African missions, however, did not diminish the black Church's prophetic voice. Frederick Douglass, Rev. Henry Garnet, and Bishop Henry Turner made clarion calls for justice as segregation continued after emancipation.

Black Baptists tried several forms of organization before forming a single convention. By 1894, most black Baptists were concentrated in the Baptist Foreign Mission Convention, the American National Baptist Convention, and the National Baptist Educational Convention. In 1895, these conventions consolidated into the National Baptist Convention of the United States (NBCUSA). Twenty years later, the leaders of the National Baptist Publishing Board (NBPB) severed their connections with the NBCUSA and formed the National Baptist Convention of America (NBCA). During the Civil Rights movement, some clergy disagreed with Dr. Joseph Jackson over his long tenure as president of the NBCUSA and his gradual approach to civil rights. Because Jackson was not willing to change his views,

Gardner Taylor, L. V. Booth, Martin Luther King Jr., and others withdrew and formed the Progressive National Baptist Convention (PNBC) in 1961. But this was not the last Baptist split. In 1988, another group left the NBCA because of differences over the governance of the NBPB. The new split called itself the National Missionary Baptist Convention of America.

Holiness organizations arose in late 19th century against what was perceived as the worldliness of the mainline denominations. The holiness movement first entered the white Methodist Episcopal Church before the Civil War and spread widely during the postbellum era. Basically, the holiness movement claimed that sanctification, another divine work, must take place in the life of the believer after conversion/salvation. Scores of Baptists and Methodists chose to associate themselves with "holiness" and thus were excommunicated from their home churches or chose to leave on their own. In 1886, Isaac Cheshier pioneered the United Holy Church of America (UHCA), the earliest black holiness group, in Method, North Carolina. Eleven years later, Charles Price Jones, a prominent Baptist preacher, founded a holiness convention in Jackson, Mississippi. Jones's convention was informally organized as the Church of God of in Christ in 1897. In 1920, Jones reorganized his group as the Church of Christ (Holiness) USA. Most holiness churches have granted much freedom to women to work as evangelists and ordained pastors and have not required educational achievements as a requirement for ordination.

Charles Parham and William Seymour were the major promoters of what has become the Pentecostal movement. They promoted another work of grace, the Baptism of the Holy Spirit, which they claimed was subsequent to salvation and evidenced by speaking in tongues. Parham, a white preacher, founded the Pentecostal movement in 1901, and Seymour, a black pastor, led the Azusa Revival (1906–1922), an international revival based in Los Angeles. Many black organizations added the Baptism of the Holy Spirit to their list of doctrines. The Pentecostal Assemblies of the World (PAW) was organized as an interracial group in 1907, but issues of power and racism forced most white ministers to leave, thus making the PAW a predominantly black Pentecostal denomination. In late 1907, Charles Mason, a holiness leader who had endorsed speaking in tongues, left Jones's organization and legally retained the name "the Church of God in Christ" (COGIC) for his new Pentecostal

Wesley Chapel on John Street, New York City, is home to the oldest Methodist congregation. The chapel was dedicated in 1768. Peter Williams, the black sexton, stands in doorway. (Library of Congress)

organization. In 1908, Magdalena Tate, a female holiness preacher, pioneered the Church of the Living God, the Pillar and Ground of the Truth. This same year, she was made bishop, the first black woman to claim such title in America. In 1924, Ida Robinson, formerly associated with the UHCA, chartered Mt. Sinai Holy Church of America, a new Pentecostal group that encouraged women to pursue the ordained ministry. Robinson also ordained men as pastors, but women clergy dominated Mt. Sinai for many decades.

During the Great Migration, Northern churches provided shelter, financial assistance, and employment to Southern migrants. Nannie Burroughs, a women's leader in the NBCUSA, followed the black prophetic tradition by speaking against black oppression in America. In 1934, Bishop Ransom led other church leaders in founding the Fraternal Council of Negro Churches, an ecumenical group designed to make a united front in tackling the social problems of the African American community.

During the Civil Rights movement of the 1950s and 1960s, the black church made a sterling contribution to the social and political advancement of the race. Local congregations served as meeting places for countless rallies and fund-raisers. Scores of local churches got involved in voter education and voter registration drives. In 1957, King and other ministers formed the powerful Southern Christian Leadership Conference. Nine years later, another group of ministers pioneered the National Conference of Black Churchmen in support of the Black Power movement. Among the prominent ministers who led the national Civil Rights movement were King, Adam Clayton Powell, Ralph Abernathy, and Jesse Jackson. Christian women also contributed as marchers, secretaries, activists, and fund-raisers. Ella Baker and Fannie Lou Hamer were the most famous female activists. Gospel stars Mahalia Jackson and Ernestine Washington sang in fund-raising concerts for the civil rights cause. Black churches later provided strong support to black presidential candidate Jesse Jackson (1984, 1988).

Any study of the black church must include those congregations that belong to white denominations. Because whites introduced the gospel to the African slaves, the early black churches either were pastored by white ministers or found themselves under white control. Nevertheless, the founding of black denominations did not mean that all blacks would leave white denominations. Today, thousands of blacks are found in the Southern Baptist Convention, the American Baptist Churches, the United Methodist Church (UMC), the Episcopal Church, the Catholic Church, and the Seventh-Day Adventist Church. Blacks can also be found in the Evangelical Lutheran Church, the United Church of Christ (UCC), the Presbyterian Church USA, the Church of God (Anderson, Indiana), the Church of the Nazarene, and the Church of God (Cleveland, Tennessee). Many black Baptist churches claim double affiliation, with both a black convention and a white group. Black clergy in white denominations, like their peers in the black denominations, also supported the Civil Rights movement. Andrew Young (UCC) and James Lawson (UMC) are the most well known among them. Also within the ranks of these white denominations must be noted the presence of large numbers of immigrants from Africa and the Caribbean.

A good number of blacks also belong to independent churches and loose fellowships. Independent churches are found in rural, urban, and suburban areas and are led by ministers who prefer independence because of personality or financial factors. Many urban storefronts and mega churches are independent. In recent years, some ministers have preferred to organize themselves as "fellowships" instead of joining the more established denominations. These fellowships do not report standards of denominationalism, such as publishing houses, Bible schools and Christian colleges, and strong foreign missions. Nonetheless, they do ordain ministers and organize national conferences. Today, the most well-known fellowship is the Full Gospel Baptist Church Fellowship, founded in 1992 and still led by its founder, Bishop Paul Morton. Another phenomenon worth mentioning is the acceptance of Pentecostal/charismatic worship styles in the more established and older denominations.

The black church has made other significant contributions to American society during the 20th century. It heavily contributed to the development of black and American Christian music. Gospel music and singing pioneers included Charles Tindley, Lucy Campbell, Thomas Dorsey, Mahalia Jackson, and others. Later, Andrae Crouch, Mattie Moss Clark, and James Cleveland were among those who developed and promoted contemporary gospel music and singing. In the area of ecumenism, blacks founded the National Black Evangelical Association (1964) and the Congress of National Black Churches (1978) and worked with the National Council of the Churches of Christ, the World Baptist Alliance, the World Methodist Council, and the World Council of Churches. It was probably this kind of ecumenism that influenced the AME (1948) and the CME (1954) to ordain women. Another interesting form of ecumenism shows in the Interdenominational Theological Center, founded in 1958, which is now a consortium of six black seminaries. In addition, black churches have built thousands of housing units for low-income and senior citizens, chartered credit unions and banks, and developed vocational programs. In the 21st century, the black church continues to receive the support of the African American community. As of 2008, the major denominations report the following memberships: AME, 1.8 million; AMEZ, 1.2 million; CME, 850,000; NBCUSA, 7.5 million; NBCA, 5 million; PNBC, 2.5 million; COGIC, 5.5 million; and PAW, 1.5 million. Overall, it must be understood that the black church is more than just Christian people who are black. It is a spiritual center, a prophetic voice, and a medium for economic empowerment.

See also: African Methodist Episcopal Church; First African Baptist Church; Slave Religion

David Michel

Bibliography

Cobbins, Otho B. *History of Church of Christ (Holiness) U.S.A.* New York: Vantage Press, 1966.

Fitts, Leroy. *A History of Black Baptists.* Nashville, TN: Broadman and Holman Publishers, 1985.

Lincoln, C. Eric, and Lawrence H. Mamiya. *The Black Church in the African American Experience.* Durham, NC: University of North Carolina Press, 1990.

Pinn, Anne H., and Anthony B. Pinn. *Fortress Introduction to Black Church History.* Minneapolis, MN: Fortress Press, 2002.

Raboteau, Albert J. *Slave Religion: The "Invisible Institution" in the Antebellum South.* New York: Oxford University Press, 1978.

Ross, Rosetta. *Witnessing and Testifying: Black Women, Religion, and Civil Rights.* Minneapolis, MN: Fortress Press, 2003.

Wilmore, Gayraud S. *Black Religion and Black Radicalism: An Interpretation of the Religious History of African Americans.* Maryknoll, NY: Orbis Books, 1998.

Black English

Black English is a dialect or language variety of American English. Also known as Black Vernacular English (BVE), African American English (AAE), African American Vernacular English (AAVE), and Ebonics, Black English is spoken by many but not all African Americans. Approximately 80–90 percent of African Americans speak Black English as least some of the time. Because of the social nature of language development and use, Black English is also spoken by many non-African Americans who live among or identify with speakers of Black English.

There are several theories posited about the origins of Black English. One of the most widely accepted theories is the creolist theory. This theory maintains that modern Black English is the result of a hybrid derived from contact between speakers of European languages and various West African languages. Slaves came in contact with Europeans, and needing to find ways to communicate, they developed an informal, simplistic way of communicating called a pidgin. This pidgin eventually became a Creole when it was the primary language of a future generation. Over time, Black English has gone through the process of decreolization, with the features of the dialect moving toward the standard form (the form used by the majority population or the population of power).

The English language includes many variations, including American dialects (varieties) such as Black English, Appalachian English, and Southern English. These dialects, including Black English, are systematically governed by linguistic rules that cross all language parameters, including the rules governing the form of language—phonology (speech sounds), morphology (word structure), and syntax (sentence structure); the rules governing word meaning—semantics (vocabulary/lexicon); and the rules governing language use—pragmatics (social rules). Each of these dialects has its own set of distinguishing features and patterns. However, a majority of the linguistic features of English are common among each of the varieties.

Common features of Black English are generally described based on phonology (those affecting pronunciation) and morphosyntax (those affecting grammar). Some phonological features of Black English include the following: changes to consonant clusters, most often seen in the final position of words, where final consonant blends such

as -st, -sk, -ft, and -ld are reduced to a single consonant such as tes'(test), des' (desk), lef' (left), and col' (cold); changes to "th" sounds, where words with a medial or final "th" are produced as the "v" or "f" sounds, as in "birfday" (birthday); changes to the "r" sound, where the "r" is not present after "o" and "u," as in "foe" (four) and "doe" (door), or is absent after consonants, as in "th'ough" (through); changes to str- words (string, street), which may become skr-words (skring, skreet); and metathesis, where the order of sounds in words is changed as in "aksed" (asked).

Some morphosyntactic features of Black English include the following: changes in tense, including the past tense, where the -ed at the end of regular verbs is not produced ("she finish_ eating fast"), or where the -ed is added to irregular verbs ("he drinked it all"); remote time construction of "been," where "been" represents an action in the distant past ("I been had one of those"); invariant use of "be," where "be" is used for "is," "are," and "am" ("he be busy all the time"); subject-verb agreement, where the subject and verb are non-complimentary ("they was walking home together"); and variable use of the copula (is/are), "they happy."

The use of dialects, including Black English, is influenced by a number of different variables. Black English is developmental. Younger and older speakers differ in the types (features) and amount (density) of dialect used, with both features and density decreasing with age and education. The exception to this observation is among adolescent males, who tend to demonstrate an increase in use of the dialect. Black English use varies between speakers from low socioeconomic and more affluent environments, with speakers from less affluent communities using a greater variety of features and more frequently. Linguistic context affects Black English use. Features are produced more frequently in natural discourse settings such as conversation than in more formal or structured contexts such as oral reading or delivering a speech. The features of Black English are not obligatory. Speakers may or may not use Black English features all the time. Features may be variable, including based on the setting (formal versus informal) and conversational partner (peer versus non-peer). Code-switching is the ability to switch between language variations, such as between Black English and more standard forms (those spoken by the majority). Some Black English speakers are more fluent at code-switching than others. Greater contact with other varieties of English, usually through school experience and mobility (close proximity to other varieties), increases the ability and likelihood of code-switching. Code-switching may also be a choice where speakers decide whether to switch based on personal choices of inclusion or exclusion (from the majority).

Black English is socially stigmatized. Individuals, whether consciously or not, elevate the language of the perceived dominant group simply because it is dominant. Given that Black English is the language of a historically, socially subordinated group in the United States, it is often negatively viewed. Negative judgments about intelligence, personal character, and status are often inaccurately made about speakers of Black English. These negative perceptions about speakers of Black English are frequently used punitively in educational and professional settings, with speakers of Black English receiving negative consequence for using the dialect.

See also: Africanisms; Gullah; Turner, Lorenzo Dow

Shurita Thomas-Tate

Bibliography

American Speech-Language Hearing Association (ASHA). *Position Statement: Social Dialects.* Rockford, MD: ASHA, 1983.

Green, Lisa. *African American English: A Linguistic Introduction.* Cambridge, UK: Cambridge University Press, 2002.

Labov, William. *Language in the Inner City: Studies in the Black English Vernacular.* Philadelphia: University of Pennsylvania Press, 1972.

Mufwene, S. S., Rickford, J. R., Bailey, G., and Baugh, J. *African American English: Structure, History and Use.* New York: Routledge, 1998.

Rickford, John. *African American Vernacular English: Features, Evolution, Educational Implications.* Oxford, England: Blackwell Publishing, 1999.

Black Folk Culture

While blacks in America long struggled against white society's efforts to keep them powerless, black folk culture—from the days of slavery through the Jim Crow and Civil Rights eras—offered blacks a vehicle by which to confront the white power structure. For instance, African American ballads and tales portrayed human heroes (such as John Henry or Shine) who challenged or resisted—and antiheroes (such as the slave John in the "John and the Master" story cycle) who outsmarted—white authority. Modeling themselves on those folk characters, blacks deepened their sense of expectation that they might eventually surmount their social marginalization.

Historically, white scholars acknowledged the British and Anglo-American influences on African American culture and yet ignored the enduring power of African and Caribbean culture on African Americans. In 1941, scholar Melville J. Herskovits asserted that this oversight (which he termed "the myth of the Negro past") was a major factor in the continuation of racial prejudice. To counter that perspective, Herskovits identified a significant number of Africanisms (African cultural survivals) in African American culture. Subsequent scholarly studies advanced general understanding of the considerable extent to which black folk culture has influenced mainstream American culture.

African American culture can be divided into three main categories: oral (verbal) folklore, customary (behavioral) folklore, and material (physical) folklore. The most renowned aspect of black folk culture is the African American oral tradition, particularly folk tales and songs. Blacks have told sacred and supernatural tales (creation legends, ghost stories, folk sermons, testimonials, and preacher tales) and secular tales (morality tales, trickster tales, and jokes). Rural as well as urban blacks have favored two types of tales: trickster tales and jokes.

The trickster figure long held a crucial if ambivalent role in African American oral tradition. Borrowing from the trickster traditions of Africa (where tricksters took on human, divine, or animal form), blacks especially valued tales involving animal trickster figures. The ultimate goal of the trickster was to subvert the corrupt and divisive moral conventions and the established order that originally enforced those morals. Fearing reprisal if they freely conveyed their grievances, slaves told tales that employed animal characters in substitution for human characters. Trickster animals, such as Brer Rabbit, symbolizing blacks, ultimately prevailed in interactions with more powerful animal characters (which, of course, represented whites). A cycle of related non-animal trickster tales, told in the years after the Civil War, concerned the ambivalent relationship between a fictional slave named John and his master. In these stories, John struggles to overcome his subservient position in racist plantation society by covertly subverting the stereotypes thrust on him by his white master.

African American jokes often took the form of competitive verbal games, which tested an individual's verbal dexterity. In these games, players leveled "sounds" (direct insults) or "signifying: (indirect insults) against an opponent, who could then respond in kind. Woofing, Signifying, and Sounding were various names for a game in which a player humorously teased his opponent. "The Dozens" referred to a game in which a player creatively poked fun at his opponent's mother. The loser of these strictly structured verbal contests was the person who allowed his verbal responses to stray from the ritualized impersonal insult expected of all players into mere personal insult.

Another type of folk tale, the toast, was a dramatic traditional narrative performed in rhymed couplets. Most frequently found in urban neighborhoods and prisons, the toast was commonly multi-episodic, chronicling the deeds of such antiheroic figures as badmen, pimps, and street people. Some well-known toasts included "The Signifying Monkey," "Stackolee," and "The Freaks Ball." By mastering the toast, one of the most complex forms within African American oral tradition, the teller gained power and prestige within black communities.

Jive is another form of traditional African American verbal communication. Historically, when they jived, blacks were engaging in playful conversations utilizing strongly African American vernacular speech. An exclusive mode of communication, jive was generally indecipherable to whites. Blacks introduced into the English language numerous words, some with clear African origins (such as *boogie, gumbo, cooter, okra,* and *goober*). Also from African sources are two familiar expressions, the affirmative phrase "uh-huh" and the negative phrase "unh-uh."

In folk tales and traditional story-songs (narrative African American songs are often referred to as "blues ballads"), blacks boasted about a host of heroes and antiheroes, both real and mythical. African American folk tales and story-songs depict mythical figures (such as the Devil and Moses), human heroes (such as John Henry, Jack Johnson, and Joe Louis), and "badmen" (such as John Hardy, Staggerlee, and Railroad Bill).

In the pre-emancipation South, slaves played traditional instrumental music at dances and sang field hollers, work songs, and spirituals (because of their power to uplift, the latter were sung during worship services and also during work). In spirituals, affirmation outweighed sorrow; confidence outweighed despair. Through singing spirituals, slaves reinforced positive beliefs (such as transcendence, ultimate justice, and personal worth) and rejected negative beliefs (such as feelings of depravity and unworthiness).

By the 1890s, these early forms of African American musical expression were influencing the development of a new folk music: the blues. Emerging as a highly localized music in the rural areas and small towns of the Deep South, particularly on large plantations and at industrial sites, the blues eventually revolutionized American music. Blues lyrics, which evoked the African American experience of social alienation in an era of restrictive Jim Crow laws, set a new standard for lyrical creativity and directness, and the music of the blues introduced new possibilities for improvisation and individual expression.

A melding of African American and white musical forms, jazz first emerged as a distinctive musical form in the late 19th century. Musicians in New Orleans—such as legendary cornet player Buddy Bolden—created jazz out of an amalgam of African American, Creole, Caribbean, and Cajun secular folk music; African American and Anglo-American sacred music; brass marching band music; and popular parlor music. The word "jazz," which in the African American vernacular originally referred to sexual intercourse, reflected the sensuality of this new style of music.

Other 20th-century musical styles first emerged in African American environments, later finding wide reception among mainstream audiences. Unlike 19th-century spirituals, which were a folk phenomenon, modern African American gospel music was commercial from the beginning, in that popular gospel music songwriters—who united religious texts with secular musical forms borrowed from blues and ragtime—earned considerable royalties by formally publishing their work.

Solo and group gospel singing influenced two later African American musical developments: (1) rhythm and blues and (2) soul. Although many performers of these related musical styles rejected the didactic spiritual messages of gospel music in order to obtain crossover popularity, instead singing secular songs about love's travails and about social issues, rhythm and blues and soul performances nonetheless retained many of the musical qualities of gospel music, including the individuality and sincerity of the singer's persona, vocal emotionalism, and vocal interaction between the lead singer and the background singers (often termed "call-and-response"). Pioneer African American rock 'n' roll musicians likewise felt the overpowering presence of gospel music.

One recent musical style, rap, is an urban version of an African American verbal tradition dating back to the pre-emancipation era. Historically, a rap was a partly spoken, partly sung poetic statement, characterized by rhymed couplets, verbal wit, and rhythmic brilliancy. Within African American society, rappers have been respected for their powerful verbal gifts and feared for their extraordinary insights into human experience.

African American customary folklore includes, among other traditional rituals and activities, behavioral expressions of religious belief (the verbal components of such expressions are part of the oral tradition). Many aspects of African American folk belief can be traced back to African sources, including the conviction that, in the realm of the supernatural, there is no dichotomy between good and evil, both being attributes of the same powers. Also African were some of the spiritual rituals of the slaves. When black conjurers attempted to arouse the spirits of dead ancestors, they sometimes used goofer—grave dirt. This term was derived from the Ki-Kongo verb *kufwa,* which meant "to die." According to a Kongo tradition, earth from a person's grave was considered to be at one with that person's spirit.

Another Africanism was the emphasis on revelation among African American folk medicine practitioners in their quest for useful plant remedies. In order to manufacture and administer folk remedies, medicine practitioners, who generally were women, collected roots, leaves, herbs, barks, and teas. These women became medicine practitioners either by apprenticeship or by being "called" to practice medicine. Some practitioners claimed that in times of crisis, they heard a voice informing them about medicines that would help people.

Black men practiced with magic as well. Generally, men became conjurers by inheritance—a man might be the son of a conjure man, obligating him to accept inherited powers or face misfortune or illness. A man could also become a conjurer voluntarily, such as if he were his father's seventh son (assuming that the father and his mate had not produced a girl).

Several types of African American folk belief involved the occult: hoodoo, a magical charm practiced by a relatively small number of people, mostly by men; signs, a more popular magical belief practiced largely by women (hoodoo was more exclusive and complex than signs); and voodoo, which developed principally in Louisiana because of that region's confluence of French, Catholic, and Haitian influences. In annual ceremonies featuring elaborate decorations (with altars surrounded by hundreds of lighted candles), the cult of voodoo invoked, among other deities, Legba, a trickster of West African and Haitian origination. Initiation into the voodoo cult involved rites of passage (seclusion, fasting, special wardrobes, dancing and possession, animal sacrifices) that closely paralleled various religious rites practiced in West Africa and Haiti. One figure associated with voodoo was Marie Laveau, whose legendary initiation into the cult involved being coaxed to join the New Orleans cult by a rattlesnake. The African American fascination with snakes can be traced back to Africa, where the serpent was an important supernatural being. For instance, in Dahomey, two rainbow-serpents (named Aido Hwedo and Damballa Hwedo) were believed to have been present at the creation of the world; similar myths concerning serpent-spirits were found in Haiti.

Another Africanism was the African American belief in *haints* (ghosts). According to many West African cultures, haints were spirits at one stage of their being. Haints could be beneficent, such as the spirits of loved ones returning from the dead to help, protect, and counsel the living. Haints could also be evil, such as the spirits of masters who returned to renew their abuse of slaves. To protect themselves from such evil spirits, slaves practiced various rituals, including putting heavy rocks on top of their masters' coffins to keep them weighted down, placing a Bible by a door to prevent spirits from entering the house, and chanting magical charms to keep evil spirits away. Believing that they were not safe from their masters even in death, slaves requested for their burial to be as far as possible from their masters.

As the slaves became Christianized, African American religious services began to combine African/Caribbean and Judeo-Christian elements. One manifestation of this fusion was the ring shout, a religious, highly ritualized dance that, in the pre-emancipation South, served as an acceptable substitute for secular dancing. After the Civil War, ring shouts increasingly came under the scrutiny of African American ministers, who judged them to be uncivilized, if not anti-Christian.

A secular African American dance originating during the days of slavery was the cakewalk, a stylized caricature of the Anglo American waltz. By 1895, the dance had become a mass cultural phenomenon and was appearing in

Broadway productions. Soon, the cakewalk was being incorporated into the high-culture musical compositions of Debussy, Sousa, and Stravinsky.

One example of African American material culture is the banjo. Slaves brought from Africa a prototype version of the banjo. By the 1840s, white audiences had been widely exposed to the banjo through the use of that instrument in minstrel shows, a new form of popular entertainment. At minstrel shows, white musicians in blackface (minstrels) imitated African American musicians by singing ersatz African American folk songs. Far from traditional (they were written commercially for the minstrel shows), minstrel songs romanticized the lives of plantation slaves. Anchoring their singing with banjo accompaniment and also performing instrumental numbers on the banjo, white minstrel performers borrowed the African American style of down-stroking across the banjo strings and utilizing the fifth (thumb) string of slave banjos.

African Americans have long constructed a variety of material objects. From Africa, slaves brought skills—especially ironworking, woodworking, and building with earth and stone—which plantation owners exploited in the New World; thus, plantation households were full of tools, furniture, quilts, pottery, and jewelry made by slaves. Similarly, plantation houses soon featured such African architectural designs as central fireplaces, steeply sloping hip roofs, wide porches with overhanging roofs, and the use of moss and earth within walls.

Another important example of African American material culture is the shotgun house. First built in New Orleans in the early 19th century by people of color (most of whom were political refugees from Haiti), the shotgun house combined African, Caribbean, and French architectural concepts. Small and rectangular—one room wide by three rooms deep, with doors at each end, and the gable end toward the street—the shotgun house is a common house design in the South today, utilized by whites as well as blacks.

Over time, African Americans developed distinctive foodways. This they accomplished by combining foodstuffs introduced from Africa (such as yams, okra, black-eyed peas, and sorghum), with Old World tastes and recipes involving African techniques of cooking and spicing, with New World foodstuffs and food preparation techniques. This fusion of foodways led to the emergence of such distinctively African American dishes as gumbo and barbecue.

A moniker often applied to African American cooking is "soul food."

Combined, all of these practices and rituals form a uniquely black folk culture.

See also: Africanisms; Animal Trickster Stories; Blues Music; Field Hollers; Goofer Dust; Grave Dirt; Hoodoo; Jazz; Laveau, Marie; Ragtime; Ring Shout; Slave Culture; Soul Food; Work Songs

Ted Olson

Bibliography

Abrahams, Roger D. *Singing the Master: The Emergence of African-American Culture in the Plantation South.* New York: Pantheon Books, 1992.

Crowley, Daniel J. *African Folklore in the New World.* Austin: University of Texas Press, 1977.

Herskovits, Melville. *The Myth of the Negro Past.* Boston: Beacon Press, 1941.

Holloway, Joseph E., ed. *Africanisms in American Culture.* Bloomington: Indiana University Press, 1991.

Hurston, Zora Neale. *Mules and Men.* New York: J. B. Lippincott, 1935.

Jarmon, Laura C. *Wishbone: Reference and Interpretation in Black Folk Narrative.* Knoxville: University of Tennessee Press, 2003.

Joyner, Charles W. *Down by the Riverside: A South Carolina Slave Community.* Urbana: University of Illinois Press, 1984.

Levine, Lawrence W. *Black Culture and Black Consciousness: Afro-American Folk Thought from Slavery to Freedom.* New York: Oxford University Press, 1977.

Puckett, Newbell Niles. *Folk Beliefs of the Southern Negro.* New York: Negro Universities Press, 1968 [1926].

Black Fraternal Societies

In contemporary society, the term "fraternal societies" conjures up images of university-based fraternities. Yet in the 19th century, fraternal societies constituted the most popular form of African American voluntary association. There were black fraternal societies as early as the 18th century, and ritual and regalia helped distinguish them from non-fraternal benevolent societies and social clubs. Such associations continue to exist today, but the heyday for the black lodge was in the late 19th and the early 20th centuries.

Although fraternalism also appealed to whites in that period, fraternal societies played a larger role in African American life. Blacks were enthusiastic joiners, and many of them affiliated with more than a single fraternal order. Deprived of opportunities for civic participation and often coping with degrading poverty, black men and women learned racial pride in their lodges, and their families could look there for material assistance at times of crisis. Despite their rhetoric about brotherhood, fraternal societies, both black and white, were notorious for quarrels, schisms, and "big men" who ruled autocratically.

Racial discrimination imposed by whites forced African Americans to organize their own segregated lodges. After the Civil War, innumerable black fraternal societies sprang up, many of them brief-lived local organizations. Fraternal societies enjoyed broad popularity in both Southern and Northern states. When they migrated to the North, Southern blacks sometimes brought their distinctive lodges with them. A great variety of lodges existed: rural lodges, urban lodges, for men only, for women only, for men and women meeting together, and for children. Although the African American elite preferred their own exclusive clubs, the lodges were cross-class organizations in which laborers, domestics, skilled workers, shopkeepers, and professionals called each other brother or sister. For instance, preachers and business entrepreneurs from Birmingham provided the leadership for lodges of Alabama coal miners.

Black lodges typically were smaller than their white counterparts. This made them financially less stable, but it also provided greater opportunity for election to office. Where else could African Americans aspire to election to numerous offices dignified by impressive titles? Deprived of political rights, blacks acquired leadership skills; they learned how to preside at meetings, keep minutes and financial accounts, and manage the activities of their societies. Fraternal societies often published their own newspapers and owned meeting halls. A few also operated retail stores, hotels or boarding houses, and farms and also established hospitals and old age homes.

Lodges' elaborate secret rituals contrasted with the simplicity of Baptist and Methodist liturgies. Ritual dominated lodge meetings, particularly for initiation ceremonies. Often they told the story of a moral pilgrimage. The fraternal societies that borrowed least from white organizations emphasized personal equality and collective service. Colorful fraternal society parades, with marchers wearing regalia or other ceremonial dress and waving lodge banners, and fraternal society funeral processions were a conspicuous part of black community life.

Black fraternal societies differed from white ones in some respects. The importance of religion and of women in the African American community help explain why, in contrast with white organizations, black fraternal societies often bore biblical names and frequently accepted men and women as members in the same lodges. The Galilean Fishermen (founded 1856) is an example of the former, the American Woodmen (founded 1901) of the latter.

The poverty of blacks encouraged their fraternal societies to emphasize mutual insurance, at first burial policies and later life insurance to support survivors. For instance, a few years before World War I, 37 fraternal societies in Virginia carried insurance policies with a face value of $4,500,000.

As an exception to the general rule of racial separation, a few partially integrated fraternal temperance societies existed in the 19th century. Typically they combined segregated local lodges with multiracial state grand lodges or national organizations. The novelist William Wells Brown waged an unsuccessful fight for racial equality first in the Sons of Temperance and later in the Good Templar fraternal order. The Independent Order of Good Samaritans and Daughters of Samaria began in 1847 as a largely white organization that admitted a few blacks. After emancipation, blacks became more numerous than whites, and the whites departed, making the Good Samaritans a black fraternal society.

The largest black fraternal societies bore names similar to that of white organizations: the Masons, the Odd Fellows, the Knights of Pythias, and the Elks. Of these parallel orders, the Prince Hall Masons were by far the oldest. In 1775, a Masonic lodge attached to a British regiment stationed at Boston initiated a group of African Americans whose West Indian leader was named Prince Hall. In 1784, the Grand Lodge of England issued the black Masons in Massachusetts an official charter, and they organized their first lodge in 1787. At first, the Prince Hall Masons could recruit only among the small number of free blacks in the Northern states. After the Civil War, they spread to the Southern states where most African Americans lived. By that time, no overall Prince Hall organization existed, so each state grand lodge was independent. Not the largest of the black fraternal societies, the Prince Hall Masons were nevertheless the most prestigious, with many middle-class members, including the first African American elected to the U.S. Senate and the first to serve on the U.S. Supreme

Court. Much of the growth in Prince Hall membership occurred in the 20th century. The related Shriner philanthropic group, founded in 1892, attracted a membership much smaller than its white counterpart. In contrast, the Prince Hall women's auxiliary, founded in 1874, was larger and more important than white Masonry's Eastern Star. At present, the Prince Hall Masons claim more than 300,000 members, including those in lodges outside the United States.

The second major parallel order, the Odd Fellows, also was organized by free blacks in the North with the help of a charter from an English grand lodge. Founded in 1843, the Odd Fellows for many years stood out as the largest black fraternal society. At its peak early in the 20th century, it claimed 300,000 members, about twice the Prince Hall membership at the time, and its lodges owned about 2 million dollars in real estate. The Odd Fellows had a sizable women's auxiliary, the Daughters of Ruth, founded in 1857. Today the Odd Fellows claim 100,000 members.

The third major parallel order, the Knights of Pythias, came into existence after the Civil War without the benefit of an English charter. Founded in 1880 in Mississippi, the Colored Knights of Pythias offered military-style formations for younger members who took the "uniform rank." Like other parallel organizations, it admitted only men, with women restricted to an auxiliary. At one time, the Pythians were a quarter-million strong, but by the beginning of the 21st century, few if any Pythian lodges survived.

The fourth major parallel order, the Elks, was founded much later, in 1898. African American women organized their own Elks society four years later. Like the Prince Hall Masons, the Elks strongly appealed to the black middle class. J. Finley Wilson, elected Grand Exalted Ruler in 1922, and holding his high office until 1953, exemplifies the "big man" who often dominated black fraternal societies. The Elks played a leading role in organizing fraternal society support for black civil rights. The Elks continue into the present day with a large membership. In the mid-1970s, there were 450,000 African American men in the Elks order, or 7 percent of all black men.

Whites resented the similar names borne by black parallel orders and their related insignia, regalia, secret handshakes, and the like. Court suits and state laws attacked in particular the black Pythians, Elks, and Shriners. The

African American organizations fought back. At considerable expense they created a network of black lawyers that foreshadowed the subsequent work of the NAACP. In 1912, the U.S. Supreme Court ruled in favor of the Pythians in their fight that had begun in Georgia, and in 1929, the high court ruled in favor of the Shriners in their struggle that had begun in Georgia and Texas. The attack on the Elks that had begun in New York State ended when the white Elks, tired of an expensive legal battle, accepted the existence of a parallel African American organization.

Many black fraternal societies had distinctive and often religious names, unrelated to those of white organizations. These black lodges typically were organized in the South. They included the United Brothers of Friendship (founded 1861, reorganized 1868) and their female partner, the Sisters of the Mysterious Ten (1878), the Mosaic Templars (1883), and the Twelve Knights and Daughters of Tabor (1871). Although few non-parallel African American societies have survived, in their prime they demonstrated the originality of black fraternalists. For instance, the True Reformers, founded in 1873 and reorganized in 1881, helped pioneer life insurance that went beyond provision for burial. Women eventually dominated the Independent Order of St. Luke, founded in 1867, with Maggie Lena Walker in charge from 1899 until her death in 1934. Both the True Reformers and the St. Luke society operated banks in Richmond, Virginia. The True Reformer bank collapsed in 1910, but the St. Luke Penny Savings Bank survived the Great Depression, and after a merger with two other black banks, it continues today as the Consolidated Bank and Trust Company. In the early 20th century, the True Reformers claimed 100,000 members, and in the mid-1920s, St. Luke claimed a similar number. None of these societies exists today.

The Knights of Peter Claver, a Roman Catholic organization founded in 1909, has a distinctive name but can be considered a society parallel to that of a white fraternal order, the Knights of Columbus. Although never large, the Knights of Peter Claver and its women's auxiliary, founded in 1922, still exist.

By the start of the 21st century, fraternal societies had gone out of fashion, and most of their members, black and white, were elderly or in late middle age. Most of the societies have become purely social organizations that patronize community philanthropies such as education and health. Embarrassed by now unfashionably flamboyant titles and costumes, most historians have neglected fraternal societies despite their historic importance.

See also: Benevolent Societies; Prince Hall Masonry

David M. Fahey

Bibliography

Fahey, David M., ed. *The Black Lodge in White America: "True Reformer" Browne and His Economic Strategy.* Dayton, OH: Wright State University Press, 1994.

Marlowe, Gertrude Woodruff. *A Right Worthy Grand Mission: Maggie Lena Walker and the Quest for Black Economic Empowerment.* Washington, D.C.: Howard University Press, 2003.

Mjagkij, Nina, ed. *Organizing Black America: An Encyclopedia of African American Associations.* New York: Garland, 2001.

Skocpol, Theda, Ariane Liazos, and Marshall Ganz. *African American Fraternal Groups, Civil Democracy, and the Struggle for Equal Rights.* Princeton, NJ: Princeton University Press, forthcoming.

Black Seminoles

The term Black Seminoles refers to escaped black slaves and free Africans in the antebellum American South who fled plantation slavery and joined indigenous Seminole communities in Florida. Independent communities composed of fugitives were known as maroons. The maroons that produced Black Seminole people began in the late 18th and early 19th centuries, as fugitive slaves headed south to Florida in greater numbers.

There were several ways in which Africans became incorporated into Seminole communities. Initially, Seminole people, particularly those in powerful political positions within the community, purchased black slaves. Seminole slavery was quite different from the plantation slavery in the American South. Blacks enslaved by Seminoles owed relatively little to their masters and often had infrequent interactions with them. Generally, Seminoles who owned slaves expected only a yearly tribute from them. Enslaved people were also sometimes captured from plantations. This happened frequently during times of conflict, when the Seminoles needed to increase their fighting forces. Finally, runaway slaves from white plantations also formed alliances with the Seminoles.

African maroon communities existed alongside Seminole communities, and cooperation developed between them. Cultural syncretism occurred between Africans and the Seminoles in this context, as Africans adopted such cultural aspects as the dress, food, and shelter style of the Seminoles. Further, there is evidence of West African influences on Seminole artwork. However, although marooned slaves did become incorporated into some aspects of Seminole communities and maroons, and Seminoles did have cultural influences on each other, this incorporation did not always occur via the creation of kinship ties. In fact, maroons often did not actually become members of indigenous Seminole communities or kinship circles. Intermarriage occurred, but infrequently. Seminole kinship is based on matrilineality, which would have meant, for instance, that babies born to black women would have been outside the bounds of Seminole kinship.

The relationship between the African maroons and the Seminoles was strengthened by their shared conflict with white Southerners and the U.S. government. Conflict between the Seminoles and Africans and the United States coalesced in the early 19th century, after proposals arose that threatened to force the removal of the Seminoles from Florida. After 1812, white Southerners, who saw the Afro-Seminole communities as threats to the slaveholding South, were determined to try to remove the Seminoles from the region. As a result, politicians conspired to relocate Native Americans to "Indian Territory," in what is now Oklahoma. This conflict resulted in the destruction of two Seminole settlements in Florida and many Seminoles and Africans fleeing into the swamplands. Other conflicts resulting from white interference ensued in the years that followed, including battles against Andrew Jackson during the First Seminole War, which occurred from 1817 to 1819.

On May 28, 1830, Congress passed the Indian Removal Act, which sought to address the concerns of white Southerners in Florida who felt that the presence of the Seminole communities encouraged slaves to abscond and that the maroons and Seminoles threatened their livelihood. Kevin Mulroy argues that the cooperative resistance mounted by Seminoles and Africans was based on two fears. First, black maroons became concerned that their freedom would be threatened by this removal, and second, indigenous Seminoles feared the loss of tributaries from their slaves if they were to be moved.

The Second Seminole War began in 1835, following the proposed Indian Removal Act. The U.S. army employed divide-and-conquer tactics that initially worked but ultimately backfired, given that whites were unsure what to do with the black Seminole maroons. It was feared that if they were returned to plantations, their knowledge of the Florida countryside would facilitate their renewed escapes, and whites were also apprehensive of their military abilities. In the end, U.S. general Thomas Jessup recommended sending the maroons west with the indigenous Seminoles.

After the removal of the Seminoles to Oklahoma, tensions grew between the indigenous groups and the maroons. In "Indian Territory," Seminoles were subject to the laws of the Creek nation, which was particularly devastating for both free and enslaved blacks in Seminole communities. Creek laws made blacks vulnerable to recapture and re-enslavement under white plantation slavery. Further, Creek laws institutionalized inequality between Native Americans and blacks, stripping blacks of some of the privileges they had previously enjoyed in Seminole society in Florida. This period gave rise to a leader among the maroons, John Horse, whose primary goal was to maintain the autonomy of Black Seminole maroons.

Separate Black Seminole maroon communities continued to exist throughout the 19th century, as did slaves and tributaries within indigenous Seminole communities. The end of the American Civil War signaled freedom for those blacks still "owned" by Seminoles. Emancipation eliminated the annual tribute they had been required to pay Seminole masters and also eliminated the constant fear of kidnap and sale into slavery outside of the Seminole community.

In the postbellum period, "freedmen" and Seminoles continued their practice of residing in separate settlements. Although the black communities were officially part of the Seminole nation, and under its governance, blacks did not culturally incorporate into indigenous Seminole clans. Relations between the two groups in the 20th century were characterized by some tension and some attempts by indigenous Seminoles to exclude Black Seminoles from the Seminole Nation's politics. Yet in contemporary society, some efforts are being made, both by scholars and by Black Seminoles themselves, to fully acknowledge the history of the Black Seminoles and to mend the relationship between them and indigenous Seminole people.

See also: Destination, Florida; Seminole Wars

Lindsay Sumner

Bibliography

Landers, Jane. "Black Community and Culture in the Southeastern Borderlands." *Journal of the Early Republic* 18, no. 1 (Spring 1998):117–34.

Mulroy, Kevin. *The Seminole Freedmen: A History.* Norman: University of Oklahoma Press, 2007.

Porter, Kenneth. *The Black Seminoles: History of a Freedom-Seeking People.* Gainesville: University Press of Florida, 1996.

A black Seminole named Abraham, one of many escaped black slaves absorbed into the Seminole nation. (Library of Congress)

Black Wedding Traditions

Black wedding traditions are as varied and as diverse as the individuals who adapt them. African Americans sometimes choose to incorporate religious, spiritual, and cultural rituals and symbols that honor their African ancestors and heritage. Black wedding traditions can be said to foster a sense of connectedness among wedding participants, as well as provide continuity between past and present circumstances.

In many world cultures, marriage is considered a union between two families who may share different wedding traditions. These might include consulting with family elders for permission to marry; exchanging dowry, livestock, or property rights; participating in a prerequisite period of supervised courtship; or a combination of these. In the United States, bridal showers, bachelor parties, and engagement parties provide occasions for family and friends to prepare the couple for marriage.

Jumping the broom is arguably the most well-known African American wedding tradition. In a number of African cultures, the broom symbolizes the beginnings of shared domestic life. During slavery, African American couples were denied the right to legally marry. The practice of jumping the broom emerged as a symbolic means of entering into marriage. In these instances, slaves would gather either in secret or with the permission of the slave owner to witness a couple's pledge of devotion. At the conclusion of the pledge, a broom would be placed on the ground in front of them, and they would jump over it to mark their transition into married life.

This custom was highly publicized in the made-for-television adaptation of Alex Haley's *Roots* and has gained in popularity since the Afrocentric cultural movements of the 1970s. Oftentimes, the broom is decorated by bridesmaids, family members, or friends. In many contemporary African American wedding ceremonies, the bride and groom may opt to jump the broom following the exchange of wedding vows or their legal pronouncement as man and wife, just prior to the recessional at the end of their wedding ceremony.

African Americans have also borrowed a number of rituals from throughout the African Diaspora. Some of the lesser known include crossing two sticks as a sign of commitment and pouring out libations in honor of the couple's ancestors. Contemporary brides and grooms often decorate the venue where their ceremony is held with flowers; those who marry in spiritual venues tend to place flowers on the altar as an offering. Elaborate hairstyles, African-inspired headpieces and fabrics (such as kente, mudcloth, or aso-oke prints) are sometimes integrated with Western attire and/or family heirlooms. African American couples may also choose to fuse Christian, Muslim, Jewish, or other religious ceremonial elements with spiritual and performative practices such as West African drumming and dance. Members of black fraternities and sororities sometimes incorporate the symbols, colors, mottos, flowers, mission, and members of their organizations into their weddings.

The wedding feast is one of the most time-honored links between peoples of African descent in the Diaspora. Wedding receptions provide opportunities for family

Jumping the broom at a slave wedding, about 1820. (Art Media)

members and friends to gather together and celebrate the festive occasion with food, drink, entertainment, and merriment. Depending on the preferences of the bride and groom, any number of ethnic and familial specialties may make their way onto African American wedding reception tables. Banquet menus may include regional specialties as diverse as Maryland crab cakes, Caribbean-inspired black cake, seafood gumbo, okra and tomatoes, red velvet cake, or palm wine. Although the wedding ceremony may have a more subdued, religious, or spiritual theme, the reception may include a live band, drummers, or DJ playing songs by black artists.

See also: Africanisms; Black Churches; Black Folk Culture

Lori Baptista

Bibliography

Cole, Harriet. *Jumping the Broom: The African-American Wedding Planner.* New York: Henry Holt, 1993.

Cole, Harriet. *Vows: The African-American Couple's Guide to Designing a Sacred Ceremony.* New York: Simon & Schuster, 2004.

Sturgis, Ingrid. *The Nubian Wedding Book.* New York: Crown Publishers, 1997.

Blackface Minstrelsy

Blackface minstrelsy was one of the central cultural forces in America from the early 19th century through the mid-20th century. It was arguably the most popular form of entertainment in the nation throughout most of the 19th century, appealing primarily to audiences that were as vast and diverse as America itself. Its primary agents were individual white performers and later troupes of four to five "Ethiopian delineators" who blackened their skin with burnt cork and performed dances, songs, and skits that they claimed were representative of genuine slave culture. In essence, minstrel shows constituted America's first national theater. It is also the source of damaging racial stereotypes that have had a devastating impact on American attitudes about African Americans and other ethnic populations.

The practice of white performers darkening their faces with makeup to perform as black characters was initially sparked by necessity in the early years of the 19th-century; black actors were not allowed to perform in white productions. The early practice of blackface also harkened back to the European traditions of the theater of misrule and festival revelry, events where clowns with blackened faces often offered parodies of and against standing social hierarchies. In early 19th-century America, white actors also had occasion to blacken their faces to perform in stage parodies of European opera. More a form of burlesque than of what would later become minstrel shows, these opera parodies might offer such fare as *Lo, Som am de Beauties* (based on Bellini's *La Sonnambula*) and *Lucy Did Sham a Moor* (based on Donizetti's *Lucia du Lammermoor*). The thrust of productions such as these was less to imitate or represent black behavior and culture than to lampoon the latest popular opera—a tradition long popular on both sides of the Atlantic. But it was an independent (and generally deeply flawed) imitation of black culture that formed the central conceit of blackface minstrelsy and sustained the tradition well into the 20th century.

The trend of distinct blackface performance was well established by the late 1820s, as musicians began to capitalize on the growing interest among Northern audiences in black culture and music. Performers such as George Washington Dixon and J. W. Sweeney found notoriety by performing musical numbers in blackface between the acts of more mainstream entertainments. Notably, it was not uncommon for street performers who actually were black to offer their routines in the byways of most Northern cities, but because white people were commonly uncomfortable about direct contact with "negroes," white performers in blackface posed a more acceptable option. Some of these earlier performers did have direct experience of black culture, either through association with free blacks or through youths spent in the slaveholding South. But many simply used blackface as a guise and offered as the music of blacks what were in fact versions and adaptations of British melodies.

Although this brand of itinerant blackface minstrelsy was a common diversion, it was the work of minstrel showman T. D. Rice that would propel the medium to a cultural phenomenon. While on tour in 1828, Rice happened to see an old, crippled black man performing for money in the street, dancing a strange step and singing, "Weel about to turn about and do jus so / Ebery time I weel about, I jump Jim Crow." Rice, a particularly capable dancer, was so taken by the routine that he resolved to learn the song and dance himself and offer it as part of a performance he was to do that night. After learning the song and the steps from the old black man (and according to some accounts, even borrowing the old man's clothes to wear as the evening's costume), Rice rushed to the theater to "blacken up." That evening, the song "Jim Crow" and the dance routine that Rice performed sparked a sensation that would quickly propel the actor from obscurity to stardom.

Rice brought to the performance a level of physicality that audiences responded to with fascination and delight; his popularity led to tours of major venues in both America and Britain. As James Kennard Jr. reported in 1845 "From the nobility in gentry, down to the lowest chimney-sweep in Great Britain, from the member of Congress, down to the young apprentice or school-boy in America, it was all: 'Turn about and wheel about and do just so / And every time I turn about I jump Jim Crow'" (James Kennard Jr. quoted in Lott, Love and Theft, 56). Although blackface performance in America before the Jim Crow phenomenon was generally offered as a between-act diversion, Rice's popularity established the material as a central entertainment worthy of a full evening's venue.

What seemed to capture the audience's fascination was the dance. There was something about the odd and exaggerated step—something about Rice's apt execution of the movements—that thrilled the crowd as the routine of no other blackface performer ever had. Rather than simply offering music and dance aligned with British folk forms, as had been the standard, Rice offered a routine based on an actual slave song and imitative of black dance. That he captured the kind of hitch and swagger the audience perceived as an embodiment of black-seeming corporality marked the routine not just as a masquerade but also as means of transgression. The song and dance were nothing new, as evidenced by the black performer Rice studied on the street. What was new was that Rice, a white man, was performing the material with startling accuracy. In effect, he made the dance visible in ways that it could not be when performed by blacks in the street; he could bring the curious and exotic dance to a white audience without bringing them into direct proximity with a "troubling" black body.

This new mode of blackface performance marked a seismic shift in the attitudes that showmen and audiences brought to minstrelsy. In an era when Americans were expected to observe a dizzying number of rules of comportment and etiquette, the flamboyance of this new variety of blackface performance offered much-needed release to white audiences. Rice (and the bevy of white performers who followed in his wake) was generally bound by the same standards of behavior that the audience was, but the pretense of performing black identity licensed him to flap his arms wildly and hoot and jump. Thus blackface became a screen on which white audiences could project their suppressed urges and repressed behavior. Unchallenged by the viable presence of black performers, minstrel performance resulted in representations of black culture that became increasingly distorted and increasingly disparaging of black people.

The transition of minstrelsy from an innocuous folk form to a transgressive cultural phenomenon was signaled by performances that became increasingly rowdy and raucous. Blackface showmen knew how to play to the crowd, dancing wildly (often suggestively) to the stomping syncopation of songs full of double entendres. The songs were sometime based on tunes from actual black folk traditions, but they were more regularly melodies created by the performers themselves and presented as authentic. With the accompaniment of the fiddle or the banjo (a new instrument derived from African musical forms), the blackface performers offered a boisterous mode of entertainment that seemed, to an often-uninformed audience, to be utterly new and exotically reckless. Performances were often so boisterous that overenthusiastic audience members routinely rushed onto the stage in spontaneous participation with the minstrel performer.

Although women had in the past been among the audiences who enjoyed earlier between-act varieties of blackface performance, the enthusiasm of crowd response quickly established this new mode as an entertainment that was too rough for proper ladies. As a result, the Jim Crow phenomenon resituated the medium as one that initially catered to an all-male crowd. Liberated from codes of propriety generally upheld in mixed company, male performers and audiences could indulge the full freedom and flamboyance the blackened guise afforded. Using the black cork as a screen of sorts, white male performers could offer their white male audiences uncensored projections of their own repressed physicality cast upon imaginary black male identity.

The effect was not lost on opportunistic printers, who cranked out the lyrics of versions and improvisations of the most popular melodies almost as quickly as performers gave them voice. Indeed, the sudden rise in the popularity of minstrelsy was in part due to print traffic of minstrel music in the form of broadsides (cheaply produced, individual pages of minstrel song lyrics that were sold on the streets for pennies per page) and later in sheet music (rough transcriptions of minstrel songs arranged for those able to play the tunes on the piano in their homes). It was in the form of sheet music, removed from the antics of the minstrel hall, that many Americans learned what to make of the images and messages of the blackface tradition.

Within a few years, blackface minstrelsy began to suffer from its initial notoriety and from its increasingly bawdy reputation. The narrowing of the audience for live performances and the increasing availability of minstrel sheet music weakened a medium that only a few years earlier had been a vibrant force. But it was the waning of the popularity of one-man minstrel shows that inspired the next shift in the evolution of minstrel performance. In the winter of 1842, a season where a weakened economy was having an ill effect on ticket sales, four individual performers decided to pool their resources and perform as a group. It was in this way that Dan Emmett, Billy Whitlock, Dick Pelham, and Frank Brower formed the Virginia Minstrels, the first minstrel troupe. Their idea for offering a full evening's

Music cover illustrated with caricatures of six minstrels in two scenes, 1830–1860. (Library of Congress)

entertainment featuring songs, dancing, and skits soon set the standard for what would become the fully realized minstrel show.

The variety of performance proved instantly popular with audiences. Previously, blackface shows had involved one man offering dances and songs, perhaps with an additional player providing music on the banjo or fiddle. But the Virginia Minstrels offered an evening of three-fold entertainment. For the first part of the show, the entire troupe sat in chairs arranged on the stage in a semicircle to play, sing, joke, and interact with each other and the audience. In addition to serving as part of the ensemble, each member of the troupe played a particular role. The "interlocutor," sitting at the center of the troupe, played banjo or fiddle and served as the comically pompous master of ceremonies and straight man to the more impish members of the team. Although he acted as the butt of many of the jokes, the actor who played the part actually served the central function of reading the reactions and energy of each audience so that he could best set up the largely improvised jokes and set the pacing of the show. To his side sat the balladeer—generally the most skilled musician of the troupe, who commonly sang lead and amazed the audience with his banjo virtuosity. In the outside chairs sat the end men (commonly named "Tambo" and "Bones"), who played percussion and served as the main jokesters of the troupe. Turning jokes and riddles against the interlocutor and each other, as well as improvising exchanges with the audience, these two players mugged and contorted to the music to assure that the performance generated a particularly high grade of frenetic energy.

The second part of the show (known as "the olio") consisted of variety acts, including acrobatics, individual song and dance routines, novelty acts (commonly featuring magicians, circus players, and drag queens), instrumental solos, and—the most central feature—the stump speech. Always a crowd favorite, the stump speech presented the interlocutor in the comic guise of a preacher, lawyer, mock politician, or quack doctor who in attempting to sound learned would offer a sermon, speech, or lecture riddled with malapropisms and inaccuracies.

The third and final part of the show offered a one-act skit, generally set on a Southern plantation. Here the troupe might offer a parody of a popular play, historical event, or opera. Often featuring elaborate sets, props, and costumes, the final act gave each member of the troupe the opportunity to show his full talents in the broadest possible context. Whatever the story or setting, the final act was punctuated with a major song-and-dance number offering a favorite melody (commonly the song "Miss Lucy Long") that the troupe and the audience might all sing together.

The success of the Virginia Minstrels not only reinvented minstrelsy but also reinvigorated it, and with the format they originated, the minstrel show came to its full realization. The new venue also provided promoters with an opportunity to expand the audience base for blackface performance. Realizing that broadening the appeal of live minstrel performance only increased sales, enterprising troupes took great efforts to clean up their acts. By the end of the 1840s, women and more refined classes began to rejoin the audience for blackface shows in increasing numbers. Although to some degree the shift can be attributed to the efforts of troupes that refashioned the traditional material to meet the exacting standards of more sensitive theatergoers, much of the change in the composition of minstrel show audiences can also be traced to the marketing of the medium through the sheet music trade.

As early as 1840, music publishers began to appreciate that by softening the suggestive edge of the lyrics and standardizing the more exotic and unfamiliar musical elements that characterized live performance of minstrel musicians, they might find among the uncertain and restricted confines of the parlor a willing and steady market. Potential consumers among the parlor set had ready income and would pay more for elegantly produced sheet music than working-class lads might pay for cheaply produced lyric sheets sold by street vendors. Also, those striving to meet the exacting standards of parlor posture and propriety appreciated the opportunity for fun and modest abandon offered by carefully recalibrated minstrel songs.

The readjustment of the market for minstrel music is reflected in a shift in the composition of minstrel sheet music covers in the early 1840s—a shift that suggests that publishers of the material had designs on parlor commerce. In the early years of the blackface show, cover art for minstrel sheet music usually offered images of the actual performers who popularized the tunes on the minstrel stage. Cover illustrations from the 1830s and early 1840s often depict an individual performer: T. D. Rice, Peter Whitlock, or any of the other artists who flocked to reproduce the wildly popular Jim Crow routine. In these early years, music publishers undoubtedly targeted male consumers,

who were more likely to have frequented performances and thus were familiar with the players who performed the rowdy, sometimes bawdy routines. To draw on that audience, publishers depended on portraits of the most popular performers in poses that suggested the dance that had become all the rage. In contrast, later in the decade, when the blackface tradition broadened, and the fully realized minstrel show became the standard, cover illustration reflected the change by offering depictions of full minstrel troupes— four or five blackened figures splayed ridiculously (often suggestively) in their chairs, instruments prominently displayed. These kinds of shows still catered primarily to male audiences, and so publishers offered sheet music covers that simply reflected the central image associated with the performances—the absurdly contorted figures of the "interlocutor," "end men," musicians, and balladeer.

However, by the mid-1840s and throughout the 1850s, a notable shift in the representation of minstrel performers occurred in the design of sheet music cover art. Depictions of upstanding, well-groomed white performers began to appear along with the grotesque, black characters they portrayed. The upright gents presented an element of elegance, of prestige, even as they perpetuated base parodies of black identity. Cover illustrations seemed to position the dapper entertainers as gentlemen callers, politely awaiting introduction into the refined space of the family parlor, or as handsome escorts inviting women to potentially join in actually attending the fun and spectacle of a performance. The white figures ushered the rollicking minstrel show into the intimate confines of the American home, and sheet music offered the means for every parlor to be transformed into a minstrel stage, every family gathering a potential opportunity to metaphorically "blacken up" and step into the limelight. Simultaneously, the potentially threatening atmosphere of the minstrel theater was neutralized even as gaudy racial misrepresentations remained in tact.

The material marks a reciprocal relationship in the latter years of the 1840s between the refined aesthetics of the parlor and the playful antics of blackface performance of the stage. This "cross pollination" between the stage and parlor (an exchange that both legitimized race parody and licensed release in refined contexts) not only expanded the market for blackface material but also broadened acceptance of pervasive racial stereotypes across the full spectrum of American society. Minstrel troupes such as E. P. Christy's Minstrels and the Virginia Serenaders performed to the most elite of mid-century society in their own lavish "Ethiopian Opera Houses." In addition to more playful (but respectful) tunes, these high-class minstrels offered beautiful love songs and sentimental ballads in four-part harmony. Master songsmith Stephen Foster composed some of his most popular (and most enduring) melodies for the minstrel stage. Even the venerated *Uncle Tom's Cabin* was absorbed into the minstrel tradition. Although some were beginning to perceive the blackface tradition as damaging and racially insulting (most notably ex-slave and abolitionist Frederick Douglass), most audiences failed to see minstrel shows as anything other than harmless entertainment. Few would have acknowledged that the satisfaction of laughing at comedic incongruity came from its power to assure audience members of their superiority over the focus of the humor—black characters. Regardless of the artistry of the performers or the cleverness of the renditions, the central comedic paradigm positioned racial superiority as the pivotal theme. But the parodies themselves were leveraged on what had already become pervasive assumptions of the racial inferiority of blacks. Paradoxically, even as white audiences indulged their sense of superiority over the representations of blacks in these productions, they were also deeply invested in the cultural practice of (un)seeing black identity. That white performers and audiences accepted that black peoples' skin served as a vacant area for playing out fantasies demonstrates again that the persistent process of blackface in America depended upon denying black identity.

Nowhere is this more evident than in the decades between the Civil War and World War I. African American performers found more opportunity to occupy the stage, but restricted by the warped perceptions of white audiences, black performers were pressured to perform the same kinds of minstrel stereotypes their white predecessors had invented. Their success depended on their own brilliant self-ridicule and their ability to assure their white audience of the validity of their own stereotypes. White audiences did not want to see black culture as it actually was and were generally not empathetic toward or interested in black issues and identity. What they wanted were songs and routines that reinforced their nostalgia for absurdly simplistic images of blacks generated decade after decade on the antebellum minstrel stage. In addition to trying to infuse more humanity into their own representations, African Americans in the post–Civil War era had to compete against

more established troupes of white performers—groups that generally monopolized the major performance stages and venues. The minstrel show in postbellum America began to expand to full-scale extravaganzas, sometimes involving as many as a hundred minstrels, sideshow acts, acrobats, circus acts, and dancing girls. These shows would by the 1880s evolve into Vaudeville.

In print music, songs from the minstrel stage continued to be popular. But in the years after the war and particularly in the post-Reconstruction era, whether songs about black figures originated from minstrelsy or not, they regularly presented the domestic lives of African Americans as woefully inadequate. Indeed, throughout the end of the 19th century, the sheet music presented and portrayed a black population incapable of maintaining the respectable bonds that were otherwise projected as bringing American families together. Even as the sanctity of family ties was being most strongly asserted as central to national identity, and even as those messages were being perpetuated in the broader-sweep popular sheet music being consumed in the domestic sphere, blacks were being denied access, excluded from the fantasy of comfort and care indulged by the rest of the population. Rather, black identity was presented as base, absurd, inferior, and uncivilized—all that was antithetical to the idealized aesthetics and aptitudes of the rest of the nation.

That sheet music offering images of failed black families became so common in post-Reconstruction America reflects a national atmosphere dubious of African Americans. Undeniably, images and messages of antebellum minstrel sheet music helped to drive into the psyche of Americans the idea that blacks were foolish, hypersexual, and (unless carefully monitored) dangerous: these were the assumptions about black behavior that Americans in the North were trying to reconcile with the behavior and attitudes of blacks now living among them in increasing numbers in urban centers. The assumptions that shaped these attitudes about black behavior were anchored to parlor culture's embrace of minstrel material in mid-century America. On the covers and in the music of antebellum sheet music, the blackface tradition had offered an endless stream of images of blacks as buffoons; as careless and carefree braggarts; as wanton women; as hot-tempered, ill-tempered, and intemperate lovers; as thieves; and as fops. Repeatedly presented as unable to maintain even the most basic standards of decorum and dignity, comic black figures amused parlor-dwelling Americans and eased middle-class uncertainty by marking the woeful extremes of social failure. Unchecked and unchallenged for decades, these images informed and influenced attitudes about black identity by importing devastatingly racist ideology into the American home in the guise of harmless entertainment.

Still, there were some ways black characters did figure into idyllic and nostalgic domestic scenes. Consider such pieces as "Old Uncle Ned," "The Old Piney Woods," or "Carry Me Back to Old Virginny"—songs that are among the most enduring melodies from the minstrel stage. In songs such at these, black characters are depicted tenderly, even lovingly, as they pine away for lost homes or absent loved ones. But in the songs, almost without exception, images of home in domestic peace are conflated with mythic plantation life—that happier time and place where the now world-weary black characters had supposedly led carefree lives under the tender care of their kindly white masters. The cover art often depicts woeful black figures who cast their longing gazes at gracious plantation scenes that seem to shimmer in the distance. The dynamic was also reproduced in sheet music covers and melodies that depict white families who have lost their beloved slaves—the dear "aunts" and "uncles" who once graced the family circle. In both situations, the domestic ideal *could* be realized for black figures, not through their own autonomous family ties but rather through filling their defined role in the completion of the idyllic domestic scenes of their white masters. The message is that blacks can be upstanding, dignified, and loyal, but only when brought into the perfecting orbit of the white family circle—that the idealized domestic atmosphere of white American families can even serve to domesticate blacks and tame their otherwise wild and unruly temperaments.

Although vaudeville would eclipse the minstrel show in the late 19th century, minstrel performance would continue to play a part in the form of virulently racist coon songs. Commonly performed by whites in blackface (but occasionally performed by African Americans), these routines presented unabashedly racist depictions of blacks as violent, oversexed, shiftless, and ignorant. This image of blacks as buffoons, braggarts, and brawlers was the distillation of minstrelsy's half-century of cultural slander and misrepresentation. Minstrelsy also played a role in many of the evolving modes of mass media. Some of Thomas Edison's earliest recordings for the phonograph were of

minstrel shows. One of the most popular shows in early radio was *Amos and Andy*, a comedy show where two white men voiced black characters drawn from the minstrel tradition. Early producers of mass-produced food products populated their labels with figures such as Aunt Jemima and Uncle Ben, carryovers from the blackface tradition. Blackface played a central part in landmark films of the early 20th century; white performers in blackface are central features of movies such as D. W. Griffith's *The Birth of a Nation* and Al Jolson's *The Jazz Singer*; blackface routines appeared regularly in Hollywood films as late as 1954 (notably, in the classic *White Christmas*).

Equally indicative of the influence of minstrelsy, roles played by African Americans throughout the mid-20th century on the stage, in films, and on the radio were commonly drawn from stereotypes from the blackface tradition. At one point, African American actor Bert Williams was one of the highest-paid performers in the Ziegfeld Follies, but the role he played (generally in blackface) was one derived from the minstrel tradition. Hattie McDaniel was the first African American to win an Academy Award (1940), but it was for playing the role of Mammy in the film *Gone With the Wind*, a character closely connected to the blackface tradition. The first television shows that featured African American characters where *Beulah* (starring Hattie McDaniel as the housekeeper for a white family) and *Amos and Andy* (starring Alvin Childress and Spencer Williams, two African American actors playing the characters originating from the earlier radio show). Although the actors playing these roles brought their very real talent to bear, the roles were undeniably tied to characters rooted in blackface minstrelsy.

During the first half of the century, the traditional minstrel show experienced a second life through countless amateur productions. Classic scripts and routines from the 19th century were mainstays for church bazaars, community theater, and school productions throughout the country. But by the Civil Rights movement of the 1960s, blackface minstrelsy was generally a stigmatized form, though stereotypes born from the tradition persist.

In the 2000 satire *Bamboozled*, filmmaker Spike Lee directly addressed the legacy of blackface minstrelsy in American culture. The plot follows the exploits of a black man who works as a writer for a major television network. Having had no luck drawing an audience for shows depicting black characters as successful members of the upper-middle-class, the writer is pressured by his superiors to generate a script about black characters that will have broad appeal. In frustration, the writer develops a pilot for what he describes as a "new millennium minstrel show," his expectation being that the courageously racist script will assure his dismissal and free him from his contract with the network. But to his surprise, not only is the pilot accepted by the network, but the show goes into production, ultimately becoming the most popular program on television. In the film, Lee explores many complex, even contradictory themes: the power of modern media, the considerable currency stereotypes of blacks still hold in American society, the ways that blacks are constrained by these stereotypes, and the ways that blacks themselves are complicit in perpetuating them. A parallel theme implicit in the film is the main character's own pantomime—a black man who strictly "performs" white behavior, speech, and mannerisms; he willingly sacrifices his own identity to assure his success in white society. In some ways the film can be read as a modern morality play in which Lee offers an important lesson about the modes and machinery of blackface that are still in operation in American culture. These stereotypes, he seems to argue, are not mere paranoid imagining of African Americans; the fantasies the minstrel tradition has etched upon our social consciousness are still present and continue to influence our attitudes about race and identity.

See also: Jim Crow; Lee, Spike; *The Birth of a Nation*; White Supremacy

Stephanie Dunson

Bibliography

Bean, Annemarie, James V. Hatch, and Brooks McNamara, eds. *Inside the Minstrel Mask: Readings in Nineteenth-Century Blackface Minstrelsy*. Hanover, NH: Wesleyan University Press, 1996.
Cockrell, Dale. *Demons of Disorder: Early Blackface Minstrels and Their World*. Cambridge, UK: Cambridge University Press, 1997.
Lhamon, W. T., Jr. *Raising Cain: Blackface Performance from Jim Crow to Hip Hop*. Cambridge, MA: Harvard University Press, 1998.
Lott, Eric. *Love and Theft: Blackface Minstrelsy and the American Working Class*. New York: Oxford University Press, 1993.
Mahar, William J. *Behind the Burnt Cork Mask: Early Blackface Minstrelsy and Antebellum American Popular Culture*. Urbana: University of Illinois Press, 1999.
Nathan, Hans. *Dan Emmett and the Rise of Early Negro Minstrelsy*. Norman: University of Oklahoma Press, 1962.
Rehin, George F. "The Darker Image: American Negro Minstrelsy through the Historian's Lens." *Journal of American Studies* 9, no. 3 (1981):365–73.
Toll, Robert C. *Blacking Up: The Minstrel Show in Nineteenth-Century America*. New York: Oxford University Press, 1974.

Blue Notes

Blues notes are tones in African American music performed at a different pitch from notes on the major scale for expressive purposes. The most commonly lowered scale degrees include the third, seventh, and fifth (by order of frequency), although any note could be lowered to produce a "bluesy" feeling in specific contexts. The pitches usually do not remain stable and frequently rise and fall, making notation within Western musical conventions difficult. The notes will usually be lowered by a quarter tone to a semitone. Blue notes have been observed in nearly all forms of African American music, including the blues, jazz, rock, gospel, work songs, spirituals, R&B, soul, and funk.

Many cite origins in sub-Saharan African music, brought over by slaves to North America, but recent studies cannot point to a single definitive source. Europeans imported slaves from many different regions and of Africa, all with very different musical traditions, making musicological detective work difficult. Further complicating research is the presence of lowered quarter and semitones in much folk music around the world, including that of Muslim and European folk music. However, it is only over a European harmonic system that the inflected notes lead to a blues tonality or feeling. Thus, all lowered thirds and sevenths are not necessarily blue notes.

Some musical theorists argue that inserting "blue notes" into a Western major/minor musical framework oversimplifies the harmonies inherit in African American music. Instead, they argue, genres such as jazz and blues should be discussed with a unique conception of harmony divorced from Western musical theory. Regardless of their origin, blue notes provide an anchoring concept in African American music that appropriately takes influences from European and African sources.

See also: Africanisms; Blues Music

Peter Carr Jones

Bibliography
Tallmadge, William. "Blue Notes and Blue Tonality." *The Black Perspective in Music* 12, no. 2 (Autumn 1984):155–65.
Weisenthaunet, Hans. "Is There Such a Thing as the 'Blue Note'?" *Popular Music* 20, no. 1 (January 2001):99–116.

Blues Music

During the 1890s, a new form of secular African American folk music—blues music—emerged among blacks in the rural areas and small towns of the Deep South, particularly on large plantations and at industrial sites in the Mississippi River valley. Initially, the blues was a highly localized music that served blacks in the aforementioned areas as a means of expressing, and possibly curtailing, their "blue" feelings as well as a mode of protest against their social marginalization during the most restrictive period of Jim Crow laws. Eventually, the blues would revolutionize American music, inspiring commercial forms of the blues and fundamentally influencing such 20th-century popular music genres as jazz, country music, rhythm and blues, and rock 'n' roll.

Uninitiated listeners have sometimes characterized blues music as possessing a predictable, simple structure, yet the genre is in fact subtly complex; performances of the blues generally balance musical articulation that is both improvisational and idiosyncratic with lyrics that exhibit a high degree of verbal creativity, individuality, emotional directness, and realism. Historically, an important component of blues music was the "blue note" (a musical note expressed with a slight deviation from its standard temperament), a distinctive musical element that would have a profound impact on virtually every genre of American music, whether traditional, popular, or classical.

The originators of blues music were blacks born shortly after emancipation. Many first-generation blues musicians had left small, family-owned, agriculturally underproducing plots of land to take temporary jobs as paid laborers on large cotton farms or as industrial workers. To express their feelings of alienation and frustration from living an insecure, nomadic existence, these musicians wrote lyrics that reflected the everyday experiences of blacks in the South, exploring such themes as the vagaries of interpersonal relationships and the predicament of being socially marginalized (i.e., as outcasts and outlaws). Incorporating musical elements from traditional African American music genres (especially from field hollers and spirituals), blues music was performed informally in public settings (i.e., on the street for tip money from passersby or at neighborhood gatherings) or more formally as entertainment in more exclusive social gatherings (for instance, in small clubs known as "juke joints" or at private parties).

Before World War I, blacks traveling across the South usually performed the blues as solo musicians, singing their interpretations of locally traditional or self-composed blues lyrics to variations of the blues tune form; such performances were generally self-accompanied on one of several instruments—initially on the fiddle, the banjo, or the one-stringed diddley bow (an Africa-derived instrument) and, with increasing frequency by the World War I years, on the piano, the harmonica, and especially the guitar. With its flexibility and portability, the guitar by the 1920s became the instrument most commonly associated with the blues. Guitar techniques utilized by blues players included finger-picking the strings in various tunings (often minor-keyed with unfretted "drone" strings); "bending" strings to produce blue notes; and using a slide (usually a bottleneck or a knife) on the strings to create a whining sound. The instrumental part on the blues guitar was often performed to sound like a second vocal.

In the early 20th century, blues musicians migrating across the Deep South transported the genre to new settings, ultimately yielding several subregional traditions of rural blues (later termed by scholars "country blues"). In east Texas, for instance, blues performed on guitar combined accentuated notes on the bass strings with floating, improvised note patterns on the high strings, whereas the blues that proliferated in the piedmont areas of Georgia, South Carolina, North Carolina, and Virginia emphasized a highly syncopated, intricate finger-picking style on the guitar and a more upbeat and harmonic approach to singing than found elsewhere in the South.

By World War I, several professional black musicians in the South had begun to compose new songs influenced by the blues. The most noteworthy among such musicians was bandleader and composer W. C. Handy, a native of Florence, Alabama, who achieved considerable commercial success through publishing his original blues compositions. After

World War I, rural blues began to be overshadowed by the more sophisticated approach to blues associated with blacks who had migrated to urban areas. At various venues (such as theaters and places selling liquor) in Southern and Northern cities, musicians performed commercial blues songs containing self-consciously urbane lyrics set to standardized rhythmic structures (especially in the popular 12-bar blues form, which incorporated the three-line A-A-B rhyme pattern). Blues singers at such venues tended to be females, several of whom—such as Bessie Smith, Ida Cox, and Ma Rainey—committed part of their blues repertoire for release on commercial records during the first half of the 1920s, attracting new audiences to the blues, including white listeners who would not otherwise have had the opportunity to hear the blues.

By the late 1920s, numerous rural blues performers were likewise making records, including "Mississippi" John Hurt, Nehemiah "Skip" James, Charlie Patton, Henry Thomas, Furry Lewis, Blind Lemon Jefferson, Blind Blake, and Thomas A. "Georgia Tom" Dorsey. Records featuring rural blues at this time rarely sold as widely as overtly commercial urban blues records, and most of the aforementioned musicians ceased performing blues by the 1930s (some—including Patton and Jefferson—died young; others—Hurt and James—gave up music entirely for decades, only to be "rediscovered" by white blues fans in the 1960s; Dorsey gravitated toward sacred music, inventing black gospel music). During the Depression, both urban and rural blues fell out of favor. Testament to the music's comparative obscurity during the 1930s was the fact that Robert Johnson—who today is arguably the most acclaimed rural blues musician of all time—recorded in the mid-1930s for a major label (Columbia), and his biggest hit record then sold only a few thousand copies.

The sound and feeling of the blues remained alive and widely heard, however, during the Depression within another black music genre, as jazz musicians—including such acclaimed instrumentalists as Louis Armstrong, Charlie Christian, Coleman Hawkins, and Charlie Parker and such jazz composers/arrangers as Duke Ellington—turned to the blues for inspiration and thus kept the genre at the forefront of musical experimentation within the United States. Similarly, the blues had a profound impact in the 1920s and 1930s on classical music composers (such as George Gershwin and Aaron Copland). Several white musicians in 1930s-era country music—particularly Jimmie Rodgers,

the Delmore Brothers, and Bob Wills—incorporated into their recordings stylistic techniques and song themes freely interpreted from the blues.

Although the blues had fallen into public neglect nationally, several blues musicians of future importance within the music genre (including Son House, McKinley "Muddy Waters" Morganfield, and Huddie "Leadbelly" Ledbetter) were "discovered" by—and made their first recordings for—folklorist Alan Lomax, who traveled through the rural South to make "field" recordings of various traditional musicians in their home locales. In the late 1940s and early 1950s, the blues experienced a surge in popularity, as a number of recording companies—primarily small labels, such as Chess, Sun, and King—released singles and albums by various practitioners of the new urban blues then being performed in cities in the North (especially in Chicago, the adopted home of such musicians as Muddy Waters and Howlin' Wolf [Chester Burnett], but also in Detroit, where John Lee Hooker was first based); in the South (principally in Memphis, home of Riley "B. B." King, and in Houston, the home location of Sam "Lightnin'" Hopkins); and in the West (for instance, in Oakland, the base for Lowell Fulson).

During the 1940s and 1950s, the blues served as a significant influence on three other emerging American musical genres: gospel, rhythm and blues, and rock 'n' roll. In the early 1960s, the rural blues received a major revival when young white music fans embraced the recordings of an older generation of black blues musicians (such as the forgotten recordings by Robert Johnson), and white entrepreneurs located several still-living rural bluesmen (including Hurt, James, House, and "Mississippi" Fred McDowell) and brought them into the international spotlight. Other black blues musicians soon became widely popular among young whites—urban blues musicians such as B. B. King, Albert King, and Junior Wells and acoustic rural blues acts such as the duo Brownie McGhee and Sonny Terry.

As a result of this new popularity, a generation of rock musicians—including such American acts as Jimi Hendrix, the Lovin' Spoonful, and the Doors and British acts such as Eric Clapton, the Rolling Stones, and Van Morrison—cited the blues as their favorite genre of music and lauded blues musicians as their main sources of inspiration. Meanwhile, emerging to considerable popularity at this time were numerous white blues interpreters—such American musicians as John Hammond Jr., Paul Butterfield, and Johnny

Winter and such British musicians as Alexis Korner and John Mayall. Although the blues' presence on the world music scene diminished somewhat in the 1970s and 1980s, a number of popular musicians—such black musicians as Taj Mahal and Robert Cray and such white musicians as Duane and Gregg Allman, Bonnie Raitt, and Stevie Ray Vaughan—continued to incorporate into their repertoires both blues compositions and blues feeling.

The 1980s and 1990s saw the blues reach new audiences. Older black performers (B. B. King, Buddy Guy, Albert Collins, Ruth Brown, and Koko Taylor, among others) and new blues interpreters (whites such as Rory Block, Roy Book Binder, and Paul Geremia and blacks such as Keb' Mo', Corey Harris, Shemekia Copeland, and Alvin Youngblood Hart) performed blues music to older as well as younger music fans. Recording companies (for instance, Alligator Records and Bullseye Blues) and magazines (most notably, *Living Blues*) were established during this period to showcase the lives and music of both living and deceased blues acts and to promote the blues as a vital, enduring art form. Visibility of the blues increased with the arrival of the new century, with the music genre serving as the subject of several major documentary productions (including *The Blues—A Musical Journey,* a 2003 series of films, with a range of accompanying CD soundtracks, produced by filmmaker Martin Scorsese). The blues as an African American music tradition was also portrayed in *O Brother, Where Art Thou?* (2000), a popular movie and best-selling soundtrack. It is evident that the blues—though emerging within black culture during an earlier era of extreme discrimination—holds significance for people of all walks of life in all eras of human history.

See also: Africanisms; Armstrong, Louis; Blue Notes; Ellington, Duke; Parker, Charlie

Ted Olson

Bibliography
Evans, David. *Big Road Blues: Tradition and Creativity in the Folk Blues.* Berkeley: University of California Press, 1982.
Ferris, William R. *Blues from the Delta.* Garden City, NY: Anchor Press, 1978.
Levine, Lawrence W. *Black Culture and Black Consciousness: Afro-American Folk Thought from Slavery to Freedom.* New York: Oxford University Press, 1977.
Palmer, Robert. *Deep Blues: A Musical and Cultural History of the Mississippi Delta.* New York: Viking Penguin, 1981.
Titon, Jeff Todd. *Early Downhome Blues: A Musical and Cultural Analysis.* Urbana: University of Illinois Press, 1977.

Bottle Trees

The unique practice of placing colored glass bottles and other luminous objects on the ends of tree limbs is a concept that ethnographers and historians link to enslaved Africans originating from the Kongo/Angola coast of West-Central Africa. Instead of glass bottles, it is likely that items such as conch shells and terra cotta pots were used in pre-colonial West-Central Africa, in association with gravesites as a means of both honoring and protecting ancestral spirits. In the American South, this practice went through a significant transformation, and in all likelihood, the introduction of Christianity and other cultural forces played a role in alterations in meanings and practices.

As early as the 18th century, this practice of placing bottles on trees specifically served a protective function—they were to trap evil spirits and prevent them from entering the user's abode. In the syncretic spiritual system that

A bottle tree, at the Pioneer Museum of Alabama. (Jeff Greenberg/ The Image Works)

accompanied the use of bottle trees, adherents believed that evil spirits would become entranced by the spectrum of colors and lights reflected on and inside the bottles by the sun, thus trapping the spirit for eternity. The howling noise the bottles created in the wind were said to be from the tormented and trapped spirits. Even the colors used for the bottles conveyed symbolic meanings. Cobalt blue bottles were noted as being particularly potent in repelling or trapping spirits.

In some cases, bottles were eventually corked and thrown into bodies of water to excise the evil spirit. In others, the bottles were exposed to sunlight as a mechanism of destroying the spirits. The very notions of "evil" spirits and spirits that could be destroyed represent significant departures from Kongo conceptualizations of the afterlife. Through the 19th century, adherents of indigenous Kongo religions in West-Central Africa believed that spirits were, at best, neutral and that ancestral spirits were immortal. Epitomized by the Kongo cosmogram and its various cognate forms (e.g., the ring shout, Capoeira, Vodun iconography), pre-colonial religions in Kongo and other regions of West-Central Africa certainly embraced the notion that spirits were invulnerable and eternal. Thus, the belief systems that undergird the creation and use of bottle trees in the American South represent notable transformations over time. However, what was once a ubiquitous practice in the black South as recently as the mid-20th century in such places as South Carolina, Georgia, Louisiana, Alabama, and Mississippi has largely disappeared with a handful of exceptions. As of the beginning of the 21st century, there is a lively amount of Internet commerce in which metal bottle "trees" using LED lights are crafted and sold—though this manifestation is largely divorced from the diverse spiritual backgrounds of this practice by slaves and their descendants.
See also: Africanisms; Slave Culture; Slave Religion

Walter C. Rucker

Bibliography
Thompson, Robert Farris. *Flash of the Spirit* New York: Vintage Books, 1983.
Thompson, Robert Farris. "Kongo Influences on African-American Artistic Culture." In *Africanisms in American Culture,* ed. Joseph Holloway, 148–84. Bloomington: Indiana University Press, 1991.
Thompson, Robert Farris, and Joseph Cornet. *The Four Moments of the Sun: Kongo Art in Two Worlds.* Washington, D.C.: National Gallery of Art, 1981.

Brer Rabbit

Brer Rabbit (or Brother Rabbit) is one of the most famous figures that appear in African American folktales. He embodies a well-known trickster character. Usually, trickster tales convey narratives of tricks played by a trickster at the expense of one (or several) of his peers. The latter usually outweigh him, but Brer Rabbit almost always outsmarts his bigger counterparts anyway. These stories constitute mimetic transpositions of a search for hope and survival, a will to find one's way out of a tricky situation or a quandary. Brer Rabbit was made notorious through the collection of stories by Joel Chandler Harris titled *Uncle Remus and Other Stories.* The first tale that casts Brer Rabbit is "Tar Baby." The tar baby is a widespread figure in African folklore. In folktales, it is known as an item made of some sticky material with a carved face, which is used to literally ensnare a person; this obviously echoes the metaphorical representations of trapping Africans. Among other meanings, the term "tar baby" has come to designate a situation or a difficulty from which it is virtually impossible to extricate oneself.

More than the quest for spiritual and physical freedom, the stories in which Brer Rabbit appears convey three types of impulse on the trickster's part. First of all, Brer Rabbit, who is lazy and whimsical, is eager to fulfill the least of his most venal needs and envies ("Brer Rabbit and the Mosquitoes?" and "Brer Rabbit Fools Sis Cow"). Second, Brer Rabbit aims at getting out of a trap. It is interesting to notice that this escaping process immutably implies the trapping of another character. This pattern may lead us to believe that Brer Rabbit, although cunning enough to think out a plan to deceive his peers, is not smart enough to avoid the ambush altogether. However, this preliminary step is inevitable in order to complete the process through which the trickster overwhelms the obstacle. There exists a correlation between the significance of achievement and the difficulties to cope with before succeeding. Third, Brer Rabbit sometimes plays tricks for the mere satisfaction of having his "compairs" look foolish ("The Elephant and the Whale") or to demonstrate that his tiny appearance is inversely proportional to his cleverness and slyness.

Brer Rabbit is very often, with just cause, held responsible for any harm done. But in spite of this, he comes up with tactics so as not to get caught. This pragmatic and protean character is indeed able to change his appearance or his voice or even become invisible in order either to mislead others or to protect himself. Brer Rabbit can also take another's identity and pretend to be someone else. The trickster tale can be considered as a contrapuntal type of answer to the quandary of invisibility and of nonrepresentation. Indeed, Brer Rabbit precisely illustrates the way one might use prejudices' face values such as symbolic invisibility and nonrepresentation in order to achieve one's goals. Brer Rabbit also relies on his victims' vices in order to lure them.

For instance, in "Some Are Going, and Some Are Coming," the Rabbit traps the Fox by revisiting on him the blurring vision he was just trapped by at the bottom of a well. He targets the Fox's gluttony. In "Brer Rabbit Earns a Dollar a Minute," the trickster bets on the Bear's belief in getting money effortlessly. In "Brer Rabbit Falls Down the Well," the eponymous character's laziness leads him to act as if he had been hurt by a briar in order to be able to take

Artist's rendition of Brer Rabbit of Joel Chandler Harris' Uncle Remus stories, 1899. (Library of Congress)

a nap. He jumps into a bucket pretending to soothe his paw but falls down the well, and Brer Fox, convinced that Brer Rabbit is playing another ruse, and sure to find out that he is hiding some treasure, wants to join Brer Rabbit; the latter pretends to be fishing, Brer Fox jumps into the bucket, falls down into the well, and both his inquisitiveness and weight extirpate Brer Rabbit from the gap. In "The False Message, Take My Place," the Rabbit was caught by a man and is hanging in a small bag at the end of a tree branch. But he soon convinces the Wolf to take his place so that the latter may reach Heaven faster. The message here is that access to Heaven has to be deserved.

According to Michael P. Carroll, the binary personality of the trickster oscillates between the image of "clever hero" and the one of "selfish buffoon." This association of antagonistic characteristics illustrates the ambivalent behavior that the trickster is liable to opt for. This is a contrasting but seemingly complementary binary pattern. Brer Rabbit invalidates social prejudices, such as negation toward African American culture, a process that is already embodied and launched by the tale itself.

See also: Africanisms; Animal Trickster Stories; Black Folk Culture

Valerie Caruana-Loisel

Bibliography

Carroll, Michael P. "Lévi-Strauss, Freud, and the Trickster: A New Perspective upon an Old Problem." *American Ethnologist* 8, no. 2 (1981):301–13.

Carroll, Michael P. "The Trickster as Selfish Buffoon and Cultural Hero." *Ethos* 12, no. 2 (1984):105–31.

Cumberdance, Daryl. *400 Years of African American Folktale from My People.* New York: Norton, 2002.

Levine, Lawrence W. *Black Culture and Black Consciousness.* London: Oxford University Press, 1978.

Brooks, Gwendolyn

Gwendolyn Elizabeth Brooks (1917–2000) was born on June 17, 1917, in Topeka, Kansas, to a former schoolteacher and the son of a runaway slave. When she was a young child, her family moved to the South Side of Chicago, the city that influenced Brooks's work throughout her career. By the age of 13, she had published her first poem, and as a young adult, Brooks corresponded with some of the most prominent poets of the Harlem Renaissance, such as James Weldon Johnson and Langston Hughes, who encouraged her writing and lauded her poetry.

In 1943, Brooks received an award from the Midwestern Writer's Conference, and in 1945, she published her first book of poetry, *A Street in Bronzeville*. Shortly thereafter, she received the Guggenheim Fellowship. In *Bronzeville*, Brooks presented, expertly, the sights and sounds of life for African Americans in her Chicago suburb. In 1949, she published another collection of poems, *Annie Allen*, for which she was the first African American to receive the Pulitzer Prize for Poetry, and she followed it with her only novel, *Maud Martha* (1953). *In the Mecca* (1968) featured Brooks's musings on Black Power as an alternative form of black activism and considered the importance of such figures as Malcolm X and the Chicago gang, the Blackstone Rangers. After *In the Mecca*, Brooks's personal engagement with Black Power developed, and she left her longtime publisher, Harper & Row, and thereafter published only with black-owned presses for the rest of her career. Also in 1968, Brooks was named the Poet Laureate of Illinois. And in 1972 and 1996, Brooks published her two-part autobiography, *Report from Part One* and *Report from Part Two*.

From the beginning of her career, Brooks refused to shy away from complicated issues. In "The Mother," she tackled the emotional trauma of abortion. Rather than take a side on the controversy, Brooks handles the personal repercussions for the mother of making a decision that she will never be able to forget because of "the children you got that you did not get." She also illustrated her engagement with the changing realities of African American life. In her most famous poem, "We Real Cool" (1960), Brooks considers the problems of alcohol, drugs, and violence as contributors to the deaths of so many young black men. Through her use of plain language and bold line breaks, Brooks posits the premature deaths of these boys as a community epidemic. And in "Gay Chaps at the Bar" and "The Progress," Brooks muses on the troubles faced by black World War II veterans upon their return home.

Gwendolyn Brooks's poems serve as a touchstone of African American history throughout the 20th century. Brooks documented the changing tenor of black activism from the Harlem Renaissance to Black Power, to begin to understand the importance of these movements for social change. In "Malcolm X," Brooks considers the significance of the former Nation of Islam leader as an enigmatic figure

Poet Gwendolyn Brooks, holding a copy of her book A Street in Bronzeville, *published in 1945, was the first African American woman to win a Pulitzer Prize. (Library of Congress)*

of black resistance and hope. In "Paul Robeson," she remembers the man, singer, and activist and the magnitude of his message for Black fraternity. And in "I Am a Black," Brooks ponders the rhetorical switch from black to African American, refusing to relinquish the importance of the term "black" as a connection to people of African descent around the world and as a powerful statement against negative stereotypes.

Although there are many recurrent themes in Gwendolyn Brooks's work, one of the most predominant is her discussion of the lives of everyday African American women. From *A Street in Bronzeville* to *In Montgomery and Other Poems*, published posthumously in 2003, Brooks considers the often-overlooked position of ordinary black women and the lives they live. She has a way of never judging her subjects and is the ultimate observer. In "Sadie and Maud," she discusses two women who, though once close, took two very divergent paths in their lives. Although the reader is supposed to feel bad about Sadie's hard life as a single mother, Brooks feels that Sadie's perseverance is commendable and leaves a legacy with her children that Maud, who went to college but lives alone, does not. These simple portraits are actually complex discussions of the black women whom Brooks encountered and knew intimately.

On December 3, 2000, Gwendolyn Brooks died at her home at the age of 83 after battling cancer. In many ways, Brooks's death spelled the end of an era. Her life and work spanned the majority of the 20th century, and she witnessed some of the most important legal, social, and cultural changes for black people in the United States. But her legacy as an artist and social critic are immense. Her innovative poetry and prose are inspiring, and all of the themes and observations in her poetry remain salient. Gwendolyn Brooks left a voluminous endowment to African American literature and history that are unmatched.

See also: Chicago Defender; Harlem Renaissance

Nicole Jackson

Bibliography

Alexander, Elizabeth, ed. *The Essential Gwendolyn Brooks.* New York: Library of America, 2005.

Bloom, Harold. *Gwendolyn Brooks: Comprehensive Research and Study Guide.* Broomall, PA: Chelsea House Publishers, 2003.

Brooks, Gwendolyn. *Annie Allen.* Westport, CT: Greenwood, 1949.

Brooks, Gwendolyn. *The Bean Eaters.* New York: Harper & Row, 1960.

Brooks, Gwendolyn. *In the Mecca.* New York: Harper & Row, 1968.

Brooks, Gwendolyn. *In Montgomery and Other Poems.* Chicago: Third World Press, 2003.

Brooks, Gwendolyn. *Maud Martha.* New York: Harper & Row, 1953.

Brooks, Gwendolyn. *A Street in Bronzeville.* New York: Harper & Row, 1945.

Wright, Steven Caldwell, ed. *On Gwendolyn Brooks: Reliant Contemplation.* Ann Arbor: University of Michigan Press, 1999.

Brown, James

Singer, dancer, songwriter, entrepreneur, and performer extraordinaire James Brown (1933–2006) appeared on *Billboard*'s Top 40 R&B chart a total of 98 times—more than any other artist; of his hits, 17 reached the top spot, and 43 charted on Pop's Top 40. His many honors include induction into the Rock and Roll Hall of Fame and a special lifetime achievement Grammy. The "Godfather of Soul," as Brown was known to millions, frequently appeared on TV talk and variety shows and made celebrated cameo appearances in several popular movies. His music has had a worldwide impact.

James Joseph Brown Jr. was born into extreme poverty in Barnwell County, South Carolina, on May 3, 1933. Deserted by his mother Susan when he was quite young, his father Joe Brown left him in Augusta, Georgia, with his aunt Handsome "Honey" Stevenson. Stevenson ran a brothel while James hustled change: shining shoes, washing cars, racking pool balls, dancing and singing for tips, leading soldiers to his aunt's brothel, and so on. Brown's training to become the "hardest-working man in show business" started early.

Arrested for breaking into cars at the age of 16, Brown was sentenced on June 3, 1949, to 8 to 16 years at the Georgia Juvenile Training Institute, a segregated reform school/prison located in Rome in northwest Georgia. In November 1951, this reform school was renamed Georgia Boys Industrial Institute and moved to Camp Toccoa, a former paratrooper training facility on Currahee Mountain near Toccoa in northeast Georgia.

Fellow inmates named him "Music Box" because he was always singing and knew all the popular songs. Through his singing, athletic ability, and reputation as a hard worker, Brown became known to the townspeople, both black and white, who helped secure his release on June 14, 1952. Brown was paroled to the family of singer and band leader Bobby Byrd (1934–2007). Brown joined Byrd's gospel group, the Ever-Ready Gospel Singers, and soon was alternating lead vocals with Byrd's sister Sarah. Byrd and Brown later featured the same alternating lead vocals on some of their biggest hits.

Brown also performed with Byrd's secular group. They sang nonstop, keeping time by clapping hands and stomping feet—a technique learned from a local gospel quartet, the MellowTones. Supplementing the guitar and piano, Byrd sang the bass part, and he and Brown sang horn parts. Eventually they added drums and bass guitar. The Flames included a number of vocalists who switched off lead and backup singing in gospel call-and-response fashion; Brown assumed the role of featured dancer. In 1953, Byrd enrolled at North Carolina A&T University, where he learned to re-conceptualize and rearrange the Flames' voices.

On February 4, 1956, the Flames first recorded for Cincinnati's King/Federal. "Please, Please, Please" (adapted from doo-wop renditions of Big Joe Williams's blues "Baby, Please Don't Go") reached the number 5 slot on the R&B chart. Brown sang lead and soon assumed permanent leadership of the band. This song eventually reflected an important event in Brown's career and in the development of black musical forms. The Africanized musical foundation Brown absorbed in South Carolina and Augusta was enhanced through the incorporation of more Euro-American concepts, preparing Brown to become a soul music pioneer, a primary creator of funk, and an essential predecessor to rap and hip-hop. "Please" began the re-Africanization of popular music through its renewed emphasis on call-and-response, the relentless repetition of words and phases as cross-rhythm, and Brown's attention to nuanced variations in vocal tone and frenzied gospel-influenced performance.

Although the Flames fell apart, Byrd eventually returned and worked with Brown off-and-on for the rest of his career—writing songs, orchestrating arrangements, managing the band, and singing and playing keyboards. Brown charted again in 1958 when "Try Me" reached the top position on the R&B chart. Brown charted 24 more times before his first crossover hit (no. 1 R&B, no. 8 Pop), "Papa's Got A Brand New Bag" in 1965. Featuring Maceo Parker on saxophone and Jimmy Nolen on guitar, "Papa's" changed popular music's emphasis on the two/four beat to a beat on the first and third, using the instruments and voices primarily as percussion in maintaining a polyrhythmic groove, with irresistible, protofunk forever changing popular music.

In 1963, Brown financed the radically innovative recording *Live at the Apollo* (the first of several of Brown's live Apollo recordings). This LP featured extended versions, complete with audience shrieks and applause; it spent an unheard-of 66 weeks on the charts. Brown and Byrd continued to refine and distill funk in subsequent hits, including "Cold Sweat" (1967), "Licking Stick" (1968), "Get Up (I Feel Like Being A) Sex Machine" (1970), "Hot Pants" (1971), "Get on the Good Foot" (1972), and others. His band, the JB's, included Parker, Byrd, and Nolen but also Fred Wesley on trombone, drummers Clyde Stubblefied and John "Jabo" Starks, and William "Bootsy" Collins on bass guitar, among

James Brown, known as the Godfather of Soul, during a live performance in 1964. (Photofest)

other superb musicians. After 1976, Brown continued to have R&B hits but not another pop hit until 1985's "Living in America."

As a spokesperson for black America, Brown met with Vice President Humphrey and controversially endorsed Nixon for president. His music also had a profound impact on black political activism; "Say It Loud—I'm Black and I'm Proud" (1968), with children chanting the title and Brown declaring, "We'd rather die on our feet than living on our knees," became an anthem for the Black Power movement.

Brown re-Africanized African American music by wryly sliding his sound on a scale between ragtime's syncopation and Africa's cross-rhythms, incorporating ideas from jazz, blues, gospel, and country and western and repeatedly sampling diverse sources from the *Petticoat Junction* theme to Elmore James to Byrd and himself, serving a role in maintaining the groove analogous to the African master drummer. Brown put on show business's most energetic performance; his dancing influenced all who followed.

In December 1988, Brown received a six-year prison sentence for illegal drug use in South Carolina; he was released in February 1991. He died of pneumonia and congestive heart failure in Atlanta on Christmas Day in 2006. Several funerals for the 20th century's greatest performer—culminating in the horse-drawn procession to Harlem's Apollo Theater—were orchestrated like Brown's stage shows, with frequent wardrobe changes and much flamboyance.

See also: Black Folk Culture

Fred J. Hay

Bibliography

Brown, Geoff. *James Brown: Doin' It to Death*. London: Omnibus Press, 1996.
Brown, James, with Marc Eliot. *I Feel Good: A Memoir of a Life of Soul*. New York: New American Library, 2005.
Brown, James, with Bruce Tucker. *James Brown, the Godfather of Soul*. New York: Thunder's Mouth Press, 1990.
Danielsen, Anne. *Presence and Pleasure: The Funk Grooves of James Brown and Parliament*. Middletown, CT: Wesleyan University Press, 2006.
Hay, Fred J. "Music Box Meets the Toccoa Band: The Godfather of Soul in Appalachia." *Black Music Research Journal* 23, no. 1/2 (2003):103–33.
Rose, Cynthia. *Living in America: The Soul Saga of James Brown*. London: Serpent's Tail, 1990.

Buckra

Of Igbo and Ibibio derivation, "buckra" and "buckraman" were terms employed by slaves to denote poor or non-slaveholding whites. Used as an expression of derision, "buckra" appears to be the only anti-white epithet created originally by enslaved Africans. Others, specifically "cracker" and "redneck," were created by the white elite to deride and ridicule poor whites. What makes the widespread adoption of "buckra" quite odd is that, given the limited number of Igbo and others from the Bight of Biafra imported into mainland North America, it would seem that other terms of derision would have been preferred. Parallel terms among numerically significant and widely distributed import groups, such as the Akan (*obruni*), the Mande (*toubab*), and the Western Bantu (*mundele*), were not adopted by African Americans in the United States. This is especially curious in the case of South Carolina, where the Igbo and others from the Bight of Biafra represented just 11 percent of all enslaved African imports during the last century of the Atlantic slave trade. Yet, it was in South Carolina that "buckra" became one of the most widely used African words.

The most likely etymology of "buckra" would be that it derives from the Ibibio term *mbakara*. Among the Ibibio and the Igbo of the Bight of Biafra, the term specifically denotes a human with the power to command others or a demon capable of wielding supernatural forces. In the assessment of historian Monica Schuler, the Igbo of Jamaica who frequently used "buckra" as a term encompassing all whites may have viewed Europeans as evil sorcerers. This concept of understanding enslavement in spiritual terms and viewing Europeans as evil spirits or demons resonates in the narratives of a number of enslaved Igbos, including Olaudah Equiano and John Jea. Thus, the Ibibio and Igbo who first used this word may have adopted it as a term of choice because of a shared belief that Europeans were essentially malevolent spirits.

In addition to its use in South Carolina and other parts of British North America, it appears that "buckra" was adopted throughout the Anglophone Americas. Specific references to the term appear in 18th-century Philadelphia, the Chesapeake, Jamaica, Barbados, and the Leeward Caribbean Islands. As Douglas Chambers contends, its widespread use throughout the Anglophone Americas represents a significant degree of Igboization among non-Igbo enslaved Africans. In addition to the use of "buckra," other significant Igboisms include the use of other Igbo-derived terms (e.g., *Obeah, okra, jonkonu*), the perseverance of discrete Igbo religious customs and beliefs (e.g., Obeah conjuration, Igbo funerary customs, the Christmas-time John Konnu masquerade), and elements of Igbo cuisine (e.g., yams, black-eyed peas, watermelon, eggplant).

See also: Igbo; Slave Culture

Walter C. Rucker

Bibliography

Chambers, Douglas. "'My Own Nation': Igbo Exiles in the Diaspora." *Slavery & Abolition* 18 (1997):72–97.
Doyle, Bertram W. "The Etiquette of Race Relations—Past, Present, and Future." *The Journal of Negro Education* 5 (1936):191–208.
Puckett, Newbell Nile. *Folk Beliefs of the Southern Negro*. Chapel Hill: University of North Carolina Press, 1926.

Schuler, Monica. "Afro-American Slave Culture." *Historical Reflections* 6 (1979):121–55.

Turner, Lorenzo Dow. *Africanisms in the Gullah Dialect.* Ann Arbor: University of Michigan Press, 1973.

Call-and-Response

The call-and-response characteristic of sub-Saharan African music is expressed both vocally and instrumentally. This call-and-response characteristic manifests the communal and dialogic nature of African music, a music whose integration into daily life and whose spiritual qualities blur distinctions between the sacred and the secular. Although all music is an important cultural expression, African music is remarkably intertwined with the maintenance, adjustment, and vitality of life on not only daily but also yearly and generational time frames. These characteristics of African music also exist in the call-and-response tradition of African American music.

In Africa, the conversational nature of call-and-response promotes group interaction and a respect for the individual, acknowledged through the attention given to the singer, the musician, and the dancer who "responds" to what came before. That dancing needs inclusion in the call-and-response tradition is not merely because people dance to music but because of the inseparability of African dance and music as indicated by *ngoma,* a word that occurs in many African languages and means both "song" and "dance" and in, for instance, Swahili, also signifies "drum." Thus, call-and-response is an essential expression of an art that brings together singing, instrumentation, and bodily movement in multigenerational ensembles whose interactions promote community while respecting individuality.

Expressions of call-and-response in Africa include the following: circular dances (ring dances) with drumming, percussive foot stomping, and the movement of individuals into the circle to dance responses to the dominant themes; the singing of songs whose cyclic tempos facilitate vocal participations that respond to previous singers; improvised songs that comment on current events and evoke responses; call-and-response Christian church ceremonies and songs; weddings, funerals, and other "life span events"; and poems in call-and-response form. In addition, much of the instrumental music of sub-Saharan Africa is composed of instruments responding to each other.

Manifestations of call-and-response in North America are equally wide-ranging. Work songs between a lead singer and a responding group not only allowed slaves to sustain energy and optimism but also allowed communication (typically using words that had multiple meanings) in the maintenance of African traditions, histories, and values. As early as the 18th century, African American church singing of hymns included improvisation, choral responses to psalms, and singing that alternated between men and women. The shout—essentially a New World version of the African ring dance—took varying forms in church, at dances, at camp singings, and in children's games (e.g., song games and jump-rope rhymes), each manifesting elements of call-and-response.

From the shout version known as "ring spiritual" derived African American spirituals, which then mixed with blues and jazz to form gospel. Gospel included call-and-response elements especially at churches that emphasized congregational spoken responses to the preacher.

Outside church, in the blues, black folk music's use of chorus refrains found expression in the call-and-response of singer and audience, of instrument and voice, and of spoken asides. Call-and-response later found musical expression not only in rhythm and blues and rap but also in the more oral and literary expressions of signifying, performance poetry (e.g., poetry slams), speeches (e.g., Martin Luther King Jr. and Malcolm X), and the percussive rhythms and structures of much African American prose.

Jazz also manifests the call-and-response of the "talking instrument" from Africa and of instrumental communication during slavery (thus the prohibition on slaves owning "loud instruments"). This "communicative" (and inherently democratic) characteristic of jazz occurs with antiphonal instrumental solos that respond to other soloists or to the group, or with section responding to section in big band music. A revealing literary expression of instrumental call-and-response is at the end of James Baldwin's short story "Sonny's Blues."

Call-and-response remains one of the characteristic elements of Africana music and, more generally, of African American culture. The protean manifestations of call-and-response attest to its continuing value in promoting vitality through the give-and-take between spiritual and physical, oral and instrumental, prescribed and improvised, society and individual.

See also: Africanisms; Black Churches; Ring Shout; Slave Culture; Slave Religion; Work Songs

Kevin M. Hickey

Bibliography

Floyd, Samuel A., Jr. *The Power of Black Music: Interpreting Its History from Africa to the United States.* New York: Oxford University Press, 1995.

Wilson, Olly. "Black Music as an Art Form." *Black Music Research Journal* 3 (1983):1–22.

Caul

The caul, or veil, is a membrane or amniotic sac covering the face of a child at birth. Although the caul has various meanings in a number of cultures, according to the folk traditions of enslaved Africans throughout the Americas, it was typically a sign that an infant would eventually be able to communicate with ghosts, predict future events, and have other uncanny abilities. The nearly identical meaning of the caul among Africans in the Kingdom of Dahomey, the Gold Coast, Dutch Guyana, Jamaica, Haiti, and the American South as a sign of otherworldly wisdom and an innate ability to commune with spiritual forces demonstrates that enduring African spiritual concepts permeated communities throughout the African Diaspora. According to noted anthropologist Melville Herskovits, there were certain aspects of abnormal births, including the caul, that predisposed certain children to be seen as developing the ability to manipulate spiritual forces. Indeed, being born with certain birthmarks, a caul, or other distinguishing congenital features often made certain children likely candidates to be future root doctors or conjurers. These notions were ubiquitous features of African American culture in the South as late as the 1930s and beyond.

The numerous interviews performed by the Georgia Writers' Project during the Great Depression illuminate the continuing significance of the caul in communities across the American South. Martha Page of Yamacraw, Georgia—an early 20th-century community of ex-slaves from both coastal South Carolina and Georgia—claimed that she

could see and interact with ghosts and other spirits because of being born with a caul. From the same community, Carrie Hamilton revealed that she also could see ghosts as a result of the veil of skin covering her face at birth. Those born with this gift believe they can see the unseeable because of their direct connection to a spirit world defined by distinctly West and West-Central African parameters.

See also: Africanisms; Black Folk Culture

Walter C. Rucker

Bibliography

Georgia Writers' Project. *Drums and Shadows: Survival Studies among the Coastal Negroes.* Athens: University of Georgia Press, 1940.

Herskovits, Melville. *Life in a Haitian Valley.* New York: Alfred Knopf, 1937.

Puckett, Newbell Nile. *Folk Beliefs of the Southern Negro.* Chapel Hill: University of North Carolina Press, 1926.

Charms

Also known as amulets, *gris-gris, juju* bags, jacks, and protective hands, these devices formed a unique category of spiritual implements employed by African- and American-born conjurers, root doctors, and diviners throughout North American history. Typically worn around the neck, wrist, or ankle and utilized for a variety of purposes, charms played an important role in the lives of enslaved and free blacks from the 17th through the 20th centuries. Because of specific African beliefs regarding causality in which "accidents" or bad fortune were understood to be caused by malevolent actions on the part of the living or the dead, protective charms became a central element in the folk culture that developed among African Americans. Notably, the use of protective charms in slave conspiracies, revolts, and other modes of resistance created a significant amount of concern among colonial- and antebellum-era whites.

Perhaps the best-documented example of charms employed in an act of slave resistance would be the 1822 Charleston, South Carolina, plot initiated and led by Denmark Vesey. His plan to destroy Charleston was greatly bolstered by an African-born conjurer named Gullah Jack. Having served as a "doctor" in Charleston for 15 years, Jack's renown as a mystic allowed him to sway enslaved Africans of all multiple ethnic backgrounds who respected him as both conjurer and "general" of the plot. Not only was Jack claimed to have a "charmed invulnerability" that would prevent him from being harmed at the hands of whites, but he also produced and distributed charms to slave combatants that were said to render them invincible. For Gullah Jack's protective charms to work, conspirators had to first fast the night before the planned revolt. The following morning, they were to place the charms, consisting of crab claws, in their mouths to be fully protected from harm. The fact that not one slave questioned the validity of Jack's powers during the course of the trials is singular testament to the continuing connection they had to African spiritual beliefs and values.

Another example of the use of protective charms n an act of slave resistance is recounted in the story of William Webb. In this case, Webb—a conjurer living in Kentucky during the 1840s—became concerned about the abusive treatment faced by slaves on a neighboring plantation. After secretly meeting with this group, he urged them to gather roots that were then placed into bags. The slaves were then instructed to walk around their own quarters a few times and to position the conjure bags in front of their owner's house during the early morning hours. These steps were taken to induce their owner to have disturbing nightmares about the slaves gaining retribution for past wrongs. In the following weeks, the owner reportedly began to treat the slaves decidedly better, and Webb's influence over them increased dramatically as a direct result.

Bags that held special items and used as protective charms were generally known as "hands" or "jacks" and were either worn or buried to work properly. A hand or jack would typically contain a variety of objects, including roots, tree bark, human hair and fingernail clippings, graveyard dirt, horseshoe nails, hog bristles, animal and insect parts, red pepper, gunpowder, and other substances. In this regard, the finding of a "conjure's cache" in an Annapolis, Maryland, house in 1996 proves instructive. Buried sometime during the 18th century in the northeast corner of this home, the items in this cache included beads, pins, buttons, a coin with a hole in it, rock crystals, a piece of crab claw, a brass ring and bell, and pieces of bone and glass. This was one of 11 such findings in Virginia and Maryland, which indicates a clear pattern—especially given the fact that the caches were always buried in the northeast corner of rooms or slave quarters. In all likelihood, these items were protective jacks buried by enslaved blacks in order to elicit the aid of powerful spiritual forces.

According to a number of African spiritual systems, certain items found in nature were imbued with an innate amount of spiritual force that could become even more potent when prepared by a conjurer. The frequent presence of charms in enslaved and free African American communities from as early as the 17th century exemplifies the perseverance of important African religious concepts. It should be mentioned that charms were not always used for benevolent purposes. A charm could also be employed to harm, inhibit, or kill others, particularly if it contained the intended victim's hair or nail clippings. In this case, "frizzled" chickens were often employed to find evil charms and *gris-gris* that were buried by conjurers. In addition to frizzled chickens, a number of counter-charms were utilized to ward off the effects of evil. Red pepper, salt, grave dirt or goofer powder, and strips of red flannel cloth were frequently used in counter-charms for a variety of reasons. In this manner, counter-charms were believed to prevent anything from insanity to death caused by evil charms.

See also: Africanisms; Black Folk Culture; Slave Culture

Walter C. Rucker

Bibliography

Blassingame, John. *The Slave Community: Plantation Life in the Antebellum South.* New York: Oxford University Press, 1972.

Georgia Writers' Project. *Drums and Shadows: Survival Studies among the Coastal Negroes.* Athens: University of Georgia Press, 1940.

Puckett, Newbell Nile. *Folk Beliefs of the Southern Negro.* Chapel Hill: University of North Carolina Press, 1926.

Raboteau, Albert J. *Slave Religion: The "Invisible Institution" in the Antebellum South.* New York: Oxford University Press, 1978.

Rucker, Walter. "Conjure, Magic, and Power: The Influence of Afro-Atlantic Religious Practices on Slave Resistance and Rebellion." *Journal of Black Studies* 32 (2001):84–103.

Coltrane, John

John William Coltrane (1926–1967), a saxophonist and composer, was most famous for playing and writing highly textured and fluid music with rapid tempos and lengthy arrhythmic phrasings. He was committed to bringing jazz, an original American music form created and influenced by African American artists, into innovative areas of composition and sound. Coltrane primarily employed the alto, tenor, and soprano saxophones to play a range of music throughout his career, including rhythm and blues, bebop, and hard bop. He also incorporated Middle Eastern instruments, Indian melodies, and African percussive rhythms into his arrangements, which firmly placed him as a major figure in the mid- to late 1960s experimental improvisational jazz movement known as "The New Thing."

Coltrane was born on September 23, 1926, in Hamlet, North Carolina, to John Robert Coltrane, a tailor, and Alice Blair Coltrane, a homemaker. He grew up with his parents, uncle, aunt, and first cousin in the home of his maternal grandparents, Reverend Walter Blair, an African Methodist Episcopal minister, and Alice Leary Blair, a homemaker. The family lived in a middle-class African American neighborhood in High Point, North Carolina. Although music was a part of his early life, with his father playing violin and ukulele recreationally and his mother playing piano and singing in the church choir, Coltrane did not begin formal musical training until playing the alto horn and clarinet in a community band that he joined at the age of 13.

Between the ages of 12 and 14, Coltrane experienced the deaths of his grandparents, father, and uncle, and by the time he reached his senior year in high school, his mother had moved to the Philadelphia area to pursue employment opportunities. However, Coltrane remained in High Point, where he joined the William Penn High School band in the first clarinetist chair. Though his band experience mostly involved the performance of marching compositions, Coltrane began exposing himself to the jazz music of alto saxophonist Johnny Hodges, who was playing with Duke Ellington's Orchestra at the time. He borrowed an alto saxophone and became remarkably adept at replicating the music of the saxophonists he admired.

In 1943, at the age of 16, Coltrane graduated from high school and moved to Philadelphia. He began working at a sugar refinery and studying saxophone at the Ornstein School of Music. Two years later, Coltrane was drafted into the U.S. Navy and stationed in Hawaii during World War II, where he played clarinet in the navy band and applied his musical skills to marching and dance music. After being released from the navy in 1946, Coltrane returned to Philadelphia, where he accepted bookings with rhythm and blues bands. However, his musical interests were focused on the jazz styles of Hodges, tenor saxophonist Lester "Pres" Young, clarinetist Artie Shaw, and trumpeter Dizzy Gillespie.

John Coltrane (photographed in 1960) possessed astonishing technical mastery, spiritual tone, and multicultural influences that stretched the boundaries of jazz and enriched its vocabulary. (Library of Congress)

In 1947, Coltrane began playing tenor saxophone in the band of alto saxophonist Eddie "Cleanhead" Vinson, a musician he greatly admired. During his tour with Vinson, Coltrane had the opportunity to connect with another idol, Charlie Parker. While meeting with Parker, he heard new melodic jazz forms that challenged him to play with the rapidity that would later inform his sound. After leaving Vinson's band, Coltrane played with trumpeter Mel Melvin's band and then in 1948 joined a group formed by the Heath brothers: saxophonist Jimmy, drummer Al, and bassist Percy. Later in the year, trumpeter Howard McGhee recruited Coltrane and Jimmy Heath to play in his band. However, Coltrane was dropped from the band after the first tour.

Coltrane joined Gillespie's band in 1949, an experience that included his introduction to Eastern music and philosophy through the guidance of tenor saxophonist Yusef Lateef. Additionally, his playing on the Afro-Cuban song "Manteca" and the Caribbean-inspired "Cubana Be Cubana Bop" presented Coltrane with insight into new ways of bringing jazz music into the realm of what is contemporarily considered "world music."

In 1951, as big bands became less economically viable, Gillespie reduced his 16-piece band to a sextet. After a short stint with the sextet, Coltrane returned to Philadelphia to study music theory and tenor saxophone at the Granoff School of Music. His music theory instructor, Dennis Sandole, advised him to listen to classical compositions and apply the multiplicity of instrumentation he heard to his single instrument. This exploration later inspired Coltrane to work toward replicating a variety of tones that were not normally associated with the saxophone's sound.

At the beginning of 1952, Coltrane joined alto saxophonist Earl Bostic's band and the following year joined the band of his idol, Johnny Hodges. However, Hodges fired him in 1954 because of Coltrane's heroin addiction, a condition that implicated the jazz culture of the time as well as Coltrane's attempt to self-medicate his chronic dental problems.

During 1954–1955, Coltrane played a regular Monday night jam session at New York's Birdland. He also continued playing rhythm and blues gigs in Philadelphia and other cities to supplement his income, performing with Daisy Mae and the Hepcats, King Kolax, and Moose Jackson, among others. Even though rhythm and blues did not reflect the musical complexity that Coltrane valued, he appreciated the means in which the form inspired a connection with its listeners.

On October 3, 1955, Coltrane married Juanita "Naima" Grubbs. Her background in music, Muslim spirituality, and daughter from a previous relationship, Syeeda, had a significant impact on Coltrane's personal life and the trajectory of his musical vocation. Throughout their relationship, he moved the family between Philadelphia and New York, depending on the circumstances of his career.

From 1955 to 1956 and then 1957 to 1960, Coltrane played alto saxophone and later tenor saxophone with the Miles Davis Quintet. During late 1955–1956 Coltrane played an incomparable solo during "Bye Bye Blackbird" and a critically acclaimed solo on Thelonious Monk's "Round Midnight" on trumpeter Davis's album, 'Round About Midnight. Coltrane experienced the freedom to explore new areas of his music with the flexibility facilitated by Davis's approach to performance.

Miles Davis fired Coltrane in 1956, most likely due to a combination of Davis's impatience with Coltrane's drug addiction and Coltrane's discontent with Davis's unpredictable band leadership. Coltrane returned home to Philadelphia and, at the beginning of 1957, commenced a spiritual quest that involved quitting drug usage, drinking, and, for a while, smoking. He also became a vegetarian.

Later in 1957, Coltrane began playing a well-received gig at New York's Five Spot with the Thelonious Monk Quartet. Coltrane had worked with pianist Monk while still with the Davis Quintet and was keen when he was asked to join him at the Five Spot. His work with Monk offered him a level of freedom not fully realized with Davis as he explored the pianist's improvisational techniques, which inspired him to experiment with his own style in new ways. Coltrane also began composing on a piano in his family's Manhattan apartment during his period with Monk.

Additionally in 1957, Bob Weinstock of the Prestige label signed Coltrane to a two-year contract. However, that same year, Coltrane obtained a special release from Prestige to record Blue Train, an album that showcased his style and strengths as a composer. A month earlier, Coltrane had been asked to rejoin Miles Davis in a sextet with alto saxophonist Julian "Cannonball" Adderley. By the end of 1958, Coltrane had started accepting bookings as a bandleader when not playing with the Davis sextet. In April 1959, Coltrane signed a two-year contract with Atlantic Records and released the classic Giant Steps, which includes "Syeeda's Song Flute" and "Naima," written for his wife and daughter, respectively. The album strengthened Coltrane's reputation as a bandleader.

In April 1960, Coltrane left Davis's band to form the John Coltrane Quartet, which, after a few personnel changes, eventually included pianist McCoy Tyner, bassist Jimmy Garrison, and drummer Elvin Jones. In 1960, Coltrane recorded My Favorite Things. The title piece, the critically and popularly acclaimed arrangement of the Broadway show song by Rodgers and Hammerstein, introduced Coltrane on the soprano saxophone and included a repetitive bass line played by Steve Davis that exemplified Coltrane's growing interest in Indian music. Davis was eventually replaced by bassist Reggie Workman in the quartet. Coltrane later attempted to use two bassists to capture Indian percussive sounds by adding bassist Art Davis to the group. Finally, there was Garrison on bass. In 1961, Coltrane added flutist, alto saxophonist, and bass clarinetist Eric Dolphy in the band, making it a quintet.

By 1961, Coltrane, known to be rather prolific in the studio, recorded Coltrane Plays the Blues and Coltrane's Sound. Additionally, he signed a contract with Impulse Records and recorded his first live album at the Village

Vanguard in New York City. In 1962, Coltrane recorded three albums: *Coltrane, Ballads,* and the acclaimed *Duke Ellington and John Coltrane.* During this period, Coltrane became further interested in the music of sitar player Ravi Shankar, as evidenced in "My Favorite Things," and the improvisational styles of avant-garde alto-saxophonist Ornette Coleman, an artist who inspired Coltrane's ventures into "The New Thing."

Coltrane separated from Naima Coltrane in 1963, subsequently divorcing in 1966 and marrying Alice McLeod, a pianist with whom he resided beginning in 1964. Coltrane and McLeod lived in Huntington, Long Island, with their three children: John Jr., Ravi, and Oran.

Coltrane recorded *A Love Supreme* in 1964. The album, considered a musical manifestation of Coltrane's spirituality, consists of a four-part suite with sections titled "Acknowledgments," "Resolution," "Pursuance," and "Psalm." In 1965, the album was awarded "Album of the Year" by the influential magazines *Down Beat* and *Jazz.* As well, he was entered into the *Down Beat* Hall of Fame and voted as "Jazzman of the Year" and best tenor saxophonist in the magazine's reader poll. Additionally, the album fortified Coltrane's mystical popular image, notably inspiring the creation of an eponymous church in San Francisco.

With *A Love Supreme* representing Coltrane's movement into new realms of musical experimentation, further exploration was evidenced in June 1965, when he assembled 10 emergent avant-garde musicians to record the album *Ascension.* By the time Coltrane recorded the five-part suite *Meditations,* he had added tenor saxophonist Farrell "Pharoah" Sanders and a second drummer, Rashied Ali, to his band. Elvin Jones, a strong drummer in his own right, eventually left the band in 1966. Further exemplifying Coltrane's musical direction, the piece "Om," recorded while the band experimented with LSD, featured Hindu chanting. As well, when McCoy Tyner left the band in 1965, Alice Coltrane replaced him as pianist.

Coltrane recorded his second live album at the Village Vanguard in May 1966. The album included only two songs: "Naima" and "My Favorite Things." In July 1966, the John Coltrane Quintet experienced a well-received tour of Japan, in which Coltrane became acquainted with his popularity when he was greeted at the airport by a crowd of Japanese fans.

Upon returning from the Japan tour, between late 1966 and early 1967, Coltrane worked in the recording studio but was inhibited by headaches and stomach pains. In 1967, he recorded the albums *Expression* and *Interstellar Space.* In March of that year, he also performed at the opening of the "Center of African Culture" in Harlem, a project developed by Nigerian percussionist Michael Babatunde Olatunji, an artist significantly influenced Coltrane's interest in African music. That same month, he renewed his contract with Impulse Records.

In April 1967, Coltrane became ill while visiting his mother's home in Philadelphia. John Coltrane died in Huntington, Long Island, from liver cancer on July 17, 1967.

See also: Black Folk Culture; Davis, Miles; Jazz; Parker, Charlie

Elisa Joy White

Bibliography

Cole, Bill. *John Coltrane.* New York: Schirmer Books, 1976.

Kahn, Ashley. *A Love Supreme: The Story of John Coltrane's Signature Album.* New York: Viking Press, 2002.

Nisenson, Eric. *Ascension: John Coltrane and His Quest.* New York: Da Capo Press, 1993.

Porter, Lewis. *John Coltrane: His Life and Music.* Ann Arbor: University of Michigan Press, 2001.

Thomas, J. C. *Chasin' the Trane: The Music and Mystique of John Coltrane.* New York: Da Capo Press, 1975.

Woideck, Carl, ed. *The John Coltrane Companion: Five Decades of Commentary.* New York: Schirmer Books, 1998.

Congo Square, New Orleans

For over a hundred years, New Orleans' Congo Square was the only venue in North America where the public performance of African drumming, music, and dance was officially sanctioned. The fusion of African and European rhythms and instrumentation that developed over the course of the square's history has led to its designation as the "birthplace of jazz."

During Louisiana's French colonial period (1718–1763), an area called the Place des Nègres, located just outside the ramparts of the original settlement, was set aside for use by enslaved Africans and people of African descent. Slaves were free from work on Sundays and holidays, and by about 1740, they had begun to congregate at the Place des Nègres to market their garden produce, wild herbs and berries, fish and game, furs, firewood, and crafts. They also used this opportunity to socialize and to make music and dance after the manner of their African nations. The market activities and dances at the Place des Nègres persisted during Louisiana's Spanish colonial period (1764–1803).

After the Louisiana Purchase of 1803, the American administration continued to allow the slaves' Sunday market activities and dances. It was during the early 1800s, when Gaetano Mariatini's traveling "Congo Circus" from Havana set up in the square during the winter season, that the site came to be called Circus Square or Congo Square.

The African cultural practices at Congo Square drew many white spectators and became a tourist attraction for American and European visitors. Many 19th-century travelers published reports of African costume, music, and dances such as the calinda, bamboula, and congo. In 1808, Christian Schultz described Africans dressed in a variety of "wild and savage fashions," who danced in circles accompanied by long, narrow drums. In 1819, Benjamin Henry Latrobe reported seeing female dancers who circled around the musicians in the center while singing a two-note refrain. Particularly valuable are Latrobe's descriptions and sketches of three drums, a banjo made from a gourd with a carved human figure atop the fingerboard, and a calabash studded with nails. These instruments have been identified as being of Yoruba, Fon, Kongo, and Ashanti origin. James Creecy wrote in 1834 of dancers adorned with fringes, ribbons, little bells, and shells and of music provided by banjos, tom-toms, jawbones, triangles, and various other instruments. By the 1840s, African instruments, dances, and apparel were being supplanted by the violin, by jigs and reels, and by European-style clothing.

Many writers from the late 19th century to the present have characterized the Congo Square phenomena as Voodoo ceremonies, said to have been presided over by the famous 19th-century priestess Marie Laveau. All African music and dance is sacred in nature, and Congo Square could certainly have been a venue for New Orleans Voodoo, a blend of African and European religious and magical traditions characterized by drumming, singing, dancing, and spirit possession.

As city authorities sought to regulate the slaves' activities, the Congo Square assemblies gradually declined. In 1820, the square was fenced and gated. In 1845, a municipal ordinance prohibited outdoor music and dancing without permission from the mayor. The festivities still occurred sporadically through the 1850s, but they were conducted under police supervision and could take place only from May through August between the hours of 4:00 and 6:30 P.M. A forest of young trees planted by the city's gardener further inhibited the dancers, and finally they ceased to congregate there.

By the time of the Civil War, what had once been the venue for authentic African cultural practices had faded into oblivion. After Reconstruction, the New Orleans City Council renamed the square for the Confederate general P. G. T. Beauregard, and it, like many other public places, was reserved for white use and remained so until the later 20th century.

In 1960, the city of New Orleans received federal urban renewal funds, which they used to purchase nine blocks surrounding the former Congo Square for a proposed cultural complex. After evicting the mostly black residents and demolishing their houses, the authorities abandoned the project. The plan was resurrected in 1971, and following the death of New Orleans jazz trumpeter Louis Armstrong, the area was named Armstrong Park. Now attractively landscaped, the park is occupied by a swimming pool, the municipal auditorium, and the broadcast facilities of radio station WWOZ. The original Congo Square is paved in concentric rings, suggestive of the slaves' dance circles, and is used for musical performances and festivals.

See also: Africanisms; Laveau, Marie

Carolyn Morrow Long

Bibliography

Cable, George W. "The Dance in Place Congo." *The Century Magazine* 31, no. 4 (1886):517–32.

Creecy, James R. *Scenes in the South and Other Miscellaneous Pieces.* Washington, D.C.: T. McGill, 1860.

Estes, David C. "Traditional Dances and Processions of Blacks in New Orleans as Witnessed by Antebellum Travelers." *Louisiana Folklore Miscellany* 6, no. 3 (1990):1–14.

Johnson, Jerah. "New Orleans's Congo Square: An Urban Setting for Early Afro-American Culture Formation." *Louisiana History* 32, no. 2 (1991):140–47.

Latrobe, Benjamin Henry. *Impressions Respecting New Orleans, Diary and Sketches 1818–1820,* ed. Samuel Wilson Jr. New York: Columbia University Press, 1951.

Schultz, Christian. *Travels on an Inland Voyage in the Years 1807 and 1808.* New York: Isaac Riley, 1810.

Conjure

Conjure is an African American form of folk healing and folk magic that involves the use of organic materials, elements of the universe, and supernatural forces to manipulate the tangible world. The "magical" forces of conjure are inexplicable and lacking in scientific grounding. However, these forces should not be equated with illusion, charlatanry, or invocatory magic. Conjure is an American tradition primarily rooted in African cosmology and herbalism. Africans on the Continent embraced a lexicon of beliefs and customs designed to help them coexist in an environment filled with animals, plants, natural elements, and unseen forces. In addition to the supreme power to whom all answered, there were deities and ancestral figures who worked together in harmony to promote balance in the universe.

During the Atlantic slave trade, many of these beliefs and customs were transported to the New World for sustenance. Nature-based customs took a stronger foothold in geographical locations with climates resembling weather conditions in Africa. Although many syncretized, African-based religions such as Santería, Shango, Candomble, and Vodun emerged in the Americas, conjure was more common in North America. Therefore, conjure took root in Louisiana, Mississippi, Alabama, Georgia, Florida, North Carolina, and South Carolina. Conjuration is informed by a fusion of African magical and medicinal herbalism, American Indian botanical knowledge, and European folk traditions. With the assistance of American Indians inhabiting areas surrounding the plantations, enslaved Africans learned the properties of local herbs and roots. Herbalism survived as a vital part of slave culture and was used to treat blacks and whites on the plantation.

Conjurers, or conjure doctors, are often described as herbalists and magicians who may practice beneficial, curative, and protective magic. Practitioners are usually paid for their services. Conjuration may be viewed as a system of black traditional medicine that cures natural and occult illnesses. Herbalism is used to treat natural illnesses; hexes are occult illnesses that can be treated only by a person who can draw on elements of the universe, spells, and personal power to uncross the hex. Contrary to popular belief, members of various ethnic and racial groups practice conjure.

Other commonly used names for conjure are *hoodoo* and *rootwork*. It has been speculated that the term *hoodoo* is a derivation of the African terms *Voodoo* and *juju*. Voodoo is a Westernized adaptation of the Fon word *Vodun*, which means "spirit" or "god"; *juju* means magic. Vodun is a West African religion that was transplanted to Haiti and eventually surfaced in Louisiana early in the 19th century after the Haitian Revolution. Hoodoo is a distinctive American tradition. Scholars have noted that beliefs and customs associated with conjure in America may be traced back to the Congo. Unlike Vodun and similar African-based practices such as Santería, Shango, and Candomble, conjure is not a religion, and therefore the practitioner, or conjurer, is not bound by a specific theology or formal initiation; conjuration may be adapted to any one of several forms of religious worship. In this tradition, personal healing and magical powers are emphasized. Conjurers empower themselves with handmade objects as an alternative to relying on the power of religious leaders or deities. Rootwork comprises a working knowledge of herbalism and nature. Therefore, the term "rootwork" is used because of the significant role of dried roots in the making of charms and casting of spells. African American practitioners and informed participants seldom use the terms "hoodoo" and "rootwork" interchangeably. In addition to roots, conjurers also use sticks, trees, stones, animals, magnets, minerals, bones, animal parts, natural waters, bodily effluvia, personal objects, ritual candles, incense, and oils.

The objectives of conjurers are often misinterpreted by the misinformed. Practitioners of conjure are consulted for spiritual cleansing, attracting affection, good health, and luck, protection, and divination. In order to achieve the desired outcomes of their clients, conjurers use techniques referred to as "laying of tricks" or "fixing tricks." The most common object used in the laying of tricks is called a bag of tricks. Sometimes it is also referred to as a mojo, nation sack, gris-gris, hand, trick bag, luck ball, or flannel. The word "mojo" may have come from the West African word *mojuba*, which means "giving praise." A mojo bag is the most commonly used talisman in conjuration, and it is extremely potent. Usually a small bag made of silk, leather, or flannel, a mojo is a bag of charms that serves as an amulet and is often concealed on the person for effectiveness and safety. Sometimes the mojo is hidden in a secret location. The basic ingredients found in a mojo are sticks, herbs, bones, and earth combined to accomplish a particular task. A nation sack is the only gender-specific mojo. It is a female-owned mojo bag worn by women under their clothes, and men were not allowed to touch them. The magical ingredients included in the nation sack depended on the desired wishes of the female who wore it. For example, egg yolks kept lovers committed, and red onion peels brought good luck.

Trees, stones, and roots are important conjuration tools. In African and African American cultural traditions, trees represent a spiritual connection between life and death. Stones are essential tools in conjuration because they hold energy and may be charged for use in specific applications. For instance, stones may be buried, placed in the sun, or immersed in a special water soak to evoke desired vibrations. Conjure stones are also known to heighten the power of conjure. Roots contain potent medicinal qualities and thus are a vital tool in conjuration. Some practitioners believe the Adam and Eve root and John the Conqueror root are two of the most frequently used roots in conjuration. John the Conqueror, or Conjure John, is recognized as the most powerful root of the forest, and its uses are diverse. This root is used in African, American Indian, and European herbalism. Adam and Eve is an American Indian root used to bring love and protection when used in conjures.

Conjurers adhere to a common set of beliefs. Conjurers believe there is one god to whom all must be held accountable for their actions, but there are also several supernatural forces working as conjuring agents for human beings, acting under the guide of the Supreme Being. To conjurers, the earth is a sacred, breathing entity that sustains and provides the sources needed for conjuration. In the African tradition of ancestral veneration, conjurers respect the beneficial powers of the dead to impart wisdom to the living because they have passed on to a spiritual plane where the past, present, and future merge. Conjurers believe that the future can be foretold and rely heavily on divination systems to assist their clients through spiritual and psychic readings. Popular divination systems are dream interpretation, playing cards, bones, shells, a candle and glass of water, and recognition of omens in nature. Conjurers must adhere to ethical standards. They must not abuse their powers.

In order to maximize the potential of conjuration, the conjurer must understand the principals of elemental magic by mastering the use of air, earth, fire, and water. Incense is often used to represent the element air. Various incenses are used for purification, protection, clarity, meditation, psychic awareness, dream intensification, and spirit communication. For instance, sage is used for meditation and purification, jasmine strengthens intuition and intensifies dreams, eucalyptus provides protection, and frankincense is used for spirit communication. In addition to incenses, a wide variety of herb-based scented oils

are employed in conjure. Like incense, oils are diffused in the air. Oils can also be used for anointing clients and for dressing candles.

The element of earth is fundamental to conjuration because it absorbs and illuminates energy. It is believed that earth from certain locations holds certain energy, and it is often used to ground spells. Earth from certain places is used to enhance certain spells. For instance, it is believed that earth from a church provides spiritual protection; earth from the top of a mountain increases psychic abilities and clarity; earth from a cemetery stimulates psychic ability and strengthens communication with the dead; earth from a bank attracts money and success; earth from a courthouse attracts success in legal matters; and earth from a garden intensifies love spells. Earth is commonly placed in a mojo to ground the spell.

Candles are used in conjuration to represent the element of fire and to release certain spirits. Specific colors are used for specific purposes. The candles must be dressed first in order to achieve a specific end. White candles are multifunctional and often represent peace; pink candles are used for attraction and healing; purple candles are used for spirituality and humility; red candles are used for desire and power; yellow candles are used for creativity and renewal; green candles are used for money and abundance; blue candles are used for insight and healing; brown candles are used for stability and focus; silver candles improve psychic ability and ease stress; and black candles promote change and increase occult power.

The fourth element, water, retains energy and is often used for cleansing and consecration. Holy water is used for clarity and consecration of sacred objects; ocean water may be used for increasing psychic abilities and bringing peace of mind; and spring rainwater may be used for healing and fertility.

After slavery, conjuration continued to exist because blacks could not afford the services of a traditional medical practitioner. However, as blacks migrated to urban areas, some of them rejected elements of conjure because of its stigma. City dwellers and educated blacks often viewed conjure as backward and unsophisticated. In an effort to assimilate into mainstream society, many blacks distanced themselves from the tradition for fear of rejection. Conjure and all that it encompassed was too closely related to the African past. Despite efforts to dismiss conjure as "Negro superstition," standard medical care did not succeed in eradicating the need for conjurers who practiced divination or crafted spells. During the late 19th and 20th centuries several conjurers gained national recognition as clients sought their services. Some of the more prominent conjurers were Doctor Buzzard of Beaufort, South Carolina; Doctor Jim Jordan of Murfreesboro, North Carolina; Aunt Caroline Dye of Newport, Arkansas; and the Seven Sisters of New Orleans. Preservation of cultural identity was also a mitigating factor in refusal of some blacks to relinquish their ties with conjure.

In the 21st century, media continues to promote negative stereotypes of conjure through images of primitive characters and rituals. Regardless of the demonization and trivialization of conjure, there has been a renewed interest in the practice and study of conjuration. In many instances, the continuation of conjure among African Americans is still perpetuated by lack of access to adequate health care. As scholars continue to explore various aspects of conjuration relative to African American healing, they are compelled to reconsider and redefine conjure beyond the realm of folklore and superstition in order to critically examine cultural dimensions of African American experiences.

See also: Africanisms; Pritchard, Gullah Jack; Root Doctors; Slave Culture; Slave Resistance

Anita L. Harris

Bibliography
Anderson, Jeffrey E. *Conjure in African American Society.* Baton Rouge: Louisiana State University Press, 2007.
Bird, Stephanie Rose. *Sticks, Stones, Roots & Bones: Hoodoo, Mojo & Conjuring with Herbs.* St. Paul, MN: Llewellyn Publications, 2004.
Chireau, Yvonne P. *Black Magic: Religion and the African American Conjuring Tradition.* Berkeley: University of California Press, 2003.
McQuillar, Tayannah Lee. *Rootwork: Using the Folk Magic of Black America for Love, Money, and Success.* New York: Simon & Schuster, 2003.
Mitchim, Stephanie Y. *African American Folk Healing.* New York: New York University Press, 2007.

Coromantee

The term Coromantee refers to an important English trading post located on the Gold Coast of West Africa during the 17th and 18th centuries. The correct appellation, Kromantine, was the name of both a key commercial village controlled by the Fante Kingdom of Fetu and a major trading fort established by the Dutch in 1598. Fort Kromantine, located near the modern-day village of Abanze, was destroyed in 1645 and rebuilt later by the English. It was to become the first English trading post along the coast of the Gulf of Guinea. From Fort Kromantine and other coastal factories like it, the English exported Africans principally to their Caribbean possessions throughout the 17th and 18th centuries. During the second Anglo-Dutch War, Fort Kromantine was seized by the Dutch West Indies Company and renamed Fort New Amsterdam—perhaps in direct response to the seizure of its namesake in North America by British forces.

As a result of the combined Fante, English, and Dutch trading activities at Kromantine, enslaved Africans exported from this region of the Gold Coast were lumped together and referred to incorrectly as "Kromantine" by European slave traders, factors, and ship captains during the 17th and 18th centuries. Although this ethnic term has its ambiguities, "Kromantine" does refer to mostly Akan-speakers from the Gold Coast who were transported to the Western Hemisphere.

Throughout the 18th century, the so-called Coromantees were a feared contingent among the many enslaved African groups in the British, Dutch, and Danish Americas. Involved as principles and leaders in more than 23 revolts and plots in locales ranging from Antigua to New York City, Coromantees were stereotyped by British planters and ship captains as being prone to rebellion, yet fiercely loyal if one could gain their respect. Importantly, the creation of Coromantee identity in the Americas was characterized by the spreading influence of Akan-speaking cultural practices, including the use of Akan day-names, Anansi the Spider stories, and Obeah—which was likely a fusion of Akan- and Igbo-speaking spiritual practices.

See also: Atlantic Slave Trade; Slave Resistance

Walter C. Rucker

Bibliography
Berlin, Ira. "From Creole to African: Atlantic Creoles and the Origins of African-American Society in Mainland North America." *The William and Mary Quarterly* 53 (April 1996):251–88.
Rucker, Walter. *The River Flows On: Black Resistance, Culture, and Identity Formation in Early America.* Baton Rouge: Louisiana State University, 2005.

Schuler, Monica. "Akan Slave Rebellions in the British Caribbean." *Savacou* 1 (1970):15–23.

Thornton, John. "The Coromantees: An African Cultural Group in Colonial North America and the Caribbean." *Journal of Caribbean History* 32 (1998):161–78.

Thornton, John. "War, State, and Religious Norms in 'Coromantee' Thought: The Ideology of an African American Nation." In *Possible Pasts: Becoming Colonial in America,* ed. Robert Blair St. George, 181–200. Ithaca, NY: Cornell University Press, 2000.

Davis, Miles

Miles Dewey Davis Jr. (1926–1991) was an influential musician who transformed the genre of jazz. Many jazz artists, ethnomusicologists, and social scientists view Miles Davis's professional career as one of constant transition. His career is highlighted by distinct periods of style that included bebop (1945–1948), cool jazz (1948–1958), hard bob (1952–1963), modal jazz (1959–1968), and electronics (1969–1991). These distinct eras in his career were quite significant within the field of jazz because of Davis's continuous effort to evolve as a musician. He introduced cool jazz, modal jazz, fusion jazz, pop, hip-hop, and rock into a musical genre (big band jazz) that held itself as conservative.

Miles Davis's contributions to the field of jazz were not anticipated at the start of his career in the late 1930s. He began performing at age 13 in East St. Louis, Illinois. Miles showed great promise as a jazz trumpeter and was given his first professional opportunity performing with the Blue Devils. A year later (1941), at age 15, he performed with Adam Lambert's Six Brown Cats. From 1941 to 1943, he performed in the St. Louis area with the Eddie Randall Band.

In 1945, Miles Davis enrolled at the Julliard School of Music in New York. His tenure at the school was short-lived; he decided to leave after one semester. Miles had been drawn to the jazz scene in New York and especially to the clubs on 52nd Street. He performed at these clubs with such future jazz greats as Charlie Parker, Tadd Dameron, Coleman Hawkins, and Bennett (Benny) Carter. For a period of five months, he played with the renowned William (Billy) Eckstine Band. His first recording session was in 1945 on the Savoy label with Herbie Fields's band, which featured "Rubberlegs" Williams.

Jazz music and performance styles had been established by such jazz greats as Louis Armstrong, Charlie Shavers, Roy Eldridge, and Rex Stewart. However, Davis's alterative style included playing within a narrower range, including a more lyric style and fast tempo, light with no vibrato. Influence for this style of performance came from his teacher—and Davenport, Iowa, jazz great—Leon (Bix) Biederbecke. Many of Miles's early performances and recordings emulate a new style that would serve as a transition for future jazz eras and trends.

In late 1948, Miles formed his own band. Through collaboration with Gil Evans, he participated in an experimental workshop that produced a series of selections that were collected and reissued as *Birth of the Cool.* A number of outstanding musicians, arrangers, and writers participated in bringing the album to fruition. A few of these individuals included Gerry Mulligan, John Lewis, Maxwell (Max) Roach, Johnny Carisi, Lee Konitz, and Kai Winding. Davis's recordings exposed the public to new styles and trends that would influence younger jazz performers who were not vested in the traditional big band sound. Miles closed out the 1940s with a performance on Christmas night at Carnegie Hall as a performer in the Stars of Modern Jazz concert. The Voice of America radio network broadcasted this performance a year later (1950).

The 1950s started with the third of five eras in Miles's career, with the fusion of cool jazz and hard bop. During this period, he introduced the Harmon mute as a performance accessory. In 1956, he recorded two bold albums, *Bye Bye Blackbird* and *'Round About Midnight.* The Harmon mute is used on a regular basis in both recordings. His performance style characteristics also expanded to include drones, half-tone oscillations, tonic-dominant alterations in the bass line, diatonic ostinatos, and a flamenco-like scale. His records titled "So What" and "Flamenco Sketches" exhibit the Flamenco style scale. Other recordings such as *Miles Ahead* 1957) were prepared in a big band format. He also produced the orchestral albums *Porgy and Bess* and *Sketches of Spain.* Both albums were influenced by composer Joaquin Rodrigo and became classics.

By 1957, Miles had assembled another group of outstanding musicians to perform with his group. Lead performers included Bill Evans, Jimmy Cobb, John Coltrane, and Cannonball Adderly. This ensemble produced two landmark recordings titled *Milestones* and *Kind of Blue* (1959). *Kind of Blue* received rave reviews from jazz critics

Miles Davis at a concert in Tel Aviv, 1987. (AP Photo)

and peers of Miles Davis. This album had a very avant-garde sound. The film score *Ascenseur Pour Lechafaud* ("Lift to the Scaffold") was completed by Miles in 1957. Louis Mulle directed this film, which was recognized as a major success in France, England, and the United States. The entire soundtrack was recorded at a Paris radio station. Each solo in the recording had its unique character. There is a strong-willed use of "echo" in "Generique" and "Chey le photograph du Motel" and a muted trumpet solo in "Diner au Motel," and "Au bardu Petit Back" incorporates a luscious improvisation, whereas "Champs-Elysees" exhibits a rock blues style. Davis shocked his followers when he moved toward partnering jazz with rock. The recording *Filles De Kilimanjaro* reinforced the partnership when Miles utilized a wak-wak pedal connected to his electronic trumpet and integrated multiple electronic keyboards and electric guitar.

One of the best recordings to feature an open fusion between soul, jazz, and rock and roll is the album *Bitches Brew* (1969). Album sales exceeded expectations, and it was the first in Davis's career to go gold. Musical elements included the use of various mutings, modal melodies, free improvisation, electronic instruments and unique harmonies. In order to deliver such an outstanding performance, Miles surrounded himself with a new core of musicians with fresh ideas. Chick Corea, Keith Jarrett, Joe Zawinal, and Herbie Hancock represent some of the new talent brought to Miles's arena. Miles also experimented with the use of improvisations in a cheerless format and a tonal ambiguous bop style during the time Wayne Shorter served as his accompanist. And the rhythm section was freed to find unique ways of expressing 4/4 rhythms.

From 1975 to 1980, Davis disappeared from the jazz scene after announcing his retirement. Many jazz critics felt that his career-ending proclamation was associated with a number of health issues, including an ongoing addiction to heroin and cocaine. However, Miles returned in early 1980 to record a series of albums that crossed a number of genres. His new release, *The Man with the Horn,* was well-received by followers of Miles as well as jazz critics. This recording became the most popular since the Grammy-winning *Bitches Brew.* Following the success of this album, Miles entered the studio to record *We Want Miles* and *Star People.* Again, Miles added a number of new performers for this recording session and public performances. Among the many performers employed were Bill Evans III on saxophone (1980–1984), Brandford Marsalis on saxophone (1984–1985), John Scofield on guitar (1982–1985), Robert Irving III on synthesizer (1980–1983), and Mino Cinelu on percussion (1982–1984).

Miles continued to experiment with different styles well into the 1980s. He recorded popular music of the rock band Scritti Politti and rock singer Cyndi Lauper. In 1985, he collaborated on the "Sun City" antiapartheid recording that protested social issues in South Africa. Following the successful release of this recording, Davis became involved in a number of new initiatives. He appeared in the television show *Miami Vice,* featured in the film *Durango,* and completed a number of commercials for New York City radio stations. Davis was the recipient of an honorary doctorate in 1986 from the New England Conservatory of Music for his longstanding achievements, which had covered a period of more than 40 years. The National Association of Recording Artists awarded him a Grammy in 1990 for lifetime achievement.

Miles Davis died in Santa Monica, California, on September 28, 1991, after suffering from a stroke and pneumonia. *See also:* Black Folk Culture; Coltrane, John; Jazz; Parker, Charlie

Lemuel Berry Jr.

Bibliography

Chambers, Jack. *Milestones*. New York: DaCapo Press, 1998.

Feather, Leonard, and Ira Gitler. *Encyclopedia of Jazz in the Seventies*. New York: Horizon Press, 1966.

Kofsky, Frank. *Black Nationalism and the Revolution in Music*. New York: Pathfinders, 1970.

Mabunda, Limpho. *Reference Library of Black America*, Vol. 4. Detroit, MI: Gale Group, 1997.

Southern, Eileen. *Bibliographical Dictionary of Afro-Americans and African Musicians*. Westport, CT: Greenwood Press, 1982.

Southern, Eileen. *The Music of Black Americans*. New York: Norton, 1997.

Taylor, Arthur. *Nates and Jones: Musician-to-Musician Interviews*. New York: Perigee, 1977.

Walton, Ortiz M. *Music: Black, White and Blue*. New York: Morrow, 1972.

Double Consciousness

In 1903, W. E. B Du Bois wrote *The Souls of Black Folk,* one of the most important and deeply profound works of African American scholarship. In the opening essay, "Of Our Spiritual Strivings," Du Bois used the concept of "double-consciousness" to describe the social, cultural, psychological, and political "contradiction" of the "American Negro" or African American in the U.S. context just four decades after the Emancipation Proclamation of 1863. Du Bois' development of this illuminating concept was grounded in his understanding of black American life from his highly original book *The Philadelphia Negro* (1896), the first of its kind, and the legacy of this understanding of what it means to be both black and American and the struggle inherent therein. Such ground is still highly relevant for our understanding of the current realities and struggles of African Americans.

For Du Bois, the souls of black folk, though highly varied, have in common the struggle to resolve this inherent contradiction—but through a resolution that works *for* African Americans and not against them. Du Bois' words

describe the dilemma of double consciousness best and show the political, cultural, and sociological struggles that continue some 100 years after the publication of *The Souls of Black Folk.* To experience and conceive of life through such a double consciousness is an undeniable dilemma and one that would, in the decades to come throughout the 20th century, define in many ways the continued struggles of Africans on American soil.

Du Bois foresaw that this concept—this dilemma, this double consciousness—that was occurring because of, alongside of, and within the central problem of the 20th century, which he identified as "the problem of the color-line," would be fundamental to the struggle for black liberation, civil rights, and equality in the United States. Indeed, some two years later, Du Bois would give a speech at the first meeting of the Niagara Movement, which would demand full suffrage, public accommodations, human rights, education for all, and ultimately, unbending enforcement of the Constitution of the United States regardless of color. The lived experiences of African Americans, as Du Bois understood it through this concept, provided undeniable evidence that the ideals of the Bill of Rights, the Constitution, and indeed the Fifteenth Amendment were *not* being realized for all Americans. The demands of the Niagara Movement were certainly grounded in a desire to reconcile the double consciousness and to explicitly attack key ideals of the United States—ideals that were not fulfilled. That the internal and external struggle of the "American Negro" was one of double consciousness, Du Bois considered to be laid directly at the hands of the government of the United States—a government rooted in white supremacy. The pursuit to unify the "soul" of the African American effectively, without losing either blackness or full American citizenship, was important for the strategies of the NAACP and other black organizations as well as in movements such as Pan-Africanism, the Civil Rights movement, and Black Power.

Not only did the idea of a double consciousness hold a central place in the strategies of important black liberation movements, but the idea also foreshadowed other important conceptual developments in African and African American scholarship. For example, Carter G. Woodson's *Mis-Education of the Negro* (1933), Frantz Fanon's *Wretched of the Earth* (1965), Stokely Carmichael and Charles V. Hamilton's *Black Power: The Politics of Liberation in America* (1967), and even Molefi K. Asante's *The Afrocentric Idea*

(1987) all were grounded in Du Bois' instructive notion of double consciousness as it manifested itself in the experiences of African Americans socially, educationally, politically, psychologically, and culturally. It truly was an idea that was ahead of its time.

See also: Du Bois, W. E. B

David L. Brunsma

Bibliography

Asante, Molefi K. *The Afrocentric Idea.* 1987. Reprint, Philadelphia: Temple University Press, 1989.

Carmichael, Stokely, and Charles V. Hamilton. *Black Power: The Politics of Liberation in America.* New York: Penguin Books, Ltd., 1969.

Du Bois, W. E. B. *The Philadelphia Negro: A Social Study.* Philadelphia: University of Pennsylvania Press, 1998 [1896].

Du Bois, W. E. B. *The Souls of Black Folk.* 1903. Reprint, New York: Dover Publications, 1994.

Fanon, Frantz. *The Wretched of the Earth.* Jackson, TN: Grove Press, 1965.

Woodson, Carter G. *The Mis-Education of the Negro.* 1933. Reprint, Lawrenceville, NJ: Africa World Press, 1990.

Ebo Landing

Among the peoples living in the Sea Islands and coastal regions of Georgia and South Carolina, a unique set of forces combined over time to produce Gullah and Geechee cultures. Both cultures were combinations of various Atlantic African language cohorts, with solidly West-Central African and Sierra Leonian foundations. Other cultures and language cohorts found expression within Gullah and Geechee, even those cultures brought to the Lowcountry by the numerically insignificant Igbo-speakers of the Niger River Delta (modern Nigeria)—who represented about 8 percent of all African imports into the region during the 18th century. Because of their alleged propensity to commit suicide, folktales about flying Africans have been linked by a range of scholars to Igbo-speaking imports in South Carolina and Georgia. However, versions of these tales can be found in other diasporic locales, including Jamaica, Cuba, and Brazil. Like many Atlantic African groups, Igbo-speakers embraced the notion of the transmigration of souls, believing that upon the death of the physical body, the soul returns to inhabit ancestral lands to await rebirth. In the case of Africans dispersed into the Western Hemisphere,

this belief in transmigration was linked to the ability of the soul to fly, swim, or find other means of conveyance across the Atlantic Ocean to, in essence, make a reverse Middle Passage.

In the context of Igbo beliefs in transmigration, the claimed ubiquity of Igbo suicides, and displacement in the Americas, tales of Africans who had the supernatural ability to fly back home were frequently told among the Gullah and Geechee of the Lowcountry. Then in the year 1803, a pivotal event occurred at Dunbar Creek, a tributary of Frederica River on St. Simons Island, Georgia, which added a new set of possibilities to folktales based on the belief in transmigration. In May 1803, a group of about 75 Igbo slaves arrived in Savannah, Georgia, by ship and were purchased by two coastal planters—John Couper of Cannon's Point on St. Simons Island and Thomas Spalding of Sapelo Island. After the purchase, the Igbo were then loaded onto another ship—a schooner named *York*—for transport to St. Simons Island. After this point, accounts vary widely regarding the ultimate fate of the Igbo. In one account, they rebelled against the ship's crew and drowned after jumping overboard. In another version, they were successfully disembarked from the ship, and while in chains and engaged in a group song, they walked into Dunbar Creek and drowned. Yet another version contends that they walked into the water after receiving a severe whipping by an overseer.

Although the actual historical accounts differ, the meanings derived from these events by Gullah and Geechee generally do not. Floyd White, an ex-slave resident of St. Simons Island recounted in the 1930s that the "Ibo" disembarked from the slave ship, engaged in a group song, and marched to Dunbar Creek on their way back to Africa. In another version told by Wallace Quarterman of Darien, the Igbo—after receiving a beating from an overseer—flew back to Africa instead of walking across the Atlantic Ocean. In both cases, the idea conveyed is that the Igbo committed mass suicide in order to release their souls from earthly bounds (Goodwine, 1998).

In conjunction with the flying African stories, the Ebo Landing account may allow for an understanding of why only African-born slaves could fly, walk, or swim back to Africa. If the soul of a deceased individual returns back to former companions and friends, that would mean that the souls of African-born slaves would have to "fly" or "swim" across the Atlantic to get back home. This was an impossible feat for slaves born in the Americas. Their families and friends were in the Western Hemisphere, not Africa, and thus they would not need the ability to take flight or "return" by other means. The phenomenon of flying Africans or analogues to Ebo Landing are absent in African folklore for similar reasons. If an individual dies in Africa, the spirit has no need to fly because it is already home. Though rooted in African metaphysical understandings, this represents an orientation that is uniquely African American in orientation and perspective.

Both the historical accounts and the folkloric renditions of Ebo Landing are what give the site known as Ebo Landing, in Glynn County, Georgia, its name. In addition to being immortalized in folk tales, the stories of Ebo Landing and flying Africans were given expression in Julie Dash's masterful reflection on Gullah life in the 1991 film *Daughters of the Dust*; in novels by Toni Morrison, Paule Marshall, and Gayl Jones—*Song of Solomon* (1977), *Praisesong for the Widow* (1984), and *Song for Anniho* (2000), respectively; and in children's stories by Virginia Hamilton, Alice McGill, Janice Liddell, Linda Nickens, and Julius Lester.

Walter C. Rucker

Bibliography

Doster, Stephen, ed. *Voices from St. Simons: Personal Narratives of an Island's Past*. Winston-Salem, NC: John F. Blair, 2008.

Georgia Writers' Project. *Drums and Shadows: Survival Studies among the Coastal Negroes*. Athens: University of Georgia Press, 1940.

Gomez, Michael A. *Exchanging Our Country Marks: The Transformation of African Identities in the Colonial and Antebellum South*. Chapel Hill: University of North Carolina Press, 1998.

Goodwine, Marquetta L. *The Legacy of Ibo Landing: Gullah Roots of African American Culture*. Atlanta, GA: Clarity Press, 1998.

Kenan, Randall. *Walking on Water: Black American Lives at the Turn of the Twenty-First Century*. New York: Knopf, 1999.

Stuckey, Sterling. *Slave Culture: Nationalist Theory and the Foundations of Black America*. New York: Oxford University Press, 1987.

Election Day

Election Day was a weeklong event involving the enslaved and free black population in the American North that began in the early 18th century. The event took place on different dates, but those dates usually correlated with the election events of the white population. The event was seen by whites as a mimicry of their election procedures, but this was not the case; "Negro" election day was much more celebratory and not only involved the election of a king or governor but also entailed music, dancing, dress, and feasts. In Massachusetts, Election Day was held on the last Wednesday of the Easter season; the festivities of election week would begin the Monday prior to Election Day and would not end until the Saturday after it.

Campaigning, planning, and preparation for Election Day would begin well in advance. The enslaved population would begin saving their pocket change in order to pay to put on some of the events that would occur. In fact, some would even make food items to sell in order to raise additional money for the festivities. Such treats as root beer and gingerbread election cakes also were prepared for election week. In addition to the money that the enslaved population earned and saved, their owners were also expected to contribute to the festivities, especially if one of the elected officials was their slave. Music and dance were a large part of the celebration throughout the Americas. Instruments such as the fiddle, banjo, fish horn, and Guinea drum were used in the celebration. The inaugural parade that followed the election showcased the musicians, the dancers, and the newly elected official dressed in bright colors and many times riding a horse with plaited hair.

When an enslaved person was elected to one of these positions, governor or king, that person's owner was expected to have an inaugural dinner in his honor. The owner was also expected to provide clothing for the events and provisions such as food and liquor. Although the positions earned were held only by blacks, the owner would also share in the prestige. The whites did not see the election festivities as being a threat because they thought that the proceedings were mimicking their own election procedures. They also wished to utilize those who were elected as enforcers of colonial policies and to maintain social order within the enslaved communities.

The title "king" or "governor" varied by location: in the royal colonies such as New Hampshire and Massachusetts, the title king was given, and in other colonies such as Connecticut and Rhode Island, the title of governor was utilized. In order to be eligible to run for office, the candidate had to be of African descent, his owner must be of some political significance, and he had to have great physical strength. The governor or king had authority over his "countrymen" and held jurisdiction over his subjects. In return, the governor or king was given respect and honor for his position. Election Day, although associated with the American North, did occur in Brazil and throughout the Caribbean. In Brazil and the Caribbean, there was one significant difference: women could be elected queens, and there could be other elected female officials.

See also: Africanisms; Black Folk Culture; Pinkster Festival; Slave Culture

Dawn Miles

Bibliography

Piersen, William D. *Black Yankees: The Development of an Afro-American Subculture in Eighteenth-Century New England.* Amherst: University of Massachusetts Press, 1988.

White, Shane. "'It Was a Proud Day': African Americans, Festivals, and Parades in the North, 1741–1834." *The Journal of American History* 81 (1994):13–50.

Ellington, Duke

Edward Kennedy "Duke" Ellington (1889–1974), born in Washington, D.C., was a jazz pianist, bandleader, and composer who, throughout the course of his life, recorded over 2,000 compositions and performed over 20,000 concerts across the globe. Ellington's music combined African American musical traditions of New Orleans jazz music and the blues of the Deep South with his own unique compositional style that borrowed ideas from the European classical musical tradition. An ability to combine different musical traditions and styles led to Ellington's enormous cross-sectional appeal and international success over the course of his life. The long-ensuing argument over whether Duke Ellington's music is African American or American music, jazz music or simply music, is misguided, for Ellington's music cannot be defined as solely one or the other; rather it is both American and African American, both jazz music and music in general—universal in its dialogue with all humanity, but also particular in the way it expresses the voice of the African American experience.

The title of "Duke" was bestowed on Ellington by a childhood friend because of the dignified way Ellington presented himself, a result of his etiquette training and socialization by his mother, Daisy Kennedy Ellington, and

his father, James Edward Kennedy, who were part of D.C.'s emerging black bourgeoisie. Although exposed to music lessons at an early age, Ellington focused more on sports and art than music throughout much of his early childhood. However, by the time he was in high school, he had realized his connection with and love for music. After hearing Harvey Brooks play ragtime piano, Ellington was suddenly inspired to begin seriously learning the instrument and the music. He learned a few tricks from Brooks and then took lessons on how to read music and improve his piano-playing techniques from Oliver "Doc" Perry and Louis Brown, other D.C.-area musicians. With confidence resulting from his training, Ellington began to play different venues throughout Washington, D.C. His sudden success gigging around town prompted him to leave high school several months prior to graduation and embark on what would be a prolific, lifelong, history-making career as a musician, bandleader, composer, and "cultural ambassador" for the United States.

In 1917, Duke Ellington formed his first band, Duke's Serenaders, which played at clubs and events in Washington, Maryland, and Virginia for approximately five years. During this time, Ellington moved out of his parents' house, bought his own home, and married Edna Thompson. In 1919, Mercer Kennedy Ellington was born, who would later follow in his dad's footsteps as leader of the Ellington Orchestra. By 1923, Ellington had made the big move to New York and set up his band "The Washingtonians," a group that gained notoriety during the Prohibition Era playing such clubs as the Exclusive Club, the Hollywood Club, and the famous Cotton Club, which nationally broadcasted The Washingtonians on a live show called "From the Cotton Club." Ellington recorded his first tunes, "East Saint Louis Toodle-Oo" and "Black and Tan Fantasy," in 1927, just prior to signing an agreement with Irving Mills, which opened doors to a number of recording companies, including Columbia, Brunswick, and Victor. His move to New York and the connections he made there helped catapult Ellington and his band onto the international stage, which increased their popularity worldwide, ultimately bringing the Ellington Orchestra—no longer The Washingtonians—both national and international acclaim.

Wynton Marsalis has described Duke Ellington as "the very greatest of great facilitators" because of his ability to play any rhythmic style and to organize, manage, and lead the 17 or so members of his orchestra. One of Ellington's gifts as a bandleader and composer was his ability to find a place and space for the different musicians' voices in his orchestra and musical arrangements, which allowed him to evoke different moods in his music and continue to generate new compositions. Ellington appreciated and worked with the different sounds, stylistic approaches, and personalities of the musicians in his band—the more hard-edge sounds of Sam Woodyard and Cootie Williams *and* the smoother sounds of Johnny Hodges and Lawrence Brown, to name a few—and they, in turn, respected and followed his lead. This type of camaraderie and musical connection among the band members was harnessed and then held together and kept in locomotion by Ellington. He was, through his leadership of the band, able to arrange and integrate the different musicians so that the music they produced together remained solid and "swinging" while still providing a variety of rich textures—tones and rhythms—that gave the orchestra its discerning sound. Many of the original band members remained in the orchestra with Ellington up until the end, playing through the latter avant-garde years and during the period of tours overseas for the U.S. State Department.

Both jazz-seasoned and classically trained composers and musicians consider "the Duke" to be one of America's (some argue the world's) greatest composers. Even a non-musician such as President Nixon recognized Duke Ellington as "America's foremost composer" and awarded Ellington the highest award issued to an American civilian, the Presidential Medal of Freedom, adding to a long list of awards, honors, and achievements garnered over the years. Duke Ellington has been awarded the President's Gold Medal on behalf of Lyndon B. Johnson; honorary doctorate degrees from America's most prestigious universities, Harvard and Yale University; the Legion of Honor, the highest honor awarded an individual by the French government; and 13 Grammy awards. Schools, festivals, parks, streets, bridges, memorials, and children across the United States have been named after Duke Ellington, a testament to his lasting impact on American music and culture and his continued importance in the hearts and minds of Americans.

See also: Black Folk Culture; Jazz; Ragtime

Sean Elias

Bibliography

Hasse, John E, Jr. *Beyond Category: The Life and Genius of Duke Ellington.* New York: Da Capo Press, 1993.

Tucker, Mike. *Ellington: The Early Years.* Urbana: University of Illinois Press, 1991.

Ethnic Randomization

Ethnic randomization is a theory that claims that slave traders and ship captains consciously selected enslaved Africans from different ethnic groups during capture and transportation so as to reduce the risk of revolts. This theory has been advanced by anthropologists Sidney Mintz and Richard Price in their book *The Birth of African American Culture: An Anthropological Perspective.*

Mintz and Price use this theory in an attempt to counter the claim of relative cultural homogeneity of the enslaved Africans advanced by Melville Herskovits, in *The Myth of the Negro Past.* According to Herskovits, there was relative cultural uniformity among West Africans, and therefore it is possible to pinpoint African cultural survivals in the New World.

Using the theory of ethnic randomization, Mintz and Price attempt to dismiss the plausibility of the argument. They argue that such survivals commonly known as Africanisms did not occur because they would require large numbers of a particular ethnic group, which was not possible because enslaved Africans had been "randomized." Mintz and Price argue that the Africans who came to the New World were drawn from different parts of Africa, from numerous ethnic and linguistic groups, and from different societies in any region. Therefore, they posit that it cannot be said that enslaved Africans shared a common culture, in which case they had nothing to transmit.

In recent times, however, while admitting that enslaved Africans indeed had diverse ethnic origins, scholars have criticized the ethnic randomization theory, stating that it goes against the logic of slave trade. John Thornton in *Africans in the New World* argues that ethnic randomization did not occur in the Middle Passage. He says that slave ships drew their entire cargo only from one or perhaps two ports in Africa and unloaded them in large lots of as many as 200–1,000 in their new Atlantic homes. He further argues that it was in the interest of the slave-ship captains to gather as many slaves as quickly as possible to reduce expenses and to keep down mortality rate. He states that once slaves were on board, in one location, the captain had little choice but to keep them on board, even if he went to other points of the coast. But if the slaves were gathered in one place, he could keep them on shore until he had to depart. Thornton further states that not only did this improve the health of slaves, but it also allowed the captain to shuffle some of the loss from death onto the sellers.

Ethnic randomization also assumes ignorance on the part of slave owners as to the identity and points of origin of slaves. Daniel Littlefield in his book *Rice and Slaves* shows that the slave owners in different regions in North America were very keen to bring in slaves of particular ethnic groups because of specific skills. He says that to argue that the white slave owners thought all slaves were the same, and therefore it did not matter where they came from, would be quite misleading. Littlefield writes about rice-growing in South Carolina and shows how some ethnic groups were preferred over others. He demonstrates that the plantation owners deliberately searched for slaves from Gambia who had rice-growing skills. If, therefore, slaves had actually been "randomized," it definitely would have presented a problem for the slave traders.

Further, Littlefield shows that the slave owners not only searched for slaves from particular regions in Africa, but also were able to identify the ethnicity of slaves by certain characteristics. Although not conclusively, they seem to have been generally able to identify origin of slaves in question. This shows that it was highly unlikely that the slave owners would be deceived as to the ethnicity of their slaves.

Additionally, the theory of ethnic randomization has influenced the debate on the formation of African American identity. Mintz and Price argue that because the enslaved Africans were ethnically mixed, they were forced to form new identities very early in their experience in the New World. They maintain that enslaved Africans became a community only as much as they experienced their new environment. Instead of drawing from their African experience, they formed new identities based on the people that surrounded them.

Douglass Chambers's book *Murder in Montpelier* addresses this issue by looking at the slave community in Montpelier in Virginia. He advances the argument that enslaved Africans reacted to crisis they encountered in the New World as Atlantic Africans as opposed to Creoles.

Moreover, he states that slaves in the Montpelier community were mainly Igbo and that although there were slaves of other ethnic groups, the Igbo influence was strong enough to influence them. So rather than the influence of the white slave owners creolizing the slaves, Chambers states that it was Igbo culture that was the dominant influence on enslaved people in that region.

Further, Chambers argues that creolization—the process of adapting to new physical and social conditions and the basic process of cultural change—was in fact a historical process as opposed to anthropological, as advanced by Mintz and Price. Chambers posits that the slave trade was more systematic and ordered than Mintz and Price want to admit. He argues, therefore, that it is plausible to state that particular ethnic groups did have the numbers enabling them to contribute significantly in the formation of African American identities.

See also: African Diaspora; Africanisms; Atlantic Slave Trade

Karen W. Ngonya

Bibliography

Chambers, Douglas. *Murder at Montpelier: Igbo Africans in Virginia.* Jackson: University Press of Mississippi, 2005.

Littlefield, Daniel. *Rice and Slaves: Ethnicity and the Slave Trade in Colonial South Carolina.* Baton Rouge: Louisiana State University Press, 1981.

Mintz, Sidney, and Richard Price. *The Birth of African American Culture, An Anthropological Perspective.* Boston: Beacon Press, 1976.

Thornton, John. *Africa and Africans in the Making of the Atlantic World, 1400–1800.* Cambridge: Cambridge University Press, 1992.

Evangelism

Evangelism, the work of spreading religious belief, was a popular and influential form of religious conversion among African Americans in the 18th and 19th centuries. In the Americas, evangelism was originally focused on the most glaring nonbelievers, namely the Native Americans and enslaved Africans. British colonists argued over the right tactics of slave evangelization. Should religious instruction for slaves be mandatory? This posed a serious dilemma to Christian slave owners. English law clearly forbade the enslavement of Christians; once slaves were converted, must they be freed? Most Anglican leaders countered such opposition by pointing out that the Bible sanctioned slavery and that Paul explicitly tells servants to obey their masters. Christianity would not make freed men, Anglican churchmen argued; rather, it would make better slaves, who would better understand their hierarchical position in the divine plan. With this message, the Society for the Propagation of the Gospel in Foreign Parts (SPG) sent missionaries to British North America. Founded in 1701, the SPG was the first organization to systematically evangelize the slaves. Southern slave owners found little to be troubled by in the SPG's tactics or message; in general, SPG evangelists affirmed the feudal hierarchy of Southern society, reiterating the morality of paternalism and rationalizing the complex slave codes that prohibited black literacy or assemblage.

Even so, the SPG achieved limited success among slaves. Few slaves could abide the tedium of the Anglican catechism without expectation of social uplift; moreover, the SPG never effectively translated the Christian message to the slave experience. It was not until Baptist and Methodist itinerant preachers spread across the rural South in the early 19th century that blacks began to convert in large numbers to Christianity. Scholars have long debated the success of Baptists and Methodist among Southern slaves, attempting to determine what made their message so appealing. Several theories have been supported: First, neither group required an educated clergy, encouraging individual slaves to preach without ecclesiastical requirement. Second, Baptists and Methodists shared an antislavery stance from their denominational beginnings and, more importantly, preached a gospel of equality that seemed to challenge the accepted social order. In addition, black evangelists such as Zilpha Elaw had a tremendous influence on converting black people to Christianity in the 18th and early 19th centuries. Subsequent black theologians would argue that Baptists and Methodism also provided a message of profound spiritual transformation and ultimate redemption, if not in this life, then in the next. Regardless of the reason, by the mid-19th century, the majority of freed blacks affiliated with either the Baptists or the Methodists as a result of this successful evangelism.

"Evangelism" is often conflated with "evangelicalism," a conservative movement in Protestantism. Evangelicalism is a specific theological strain sourced in the Wesleyan movement of the 18th century. Evangelical Christians emphasized the role of the individual in his or her own conversion. Whereas all Protestants shared an investment in personal salvation and sanctification, evangelicals believed that an individual had the right to accept or reject salvation. In 19th-century America, evangelicalism was the mainline religion, usefully describing the attitude of most Baptists and Methodists. Historians have long conflated this evangelical majority with the eventual success of the abolitionist movement. Because such inordinate responsibility was placed on the individual in his or her own conversion, individual activity was seen more broadly as a key demonstration of God's grace. Social reform, like abolition, was therefore a major evangelism of American evangelicals, who sought to perfect the world to match their perfected souls. The majority of Northern abolitionists would aptly be described as evangelical.

The effects of Christian evangelism on African Americans are widely debated. For some, black conversion to Christianity facilitated the growth of independent black institutions (such as the African Methodist Episcopal Church and the Southern Christian Leadership Conference) and the development of wide-ranging social service and educational networks. Others contend that Christianity was another tool of white oppression; such critiques would spawn such 20th-century movements as Marcus Garvey's United Negro Improvement Association (UNIA), the Nation of Islam, and alternatives led by religious leaders such as Daddy Grace and Father Divine. Such assessments aside, the demographic and sociological impact of Christian evangelism within African America is indisputable.

See also: African Methodist Episcopal Church; Daddy Grace; Elaw, Zilpha; Father Divine; Society for the Propagation of the Gospel in Foreign Parts

Kathryn Emily Lofton

Bibliography

Butler, Jon. *Awash in a Sea of Faith: Christianizing the American People.* Cambridge, MA: Harvard University Press, 1990.

Frey, Sylvia R., and Betty Wood. *Come Shoutin' to Zion: African American Protestantism in the American South and British Caribbean to 1830.* Chapel Hill: University of North Carolina Press, 1998.

Heyrman, Christine. *Southern Cross: The Beginnings of the Bible Belt.* Chapel Hill: University of North Carolina Press, 1997.

Raboteau, Albert. *Slave Religion: The "Invisible Institution" in the Antebellum South.* New York: Oxford University Press, 1978.

Family Patterns

Family studies have identified characteristic family patterns—broadly defined as general value orientations and structures transmitted intergenerationally through socialization—in most cultural groups. In the case of African Americans, family scholars have noted that, in spite of their diversity stemming from immigration experiences, regional residence, political views, income differences, and phenotypic characteristics, one can identify several family patterns based on African Americans' shared history and common cultural bonds. Two perspectives have dominated the study of these characteristics, at times highlighting different patterns and generating intense debate and controversy: a social pathological (or ethnocentric) approach versus a strength (or culturally relative) paradigm.

In the social-deficit tradition, African American family life, from its beginning up to the present, has not adhered to the norm or the ideal family structural model, defined as a man and a woman with their children living in the same home and endorsing a European American middle-class set of values and ways of being. The ethnocentric approach, therefore, has highlighted what it considers to be pathological and dysfunctional family patterns because of their variation from the expected Eurocentric Christian norm. It has criticized the African American family as a unit lacking a consistent and cohesive structure that moves in a constant state of turmoil. It argues that some of these family deficits existed originally in Africa prior to the capture and enslavement of Africans. It assumes that African slaves brought with them these family deficiencies to the New World and have remained part of the family structure to this day. Also, it maintains that African values, customs, and cultural norms were destroyed during slavery and to some extent by contemporary racism.

The family studies of sociologist E. Franklin Frazier (1894–1962) are prototypical of the deficit perspective and he considers the African American family deeply pathological, a condition stemming in part from the historical legacy of racism and contemporary impact of racism and discrimination. From a similar perspective, in his book *Dark Ghetto,* social psychologist Kenneth B. Clark (1895–1963) summarized what he considered some distinctive family patterns: low aspirations, poor education, family instability, illegitimacy, unemployment, crime, drug addiction, alcoholism, frequent illness, and early death. This approach entered mainstream popular discourse in 1965 with the publication of *The Negro Family: The Case for National Action,* in which Daniel P. Moynihan (1927–2003) described the disintegration of black families as part of a "tangle of pathology" ultimately attributed to three

hundred years of injustice and culminating in high levels of unemployment, welfare dependency, and high rates of nonmarital births.

In contrast to the social-pathology paradigm, which tends to see some of the family patterns as deeply embedded in the history of African American families, the cultural relative approach emerges out of the work of William Edward Burghardt Du Bois (1868–1963) and Melville J. Herskovits (1895–1963) and sees patterns such as low marriage rates, high rates of teen pregnancy, and single-parent, female-headed households as evidence of the inherent strength of African American families, especially women who raised their children and kept their families together during slavery, through Jim Crow and contemporary racism and discrimination. It argues, for example, that the high rate of single mothers leading African American families indicates a resistance, symbolic at times, to the oppressive conditions of both racism and patriarchy. Robert B. Hill is an articulate spokesperson for the strength approach, and he has identified five strengths that had been culturally transmitted through African ancestry to contemporary African American families: strong kinship bond, strong work orientation, strong achievement orientation, flexible family roles, and a strong religious orientation. In his monumental study *The Black Family in Slavery and Freedom, 1750–1925,* historian Herbert Gutman (1928–1985) argued that due to highly adaptive and resilient family patterns, the African American families survived the slave system and then legal segregation, discrimination, and enforced poverty with remarkable strength and solidarity.

From a more holistic approach, sociologist Andrew Billingsley sees African American family patterns as including both weaknesses and strengths. He has argued that their strengths are far greater, and they are distinguished by their adaptive and regenerative powers. He also has identified several distinctive African family patterns that have survived the American experience: consanguinity or blood ties taking precedence over all types of relationships; extended family versus nuclear families; child-rearing considered as the responsibility of parents and the extended family; respect and reverence shown to family elders and others; reciprocity among family members; and cooperation or shared responsibility for the well-being of others. The survival and development of African American families on American shores since 1619 is seen as a testament to their adaptability, viability, and resilience derived from these strengths.

Five generations of a slave family in Beaufort, South Carolina, in 1862. (Library of Congress)

The U.S. Census Bureau recently published some statistics that provide an insight into the contemporary structural reality and patterns of average African American families. There are currently 8.4 million African American households in the United States, with 46 percent living in owner-occupied homes, with a $31,969 annual median income, an increase up from a $26,468 median income in 1986. Sixty-four percent of homes contain a family, and 45 percent contain a married-couple family. Additionally, 1.2 million African American grandparents are living with their own grandchildren younger than 10 years of age, and 51 percent of these grandparents are also responsible for their care.

See also: Frazier, E. Franklin; Herskovits, Melville; Slave Culture

Fernando A. Ortiz

Bibliography

Bennett, Lerone. *Before the Mayflower: A History of Black America.* New York: Penguin, 1997.

Billingsley, Andrew. *Climbing Jacob's Ladder: The Enduring Legacy of African-American Families.* New York: Simon & Schuster, 1992.

Clark, Kenneth B. *Dark Ghetto: Dilemmas of Social Power.* 1965. Reprint, New York: Harper & Row and Wesleyan University Press, 1989.

Frazier, E. Franklin. *The Negro Family in the United States.* Chicago: University of Chicago Press, 1939.

Gutman, Herbert. *The Black Family in Slavery and Freedom, 1750–1925.* New York: Pantheon, 1976.

Hill, Robert. *Strengths of Black Families.* New York: Emerson Hull, 1972.

Martin, Joanne M., and Elmer Martin. *The Helping Tradition in the Black Family and Community.* Washington, D.C.: National Association of Social Workers Press, 1985.

Moynihan, Daniel. *The Negro Family: The Case for National Action.* Washington, D.C.: U.S. Department of Labor, Office of Policy Planning and Research, 1965.

Field Hollers

Field hollers—also known as whooping, arhoolies, cries, and hollers—were a form of communication between enslaved people on cotton, rice, and sugar plantations. Along with work songs, field hollers were vocal expressions that allowed slaves to articulate religious zeal, feelings of frustration, and even secret messages about escaping slavery. Yet unlike collective work songs, field hollers were a solitary expression, sung for one's own joy, grief, relief, and so on; to communicate one's location or other information to others; to call the hunting dogs; to let one's family and neighbors know one is returning home, and so on. Even so, there was often a call-and-response component to field hollers, in which the holler might be echoed by other workers or passed from one to another.

Drawing on African musical styles, field hollers followed specific patterns; they were sung with recognizable lyrics or as meaningless embellished sounds, they tended to be highly improvisational, and they were characterized by a nuanced control of tone and pitch. Early writers, including renowned black abolitionist Frederick Douglass, wrote of the hollers' vocal gymnastics and their characteristic melancholic cast. Scholars have likewise suggested that antebellum hollers, which whites often described as "meaningless," may, in fact, have been sung in African languages not recognized by the overseers, thus serving as subversive and clandestine communication among the enslaved.

Moreover, music educator Willis Laurence James recognized that field hollers possessed a common African origin with other types of black vocal expression. He grouped field hollers with other African American cries, from street peddler's calls to the hollers of black drill sergeants and baseball umpires, and classified hollers into three categories: "plain cries," the simplest in form and structure; "florid cries," the most favored type, featuring elaborate vocalizing that cannot be recorded with standard musical notation; and "coloratura cries," the most amazing and remarkable feats in folk music. As agriculture and other manual labor in the South became mechanized, the holler became increasingly rare. Even so, it lived on in folk preaching, dance calling, and gospel, blues, and jazz singing, and according to James, its influence is even to be heard in the singing of popular white crooners.

The holler's influence is nowhere stronger than in the blues. Enslaved Africans used their culturally more sophisticated understanding of tone to vocally simulate sounds from the world around them. This included vocal simulations of European musical instruments, especially horns. Later, when African Americans were able to obtain European instruments, they adapted them to the aesthetic of the holler by muting and plunging them, bending notes, and so forth. Like the holler, blues is solo vocalizing, of a melancholic character, which emphasizes tone quality and variation. As a vocal genre, the blues, like the holler, allow for and displays great freedom. It is through the blues and black gospel that African American music of the second half of the 20th century absorbed this aesthetic, perhaps witnessed nowhere more spectacularly than in the live performances of James Brown and the carefully controlled and tonally complex shrieks and hollers they featured.

See also: Africanisms; Blues Music; Call-and-Response; Douglass, Frederick; Field Hands; Slave Culture

Fred J. Hay

Bibliography

Courlander, Harold. *Negro Folk Music U.S.A.* New York: Columbia University Press, 1963.

Douglass, Frederick. *My Bondage and My Freedom.* New York: Miller, Orton & Mulligan, 1855.

James, Willis Laurence. "The Romance of the Negro Folk Cry in America." In *Mother Wit from the Laughing Barrel: Readings in the Interpretation of Afro-American Folklore,* ed. Alan Dundes. Englewood Cliffs, NJ: Prentice-Hall, 1973.

Fitzgerald, Ella

Known as the First Lady of Song, Ella Fitzgerald (1917–1996) was an accomplished jazz musician who charmed audiences and critics alike from the time she won the Apollo

Amateur Night in 1934 to her final concert in 1992. She lent her voice, characterized by impeccable pitch, superb diction, and a sweet and clear quality, to a range of musical styles that appealed to a variety of audiences. By one count, she recorded 1,117 different songs.

Fitzgerald was born April 25, 1917, to the unwed couple of William Fitzgerald and Tempie Williams Fitzgerald in Newport News City, Virginia. By the time she was four, her father had left, and her mother was living with Portuguese immigrant Joseph Da Silva. The family moved to Yonkers, New York, where Fitzgerald grew up listening to popular music and especially adored Louis Armstrong and Connee Boswell, an early and innovative white jazz singer whom Fitzgerald strove to emulate at her first Apollo appearance.

Fitzgerald's mother died in 1932. Her mother's sister, Virginia, soon removed her from her stepfather's home, fearing she was being mistreated. Her half-sister soon joined them when Da Silva died as well. Fitzgerald found work running numbers and alerting a prostitution house to police presence. The authorities caught her and sent her to a reform school, where at the time black girls were placed in the worst housing, beaten, held in basements, and perhaps even tortured, according to a 1936 government report and a 1990s journalistic investigation. Fitzgerald later became known for her work on behalf of children and helped establish the Ella Fitzgerald Child Care Center in Watts, Los Angeles, in 1977.

In the fall of 1934, Fitzgerald escaped from the reform school and lived homeless in New York City to evade the authorities. By November 21 of that year, she was on stage at the Apollo, where, as the story goes, she planned to dance but decided at the Monday screening to sing. Her top prize of a week's worth of singing engagements was not honored, possibly because of her appearance from living on the streets. Her unkempt condition later reportedly put off bandleader Fletcher Henderson. It also put off bandleader Chick Webb when he first met her. His male singer, Charles Linton, persuaded him to try her out in front of an audience.

Webb quickly came to see Fitzgerald as key to his aspirations to greater commercial success. In 1935, Fitzgerald and his band made her first record, "Love and Kisses," and after that, Webb barely recorded without her. In 1938, Fitzgerald had her first big hit with "A-Tisket, A-Tasket," a nursery rhyme she wanted to record against the judgment of Decca recording executives. She continued to write many of her own novelty songs—with such names as "Gotta Pebble in My Shoe" and "Chew, Chew, Chew, Chew Your Bubble Gum"—and in 1940 became one of the youngest members of the American Society of Composers, Authors and Publishers (ASCAP). In 1939, Chick Webb, whose growth had been stunted and back hunched from a childhood disease, died of spinal tuberculosis at age 30. Fitzgerald became the leader of her own big band, an astounding feat for a female or for a vocalist, though trumpeter Taft Jordan took over most of the traditional duties. The band split up in 1942 as the big band heyday drew to a close.

Fitzgerald became interested in the emerging bop sound exemplified by Dizzy Gillespie, and indeed, biographer Stuart Nicholson calls her the only musician to successfully cross over from swing to bop. Her record "Flying Home" (1945) combined scat singing—popularized by Louis Armstrong—with bop sensibilities and became a landmark of scat, and her records "Smooth Sailing" and "How High the Moon" also exemplified bop. Such recordings also demonstrate why musicians praised the hornlike quality of her voice.

Jazz vocalist Ella Fitzgerald in 1940. (Library of Congress)

In the 1950s, Norman Granz, upset with Fitzgerald's treatment at Decca, got her out of her contract a year early through a trade and began recording her on Verve. This led to the 19-volume *Song Book* series, in which Fitzgerald recorded songs by such composers as Cole Porter, George Gershwin, Duke Ellington, and Johnny Mercer. She also became a prominent draw at Granz's Jazz at the Philharmonic concert tours. During this period she recorded three albums of duets with Louis Armstrong, which are characterized by the singers' playfulness and the contrast between their voices.

Fitzgerald dated a series of musicians. In 1941, she married Ben Kornegay but followed her managers' advice in seeking an annulment when they became convinced Kornegay was after her money. In 1947, she married bassist Ray Brown. Together they adopted her sister's newborn, whom they named Ray Brown Jr. When the marriage broke up in 1953, Ray Jr. lived with Ella but effectively was raised by her Ella's aunt Virginia while his adoptive parents toured.

Perhaps one of the most enduring contrasts in jazz is between Fitzgerald and Billie Holiday, who, only two years Fitzgerald's senior, was already making a name for herself when Fitzgerald arrived in Harlem. Holiday fans appreciate her method of internalizing the emotions of a song and creating a subjective experience for the listener. By contrast, Fitzgerald fans often applaud her focus on melody and technique over feeling. Many have commented that Holiday acted out her songs, living and dying tragically. Yet Fitzgerald also lived her more detached musical style, making few close friendships over the years.

In the *Down Beat* readers poll for top vocalist, Fitzgerald placed first from 1937 to 1939 and again from 1953 to 1970. In the magazine's critics poll, instituted later, she placed first from 1953 to 1971 and again in 1974. In 1974, the University of Maryland Eastern Shore named its performing arts center after her, and in 1979, she received a Kennedy Center Honors Medal. She won 14 Grammys, and in 1989, the Society of Singers named its lifetime achievement award the "Ella."

See also: Black Folk Culture; Jazz

Brooke Sherrard

Bibliography

Colin, Sid. *Ella: The Life and Times of Ella Fitzgerald.* London: Elm Tree Books, 1987.
David, Norman. *The Ella Fitzgerald Companion.* Companions to Celebrated Musicians. Westport, CT: Praeger, 2004.
Nicholson, Stuart. *Ella Fitzgerald: The Complete Biography.* New York: Routledge, 2004.

Flying African Stories

Flying African stories were tales shared among enslaved people on plantations that drew on African spiritual beliefs to give the enslaved people hope that they could escape bondage and return to their African homeland.

Numerous stories collected in *Drums & Shadows*, a compilation of tales collected by the Georgia Writers' Project (a branch of the Works Progress Administration) in 1940, describe instances of extreme suffering on the slaves' part, or the immediacy of tragic outcome, when some instances of mystic relief unexpectedly prevent the tragedy to occur. A ghost or a spirit suddenly provides the slave with wings, and the latter thus flies immediately back to his native soil. In another example, a legend told of an old man who would come to the plantations and would support the slaves with their unbearable pains. To do so, he would come close to them and blow magic words to them. Right after that, the slaves would be transformed into winged creatures and would fly back to Africa.

Significantly, flying African stories have often been linked to African spiritual beliefs, particularly the notion of transmigration, the idea that one's soul would return to Africa after physical death. Perhaps the most compelling connection between concepts of death, transmigration, and flying African stories came in the story of Ebo Landing, an event in which a group of Africans, after getting a vicious beating from their masters, marched into the ocean and drowned themselves. From then on, the story was told that they had "flown" back to Africa. Scholars now believe that folktales involving flying Africans are actually stories about transmigration and a soul-return to Africa.

Beyond the connection to transmigration, however, the flying African stories have other significant recurring elements—such as spirits' power of invisibility; power of clear-sightedness; power to blind and to restore sight; power to cure; and power to cast magic charms, spells, and evil charms—but we also find the symbol of taboo food laid on people, including salt. Indeed, the salt that was used to preserve food shipped from abroad to America was linked both with the themes of forced exile and with the food eaten by the white tormentors. Thus, eating salt or salty food meant submitting to the whites. As opposed to that, protecting oneself from absorbing salt reflected one's ability to escape domination and thus one's power to fly. What is more, the act of refusing to eat salt was a way of expressing one's faith. This is why the symbol of salt is recurrent in flying African stories, as Monica Schuler analyses it in *Drums & Shadows.*

Flying African stories, orally transmitted from generation to generation, provided the means to bypass the official version of history and the dominant culture. The symbol of the flying African reveals a power of imagination and a creative drive on the African Americans' part. It also permits transcendence of the absence of representation and the denial of orality in the cultural landscape. Eventually, the symbol of the flying African came to illustrate the widely significant theme of a return to the roots, as in, for instance, the case of "Flying Home" by Ralph W. Ellison, who titled his short story after the famous jazz piece by Lionel Hampton. In this story, Ellison provides the reader with a transposition of the myth of flying Africans by confronting its signification with the themes of the color line, forbidden social ascension, and the perilous denial of one's roots.

The flying African stories present a mimetic transposition of the search for transcendence. They also evoke the theme of disappearance as a contrapuntal answer to bondage and earthly suffering.

See also: Africanisms; Ebo Landing; Gullah; Transmigration

Valerie Caruana-Loisel

Bibliography

Courlander, Harold. *A Treasury of Afro-American Folklore.* 1976. Reprint, New York: Marlowe, 1996.

Cumberdance, Daryl. *400 Years of African American Folktale from My People.* New York: Norton, 2002.

Gates, Henry Louis, and Nellie Y. McKay. *The Norton Anthology of African American Literature.* New York: Norton, 1996.

Georgia Writers' Project. *Drums and Shadows: Survival Studies among the Georgia Coastal Negroes.* Savannah: University of Georgia Press, 1986.

Hamilton, Virginia. *The People Could Fly: American Black Folktales.* New York: Knopf, 1985.

Schuler, Monica. "Afro-American Slave Culture." *Historical Reflections* 6 (1979):121–55.

Frazier, E. Franklin

Dr. Edward Franklin Frazier (1894–1962), a black sociologist and educator, became one of the principal voices in the Africanisms debate, which included such notable scholars as Melville Herskovits, Lorenzo Dow Turner, and W. E. B. Du Bois. Born in Maryland at the height of the black nadir, Frazier graduated from Baltimore's Colored High School in 1912 and attended Howard University to study Latin, Greek, German, and mathematics. After graduating from Howard, he taught throughout the South until 1919, when he enrolled in graduate school at Clark University in Worcester, Massachusetts. Frazier earned a master's degree in sociology and became a research fellow at the New York School of Social Work in 1920. In 1922, he began a two-year teaching stint at Morehouse College before serving as the director of the Atlanta School of Social Work until 1927. After earning a PhD in sociology at the University of Chicago in 1931, Frazier taught at Fisk University for three years. In 1934, he became chair of Howard University's sociology department, a position he held until his retirement in 1959.

Author of more than 10 books and dozens of journal articles, Frazier contributed to a number of scholarly debates and was widely recognized as the leading authority on the black family in America. His distinguished career led to a number of achievements. Frazier earned a Guggenheim Fellowship in 1940; he became the first black president of the American Sociological Association (ASA) in 1948; and for his lifetime contributions to the field of sociology, Frazier was a recipient of the ASA's MacIver Award. Despite the universal acclaim for his contributions, Frazier was not averse to controversy and took a number of unpopular stances throughout his long career. While an instructor at Morehouse College, Frazier published an article titled "The Pathology of Race Prejudice," which associated racism with mental illness. Although this conclusion has become accepted by many social scientists, in 1927, it cost Frazier his teaching position at Morehouse and was one of the factors that prompted his move to Chicago.

Perhaps the most significant controversy Frazier was involved in was the so-called Africanisms debate and his long-standing rivalry with anthropologist Melville Herskovits. The opening salvo in the debate was launched in 1939 with the publication of Frazier's *The Negro Family in the United States.* Championing what became known as the "catastrophist school," Frazier argued that slavery had effectively destroyed the black family, and this reality facilitated the "Americanization" of slaves and the complete annihilation of African culture in the United States. Even after the publication of Herskovits' monumental *The Myth of the Negro Past* two years later, Frazier refused to waiver in his contention that African culture had largely disappeared in North America.

In a 1949 work titled *The Negro in the United States,* Frazier dedicated the first chapter to attacking Herskovits's thesis that the African contributions to African American culture were substantial. Although Frazier, for the first time, acknowledged the presence of certain Africanisms, he also contended that the significance of African heritage had been diminished by conditions in American society. It is important to note that Frazier was likely responding to the social environment around him more than to the particulars of his ongoing debate with Herskovits. He was born in the midst of the black nadir, when African Americans had to face the brutal combination of legally sanctioned segregation, political disenfranchisement, unprecedented levels of racial violence, and an anti-black propaganda campaign in the media. In this hostile climate, any claims that African Americans were somehow different from whites would further justify their debased treatment. Even as late as the 1960s, in *The Negro Church in America,* published posthumously in 1963, Frazier would continue the Africanisms debate. Although he made important contributions in a number of areas, it is now clear that Frazier was wrong when he claimed that enslaved Africans in North America were completely stripped of their cultural heritage.

See also: Africanisms; Family Patterns; Herskovits, Melville; Turner, Lorenzo Dow

Walter C. Rucker

Bibliography

Edwards, G. Franklin, ed. *E. Franklin Frazier on Race Relations: Selected Papers.* Chicago: University of Chicago Press, 1968.

Frazier, E. Franklin. *The Negro Church in America.* New York: Schocken Books, 1963.

Frazier, E. Franklin. *The Negro Family in the United States.* Chicago: University of Chicago Press, 1939.

Frazier, E. Franklin. *The Negro in the United States.* New York: Macmillan, 1949.

Herskovits, Melville. *The Myth of the Negro Past.* 1942. Reprint, Boston: Beacon Press, 1958.

Full Immersion Baptism

Full immersion baptism is an initiation rite into the Christian church. Theologians have hypothesized that immersion baptism is a derivative of Jewish ritual washings, whereby the participant bathed in collected rainwater to perform personal ritual purification. The significance of this is that the tub contained flowing water that possessed qualities that sustain life. Likewise, for enslaved Africans, theologians have theorized that immersion baptism could have evinced distinctive memories of God and the significance and sacredness of water to them. Hence, many African Americans joined denominations such as the Methodists and Baptists that practiced baptism in this manner. Because Jesus himself modeled this mode of baptism, Christians practice full immersion baptism as a means of identifying with the life, death, and resurrection of Christ. Black liberation theologians have concluded that because Jesus identified with the poor and oppressed, and African Americans have historically been disenfranchised and oppressed, immersion baptism not only symbolizes freedom and purification from sin but also signifies one's affirmation of his or her human worth, dignity, and willingness to submerge oneself in the black church's commitment to continuing Christ's mission of liberation from an unjust and immoral world, in addition to affirming an anticipation of future redemption by Christ. Consequently, participants in this mode of baptism are usually young adults or adults who have the capacity to consent to the decrees and mandates of the church.

See also: Slave Culture; Slave Religion

Pearl Bates

Bibliography

Costen, Melva Wilson. *African American Christian Worship.* Nashville, TN: Abingdon Press, 1993.

Evans, James H. *We Have Been Believers.* Minneapolis, MN: Augsburg Fortress, 1992.

White, James F. *Introduction to Christian Worship.* Nashville, TN: Abingdon Press, 2000.

Goofer Dust

Goofer dust, also known as grave dirt, is earth taken from graves for use by practitioners of the African American spiritual practice known as hoodoo. The term "goofer" may have evolved from the Kikongo word *kufwa,* meaning "to die." Grave dirt has been popular since at least antebellum days, and users have employed it for diverse purposes, ranging from winning love to killing enemies. Its power comes from the spirit of the person from whose burial place it is taken. Thus, the choice of graves could be very important. For instance, hoodoo practitioners often seek plots filled with the remains of beloved family members when their object is obtaining protection from evil. On the other hand, if one wants to harm an enemy, the graves of the wicked are preferable. Most collect the dirt in rituals that culminate in payments of small change to the spirits of the deceased.

By the 20th century, goofer dust did not always literally come from graves. Some unethical hoodoo supply manufacturers have obtained soil from more convenient sources or substituted colored minerals for grave dirt. In other cases, goofer dust has developed into a compound of multiple ingredients. According to one modern hoodoo manual, goofer dust is a mixture that should incorporate graveyard dirt, sulphur, powdered snails, snake skins, and powdered herbs.

See also: Africanisms; Grave Dirt; Hoodoo; New York Conspiracy of 1741; Slave Culture

Jeffrey Elton Anderson

Bibliography

Anderson, Jeffrey Elton. *Conjure in African American Society.* Baton Rouge: Louisiana State University Press, 2007.

Long, Carolyn Morrow. *Spiritual Merchants: Religion, Magic, and Commerce.* Knoxville: University of Tennessee Press, 2001.

Yronwode, Catherine. *Hoodoo Herb and Root Magic: A Materia Magica of African American Conjure and Traditional Formulary Giving the Spiritual Uses of Natural Herbs, Roots, Minerals, and Zoological Curios.* Forestville, CA: Lucky Mojo Curio, 2002.

Grave Decorations

African Americans have a unique tradition of gravesite decoration, most often found in rural Southern cemeteries, in which family and friends leave personal objects belonging to the dead for their subsequent use in the spirit world. These "grave goods" may include cups and saucers, candy dishes, pitchers, medicine bottles, figurines, clocks, lanterns, automobile parts, and bed frames. Graves are sometimes ornamented with seashells and outlined with bottles driven neck-down into the earth. Dishes and medicine bottles, in particular, are often selected as grave decorations because they were the items used by the deceased during their last illness, and they must be cracked so that the spirit of the vessel is released to serve its owner in the next world.

Such practices have an African origin. The Kongo people of Central Africa, a great many of whom were imported to North America as slaves, placed metal cooking pots, crockery, and glass bottles on graves to ensure that the spirit would not return in search of these necessary items. Earth from a grave was often an ingredient in Kongo *nkisi* charms, as were white objects, representing the "white realm of the dead," and seashells, which symbolize the water from whence the spirits came and to which they will return. Just as Africans sought spiritual aid from the ancestors, African Americans use the cemetery and the spirits of the dead for supernatural power.

Researchers such as author Zora Neale Hurston, the independent folklorist Harry Middleton Hyatt, and fieldworkers for the Federal Writers' Project documented such practices in the late 1920s through early 1940s. They found a wide variety of graveyard customs in the Upper South and Atlantic coastal regions in particular: graveyard dirt and bits of bone were incorporated into magical charms; an image of the intended target of the charm or a bottle containing his or her bodily products might be buried in the cemetery; a silver dime or a handful of rice was left to pay the dead for their assistance. In New Orleans, where most interments are in above-ground tombs, the spirits of the dead were solicited by leaving cooked food, fruit, candies, flowers, whiskey, and coins; by burning a candle; and by drawing a cross mark (the "Kongo cosmogram") on the tomb of persons believed to possess great spiritual power. From the late 19th century until the present, the tomb of Voodoo priestess Marie Laveau and a wall vault in St. Louis Cemetery No. 2, also associated with Laveau, have been the recipients of offerings and cross marks.

See also: Africanisms; Black Folk Culture; Hurston, Zora Neale; Kongo Cosmogram; Laveau, Marie; Slave Culture

Carolyn Morrow Long

Bibliography

Fenn, Elizabeth. "Honoring the Ancestors: Kongo-American Graves in the American South." *Southern Exposure* 13 (September/October 1985):42–47.

Georgia Writers' Project (Savannah Unit). *Drums and Shadows: Survival Studies among the Georgia Coastal Negroes.* 1940. Reprint, Athens: University of Georgia Press, 1986.

Hurston, Zora Neale. *Mules and Men.* 1935. Reprint, New York: Harper and Row, 1990.

Hyatt, Harry Middleton. *Hoodoo-Conjure-Witchcraft-Rootwork,* 5 vols. Hannibal, MO: Western Publishing, 1970–1978.

Long, Carolyn Morrow. "Folk Gravesites in New Orleans: Arthur Smith Honors the Ancestors." *Folklore Forum* 29, no. 2 (1998):23–50.

Long, Carolyn Morrow. "Voodoo-Related Rituals in New Orleans Cemeteries." *Louisiana Folklore Miscellany* 14 (1999):1–14.

Thompson, Robert Farris. *Flash of the Spirit: African and Afro-American Art and Philosophy.* New York: Vintage Books, 1983.

Vlach, John Michael. "Graveyard Decoration." In *The Afro-American Tradition in Decorative Arts.* Cleveland, OH: Cleveland Museum of Art, 1978.

Grave Dirt

Also known as goofer dust, grave dirt was the most powerful ingredient in the arsenal of African American conjurers. In combination with blood, animal parts, plant matter, and other items, graveyard dirt was included in charms, counter-charms, and remedies. It was also a prominent ingredient in oathing ceremonies throughout the African Diaspora. With origins among multiple Atlantic African groups, the significance of so-called goofer dust in African American spiritual beliefs is connected to their reverence for ancestors. The belief that the world of the living is connected to that of the dead is found among a number of African cultural groups brought to North America during the era of the Atlantic slave trade.

Graveyard dirt was used in a range of spells and charms created by African American conjurers. Many believed that rubbing goofer dust on their limbs, combining it with other items and wearing it in a bag around the neck, or burying clumps of graveyard dirt around their homes could be effective methods of warding off harmful conjuration. In the example of a love-charm, graveyard dirt was combined with one quart of vinegar, one quart of rainwater, and nine iron nails. After this mixture was boiled and then cooled for nine days, it was combined with more vinegar and rainwater, bottled and corked for nine days, and sprinkled in the target's yard. Supposedly the target would be amenable to a marriage proposal on the 10th day.

In another example, a "trick bag" could be prepared by combining the ashes of a jaybird's wing, a squirrel's jaw, a rattlesnake's fang, and the dirt from the grave of a criminal. Once this concoction was mixed with a "pig-eating" sow and made into a cake, three feathers from a crowing hen were added, along with the hair of the person employing the charm. After all of these preparations, everything would be placed in a cat-skin bag and buried under the house of the intended victim. The trick bag would cause disease, bad luck, and sorrow. In similar fashion, harmful conjure bags used in coastal Georgia often contained grave dirt, sulphur, and the hair of the victim and were believed to cause insanity.

Another use for grave dirt was as an oathing ingredient. A number of conspiracies, particularly those involving Akan-speaking slaves from the Gold Coast, involved the consumption of an "oath drink," which typically included human blood, rum, and grave dirt. Because of the idea that ancestral spirits were an active force in the affairs of the living, imbibing an oath drink created an unbreakable bond between the ancestral spirits and the living. Examples of this use of graveyard dirt abound in the British, Danish, and Dutch Caribbean. In North America, Akan-speaking slaves inspired by loyalty oaths were involved in both the 1712 New York City revolt and the 1741 New York City conspiracy.

Although applications varied, there were certain beliefs regarding the power of graveyard dirt that were almost universal. The majority of charms contained goofer dust as an ingredient, perhaps because of the belief that gravesites contained the spiritual essence of the deceased. Among African American spiritualists, there was seeming consensus that angry spirits increased the strength of harmful charms. Thus, hoodoo doctors in New Orleans believed that dirt from the grave of a sinner or a murder victim was the most effective component to add to harmful spells or charms. Likewise, goofer dust from an infant's grave was extremely potent. Dirt from the grave of a sinner, a murdered person, or an infant were said to be the only ingredients that could make a charm powerful enough to kill.

See also: Africanisms, Black Folk Culture; Goofer Dust

Walter C. Rucker

Bibliography
Georgia Writers' Project. *Drums and Shadows: Survival Studies among the Coastal Negroes.* Athens: University of Georgia Press, 1940.

Puckett, Newbell Nile. *Folk Beliefs of the Southern Negro.* Chapel Hill: University of North Carolina Press, 1926.

Thompson, Robert Farris. "Kongo Influences on African-American Artistic Culture." In *Africanisms in American Culture,* ed. Joseph Holloway, 148–84. Bloomington: Indiana University Press, 1991.

Gullah

"Gullah" refers to the culture, language, and inhabitants of the Sea Islands of South Carolina, Georgia, and northern Florida, where economic and social isolation bred a unique Creole culture and society. In Georgia, Gullah people are sometimes referred to as the Geechee, a name derived from the nearby Ogeechee River.

The history of the Gullah people began with the large-scale migration of West Indian planters to the South Carolina and Georgia Sea Islands in the 17th and 18th centuries. Relocating en masse, with their newly enslaved Africans and seasoned slaves, planters reestablished absentee plantations, where interactions between blacks and whites were limited. As early as the first decade of the 17th century, slaves and free black people outnumbered whites in the region; and by the 19th century, the number of slaves inhabiting the islands had grown to 80 percent of the local population and over 95 percent in rural pockets along the coast. Plantation agriculture—particularly cultivation of indigo, rice, and long-staple cotton—contributed to the increase in the number of slaves. In 1860, the average Sea Island plantation had two hundred bondsmen and women residing on plantations of 90,000–100,000 slaves. The unusually large numbers of Africans and African Americans in the region played a central role in the development of the Gullah culture and language.

This black majority combined with other factors, such as the relative isolation of the Sea Islands, to foster the development of Gullah culture and language. The Sea Islands, which consist of several hundred low, flat isles that hug the South Carolina and Georgia coast, range in size from the small and uninhabitable to larger islands located off the coast of urban centers, such as Charleston, South Carolina, and Savannah, Georgia. Well into the 19th century, the islands had limited contact with the mainland, creating a cultural hot spot for the various peoples that gathered there. The coastal isolation of the islands also facilitated the continued importation of illegally imported Africans, who were sold to Sea Island planters as late as 1858. When folklorists surveyed residents as part of the 1930s Works Progress Administration (WPA) Georgia Writers' Project, native Africans and other former slaves were still alive to share folkways passed down from recent African ancestors.

The Gullah people's contact with Africans reinforced beliefs and practices passed down centuries before; however, dramatic events of the 19th century also contributed to the development of Gullah culture. Immediately following the American Civil War, many whites abandoned their Sea Island plantations, leaving large numbers of slaves and freedmen with unregulated access to land. Precipitated by the arrival of Union troops and Northern aid workers, the islands became a testing ground for postwar programs that sought to integrate freedmen into free society. As white flight to the mainland further isolated the islands, inland blacks seeking land brought language and culture from the outside to the region. Although some whites regained rights to their land after the war, the experiences of wartime land ownership helped limit the effects of black out-migration after emancipation. The Gullah language consists of a mixture of English and African grammar and vocabulary. Scholars are divided as to the origins of the word; some trace "Gullah" to the Gola people of present-day Sierra Leone, and others to the Central African republic of Angola. Whatever its origins, the Gullah language represents a blend of European, Caribbean, and African elements acquired during three centuries of Atlantic trade. Contrary to the beliefs of 19th-century Whites, Gullah is not a simplified version of English, but a complex blend of English and several African languages. It is distinct from African American Vernacular English and Standard English, and in it linguists have identified elements of African languages, including Ewe, Hausa, Igbo, Kikongo, Mende, and Yoruba. Scholars have also identified similarities between Gullah and Krio, a West African English-based Creole language spoken in present-day Sierra Leone.

Gullah consists of several regional dialects and is generally unintelligible to English speakers. Colonel Thomas Wentworth Higginson, abolitionist and author of *Army Life in a Black Regiment,* was among the many Northerners who remarked on the unique grammatical cadence and vocabulary of the Gullah people during and immediately after the Civil War. Higginson cited a "spicy" and "head-over-heels" arrangement of pronouns in speeches and songs such as "Ride in, Kind Saviour." He noted that renditions of the song's final stanza vacillated between "we" and "me." By forming plurals and negations differently than in English, Gullah retained grammatical elements of African dialects that facilitated communication between speakers of various African languages.

Pronoun tenses and numbers are equally fluid in Gullah. According to Reed Smith, one early observer of the language, the following Gullah phrase—"Uh yeddy 'um but 'uh ent shum"—could be translated into English in over a dozen ways: "I (hear/heard) (it/her/him/them) but I (didn't/don't) see (it/her/him/them)." By distinguishing between actions that were continual and those that were momentary, rather than specifying the relative time of an action per English custom, Gullah retained grammatical rules similar to the Ewe, Yoruba, and other African linguistic groups.

In addition to grammatical variations, African vocabulary also differentiates Gullah from English. Documentation of Gullah speech from the mid-20th century, when decreolization was already underway, uncovered thousands of words with African origins, such as "goober" (peanut) and "kuta" or "cooter" (turtle), which were gradually adopted into English usage. In 1949, anthropologist and Gullah scholar Lorenzo Dow Turner documented 4,000 African words, including several hundred African names used frequently by Gullah speakers.

The use of non-African phrases, shortened over time, also characterizes the language and demonstrates how efforts to communicate shaped Gullah speech. According to another early scholar of Gullah, Mason Crum, terms such as "tebl tapa," or "preacher," derived from the descriptive phrase "one who taps on the table." Similarly, "swit maut," or "to flatter," came from the phrase "to sweet mouth."

Elements of nonverbal communication among the Gullah were also rooted in African patterns. A common Gullah gesture of averting one's gaze by turning the head with pursed lips is reminiscent of a similar gesture from the Kongo. Other Gullah signs, unique to individual genders, share qualities common to various African cultures.

Gullah culture closely followed the pattern of language, borrowing heavily from African folkways. Anthropologists and folklorists have identified strong ties to African folk beliefs regarding family organization, religious practice, work patterns, and artistic expression. Gullah slaves in rice-producing regions of the coast, for example, worked rice fields in an African manner, using African-style baskets and fans to process the commodity. They also used baskets to carry goods in a style reminiscent of African peddlers and produced coiled pottery and household items identical to those produced in West Africa. With respect to religion, the Gullah, who are primarily Christian, also incorporated elements of African song and dance into religious practices, such as the "ring shout." In the Gullah's understanding of magic, conjuring, and mysticism, Gullah practices were similarly derived from African and Afro-Caribbean rituals.

Despite continued isolation in the decades following the Civil War, by the 1920s and 1930s, anthropologists and folklorists recognized the potential impacts of economic and social transformation on the Gullah. In recent years, these transformations—particularly the influx of tourists in the region—have led to the gradual decline of Gullah ways. Today, less than 25,000 Gullah speakers remain in Lowcountry enclaves, and 10,000 outside of the region, primarily in the New York City area. Yet, even as the number of Gullah ebb, their lasting impact on culture and history of the region is clear. Their language and culture provide a rare window into the transplantation and recreation of African folkways among peoples of African descent in the Americas.

See also: Black English; Pritchard, Gullah Jack; Ring Shout; Sierra Leone; Slave Culture; Sweetgrass Baskets; Task System; Turner, Lorenzo Dow

Erica Ann Bruchko

Bibliography

Bennet, John. "Gullah: A Negro Patois." *South Atlantic Quarterly* 7: (1908) 332–47.

Crum, Mason. *Gullah: Negro Life in the Carolina Sea Islands.* Durham, NC: Duke University Press, 1940.

Gordon, Raymond G. *Ethnologue: Languages of the World.* 15th ed. Dallas, TX: SIL International, 2005.

Higginson, Thomas Wentworth. *Army Life in a Black Regiment.* New York: Houghton, Mifflin, 1900.

Joyner, Charles W. *Down by the Riverside: A South Carolina Slave Community.* Urbana: University of Illinois Press, 1984.

Littlefield, Daniel C. *Rice and Slaves: Ethnicity and the Slave Trade in Colonial South Carolina.* Baton Rouge: Louisiana State University Press, 1981.

Rose, Willie Lee. *Rehearsal for Reconstruction: The Port Royal Experiment.* New York: Vintage Books, 1964.

Smith, Reed. *Gullah.* Columbia: University of South Carolina Press, 1926.

Tindall, George Brown. *South Carolina Negroes, 1877–1900.* Columbia: University of South Carolina Press, 2003.

Turner, Lorenzo D. *Africanisms in the Gullah Dialect.* New York: Arno Press, 1969.

Wood, Peter H. *Black Majority: Negroes in Colonial South Carolina from 1670 through the Stono Rebellion.* New York: Norton, 1974.

Gumbo

The hearty stew known as gumbo is considered a hallmark of New Orleans cuisine and is also quite popular in the Gulf Coast region of the United States. Gumbo can be attributed to Spanish, English, German, Italian, French, Native American, West Indian, and African cultural and culinary influences that converged as a result of waves of European settlement of the American South, the transatlantic slave trade, and intermarriage.

The word "gumbo" or "gombo" is of West African origin, ascribed to the Bantu word for okra and "kombo," the word for sassafras leaf used by the Choctaw, Chetimache, and Houma Indians who once populated southern Louisiana in great numbers. Okra was transported to the New World along with African slaves; sassafras was native to the coastal regions of the American South and introduced to settlers by the Native Americans. Both ingredients function as thickening agents within the dish; okra is added during the cooking process, whereas gumbo filé (ground sassafras leaves) is sprinkled on top of a dish after it has been prepared and is ready to be served.

There are an infinite number of recipes and varieties of gumbos: seafood, wild game, chicken, and andouille sausage are a few of the more popular varieties. The stew is alternately attributed to Cajun and Creole culinary traditions. Gumbos traverse the two cuisines and rely on the availability of local ingredients as well as the innovative spirit, skill, taste preferences, and historical memory of the cook. Although there are few hard and fast rules about gumbos, most gumbos are accompanied by rice and do include some variation of the following basic ingredients: Roux, a classical French technique and base for thickening soups and stews, roux is comprised of a mixture of equal parts flour and fat (usually butter, lard, or oil). It is constantly stirred and cooked over medium heat until it reaches the desired color (light, medium, or dark) and the raw taste of the flour is cooked off. Stock or broth, usually chicken or seafood, to which the roux is added; and trinity, a combination of equal parts diced bell pepper, onion, and celery that provides a flavor base.

Acadian or Cajun gumbos are arguably the more rustic of the two schools of cookery. Cajuns, the descendants of exiled French refugees from Nova Scotia, Canada, began to settle in the swamps and bayous of southern Louisiana during the mid-18th century. Native Americans introduced them to much of the wild game and vegetation of their habitat, and German settlers passed along sausage-making and curing techniques that Cajuns adapted to make culinary staples such as andouille and boudin sausages and tasso ham. Cajun gumbos are generally characterized as having a darker roux and a tendency to use gumbo filé instead of okra.

Creole culinary traditions originated in the kitchens of New Orleans' elite owner classes during the early 1700s, where meals were expertly prepared by Creole housewives and African slave-cooks. As adaptations of classical Spanish, Italian, and French recipes (such as *bouillabaisse*), Creole gumbos are indebted to German butchery and sausage-making techniques as well as to West Indian, Native American, and African produce and cooking methods. Lighter roux and the use of okra are sometimes characteristic of (but not exclusive to) Creole gumbos.

Contemporary Creole cookery is especially indebted to African Americans, the descendants of enslaved Africans who continue to refine and develop the cuisine. Gumbo Zhèbes, a stew of fresh spring greens seasoned with salt pork or ham, is also attributed to Creole cooks.

See also: Black Folk Culture; Jambalaya

Lori Baptista

Bibliography

Bower, Anne L., ed. *African American Foodways: Explorations of History and Culture.* Champaign and Urbana, IL:: University of Illinois Press, 2007.

Hearn, Lafcadio. *La Cuisine Creole: A Collection Of Culinary Recipes from Leading Chefs and Noted Creole Housewives, Who Have Made New Orleans Famous for Its Cuisine (1885).* Whitefish, MT: Kessinger Publishing, 2008.

McKee, Gwen. *The Little Gumbo Book.* Brandon, MS: Quail Ridge Press, 1986.

Thorne, John, with Matt Lewis Thorne. *Serious Pig: An American Cook in Search of His Roots.* New York: North Point Press, 1996.

Herskovits, Melville

Melville Jean Herskovits (1895–1963) was an anthropologist and folklorist noted for constructing a model of acculturation and cultural development in examining the absence or presence of African culture in contemporary African American life. Herskovits, one of two children, was born in Bellefontaine, Ohio, to Herman and Henrietta Hart Herskovits on September 10, 1895. His father, a merchant, emigrated from Austria-Hungary in 1872, and his mother emigrated from Germany in 1882. After his mother's death in 1941, he and his family moved to Erie, Pennsylvania, where he graduated from high school in 1912.

Herskovits studied concurrently at University of Cincinnati and Hebrew Union College in 1915, but his studies were interrupted by 15 months of service in World War I. In 1919, he was discharged from the U.S. Army Medical Corps; prior to returning to the United States, he studied at the University of Poitiers in France. His education continued in the United States at the University of Chicago, where he received a PhD in history in 1920. Subsequently, at Columbia University, Herskovits transitioned from history to anthropology. Franz Boaz served as his academic advisor, and in 1921, he received an MA, completing a PhD in 1923 in anthropology; his dissertation was titled "The Cattle Complex in East Africa." While in New York, Herskovits's social theories were influenced by A. A. Goldenweiser and Thorstein Veblen at the New School for Social Research, in addition to Margaret Mead, Ruth Benedict, and his future wife, Frances Shapiro, whom he later married in 1924.

In 1923, Herskovits received a three-year research fellowship from the National Research Council Board of Biological Sciences to conduct research on the "New World Negro." While researching the physical anthropology of African Americans for the fellowship, he simultaneously taught at Columbia, from 1923 to 1927; however, in 1925, he worked at Howard University as assistant professor in anthropology, at which time he became acquainted with Alain Locke, E. Franklin Frazier, Ralph Bunche, and Sterling Brown. In 1927, he moved to Northwestern University as an assistant professor in sociology. Initially, he was the only anthropologist at Northwestern; he later established an anthropology department, of which he became chair in 1938. He contributed to the study of African Americans by establishing the first African American program in 1948 and was appointed chair in 1961. Later he formed the African Studies Association and became its first president.

Herskovits's scholarship was advanced through several field trips to Suriname, Nigeria, Haiti, Trinidad, Benin, Ghana, and Brazil to conduct ethnographic studies of African diasporic civilization and evaluate African traits remaining in these cultures. The 1928 and 1929 fieldtrips to Suriname resulted into two publications coauthored with Frances Herskovits: *Rebel Destiny* (1934) and *Suriname Folk Lore* (1936). His fieldtrip to West Africa resulted in the publication of *An Outline of Dahomean Religious Belief and Dahomey: An Ancient West African Kingdom.*

In the mid 1920s, Herskovits initially followed Boaz's theory that there was an absence in the continuity of Africa's past to contemporary African Americans' lives. After his ethnographic study of African cultures, Herskovits argued that African cultural elements remained in New World African descendents throughout the Diaspora. Furthermore, his research focused on the acculturation and the process associated with cultural changes. By examining "Africanisms," he created cultural categories for Africans and Europeans to explore metaphors that could substantiate their cultural formation. Herskovits's classic thesis in *Myth of the Negro Past* (1941) postulates that Europeans tried to destroy African historical contributions to the formation of culture globally, and African cultural traits were retained in the African American culture; moreover, these traits were acculturated into Anglo-Americans as well. Herskovits linked African American linguistics, music, dance, folklore, folk medicine, and funeral practices to African cultures as evidence in his thesis. In addition, Herskovits argued that African traits were more common in Brazil and the Caribbean because of their relative isolation from Europeans; similarly, the inhabitants of the coastal islands of Georgia and South Carolina retain the highest African traits in the United States. Consequently, Herskovits was noted for his argument on ethical relativism in politics; he maintained that there was no objective order of justice and that what is moral in one culture may not be moral in another; therefore, Herskovits questions legitimating one culture and invalidating another culture.

During his long academic career, he held numerous offices and memberships, including the following professional affiliations and positions: editor of *The American Anthropologist* (1949–1952) and *The International Directory of Anthropologist* (1950), vice president of the American Association for the Advancement of Science (1934), president of the American Folklore Society (1945), and membership on the permanent council of the International Anthropology Congress. Herskovits's works include *The Myth of the Negro Past* (1941), in which he traces African American roots to West Africa to examine racial myths; *The Economic Life of Primitive People* (1940), an anthropological study of primitive culture's economics; and *Man and His Works* (1948), a survey that was descriptive and theoretical in examining cultural anthropology. Three of Herskovits's last books, *Continuity and Change in African Culture* (1959), *Economic Transition in Africa* (1964), and *The Human Factor in Changing Africa* (1962), reflect both the rapid development of Africa's place in the world and the increased academic interest in African studies.

See also: Acculturation; Africanisms; Frazier, E. Franklin; Locke, Alain; Turner, Lorenzo Dow

T. Alys Jordan

Bibliography

Gershenhorn, Jerry. *Melville J. Herskovits and the Racial Politics of Knowledge.* Critical Studies in the History of Anthropology. Lincoln: University of Nebraska Press, 2004.

Price, Richard, and Sally Price. *The Root of Roots: Or, How Afro-American Anthropology Got Its Start.* Chicago: Prickly Paradigm, 2003.

High John the Conqueror Root

High John the Conqueror is a spirit-embodying root popular among practitioners of African American conjure and hoodoo. It is employed for protection from enemies and malevolent spirits, for luck in gambling and money matters, to obtain a favorable outcome in court cases, and for success with women. The root is carried in the pocket and rubbed when needed; "fed" or "dressed" with various substances; boiled to make baths and floor wash; soaked in whiskey, oils, and perfumes for an anointing substance; or incorporated into the charm packets called mojo bags and lucky hands.

Conjurers and hoodoo doctors harvested High John the Conqueror root in the wild until the mid-20th century. The large, twisted or swollen tubers, rhizomes, or taproots of Jack-in-the pulpit (*Arisaema triphyllum*), Solomon's seal (*Polygonatum odoratum*), beth root (*Trillium*), or some species of wild morning glory (*Ipomoea*), all native to the southeastern United States, may originally have served as John the Conqueror. Present-day spiritual supply stores offer a morning-glory relative, Mexican jalap root (*Ipomoea jalapa*), as High John the Conqueror. St. John's wort (*Hypericum perforatum*) has been cited by some writers as the source of High John the Conqueror, but its branching, fibrous root system in no way resembles the original John the Conqueror root.

In many West and Central African belief systems, every natural object is believed to have an indwelling spirit that can be summoned to the aid of human beings. The name "High John the Conqueror" suggests that a potent personality inhabits this magical root. High John has been equated with Funza, the Central African Kongo spirit of power and masculinity embodied in twisted, swollen, phallus-shaped roots. High John may also have West African Fon and Yoruba antecedents. In his role as a protector against human enemies, authority figures, and malevolent spirits, he resembles Gu, the warrior spirit of iron and warfare. His function as a bringer of luck in gambling, business, and money matters relates him to Eshu, the trickster spirit who governs chance and the crossroads. In his role as a "conqueror" of women, he is related to Shangó, the handsome and virile spirit of thunder and lightning.

Zora Neale Hurston associated the indwelling spirit of High John the Conqueror root with the African American slave trickster hero Old John, a man of great strength and cunning. Stories of Old John and his adversary Old Marster constitute a cycle of folk narratives that parallel the better-known tales of Brer Rabbit. Other folklore texts assert that the character of High John is synonymous with St. John the Baptist, the biblical character who baptized Jesus, preached in the wilderness, and conquered Satan.

The prototype for High John the Conqueror could also have been a historic person, possibly a powerful hoodoo doctor who became associated in the minds of believers with this African spirit. The word "high" connotes authority, strength, and potency, and in coastal Maryland and Virginia, a conjurer was called a "high man."

In all of these possible aspects, High John the Conqueror personifies a strong, dark, virile, masculine spirit who protects his devotees and brings them success, wealth, and luck. He represents the resiliency and empowerment of black people in surviving slavery and its aftermath of poverty and racism.

See also: Black Folk Culture; Conjure; Hoodoo; Hurston, Zora Neale; Root Doctors

Carolyn Morrow Long

Bibliography

Anderson, Jeffrey Elton. *Conjure in African-American Society.* Baton Rouge: Louisiana State University Press, 2007.

Hurston, Zora Neale. "High John de Conker." *American Mercury* 57 (1943):450–58.

Hyatt, Harry Middleton. *Hoodoo-Conjuration-Witchcraft-Rootwork.* Hannibal, MO: Western Publishing, 1970–1978.

Long, Carolyn Morrow. *Spiritual Merchants: Religion, Magic, and Commerce.* Knoxville: University of Tennessee Press, 2001.

Hoodoo

Hoodoo, also known as conjure, tricking, goofer, and rootwork, is a spiritual system long practiced by some African Americans, particularly in the South. Adepts—known as hoodoo doctors, conjurers, trick doctors, goofer doctors, and root doctors—told fortunes, healed illnesses, performed spells, and made charms for paying clients. Conjure originated during the colonial era as a Creole adaptation of African spirituality. By the 19th century, it had developed into a rich syncretistic practice that incorporated African, European, and Native American beliefs. Hoodoo continues to survive today in the form of spiritual supply stores.

Conjure did not evolve from any single African forebear. Instead, it combined practices of many ethnicities, including the Yoruba, Fon, and Kongo. Moreover, hoodoo differed depending on the area examined. For example, along the banks of the Mississippi River, the original French colonists imported many West Africans from the Fon, Yoruba, and neighboring peoples during the early 18th and 19th centuries. In consequence, West African influences predominated in the hoodoo of the area until well into the 20th century. On the other hand, English settlers along the Atlantic Coast preferred slaves from West-Central Africa, importing large numbers from the Kongo and related groups but comparatively few West Africans. Thus, the elements of conjure in areas originally peopled by Anglo settlers tended to be West-Central African in origin.

Regional distinctions are clear in the words used for African American magic in each area. In the region settled by the French, "hoodoo" was originally the word used by blacks to represent what whites called Voodoo. Both "hoodoo" and "Voodoo" appear to have derived from the Fon and Ewe word *vodu,* meaning "god" or "worship of the gods." In the areas settled by the English, particularly the coastal areas of South Carolina and Georgia, a favored term was "goofer," a word that appears to be of Kongo derivation. Eventually, "hoodoo" would come into general use to represent all African American magic, most likely because of its popularization as a result of late 19th-century media attention to New Orleans–area Voodoo. "Goofer," in contrast, would largely disappear from common usage by the mid-20th century.

Another major distinction between the regions settled by the French and English was that hoodoo survived as a religion longer in the former. Until the late 19th century, for instance, New Orleans Voodoo/Hoodoo was a full-fledged religion, complete with a pantheon of West African gods, a priesthood, and ritual worship and initiations. Over time, the religious elements of hoodoo fell away or were forcibly suppressed by whites. But according to some observers, including Zora Neale Hurston and employees of the Federal Writers' Project, many black Americans remembered the names of African deities until at least the 1930s. Initiation ceremonies also persisted until about the same time. In the English area, however, almost all the communal rituals and deities that survived the Middle Passage had disappeared before the Civil War.

In both regions, European and Native American beliefs mingled freely with the African practices on which conjure was originally based. Perhaps the best examples of this syncretism come from Louisiana hoodoo. In New Orleans, altars, images of saints, and candles made their way into the magic of African Americans by at least the early 19th century. Also, although many blacks practiced Creole faiths and worshipped such beings as Blanc Dani, the serpent god, and Monsieur Assonquer, deity of good fortune, they were likely to consider themselves good Christians. This dual belief system reportedly extended even to hoodoo priests and priestesses. Marie Laveau, the most famous of all Voodoo leaders, was reputedly a devout Catholic. In places where the dominant form of Christianity was of a Protestant variety, conjurers commonly used Bibles in their performance of spells and making of charms, and many practitioners also served as ministers. Native Americans' chief contributions took the form of herbal curios. One example was puccoon root, which some African Americans believed conferred good luck on those who possessed it. Native Americans originally used it as a ritual paint.

Hoodoo has survived to the present. A smattering of practitioners who gather herbs and roots continue to serve clients in rural areas. More notable, however, has been the rise of conjure shops, also known as spiritual supply stores, which first appeared in the decades following Emancipation. By the 1930s and 1940s, such shops were common in urban areas. Instead of herbal curios, their shelves were filled with oils, incenses, bath crystals, and later, magical aerosol sprays. Along with the consumer-oriented conjure stores, large manufacturers and distributors of hoodoo supplies appeared, which provided most of the products that appeared in the shops and frequently conducted direct-to-consumer mail-order businesses. Spiritual supply shops and large manufacturers remain a part of many African American communities today.

See also: Black Folk Culture; Conjure; Hurston, Zora Neale; Laveau, Marie; Root Doctors

Jeffrey Elton Anderson

Bibliography

Anderson, Jeffrey Elton. *Conjure in African American Society.* Baton Rouge: Louisiana State University Press, 2007.

Chireau, Yvonne Patricia. *Black Magic: Religion and the African American Conjuring Tradition.* Berkeley: University of California Press, 2003.

Hurston, Zora Neale. "Hoodoo in America." *Journal of American Folklore* 44 (1931):318–417.

Long, Carolyn Morrow. *Spiritual Merchants: Religion, Magic, and Commerce.* Knoxville: University of Tennessee Press, 2001.

Puckett, Newbell Niles. *Folk Beliefs of the Southern Negro.* Chapel Hill: University of North Carolina Press, 1926. Reprint, Montclair: Patterson Smith, 1968.

Hurston, Zora Neale

Zora Neale Hurston (ca. 1901–1960), scholar and novelist, was a major figure of the Harlem Renaissance whose writing career moved comfortably between the linguistically rich black vernacular of her Southern upbringing and the scholarly tone of her anthropological training at the prestigious Barnard College. A folklorist and creative writer, Hurston was born in Eatonville, Florida, the first incorporated all-black town in America. She was the fifth of eight children born to John Hurston, a mulatto from Macon County,

Alabama, and Lucy Ann Potts, a schoolteacher. Hurston's writing was heavily influenced by her historical and cultural circumstances, with Eatonville and the tales of local storytellers often taking prominence in her texts. Hurston once said that she had the "map of Dixie" on her tongue, a trademark implicit throughout much of her literary works.

During her youth, Hurston's father served three terms as mayor of Eatonville and was a Baptist minister and carpenter. The death of her mother when she was nine marked a turning point that redirected her life and that forced Hurston to find a means of supporting herself when her father remarried a woman who did not like her. She landed a job working for a singer who was touring the South in *H.M.S. Pinafore,* with a Gilbert and Sullivan repertory company. While working for the touring group, Hurston was teased mercilessly about her Southern accent. When her employer 'Miss M-' got married, Hurston began working her way through school by sheer determination. First, she attended high school at nights in Baltimore, studying English with Dwight O. W. Holmes. She then attended Morgan for two years before transferring to Howard University (1919–1923). While at Howard, Hurston participated in The Stylus, a literary society that published her first short story, "John Redding Goes to Sea," in 1921. Hurston was beginning to discover the literary potential of a cultural milieu and the artistry of the folk idiom that would launch a remarkable career as a creative writer. Hurston's association with The Stylus, whose membership included professor and editor of the revolutionary *New Negro* Alain Leroy Locke, garnered an invitation to contribute to *Opportunity Magazine,* a new publication that she credited as "the root" of the Harlem Renaissance.

In early 1925, Hurston moved to New York City, where she met Charles S. Johnson, editor of *Opportunity,* who published her story "Drenched in Light." In 1925 and 1926, Hurston submitted the short story "Spunk" and the play "Color Struck" to *Opportunity,* and both won prizes. Through Johnson, Hurston met many black writers and reconnected with the former Morgan dean, William Pickens, who worked for the NAACP. By November 1926, Hurston was an editor, along with Langston Hughes and Wallace Thurman, of the short-lived magazine *Fire!!*

After arriving in New York, Hurston quickly secured a job as secretary to writer Fannie Hurst and garnered a scholarship to Barnard College through the efforts of Annie Nathan Meyer. Hurston entered the prestigious university as the only black student in the fall of 1925. While at Barnard, Hurston studied anthropology under the guidance of famed anthropologist Dr. Franz Boas, who arranged, upon her graduation in 1928, for a fellowship to collect Negro folklore in the South. Supported by the Association for the Study of Negro Life and History, this initial trip left little to show for her efforts. However, in future trips, Hurston developed into a more mature and thoughtful scholar who gained success in her ventures and was able to discover the literary potential in celebrating the culture that had birthed her.

Support for additional research trips came to Hurston through Mrs. Rufus Osgood Mason, a patron of the arts (called "Godmother" by black artists Mason supported financially) who provided a stipend of $200 a month for two years and additional sporadic support for five years. It was also during this time that Hurston met the first of her two husbands, Herbert Sheen, whom she married on May 19, 1927. Although they did not divorce until July 7,

Zora Neale Hurston, renowned scholar and author, was a celebrated figure of the Harlem Renaissance (Library of Congress)

1931, Hurston's relationship with Sheen ended in early 1928. Her second marriage to Albert Price III, who was 23 years old when they married in June 1939 in Fernandina, Florida, was short-lived also. Divorce papers were filed in early 1940, and after a brief reconciliation, the divorce was finalized on November 9, 1943. There has been speculation that both marriages ended as a result of her fierce independence and commitment to her career.

The 1930s were Hurston's most prolific and productive years as a writer, although much of her writing received mixed reviews. Many of her major works were published during this decade, including *Jonah's Gourd Vine* (1934), *Mules and Men* (1935), *Their Eyes Were Watching God* (1937), *Tell My Horse: Voodoo and Life in Haiti and Jamaica* (1938), and *Moses, Man of the Mountain* (1939). Hurston possessed an exuberant personality, which she was able to bring to bear in her writing. She often elected to write in a narrative style that combined the scientific voice of her formal training with a voice of a writer who had no qualms about taking creative license with the stories of her informants. Some critics frowned on this practice, finding it difficult to ascertain where Hurston's creative writing stopped and the authentic lore began.

Hurston's writing embodies storytelling as a distinct cultural marker of the communities she describes. While carrying on the traditions of orality, Hurston skillfully translates spoken communication into the written medium of literature. Performing stories through written texts is ultimately Hurston's genius. Hurston was able to set down on paper the performed behaviors she observed while moving between the role of insider (subject) and outsider (one who objectifies).Hurston adopted a storytelling strategy to mimic the very folklore she sought to articulate for a mass audience by positioning herself as an insider and product of the environment she researched. Hurston's choices were rebuffed by many of her fellow contemporaries of the Renaissance, who also sometimes accused Hurston of maintaining a sense of ambiguity and silence when confronting issues of race and politics. She often elected to focus on individual potentiality, while avoiding the larger problems of race that many of her contemporaries were dedicated to exposing.

Hurston traveled extensively, negotiating territory between Florida, New Orleans, and the Caribbean as she set about the work of collecting tales, jokes, dances, and music on front porches and in jook joints as both participant and observer. She was awarded two Guggenheim Fellowships that assisted in her efforts to document black folklore. Hurston published a collection of folktales in 1931, "Hoodoo in America," in the *Journal of American Folklore*, and subsequently in 1935 repeated some of the same material in the book *Mules and Men*. Written in two parts, *Mules and Men* is a narrative of Hurston's journey back home to Eatonville to collect folklore and is a compilation of tall tales, songs, sermons, and stories that both Hurston and her informants call "lies"; part 2 of the book is both a travelogue and the first scholarly treatment by a black American scholar of New Orleans hoodoo culture. Hurston's journey into hoodoo involved undergoing five separate initiations by religious practitioners and included study with a supposed relative of New Orleans' most famous practitioner, Marie Laveau. In *Mules and Men* and *Tell My Horse: Voodoo and Life in Haiti and Jamaica* (published in England under the name *Voodoo Gods*), Hurston links American and Caribbean practices and treats voodoo as a complex, old religion, worthy of spiritual possibilities and serious study and respect.

In 1930, Hurston collaborated with her friend Langston Hughes on a three-act play, which was not produced or published in their lifetimes because of what Hughes would label as a falling-out. *Mules Bone*, a comedy adapted from Hurston's collected folktale "The Bone of Contention," was written in hopes of portraying black characters in a spirited and favorable light. However, after contentious arguing over rights to the play, the longtime friendship between Hurston and Hughes dissolved, and the drama was largely forgotten until 1991, when the Lincoln Center Theatre in New York staged the play.

Hurston was drawn to the theater at various points in her life as a writer, director, and performer. On January 10, 1932, with borrowed money, she mounted a show at the John Golden Theatre consisting of the work songs, blues, and spirituals collected during her fieldwork. Although she went on to produce additional versions of this show under various names throughout her career, Hurston is not remembered as much for her dramatic texts as she is for her novels, short stories, and magazine and newspaper articles.

The short story "The Gilded Six-Bits" was published in *Story Magazine* in August 1933. Shortly thereafter, Hurston, who was living in Florida at the time, was approached by the J. B. Lippincott Company about whether she had a book-length project. This inquiry prompted Hurston to move to Sanford, where she wrote *Jonah's Gourd Vine* (1934) over a three-month period. Lippincott subsequently bought the manuscript and paid Hurston a $200 advance. This book marked a breakthrough for Hurston, and she went on to write the important American novel *Their Eyes Were Watching God* (1937) in Haiti over the course of seven weeks. Today, this work is seen as depicting an early feminist protagonist, Janie Crawford. The central character experiences several love relationships, including a most passionate love affair with Tea Cake, only to see the affair dissolve under tragic circumstances. In the end, it becomes a story about Janie's journey and discovery of "self." Oprah Winfrey produced *Their Eyes Were Watching God* for television in 2005. Starring Halle Berry as Janie Crawford, the novel was adapted by Suzan-Lori Parks, the first African American woman to win a Pulitzer Prize for Drama.

After a period of prolific writing, Huston spent her final years in Florida, where she worked as a librarian, newspaper freelancer, substitute teacher, and maid. In the literary world, she all but vanished into obscurity during her later life. Publishers rejected her final attempt at a full-length project based on the life of the biblical Herod. By early 1959, Hurston, already suffering from high blood pressure, gall bladder attacks, an ulcer, and malnutrition, had a stroke. In October of that year, Hurston was moved from her home at 1734 School Court Street in St. Pierce, Florida, to Saint Lucie County Welfare Home, where she died on January 28, 1960. Hurston was buried in an unmarked grave in the segregated Garden of the Heavenly Rest Cemetery in St. Pierce. In 1973, writer Alice Walker traveled to Florida and placed a gravestone on her burial site that reads, "Zora Neale Hurston, A Genius of the South, Novelist, Folklorist, Anthropologist, 1901–1960." In all, Hurston published seven full-length books and over 75 short stories, plays, and articles and wrote numerous pieces of unpublished materials.

See also: Black Folk Culture; Harlem Renaissance; Hoodoo; Hughes, Langston; New Negro Movement

Jayetta Slawson

Bibliography

Cronin, Gloria L., ed. *Critical Essays on Zora Neale Hurston*. New York: G. K. Hall, 1998.

Hemenway, Robert E. *Zora Neale Hurston: A Literary Biography*. Urbana: University of Illinois Press, 1977.

Hughes, Langston, and Zora Neale Hurston. *Mule Bone: A Comedy of Negro Life*. New York: HarperPerennial, 1991.

Hurston, Zora Neale. *Dust Tracks on a Road*. 1942. Reprint, New York: HarperPerennial, 1996.

Hurston, Zora Neale. *Mules and Men.* 1935. Reprint, New York: HarperPerennial, 1990.

Hurston, Zora Neale. *Tell My Horse: Voodoo and Life in Haiti and Jamaica.* 1938. Reprint, New York: HarperPerennial, 1990.

Walker, Alice. *In Search of Our Mothers' Gardens.* San Diego, CA: Harvest, 1984.

221–41. Carbondale: Southern Illinois University Press, 2004.

Raboteau, Albert J. *Slave Religion: The "Invisible Institution" in the Antebellum South.* New York: Oxford University Press, 1978.

Hush Harbors

Often referred to as invisible institutions or underground religions, hush harbors acted as critical locations where enslaved individuals would come together in secret to practice Christianity, sing spirituals, and worship with one another. Hush harbors took place not only in slave quarters, but also in wooded areas, swamps, ravines, and other remote places thought to be outside of a master's gaze or the hearing range of nearby slave owners. Believers were called to participate through specific signals and passwords—encoded messages reminiscent of the layered meanings that could be found in some of the songs of freedom that they sung—with iron pots, kettles, and wet rags sometimes used to muffle their voices and protect their secrecy. These clandestine spaces allowed for and encouraged the development of religious spirituals and the growth of black preachers long before many African Americans were able to widely practice religion freely in the United States.

Taking part in communal forms of worship was prohibited for most antebellum American slaves, and doing so meant possibly being whipped, beaten, sold, or subjected to another form of harsh punishment, including death. Nonetheless, many risked these potential consequences so that they could gather in a place that would offer them hope, healing, and a sense of spiritual and personal connection within an institution that attempted to deny them all that and more. To many of those enslaved, hush harbors served as havens of community and as necessary, if not subversive, spaces of resistance and refuge.

See also: Slave Culture; Slave Religion

Amanda J. Davis

Bibliography

Nunley, Vorris, L. "From the Harbor to Da Academic Hood: Hush Harbors and an African American Rhetorical Tradition." In *African American Rhetoric(s): Interdisciplinary Perspectives,* ed. Elaine B. Richardson and Ronald L. Jackson,

Infanticide

Infanticide is the practice of killing one's own child, a form of resistance employed by enslaved women to prevent their children from being enslaved. Having experienced multiple forms of oppression in the institution of slavery, because of their race and sex, enslaved women engaged in many forms of resistance to combat the harsh realities of slavery. Specifically, there are several methods of resistance that enslaved women utilized to combat sexual abuse and to prevent unwanted pregnancies that often resulted from unwanted sexual interactions with their masters. These methods included abstinence, abortions, various means of birth control, and infanticide.

Much contention has surfaced around infanticide and the reason a mother would kill her child. However, infanticide was an intentional act performed by enslaved women for many reasons. More specifically, a woman performed infanticide to prevent her child from experiencing the harsh realities of slavery—physical, sexual, and psychological abuse.

In the case of slavery in the United States, a slave did not own his or her body. Rather, enslaved women and men were considered to be the property of their master. In the case of a child born to a slave woman, the child inherited the status of his or her mother; therefore, the child too was a slave and belonged to the master, not the mother. Hence, given that the master owned the child, he had the liberty to sell the child from the mother or vice versa; he also had the freedom to treat the child in any manner that he deemed appropriate. However, in any case, the status of a child as the master's property was not readily accepted by enslaved women. Ownership of a child resulted in tensions and a constant power struggle between the enslaved women and their masters.

Infanticide was used as a mechanism for enslaved women to negotiate their power and to maintain a certain amount of autonomy over the trajectory and realities of their own lives and the lives of their children. The constant threat of potentially having a child sold from her or vice versa fueled infanticide; therefore, to avoid separation, women utilized their power to prevent separation. A mother displayed and reclaimed ownership over her child by exhibiting her ability to bring it into and out of the world through infanticide. The most famous example of this behavior was displayed by Margaret Garner, a fugitive slave who killed her daughter rather than have her returned to bondage. In cases where the master fathered a child with a slave woman, she would kill the child so that the child would avoid being mistreated by the jealous mistress.

Moreover, infanticide was practiced to avoid other forms of sexual exploitation; specifically, infanticide was conducted as a means to control reproduction on plantations. Many masters promoted and encouraged pregnancies among their enslaved women to increase their holdings of slaves. Reproduction among slaves meant that slaves' levels of productivity would increase, and consequently, the plantation's monetary returns, effectiveness, and efficiency would too increase, without the master having to invest in purchasing additional slaves. Hence, enslaved women were viewed as economic profits for their masters because of their ability to reproduce more slaves.

From the perspective of white masters, the death of a child a result of carelessness on the mother's behalf. In one instance, a master attributed the death of an infant to recklessness on the part of his or her mother. Another master claimed that during the winter months, enslaved women had the tendency to smother or roll over onto their child in the effort to keep the child warm; and in other cases, white men attributed the death of a child to the idea that enslaved women neglected maternal feelings. Some masters, however, noticed that levels of reproduction were relatively low among their enslaved women, and they attributed this to intentional forms of abortion. In any case, regardless of how people perceived enslaved women and their relationships with their children, enslaved women loved their children. This love was depicted in a mother's willingness to lose her child rather than have the child under the constant gaze of the master and raised in the institution of slavery. A slave woman was known to have said that she would rather turn her child over to the hands of God than to her white master.

Infanticide was masked in various ways, and multiple persons participated in such acts. Infanticide was covered by a legitimate or fabricated illness that a child was said to have had; it was also disguised by poisoning, smothering, or strangulation. Moreover, women, men, and midwives participated in covering up infanticide. Midwives, for example, made significant contributions to abortions and other ways for a pregnant woman to conceal or terminate her pregnancy and end the life of her born child. Furthermore, husbands and wives were known to have participated in killing their children and then themselves.

Regardless, not all mothers committed infanticide or intentionally terminated their pregnancy or the life of their young child. In fact, accounts of infanticide were relatively low. Recent scholarship and technology, for example, has revealed that many infants may have succumbed to sudden infant death syndrome (SIDS)—a syndrome among infants that causes them to mysteriously die in their sleep.

Infanticide was practiced among enslaved women for a number of reasons; regardless of the reason, however, enslaved women engaged in such conspiracies with the child's interests in mind. Given that these women were living in the unrelenting institution of slavery, they knew the heartbreak and abuse that their children would encounter if raised in such an institution.

See also: Garner, Margaret; Slave Resistance

Ashley C. Bowden

Bibliography

Hine, Darlene Clark. *Hine Sight: Black Women and the Re-Construction of American History.* New York: Carlson Publishing, 1994.

Hine, Darlene Clark, and Kathleen Thompson. *A Shining Thread of Hope: The History of Black Women in America.* New York: Broadway Books, 1998.

White, Deborah Gray. *Ar'n't I A Woman? Female Slaves in the Plantation South.* New York: Norton, 1985.

Jambalaya

Jambalaya is a rice-based dish that emerged during the 18th century in modern-day Louisiana. The dish normally consists of chicken, ham, hot sausage, shrimp, green peppers, onions, garlic, tomatoes, celery, and numerous spices, although there are many variations. The base of the dish is always rice, and the rice is cooked with the ingredients, not added to them as in many other rice-based dishes. There are two major variations of the dish, Creole jambalaya or red jambalaya and Cajun jambalaya or brown jambalaya. The differentiation in color comes from the variant methods used in cooking the dish.

There is debate over the word "jambalaya" and its origins. Some believe that the word comes from the combination of "jambon," meaning ham in French; "a la," meaning "in the style of"; and "ya," which some believe to be a West African word for rice. Others believe it may be a combination of "jambon" and "paella," which is a Spanish dish that also has rice as its base. The dish has become well known, and variations of it are present in the Caribbean and Brazil.

Louisiana was originally a colony that survived off of convict labor and the labor of enslaved Native Americans, from its establishment in 1682. The first enslaved Africans were not brought to Louisiana until 1719, and upon their arrival, they were sent immediately to purchase rice to plant. A large percentage of the enslaved Africans brought to Louisiana from this point on came from the Senegambia region of West Africa, which is part of the rice belt of West Africa. These persons played a large part in the development of the culture of the area, including the food culture.

The enslaved Africans had immense knowledge of rice-planting techniques. African technology in planting and cultivating rice is what allowed areas such as Louisiana and South Carolina to not only survive but even flourish. The technology provided by the enslaved Africans was used to transform dismal swamplands into areas appropriate for the cultivation of rice. Europeans generally had no rice cultivation skills and therefore had to rely solely on the enslaved Africans to support them with their expertise in this area.

Another influence from African cultures was the seasoning of the jambalaya. The seasoning generally has a bite to it or is spicy in a way that has been noted to be West African in nature. This lending of cultural food traits was seen in foods eaten by both the enslaved and their European enslavers, given that the enslaved women cooked for the whites. Many of the ingredients in jambalaya may not have been easily accessible for the enslaved themselves. Dishes such as jambalaya were cooked for the slave owners, and because of this, African culinary skills became interwoven in the defining of a food culture in the Americas.

See also: Africanisms; Black Folk Culture; Gumbo

Dawn Miles

Bibliography

Hall, Gwendolyn Midlo. *Africans in Colonial Louisiana: The Development of Afro-Creole Culture in the Eighteenth Century.* Baton Rouge: Louisiana State University Press, 1992.

Harris, Jessica. "Same Boat, Different Stops: An African Atlantic Culinary Journey." In *African Roots/American Cultures: Africa in the Creation of the Americas,* ed. Sheila Walker. Lanham, MD: Rowman & Littlefield Publishers, 2001.

Klein, Sybil. "Louisiana Creole Food Culture: Afro-Caribbean Links." In *Creole: The History and Legacy of Louisiana's Free People of Color,* ed. Sybil Klein. Baton Rouge: Louisiana State University Press, 2000.

Walker, Shelia. "Are You Hip to the Jive? (Re)Writing/Righting the Pan-American Discourse." In *African Roots/American Cultures: Africa in the Creation of the Americas,* ed. Shelia Walker. Lanham, MD: Rowman & Littlefield Publishers, 2001.

Jas

The precursor of the word "jazz" was the shortened, staccato-pronounced "jas," commonly used in the New Orleans, southern Louisiana, region where the music first evolved. Many scholars, jazz musicians, and critics have speculated about the origins of the word "jazz" and its meaning. Significations have variously come down as "hot," "lively," "to spice up," "flashy," "to copulate," "vulgar," "devil music." The word seems to have taken on as many connotations as its improvisational modes. Generally, "jas" was believed to be a slang word that had no formal linguistic ties with English or African languages. However, like many slang words whose origins have been traced back to an African language, "jas," according to Black English expert Dr. Geneva Smitherman, is a word of Mandenka origin that means "to speed up," "to act out of the ordinary," or "unpredictable behavior." The word also has Arabic language roots meaning "to break" or "to cut."

For decades and for reasons understandable, given the spurious appropriation and designation of jazz as an amalgamated American music, jazz musicians often renounced the term as an ambiguous word loaded with stereotypic nuances and argued instead for explanatory terminologies that make references to its ethnic origins. Duke Ellington decried "jazz," a word he mistrusted, and called his music "freedom of expression." Yusef Lateef preferred "auto-physio-psychic music." Cecil Taylor and Ornette Coleman referred to their art as "Black classical music," and the Art Ensemble of Chicago called it simply "Great Black Music."

No single word has concisely been substituted for the word "jazz," and no matter how much musicians and critics try to extricate the word from that great musical genre, the term seems to stick. In African cosmology, language possesses numinous qualities, and a word is perceived as a living entity that naturally attaches itself to the object or idea it signifies. Perhaps it is for this reason that the word "jazz," like living seeds, thrives and persists. The meaning of "jas" is a succinct explication of the improvisational nature and style of the music. It is spontaneous and unpredictably improvised with unexpected breaks and cuts—that is to say it is syncopated. "Jas" or "jazz," therefore, denotes improvisation and syncopation in the Mandenka/Mandingo language. Furthermore, according to Louisianan writer George Washington Cable, who wrote about the activities of 19th-century ethnic groups of New Orleans, jas was a style of singing used by Mandenka lead singers when they broke away from the base melodic line of a song and then improvised around the melody, a technique later simulated by jazz soloists. The lead singers of the Mandenka and the jazz singers and soloists "break up" the original melody and extemporaneously compose a new arrangement using the same notes. The same technique was employed in work songs and spirituals, and before the evolution of jazz, "jas" was associated with slave songs and dances. "Jas," then, is an African word and aesthetic technique describing the structural elements of what became known as jazz.

See also: Africanisms; Black Folk Culture; Jazz

Nubia Kai

Bibliography

Feather, Leonard. *The Pleasure of Jazz.* New York: Bell Publishing, 1976.

Jones, Leroi (Amiri Baraka). *Black Music.* New York: William Morrow, 1970.

Major, Clarence, ed. *Juba to Jive: A Dictionary of African American Slang.* New York: Penguin Books, 1990.

Peretti, Burton W. *The Creation of Jazz: Music, Race and Culture in Urban America.* Urbana: University of Illinois Press, 1992.

Smitherman, Geneva. *Talkin and Testifyin: The Language of Black America.* Boston: Houghton Mifflin, 1977.

Spellman, A. B. *Four Lives in the Bebop Business.* New York: Limelight Editions, 1988.

Tucker, Mark, ed. *Duke Ellington Reader.* New York: Oxford University Press, 1992.

Jazz

Described as "America's classical music," jazz is the first indigenously developed musical expression of America.

The origin of the word "jazz" is as conjectural and conflicting as its birthplace. Although some theories suggest jazz as a result of the changing name of the early Mississippi drummer Charles, others claim its descent from the French word *jaser,* meaning "to speed up, to stimulate," vaguely signifying sexual copulation.

Developed by the black Americans, jazz is a unique synthesis of the best elements from European and West African musical heritage and the African American forms of ragtime, minstrelsy, and the blues. But what differentiates jazz from its cultural predecessors is the widespread use of complex rhythms and improvisation. Jazz improvisation refers to an artist's creative response to a repertoire of songs mostly drawn from blues, jazz tunes, or entirely new melodies. Henry Louis Gates Jr. and Houston A. Baker Jr., in *The Signifying Monkey: Towards A Theory of Afro-American Literary Criticism* and *Blues, Ideology and Afro-American Literature,* identify improvisation as fundamental to African storytelling and signifying traditions. Closely related to the call-and-response of African expressive cultures, jazz improvisations are based on chord progressions and the piano scales that correspond to the piano chords. The New Orleans cornetist Charles "Buddy" Bolden is considered the first improvising jazz musician. Syncopated rhythms (rhythms with offbeat accents), call-and-response patterns, harmonic structures, and kinetic orality are other invariable features of jazz music. A typical jazz orchestra employs trumpet, trombone, saxophone, and piano, though no instrument is foreign to jazz today.

Even though there are many conflicting theories, there is a general consensus about the preeminent role of the New Orleans, particularly Storyville, between 1890 and 1910 in the growth and development of jazz music. During this period, Joe "King" Oliver and his star trumpeter disciple Louis Armstrong, taking cues from earlier masters, refined and enlarged jazz music. In 1923, King Oliver's orchestra became the first African American band to record for a major label. The other key architects of this formative period were Jelly Roll Morton, Freddie Keppard, Bunk Johnson, and Clarence Williams. With the fall of Storyville, the Red Light district of New Orleans, during the World War I, jazz migrated to Chicago and New York, developing new musical idioms there.

The late 1920s and 1930s saw an unprecedented growth of jazz music and can be seen as a progressive phase of black popular music. Louis Armstrong's Hot Five and Hot

Seven, blues singers such as Ma Rainey, Ida Cox, and Bessie Smith, and the big musical bands of Duke Ellington, together with the rise of new electronic mass media (phonographs, jukeboxes, and radio) and jazz clubs, consolidated and brought jazz to greater visibility and immense popularity. Dominated by the big bands (constituting of 12 to 16 members), the 1930s witnessed an invigorating and boisterous variety of jazz called swing. Used mostly for dancing, swing, though less complex than the later forms of jazz, expanded the rhythmic patterns of ragtime and emphasized strong rhythmic section. Bandleaders such as Benny Goodman ("The King of Swing"), Count Basie, Benny Carter, Earl Hines, Artie Shaw, Chick Webb, and Charlie Barnet and the famous black swing bands the Savoy Sultans (Count Basie's band), the Chick Webb band, and the Jay McShann band upheld and popularized swing tradition. It was during this time that Billie Holiday ("Lady Day"), with her husky and buoyant voice, impressed the jazz lovers, later on becoming one of the prominent figures in the history of jazz. Beyond its genuine expression of the experiential realities of black life, jazz and its variants increasingly became a vital cultural and social force of this period. It is this all-pervasiveness of jazz in the early decades of the 20th century that provoked F. Scott Fitzgerald to christen the twenties as "the Jazz Age" (also referred to as "the Roaring Twenties"). Today the expression refers to the years between the end of World War I (1918) and the Stock Market crash (1929) and is related to the Harlem Renaissance.

The Great Crash (1929) and general worsening of American condition, together with the closure of many jazz clubs, dramatically declined the appreciation of jazz music. The big bands of the swing era eventually gave way to an acerbic and fiery style of jazz called bebop (shortened form "bop"). Performed primarily in small groups, bebop captivated audiences with its rhythmic intricacies and long melodies and through an emphasis on new musical idioms. Though this progressivistic desire of bebop met with fiery criticism from the purists of jazz music, who favored a revival of Dixieland jazz, it was bebop with its exacting repertoire of music that elevated jazz into classical status. The trumpeter Dizzy Gillespie, the alto saxophonist Charlie Parker, and pianists Thelonius Monk and Bud Powell—along with swing-era artists, notably the tenor saxophonist Lester Young and the trumpeter Roy Eldridge—were instrumental in developing this dialect. Other practitioners include Sonny Stitt, Dexter Gordon, J. J. Johnson, Kenny Clarke, Max Roach, and Charles Mingus; but it was Charlie Parker (nicknamed "Yardbird" or "Bird"), with his dazzling musicianship and astounding technical virtuosity, who basked in the limelight.

The postwar era saw the rise of two new styles: cool jazz and hard bop. Blending the scored principles of swing and rhythmic progress of bebop, cool jazz was mute, light, and sometimes emotionally detached. Influenced by Stravinsky and Debussy, cool jazz disdained innovations in favor of closeted solo style and subtle rhythms. The trumpeter Miles Davis and the pianist John Lewis were of paramount importance in influencing the harmonic and rhythmic direction of bop. The first cool jazz album was by a nonet (or nine-piece) group led by Miles Davis and came to be known as "The Birth of the Cool." The ensembles of cool jazz, besides involving typical jazz instruments, also experimented with new musical instruments such as baritone saxophone, flugelhorn, and French horn. Furthermore, modal music (the unchanging harmony played over a period of time) developed and popularized by Miles Davis eventually paved way for the fusion of jazz with rock music, referred to as jazz-rock.

If cool jazz revealed the unusual melodic aspect of jazz music, hard bop diverged from the funkier side of it. In fact, hard bop, with its emphasis on phrases and rhythms, can be described as an extension of bebop and the opposite of cool jazz. With an unmistakable influence of gospel and blues music, predominantly in the persons of Horace Silver and Donald Byrd, the hard bop was characterized by aggressive and explosive music. Particularly, this strand of jazz refracted the black experience in eastern cities, including New York, Philadelphia, and Detroit. Such diversity led to the development of such classic songs as Clifford Brown's "Joy Spring," Benny Golson's "Blues March," and Cannonball Adderley's "Work Song." The hard bop artists Elvin Jones, Art Blakey, and Philly Jo Jones, among others, were quite successful. But what dominated the attention of the black audience in this era was a danceable style of jazz called rhythm and blues (R&B) and its later version, rock and roll. Effervescent black saxophonist Louis Jordan was the chief architect of rhythm and blues, and the white Southerner Elvis Presley, with his sophisticated dance steps and strong dose of country and gospel music, was the most influential performer of rock and roll. Other important black rock and roll musicians include Ray Charles, Chuck Berry, and Clyde McPhatter.

After the 1950s, informed by black radicalism and cultural nationalism, jazz became a significant component of the Civil Rights movement. Inaugurated by such warriors as John Coltrane and Ornette Coleman, this decade particularly witnessed the dissonance within and between solos and chaotic group improvisations, giving momentum to the "protest" aspect of jazz music. Although there were many major performers, such as Jimi Hendrix, Wilson Pickett, Curtis Mayfield, and Curtis Redding, it was John Coltrane echoing the utter disillusionment and affluent optimism of the era who captivated the audience. Ornette Coleman's "Free Jazz" and John Coltrane's "Ascension" set the tone of the decade. In addition, the rise of the women's liberation movement and feminism in the late 1960s benefited women bands and veteran performers such as Mary Lou Williams, Melba Liston, and Betty Carter.

Fusion, pluralism, and fragmentation characterized the later jazz. If the 1970s saw significant cross-cultural influences and the use of sophisticated instrumental pop mixes resulting in the birth of new styles of jazz music, the post-1980s witnessed a revival of interest in traditional jazz music and big-band style in Thad Jones, Mel Lewis, and Woody Herman. Today, jazz thrives in the form of post-bop, retro swing, neobop, rap, gangsta rap, and smooth jazz. The contemporary performers, unlike the past masters, are trained artists and utilize the strengths of the electronic medium. However, the bulk of mass media (movies, television) and popular culture, the splintering of jazz into many styles, avant-garde self-indulgence, and entrenched racism robbed the relevance and urgency of jazz over the years.

Interestingly, jazz as an aesthetic model did not remain solely in the domain of music but influenced virtually all the national culture, such as photography (William Claxton, Roy DeCarava), film (*The Jazz Singer, Blues in the Night*), classical music (Aaron Copland), and painting (Romare Bearden, Jackson Pollack, Stuart Davis). Most notably, with its spontaneity and deep spiritualism, jazz has always fascinated black American authors, leading to its features being meaningfully syncretized as a dominant interest of the narrative. Some of the prominent literary texts that tap the metaphoric strength and multifacetedness of jazz include Langston Hughes's poem "Jazzonia," from his 1926 collection of poems *The Weary Blues;* James Baldwin's *Sonny's Blues* (1957); and James Weldon Johnson's novella *The Autobiography of an Ex-Colored Man* (1912). Deeply influenced by jazz musicians such as John Coltrane and Ornette Coleman, Amiri Baraka's poems perhaps would be the closest verbal translation of jazz music. Most recently, Ishmael Reed's *Mumbo Jumbo* (1972) and Toni Morrison's *Jazz* (1993) utilize the codes of jazz music with felicity. Morrison's *Jazz* in particular not only capitalizes on the term "jazz" to explore the ethos of the Harlem period, which provides the setting of the novel, but also profits from its presumed sexual origins. Furthermore, improvisation and call-and-response patterns of jazz music are brought to bear on the text in order to delineate the contingency of identity and the sensual nature of the characters in the novel. Even Morrison's recent novel *Love* (2003) references the stupendous jazz players of the previous century, such as Joe "King" Oliver and Thomas "Fats" Waller. Louis Armstrong's *Satchmo: My Life in New Orleans* (1954), Sidney Bechet's *Treat It Gentle* (1960), and Charles Mingus's *Beneath the Undergo* (1971) are some influential jazz autobiographies, among others. Jazz festivals (New Orleans Jazz and Heritage Festival), jazz studies departments, and formal academic courses, as well as numerous sociological and anthropological treatises, all indisputably testify to the centrality of jazz in the American cultural terrain.

Through addressing realities and shaping perceptions, jazz remains one of the greatest expressive cultures and social forces of America. Furthermore, through its dedicated articulation of the anxieties, attitudes, chaos, and optimism of American society, jazz remains, as Paquito D'Rivera explained, a way to view life. To say this is to insist on indescribable and interpretative challenges offered by jazz, which compels one to agree with Louis Armstrong's definition: "If you gotta ask, you'll never know."

See also: Africanisms; Armstrong, Louis; Bebop; Black Folk Culture; Coltrane, John; Davis, Miles; Jas; Ragtime

Sathyaraj Venkatesan

Bibliography

Baker, Houston, A., Jr. *Blues, Ideology and Afro-American Literature.* Chicago: Chicago University Press, 1984.

Collier, James Lincoln. *Jazz: The American Theme Song.* New York: Oxford University Press, 1993.

Collier, James Lincoln. *The Making of Jazz.* New York: Delta, 1978.

Gates, Henry Louis, Jr. *Signifying Monkey: A Theory of African-American Literary Criticism.* New York: Oxford University Press, 1988.

Gioia, Ted. *The History of Jazz.* New York: Oxford University Press, 1997.

Hodeir, Andre. *Jazz: Its Evolution and Essence.* New York: Grove, 1956.

Ogren, Kathy J. *The Jazz Revolution: Twenties America and the Meaning of Jazz.* New York: Oxford University Press, 1989.

Townsend, Peter. *Jazz in American Culture.* Jackson: University Press of Mississippi, 2000.

John the Slave Tales

John the Slave Tales or John Tales are a type of African American folklore that focuses on the enslaved trickster character, John. In these stories John, also named "High John" or "Jack," frequently outsmarts and humiliates his oppressor, Ole Master, and sometimes his fellow laborers. Although John's acquisition for food, clothing, and leisure time are highlighted in the tales, a common theme is his ability, sometimes unintentional, to outwit his oppressor. In some instances, John is successful in his efforts and overcomes punishment, whereas in others, he is not portrayed as the victor and instead suffers the wrath of Ole Master. The varying achievements of John in these stories represent a more realistic representation of the experience of slavery for African Americans than animal trickster tales. Although scholars are uncertain of the origin of these stories, they believe that enslaved Africans told John the Slave Tales among themselves for entertainment.

Whereas the characters in animal stories pursued material acquisitions, John the Slave Tales focused more on John's sometimes-unknowing ability to defy white superiority. One such story recounts John telling Ole Master that he could tell fortunes. Ole Master told another man, who, in disbelief, bet his entire plantation that John was lying. In preparation, the man got a raccoon and put it in a box. The next morning, John and Ole Master came to the man's plantation. John, who was lying about his ability to tell fortunes, slowly conceded and reluctantly stated, "Well, white folks, you got the old coon at last." Even though he was referring to himself, everyone cheered and claimed that John could tell fortunes. After the spectacle, John told Ole Master that he would never tell fortunes again, and Ole Master did not care because John had made him a rich man.

John also often embarrasses Ole Master in front of his counterparts. For example, one day, Ole Master claimed to a traveler that John had never lied to him in his life. The man bet Ole Master 100 dollars to 50 cents that he could catch John in a lie. The next day after breakfast, the traveler instructed Ole Master to put a live mouse in a covered dish on the breakfast table and tell John that he could eat any leftovers on the table but not to open the dish. After the men returned, Ole Master asked John if he had obeyed his orders, and John swore he had. The traveler then uncovered the dish, but the mouse was gone. He then boasted to Ole Master that John was lying to him all the time. Ole Master was proven wrong and undoubtedly humiliated in front of the stranger.

African American folklorist Zora Neale Hurston, in particular, refers to him as "High John the Conqueror," an African prince and root doctor enslaved in the Americas. Hurston was among the first to record John Tales in 1927 from rural black interviewees in Alabama and Florida.

John the Slave Tales provided enslaved Africans with pride, humor, and ideas about how to resist slavery. The tales are a significant part of African American folklore, and John remains a celebrated hero among African Americans. *See also:* Black Folk Culture; Hurston, Zora Neale; Slave Culture

Zawadi I. Barskile

Bibliography
Hurston, Zora Neale. *Every Tongue Got to Confess: Negro Folktales from the Gulf States.* New York: HarperCollins, 2001.

Hurston, Zora Neale. *The Sanctified Church: The Folklore Writings of Zora Neale Hurston.* Berkeley, CA: Turtle Island, 1981.

Levine, Lawrence W. *Black Culture and Black Consciousness: Afro-American Folk Thought from Slavery to Freedom.* New York: Oxford Press, 1977.

Joplin, Scott

Scott Joplin (1868–1917) was born in Texas, the son of Florence Givens and Giles Joplin, during the period in American history when the peculiar institution of slavery was being dismantled, with the resultant violence against African Americans during this period being pervasive.

Through his parents, a young Scott Joplin learned the importance of possessing a strong work ethic, as well as a formal education. The condition of African American lives during the Reconstruction period necessitated that the African American rise above the imposed illiteracy and other forms of subjugation in order to preserve the

African American self. Scott Joplin learned to embrace African American traditions of dress, body language, and speech—he was also exposed to traditional African American folk music. Folk music born out of a legacy of oppression and spiritual maintenance within the United States of America and beyond would be embraced, melded, and developed into a unique African American musical art form called ragtime.

During the 1870s and 1880s, Scott Joplin attended school and learned to read and write while residing in Texarkana, Texas. His mother, Florence, was a domestic servant who worked for an employer who owned a piano. It was at the home of the W. G. Cook family that Scott Joplin was introduced to the piano. Scott Joplin developed his aptitudes and soon thereafter attracted the attention of a German music teacher, who offered Joplin training in the reading and composing of music. It was during this period that Joplin was introduced to some of the important compositions of classic European musicians.

Joplin played at churches, bars, homes, fairs, and any other venue. As an African American male, he managed to cultivate his intellectual and musical aptitudes in a period of rife with violence and hostility against African Americans. He was able to cultivate his aptitudes across racial, class, and ethnic lines during this period.

Exactly when Scott Joplin left Texarkana, Texas, is uncertain, but he turned up in Missouri in 1890. It is assumed that during the 8 to 10 years prior, Joplin traveled the South, playing his music for all to hear. A continuous student of traditional African American folk music, or "coon songs," Scott had begun to compose and play an up-tempo, heavily syncopated musical form that would be named ragtime.

The Columbian Exposition of 1893 in Chicago, Illinois, marked the emergence of Scott Joplin as the "King of Ragtime." It was at the Exposition that Scott Joplin and his contemporaries began critically writing ragtime sheet music, offering their compositions to the masses. As an "unofficial" musician at this exposition, Scott Joplin introduced the non-African American attendees to the world of ragtime's richly textured music. The exposition also gave Scott Joplin an opportunity to hear the works of some of the best contemporaries of his time and to forge friendships with such important musicians as Otis Saunders.

Scott Joplin formed a band in 1893 and toured with Otis Saunders for years afterward. Saunders encouraged Joplin to further nurture his ability to compose music.

Joplin's ragtime music was heavily syncopated and complex, quite contrary to prevailing musical compositions of the time.

By 1894, Scott Joplin was residing in Sedalia, Missouri. He played his music in spheres and establishments of all sorts in order to earn a living, all the while continuing to compose his own music. In 1897, while living in Sedalia, Scott Joplin composed the most important ragtime tune, or "rag," of all time, the "Maple Leaf Rag"—some say with the assistance of Otis Saunders. The song was named after the Maple Leaf Club, where Scott Joplin usually entertained with his compositions and piano play. While composing and playing at the Maple Leaf Club, among others, Joplin enrolled in the Smith School of Music, a division of the George R. Smith College for Colored People. He never forgot the importance of a formal education.

While playing the "Maple Leaf Rag" one day at its namesake club, Scott Joplin was heard by music publisher John Stark. The two men formed a publishing partnership, and in 1899, "Maple Leaf Rag" was published through a publishing house. Over the next century, its sales and

Musician Scott Joplin was known as the King of Ragtime. (Michael Ochs Archives/Getty Images)

popularity would secure the legacy of Scott Joplin and lend credence to ragtime as a unique, African American musical complexity. The inherent complexities of Scott Joplin's "Maple Leaf Rag" made it an intellectualized statement of African American musical ingenuity and sociopolitical assertiveness. The popularity of this tune afforded its composer recognition well beyond the local walls of Sedalia, Missouri.

From 1885 to 1916, Scott Joplin would continue to compose, and sparingly play, "rags." From 1911 to 1916, he worked on opera composition. During these years, he also taught music and continued to influence his contemporaries; Joplin launched the careers of several other musicians, who then expanded on the social discourse between African American music and the collective consciousness of all Americans. Scott Joplin's music echoed the chants of social, political, and economic justice.

Joplin infused the American musical lexicon with complex musical compositions born out of the experiences of field hands, house servants, and other indigenous African people from all parts of the world. He died in New York in 1917; in 1976, he was awarded a special posthumous Pulitzer Prize. Ragtime music continues to persist as both an art form and an intellectual and musical curiosity—mainly because of the legacy of Scott Joplin.

See also: Ragtime

Bruce Ormond Grant

Bibliography
Berlin, Edward A. *King of Ragtime: Scott Joplin and His Era.* New York: Oxford University Press, 1994.
Berlin, Edward A. *Ragtime: A Musical and Cultural History.* Berkeley: University of California Press, 1980.
Gammond, Peter. *Scott Joplin and the Ragtime Era.* New York: St. Martin's Press, 1975.
Gracyk, Tim, and Frank W. Hoffman. *Popular American Recording Pioneers, 1895–1925.* New York: Haworth Press, 2000.

Juba Dance

Juba is a dance popularized by enslaved Africans in the American South, though examples of it or its cognate forms were witnessed in the Dutch Guiana and the British Caribbean during the 19th century. Like so many expressive forms created in slave communities throughout the Americas, the Juba was a multidimensional concept involving a dance, a type of song and group singing, a rhythmic "patting" of body parts in emulation of musical instruments, and a method of competitive banter. In a typical demonstration, a circle of performers—engaged in singing, creating improvised rhymes, dancing, and bodily patting—would form around two dancers who would engage in semi-competitive dance play. The circle of dancers would sometimes move counterclockwise while the two Juba dancers inside the circle would turn counterclockwise with one leg raised, engage in stomping and thigh slapping, and perform a variety of dance steps popular on Southern plantations, including the Pigeon Wing, the Long Dog Scratch, Blow the Candle Out, and the Yaller Cat, among many others.

Because of the multiple references and connections to counterclockwise circularity, the Juba dance is often linked to the Kongo cosmogram, the ring shout, and even Brazilian Capoeira. As such, the origin of this form might be found among enslaved West-Central Africans who made up the majority of those brought to North America via the Atlantic slave trade. Though the origins of this form may not be clear, it is quite certain that from the various Juba circles formed in the plantation South during the 19th century sprang highly popular dances and dance styles such as the Charleston, hambone, Black Greek step-dancing, and tap dancing.

See also: Angolan/Kongolese; Black Folk Culture; Kongo Cosmogram; Ring Shout; West-Central Africa

Walter C. Rucker

Bibliography
Knowles, Mark. *Tap Roots: The Early History of Tap Dancing.* Jefferson, NC: McFarland, 2002.
Obi, T. J. Desch. *Fighting for Honor: The History of African Martial Arts Traditions in the Atlantic World.* Columbia: University of South Carolina Press, 2008.
Stuckey, Sterling. *Slave Culture: Nationalist Theory and the Foundations of Black America.* New York: Oxford University Press, 1987.

Kongo Cosmogram

The Kongo cosmogram (*Yowa*) is a ritual symbol that represents the Kongo sign of the cosmos and the continuity of human life. Although its design is similar to the Greek cross (+), the Kongo cosmogram does not symbolize the

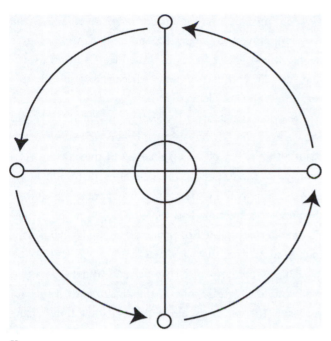

Kongo cosmogram

crucifixion of Jesus Christ. The BaKongo (Kongolese persons) believe that the continuity of life is circular. The horizontal bar of the cosmogram represents the divide between the mountain of the living world and the world of the dead. The BaKongo believe that these two worlds are counterparts, where the mountain of the living is called "earth" (*ntoto*) and the mountain of the dead is called "white clay" (*mpemba*).

The four disks at the points of the cross stand for the "four moments of the sun," and the continuity of the circumference represents the certainty of reincarnation. The vertical ends signal the summits of each world. The north point symbolizes noon, maleness, and the peak of a person's strength on earth. The south point represents midnight, femaleness, and the peak of a person's strength in the world of the dead. BaKongo believe that the righteous person will never be destroyed but will continue to return to earth in the name or body of progeny, or as water, a stone, or a mountain.

The cosmogram is a symbol of crossroads and is used in various spiritual ceremonies. The point of intersection symbolizes the passage and communication between the world of the living and the world of the dead. When drawn on the ground, the cosmogram is used as a ritual space for oath-taking. When taking an oath, a person stands on the cross, situating him or herself between both worlds, and invokes the powers of both. Cosmograms were also used

when reading the soul of a person or in rituals that invoked the dead. The various purposes of the Kongo cross reflect the many ways in which it can be drawn. The form the cross takes depends on who draws it and what type of ceremony it will be used for. The designs are sometimes elaborate and include arrowheads at the ends of the four points and designs within the quadrants. The more simple designs have four points at the tips connected by a line representing a counterclockwise motion.

For Kongo priests, drawing the cosmogram is only a part of ritual ceremonies. Singing or chanting in Ki-Kongo (a Kongo language) is another integral part. The BaKongo believe that drawing the cosmogram and singing join together to bring God's power to the designated spot. These practices and rituals can be found among different groups throughout the African Diaspora.

In places such as the Southern United States, Puerto Rico, Cuba, and Brazil, where enslaved Kongolese were taken, cosmograms were found painted on walls and engraved in bowls. In the U.S. South, some of these bowls were found at the bottoms of rivers and date back to the 18th century. Many scholars believe that the Kongo cosmogram's ubiquity suggests that African captives retained their African beliefs in the New World.

See also: Flying African Tales; Juba Dance; Kongo Kingdom; Ring Shout; Transmigration

Jarett M. Fields

Bibliography

Ferguson, Leland G. *Uncommon Ground: Archaeology and Early African America, 1650–1800.* Washington, D.C.: Smithsonian Institution Press, 1992.

MacGaffey, Wyatt. *Religion and Society in Central Africa: The BaKongo of Lower Zaire.* Chicago: University of Chicago Press, 1986.

Thompson, Robert F. *Flash of the Spirit: African and Afro-American Art and Philosophy.* New York: Vintage Books, 1984.

Kwanzaa

Kwanzaa is a Pan-African holiday started in the United States in 1966 during the midst of African struggles for equality and liberation worldwide. The holiday is a cultural celebration of African beliefs and values celebrated annually from December 26 through January 1. Patterned after African harvest festivals, Kwanzaa gets its name from the Swahili phrase "matunda ya kwanza" or "first fruits." Though the holiday was begun in the United States during the Black Power movement, it is based on communitarian value systems practiced in Africa for thousands of years and therefore available to all descendants of Africans, regardless of where they live. As part of a larger Kawaida cultural theory, Kwanzaa is usually celebrated by people of African ancestry who are interested in reclaiming and reconstructing their cultural heritage.

Kwanzaa was started by Maulana Karenga through the US Organization and is based on five fundamental activities performed by its practitioners: (1) ingathering of the people, (2) reverence for the creator and creation, (3) commemoration of the past, (4) recommitment to the highest cultural ideas, and (5) celebration of the good. The cultural holiday is not religious and can be celebrated by Africans regardless of religious affiliation.

At its core, Kwanzaa is based on a matrix of seven governing principles that are meant to help Africans build up and reinforce the African culture and worldview. Collectively known as the Nguzo Saba, the seven principles were selected for their recurrence in communitarian African societies, their relevance to the African American struggle for equality, the cultural and spiritual importance of the number seven in African cosmology, and the manageability of this number in learning and teaching the principles. Created as an Afrocentric value system, the Nguzo Saba is also regarded as contributing to the building up and reinforcing of family within the Pan-African community. The seven principles of Kwanzaa are as follows:

Umoja (unity): Umoja is the first principle; it is considered foundational in the celebration of Kwanzaa because without it, the remaining six principles suffer.

Kujichagulia (self-determination): Succinctly, kujichagulia expresses the importance of self-definition and the right of a people to define and develop themselves outside of external influences.

Ujima (collective work and responsibility): This third principle emphasizes the need for all Africans to work together on issues affecting the entire collective. As defined by Karenga, this principle regards "African" as more than an identity; it is also a duty and a responsibility.

Ujamaa (cooperative economics): This principle of the Nguzo Saba stresses the relevance of shared wealth and social responsibility and is based on communitarian values.

Nia (purpose): As the fifth principle of Kwanzaa, Nia is a commitment to the understanding that Africans are a people whose legacy has contributed to the world as it is known today and thereby links Africans to a specific cultural and historical identity.

Kuumba (creativity): The sixth principle of the Nguzo Saba is based on African spiritual beliefs that view creativity as an imitation of the original act of the Creator. As a principle of Kwanzaa, Kuumba addresses the responsibility of Africans in making the community more beautiful than the previous generation had.

Imani (faith): The final principle of the Nguzo Saba is to remind Africans that they are capable of victory.

During the week of December 26 through January 1, celebrants meditate on one of the Nguzo Saba principles each day. The family usually gathers at some time during the day to discuss the principle, recommit to its basic value, and practice *tambiko,* or the pouring of libation from the *kikombe cha umoja,* or unity cup. During this gathering, the family congregates in a space decorated according to Kwanzaa practice.

In a central location in the family home or community institution, a *mkeka* (or straw mat) is placed to symbolize the cultural and historical foundation on which Kwanzaa is based. On top of this *mkeka* are placed *mazao* (the crops) that symbolize the rewards of collective labor; the *kinara* (candleholder) symbolizing the roots of African people found on the African continent; the *muhindi* (ears of corn) to symbolize the children; the *mishumaa saba* (seven candles) to symbolize the seven principles of Kwanzaa; the *kikombe cha umoja* (unity cup) to symbolize unity; *zawadi* (gifts) to symbolize the reciprocal relationships between parents, through labor and love, and their children, through their commitments made and kept; and occasionally the *bendera* (flag) to symbolize the struggle (red), people (black), and the future (green).

Once everyone has gathered, it is common for one to ask *"Habari gani?"* or "What is the news?" A one-word response is given according to the principle of the day, for example, *"umoja."* Each day, candles are lit to commemorate the value of the day. Each candle in the *kinara* represents a single principle. The center candle is black and represents the people. This is the first candle lit during the celebration and symbolizes the principle of *umoja,* or unity. To the left of this candle are three red candles symbolizing the principles *kujichagulia, ujamaa,* and *kuumba.* To the right of the black candle are three green candles symbolizing the principles *ujima*, *nia*, and *imani*. The black candle is always lit first to illustrate the understanding that the people come first. Candles are then lit left to right to show that the people come first, followed by the struggle, but that from the struggle comes hope.

During the Kwanzaa celebration, if gifts are exchanged, they are usually given to children. Included in these *zawadi* (gifts) are always a book and some symbol of the child's cultural heritage. Commercialization of Kwanzaa is a concern for many of its practitioners, and for that reason many *zawadi* are handmade to avoid corporate exploitation of the holiday. The final day of celebration, January 1, is reserved for somber reflection and assessment of the preceding principles and the work of the individual in the coming year. Kwanzaa's emphasis here is on recommitment to the restoration of African culture and sovereignty globally.

See also: Afrocentricity; Black Power; Karenga, Maulana; US Organization

Tiffany Pogue

Bibliography

Copage, Eric V. *Kwanzaa: An African American Celebration Of Culture And Cooking.* New York: Harper Collins, 1993.

Karenga, Maulana. *Kwanzaa: A Celebration of Family, Community and Culture.* Los Angeles: University of Sankore Press, 1996.

Karenga, Maulana. *Kwanzaa: Origin, Concepts, Practice.* San Diego, CA: Kawaida Publications, 1977.

Riley, Dorothy Winbush. *The Complete Kwanzaa: Celebrating Our Cultural Harvest.* New York: Book Sales, 2003.

Laveau, Marie

Marie Laveau (1801–1881), generally referred to as a "Voodoo queen," was a leading figure in New Orleans throughout much of the 19th century. In part because mystical self-representation was key to Laveau's life, in part because she seems to have been illiterate, and in part because rumors continue to swirl around her memory (her tomb remains a popular New Orleans tourist stop), many of the details of her biography remain confused or unknown, including the spelling of her name, which is often spelled either "Laveau" or "Leveaux." During the late 19th century, Laveau and her family, for example, regularly listed her age in the 90s— suggesting a birth date in the 1780s. Her father, Charles

Laveau[x], is sometimes listed as white—even though he was much more likely of mixed race. Some accounts indicate that her mother, Marguerite D'Arcantel, was also a *voodooienne*, though very little is known about her. Several other women used Laveau's name—including at least one of her daughters—and their exploits are sometimes collapsed into the Marie legend.

Recent scholars, though, have found baptismal records (as well as an August 1819 marriage record documenting Laveau's brief marriage to Jacques Paris) that mark her birth as a free Creole of color in 1801. Little is known of her Haitian-born husband Paris, who died soon after the wedding under mysterious circumstances. Laveau spent much of the next 40 years with Jean Cristophe Duminy de Glapion, a War of 1812 veteran who died on June 26, 1855, and who some continue to assert was of mixed race even though public documents consistently place him as white. The two never officially married but had several children (probably 5—2 boys and 3 girls—though some more fanciful sources suggest as many as 15). Laveau used Glapion as her last name—and as the last name of her children—for most of the rest of her life.

By the 1840s, Laveau was already prominent in New Orleans' spiritual culture. She was a participant in the ceremonial dances in New Orleans' Congo Square as well as in St. John's Eve festivals at Lake Pontchartrain, and her leadership in such ceremonies, which borrowed from (and heavily sexualized) both Roman Catholic and African diasporic traditions, became central to her legend. She combined the growing public sense of her supernatural abilities with knowledge gained from working as a hairdresser to New Orleans' white elite to position herself as one of the city's most important practitioners of Voodoo and also a dealer in charms and home remedies. (This combination was also likely the reason that she avoided harassment during the periodic crackdowns on Voodoo by the New Orleans authorities, especially in the 1850s.)

As she was building this public persona, Laveau was also raising her family. Her two sons (François and Archange) and one daughter (Marie Louise) died young, but at least two daughters—Marie Heloise and Marie Philomene (spelled variously)—eventually joined their mother in the world of voodoo. Some scholars note Marie Heloise as "Marie the Second" and suggest that she joined her mother as a "Voodoo queen." Philomene, who had a long-term relationship with the white Alexandre Legendre, similar to her mother's with Glapion (they had at least three children and were even listed together in the 1870 census), did much to advance her mother's legend by producing a widely cited obituary when Laveau died in 1881. All seem to have lived in the vicinity of Laveau's St. Ann Street home, and some census records list Philomene and her children as living with Laveau late in the 19th century.

Some accounts suggest that Laveau used her power to help the community; select recent biographers depict her alternately as an antislavery activist (even though both she and Glapion owned slaves), an antipoverty crusader, and a nurse in yellow fever and cholera epidemics. On the other hand, some claim that she used her role mainly for personal gain and that she kept a brothel on Lake Pontchartrain that catered to rich whites. Little direct evidence supports these assertions. Laveau never became wealthy because of her role among New Orleans voodooiennes; recent evidence suggests that she did not even own the house on St. Ann Street that she made famous.

Laveau's youngest daughter Philomene died June 11, 1897, and essentially ended her immediate family's large-scale public promotion of Laveau's legend—though some women who held (and more who claimed) the Laveau name continued to be active in New Orleans. A number of interviews conducted by the Louisiana Writers Project contain stories about Laveau, but two 20th-century figures shaped the modern sense of Laveau most heavily. Zora Neale Hurston spoke in depth on Voodoo culture (and sometimes specifically on Laveau) in an extended 1931 article in the *Journal of American Folklore* and in her 1935 *Mules and Men*. Hurston's depictions—shaped by both her training as an anthropologist and her deep love of story—are of arguable credibility even though they are fascinating and lively; late 20th-century efforts to reconsider Hurston led naturally to additional examination of her work on Voodoo. Much less trustworthy, much more sensationalistic, and much more popular when it was released is Robert Tallant's 1946 *Voodoo in New Orleans*, which recounts a number of (highly sexualized) stories of Laveau.

See also: Conjure; Hoodoo; Hurston, Zora Neale

Eric Scott Gardner

Bibliography

Fandrich, Ina Johanna. *The Mysterious Voodoo Queen, Marie Laveaux: A Study in Powerful Female Leadership in Nineteenth-Century New Orleans.* New York: Routledge, 2005.

Long, Carolyn Morrow. *A New Orleans Voodou Priestess: The Legend and Reality of Marie Laveau.* Gainesville: University Press of Florida, 2006.

Ward, Martha. *Voodoo Queen: The Spirited Lives of Marie Laveau.* Jackson: University Press of Mississippi, 2004.

Locke, Alain

History remembers Alain Locke (1885–1954) as the first African American Rhodes Scholar (1907) and, more famously, as the "dean" of the Harlem Renaissance (1919–1934). Locke edited *The New Negro* (1925), acclaimed as the "first national book" of African Americans. In this way, Locke's role is analogous to that of Martin Luther King: whereas King championed the civil rights of African Americans through nonviolent civil disobedience, Locke did so through a process known as "civil rights by copyright."

In the Jim Crow era, when blacks had no effective political recourse, Locke used the arts as a strategy to win the respect of the white majority and to call to their attention the need to fully democratize democracy and Americanize America by extending full equality to all minorities. Recent scholarship has brought Locke back to life, and his philosophy of democracy, in particular, lends him renewed importance.

Harvard, Harlem, Haifa—place names that represent Locke's special involvement in philosophy, art, and religion—are keys to understanding his life and thought. Harvard prepared Locke for distinction as the first black Rhodes Scholar in 1907 and, in 1918, awarded Locke his PhD in philosophy, thus securing his position as chair of the Department of Philosophy at Howard University from 1927 until his retirement in 1953. Harlem was the mecca of the Harlem Renaissance, whereby Locke, as a spokesman for his race, revitalized racial solidarity and fostered the group consciousness among African Americans that proved a necessary precondition of the Civil Rights movement. Haifa is the world center of the Bahá'í Faith, the religion to which Locke converted in 1918, the same year he received his doctorate from Harvard. Until recently, this has been the least understood aspect of Locke's life. During the Jim Crow era, at a time when black people saw little possibility of interracial harmony, this new religious movement offered hope through its "race amity" efforts, which Locke was instrumental in organizing. These three spheres of activity—the academy, the art world, and spiritual society—converge to create a composite picture of Locke as an integrationist whose model was not assimilation, but rather "unity through diversity" (the title of one of his *Bahá'í World* essays).

Born in 1885, Locke was sent by his mother to one of the Ethical Culture schools—a pioneer, experimental program of Froebelian pedagogy (after Friedrich Froebel [d. 1852], who opened the first kindergarten). By the time he enrolled in Central High School (1898–1902), Locke was already an accomplished pianist and violinist. In 1902, Locke attended the Philadelphia School of Pedagogy, graduating second in his class in 1904. That year, Locke entered Harvard College with honors at entrance, where he was among only a precious few African American undergraduates.

During the "golden age of philosophy at Harvard," Locke studied at a time when Josiah Royce, William James, George Herbert Palmer, Hugo Münsterberg, and Ralph

Alain Locke was a writer, philosopher, educator, and patron of the arts. He is best known for his writings on and about the Harlem Renaissance. (National Archives)

Barton Perry were on the faculty. Elected to Phi Beta Kappa, in 1907 Locke won the Bowdoin Prize—Harvard's most prestigious academic award—for an essay he wrote, "The Literary Heritage of Tennyson." Remarkably, Locke completed his four-year undergraduate program at Harvard in only three years, graduating magna cum laude with his bachelor's degree in philosophy. Then, Locke made history and headlines in May 1907 as America's first African American Rhodes Scholar. Although his Rhodes scholarship provided for study abroad at Oxford, it was no guarantee of admission. Rejected by five Oxford colleges because of his race, Locke was finally admitted to Hertford College, where studied from 1907 to 1910.

Jewish philosopher Horace Kallen describes a racial incident over a Thanksgiving Day dinner hosted at the American Club at Oxford. Locke was not invited because Southern men refused to dine with him. Kallen and Locke became lifelong friends. In the course of their conversations, the phrase "cultural pluralism" was born. Although the term itself was thus coined by Kallen in this historic conversation with Locke, it was really Locke who developed the concept into a full-blown philosophical framework for the melioration of African Americans. Distancing himself from Kallen's purist and separatist conception of it, Locke was part of the cultural pluralist movement that flourished between the 1920s and the 1940s. Indeed, Locke has been called the "father of multiculturalism."

So acutely did the Thanksgiving Day dinner incident traumatize Locke that he left Oxford without taking a degree and spent the 1910–1911 academic year studying Kant at the University of Berlin and touring Eastern Europe as well. During his stay in Berlin, where he earned a B.Litt, Locke became conversant with the "Austrian school" of anthropology, known as philosophical anthropology, under the tutelage of Franz Brentano, Alexius von Meinong, Christian Freiherr von Ehrenfels, Paul Natorp, and others. Locke much preferred Europe to America. Indeed, there were moments when Locke resolved never to return to the United States. Reluctantly, he did so in 1911.

As an assistant professor of the teaching of English and an instructor in philosophy and education, Locke taught literature, English, education, and ethics—and later, ethics and logic—at Howard University itself, although he did not have an opportunity to teach a course on philosophy until 1915. In 1915–1916, the Howard chapter of the National Association for the Advancement of Colored

People (NAACP) and the Social Science Club sponsored a two-year extension course of public lectures, which Locke called, "Race Contacts and Inter-Racial Relations: A Study in the Theory and Practice of Race."

In the 1916–1917 academic year, Locke took a sabbatical from Howard University to become Austin Teaching Fellow at Harvard, where he wrote his 263-page dissertation, *The Problem of Classification in [the] Theory of Values*, evidently an extension of an earlier essay he had written at Oxford. It was Harvard professor of philosophy Josiah Royce who originally inspired Locke's interest in the philosophy of value. Of all the major American pragmatists to date, only Royce had published a book dealing with racism: *Race Questions, Provincialism, and Other American Problems* (1908). In formulating his own theory of value, Locke synthesized the Austrian school of value theory (Franz Brentano, Alexius von Meinong, and later on, Rudolf Maria Holzapfel) with American pragmatism (George Santayana, William James, and Josiah Royce), along with the anthropology of Franz Boas and Kant's theories of aesthetic judgment.

When awarded his PhD in philosophy from Harvard in 1918, Locke emerged as perhaps the most exquisitely educated and erudite African American of his generation. The year 1918 was another milestone in Locke's life, when he found a "spiritual home" in the Bahá'í Faith, a new world religion whose gospel was the unity of the human race. The recent discovery of Locke's signed "Bahá'í Historical Record" card (1935), in which Locke fixes the date of his conversion in 1918, restores a "missing dimension" of Locke's life. Locke was actively involved in the early "race amity" initiatives sponsored by the Bahá'ís. "Race amity" was the Bahá'í term for ideal race relations (interracial unity). The Bahá'í "race amity" era lasted from 1921 to 1936, followed by the "race unity" period of 1939–1947, with other socially significant experiments in interracial harmony (such as "Race Unity Day") down to the present. Although he studiously avoided references to the faith in his professional life, Locke's four *Bahá'í World* essays served as his public testimony of faith. But it was not until an article, "Bahá'í Faith: Only Church in World That Does Not Discriminate," appeared in the October 1952 issue of *Ebony* magazine that Locke's Bahá'í identity was ever publicized in the popular media.

In 1925, the Harlem Renaissance was publicly launched. It was conceived a year earlier, when Locke was asked by the editor of the *Survey Graphic* to produce demographics on Harlem, which is in the district of Manhattan in New York. That special issue, *Harlem, Mecca of the New Negro*, Locke subsequently recast as an anthology, *The New Negro: An Interpretation of Negro Life*, published in December 1925. A landmark in black literature, it was an instant success. Locke contributed five essays: the foreword, "The New Negro," "Negro Youth Speaks," "The Negro Spirituals," and "The Legacy of Ancestral Arts." *The New Negro* featured five white contributors as well, making this artistic tour de force a genuinely interracial collaboration, with much support from white patronage (not without some strings attached, however). The last essay was contributed by W. E. B. Du Bois.

Locke hoped the Harlem Renaissance would provide "an emancipating vision to America" and would advance "a new democracy in American culture." He spoke of a "race pride," "race genius," and the "race-gift." This "race pride" was to be cultivated through developing a distinctive culture, a hybrid of African and African American elements. For Locke, art ought to contribute to the improvement of life—a pragmatist aesthetic principle sometimes called "meliorism." But the Harlem Renaissance was more of an aristocratic than democratic approach to culture. Criticized by some African American contemporaries, Locke himself came to regret the Harlem Renaissance's excesses of exhibitionism as well as its elitism. Its dazzling success was short-lived.

Strange to say, Locke did not publish a formal philosophical essay until he was 50. "Values and Imperatives" appeared in 1935. In fact, this was Locke's only formal philosophical work between 1925 and 1939. Apart from his dissertation, Locke published only four major articles in a philosophy journal or anthology: "Values and Imperatives" (1935), "Pluralism and Intellectual Democracy" (1942), "Cultural Relativism and Ideological Peace" (1944), and "Pluralism and Ideological Peace" (1947).

In 1943, Locke was on leave as Inter-American Exchange Professor to Haiti under the joint auspices of the American Committee for Inter-American Artistic and Intellectual Relations and the Haitian Ministry of Education. Toward the end of his stay there, Haitian president Élie Lescot personally decorated Locke with the National Order of Honor and Merit, grade of Commandeur. There Locke wrote *Le rôle du Négre dans la culture Américaine*, the nucleus of a grand project that Locke believed would be his magnum opus. That project, *The Negro in American Culture,* was completed in 1956 by Margaret Just Butcher, daughter of Howard colleague and close friend Ernest E. Just. It is not, however, considered to be an authentic work of Locke.

In 1944, Locke became a charter member of the Conference on Science, Philosophy and Religion, which published its annual proceedings. During the 1945–1946 academic year, Locke was a visiting professor at the University of Wisconsin, and in 1947, he was a visiting professor at the New School for Social Research. For the 1946–1947 term, Locke was elected president of the American Association for Adult Education (AAAE), as the first black president of a predominantly white institution. His reputation as a leader in adult education had already been established by the nine-volume *Bronze Booklet* series that he had edited, two volumes of which he had personally authored as well.

He moved to New York in July 1953. For practically his entire life, Locke had sought treatment for his rheumatic heart. Locke died of heart failure on June 9, 1954, in Mount Sinai Hospital. On June 11 at Benta's Chapel, Brooklyn, Locke's memorial was presided over by Dr. Channing Tobias, with cremation following at Fresh Pond Crematory in Little Village, Long Island.

As a cultural pluralist, Locke may have a renewed importance as a social philosopher, particularly as a philosopher of democracy. Because Locke was not a systematic philosopher, however, it is necessary to systematize his philosophy in order to bring its deep structure into bold relief.

Democracy is a process of progressive equalizing. It is a matter of degree. For blacks, American democracy was largely a source of oppression, not liberation. America's racial crisis was not just national—it was a problem of world-historical proportions. As a cultural pluralist, Alain Locke sought to further Americanize Americanism and further democratize democracy. In so doing, he proposed a multidimensional model of democracy that ranged from concepts of "local democracy" all the way up to "world democracy." This multidimensional typology is developed further in the penultimate chapter of Christopher Buck's *Alain Locke: Faith and Philosophy* (2005). We know that Alain Locke *was* important. If his philosophy of democracy has any merit, we know now that is Locke *is* important, especially if it is time to transform democratic values into democratic imperatives.

See also: Du Bois, W. E. B; Harlem Renaissance; New Negro Movement; Woodson, Carter Godwin

Christopher Buck

Bibliography

Buck, Christopher. "Alain Locke." In *American Writers: A Collection of Literary Biographies,* ed. Jay Parini. Farmington Hills, MI: Scribner's Reference/Gale Group, 2004.

Buck, Christopher. "Alain Locke: Baha'i Philosopher." *Baha'i Studies Review* 10 (2001/2002):7–49.

Buck, Christopher. *Alain Locke: Faith and Philosophy.* Los Angeles: Kalimát Press, 2005.

Buck, Christopher. "Alain Locke and Cultural Pluralism." In *Search for Values: Ethics in Baha'i Thought,* ed. Seena Fazel and John Danesh. Los Angeles: Kalimát Press, 2004.

Harris, Leonard, ed. *The Philosophy of Alain Locke: Harlem Renaissance and Beyond.* Philadelphia: Temple University Press, 1989.

Kallen, Horace Meyer. "Alain Locke and Cultural Pluralism." *Journal of Philosophy* 54, no. 5 (1957):119–27. Reprinted in Kallen, *What I Believe and Why—Maybe: Essays for the Modern World.* New York: Horizon Press, 1971.

Locke, Alain. *The Negro and His Music.* Washington, D.C.: Associates in Negro Folk Education, 1936. (Bronze Booklet No. 2).

Locke, Alain. *The Negro Art: Past and Present.* Washington, D.C.: Associates in Negro Folk Education, 1936. (Bronze Booklet No. 3).

Locke, Alain. "Negro Spirituals." *Freedom: A Concert in Celebration of the 75th Anniversary of the Thirteenth Amendment to the Constitution of the United States* (1940). Compact disc. New York: Bridge, 2002. Audio (1:14).

Locke, Alain, ed. *The New Negro: An Interpretation.* New York: A. & C. Boni, 1925. Reprint, New York, Simon & Schuster, 1927; New York: Touchstone, 1999.

Locke, Alain. *Race Contacts and Interracial Relations: Lectures of the Theory and Practice of Race.* Ed. Jeffery C. Stewart. Reprint. Washington, D.C.: Howard University Press, 1992.

Locke, Alain. "The Unfinished Business of Democracy." *Survey Graphic* 31 (November 1942):455–61.

Locke, Alain. "Values and Imperatives." In *American Philosophy, Today and Tomorrow,* ed. Sidney Hook and Horace M. Kallen. New York: Lee Furman, 1935. Reprint, Freeport, NY: Books for Libraries Press, 1968.

Locke, Alain. *Le rôle du Négre dans la culture Américaine.* Port-au-Prince: Haiti Imprimerie de l'état, 1943.

Locke, Alain, and Montgomery Davis, eds. *Plays of Negro Life: A Source-Book of Native American Drama.* New York: Harper and Row, 1927.

Locke, Alain, Mordecai Johnson, Doxey Wilkerson, and Leon Ransom. "Is There a Basis for Spiritual Unity in the World Today?" *Town Meeting: Bulletin of America's Town Meeting on the Air* 8, no. 5 (1942):3–12.

Locke, Alain, and Bernhard J. Stern, eds. *When Peoples Meet: A Study of Race and Culture Contacts.* New York: Committee on Workshops, Progressive Education Association, 1942.

Mason, Ernest. "Alain Locke's Social Philosophy." *World Order* 13, no. 2 (Winter 1979):25–34.

Washington, Johnny. *Alain Locke and Philosophy: A Quest for Cultural Pluralism.* New York: Greenwood Press, 1986.

Mardi Gras

Mardi Gras is an annual celebration, historically held in New Orleans, Louisiana, that draws tourists from around the world; it is the culmination of 10 days of street festivities that include musical performances, dancing, costume displaying, extravagant parades, and fancy balls. Mardi Gras marks the last day of feasting prior to the beginning of Lent. The holiday is always scheduled 47 days before Easter Sunday and falls between February 3 and March 9. Surrounding Mardi Gras are multicultural and boisterous public spectacles that have maintained particular significance and distinction in the communities of African Americans and Creoles of Color. Two of the most prominent events associated with the merriment, and having deep cultural and historical roots, are the parades of the Mardi Gras Indians and the Zulu Krewe. As such, similar festivals, such as Carnival, are celebrated around the world in places such as Rio de Janeiro, Bolivia, and the Caribbean.

In the early 1700s, Code Noir, an official regulation of conduct between slaves and slave owners, had both positive and negative consequences in New Orleans. One benefit of the code was the margin of freedom it provided for slaves, which aided in the sanctioning of a public space that would later be called Congo Square. By the mid 1730s, Congo Square was a public market where African singing, dancing, and costuming were commonplace occurrences. These artistic expressions were forerunners to and aided in the establishment of African American Carnival traditions. All social classes in New Orleans celebrated Mardi Gras (French for "Fat Tuesday"), although for a brief period, blacks were prohibited from masking because of fear that the maskers might aid the king's enemies in gaining access to dances or might commit robberies.

Revelers beg for prized Zulu coconuts from Zulu Rascals member Benjamin Bennett, left, during the Krewe of Zulu Mardi Gras parade in New Orleans, February 5, 2008. (AP/Wide World Photos)

Carnival has long been identified with New Orleans street performance. A form of street dancing called "Second Line" originated in the mid 1800s. The phrase was originally coined to refer to the crowd that followed the musicians and mourners in a street celebration for a funeral. Another influence on the evolution of Mardi Gras in African American communities was Buffalo Bill's Wild West Shows that, in the late 1800s, introduced New Orleans audiences to the pageantry of Native American costuming. These shows may have affected a street spectacle that formed as an outgrowth of a cultural bond between runaway slaves and the Native Americans that hid them: the parading of various Mardi Gras Native American groups headed by chiefs and "shrouded in secrecy." Africans and Native Americans had found commonality as oppressed subcultures and forged connections. When groups of black men, sometimes referred to as "gangs" or "tribes," began dressing up like Native Americans and parading on improvised street routes during celebration, there were sometimes violent encounters among the various groups.

Today, the complex and ornamental costumes worn by the revelers are central to the identity of Mari Gras Indians. These costumes are magnificent constructions that are hand-sewn at great expense by individuals who spend several months every year preparing the intricate beading and feathered regalia with great care. These colorful costumes, when worn during Carnival in contemporary society, became a source of celebration and competitiveness between the various groups. Costume competitiveness has replaced much of the violence formerly associated with the Mardi Gras Indian celebrations. These syncretistic practices coupled with Caribbean influences evidence cultural traditions that survive in contemporary New Orleans culture and are displayed publicly during Mardi Gras celebrations by men who dress as Native Americans during street reveling.

Other events of historical significance to New Orleans Mardi Gras include the Illinois Club formed during Jim Crow for purposes of providing a ball for people of color. Although women were initially allowed to join the club, it soon became an all-male organization. This formal ball stood in sharp contrast to the Baby Dolls, a group of prostitutes who, beginning in 1912, dressed up and paraded through the streets dressed in bonnets and ribbons. Yet another Mardi Gras tradition that formed in the first part of the 20th century was the Krewe of Zulu, a group originally established in 1909 under the name "The Tramps,"

but reorganized in 1916 under the auspices of Zulu Social Aid and Pleasure Club. The Zulu parade is the oldest and largest African American parade connected to Mardi Gras, and it is widely known for the coconuts that the float riders, dressed in grass skirts and blackface, throw to parade watchers. In 1949, wearing a red velvet robe and traditional blackface, Louis Armstrong became the most famous king to lead the Zulu Parade.

Some of the activities associated with Mardi Gras have become outdated but are still recreated each year. For instance, flambeaux carriers were men of color who initially carried torches to light parade floats before electricity was available to do so. Even though this tradition is still alive at present, fewer flambeaux carriers are seen at each Mardi Gras celebration. The few remaining carriers stand as bearers of historical memory.

See also: Armstrong, Louis; Black Folk Culture; Congo Square, New Orleans

Jayetta Slawson

Bibliography

Schindler, Henri. *Mardi Gras New Orleans*. Paris: Flammarion, 1997.

Smith, Michael. *Mardi Gras Indians*. Gretna, LA: Pelican Publishing, 1994.

Miscegenation

The term "miscegenation" refers to the sexual union and cohabitation between persons of different racial origin and was used in laws passed in the United States that prohibited interracial marriage. It also refers to persons who believe racial intermarriage is fundamentally wrong. The term is derived from the Latin *miscere,* meaning "to mix," and *genus,* meaning "race," and it replaces the term "amalgamate," which was not accurate or scientific. In short, it means simply "to mix race," a phenomenon that has been in existence since the early colonial times in American history, to the present day. The word was coined, or at least became popularized, in 1863 by the anonymous authors of a pamphlet at Christmas time in New York City, titled *Miscegenation: The Theory of the Blending of Races Applied to the White and Negro,* who argued in favor of African American and white intermarriage. The real authors were discovered to be

David Goodman Croly, managing editor of the *New York World*, a staunchly Democratic Party paper, and George Wakeman, a reporter for the same newspaper. The pamphlet was soon exposed to be a hoax, essentially a political ploy aimed at discrediting the Republican Party, Abraham Lincoln's presidency, and the abolitionist movement, only months away from a presidential reelection in 1864. Nonetheless, this pamphlet and others like it resurfaced regularly throughout the American Civil War by opponents of the Republicans. At that time, the notion of interracial marriage between blacks and whites was indeed highly controversial, and it certainly would have angered some voters.

The first anti-miscegenation law was enacted in 1664 in Maryland, likely in response to sexual liaisons and marriages between white indentured servants and black slaves. At that time, virtually all blacks were slaves and whites free. As a result, race and legal status were intertwined. Unions between whites males and black slave women were not a concern for the law because the resulting progeny were forever black and slaves under the matrilineal principle of identity. However unions between black male slaves and free white women complicated social boundaries for that day and produced mixed-race progeny who were legally white for all purposes of the law. This undermined the very institution of slavery, both legally and economically. Thus, early anti-miscegenation laws were aimed at discouraging racial intermarriage that created the mirage of "racial equality" and at maintaining a system were blacks were forever property and at the bottom. Henceforth, most states, one after the other, passed laws banning interracial intermarriage. These laws chiefly targeted blacks but sometimes applied to Native Americans and Asians, but never Latinos. As a result, some non-white groups were able to intermarry with each other, whereas others were not. There were even cases of persons with a triracial identity (black, white, and Native American) who were unable to marry anyone. Some states enforced their own anti-miscegenation laws comprehensively, whereas others did not enforce them at all or only selectively. These variations existed because marriage was a state responsibility and tended to reflect local custom and attitudes. Moreover, definitions of "blackness" and "whiteness" also varied from state to state and over time. Someone considered legally white in one state might be considered black in another and vice versa and thus unable to contract marriage with anyone outside his or her perceived racial group. Civil authorities such as town marriage clerks, the police, and even clergy licensed to perform marriages had wide discretion when determining racial classification and served as watchdogs and enforcers of white supremacy. During the Reconstruction era immediately following the Civil War, many Southern states temporarily abandoned their anti-miscegenation laws in light of political and economic ruin caused by the war and the Union's victory over the Confederacy under the banner "equality for all." But by about 1880—the onset of the Jim Crow era that brought about legalized segregation throughout the United States—many states reenacted laws banning interracial marriages, and this caused a chain reaction of sorts, leading to many states, not limited to the South, either reenacting previous passed legislation or tightening existing laws on anti-miscegenation, making them far more universal and exclusive, in terms of racial definitions, than ever before.

Those accused of miscegenation faced the strong possibility of a felony-misdemeanor conviction, resulting in a fine or imprisonment for one to five years or sometimes both. The state of Virginia punished violators with banishment from the state. Criminal penalties such as hefty fines also extended to civil authorities, such as officiants at wedding ceremonies and town clerks who issued marriage licenses. Sometimes immunity for interracial couples was as simple as crossing the state line to a jurisdiction that permitted mixed-race marriages. Yet some states, such as Virginia, did not recognize interracial marriages contracted in other states, so there was no guarantee. Even those who did not get caught felt the sting of these laws. The interracial nature of a marriage was sufficient grounds to have a marriage declared null and void and was sometimes used by relatives to deny the surviving black spouse of his or her rightful inheritance.

The best-known victim and resister of the anti-miscegenation regime was Jack Johnson (1878–1946), the first African American heavyweight boxing champion. Throughout his professional career, 1897–1915, Johnson earned considerable wealth fighting black and then white boxers. His flair, narcissism, athletic prowess, outspoken contempt for racism, and public pursuit of white women (he married three) breached social convention and made him a target. As a result of Johnson's success in the ring as well as the bedroom, he was hated and feared by American white males, and this almost led to Congress's passing a law banning interracial marriages, which would have been an invasion of states' rights. Unable to charge Johnson with any existing anti-miscegenation law, in 1913 his enemies conspired to find him guilty of violating the Mann Act (1912), which prohibited transporting a white woman across state lines Johnson had bought a train ticket from Pittsburgh to Chicago for his 19-year-old white wife. The case was dubbed "the evils of miscegenation." Fleeing his conviction, Johnson went into exile. In 1915, he fought Jess Willard in Cuba and lost his heavyweight championship. In 1920, he returned to the United States, surrendered himself to authorities, and served one year in jail.

During the height of the anti-miscegenation regime, 1880 to 1950, courts and politicians at all levels upheld the constitutionality of these laws. There were several important court cases, specifically, *Pace v. Alabama* (1883) and *Loving v. Virginia* (1967). In the former, the Supreme Court reaffirmed its position on miscegenation and denied the interracial couple the right to a legal marriage based on the "equal protection" clause of the Fourteenth Amendment to the U.S. Constitution. Anti-miscegenation laws and their associated criminal penalties in theory applied equally to all persons, black, white, yellow, and so on, and hence did not discriminate; therefore, they were considered constitutional. The watershed case was *Loving v. Virginia* (1967), in which an interracial couple, Mildred Jeter, a black woman, and her white husband, Robert Loving, were arrested in their home state of Virginia for violating that state's anti-miscegenation laws. The couple temporarily relocated to the District of Columbia, which had long since repealed its own anti-miscegenation laws. Upon their return to Virginia, the Lovings found their marriage and cohabitation in violation of state law. They were ordered to leave the state and never return, on pain of imprisonment. The couple moved back to the District of Columbia and filed action against Virginia. After a long and hard-fought battle, the couple was successful in the Supreme Court, which struck down anti-miscegenation laws as unconstitutional in breach of the same clause that was used to up hold the *Pace* case. It was not until 2000, however, that Alabama became the last state to repeal its anti-miscegenation law (which formed part of the state constitution).

It is ironic that African Americans gained civil rights (1965) before they gained the right to marry outside their own racial group (1967). In some respects, interracial marriage was more significant than civil rights. The ability to marry outside one's race, but within the dominant culture, was less a legal right than a fundamental human right symbolizing true racial equality. Civil rights gained in the 1950s

and 1960s did not extend to interracial marriage. African Americans could still be second-class citizens despite having acquired full citizenship rights—a strange paradox that speaks volumes of race relations.

See also: Amalgamation; Mulatto; Quadroon

Justin Marcus Johnston

Bibliography

Robinson, Charles. *Dangerous Liaisons: Sex and Love in the Segregated South.* Fayetteville: University of Arkansas Press, 2003.

Romano, Renee Christine. *Race Mixing: Black-White Marriage in Postwar America.* Cambridge, MA: Harvard University Press, 2003.

Wallenstein, Peter. *Tell the Court I Love My Wife: Race, Marriage, and Law—An American History.* New York: Palgrave Macmillan, 2004.

Mulatto

"Mulatto" (often assumed to be derived from the Spanish *mulato,* or "little mule") typically refers to someone of mixed racial heritage; however, the term commonly refers to a person of mixed Caucasian and Negro ancestry or, in late 20th-century parlance, a "biracial" individual. In the American context, "race mixing," or miscegenation, occurred regularly. The one-drop rule (defining who was black) can be traced back to the colonial period, when miscegenation occurred largely between white indentured servants and both slave and free blacks. In most colonies, the mulatto children from these unions were considered black (with exceptions—e.g., Virginia, where they were sometimes considered white). In areas of the South, when interracial intercourse occurred, it was generally between white men and both enslaved and free black women. Some areas, such as Charleston and New Orleans, saw free mulattos forming alliances with whites and serving as a buffer group (economically and socially) between whites and blacks, possessing a unique in-between status within the existing racial hierarchy.

However, these are the exceptions to the rule. The institution of slavery, built on white supremacist ideology and absolute prohibition of miscegenation, brought whites and blacks into close physical proximity on a daily basis. As a result of the mentality that white male slave owners could "rightfully" use their black female slaves at will, the vast majority of interracial sex consisted of exploitative unions between white male slave owners and their black female slaves (whereas sex between white women and black men was strictly forbidden). To have a mulatto child in a white family was scandalous and threatened the entire ideological logic of the slave system. A mixed-race child in the slave quarters, however, was not only tolerated but often considered an asset. Either way, light-skinned mulatto children were often given special privileges: positions as "house servants," education, training, and access to white culture, to name a few.

The Civil War, due to increasing Southern defense of slavery and the one-drop rule, created a climate of distrust and hostility toward free mulattos and permanently altered the relationship between whites and mulattos in many places. Free mulattos sought alliances with blacks and shifted their sense of identity accordingly—this alliance, though not unproblematic, continued well into the mid-20th century. Because of the many privileges mulattos were allowed prior to the Civil War, many emerged as leaders of Southern blacks through Reconstruction and into Jim Crow and served critically important roles in the black struggle (e.g., see prominent mulattos such as W. E. B. Du Bois, William Monroe Trotter, James Weldon Johnson, A. Philip Randolph, and Walter White). Interestingly, throughout the Harlem Renaissance, the work of many mulatto artists, musicians, dancers, poets, and writers represented *the* articulation of the black experience (e.g., Zora Neale Hurston, Langston Hughes, Claude McKay, and Jean Toomer) to white audiences.

A generation after the passage of *Loving v. Commonwealth of Virginia* (1967), which made laws prohibiting miscegenation illegal, by the mid-1980s, the United States had seen the rise of multiracial, biracial, and mixed-race individuals and groups of individuals demanding a change in the way that the United States racially classifies its citizens. Dubbed by some scholars as the "neo-mulattos," the multiracial movement is attempting to deal serious blows to the one-drop rule; however, the reasons behind these movements and the implications for the struggle for black liberation in the United States remain little understood.
See also: Amalgamation; Miscegenation

David L. Brunsma

Bibliography
Davis, F. James. *Who Is Black: One Nation's Definition.* University Park: Pennsylvania State University Press, 1991.
Reuter, Edward Byron. *The Mulatto in the United States.* Boston: Richard G. Badger, 1918.
Williamson, Joel. *New People: Miscegenation and Mulattoes in the United States.* New York: Free Press, 1980.

Names Debate

The names debate refers to the conflict among African Americans over which term they wanted to use to describe themselves racially. Many terms—both positive and derogatory—were used to describe people of African descent in the United States, including "Afric," "African," "colored," "black," "Niger," "Negro," and so on.

Yet by the 1830s, African Americans sought to exercise self-determination and wanted to name themselves on their own terms. Thus, the names debate began in 1835 when William Whipper, a wealthy Philadelphian, introduced a controversial resolution at the fifth gathering of the Colored Convention. Prior to 1835, most black organizations used "African" as a way of demonstrating their distinct identity and cultural pride. However as opposition to African colonization prompted black activists to claim America as their homeland, some leaders pondered the ramifications of their naming tradition. In particular, men such as William Whipper argued that black people should break down the barriers of racial separation by removing racial designations and eradicating separate black organizations and institutions. This belief led Whipper to propose that African Americans should abandon the use of the term "colored" and remove the term "African" from their organizational titles.

Not surprisingly, there was significant debate over Whipper's proposal at the 1835 Colored Convention. However, the resolution finally passed. In the end, however, it is important to note that African Americans were reluctant to abandon the use of racial designations entirely. Although they eventually ceased using the term "African," they retained the use of "colored" as well as other racial signifiers. Reflecting their early commitment to Black Nationalism, most black activists were not yet ready to adopt Whipper's vision of complete assimilation into American society, and therefore, black leaders continued to create and support separate black organizations and institutions long after the 1835 convention. They supported their decision so strongly that, in 1838, when Philadelphians continued to press the issue of removing racial distinctions, Samuel Cornish, editor of the *Colored American* newspaper, became enraged and criticized the Philadelphians for arguing about minor issues rather than focusing on the real issues, such as slavery and the denial of citizenship, that plagued the black community.

Even so, the debate over names that commenced in the 1830s haunted African Americans well into the 21st century, as activists struggled to determine how they wanted to define themselves as a race.

See also: Cornish, Samuel; Whipper, William

Leslie M. Alexander

Bibliography

Alexander, Leslie. *African or American? Black Identity and Political Activism in New York City, 1784–1861.* Urbana: University of Illinois Press, 2008.

Rael, Patrick. *Black Identity and Black Protest in the Antebellum North.* Chapel Hill: University of North Carolina Press, 2002.

Stuckey, Sterling. *Slave Culture: Nationalist Theory and the Foundations of Black America.* New York: Oxford University Press, 1987.

Negritude

Negritude was a Pan-African literary, philosophical, cultural, and sociopolitical movement characterized by the writings of young, black, French intellectuals from the 1930s well into the 1950s. Fostered by some of France's leading intellectuals through the 1940s and 1950s, Negritude grew to worldwide recognition as a pivotal moment in the historical trajectory of black consciousness thought. Inspired by the artists, writers, and thinkers of the Harlem Renaissance as well as black writers of various disciplines from the French colonies, Negritude intellectuals advocated the search for an authentic black voice that stemmed from the awareness of a rich African cultural heritage. Negritude writers implored Africans and African descendents from all over the world to throw off the shackles of European colonial imperialism, which they considered not only devastating to their African inheritance but also stifling to the artistic creation and cultural and social autonomy that this history precipitated. Negritude manifested itself in the form of philosophical, social, and political tracts in addition to a magnitude of literary works in poetry, prose, theater, and fiction. Distinguished by multifarious interpretations of the methods and meanings of black consciousness and black humanism, the Negritude writers did not subscribe to a unified theory for black cultural advancement. Even in the midst of its development, Negritude faced criticism from within and outside the movement for what appeared to be an essentialist outlook on black identity. Despite the critiques of Negritude, which have consistently questioned its methods for the past 65 years, it is widely recognized as a paramount literary, cultural, and sociopolitical movement.

Students from the West Indies islands of the French Antilles, who were attending universities in Paris, founded the Negritude movement. The publication of two student journals, each of which produced only a single issue, punctuated the early history of Negritude. The first, *Légitime Défense,* written by René Ménil, Jules Monnerot, and Etienne Léro in 1932, represented the more politically oriented facet of Negritude. The Marxist-Leninist theory that was popular among the French intelligentsia of the time and the surrealist circle of André Breton heavily influenced the writing of *Légitime Défense.* Addressed to their fellow students, the *Légitime Défense* group's manifesto was a shocking cry against their very own French bourgeois backgrounds and the capitalist oppression of the proletariat in the Caribbean. Reaching both West Indian and African immigrants in Paris and causing quite a stir in the Caribbean, *Légitime Défense* was one of the inspirations behind the publication of the second student journal that defined Negritude's early years. Titled *L'Etudiant noir,* and published in 1935, it contained contributions by Antilleans Aimé Césaire and Léon Damas and the Senegalese Léopold Sédar Senghor. In the pages of *L'Etudiant noir,* these three writers, who became the central voices of the Negritude movement, appealed to a Pan-African community, both locally and abroad, fractured by the tactics of assimilation used by European colonizers to assert their own cultural superiority over that of the cultures they colonized. *L'Etudiant noir* served as a foundation for the unification of colored people from diverse backgrounds, supported by the Negritude writers in the form of a search for cultural memory and a revitalization of authentic, African cultural forms. Unlike the writers of *Légitime Défense,* Senghor, Césaire, and Damas did not believe that communism or surrealism were effective tools for bringing about the changes they desired for communities of disenfranchised blacks. In contrast to the political content of *Légitime Défense*, *L'Etudiant noir* advocated social and cultural methods through which African descendants could rediscover their lost cultures and exercise their unique creative potential.

The students who authored these early formulations of Negritude found inspiration in a variety of sources indigenous to their countries of origin, as well as important texts to which they were introduced through their French educations. A number of journals and newspapers circulating in Paris in the 1930s catered to black audiences and treated issues of race in the colonial situation, such as *La Voix des Nègres, La Race nègre,* and *La Dépêche africaine.* Although these periodicals were not as inflammatory as Negritude theory intended to be, they were a model platform for the discussion of cultural conflict. The Negritude writers also admired the work of such anthropologists and ethnologists as Leo Frobenius and Maurice Delafosse, who, during the first quarter of the 20th century, began to critically explore the social and cultural achievements of precolonial African societies. Such studies posed a threat to the French program of assimilation because they asserted the existence of a unique African culture, and thus their

Léopold Sédar Senghor was a Senegalese writer and statesman, and key figure in the Negritude movement. (Sophie Bassouls/ Sygma/Corbis)

impact and content appealed to young black scholars. The work of the writer and African colonial administrator René Maran, whose novels, articles, and journal *Les Continents* elucidated the mismanagement of the French authorities in Africa and supported black cultural production, was of particular importance to an intellectual community of African descendents in Paris and was especially foundational to Senghor's theorization of symbiosis of African and European civilizations. Maran was an important figure in the promotion of the literature and social movement surrounding the Harlem Renaissance in France, through critical articles and in encouraging translations of African American works. Maran hosted W. E. B. Du Bois, Langston Hughes, Claude McKay, and others in Paris throughout the 1920s and 1930s, introducing black French scholars to the works of their American compatriots. Paulette and Jeanne Nardal's *La Revue du monde noir* similarly promoted African American writers of the Harlem Renaissance and advocated Pan-African unification around the sharing and exchange of cultural production, a goal that the Negritude writers later championed. The biting tone and sense of urgency presented by the "New Negroes" of the Harlem Renaissance particularly appealed to the Parisian students who would compose the Negritude movement. During the pre-Negritude period, the cultural exchange between African Americans and French blacks was one-sided, yielding the translation of many Harlem Renaissance writers into French, but few French texts into English. One of the most influential works translated into French was Claude McKay's novel *Banjo,* which depicted realistic race relations in the African Diaspora, attempted to dispel interracial prejudices propagated by colonial hegemony, and sought to reconcile the supposed distinction between primitive and civilized societies. McKay's work was a common inspiration for the varied foundations of Negritude in Nardal's revue, *Légitime Défense,* as well as the writings of Césaire, Damas, and Senghor.

Although the Negritude movement gained considerable momentum in 1930s Paris through the activities of the West Indian students, the writings of its major figures did not reach a wider French audience until the late 1940s. In many cases, the promotion of Negritude relied on the elite French intellectual community to embrace its outpouring and support its publication. Damas's seminal 1937 book of poems, *Pigments,* was the notable exception, although it still carried, in the form of a preface, the stamp of approval of the surrealist author Robert Desnos. Césaire's *Cahier d'un retour au pays natal,* the most highly regarded work of Negritude poetry, did not appear in a full edition until 1947, with the endorsement of André Breton. In 1948, Senghor published two books of his own poetry, *Hosties noires* and *Chants d'ombre,* in addition to an anthology of French-language black poetry, prefaced by the philosopher Jean-Paul Sartre's controversial essay "Orphée noir." Negritude appealed to the postwar French literati because it shared in common with European modernism sentiments of alienation, fragmentation, and a distrust of enlightenment philosophy and inherited cultural norms. Negritude's perceived link to primitive expression also reinforced a classic theme of modernism, which sought to expose cultural difference and posit a universal primitivism at the heart of European culture. Another reason for the postponed reception of the Negritude writers was the climate of interwar France. It was not until after World War II that the French colonial administration and the public at large were ready to start accepting decolonization. Black voices began to be heard after the war, not because they were previously silent, but because the world was finally ready to listen to them.

Aside from the initial split between Negritude's politically and culturally minded camps, the three canonical Negritude theorists—Damas, Césaire, and Senghor—themselves differed in their approaches to the questions of black identity. Damas and Césaire mounted scathing, anguished critiques of slavery, colonialism, and the terminal condition of assimilation, insisting instead on an authentic black identity rooted in the West Indies and pre-colonial Africa. Assimilation amounts, for Damas, to the negation of indigenous African culture and casts whoever participates in a conspiratorial role, one guilty of the bloodshed in the name of colonial domination. Césaire hails the purportedly savage, fictively brutal tendencies ascribed to blacks over the reason and logic of Western civilization in an effort to radically combat assimilation. These racial stereotypes, readily accepted by many Westernized blacks, become ridiculous tropes in Césaire, exposing the fallacious assumptions inherent in a discourse sympathetic to assimilation. Césaire would rather embrace the negative racial stereotype imposed on him and in turn relish in a seemingly more authentic blackness that participate in a culture that dismissed and tried to eradicate his heritage. Senghor, on the other hand, had grown up in Senegal, and his poetry reflected a close tie to African roots while at the same time lamenting

a mythic, romantic vision of a lost Africa that represented both his youth and Africa's pre-colonial innocence. Senghor maintained a belief in the harmonious coexistence and integration of Western and African cultures, where each mutually benefited from the other.

The enhanced audience that Negritude writers began to receive in the late 1940s brought with it a concomitant critical eye that accounts for the relative downplay the movement has experienced ever since. The most notable critique was Sartre's dialectical, Marxist take on Negritude in his "Orphée noir," which labeled Negritude a form of "antiracist racism" that, though constituting an invaluable phase in the triumph over racial oppression, would have to eventually be superceded by a raceless worldview. Senghor would later agree with Sartre on the racism inherent in Negritude that led the writers to adopt the rhetoric of the colonizers in order to spur the black masses into a consciousness of their own state. Rather than point out how whites actively portrayed stereotypic characteristics of assimilated blacks, Negritude sought to liberate these guises that had unconsciously been internalized by blacks. By angrily and viciously affirming their authentic cultural achievements and potentials, as well as pointing out the methods through which those qualities had been systematically erased from cultural memory, the Negritude writers sought to revitalize and reestablish black culture as a worthy and natural form of production. However, the Negritude writers (Senghor in particular) are often criticized for adopting an essentialist view of black experience where, in order to unite a Pan-African community, they neglect the specific, diverse, and localized situations faced by subaltern subjects. Whatever its shortcomings, Negritude stands as an important precursor to post-colonial thought, and it is recognized today as being a vital force in the advancement of black consciousness.

See also: Harlem Renaissance; New Negro Movement

Matthew Evans Teti

Bibliography

Fabre, Michel. *From Harlem to Paris: Black American Writers in France, 1840–1980.* Urbana: University of Illinois Press, 1991.

Jack, Belinda Elizabeth. *Negritude and Literary Criticism: The History and Theory of "Negro-African" Literature in French.* Westport, CT: Greenwood Press, 1996.

Kasteloot, Lilyan. *Black Writers in French: A Literary History of Negritude.* Trans. Ellen Conroy Kennedy. Philadelphia: Temple University Press, 1974.

Kennedy, Ellen Conroy, ed. *The Negritude Poets: An Anthology of Translations from the French.* New York: Viking Press, 1975.

Michael, Colette V. *Negritude: An Annotated Bibliography.* West Cornwall, CT: Locust Hill Press, 1988.

Richardson, Michael, ed. *Refusal of the Shadow: Surrealism and the Caribbean.* Trans. Krzysztof Fijalkowski and Michael Richardson. London: Verso, 1996.

Sharpley-Whiting, T. Denean. *Negritude Women.* Minneapolis: University of Minnesota Press, 2002.

Obeah

Obeah is a sacred healing practice identified with the Caribbean and Caribbean-based communities. It is rooted in West African belief systems and characterized by the syncretism, or mixture, of African and European elements. The word "obeah" stems from the Gold Coast region of Africa, from the Ashanti word *obay-ifo* or *obeye,* for witch or wizard, which was, through the enslavement of large African populations and the subsequent imposition of British culture, anglicized into "obeah," "obiah," and "obia." In contemporary terms, Obeah is conceptually most closely linked to witchcraft; Obeah also carries with it the same myriad of misrepresentations and pejorative connotations as witchcraft. This accounts, in part, for the secretive nature of Obeah practice. The Obeah practitioner, most often called an Obeah man, Obeah woman, bush man, or bush woman, consults with an individual client in order to secure for him or her a desired effect associated with the client's real and perceived health and personal welfare. The Obeah practitioner then uses his or her knowledge of herbal and animal medicinal properties or ability to invoke ghosts of the dead and other spirits to produce the desired effect.

Obeah is often linked, or thought to be synonymous with, other African-derived religious practices of the region, specifically Vodou (often known as "Voodoo") and Santeria. Although they are all similar in terms of their African origin, syncretic manifestation, and coexistence within Caribbean cultures, they are not the same. Some differences stem from the dissimilarities in the cultures and political histories of the colonizing powers. Other differences stem from varying spiritual and stylistic preoccupations within the belief systems. Both Vodou and Santeria are practiced through community-based ceremonies characterized by group rituals, drumming, singing, and dancing. They also acknowledge a primarily fixed pantheon of deities or ancestors who guide practitioners and manifest themselves through possession. Although Vodou and Santeria priests and priestesses are trained with specialized knowledge, any believer can participate in these religious practices to some degree. On the other hand, Obeah is individualistic by nature, and practitioners are trained through a lengthy process of apprenticeship. Not everyone can practice Obeah. There is also no group ritual involved in Obeah, except in the case of Myalism, a unique form of Obeah practiced solely in Jamaica. The supernatural in Obeah are not deities who guide; rather, they are primarily spirits of the dead manifested in ghosts and nature, called on for a desired end, both good and bad. Obeah is not a religion but rather a sacred healing practice that acknowledges a spiritual belief system.

In the British imagination, Obeah has historically been the umbrella term for any African-based spiritual practice unknown to the European tradition that purports to give the black population a sense of agency or authority. Most often dismissed by the colonial power as the superstitious beliefs of backward people, the legal impositions put on Obeah speak to a more complex, ambivalent relationship to it. Since the earliest days of slavery, Obeah has in fact proven to be a source of anxiety for the British population. Its practice, as well as all the cultural practices associated with it such as drumming, was continually banned throughout the region at various moments from the 17th through 19th centuries, forcing it underground. Obeah was seen as potentially dangerous, the source of potential insurrection. Despite the individualistic nature of Obeah, the Obeah practitioner was considered a community leader with the power to incite slaves to rebellion and to poison slaveholders and their families. Two of the most notorious rebellions in Jamaica were led by those associated with Obeah. Nanny, also called Queen Mother of the Blue Mountains, or Granny Nanny, led the resistance against the British during the First Maroon War (1730–1739). She was known to be an Obeah woman. Tacky, the leader of the Easter Sunday Rebellion of 1760, claimed African royalty and aid from an Obeah man while in battle. The spirit of resistance inherent in these rebellions and others only heightened British apprehension about Obeah, which reached its peak in the late 18th century. Obeah also became a popular motif in British literature and performance at this moment. Through literature and performance, through fear and mocking, the complexities of Obeah were made more manageable for a British audience.

Further syncretized with Hindu mysticism during the post-emancipation importation of South Asian laborers to Trinidad and Guyana, Obeah has grown and changed since the end of slavery in the Caribbean. Nonetheless, in contemporary Caribbean society and Caribbean communities throughout the world, Obeah remains an underground practice that captures the popular imagination. It is a standard motif in literature, art, and music. Artists such as Nina Simone, the Mighty Sparrow, Jamaica Kincaid, and Jean Rhys have all employed the motif of Obeah at some point in their work. For most of these artists, Obeah symbolizes an alternative to Western understandings about the world. Obeah represents a resistance to oppression and an insistence on African-based notions of personal and political autonomy.

See also: Conjure; Coromantee; Igbo; Slave Religion

Renée M. Baron

Bibliography

Fernandez Olmos, Margarite, and Lizabeth Paravisini-Gebert. *Creole Religion of the Caribbean: An Introduction from Vodou and Santeria to Obeah and Espiritismo.* New York: New York University Press, 2003.

Richardson, Alan. "Romantic Vodoo: Obeah and British Culture, 1979–1807." In *Sacred Possessions: Vodou, Santeria, Obeah, and the Caribbean,* ed. Margarite Fernandez Olmos and Lizabeth Paravisini-Gebert. New Brunswick, NJ: Rutgers University Press, 1997.

Octoroon

Sexual activity among Euro-Americans, Native Americans, and enslaved and free African Americans led to children of "mixed" parentage. Observers, particularly in the dominant culture, created legal and social categories into which they placed these individuals. More than a dozen terms existed; a few become standardized in the United States: "mulatto" for someone with one black and one white parent, "quadroon" for someone with one black and three white grandparents, and "octoroon" for an individual with seven white great-grandparents and one black great-grandparent.

"Octoroons" were assumed to physically resemble stereotypical white Americans so closely that few observers would ascribe to them an African American identity. Especially in the pre–and post–Civil War period, but throughout U.S. cultural history, white and African American writers and filmmakers have produced works based on the supposed condition of life for octoroons. When the protagonist is a male, this literature may explore the ways in which "passing for white" could lead to significant economic and other benefits. More commonly, the protagonist is a "tragic octoroon," a young woman who at first may not even know her lineage. Some accident or happenstance uncovers her parentage, and the heroine is faced with new circumstances—she might be enslaved or lose her inheritance or her fiancé or, especially in post-slavery material, face issues of discrimination and questions of self-identity. In many cases, the ending is tragic: suicide, murder, or a sudden illness ends the octoroon's life. Occasionally, even in pre–Civil War works, there is a happier ending—in *Caste* (1856) the "white" hero does not recoil from the news of his beloved's ancestry, and they leave the United States for a happier married life in France.

In both popular culture and serious literature, the octoroon has been a useful construction through which society can explore racial attitudes and experiences. In real life, those who were defined as octoroons sometimes defined themselves as "white" and sometimes as "black" and today might define themselves as "multiracial."

See also: Amalgamation; Miscegenation; Mulatto; Quadroon

JoAnn E. Castagna

Bibliography

O'Toole, James M. *Passing for White: Race, Religion, and the Healy Family, 1820–1920.* Amherst: University of Massachusetts Press, 2002.

Pike, Mary Hayden Green. *Caste: A Story of Republican Equality.* Boston: Phillips, Sampson, 1856.

Rothman, Joshua D. *Notorious in the Neighborhood: Sex and Families across the Color Line in Virginia, 1787–1861.* Chapel Hill: University of North Carolina Press, 2003.

Sollors, Werner. *Neither Black or White Yet Both: Thematic Explorations of Interracial Literature.* New York: Oxford University Press, 1997.

Williamson, Joel. *New People: Miscegenation and Mulattoes in the United States.* New York: Free Press, ca. 1980.

Zanger, Jules. "The 'Tragic Octoroon' In Pre-Civil War Fiction." *American Quarterly* 18, no. 1 (Spring 1966):63–70.

Parker, Charlie

Charles Christopher "Bird" Parker Jr. (1920–1955), born in Kansas City, Missouri, and known also by the nicknames

"Yardbird" and "Yard," was a jazz saxophonist, composer, and leader in the development of bebop, a radical movement in jazz away from the popular, orchestrated swing music of big bands to smaller ensembles that relied more on improvisation and complicated, rapidly played melodies and rhythms. Parker's distinctive, influential approach to music took shape during the 1940s and 1950s, when he, along with such musicians as Thelonius Monk, Bud Powell, Kenny Clarke, Miles Davis, Charles Mingus, Max Roach, and Dizzy Gillespie, revolutionized jazz music and challenged the sensibilities of what was acceptable musically and socially in the mid-20th century. Parker and the other bebop innovators directed jazz music away from the realm of entertainment and into the arena of cultural, political, and social critique and "high art" to voice a pro-black, race-conscious perspective on the world and present a complex, sophisticated art equal to or better than any of the great European artistic creations. The bebop revolution, with Parker at the helm, sought to disrupt the status quo, musically and intellectually, to reprogram jazz and reestablish African American influence and presence in jazz, and to challenge the way big-band jazz was being appropriated by white musicians and protest the ways the older swing-era jazz was losing its African American "voice" by accommodating to white audiences.

Charles and Addie Parker's only child, Charlie Parker, began playing saxophone in 1931, at the age of 11. By the time he was a teenager, Parker was playing sax in the high school band and immersing himself in the thriving local musical scene of Kansas City. By 1935, he was gigging around town with a number of jazz and blues ensembles and, at the same time, taking in the music of Count Basie (as well as other talented, well-established jazz groups playing around Kansas City) and learning various techniques and ideas from Buster Smith. He married his first wife, Rebecca Ruffin, in 1936. And in 1938, Parker joined the pianist Jay McShann's group and began to tour across the United States. After playing in Chicago and New York and throughout the southwestern United States with McShann, Parker moved to New York in 1939, where he took odd jobs to support himself; participated in jam sessions with other African American musicians at Monroe's Playhouse, Minton's Playhouse, and other "uptown" African American clubs; and continued to perform and record on and off with McShann.

In 1942, Parker left McShann to play with Earl Hines, and by 1945, he was leading his own band and collaborating

with Dizzy Gillespie, Miles Davis, Thelonius Monk, and other up-and-coming bebop musicians. In the middle of this period, in 1943, Parker married his second wife, Geraldine Scott. In 1945, Parker went on the road with Gillespie, hoping to make something happen in California. But the project went sour, the band broke up, and all the musicians headed back to New York, except for Parker, who decided to stay on the West Coast. While living in Los Angles, Parker began to use heroin and quickly became addicted. In 1946, shortly after recording "Lover Man" for the Dial record label, Parker was committed to Camarillo State Hospital following an alcohol- and drug-related "nervous breakdown." After his release from the hospital in 1947 and return to New York, Charlie Parker was able to stay clean for only a short period of time, a period that, some claim, facilitated his best playing and most solid recordings.

During what might be considered the high point of his musical career, the years 1947–1951, Charlie Parker, by all accounts, was playing at his best and recording his most memorable work. In 1947, Parker released *Yardbird Suite,* a group of recordings that included a number of different lineups of musicians, including the legendary Charlie Parker Quintet he formed with such jazz powerhouses as Max Roach, Tommy Potter, Duke Jordan, and Miles Davis. In addition to his quintet, Parker formed several other ensembles that also appear on the record: the Charlie Parker Septet, the Charlie Parker Quartet, Charlie Parker's New Stars, Charlie Parker's All Stars, and Charlie Parker's Re-Boppers. Parker married his third wife, Doris Snyder, in 1948, and then married his final wife, Chan Richards, in 1950. Parker fathered five children, two with Richards and three in his other marriages. In 1949–1950, Parker traveled to Europe to perform and was well received. Back home in the United States, Parker continued to record and play venues throughout New York. But in 1951, Parker's cabaret license was revoked due to a drug-related issue, banning him from seeking employment at nightclubs around town. From 1952 to 1953, Parker struggled with unemployment, which likely contributed to his excessive drug and alcohol use and mental illness. Nevertheless, he was still able to produce valuable music during this period.

In 1953, the same year his license was reinstated, Parker, along with Max Roach, Bud Powell, Charles Mingus, and Dizzy Gillespie, was invited to perform at Massey Hall in Toronto, Canada. This performance recorded by Mingus, *Jazz at Massey Hall,* has been described as one of the best live jazz recordings ever made. Although Parker was still generating his musical genius in recordings and performances such as that at Massey Hall, he was in poor health, and in 1955, Parker died from a bleeding ulcer and pneumonia, complications no doubt related to hard living. According to musicians and jazz critics alike, Charlie Parker is considered to be one of only a few true innovators in jazz and the key player and guiding force in the bebop revolution of jazz music. Parker's music is required learning for any aspiring jazz musician, and his role as a tragic hero is a lesson for anyone interested in the history of jazz.

See also: Bebop; Black Folk Culture; Jazz

Sean Elias

Bibliography

Giddens, Gary. *Celebrating Bird: The Triumph of Charlie Parker.* New York: De Capo Press, 1998.

Russell, Ross. *Bird Lives! The High Life and Hard Times of Charlie (Yardbird) Parker.* New York: Charter House, 1973.

Woideck, Carl. *Charlie Parker: His Music and Life.* Ann Arbor: University of Michigan Press, 1996.

Pinkster Festival

Pinkster is the name that the Dutch gave to the holiday known as Pentecost, a holiday that developed into an influential African American festival in the 17th and 18th centuries. Pentecost refers to the seventh Sunday after Easter (the day commemorating the resurrection of Jesus Christ), when the apostles received the gift of the Holy Spirit. Among medieval and early modern Europeans, the day of Pentecost (Whit Sunday) and the season of its celebration (Whitsuntide) constituted an important part of popular Christianity, marked by a variety of festivities.

In the 17th century, Dutch immigrants came to North America to settle the New Netherland colony, the area from Delaware Bay to the Connecticut River that comprises present-day New York, New Jersey, Connecticut, and Massachusetts. The Dutch émigrés brought with them the religious and secular celebrations of their homeland. Pinkster emerged as the dominant public holiday, where settlers gathered in town squares and the countryside to celebrate Pentecost in festival. Interestingly, Pinkster transformed from a religious, European celebration to a secular festival

characterized by West African–style music, dance, and pageantry, featuring an African "king" who presided over the revelry. The emergence of the Pinkster celebration as a predominantly African American festival in character attests to the ability of enslaved Africans to syncretize various West African cultural forms with those of Europeans—in this case the culture of the Dutch colonists—to invent tradition under the oppressive strictures of slavery.

In 1609, the Dutch sent English sea captain Henry Hudson to explore North America in search of the Northwest Passage. Hudson explored Delaware Bay and the river that would later bear his name. He made contact with the Mohawk branch of the Iroquois Nation and with their help established a lucrative fur trade. The trade facilitated the immigration of Dutch men and eventually the founding of a colony under the control of the Dutch West India Company.

The Dutch West India Company, however, did not relegate its activities to fur trading. As early as 1596, the Dutch participated in the trading and enslaving of Africans. Yet it was not until the Dutch owned several colonies in the Americas (i.e., the Netherland Antilles, Virgin Islands, Tobago, Suriname, Guyana, and parts of Brazil and Chile) that slave trading represented a significant portion of the Dutch Atlantic economy. All of these colonies required a constant labor source to maximize profits for the settlers, company, and Dutch empire—namely slaves. New Netherland (New Amsterdam) did not exempt itself from trafficking in the slave trade and utilizing slave labor in Albany (Fort Orange), the Hudson Valley, Long Island, East New Jersey, and Manhattan (New York City). The importation of enslaved Africans directly from Africa, as well as from South America and the Caribbean, altered the cultural map of Dutch North America—most evidently in public celebrations such as Pinkster.

When the Dutch lost control of their mainland North American colony to the British in 1664, slavery had already taken root in New England and the Middle Colonies. Although now populated with predominantly British settlers, Dutch families and Africans continued to observe Pinkster in the region. In the mid-18th century, the African-born population in New York increased significantly, coinciding with their participation in Pinkster. As dramatized by the writer James Fenimore Cooper in his novels *Spy* (1823) and *Satanstoe* (1845), African Americans dominated "pinkster frolics" in New York by the early 19th century.

An 1803 description of the Pinkster festival celebrated in Albany, New York, proves instructive in revealing the African transformation of a Dutch holiday into a distinctly African American cultural product. According to contemporaneous reports, African Americans patrolled the streets of Albany the week before Pinkster, during which time residents could hear the beating of drums. This activity coupled with the encampment of Pinkster Hill by enslaved Africans signaled the advent of Pinkster. On the actual day of the festival, the Monday after Pinkster, residents (both black and white) of the city and the surrounding countryside gathered at the hill to witness and participate in the festival. The white audience amounted to spectators who came to watch the "Negroes" frolic. However, the black onlookers were more often than not active participants in the festivities.

The Africans altered the hill, a site where public hangings took place, by constructing arbors of bushes and branches and adorned with azaleas (also known as the Pinkster Blummachee) in the form of an amphitheatre. The use of bushes to construct these coverings harkened back to West African cultural practices. In the arbors revelers could find a variety of foodstuffs and spirits. The celebration included sports, games, and dancing. The African king, referred to as the "captain-general and commander in chief of the pinkster boys," presided over the events. As a rule, the king had to be African-born, and he usually traced his lineage back to one of the ethnic groups on the so-called Guinea Coast—the west coastal region of Africa from present-day Sierra Leone to Benin. The most famous king was King Charles (aka King Charley or Carolus Africanus Rex).

King Charles, like his African subjects, dressed in a manner that set him apart from the white revelers. The king wore a flamboyant outfit: a British brigadier's red jacket of ankle-length, trimmed with gold lace; yellow buckskins; blue stockings; and black shoes with gleaming silver buckles. A hat, also trimmed with gold lace, complemented the ensemble. The African participants wore vibrantly colored cloths emblematic of their African heritages. Although King Charles wore European-style clothing in mockery of the defeated British, his identity as an African was unquestionable to the active and passive participants. Similarly, the clothing of the African-descended population bespoke their connection to the land of their ancestors.

It was not simply the raiment of the Africans that reflected the transformation of the Dutch holiday, but the content of the celebration as well. Three central components of African American culture—songs, oration, and dance—infused the fête. Orators and songstresses performed in a variety of African languages, of which the white audience would have had little to no knowledge. Such practices revealed not only the polyglot nature of the African-descended population but also the insular messages of the songs and speeches. The lyrics and words were meant to be understood by those in the black community with cultural memories of West Africa. In addition to the oral tradition, the somatic or bodily performance in dance reflected the African provenance of the festival. Most noted by spectators was the "Toto" or "Guinea dance" characterized by gesticulations alien to the European and white colonial dance forms. Criticized by whites as either "lewd" or "indecent," this dance unabashedly proclaimed the enslaved Africans' desire to tap into their African roots. Thus, the dance itself was an act of resistance to white attempts to diffuse and negate African cultural retentions. Clothing, dance, song, speech, material culture, food—all affirmed the African-derived nature of the Pinkster experience.

On the eve of the Albany Common Council's decision to ban the Pinkster festival in 1811, Africans continued to celebrate the holiday according to their own dictates. Although the festivities themselves became increasingly commercialized and child-oriented (in terms of audience), the content of the performances changed little. Although white children and their parents may have interpreted the African king as an Uncle Remus figure (the wise storyteller) for their own amusement, the African American population revered him as an important figure in their community. The secularization of Pinkster, though perhaps viewed as blasphemous or at best a championing of a world turned upside down, allowed blacks to create their own cultural space and tradition in New York. It was this exercising of black autonomy that alarmed the council most, despite white protestations that the festival promoted immorality, which led to the dismantling of Pinkster celebrations in the city. As in Albany, by the 1820s, Pinkster had disappeared from the African American cultural landscape in the North. This celebration was supplanted by abolition parades and General Training Day (the parade of black Revolutionary War veterans).

Scholars continue to debate to what extent African cultural patterns influenced the formation of African American culture. Analyses of Pinkster are not exempt from the controversy over retention, syncretism, and borrowing in the African American tradition. Clearly Pinkster had its roots in Dutch culture, but through the process of cultural contact, it ceased to be something purely "Dutch." Indeed, the absence of whites in performance roles and the relegation to them as spectators signaled the processes by which whites slowly acculturated to African American ritual. It is not clear why or how the African king emerged as the symbolic figure of the Pinkster boys. However, historic evidence suggests that African determination rather than Dutch colonial paternalism was responsible for the reinvention of Pinkster as an African American celebration.

See also: Dutch New Netherland; Middle Colonies

Jeannette Eileen Jones

Bibliography

Emmer, Pieter C. "The History of the Dutch Slave Trade, A Bibliographical Survey." *The Journal of Economic History* 32 (1972):728–47.

Fabre, Geneviève. "Pinkster Festival, 1776–1811: An African-American Celebration." In *Feasts and Celebrations in North American Ethnic Communities,* ed. Ramón A. Gutiérrez and Geneviève Fabre. Albuquerque: University of New Mexico Press, 1995.

Hill, Patricia Liggins. *Call & Response: The Riverside Anthology of the African American Literary Tradition.* Boston: Houghton Mifflin, 1997.

Maultsby, Portia K. "Africanisms in Africa-American Music." In *Africanisms in American Culture,* ed. Joseph E. Holloway. Bloomington: Indiana University Press, 1990.

Stuckey, Sterling. *Going through the Storm: The Influence of African American Art in History.* New York: Oxford University Press, 1994.

Stuckey, Sterling. *Slave Culture: Nationalist Theory and the Foundations of Black America.* New York: Oxford University Press, 1987.

White, Shane. "'It Was a Proud Day': African Americans, Festivals, and Parades in the North, 1741–1834." *Journal of American History* 81 (1994):13–50.

White, Shane. "Pinkster: Afro-Dutch Syncretization in New York City and the Hudson Valley." *Journal of American Folklore* 102 (1989):68–75.

Poisonings

Throughout the history of slavery in the Americas, and especially in the 18th century, enslaved Africans drew on indigenous African, European, and Native American cultural and religious knowledge to resist the conditions of slavery through the use of poisons and other deadly substances. Victims of poisoning were not only white masters and overseers; more often, they were other enslaved people or animals. Although many poisons were made from deadly substances, such as arsenic, ground glass, or toxic plants, poisoners also sought to inflict harm by manipulating the supernatural through religious rituals and conjuring. Whether magical or material, whites and blacks used the term "poisoning" to describe a range of activities and substances designed to injure their target. One of many tools creatively used to resist enslavement, poisons were also employed by slaves to exact power, express frustration, punish wrongdoers, and wield social control.

The practice of poisoning took hold as a form of slave resistance because it proved to be an effective tool for slaves to retaliate against whites and to gain positions of power in their own communities. Though African religious and cultural practices did include the use of poisons and harmful magic, it was the particular conditions of slavery that led to poisoning's popularity. Because slaves were responsible for agriculture, livestock, and food preparation, their daily work gave them access to goods that could be poisoned or could deliver poison. Thus, rather than poison slaveholders, slaves often used poison to kill livestock. Poisoning livestock was safer than killing whites but still undermined white authority and delivered a financial blow. As the animal's caretakers, slaves could portray poisonings as sickness or epidemic. Furthermore, slaves sometimes poisoned or killed livestock when their own food supplies were meager as a way to procure meat that would be rejected by whites for fear of disease.

It is important to remember, however, that poisonings were targeted not only at those outside of the slave community. Intra-black poisonings dominate reports and illustrate the complex conditions of slavery. As with any community, tensions existed between slaves. Whether those conflicts occurred in the Americas or originated from individual or national conflicts in Africa, poisons were one of the few weapons available to slaves looking to harm or kill each other. Intra-black poisonings also occurred when individuals were perceived as threats to the slave community. Slaves, particularly domestic slaves, who were favored by masters, who gave information to whites, or who collaborated with whites were likely targets. In this way, poison-induced death or sickness was a form of social control intended to discourage slaves from cooperating with masters and eliminate individuals who were a threat. In addition, these actions undermined masters by exacting financial loss.

Though noxious substances were used throughout the Americas to harm people and animals, reports of poisonings also document a pervasive belief that Africans and natives effectively used magic and conjuring to produce sickness and death. The term "poisoning" was used just as frequently to describe these supernatural events. In some ways, the threat of supernatural harm was more unsettling to potential victims because it was quite difficult to detect or prevent the ill effects of magic. Many whites had little doubt about Africans' inherently devilish dispositions and easily believed that their slaves were able to harm them using these powers. Religious leaders, often referred to as Obeah men and women, found themselves in powerful social positions. Often individuals who had recently lived in Africa, Obeah practitioners were said to have the power to make someone invincible, cure diseases, resurrect the dead, and cause harm to anyone they wished. These religious experts possessed knowledge of poisons, whether magical or material, and offered their services through reciprocal exchange. In the slave and white communities, known Obeah practitioners were feared and revered. Whites, apprehensive of an Obeah leader's power to organize slaves in rebellion, cause harm, provide leadership, and transmit knowledge, attempted to identify and remove an Obeah man from their labor force.

Historical documents illustrate clearly that slaves used poisons; however, it is unlikely that poisonings occurred as frequently as they were reported. Living in fear of their slaves' religious and worldly powers, whites were apt to attribute sickness, death, and other destructive events to poisonings or malevolent religious activity. It was even believed that the Obeah practitioner could slowly dispense poison from afar and, therefore, mimic the natural progression of sickness. In this way, whites' obsession with poisoning was largely self-sustaining. As whites accepted and shared stories of slave revolts and poisonings, they simultaneously reinforced the power of Obeah leaders in the eyes of whites and Africans. Rumors of potential poisonings or curses could send an entire white population into panic, and in many cases, dozens of slaves were punished or killed for their alleged involvement. Some communities even passed laws mandating that slaves' quarters be searched regularly in the interest of public safety. Even as late as 1826, when reports of slave poisonings had almost disappeared, nearly 30 slaves accused of poisoning were brought to trial in Martinique, an island in the French Caribbean.

Though reports of poisonings by slaves occurred all across the Americas, they were most pronounced in the Caribbean, where slavery was particularly harsh, slaves vastly outnumbered Europeans, African cultural and religious practices survived, and contact with natives provided information about indigenous poisons. Until the end of the Atlantic slave trade in the 19th century, the Caribbean was a major economic center of the New World, and most African slaves brought into the Americas entered through Caribbean ports. As slaves were taken from the Caribbean and sold throughout the Americas, knowledge about poisons and the religious practices associated with poisonings spread. Of course, differing conditions of enslavement and slave population sizes affected the ways this knowledge was used in new environments.

Accounts of poisonings during slavery are a fascinating blend of fantasy and fact. As enslaved Africans adjusted to life in the New World, poisonings—and the threat of poisonings—were a way to exert control on a world that was profoundly uncontrollable. By disrupting operations, undermining discipline, challenging white power, and exerting agency, poisoners posed a threat that went to the foundations of colonial order. Whether used to punish whites, gain social power, or produce fear, Africans poisoned, threatened poisoning, and took credit for poisonings as a means of exerting agency and resisting enslavement. Of course, the cultural drama surrounding poisoning did not always favor slaves, given that white fears of black power led to false accusations and increased supervision, punishments, and paranoia. By the beginning of the 19th century, a decline in the Atlantic slave trade paralleled a decline in reported poisonings. As the slave trade became a domestic affair, African Americans turned toward different forms of religious and social resistance.

See also: New York Conspiracy of 1741; Pritchard, Gullah Jack; Slave Resistance

Kathleen Hladky

Bibliography

Morgan, Philip. *Slave Counterpoint: Black Culture in the Eighteenth-Century Chesapeake and Lowcountry.* Chapel Hill: University of North Carolina Press, 1998.

Rucker, Walter. "Conjure, Magic, and Power: The Influence of Afro-American Religious Practices on Slave Resistance and Rebellion." *Journal of Black Studies* 32, no. 1 (2001):84–103.

Rucker, Walter. *The River Flows On: Black Resistance, Culture, and Identity Formation in Early America.* Baton Rouge: Louisiana State University Press, 2007.

Savage, John. "Black Magic and White Terror: Slave Poisoning and Colonial Society in Early 19th Century Martinique." *Journal of Social History* 40, no. 4 (2007):635–62.

Prince Hall Masonry

The African American Masonic order known as Prince Hall Masonry was established in the United States in 1787 under a British Masonic charter and takes its name from Prince Hall, a former Boston slave who obtained his freedom around 1770. An ardent patriot, a veteran of the American Revolution, and an active abolitionist, Hall found it necessary to take an unusual route to establish this brotherhood organization for African Americans.

Hall established the first brotherhood organization for African Americans in Boston in the 1770s, under the name of the African Grand Lodge of North America. Locally, it was called the Prince Hall Masons. In 1775, he had applied to the Boston Masonic Lodge for membership and was rejected on the basis of his African ancestry. As a result, Hall petitioned a British lodge associated with British army troops then occupying Boston for membership. Hall and several other free men of color in Boston were then initiated into the Irish Army Lodge #441. Even after the American Revolution, Hall was unable to gain a full charter for the African Lodge through Masonic orders in the United States. In 1784, Hall obtained a limited license by a British order to establish African Lodge #1, with Hall as its first grand master. Hall turned to the same British order for help once again in 1787 when the British granted a full charter for the African Lodge #459, and in 1791, Hall became the provincial grand master of North America. With his new authority, Hall began to authorize black lodges in other American cities, including New York, Philadelphia, and Providence. The Prince Hall Masonic orders worked to improve personal, interpersonal, and community relationships skills—as well as to promote tolerance, charity, and improve the welfare of all.

In Boston, the African Meeting House, the African Society, and the African Lodge worked closely on social issues to better the lives of African Americans. As Prince Hall Masonry began to expand, the groups worked alongside Methodist congregations as well as other benevolent aid societies to further social causes on behalf of both free and enslaved blacks. To a great extent, the causes reflected those that their founder, Prince Hall, had begun to fight upon establishing his personal freedom prior to the American Revolution.

Upon becoming free, Prince Hall had become an activist almost immediately as he, along with others, petitioned the Massachusetts Colonial Legislature, urging them to end slavery in the state. His philosophy borrowed from the same rhetoric used by the founding fathers who were pushing for independence from the Crown—natural rights. In his determination to effect change, Hall established two modes of attack. The first mode involved direct activism, such as petitioning the legislature—he challenged the existing order and protested for specific change. Hall's other method employed to create change was to work through institutional development—using organizations such as the Masons, churches, and other voluntary associations.

Prince Hall used his Masonic organization to promote community-building activities. Besides speaking out against slavery and violence to blacks and promoting rights for free Africans, Hall used his position (first as "worshipful master" and later as "grand master") as a platform to fight for education for black children, citing that free people of color were taxed as were white citizens, thereby qualifying black children for public education. He eventually established a school in his own home.

By 1786, Prince Hall and his Masonic Orders began to demonstrate their support of the fledgling United States and to establish the place of free Africans within the new system. Hall went as far as offering assistance to the government in putting down Shays Rebellion. The government rejected their offer. The government also rejected Hall's petition for funding the "repatriation" of African Americans to Africa, utilizing their own government and structure once settled—one of the earliest expressions of colonization to come from a major African American leader.

By Hall's death in 1807, black Masonic orders were spread throughout cities in the Northeast and the Midwest, and many stable orders existed in the Upper South. Many African lodges were casually referred to as "Prince Hall" orders during Hall's lifetime; many groups officially changed their name in his honor after his passing. Some orders have merged into the white American Masonic structure, some still hold British charters, and many are independent organizations without an official affiliation with either country's Masonic orders.

See also: Black Fraternal Societies; Hall, Prince

Jane M. Aldrich

Bibliography

Walkes, Joseph A. *Black Square & Compass: 200 Years of Prince Hall Freemasonry.* Richmond, VA: Macoy Publishing & Masonic Supply, 1989.

Wilder, Craig. *In the Company of Black Men: The African Influence on African American Culture in New York City.* New York: New York University Press, 2002.

Pryor, Richard

Richard Pryor (1940–2005) began his comedic career with relatively race-neutral comedy modeled after his idol Bill Cosby, but he eventually brought an African American folk sensibility tinged with a sometimes foul-mouthed vulgarity to his humor. His stage act often drew on the pathos of the African American working class and the dispossessed, such as pimps, prostitutes, and winos, in an overt and unapologetic way. His comedic styling opened up African American language and customs to the American mainstream. An article in *Ebony* magazine written in 2006, said that Pryor mirrored the black condition without exploiting it and that his comedy contributed to the evolution of a true black humor in the United States (Ebony, February 2006).

Initially, his comedic style after a self-imposed exile in California's Bay Area was considered black hipster chic. However, Pryor's outrageous stage persona and unique style of looking at the world eventually exerted a lasting influence on the nation's humor and cultural life. At the time of his death from a heart attack on December 11, 2005, news outlets across the country noted that Pryor's comedy had given numerous entertainers, including Eddie Murphy, Robin Williams, Chris Rock, and Steve Martin, license to inject social commentary into their comedy, acting, or art.

Richard Franklin Lenox Thomas Pryor III was born on December 1, 1940, in Peoria, Illinois. His father, Leroy "Buck" Pryor, was a pimp; his mother, Gertrude Thomas Pryor, was a prostitute; and his grandmother who raised him, Marie Carter, was a madam who ran a brothel.

Although Pryor's parents were not married when Richard was born, they did marry briefly three years later, but from an early age, he was left in the care and custody of his father's mother at the brothel on north Washington Street. The *Official Biography of Richard Pryor* says that at age six, he was raped by a teenage neighbor and was later molested by a Catholic priest during catechism. His home life was not much better. He was later molested again as a teenager by one of the brothel's customers and allegedly witnessed his mother performing sexual acts for money with the town's mayor. Many of those closest to him attribute his legendary problems with booze, sex, and alcohol to his inability to escape the traumas of his early life.

Bishetta D. Merrit says in her profile of Pryor for the *Museum of Broadcast Communications* that his public performing career began in high school when a teacher convinced him to stop cutting and disrupting classes by giving him the opportunity to perform his comedy routine once a week for his classmates. Later, Pryor dropped out of high

Comedian Richard Pryor performs at the Hollywood Bowl on September 19, 1977, in Los Angeles, California. (AP Photo/Lennox McLendon)

school and enlisted in the army, and when he was dishonorably discharged for allegedly stabbing another soldier in a fight, he began playing in small strip and jazz clubs along the infamous "chittlin' circuit" throughout the Midwest. The earlier phases of his notoriety found him playing clubs in New York as the opening act for Bob Dylan and Richie Havens among others, but his routines did not contain the razor's-edge social commentary for which he would later become famous. It was not until after a two-year hiatus spent in exile in the politically charged atmosphere of Berkeley, California, hanging out with such iconic figures as Ishmael Reed and Huey P. Newton, reading the *Autobiography of Malcolm X,* and observing people in bars and clubs and on street corners, that he returned to the stage.

This new Pryor no longer mimicked the clean-cut Cosby's image. In his *Washington Post* obituary, Mel Watkins says that Pryor's body language conveyed the ambivalence—at once belligerent and defensive—of the African American male's provisional stance in society. His monologues evoked the passions and foibles of all segments of black society, including working-class, churchgoing people and prostitutes, pimps, and hustlers. He began to create side-splitting comedy out of blatant racism, sex, and his bizarre upbringing in a house of prostitution in his native Peoria, Illinois.

Eventually, his popularity skyrocketed, and his career as a stand-up comedian expanded to that of television and film star. Pryor appeared in, wrote, or directed a variety of films, including the following: *The Busy Body* (1967), *Wild in the Streets* (1968), *The Green Berets* (1968), *Lady Sings the Blues* (1972), *Car Wash* (1977), *Superman* (1983), and *Brewster's Millions* (1985). Throughout his career, he won five Grammy Awards and one Emmy. In 1998, he was awarded the Kennedy Center's Mark Twain Prize for American Humor.

On December 11, 2005, Richard Pryor died after a lengthy battle against multiple sclerosis.

See also: Cosby, Bill; Poitier, Sidney

Raymond Janifer

Bibliography

Acham, Christine. *Revolution Televised: Prime Time and the Struggle for Black Power.* Minneapolis: University of Minnesota Press, 2004.

Merrit, Bishetta. "Pryor, Richard." *The Museum of Broadcast Communications.* February 20, 2009, http://www.museum.tv/archives/etv/.

Pryor, Richard. The Official Biography of Richard Pryor. Accessed February 20, 2009. http://www.richardpryor.com.

Pryor, Richard. *Pryor Convictions: And Other Life Sentences.* New York: Pantheon Books, 1997.

Watkins, Mel. "Richard Pryor, Iconoclastic Comedian, Dies at 65." *Washington Post* December 11, 2005.

Williams, John A., and Dennis A. Williams. *If I Stop, I'll Die: The Comedy and Tragedy of Richard Pryor.* New York: Thunder's Mouth Press, 2006.

Quadroon

The word "quadroon" comes from the Spanish word *cuarteron,* which was a racial category given to people with one-quarter, or one *cuarto,* of black ancestry. With the rise of the Atlantic slave trade during the 16th and 17th centuries, many people of African and European descent engaged in sexual acts that produced mulatto offspring, or children of mixed race. Most European lawmakers, in both Africa and North America, looked down on such activities as "shameful" and "unnatural." Ultimately, colonial leaders enacted miscegenation laws that forbade or limited sexual interaction and marriage between people of different races. Many of these laws remained intact into the 20th century.

Although people of European and African descent sometimes chose to develop unions, more often, white slaveholders forcibly engaged in sexual intercourse with enslaved women. This combination of factors produced a diverse spectrum of racial categories and skin colors. Many "free people of color," as they came to be known, established communities in urban areas in both the North and the South. Free people of color might be quadroons, octoroons (one-eighth black), or any other percentage of blackness, but they were almost always considered black by society's standards. After the American Revolution, many people of European descent, particularly in the South, began to equate whiteness with freedom and blackness with slavery. Though it was sometimes possible for people of African descent to "pass" as white, the emerging tensions between the North and South compelled many white slaveholders to insist on a strict legal separation based on race.

After the Civil War and Reconstruction, emancipated people of African descent still experienced the burden of racial categorization. Segregation laws were the most poignant example of the U.S. government's unwillingness or inability to treat people of all races with equal consideration. Even after the Civil Rights movement, racial categories such as "quadroon" still shape the way some people think about human differences.

See also: Amalgamation; Miscegenation

Michael Pasquier

Bibliography

Berlin, Ira. *Many Thousands Gone: The First Two Centuries of Slavery in North America.* Cambridge, MA: Belknap Press of Harvard University Press, 1998.

Ragtime

Ragtime is a popular musical genre originated by African Americans that emerged in the United States during the late 19th century. One set of the genre's roots resides in the African American work songs and spirituals from the American South. Ragtime was first prominent during the years 1897–1919 and was notably associated with composer Scott Joplin. The genre of ragtime was considered by some to be an early form of jazz, and although also considered by many to be primarily composed for the piano (i.e., instrumental, ragtime also existed in vocal form.

Classic piano ragtime compositions were composed mostly of three or four themes. Each theme was conceived to be a complete, independent, 16-measure musical entity, with the measures of each theme combined and recombined in order to produce sound. Melodically and structurally, ragtime compositions resemble the march. In addition to the march, the foxtrot, cakewalk, "coon-song," and various African rhythms have each served as a source for early ragtime compositions.

Most ragtime compositions were distinguished by their elaborate syncopated rhythms. The act of musical syncopation involves placing an emphasis on a usually unstressed beat. In ragtime music, primarily delaying or advancing a melodic note accomplishes syncopation. The important types of syncopations within ragtime music are "tied," "untied," and "augmented." Syncopation is an enduring, distinctive element of ragtime music, but syncopation is by no means the primary defining element. Although there are many ragtime compositions that do not contain syncopated rhythms, syncopation and syncopated rhythms are defining features of African American music.

The syncopation of ragtime music served as a starting point for some who were curious of the origin of the word "ragtime." The elaborate syncopated rhythms led some to believe that the word "ragtime" is descriptive of the type of physical reaction one had to the elaborate rhythms. Others proposed that the word "rag" was descriptive of the clothing of its performers, with "rag-time" denoting the fact that this music was played by African Americans individuals and bands from the American South. Consequently, the active use and interpretation of the word "ragtime" implied that it was time for the "ragged" entertainment of African American ragtime bands. What is certain, however, is that the dynamic yet unclear origins of the word reflected the African American social, cultural, political, and economic reality of the times from which it emerged.

The popularity of ragtime music in a time of intense American racism was cause for concern to some. Some critics of ragtime asserted that the music appealed to the worst of human tastes because the content of the early tunes reflected the African American people as racialized social products of the times. Ragtime was thus viewed as an extension of the "coon song" and thus was not appealing to mainstream white America because it allegedly represented a musical production of the lowest cultural kind.

Being an African American invention, ragtime music was further derogated because of that fact alone. Further, piano ragtime music was derogated because it first found life in social establishments not very respected by mainstream white America, further providing impetus for criticism of the genre as a legitimate art form. Ragtime music, however, would enjoy sustained popularity for this very reason.

The sustained popularity of ragtime was partly due to the creative ways in which African Americans allowed the genre to expand and become inclusive. African Americans composed and performed ragtime, but they also allowed other racial groups and women to compose and perform their art, allowing for a sustained longevity of the complex and elaborate art form in various derivations.

Ragtime music was innovative, complex, rich, and textured; it was a sophisticated way through which African Americans critiqued the social, political, and economic realities of the times. Ragtime provided a medium through which African Americans could communicate to each other and to the world; ragtime communicated ideas about liberty, freedom, love, community, and family. Its elaborate melodic and compositional makeup stood as testament to the ingenuity of African Americans; it stood as a reminder of eternal African American inner strength, resilience, persistence, and genius.

Ragtime music has endured over the years and most recently has experienced a renewed scholarly interest with the African American musical community. Some important ragtime compositions include "Harlem Rag," "Frog Legs Rag," "Sunflower Slow Drag," and "Maple Leaf Rag." *See also:* Black Folk Culture; Jazz

Bruce Ormond Grant

Bibliography

Berlin, Edward A. *King of Ragtime: Scott Joplin and His Era.* New York: Oxford University Press, 1994.

Berlin, Edward A. *Ragtime: A Musical and Cultural History.* Berkeley: University of California Press, 1980.

Gracyk, Tim, and Frank Hoffmann. *Popular American Recording Pioneers, 1895–1925.* New York: Haworth Press, 2000.

Hasse, John E. "Ragtime from the Top." In *Ragtime: Its History, Composers and Music,* ed. John E. Hasse. New York: Schirmer Books, 1985.

Jasen, David A., and Jay Tichenor. *Rags and Ragtime: A Musical History.* New York: Dover Publications, 1978.

Ring Shout

The ring shout is a kind of holy dance in which the participants move counterclockwise in a circle, hardly lifting their feet from the floor, knees bent, leaning slightly forward from the hips, and making movements expressive of the lyrics sung by a "leader" and "basers," or chorus, in call-and-response fashion, propelled by cross-rhythms produced by foot stomping, hand clapping, and often a "sticker," a person who beats a broom handle or other stick on the wood floor. The shout usually begins slowly and gradually builds in intensity. Sometimes a shout might last an hour or more and a shout service for hours. Drums, common to the ring dances of Africa and elsewhere in the African Diaspora, were usually absent from the North American ring shout, their use by slaves having been forbidden. The persistence and complexity of the African rhythmic base was maintained through these other percussive techniques.

Once found throughout the slave states, the shout survived longest along the rice coast stretching from the North Carolina–South Carolina border to north Florida. This was an area with a greater concentration of African Americans and one in which a number of the slaves at the time of emancipation were African-born. It was thought that the ring shout had completely disappeared in North America until 1980, when a surviving shout group was discovered in coastal Georgia. This group organized themselves as the McIntosh County Shouters for festival performances. The McIntosh County Shouters are documented in sound recordings, videos, and a scholarly book.

Slave owners sometimes tolerated but often were unaware of the shouts. Many clergy, black and white, disapproved of this mode of worship that was of such obvious African origin; they often referred to the shout as "heathenish" or "barbaric." For these reasons, slaves, and later freed blacks, often performed the shout ritual in secrecy. Though syncretized with Christian themes and motifs, the ring shout stemmed from sacred dance and ritual of West Africa—its counterpart still to be commonly found in Jamaican Afro-Christian cults, in Haitian Voodoo, and throughout the Afro-Caribbean culture area.

There exist a few descriptions of the shout made by white observers prior to emancipation, but most descriptions of the shout are postbellum, including numerous ones collected in the Federal Writers' Project ex-slave narratives. According to Dena Epstein, the first known description of the ring shout dates from 1845—Sir Charles Lyell's description of slaves in coastal Georgia. The earliest use (1860) of the term "shout" was in an unidentified Englishman's description from Beaufort, South Carolina. During Reconstruction, descriptions of the shout appeared more frequently.

In the 20th century, Robert W. Gordon published important descriptions of the shout in Georgia (1927) and South Carolina (1931). New Jersey native Lydia Parrish collected a number of shout songs in coastal Georgia in the decades prior to World War II, publishing them with descriptions and photographs of the shout in *Slave Songs of the Georgia Sea Islands* (1942). John and Alan Lomax recorded shouts as far west as Louisiana for the Library of Congress over a period of several decades. The Rosenbaums (Art and Margo Newmark) and Johann Buis published a study of the McIntosh County ring shout, complete with song texts, drawings, photographs, an ethnographic study of the shouters, and a biographic profile of their leader, Lawrence McKiver, in their essential work, *Shout Because You're Free: The African American Ring Shout Tradition in Coastal Georgia* (1998). The Rosenbaum's book includes the most detailed and complete historical overview of the shout tradition and the most extensive Bibliography.

The shout should be understood as community dance and ritual rather than in terms of the English word "shout." Of undoubted African origin, the shout as practiced by African Americans along the rice coast in the 20th century did not include actual vocalized shouting. Earlier accounts of the shout sometimes describe participants becoming possessed, shouting, and "falling out" of the circle. Rosenbaum suggested that this spirit possession was due to the influence of the Great Revival, but these instances are more likely reinterpretations of African spirit possession as is still found in the circular dancing of Afro-Caribbean religion. The term "shout" itself may have come from Africa: linguist Lorenzo Dow Turner suggested the word's origin could be found in the Arabic word *saut*—a term used to denote circular ritual movement as practiced in parts of Islamic western Africa. Rosenbaum and other 20th-century observers discovered a separate category of mostly religious-themed songs for the shout, "shout songs" or "running spirituals."

Historians such as Sterling Stuckey who have examined the shout primarily through the historical literature argue that spirituality was central to the ring dance. The ring shout has a connection to many different ring dances throughout West and West-Central Africa and can be found throughout the African Diaspora. Perhaps the most compelling spiritual connection is the ring shout's similarity to the Kongo cosmogram, which symbolizes the four major phases of the lifecycle—birth, adolescence, adulthood, and the afterlife. Thus, both the ring shout and the cosmogram were important symbols in African American culture that reflected the belief in the connection between the living and the ancestral worlds.

Because the ring shout had a distinctly African spiritual origin, the shout was typically held apart from the regular Christian worship service as a distinct activity, either after regular worship had concluded or as specially scheduled events. Participants were careful to never cross their legs because it was believed that to do so was dancing rather than shouting, of Satan rather than of God. Those who crossed their legs or danced too lasciviously were removed from the ring if not the building. The shout was also performed at funerals and on secular occasions such as corn shuckings and post-harvest celebrations, and the lyrics were not always on sacred topics, but rather sometimes on demonstrably secular topics. To apply the premises of Euro-American religious thought to African American practice forces the latter into a false dichotomy of the sacred and secular that does not exist in traditional African and African Diasporan culture. The ring as symbol of community and respect for the ancestors is of many dimensions, reflecting both sacred and profane aspects of life.

Johann S. Buis identifies the underlying rhythm of the shout as the 3+3+2 pattern—the African rhythmic pattern that is the basis of African American music, from the blues, gospel, and jazz to all that followed. The tools of Western musical analysis are insufficient not only to study the rhythmic sophistication of African and African-derived music but also to study its characteristic nuance of tone. It is in these two dimensions that the ancestral spirituality of Africa survives in the ring shout and in its musical progeny: the popular music of black America.

In New Orleans, the ring shout was used in burial rituals, and the ring was straightened out to become the second line of jazz funerals. There is also evidence of the shout's influence in bop jazz and rhythm and blues hits, such as Paul Williams's "The Hucklebuck." The emergence of funk in mid-20th century was nothing less than a full-blown revival of the ring in modern garb.

The shout has also survived in secular dance. A number of observers have mentioned the shout's influence on the minstrel shows' "walk around" and "cake walk," as well as it adaptation into the Charleston. Floyd adds to these the breakdown, buzzard lope, and slow drag of the late 19th century on through the 20th century's black bottom and lindy hop, to the line dances of the late 20th century.

See also: Kongo Cosmogram; Slave Culture; Slave Religion

Fred J. Hay

Bibliography

Epstein, Dena J. *Sinful Tunes and Spirituals*. Urbana: University of Illinois Press, 1977.

Floyd, Samuel A. *The Power of Black Music*. New York: Oxford University Press, 1995.

Floyd, Samuel A. "Ring Shout! Black Music, Black Literary Theory, and Black Historical Studies." *BMRJ* 11, no.2 (1991):267–89.

Gordon, Robert Winslow. "Negro 'Shouts' from Georgia." 1927. Reprint in *Mother Wit from the Laughing Barrel: Readings in the Interpretation of Afro-American Folklore*. Ed. Alan Dundes, 445–51. New York: Garland, 1981.

Gordon, Robert Winslow. The Robert Winslow Gordon Collection. Special Collections & University Archives, The University of Oregon, Eugene, Oregon.

Parrish, Lydia. *Slave Songs of the Georgia Sea Islands.* Athens: University of Georgia Press, 1992.

Rosenbaum, Art and Margo Newmark Rosenbaum, and Johann Buis. *Shout Because You're Free: The African American Ring Shout Tradition in Coastal Georgia.* Athens: University of Georgia Press, 1998.

Stuckey, Sterling. *Slave Culture: Nationalist Theory and the Foundations of Black America.* New York: Oxford University Press, 1987.

Rogers, Joel Augustus

Joel Augustus (J. A.) Rogers (1880–1966) was a prolific self-trained historian, photo-anthropologist, novelist, and journalist who fluently spoke and read fluently four different languages (Spanish, French, German, and Portuguese). During his lifetime, Rogers did more to popularize African, African American, and African Diaspora history than any other American scholar in the 20th century. Rogers was born on September 6, 1880, in Negril, B.W.I., Jamaica, to Samuel Rogers and Emily Johnstone. As a child growing up in Jamaica's color class-consciousness, Rogers was taught by the British ruling class that unmixed black people were inferior to them and to biracial light-skinned colored blacks. Fortunately, Rogers, a light-skinned black Jamaican, found it very hard to believe such racist sentiments.

Before immigrating to the United States, Rogers served in the British Army with the Royal Garrison Artillery at Port Royal but was discharged because of a heart murmur. Shortly after arriving in New York on July 23, 1906, Rogers experienced his first taste of American racism when he was discriminated against at a small restaurant in Times Square, something he never forgot for the rest of his life. Rogers stayed briefly in New York and Canada before relocating to Chicago on July 4, 1908. In 1909, Rogers enrolled in the Chicago Art Institute, where he studied commercial art and worked as a Pullman porter during the summers from 1909 to 1919. Rogers tried to enroll at the University of Chicago but was denied entry because he did not possess a high school diploma. The irony of Rogers being denied entry to this prestigious institution is that Zonia Baber and George B. Foster, a couple of distinguished professors, were using his self-published novel *From "Superman" to Man* (1917) in their classes. In fact, after finding out about Rogers's rejected application at the University of Chicago, Foster invited Rogers to lecture in one of his classes.

While living in Chicago, Rogers officially became a naturalized U.S. citizen on February 21, 1918. In 1921, Rogers relocated to Harlem, where he met and befriended Hubert Harrison (1883–1927), the Caribbean black radical and George Schulyer (1895–1977), journalist and satire novelist. New York and later Paris (late 1920s and various times afterward) became the two places where Rogers would live throughout his life, while doing research at important libraries, art galleries, museums, and cathedrals in America, Europe, and Africa. Even though Rogers never attained an academic degree, he was respected for his work in France and England. In 1930, he was elected to membership in the Paris Society of Anthropology, the oldest anthropological society in the world. In 1931, Rogers also gave a paper on "race mixing" at the International Congress of Anthropology in Paris, France, which was opened by President Paul Doumer (1857–1932) of the Third French Republic. To Rogers's surprise, his paper was later published in several French newspapers and the *London Times*. Roger also became a member of the American Geographical Society in 1945.

Rogers is mostly known for his historical writing on history and race, but he is rarely given credit for being an exceptional journalist. During the 1920s, Rogers became a newspaper columnist and reporter for the *Pittsburgh Courier* and the *New York Amsterdam News* and wrote many essays and commentaries for *The Messenger Magazine*. Rogers worked for the *Pittsburgh Courier* from approximately 1923 to 1966. His weekly comic column, "Your History," which began in 1934, became a medium for popularizing African and African Diaspora history to the masses of African Americans throughout America. Rogers used the "Your History" column not only to disseminate history but also to popularize prominent contemporary people of African descent. In 1962, the "Your History" column name was changed to "Facts About the Negro." Rogers also wrote social commentaries in the *Pittsburgh Courier* titled "Rogers Says" and "History Shows."

As a newspaper correspondent for the *Pittsburgh Courier,* Rogers became a household name among African Americans as an overseas newspaper correspondent. He wrote about his travels in Europe and Africa. During the late 1920s, and while living in Paris, he wrote a short-lived column titled the "Paris Pepper Pot," which covered race relations in France and how African Americans fared in Paris compared to America. The "Paris Pepper Pot" was also syndicated in the *New York Amsterdam News* and the *Chicago Defender*. In 1930, Rogers attended the coronation of Haile Selassie of Ethiopia, yet his most rewarding overseas job was going to Ethiopia in 1935 to cover the Italo-Ethiopian War (1935–1936). Through the *Pittsburgh Courier*, Rogers was the only African American to report back firsthand accounts of war activities in Ethiopia.

After leaving in Ethiopia in 1936, Rogers traveled to Geneva to attend the League of Nations hearings on the Italo-Ethiopian war and reported through the *Courier* what the Leagues' Committee of Thirteen had proposed to do about the war. A few days later, Rogers traveled to London and lectured before Sir Percy Vincent, Lord Mayor of London, and other British dignitaries about the crisis confronting the Ethiopians. After settling back in New York, Rogers became a major contributor and advisor for the Writers' Program. As a historian and journalist, one of Rogers's biggest compliments came from the American journalist and social critic H. L. Mencken, who paid Rogers $500 to publish "The Negro in Europe" in the *American Mercury* (May 1930) and who in 1945 personally praised Rogers for writing his pioneering work about black and white miscegenation, *Sex and Race*.

As a self-trained historian, Rogers did pioneering archival historical research that many scholars today would classify as African Diaspora history. Rogers's contribution to world history was so influential that, in 1954, he was presented with a gold medal at New York's Waldorf-Astoria by Ethiopia's Emperor Haile Selassie (Ras Tafari) in recognition of his contribution to the study of African history. Considering the handicaps of not having a research assistant and traveling throughout Europe, Africa, and America at his own expense without any philanthropic or institutional support, it is amazing that he accomplished as much as a scholar before he passed away in New York on March 26, 1966.
See also: African Diaspora; Harlem Renaissance; Woodson, Carter Godwin

Thabiti A. Asukile

Sources

Asukile, Thabiti A. "J. A. Rogers: The Scholarship of an Organic Intellectual." *The Black Scholar* 36, no. 2–3 (Summer–Fall 2006):35–50.

Turner, W. Burghardt. "J. A. Rogers: Portrait of an Afro-American Historian." *The Black Scholar* 6, no. 5 (1975):38–55.

Root Doctors

Root doctors, also known as rootworkers, were African American practitioners of magic and herbal medicine who appeared during the colonial and antebellum eras, partly in response to inadequate medical care and the injustices of slavery. The title "root doctor" refers to practitioners' tendency to rely heavily on roots in their treatments. Historically, there have been two types of root doctors: those who also practiced magic and those who did not. For African American magic workers, known as conjurers or hoodoo doctors, treating illnesses with roots and herbs was merely part of their repertoire. Some root doctors, however, focused on healing without engaging in other activities commonly practiced by hoodoo doctors, such as fortune-telling and making luck charms.

In actual practice, the lines between the two categories of root doctors are blurry, especially before the late 19th century, when the efforts of black educators to eradicate so-called superstition from the black community succeeded in convincing many African Americans of conjure's supposed backwardness. For example, early root doctors frequently saw their healing as a magical pursuit and relied on the aid of animistic spirits that purportedly inhabited the botanical and zoological elements that practitioners employed in their cures. The role of magic is best illustrated by the ailments that root doctors were called on to treat. Some were commonly recognized medical concerns, such as headaches or sore throats. Others, however, were clearly magical illnesses. Among the most common of the latter were reptilian inhabitants of the body, insanity brought on by curses, and locked bowels, a kind of terminal constipation.

Regardless of their acceptance or rejection of magic, root doctors possessed notable abilities to help with both physical and mental complaints. In the days before emancipation, when gaining access to medical professionals was difficult for many slaves, rootwork was a viable alternative. Among the slaves' many herbal remedies were the use of horehound to treat colds, dried watermelon seeds to expel kidney stones, and mullein for swollen joints. After the demise of slavery, rootworkers survived as a comparatively inexpensive substitute for doctors. Of course, although some of the root doctors' magic-based cures were no more medically efficacious than placebos, others have since been scientifically proven to have beneficial effects. Modern mental health care professionals have also pointed out that rootwork could act as a form of psychological therapy as well, especially for those who believed that they were victims of evil magic. Some psychiatrists and psychologists have suggested that today's health care professionals should seek out root doctors to help treat African Americans who believe they are suffering from hoodoo curses.

On the other hand, rootworkers could also be a source of maladies. As the reputed existence of magical illnesses implies, some also practiced malevolent sorcery. Many examples of slaves employing magical "poisons" to harm their masters have survived. More recently, some African Americans have considered rootwork an effective method of eliminating enemies. Thus, although root doctors could cure such ailments as reptiles in one's body and locked bowels, they might have caused them in the first place.

See also: Conjure; Hoodoo; Slave Religion

Jeffrey Elton Anderson

Bibliography

Anderson, Jeffrey Elton. *Conjure in African American Society.* Baton Rouge: Louisiana State University Press, 2007.

Fett, Sharla M. *Working Cures: Healing, Health, and Power on Southern Slave Plantations.* Chapel Hill: University of North Carolina Press, 2002.

Hurston, Zora Neale. "Hoodoo in America." *Journal of American Folklore* 44 (1931):318–417.

Mitchell, Faith. *Hoodoo Medicine: Gullah Herbal Remedies.* Columbia, SC: Summerhouse Press, 1999.

Salt-Water Negroes

"Salt-water Negroes" is a derogatory term assigned to slaves who were brought from Africa, across the Atlantic Ocean, during the Atlantic slave trade. They were given this term to differentiate them from the American-born slaves. The "salt-water" part of the phrase is derived from the salty nature of the Atlantic Ocean waters, and the term was probably used by both white slave owners and American-born slaves. Some sources claim that American-born slaves used this term because they saw themselves as better than the newcomers, given that they were familiar with the functioning of the American system. However, other scholars have argued that such terminology was mainly a creation of the white slave owners, and if it was ever adopted by the slaves, it likely did not carry the same connotation. Further, they argue that American-born slaves held newcomers in high esteem because they represented the connection with

Africa, their common homeland, which those born in the Americas had never seen.

Regardless, most scholars agree that African-born slaves rejuvenated African American cultures in the New World and prevented Africa from fading from the minds of enslaved Africans. Moreover, they note that African-born slaves usually played a significant role in revolts and conspiracies, a fact that most white slave owners recognized as well. For example, after the eruption of the Stono rebellion in 1739, colonial officials deemed it prudent to reduce the numbers of Africans in the colony.

The influx of "salt-water" slaves did not stop until after the ban on the slave trade was put in place in 1808. Meanwhile, their influx contributed greatly to the demographic pattern of slaves in the New World. This continuous influx gave the African Diaspora its distinctive feel and influenced the formation of African American identity.

See also: Atlantic Slave Trade

Karen W. Ngonya

Bibliography

Mullin, Michael. *African in America: Slave Acculturation and Resistance in the American South and the British Caribbean 1736–1831.* Urbana: University of Illinois Press, 1994.

Pearson A. Edward, ed. *Designs against Charleston, the Trial Record of the Denmark Vesey Slave Conspiracy of 1822.* Chapel Hill: University of North Carolina Press, 1999.

Smallwood, Stephanie E. *Saltwater Slavery: A Middle Passage from Africa to American Diaspora.* Cambridge, MA: Harvard University Press, 2007.

Thornton, John. *Africa and Africans in the Making of the Atlantic World, 1400–1800.* Cambridge: Cambridge University Press, 1992.

Young, Jason. *Rituals of Resistance: African Atlantic Religion in Kongo and the Lowcountry South in the Era of Slavery.* Baton Rouge: Louisiana State University Press, 2007.

Sambo

"Sambo" is a derogatory racial stereotype that ridicules and belittles African Americans; it was created by the slave-owning plantocracy of the antebellum South to characterize the typical slave and, thereby, justify the institution of slavery. Sambo was a caricature rather than an apt characterization; it portrayed the slave as happy-go-lucky, docile, childish, and dependent on and loyal to his master, yet lazy and irresponsible. The happy-go-lucky, docile, and loyal aspects of this highly distorted image suggested that slaves were contented with their lot. Sambo's alleged child-like, dependent, lazy, and irresponsible traits were invoked by the plantocracy to justify the bondage of infantile blacks to paternalistic white masters. In sharp contrast to the feared and hated brute or savage—a rival stereotype of the violent and sexually threatening black male that emerged in the Reconstruction era—the silly-acting Sambo was viewed as a lovable, if sometimes exasperating, character. Even as rival black stereotypes emerged, the Sambo stereotype persisted in Southern folklore as an example of black inferiority.

The Sambo stereotype crossed -over into mainstream American culture with the publication, in 1898, of Helen Bannerman's illustrated children's book, *The Story of Little Black Sambo*. Sambo (often depicted as a tattered, grinning, watermelon-eating fool) and other "darky" images, such as the Coon, Mammy, Uncle, and Pickanniny, became mascots of the white supremacist South. These caricatures appeared ubiquitously on everyday items—for example, sugar bowls, saltshakers and other kitchen utensils, postcards, lawn statuettes, and business logos. They were symbols that reinforced white dominance and black subordination during the Jim Crow era. The offensive practice of publicly displaying such caricatures in the South continued into the late 20th century, gradually diminishing as a result of black protest. Many African Americans now collect such items as memorabilia of a painful yet never-to-be-forgotten past.

Boskin traces the etymology of the name Sambo either to the West African Mende and Vai languages, where the word means "shameful" or "disgraced," or to Hispanic and Portuguese sources, where *zambo* means "bow-legged" or "knock-kneed" and denotes a person who resembles a monkey. Boskin notes that Sambo, as a proper name given to slaves, appears in records as early as the 1600s. It gained increasing popularity in the 1700s and 1800s, eventually becoming a nickname used by whites to designate any anonymous slave. Ultimately, Sambo became a generalized racial slur that was hurled at any African American.

Sambo made a dramatic appearance in the hallowed halls of academia when the historian Stanley Elkins unleashed a firestorm of scholarly debate and criticism with the publication of a controversial thesis concerning the impact of slavery on the African American personality. Elkins argued that Sambo was a real historical personality type, not a fictive caricature, and that the docile (non-rebellious),

infantile Sambo was the most prevalent personality type occurring among African American slaves. Furthermore, he asserted that this dysfunctional Sambo personality type was uniquely the product of the oppressive "total institution" or "closed system" of North American slavery and that the Sambo type did not occur in the relatively "open" (i.e., less oppressive, less restrictive) slave systems of Latin American and the Caribbean, where normal human aspirations for freedom resulted in long-standing traditions of slave revolt. He stressed, however, that a comparable prevalent dysfunctional docile personality type did occur among Jews interred in Nazi concentration camps, which were similar in oppressive structure to North American slave plantations.

Scholars contended with Elkins on several issues, including the following: (1) a reinterpretation of historical evidence minimizing his crucial distinctions between North American and Latin America slavery, slave docility, and rebelliousness; (2) the existence of other prevalent African American slave personality types, most notably a rebellious "Nat" (i.e., Nat Turner) type; (3) the evidence of a "Quashee" personality type, analogous to Sambo, in the Caribbean slave system; (4) the evidence that Sambo was a dissemblance or masquerade, not an internalized personality type; and (5) the questionable analogy between North American plantation slavery and Nazi concentration camps.

Television and film provide further instances of, or commentary on, Sambo and other distorted black images. Most notable are the banned 1950s sitcom *Amos 'n' Andy;* the PBS documentaries *Ethnic Notions* by Marlon Riggs and *The Black Caricature* by Deidre Leake Butcher; and Spike Lee's film *Bamboozled* (2002). Haile Gerima's film *Sankofa* (1993), focusing on the dynamic transformation of the slave personality from docility to rebelliousness, presents a critical and corrective commentary on the controversial Elkins thesis.

See also: Slave Resistance

Yusuf Nuruddin

Bibliography

Blassingame, John. *The Slave Community: Plantation Life in the Antebellum South*. New York: Oxford University Press, 1972.

Bogle, Donald. *Toms, Coons, Mulattoes, Mammies and Bucks: An Interpretive History of Blacks in American Films*. New York: Continuum International Press, 2003.

Boskin, Joseph. *Sambo: The Rise and Demise of an American Jester*. New York: Oxford University Press, 1986.

Elkins, Stanley. *Slavery: A Problem in American Institutional and Intellectual Life.* Chicago: University of Chicago Press, 1959.

Fredrickson, George, and Christopher Lasch. "Resistance to Slavery." In *The Debate over Slavery: Stanley Elkins and His Critics,* ed. Ann Lane. Urbana: University of Illinois Press, 1971.

Genovese, Eugene. "Rebelliousness and Docility in the Slave: A Critique of the Stanley Elkins Thesis." In *The Debate over Slavery: Stanley Elkins and His Critics,* ed. Ann J. Lane. Urbana: University of Illinois Press, 1971.

Nuruddin, Yusuf. "The Sambo Thesis Revisited: Slavery's Impact upon the African American Personality." *Socialism and Democracy* 17, no. 1 (2003):291–338.

Patterson, Orlando. "Quashee." In *The Debate over Slavery: Stanley Elkins and His Critics,* ed. Ann J. Lane. Urbana: University of Illinois Press, 1971.

Stampp, Kenneth. "Rebels and Sambos: The Search for the Negro's Personality in Slavery." *Journal of Negro History* 37, no. 3 (1971):367–92.

Sanchez, Sonia

Sonia Sanchez (1934–) is an author and activist who played a significant role in the black arts movement and continues to agitate for black civil rights in the 21st century. Born Wilsonia Benita Driver in Birmingham, Alabama, Sonia Sanchez's parents were Wilson L. and Lena (Jones) Driver. She has one sibling, Pat, and her mother died while attempting to deliver twins when Sonia was one year old. Sonia and Pat were raised by their paternal grandmother and relatives until Sanchez was six.

In the late 1930s, Birmingham, Alabama, was segregated, and African Americans routinely had to endure violence, ridicule, cruelty, and continuing harassment at the hands of whites. One day, while Sanchez was riding the bus with her aunt Pauline, the bus continued to become crowded with white passengers, pushing the African Americans riders to the back of the bus. The bus driver told all of the African American passengers to exit the bus, and when Sanchez's aunt refused to get off the bus, the driver threatened to physically remove her. Sanchez's aunt spit on the driver and was arrested. Sanchez's family felt that her aunt had to leave Birmingham that night in order for the rest of the family to stay there without harassment.

By 1943, Sanchez had lost her mother and her grandmother and had consistently dealt with the annals of racism and white supremacy in the South. It was also within that same year that Sanchez and her sister Pat had to move to Harlem, New York, to live with their father and his third wife. These life-changing events became the catalyst for Sanchez to begin writing. The library became a regular field trip for Sanchez, and a black female librarian introduced her to a book called *Negro Poetry.* Sanchez continued to study and write using the pen, as opposed to her voice, to express her deepest feelings about white supremacy, black unity, and the relationships between black women and men.

Sanchez earned a bachelor's degree from Hunter College. Later, Sanchez received a postgraduate degree, studying poetry with Louise Bogan, at New York University in 1958. This is also where she formed a writers group with other poets from in and around Greenwich Village. Other members of the poetry group included Amiri Baraka (LeRoi Jones) and Askia Muhammad Touré. Newly divorced from Puerto Rican immigrant Albert Sanchez, Sanchez began to perform her first poetry readings at local bars and clubs. Her group wanted to take its poetry to places that it was not normally heard. While Sanchez worked with this particular group, she was able to publish her first poem.

Shortly thereafter, Sanchez, Haki R. Madhubuti (Don L. Lee), Nikki Giovanni, and Etheridge Knight formed the "Broadside Quartet," a group of black poets known for their strident political beliefs. This same group produced Broadside Press, an African American–owned and operated press. Sanchez and the other members of the group often put their royalties back into the press to continue publishing and investing the company. The group held the conviction that African American arts were a needed form of expression within the larger African American community. Sanchez went onto to marry Etheridge Knight and later had three children with him, Anita, Morani Neusi, and Mungu Neusi, although the marriage ultimately ended in divorce.

With the unfolding Black Nationalist movement in the United States, the tones and sentiments within Sanchez's poetry began to change. Her ontological stance began to take on the rhetoric and energy of the budding nationalist movement in the United States and abroad. For the first time, Sanchez's as well as other African American poets' work began to sing the praises of Malcolm X, to call for African Americans to begin to reclaim and reconnect with their African heritage, and to allow African Americans to conceive of a world and life without the presence of white supremacy and fear. One of the most intricate revolutionary stances Sanchez adopted in her poetry was her rejection of Western academic jargon and her embracing of the "language of the streets." Sanchez often used lowercase letters, hyphens, different spellings, and different phonetic structures in her poetry, which made her poetry stand out for its originality and passion for an alternative way of writing.

Sanchez also had a long career as an academic, helping form the first Black Studies program in the nation at San Francisco State in 1965. She later went on to teach at the University of Pittsburgh and became an assistant professor at Rutgers from 1970 to 1971. Separating from the Broadside Quartet, Sanchez reformulated as an independent artist, focusing more on black women and continuing to teach courses at Manhattan Community College and City College of the City University of New York.

In 1972, Sanchez went on to become an associate professor at Amherst College. Being that Sanchez was a poet, academic, and activist, she struggled to maintain her public and personal life. Her radical views, and her subsequent arrest at a strike at Manhattan Community College, caused Sanchez to lose employment in the academic realm. In 1977, Sanchez moved out of New York to settle in Philadelphia, where she still lives today. She obtained a job teaching at the University of Pennsylvania and later at Temple University, where she became the chair of the women's studies program.

Sanchez has delivered lectures and performed her poetry at more than 500 universities and colleges. Her books of poetry, *Homegirls* and *Handgrenades,* won an American Book Award in 1985, and in 1997, *Does Your House Have Lions,* which was about her stepbrother, who died of AIDS complications, was nominated for both an NAACP Image Award and the National Book Critics Circle Award. Her ability to talk about such hard-hitting issues as poverty, racism, sexism, and rage has earned Sonia Sanchez the reputation of one of the most revered and accomplished poets of our time.

See also: Black Arts Movement; X, Malcolm

Kaila A. Story

Bibliography

Bean, Annemarie. *A Sourcebook of African-American Performance: Plays, People, Movements.* New York: Routledge, 1999.

Nelson, Emmanuel Sampath. *African American Dramatists: An A-to-Z Guide.* Westport, CT: Greenwood Publishing, 2004.

Sanchez, Sonia. *Does Your House Have Lions?* New York: Beacon Press, 1998.

Sanchez, Sonia. *Shake Loose My Skin: New and Selected Poems.* New York: Beacon Press, 2000.

Sanchez, Sonia. *Wounded in the House of a Friend.* New York: Beacon Press, 1995.

Sanchez, Sonia, and Joyce Ann Joyce. *Conversations with Sonia Sanchez.* Jackson: University Press of Mississippi, 2007.

Poet Sonia Sanchez speaks during a news conference at the opening of the "Freedom's Sisters" exhibition at the Cincinnati Museum Center, March 14, 2008. The Smithsonian traveling exhibit tells the story of 20 African American women who helped shape the Civil Rights movement. (AP Photo/David Kohl)

Shakur, Tupac

Tupac "2Pac" Amaru Shakur (1971–1996) was a prominent American rapper and actor who, though born and raised in New York and Baltimore, became synonymous with West Coast "gangsta" rap during the 1990s.

Born Lesane Parish Crooks on June 16, 1971, his name was quickly changed to Tupac Amaru Shakur by his mother, prominent Black Panther activist Afeni Shakur. Many critics and scholars have noted the contradictory or fragmented nature of Tupac's music, namely the tension between sensitive social and political awareness and the need to be a hardened "gangsta." Through the continuous release of posthumous albums, and the establishment of the Tupac Amaru Shakur Foundation by his mother, Tupac's legacy has been profound. The intelligence, astute social commentary, and keen political awareness—all a product of his unique upbringing—combined with the swagger, continued legal troubles, and violence of his public persona, have all contributed to the mythologizing of Tupac into a black folk hero or martyr for the hip-hop generation. Like no other musician save Elvis, the mythology surrounding Tupac has given rise to the belief that he still lives.

Afeni Shakur, a member of the Black Panther Party, became pregnant with Tupac while out on bail, having been arrested in April 1969, along with 20 other New York Black Panthers, for allegedly conspiring to bomb several New York locations, including police and train stations. Midway through her pregnancy, the bail was revoked, and she was again incarcerated. At trial, Afeni—though 8 months pregnant and lacking a high school diploma—acted as her own lawyer and succeeded in getting herself acquitted for lack of evidence.

Once out of jail, Afeni married fellow black revolutionary, Mutulu Shakur, who was later accused of orchestrating

Tupac Shakur in a scene still from Gang Related *(1997). (Photofest)*

a 1981 Brinks armored car robbery that left two New York policemen and a Brinks guard dead. Mutulu went underground for several years, maintaining his innocence, but was arrested in 1986 and found guilty of the robbery and attempting to break famed African American activist Assata Shakur out of prison.

With Mutulu on the run, Afeni and her children moved between Harlem and the Bronx during the 1970s and mid-1980s. Hip-hop was developing in the Bronx at this time, potentially offering Tupac his first exposure to the culture in which he would later become a legend. In 1983, Tupac enrolled in the Harlem-based 127th Street Ensemble theater group, where he played Travis in Lorraine Hansberry's "A Raisin in the Sun." That same year, Afeni Shakur was introduced to crack cocaine by her boyfriend "Legs," a gangster and street hustler. As a result, Afeni and her family spent many of the next few years living in homeless shelters while on welfare.

In 1985, Afeni moved her family to Baltimore, where Tupac enrolled in the Baltimore School for the Arts. In addition to studying jazz, ballet, and poetry, he continued acting and performed in various Shakespeare plays before landing the role of the Mouse King in "The Nutcracker." Tupac also began his rap career while in Baltimore. With his friend Dana "Mouse" Smith as his beatbox, Tupac began competing with the other kids in his school, quickly gaining recognition as one of the best. Around this time, he also wrote his first rhyme, inspired by the fatal shooting death of a friend, under the name MC New York. Despite his obvious poverty, Tupac used his significant charisma and sense of humor to parlay his connection to New York into a tough-guy reputation, adding a swagger and air of cool to his already-popular school persona. While at school, Tupac also first met Jada Pinkett (later wife of Will Smith), who would be a close friend until his death.

Afeni again moved her family in 1988, taking them to Marin City, California. In Marin City, a poor and predominantly African American section of the otherwise affluent Marin County, Tupac underwent one of the most painful parts of his life. Afeni's drug addiction grew worse, and Tupac became increasingly responsible for his family's well-being. Although he tried to stay involved in the performing arts, he eventually dropped out of high school, moved from his mother's house, and began selling drugs.

By the end of the 1980s, Tupac dropped MC New York in favor of his given name and was rapping with a local group, "Strictly Dope." In 1990, Tupac caught a break when he was hired as a roadie and backup dancer/rapper for the Oakland-based rap group Digital Underground. Tupac's first appearance on a record came with Digital Underground's 1991 album *This Is an EP Release*. While on tour, Tupac also read for the part of Bishop in Ernest Dickerson's 1992 film *Juice*, landing the role and launching a short but successful acting career.

In November of 1991, Tupac released his debut solo album, *2Pacalypse Now*. The album reached number 13 on the *Billboard* R&B chart, eventually going gold, but quickly drew fire from politicians, police, and some African American leaders for its violent imagery and critique of law enforcement. Not all of the songs on this largely gangsta rap album were violent. "Brenda's Got a Baby," the socially aware story of a pregnant 12-year-old inspired by a newspaper article Tupac read, became one of the album's most popular tracks.

Tupac released *Strictly 4 My N.I.G.G.A.Z.* in 1993, which hit number 4 on the R&B charts before going platinum. The album was a blend of powerful social commentary and good-time music, as exemplified by the two hits, "Keep Ya Head Up" and "I Get Around," which peaked on the pop charts at numbers 12 and 11, respectively. Following the earlier acclaim of *Juice*, in 1993 Tupac landed a role in John Singleton's *Poetic Justice* alongside Janet Jackson, followed by a role in *Above the Rim* later that year. In 1994, after his near-fatal shooting and while imprisoned for sexual assault, Tupac released *Me Against the World*. Filled with new depth and emotion fueled by his shooting and ongoing legal troubles, the record was a success, debuting at number one on the U.S. charts and making him the first artist to have a number 1 record while incarcerated.

Though sentenced to four and a half years, Tupac was released on parole after serving eight months when he signed to Marion "Suge" Knight's Death Row records and Knight posted a $1.4 million bond. Having been productive in jail, Tupac's next release was *All Eyes on Me*, hip-hop's first two-disc album of original material. Debuting at number 1 on the charts, and going quintuple platinum by fall, *All Eyes on Me* represented a harder album, with Tupac unashamedly embracing his thug-icon status. It contained several popular singles, including the mega-hit "California Love," and was quickly regarded as a classic example of gangsta rap style. After moving to Death Row, Tupac expressed a growing dissatisfaction with hip-hop and an

interest in pursuing acting full-time. In the summer of 1996, he starred in *Bullet* and began filming for *Gridlock'd* and *Gang Related*, the last two of which would be released after his death later that year.

At the time of his death, Tupac was recording his second Death Row album. Released eight weeks after he died, *Don Kiluminati: The 7 Day Theory* was widely seen as an attempt by Knight to exploit Tupac's death. More significantly, it was released under the alias "Makaveli," a clear nod to Italian political theorist Niccolo Machiaveli, who faked his own death in order to take revenge on his enemies seven days later. Thus, the album was less influential as music than it was in perpetuating the myth that Tupac still lives.

Tupac's legal troubles began with his rap career. In 1991, Tupac filed a $10 million civil suit against the Oakland Police, claming he was beaten after a jaywalking citation. The suit was settled out of court. In 1992, Tupac's entourage was involved in an altercation in Marin City that escalated into a shootout, leaving a six-year-old child dead from a stray bullet. Although ballistics cleared him of responsibility, the child's family brought a wrongful death suit against him in 1995. Tupac was arrested in 1993 for shooting two off-duty Atlanta police officers whom he saw harassing a black motorist. The charges were dropped when it was found that the officers had been drunk and in possession of weapons stolen from the evidence locker. Later that year, Tupac and several members of his entourage were charged with sexual assault. Though Tupac admitted to having consensual sex with the woman several days before, he denied the charges that he or his entourage gang-raped her when she visited his room, claiming that he had been asleep. One day prior to being found guilty on three accounts of molestation, though found innocent on six greater charges, Tupac was robbed and shot five times while entering a Manhattan recording studio. In jail, Tupac claimed that Sean "Puff Daddy" Combs, Biggie Smalls (the Notorious B.I.G.), and Tupac's close friend and producer Randy "Stretch" Walker had set him up. Once released from jail, Tupac recorded "Hit 'Em Up." On it Tupac claimed he had slept with Smalls's wife, Faith Evans, and publicly accused Smalls of orchestrating the shooting. This altercation sparked the famed East Coast–West Coast rivalry that ended only after the murders of both Smalls and Tupac.

Tupac Shakur was shot on September 8, 1996, in Las Vegas, Nevada, following the Tyson–Seldon fight at the MGM Grand. Before leaving the hotel, Tupac and his entourage were involved in the beating of Southside Crips gang member Orlando "Baby Lane" Anderson, in response to Anderson's earlier robbery of a Death Row employee. After the beating, Tupac and Knight started driving to the Death Row–owned Club 662. On the way, a white Cadillac opened fire on Knight's car, hitting Tupac four times: once each in the chest, pelvis, right hand, and right thigh, with one of the bullets ricocheting into his right lung. He died five days later from internal bleeding and was cremated. Knight suffered minor head wounds caused by shrapnel.

The case remains unsolved, leaving a wake of popular theories. Some believe that Smalls and Combs arranged the shooting in an escalation of their public rivalry. Others suggest it was Knight or Death Row's mob or gang connections. The most enduring theory links it to Anderson's beating, a claim made more popular by Anderson's mysterious shooting death less then two years later. The case, thought to be cold, was reopened in 2007 following new evidence presented by Tupac's former bodyguard, Kevin Hackie, implicating Knight and the allegedly corrupt retired Compton policeman Reginald Wright Jr. The two maintain their innocence, and the case remains unsolved.

See also: Black Panther Party; Hip-Hop

Aaron D. Sachs

Bibliography

Dyson, Michael. *Holler If You Hear Me.* New York: Basic Civitas Books, 2001.

Hoye, Jacob, and Karolyn Ali. *Tupac: Resurrection.* New York: Atria, 2003.

Monjauze, Molly, Gloria Cox, and Staci Robinson. *Tupac Remembered.* San Francisco: Chronicle Books, 2008.

Shakur, Tupac. *The Rose That Grew from Concrete.* New York: MTV, 1999.

Vibe. *Tupac Amaru Shakur, 1971–1996.* New York: Three Rivers Press, 1998.

Shrine of the Black Madonna

The Shrine of the Black Madonna is part of the Pan African Orthodox Christian Church (PAOCC), founded by Rev. Albert B. Cleage Jr. (Jaramogi Abebe Agyeman) in Detroit, Michigan. The Shrine gained national fame in 1967 when on Easter Sunday, Cleage unveiled an 18-foot-high and 9-foot-wide black Madonna and Child, which replaced a stained glass window depicting the Pilgrims' landing at Plymouth Rock. With the Shrine as his institutional base, Rev. Cleage called for black churches to reinterpret the teachings of Christianity to address the social, economic, and political needs of the contemporary African American community. The Shrine thus provided a crucial physical and metaphysical space that fostered the emergence of Afrocentric black theology in the late 1960s and 1970s.

Formerly known as the Central Congregational Church, founded by Cleage in 1953, the Shrine of the Black Madonna has provided theological, philosophical, and institutional support for the African American community in Detroit and beyond. It had 50,000 members at its peak, and although membership has declined in recent years, the Shrine has expanded with new congregations in other locales, including Flint, Michigan; Kalamazoo, Michigan; Houston; Atlanta; New York; Philadelphia; and South Carolina. Featuring a strong focus on economic self-sufficiency and religious reawakening, the Shrine envisions the church as a focal point of the African American community, playing an important role especially in political, cultural, and educational life. Combining black separatism with biblical inspiration, the Shrine stands firmly in the long tradition of leaders who blended religion and Black Nationalism; indeed, Cleage publicly acknowledged his debt to such ideological predecessors as Malcolm X and Marcus Garvey.

The Shrine became particularly prominent for its role in city politics following the 1967 riots in Detroit. As many whites fled the city to the suburbs, membership in black social and political organizations exploded, and the Shrine became one of the most important religious and civic organizations in the city. The Shrine actively campaigned to elect black public officials and was instrumental in the 1973 election of Detroit's first African American mayor, Coleman Young. It also helped launch the political careers of U.S. representative Carolyn Cheeks Kilpatrick and former U.S. representative Barbara-Rose Collins.

Over the years, the Shrine has offered a number of institutional programs, including bookstores, community service centers, youth centers and academies, a neighborhood supermarket, and Beulah Land Farms in South Carolina. The Shrine of the Black Madonna Culture Center and

Bookstore, established in 1970, has served as an outlet for black writers, historians, and artists to share their work and as a place where members of the black community can learn their history and culture. All of these institutions are designed to enhance the goal of black economic development.

In the midst of the social and cultural upheavals of the 1960s, many black activists began to question whether Christianity was a source of liberation or oppression for African Americans. Cleage was quite critical of the role played by white Christians in fostering racism, colonialism, and imperialism, but he forcefully countered the claims of those such as Elijah Muhammad and Stokely Carmichael that Christianity was a white man's religion with a white man's God, inherently bankrupt and serviceable only in the propagation of white supremacy. Asserting that Christianity was rightfully a black religion, Cleage redefined Jesus and Christianity in new terms that sought to assure their continuing relevance in the modern black community. The Shrine of the Black Madonna served as the institutional base for Cleage's ideas.

Born in 1911 in Indianapolis and then raised in Detroit, Cleage was ordained a minister in the Congregational Church in 1943. His early efforts at building interracial fellowships among Congregationalists and Presbyterians were failures, and he grew increasingly frustrated with the integrationist approach of the mainstream Civil Rights movement. By the late 1960s, he had become the most vocal Christian clergyman calling for a more radical approach to the question of racial equality. After unsuccessful attempts to win elected office, he launched the Black Christian National Movement (the name was later changed to the Pan African Orthodox Christian Church) in 1967 and transformed his Congregational church to the Shrine of the Black Madonna, with the Easter Sunday unveiling of the Black Madonna as the dramatic signifier of the change.

In 1968, Cleage expressed his theological views in a collection of sermons and other writings titled *The Black Messiah*. He further articulated his views in *Black Christian Nationalism: New Directions for the Black Church* (1972). He also changed his name to Jaramogi Abebe Agyeman, Swahili for "liberator, holy man, savior of the nation."

The Shrine of the Black Madonna has continued its active ministry and community work, even after the death of its founder in 2000. The current leader of the Shrine, and patriarch of the PAOCC, is Jaramogi Menelik Kimathi (Demosthene Nelson).

See also: Black Churches; Black Nationalism; Pan-Africanism; Republic of New Afrika

Patrick Q. Mason

Bibliography
Cleage, Albert B. Jr. *The Black Messiah*. 1968. Reprint, Trenton, NJ: Africa World Press, 1989.

Signifying

The act of signifying is a verbal art form in which a person puts down or talks negatively about (signifies on) someone, to make a point or sometimes just for fun. The notion of signifying was also made famous and analyzed by Henry Louis Gates Jr. in *The Signifying Monkey*. It refers to an instrument for eloquent swerving that exploits stylistic devices such as double entendre and irony. Indeed, the concept itself designates the ambivalent art of concealing, hiding, and veiling, in order to highlight and underline one's discourse and intended message.

The signifying principle is pregnant with cultural and historical values. The recurrent trickster figure of the Monkey in the Signifying Monkey series of tales embodies the concept and the act of signifying. Henry Louis Gates Jr. traces the Signifying Monkey's origins back to the mythological figure of Esu. Belonging to the Fon mythology and standing as the equivalent to the Greek mythological figure of Hermes, Esu-Elegbara stands as the figure of interpretation and therefore the figure of representation. Esu, the ubiquitous messenger gifted with the ability to speak any language, thus stands as the best mediator. Esu is also known as a trickster and as such is likely to play tricks, to blur, and to trap, for instance, through words. Therefore, one better understands the mythopoetic status of the Signifying Monkey.

Moreover, a character such as the Signifying Monkey reminds us of a "playful" semantic dimension that one also finds in verbal games such as the call-and-response or confrontations, as in playing the dozens (a kind of game meant to test one's ability to resist insult). The blurring and misleading aspect of the instance of signifying also reminds us of the first gospels and blues songs whose content sounded either happy and rejoiced to express sorrow or sad and longing to convey feelings of joy. African American slaves used to employ this process of codification in order to communicate without having white masters spy on them.

The act of signifying consists of a three-step informative process and a double didactic challenge. First, the signifier targets his "momentary victim." Second, the latter receives the two-layered message, which contains both the blurring content and its "real" significance to be deciphered. The process of signifying both conceals the message and provides the receiver with the necessary clues to decode it. Thereafter, the temporary prey figures the message out and gains a better awareness at the same time. On the other hand, the act of receiving the message itself unfolds according to three phases: first, the addressee gets the misleading message; then he undergoes the humiliating effects of its blurring content, for instance, misunderstanding or a feeling that he is being laughed at. And last, the signifier's target starts figuring out the keys the message also contains before grasping its initially intended meaning. Thus, the process of signifying aims both to convey some information and to teach how to decode its blurred content, thanks, for example, to tonal connotation or implausible aspects of the message itself. This allows us to add two more remarks. On one hand, the information conveyed is not the sole element whose origins are veiled. Indeed, the signifier's target may also remain difficult to identify until the signifying process has concluded. The addressee could be, for instance, a third person attending the instance of signifying without realizing he or she is the actual receiver. On the other hand, the signifier's purpose could consist of both a didactic attempt toward the addressee and a way for the signifier to express his disbelief toward a set of circumstances thanks to the ironic dimension of the act of signifying.

See also: Anansi the Spider; Animal Trickster Stories; Brer Rabbit; John the Slave Tales

Valerie Caruana-Loisel

Bibliography

Courlander, Harold. *A Treasury of Afro-American Folklore.* New York: Marlowe, 1996.

Gates, Henry Louis Jr. *The Signifying Monkey, A Theory of African-American Literary Criticism.* New York: Oxford University Press, 1988.

Levine, Lawrence W. *Black Culture and Black Consciousness.* London: Oxford University Press, 1978.

Mitchell-Kernan, Claudia. "Signifying." In *Mother Wit, From the Laughing Barrel,* ed. Alain Dundes. Jackson: University Press of Mississippi, 1996.

Smitherman, Geneva. *Black Talk, Words and Phrases from the Hood to the Amen Corner.* New York: Houghton, 2000.

Slave Culture

Slave culture refers to the totality of shared learned behavior and system of meanings that were historically inherited by slaves from their ancestral past, socially constructed and adapted during their enslavement and transferred to new generations. Their culture encompassed all dimensions of their human existence, shaped and constructed their realities and worldviews, and often served an adaptive and supportive role. Culture is internally represented as the cherished symbols, goals, beliefs, and values of slaves. As an external representation, it includes the arts, rituals, artifacts, institutions and social structures of the slave period.

The ancestral African past of slave culture has been debated by historians. E. Franklin Frazier (1894–1962) noted in *Race and Culture Contacts in the Modern World* that few remnants of African culture survived slavery. Dissenting with this view, Melville J. Herskovits (1895–1963) documented many Africanisms, or African expressive cultural practices, in *The Myth of the Negro Past* (1941), which he found in the costume, culinary and funerary practices, hair braiding, musical instrument making, naming and traditions related to childbirth, proverbs, techniques of planting and harvesting, architecture, and ways of speaking. Herskovits described vestiges of West Africa in slave culture such as the significance and homage paid to ancestors, the use of song for social derision, extensive employment of magic, the use of animal tales as devices of enculturation and moral education, African linguistic patterns, and a major role for women in economic life. Newbell Niles Puckett (1898–1967), in his classic *Folk Beliefs of the Southern Negro* (1926), also studied slave culture and discussed the preservation of African traits in slave burial customs and religious beliefs in ghosts, witchcraft, and voodoo. Many slaves continued to hold onto these African worldviews in which spirits, charms, and spells had potent power. For historian Sterling Stuckey, the ring shout is another example of a carryover of cultural and religious practice from Africa where a sense of identity was celebrated and formed.

The breadth and depth of slave culture is extensive. Slaves had a rich repertoire of folktales, which included trickster tales and tales of metamorpheses. Animals of African ancestry were acculturated, and so the African hare became Brer Rabbit, the jackal became the American fox, and the tortoise became a turtle or terrapin. The structure and purpose of folktales often answered why and how questions, as illustrated in the well-known tales *Why the Lizard Often Nods, Why the Owl Never Sleeps at Night, Why Women Always Take Advantage of Men,* and *Why the Sister in Black Works Hardest.* John Wesley Blassingame (1940–2000) noted that slave culture acted as a form of resistance to enslavement and that this folklore lightened the burden of oppression, promoted group solidarity, provided ways for verbalizing anger, sustained hope, and built self-esteem. The protagonists of these tales often outsmart the enemy and inspire unity, as in the story of *Why the Hare Runs Away* and the *King Buzzard* tales. Joel Chandler Harris (1845–1908) published *Uncle Remus: Songs and Sayings* (1880), which contains the first collection of these slave tales.

Slaves also retained and practiced some of their folk arts and crafts at the plantations, such as sweetgrass basketweaving, quilting, and woodwork and metalwork. Slave women often got together at night, after a day's work in the rice fields, to make warm and beautiful quilts. Quilting became an occasion of social interaction as well as an occasion of work, thus helping to ease the burden of bondage. The North Star, crossroads, and the wagon wheel are some celebrated quilting coded symbols used by slaves to mark safe houses and escape routes on the Underground Railroad. Male slaves living on the plantation became skilled craftsmen and crafted beautiful and functional furniture from local wood, often cypress and oak, as the intricate woodwork of old plantation houses erected by slave labor still indicates.

Africans also brought music that served as an expression of hope and religious faith. In his autobiography *Narrative of the Life of Frederick Douglass* (1845), Frederick Douglass described how slaves would often sing while working. These work songs kept slaves working in rhythm and are purported to be the source of the musical genre of the blues. In many parts of Africa, music was not primarily a form of entertainment but rather a means for people to connect with each other and to communicate with the spirit world. Chanting and singing were designed to facilitate such communication by creating trance states or inducing a shared emotional climate among the participants.

Slaves would often gather in rural settings and listen to fiery speeches by slave preachers and sang songs, which eventually developed into the form called Negro spiritual. Some of the stylistic features of these musical expressions in slave culture—for example, harmonization, singing in thirds, emotionalism, and the call-and-response—are also purported to be some of the foundations of gospel music.

Slave culture has also left a rich legacy of literature and writing. Some of the landmarks include the ballad *Bars Fight* (1855) by Lucy Terry (circa 1730–1821), considered the oldest known work in literature by an African American; *The Narratives of the Uncommon Sufferings and Surprising Deliverance of Britton Hammon, a Negro Man* (1760) by Britton Hammon (birth and death dates unknown), the first voyage account published by an African American; *An Evening Thought, Salvation by Christ, with Penitential Cries* (1760) by Jupiter Hammon (1711–1806), the first known poem by an African American male; and *On Messrs. Hussey and Coffin* (1766) by Phillis Wheatley (1753–1784), an enslaved African in Boston who became the first published female African American poet. The slave narrative, a literary form used by former slaves to recount their stories of oppression, is part of this impressive heritage.

See also: Africanisms; Animal Trickster Stories; Black Folk Culture; Conjure; Ring Shout; Slave Diet; Slave Religion; Work Songs

Fernando A. Ortiz

Bibliography
Blassingame, John. *The Slave Community: Plantation Life in the Antebellum South.* New York: Oxford University Press, 1972.
Frazier, E. Franklin. *Race and Culture Contacts in the Modern World.* New York: Alfred A. Knopf, 1957.
Herskovits, Melville. *The Myth of the Negro Past.* New York: Harper and Brothers, 1941.
Levine, Lawrence. *Black Culture and Black Consciousness.* New York: Oxford University Press, 1977.
Puckett, Niles Newbell. *Folk Beliefs of the Southern Negro.* 1926. Reprint, Whitefish, MT: Kessinger Publishing, 2003.
Stuckey, Sterling. *Slave Culture: Nationalist Theory and the Foundations of Black America.* New York: Oxford University Press, 1987.

Slave Religion

Slave religion refers to the spiritual practices of enslaved Americans who combined African culture and religion with Christian principles to create a unique form of Christianity that emphasized physical and spiritual liberation.

The messages of freedom and Christian deliverance at the core of slave religion emerged in mid-18th-century North America when a series of religious revivals swept both the Northern and Southern colonies. Emotionally charged and egalitarian in nature, the revivals attracted large numbers of slaves, who saw elements of African religious practices in the expressive nature of evangelical worship. Hundreds of blacks, remarked itinerant Methodist minister Devereux Jarratt, were moved to tears during a revival that swept Virginia and North Carolina in the late 1770s (Raboteau, 1999). Through emphasis on personal experience instead of rigorous and ascetic moral instruction, social divisions rooted in race, education, and status that had previously separated black and white congregants diminished.

As black and white attitudes toward religion shifted, increasing numbers of slaves joined evangelical churches. By the 1790s, thousands of black congregants across the South had become members of the two fastest-growing evangelical denominations among blacks and whites—Methodist and Baptist. In 1797, the Methodist Church recorded over 12,000 black congregants—one-fourth of total church membership. Similar numbers of slaves joined Baptist churches, especially in rural areas. Spurred by revival and the decentralized nature of the Baptist Church, the number of black Baptists in early America increased from 18,000 in 1793 to 40,000 in 1813.

As slave membership increased and religious revivals subsided, the presence of African elements in religious worship gradually distinguished slave religion from mainstream Christianity. "Ring shouts" of the South Carolina and Georgia Lowcountry incorporated vocal responses, clapping, and shuffling into worship, reminiscent of African religious dance. Other African-influenced practices, such as call-and-response" singing, also characterized the religious worship of slaves. By using African cultural forms to express Christian themes, slaves reaffirmed their claims to the Christian faith.

Black preachers, numbers of whom grew alongside converts, also helped define slave religion in important ways. Although Southern law required white supervision of black religious gatherings, licensed black Methodist and Baptist ministers created congregations within white churches and fostered the creation of independent black churches in the early decades of the 19th century. Often having firsthand knowledge of slavery, these black leaders were fundamental in bringing Christianity to the quarters.

Indeed, black preaching in Methodist and Baptist churches and institutional church membership represented only one manifestation of slaves' growing interest in Christianity. On plantations where masters circumscribed slaves' ability to create independent religious institutions, slaves looked outside of the formal church for spiritual guidance free of proslavery propaganda. These "invisible institutions," as one scholar has called them, lacked denominational structure and formal membership, but nonetheless provided slaves with spiritual support and guidance. As slaves "stole away," gathering in cabins and brush harbors or "hush harbors" that were free from the prying eyes of masters, slave preachers extolled messages of physical and spiritual liberation. The result was a variation of Protestant Christianity that resembled the emotionalism of earlier revivals and integrated slave culture and African religions into slave worship.

Part of slaves' appropriation of Christianity also grew out of the themes extolled in slave sermon and song. Old Testament figures such as Moses achieved particular prominence in slave preaching. Slaves saw themselves as the wandering children of Israel, prisoners of Egypt who suffered bondage under the Pharaoh and sought exodus. This spiritual journey from slavery to freedom, as well as New Testament messages, struck a chord among slaves. Indeed, spirituals were perhaps the clearest expression of slave faith and a desire to be relieved of the suffering of their world.

Immediately following the Civil War, one close observer of slave religious practices heard one of the many songs of freedom that epitomized the core message of slave religion. As slaves sung of being set free and rising from the valley, they personified the difficult journey from slavery to freedom.

After emancipation, the religion slaves created would remain a cornerstone of black life and faith amid continued struggles for social equality in the U.S. North and South.

See also: Black Folk Culture; Hush Harbors; Ring Shout; Slave Culture

Erica Ann Bruchko

Bibliography

Genovese, Eugene D. *Roll, Jordan, Roll.* New York: Pantheon Books, 1974.

Higginson, Thomas Wentworth. *Army Life in a Black Regiment.* Boston: Fields, Osgood, 1870.

Lyell, Charles. *A Second Visit to the United States of North America.* London: J. Murray, 1850.

Raboteau, Albert J. *African American Religion.* Oxford: Oxford University Press, 1999.

Raboteau, Albert J. *Slave Religion: The "Invisible Institution" in the Antebellum South.* Oxford: Oxford University Press, 2004.

Soul Food

Soul food refers generally to the style of cooking and eating developed by enslaved Africans on Southern plantations. It represents a synthesis of African culinary sensibilities with the practicalities of African survival in the American South. It also embodies the taste traditions of the various cultures to which Africans in the New World were exposed.

Before arriving in the New World, sub-Saharan Africans had a diet primarily emphasizing such vegetables as okra, yams, squash, pumpkins, eggplant, leafy greens, and peppers. These were prepared in rich soups and stews along with meat, fish, or fowl and often served with a starch. The starchy accompaniment to these meals, known by many names, might consist of pounded yam (also known as FuFu) or stiff cornmeal porridge (also known as Sadza) and was essentially used as a bread-like eating utensil. Other food staples included palm oil, in which foods were fried, as well as groundnuts and seeds.

The enslavement of African people between the 15th and 19th centuries had a significant impact on the quality and substance of their diet. Enslaved Africans traveling to the Americas were typically malnourished, subsisting on small quantities of beans and rice and low-quality food rations. On American plantations, enslaved Africans were sometimes able to grow local vegetables that in some instances were similar to those found in Africa. Over time, American "sweet potatoes" replaced African "yams," and collard greens replaced leafy greens found on the African continent. In addition to local vegetables, enslaved Africans caught fish and seafood or hunted such small easily caught game as squirrel, rabbit, and possum. Periodically, enslaved Africans might also receive food rations from their owners consisting of such items as cornmeal, flour, milk, and molasses. These items in combination with others were used to produce such filling staples as cornbread and hushpuppies. Many enslaved Africans, particularly those who worked in the homes of their owners, also received scraps of meat that were left over from choicer portions. These included fatty pieces of pork sometimes called fatback or salt pork, which was typically used to season and cook vegetables. Enslaved Africans also had access to other remains from the pig, such as the feet, tails, ears, intestines and skin. These were typically fried or pickled, becoming such favored items as scrapple, chitlins, and pork rinds. Over time the culinary innovations and adaptations introduced by enslaved Africans became popular with whites as well.

Today, a typical "soul food" dinner might consist of some combination of the following, for example: fried chicken, baked ham, smothered pork chops, fried catfish, macaroni and cheese, baked beans, collard greens, candied yams, black-eyed peas, corn bread, sweet potato pie, and peach cobbler. Other popular soul food items include gumbo (a hearty Creole stew combining sausage, seafood, and vegetables), jambalaya (a Creole dish similar to gumbo), grits (an enriched corn porridge), and potato salad.

The term "soul food" became popular during the 1960s and 1970s in the United States during a time when the Civil Rights and Black Power movements measurably influenced the way that Americans thought about African American culture. In an era when such terms and ideas as "Black Power" and "black is beautiful" came into usage in relation to African Americans, so did the concept of "soul." Soul in relation to African Americans refers to an intangible, yet validating spiritual essence or style that is seen as permeating African American culture. Thus, it is not uncommon for the concept of soul to be applied to African American music, art, dance, and food.

In recent years, the soul food diet, particularly the aspect that deals with the heavy consumption of fried, processed, salty, high-fat, and high-cholesterol foods, has been increasingly criticized for contributing to rising rates of obesity and morbidity among African Americans as well as related health ailments such as diabetes (sometimes referred to as "sugar"), high blood pressure, and heart disease. In response, cooks, dieticians, and nutritionists in consultation with medical personnel have begun to publish cookbooks touting healthier versions of many popular soul food dishes. The soul food diet persists in African American communities because of the comfort and sense of community with which the food is associated. Often served at churches, family gatherings, and neighborhood events, soul food has become fundamentally linked to the African American experience.

See also: Africanisms; Black Folk Culture; Rice Cultivation; Slave Culture; Slave Diet

Chishamiso Rowley

Bibliography

Liburd, Leandris C. "Food, Identity, and African-American Women with Type 2 Diabetes: An Anthropological Perspective." *Diabetes Spectrum* 16 (2003):160–65.

Whitehead, Tony Larry. "In Search of Soul Food." In *African Americans in the South*, ed. H. Baer and Y. Jones. Athens: University of Georgia Press, 1992.

Sweetgrass Baskets

Sweetgrass baskets, coil form—or sewn—baskets, are named for the materials used in their construction. Sweetgrass (*Muhlenbergia filipes*) is a perennial grass that grows from underground runners in nutrient-poor, sandy soil, often near the edge of tidal marshlands of the mainland, barrier islands, and sea islands of Lowcountry, South Carolina. The plants, which produce distinctive, ornamental mauve flowers in the autumn, prefer full to partial sun and are made up of long, smooth grass blades that are strong, yet supple enough to be woven into functional baskets. A thin, continuous bundle of the dried sweetgrass is woven around itself and tied—or sewn—down by a second medium, such

Weavers in Mount Pleasant, South Carolina, make sweetgrass baskets. (AP Photo/Evan Berland)

as split palmetto leaves, raffia, or even pine needles, to form an "eye" in the middle of the basket and wound outward to form the desired size and shape of the basket being created. Baskets of similar design, but of varying materials, are made throughout the Lowcountry with bulrushes or other local grasses used in place of the sweetgrass.

Utilitarian baskets of this style were brought from the rice coast of West Africa to the rice-growing regions of the colonies as early as the 17th century. These sewn baskets were strong yet flexible and made in a variety of shapes and sizes depending on the task for which the basket was intended. One specific basket style was the fanner basket, which played an important role in the processing of rice on both sides of the Atlantic Ocean. Once the rice had been pounded to loosen the husk from the kernel, the rice was placed in the large, flat fanner basket, and workers would repeatedly toss the pounded rice into the air. The wind would blow away the chaff while the worker caught the cleaned rice back in the basket. These fanner baskets, as well as other functional baskets, were vital tools on the rice plantations, and planters' records from the antebellum period reveal that collecting materials for and making sweetgrass baskets was an important activity performed by the enslaved population, typically the men.

As rice production came to an end due to labor changes after the Civil War and natural disasters that altered the saline content of the former rice paddocks, the creation and use of sweetgrass baskets in Charleston declined dramatically. However, within many African American households, the craft continued, often with women taking over the collecting of materials and the sewing of baskets. The craft was most often passed from mother or grandmother to daughters and granddaughters. Although sweetgrass basket making almost disappeared to a great extent throughout the Lowcountry, a small group of women in the Mt. Pleasant area kept the skill alive and passed it down through the generations. Many of them descended from the enslaved populations on Boone Hall Plantation or Snee Farm and were able to make an income from producing these baskets in the 20th century and selling them to tourists in small stalls along the Ocean Highway (Route 17) or in the market and street corners of historic downtown Charleston.

Mt. Pleasant, formerly a small town just up the coast from Charleston, is still the hub of the sweetgrass basket makers—many of whom have placed baskets in the Smithsonian Institution or other prominent museums and whose baskets command great prices as works of art. The knowledge of finding and preparing the sweetgrass—as well as the technique of making baskets—is still mainly passed down through families. Basket styles range from the traditional utilitarian types during the plantation era to new, elaborately decorative forms created by the artistic. Sweetgrass baskets can still be purchased at private stands along Highway 17 above Mt. Pleasant and from vendors in the market or on street corners of the main tourist areas of Charleston.

See also: Black Folk Culture; Carolinas; Gullah; Rice Cultivation; Sierra Leone; Task System

Jane M. Aldrich

Bibliography

Cross, Wilbur. *Gullah Culture in America.* Westport, CT: Praeger, 2008.

Rosengarten, Dale. *Row upon Row: Sea Grass Baskets of the South Carolina Lowcountry.* Columbia: University of South Carolina Press, 1994.

Rosengarten, Dale, Theodore Rosengarten, and Enid Schildkrout. *Grass Roots: African Origins of an American Art.* New York: Museum for African Art, 2008.

Syncretism

Anthropologists, folklorists, and cultural historians use the term "syncretism" to explain the merging of cultural forms or practices from different cultures to produce a new cultural product. This process of cultural blending involves both retention and reinterpretation—that is, the maintenance of preexisting traits distinct to one's own culture as well as the synthesis of those traits with new ones encountered through the experience of cultural contact. Cultural encounters can occur in a relationship of either domination and subordination or willing coexistence. Yet syncretism reflects the ability of individuals to consciously mix, borrow, or modify seemingly irreconcilable or incongruent cultural practices in order to create a new product meaningful to and functional in their lives.

Syncretism as a concept for understanding cultural formation is closely related to the terms "creolization" and "hybridity." Somewhat synonymous, the three terms contain slight variations in meaning. Thus, taken collectively, syncretism, creolization, and hybridity allow scholars to explain the complex phenomena of cultural interpenetration by acknowledging but not deriding mixture. Linguists (scholars who study language) initially used creolization to explain the emergence of new languages—pidgins and creoles—when two or more distinct linguistic groups came into contact. Pidgin was the simple form of a language first spoken by people who came into contact with one another but did not share a common language. For example, first-generation Africans enslaved in the Americas developed pidgins to communicate with their European enslavers. Those Africans passed those languages down to their children, so that the next generation spoke them as "native" languages—creoles. Although scholars use creolization predominantly to explain linguistic mixture or syncretism, the term is also used to explain identity formation. As indicated in the preceding example, not only were new languages formed (i.e., patois, Black English, and so on), but new identities were formed as well (African Americans, West Indians, Creoles).

Hybridity also explains cultural mixture. Although initially used pejoratively to denote racial mixture (miscegenation or "mongrelization"), scholars now use hybridity to explain the mixture of two cultural elements. Like syncretism, hybridity recognizes deliberate choices made by individuals to blend identities or cultural elements to their benefit. For example, the term African American recognizes the hybrid identity of peoples of African descent in America. Ostensibly, it does not privilege either the American or African component of black identity in America. It views black identity as a hybrid of two cultural experiences, broadly speaking. It acknowledges the African origin and past and the American past and present that inform the African American experience.

With regard to the history of Americans of African descent, scholars employ syncretism to explain not only the "birth" or emergence of African American culture, but also its specific elements as they evolved in the context of race-based slavery and white supremacy. For example, some scholars of the colonial and antebellum African American experiences invoke syncretism to explain such myriad cultural phenomena as slave naming practices, religion, parades, burial rituals, family patterns, marriage rites, language, music, dance, diet, and dress. In their examination of these cultural elements, these scholars call attention to the African retentions found in slave adaptations of dominant cultural forms. Thus, syncretism as a model for understanding African American cultural formation does not dismiss the African influences on black culture, but acknowledges the real limitations that isolation from Africa and bondage placed on that development.

One noted example of cultural syncretism among enslaved Africans in the Americas was their conversion to Christianity. In the British North American colonies, which later became the United States, that conversion involved a blending a various religious beliefs and rituals from West and Central Africa with Protestant Christianity. The product of that fusion is what scholars and lay people alike refer to as black Christianity. In this illustration, African beliefs in spirit possession rationalized the Christian belief in the Holy Spirit to the slave's worldview. Similarly, African religious practices that incorporated dance and the playing of multiple musical instruments validated for converted slaves the Psalmist's entreaty to worship the creator with dance and music. Thus, ecstatic worship, dance, spirit possession, and shouting rooted in the varied heritages of enslaved Africans transformed not only their religious identity as African Americans but also the worship style of white evangelical Christians. In this case, religious syncretism was reciprocal.

Syncretism allows scholars to explain not only the historic development of African American culture but also contemporary configurations of black culture, particularly in the age of globalization. Syncretism helps explain a new era of cultural cross-pollination in the African Diaspora, where Latino, Caribbean, African, and African American cultures combined to produce new vibrant cultural expressions, such as hip-hop.

See also: Acculturation; Africanisms; Amalgamation

Jeannette Eileen Jones

Bibliography

Hall, Robert L. "African Religious Retentions in Florida." In *Africanisms in American Culture,* ed. Joseph E. Holloway. Bloomington: Indiana University Press, 1990.

Herskovits, Melville J. *The Myth of the Negro Past.* Boston: Beacon Press, 1941.

Mintz, Sidney W., and Richard Price. "The Birth of African-American Culture." In *African-American Religion: Interpretive Essays in History and Culture,* ed. Timothy E. Fulop and Albert J. Raboteau. New York: Routledge, 1997.

Stewart, Charles. "Syncretism and Its Synonyms: Reflections on Cultural Mixture." *Diacritics* 29, no. 3 (1999):40–62.

Stuckey, Sterling. *Slave Culture: Nationalist Theory and the Foundations of Black America.* New York: Oxford University Press, 1987.

Wright, Donald R. *African Americans in the Colonial Era: From African Origins through the American Revolution.* Arlington Heights, IL: Harlan Davidson, 1990.

Tituba

Tituba (birth and death unknown), also known as Tituba Indian, was the slave of Samuel Parris, the minister of Salem Village, Massachusetts, from 1689 to 1697. Her birth date and her age during her time of residence in Salem are unknown. She was one of the first three people to be accused of witchcraft by Minister Parris's 9-year-old daughter, Betty, and Betty's 11-year-old cousin, Abigail Williams, during the Salem Witch Trials (1692–1693). Despite the key role she played during the trials, Tituba's involvement is often overlooked in official histories of the period. Her story has long been characterized by debate and speculation, and she has acquired an almost mythical status.

Tituba's origins and racial identity are largely unknown and continue to be heavily debated among critics and historians. In historical documentation, Tituba is described interchangeably as Indian or African. In 1868, the poet Henry Wadsworth Longfellow wrote the verse-drama *Giles Corey of the Salem Farms,* in which he identifies Tituba as half-Indian and half-African. Other literary and critical interpretations have sought to specifically pinpoint Tituba's origins to one of these racial groups. In both Arthur Miller's play *The Crucible* (1953) and Ann Petry's novel *Tituba of Salem Village* (1964), Tituba is portrayed as African. Novelist Maryse Condé believes Tituba to have been born in Barbados, the daughter of an African slave who was raped by an Englishman during her crossing from Africa to the Caribbean. However, Elaine Breslaw, author of *Tituba, Reluctant Witch of Salem* (1996), posits that she is an Arawak Indian from Guiana. She argues that Tituba traveled from Guiana to Barbados, either as the victim of kidnap or through the migration of her community.

Samuel Parris was born in Barbados but immigrated to America to take up a place at Harvard University. He returned to the island in 1673 to claim his inheritance. Although no direct historical evidence exists, it is thought that he bought Tituba and her husband, John Indian, as domestic slaves on this trip. Tituba and John moved with the Parris family to Salem Village in July 1689. The accusations of witchcraft aimed at Tituba began in February 1692. Betty Parris and Abigail Williams began complaining that they had been bitten during their sleep and began to suffer from a series of strange seizures and trances. The Parris's neighbor, Mary Sibley, asked Tituba and John Indian to help her make a witch cake, a practice that would supposedly protect the girls and reveal the names of their afflicters. Tituba did so; however, the girls' symptoms became worse after the use of the witch cake. After the village doctor, Dr. Griggs, could find no apparent medical cause for these physical afflictions, witchcraft was declared to be responsible, and the girls named Tituba and their neighbors Sarah Good and Sarah Osbourne as the perpetrators. All three women were cross-examined in the Salem town court by Judge John Hathorne in March 1692.

A number of interpretations have been put forward to suggest why the girls began to demonstrate such strange behavior. Popular legend held that the girls had made frequent trips with Tituba to the Salem woods, where she had demonstrated to them, and they had participated in, various kinds of voodoo magic, and that their accusations toward her resulted from the guilt they felt at participating in such "heathen" activities. However, many historians, including Mary Beth Norton and Elaine Breslaw, have since proved this story to be a fabrication of 19th-century stories about the trials. A complex mix of personal grudges, social unease, political instability in the area, and a culture of fear generated from the threat of American Indian attacks is the most likely explanation for what became an outbreak of accusations. The fact that Tituba was of a different ethnicity that was, whether Indian or African, associated in the Puritans' mind with unfamiliar pagan and voodoo practices most likely made her an appropriate and believable target or scapegoat for the girls' initial accusation.

At first, Tituba denied having any involvement in witchcraft. During her trial, however, which lasted for several days, she eventually not only confessed, declaring herself to be under the influence of the devil and confirming the community's fears, but also accused other people from inside and outside Salem village as being witches and of tormenting her, including Good and Osbourne. Her testimony and the language that she used to describe the supernatural occurrences she had witnessed played on the deepest fears of Salem's Puritan population and thus

Depiction of West Indian slave Tituba "bewitching" children in Salem in 1692. Tituba was the first woman accused of witchcraft preceding the Salem Witch Trials. She admitted to the practice and implicated others in her confession. (North Wind Picture Archives)

contributed to the escalation of the crisis. It is thought that Minister Parris may have beaten her in order to get her to confess.

If a person accused of witchcraft during this period pleaded guilty, part of he person's punishment was the seizing of his or her property and assets. Because Tituba was a slave, she had no property or assets to lose. After her confession, she was placed in Salem jail, where she remained for 13 months. Minister Parris refused to pay her jail fees. It is thought that Tituba was acquitted of her "crimes" on May 9, 1693. It is not known precisely when Tituba was released from prison or whether upon her release she was reunited with John Indian. Although historians continue to debate the details of her life, the circumstances surrounding her actions after the witch trials and concerning her death remain unknown, contributing to her status as an elusive historical figure.

See also: Conjure; New England Colonies; Slave Religion

Rebecca L. K. Cobby

Bibliography

Breslaw, Elaine G. *Tituba, Reluctant Witch of Salem: Devilish Indians and Puritan Fantasies.* New York: New York University Press, 1996.

Condé, Maryse. *I, Tituba: Black Witch of Salem.* New York: Ballantine Books, 1992.

Hoffer, P. C. *The Devil's Disciples: Makers of the Salem Witch Craft Trials.* Baltimore, MD: John Hopkins University Press, 1996.

Norton, Mary Beth. *In the Devil's Snare: The Salem Witchcraft Crisis of 1692.* New York: Alfred Knopf, 2002.

Tucker, Veta Smith. "Purloined Identity: The Racial Metamorphosis of Tituba of Salem Village." *Journal of Black Studies* 30, no. 4 (2000):624–34.

Transmigration

The notion that the human spirit or soul is indestructible and eternal can be found in a number of religions and spiritual systems in Atlantic Africa and throughout the Atlantic African Diaspora in the Americas. At the heart of such folkloric traditions as the "flying African" tales and the story of Ebo Landing, this concept—akin to reincarnation—prefigured a number of phenomena in African American religious worldviews. In Atlantic Africa, transmigration is at the heart of the Kongo cosmogram—a continuously moving, counterclockwise circle that reflected both the east-to-west motion of the sun and the movement of human souls to and from the earthly plane of existence. In the particular context, an ancestral spirit could often be reborn with its kinship group. The link between the Kongo cosmogram and transmigration may have prefigured the idea within African American folkloric traditions that dreaming of a fish equates to an imminent pregnancy within the family. Beings residing below the Kalunga Line—a horizontal line in the Kongo cosmogram separating the earthly and spirit realms—were envisioned as *simbi* spirits, or chalk-white fish. These disembodied *simbi* spirits, bound to be reborn, indeed represented potential pregnancy, birth, and the continuation of the perpetual cycle of life.

Transmigration was also embodied within the ring shout, which itself was a reflection of the Kongo cosmogram. Though individuals engaging in the ring shout by the late 19th and early 20th centuries may have lost touch with the spiritual underpinnings of this practice, the form itself—a counterclockwise circle in emulation of the cosmogram—captures the very concept of the immortality of the human spirit.

Belief in transmigration likely played an important role in slave rebelliousness and resistance. In the course of

the 1733–1734 Danish St. John slave revolt, a movement in which slaves held the island for nearly six months, the leaders were inspired by notions of the eternal soul. During the subsequent court trials, one anonymous slave testified, "When I die, I shall return to my own land." It is clear that the rebels involved in this particular attempt to cast off the chains of enslavement originated from West Africa's Gold Coast and were likely Akan-speakers from the collapsed state of Akwamu. Other Akan-speakers used similar conceptualizations of transmigration to engage in acts of resistance or shaped community values regarding burial practices. A sizable number of suicides or suicidal resistance efforts engaged in by Akan-speakers in 18th-century Jamaica, New York, Antigua, and Barbados were likely shaped by a strong belief in transmigration. In addition, a symbol that implies the impervious and eternal nature of the human soul—the Akan *Adinkra* known as *Sankofa*—was found on a coffin lid buried at some point in the early 18th century in New York City's African Burial Ground. The use of conch shells and other seashells—as a replication of the Kongo cosmogram—conveyed similar values at gravesites in South Carolina, Brazil, and Haiti, among many other locales.

Within African American folklore, the ubiquitous "flying African" tales and the story of Ebo Landing embody both resistance to slavery and spiritual transmigration. Both sets of folktales are based on cases of suicide or death through other means that lead to the releasing of human spirits from earthly limitations in order to fly, walk, or swim back to Atlantic Africa. Within these stories, only those born in Africa had the ability to fly or walk back to Africa. Verification that slaves in the American South embraced transmigration and the ability of Africans to return home can be found in the narratives of Charles Ball and Olaudah Equiano. If the soul of a deceased individual returns back to former companions, friends, and kin, that would mean that the souls of African-born slaves would have to "fly" or "swim" across the Atlantic to get back home. This would not work for slaves born in the Americas. Their families and friends were in the Western Hemisphere, not Africa, and thus they did not have the ability to take flight. The phenomenon of flying Africans is absent in African folklore for similar reasons. If an individual dies in Africa, the spirit has no need to fly because it is already home. Though rooted in African metaphysical understandings, this represents an orientation that was uniquely African American and perhaps, in other ways, epitomizes the creolization process.

See also: Ebo Landing; Flying African Stories; Slave Religion

Walter C. Rucker

Bibliography

Gomez, Michael. *Exchanging Our Country Marks: The Transformation of African Identities in the Colonial and Antebellum South.* Chapel Hill: University of North Carolina Press, 1998.

Heywood, Linda, ed. *Central Africans and Cultural Transformations in the American Diaspora.* New York: Cambridge University Press, 2002.

Rucker, Walter. *"The River Flows On": Black Resistance, Culture, and Identity Formation in Early America.* Baton Rouge: Louisiana State University Press, 2005.

Stuckey, Sterling. *Slave Culture: Nationalist Theory & the Foundation of Black America.* New York: Oxford University Press, 1987.

Thompson, Robert Farris. *Flash of the Spirit.* New York: Vintage Books, 1983.

Turner, Lorenzo Dow

Named the "Father of Gullah Studies," African American linguist Lorenzo Dow Turner (1890–1972) was born on August 21, 1890, in Elizabeth, North Carolina. His father, Rooks Turner, was a free black man who, after attending Howard University, became an educator. Before Lorenzo Dow's birth, Rooks purchased three acres of land in North Carolina, where he later built the Rooks Turner Normal School. His mother, Elizabeth Sessoms Freeman, was born enslaved and later raised by her African American stepfather, Anthony Freeman.

In 1910, Lorenzo Dow, like his father, entered Howard University where he studied German, French, Latin, and Greek and received bachelor's degree in English. In 1917, he received a master's in English from Harvard University. Seven years later, he received a PhD in English from the University of Chicago. During the summer of 1929, while taking time from teaching at Fisk University in Nashville, Turner ventured to another historically black university, South Carolina State, located in Orangeburg. It was during this summer teaching experience that he heard "Gullah" for the first time, marking his initial interest in the language

and culture that would become paramount in the development of his career and legacy.

From June to December 1932, and again in the summer of 1933, Turner studied the South Carolina Sea Islands through ethnographic interactions. Turner interviewed 21 Gullah speakers in South Carolina on Johns, Wadmalaw, Edisto, and St. Helena Islands; in Georgia on Sapelo and St. Simons Islands; and on Harris Neck and Brewer's Neck, parts of a peninsula mainland area. In 1935, he immersed himself in the study of African languages that he believed were crucial to understanding the background of the Gullah culture and language. Between 1936 and 1941, Turner traveled across three continents to study the language patterns of Africans throughout the Diaspora. He learned five languages, including those of Krio, Twi, Kimbundu, Efik, Fante, Ewe, Yoruba, and other groups while in England. In Brazil, he found pride among diasporic Africans toward their contribution to the region's cultural elements, especially dance and language.

In 1949, his book *Africanisms in the Gullah Dialect* was published and recognized as an unprecedented analysis of the Gullah people and their language. In his work, he debunked the dominant myth of Gullah as "baby talk" English from the mouths of uncivilized, enslaved Africans. Instead, he asserted that Gullah is a creolized form, blending elements from numerous languages of enslaved Africans who were transported to South Carolina and Georgia during the 18th century and the first half of the 19th. He provided exhaustive lists of sounds, intonations, names, and words in Gullah that are parallel to those in West African languages, demonstrating that Gullah is a language, adhering to grammatical rules and sentence structures. *Africanisms* served as a model for multidisciplinary studies ranging from anthropology to history and especially linguistics. Historians used the manuscript in the development of their works regarding African Americans; such is the case with Melville Herskovits's *Myth of the Negro Past.*

Although Turner published two more works, *The Krio Language of the Sierra Leone* (1963) and *Krio Texts: With Grammatical Notes and Translation in English* (1965), *Africanisms* is noted as one the most influential works in African American and African studies. In 1972, Lorenzo Dow Turner died, leaving behind his two sons and widow Lois Turner Williams, who continued the dissemination of his works to various archives and research centers across the United States.

See also: Africanisms; Gullah; Herskovits, Melville

Tamara T. Butler

Bibliography

Turner, Lorenzo Dow. *Africanisms in the Gullah Dialect.* Ann Arbor: University of Michigan Press, 1973.

Wade-Lewis, Margaret. *Lorenzo Dow Turner: Father of Gullah Studies.* Columbia: University of South Carolina, 2007.

Walker, Margaret

Margaret Abigail Walker (1915–1998), a poet, novelist, and essayist, was born in Birmingham, Alabama. Her father, Sigismond, was a native of Jamaica who earned a theological degree and was ordained as a black Methodist minister, and her mother, Marion, was a college-educated musician. Walker was one of four children born to them. Together they instilled in their daughter an awareness of and respect for the power of words. Walker found her communicative talent in poetry, which she began writing at age 12. She enrolled at Northwestern and earned her bachelor's degree in 1935. After graduation, she remained in Chicago for the next four years to work, holding various publishing jobs as a typist, a newspaper reporter, an editor of a magazine, and a member of the Works Progress Administration's Federal Writers' Project. Her participation in this latter group led to her introduction to several politically active writers of the Chicago Renaissance, such as Nelson Algren, Richard Wright, James Farrell, Studs Terkel, and Gwendolyn Brooks.

In 1939, she started a master's program at the University of Iowa, and she earned her MA in 1940 by submitting a collection of poems she had written as her thesis. In 1942, when Walker was 27 years old, she published a volume of poetry titled *For My People,* her first book. She received immediate recognition and praise for this book when she was awarded the Yale University Younger Poets Competition for the title poem, which also earned her the distinction of being the first African American ever to win the prize. In *For My People,* Walker incorporates jazz and blues rhythms, figures from folklore, religious imagery, and U.S. history to evoke the devastating effects of racism on African Americans. Like Langston Hughes's "The Negro Speaks of Rivers," Walker's titular poem became an oft-quoted verse of civil rights protest. This poem is all the more remarkable when one considers Walker's assertion that it took her only 15 minutes to compose it on her typewriter.

Walker's writing and her academic responsibilities kept her busy during the 1940s; in 1942, she was given a professorship at Livingston College in North Carolina, in the English department, and she also lectured at Jackson State University in Mississippi, where she was made a faculty member in 1949. In 1944, she won a Rosenwald Fellowship for creative writing. From 1943 through 1948, she was a lecturer with the National Concert Artists Corporation. In 1943, she married Firnish James Alexander and had four children—two boys and two girls.

In her late 40s, she enrolled in a PhD program at Iowa University, where she earned her degree in 1965, when she was 50 years old. Her doctoral dissertation was the manuscript of her novel *Jubilee.* This book was published by Houghton Mifflin in 1966, and that same year, Walker was named a Houghton Mifflin literature fellow. Though she published a handful of poems in the 1940s and 1950s, there is a glaring gap in her publishing activity from 1942 until the appearance of *Jubilee* in 1966. This silence can be attributed to the fact that she was raising her family, teaching at various colleges, and researching information for *Jubilee,* which was set during the Civil War and contains significant biographical and historical data. A large part of this work is based on the life of Walker's great-grandmother, Margaret Duggans Ware Brown. It focuses on the antebellum period through the Reconstruction and provides accurate details about the plantation system and slavery in the South during this time.

The bulk of this book's content is based on the stories Walker's grandmother told her about her great-grandmother; her family's oral history forms the backbone of the novel. Walker began to flesh out her story by researching Civil War history and other black slave narratives when she was an undergraduate at Northwestern, and she continued to work on her book in between her teaching and family duties.

Unlike traditional coming-of-age novels, *Jubilee* traces the gender, class, and race awareness and evolution of Vyry, a mulatto house servant. Vyry's father is the master of the plantation she lives on, and her mother was his mistress. Her mother dies when she is seven years old, and she goes to live in her father/master's house, where she becomes the servant of his daughter, Lillian, and the object of loathing of his wife, Big Missy Salina. As a teenager, Vyry becomes the house cook. Randall Ware, a freeborn black man who works as a blacksmith, unsuccessfully tries to buy Vyry's freedom. On the eve of the Civil War, and before her 20th birthday, Vyry births three of Ware's children. Ware becomes a blacksmith for the Union Army in 1862, and Vyry remains on the plantation. After the war, Vyry marries Innis Brown, and the couple work as sharecroppers in Alabama. The Ku Klux Klan burns down their home, forcing them to flee. They eventually find a town in which to live, where their white neighbors help them build a new house, and Vyry and Innis are able to start a new life.

Not only is the book well researched and poignantly written, but it is also a novel about a black woman's experience, written by a black woman writer, and this element of the novel cannot be overemphasized.

Walker is also the author of *How I Wrote Jubilee* (1972), *A Poetic Equation: Conversations between Margaret Walker and Nikki Giovanni* (1974), *The Daemonic Genius of Richard Wright* (1982), *This Is My Century: New and Collected Poems* (1988), and *How I Wrote Jubilee and Other Essays on Life and Literature* (1990). Other awards and honors she received include a Fulbright Fellowship in 1971, a National Endowment for the Humanities in 1972, an honorary doctorate in literature from Northwestern University in 1974, an honorary doctorate of letters from Rust College in 1974, an honorary doctorate of fine arts from Dennison University in 1974, and an honorary doctorate of humane letters from Morgan State University in 1976. Walker died in Chicago, in 1998.

See also: Brooks, Gwendolyn; Haley, Alex; Wright, Richard

Jessica Noelle Apuzzo

Bibliography

Barksdale, Richard K. "Margaret Walker: Folk Orature and Historical Prophecy." In *Black American Poets between Worlds, 1940–1960*, ed. R. Baxter Miller. Knoxville: The University of Tennessee Press, 1986.

Davies, Arthur P. *From the Dark Tower. Afro-American Writers 1900–1960*. Washington, D.C.: Howard University Press, 1974.

Emanuel, James A., and Theodore L. Gross, eds. *Dark Symphony. Negro Literature in America*. New York: Free Press, 1968.

Evans, Mari. *Black Women Writers (1950–1980). A Critical Evaluation*. Garden City, NY: Anchor Press/Doubleday, 1984.

Gwin, Minrose C. "Jubilee: The Black Woman's Celebration of Human Community." In *Conjuring. Black Women, Fiction, and Literary Tradition,* ed. Marjorie Pryse and Hortense J. Spillers. Bloomington: Indiana University Press, 1985.

Miller, R. Baxter. "The 'Intricate Design' of Margaret Walker: Literature and Biblical Re-Creation in Southern History." In *Black American Poets between Worlds, 1940–1960*, ed. R. Baxter Miller. Knoxville: The University of Tennessee Press, 1986.

Wonder, Stevie

An internationally renowned musician, composer, producer, humanitarian, and social activist, Stevie Wonder (1950–) is one of the most well-known and successful artists on the original Motown label. Wonder's career, beginning in his early teens, spans over four decades and has earned him international acclaim. The multitalented artist plays at least seven instruments and continues to draw new and younger listeners while maintaining a solid international fan base. His activism and concern with humanitarian issues, which is reflected in both his actions and his music, has also contributed to his enduring appeal.

Stevie Wonder was born Steveland Hardaway Judkins in Saginaw, Michigan. He later moved to Detroit, where he changed his last name to Steveland Morris, a name that he uses today. As a premature infant, Wonder was exposed to excessive levels of oxygen in his incubator that rendered him blind. He developed a refined hearing sensibility and a gift for music. By the time he was 12 years old, Stevie had learned to play a number of instruments, including the piano, drums, and harmonica. After being discovered by Ronnie White of the Miracles, Stevie was signed to Motown Records. Motown mogul Berry Gordy, quickly renamed the youth "Little Stevie Wonder," and by age 13, Wonder had scored his first major hit with the song "Fingertips." As a teen, Stevie Wonder went on to score a number of hits for the Motown record label, including "Uptight (Everything's Alright)," "With a Child's Heart," and many others. He also began to compose and produce hit songs for other Motown artists.

Although Wonder scored numerous hit records with Motown as a teen, either himself or as a songwriter for others, it was when he reached adulthood that his artistic genius began to flourish. When Stevie Wonder turned 21, he brokered a deal with Motown that gave him full artistic control over his music as well as ownership of his work.

He financed and produced two albums featuring his own material and began working with such artists as Deniece Williams and Syreeta White, whom he later married. The album *Talking Book,* released in 1972, was a critical and commercial success that featured the hits "Superstition" and "You Are the Sunshine of My Life." The album *Innervisions,* released in 1973, extended the themes of social consciousness reflected in some of Wonder's earlier work. Hit singles from *Innervisions* include "Living for the City" and "Higher Ground." Other critically acclaimed and hit albums produced during the 1970s include *Music of my Mind* (1972); *Fulfillingness' First Finale* (1974); what is considered by some to be a crowing achievement of this era, the double album *Songs in the Key of Life* (1976); and a movie soundtrack, *Journey through the Secret Life of Plants* (1979).

During the 1980s, Stevie Wonder continued to produce successful albums, including the platinum-selling *Hotter Than July* (1980), which featured hit tributes to Dr. Martin Luther King Jr. and Bob Marley; *Original Musiquarium* (1982), which featured a hit tribute to Dizzy Gillespie; the soundtrack for the film *The Woman in Red,* which produced the number 1 hit "I Just Called to Say I Love You" (1984); *In Square Circle* (1985), featuring the number 1 pop hit "Part-Time Lover"; and *Characters* (1987).

After *Characters,* Stevie went on a four-year hiatus. He resurfaced in 1991 with the soundtrack for Spike Lee's film *Jungle Fever* (1991), a mellow production exploring the theme of interracial relationships. During the 1990s, he also produced *Conversation Peace,* which attempted to address how themes of love, forgiveness, and communication could be used to prevent human violence. He also produced a live album, *Natural Wonder,* which featured energized renditions of his classic hits.

In addition to his own work, Stevie Wonder has also written and produced numerous hit songs or collaborated with other artists, including Michael Jackson, Roberta Flack, Chaka Khan, Barbara Streisand, Paul McCartney, the Eurhythmics, Julio Iglesias, and others. He has also influenced multiple generations of musicians, including most recently such artists as India Arie, John Legend, Jodeci, and Alicia Keys.

Stevie Wonder's contributions extend beyond music. Although many consider him a remarkable person because of his artistic gifts, it is his consistent commitment to dealing with themes of social justice that has earned him humanitarian status.

Songs produced by Stevie Wonder during the 1960s and 1970s, including a remake of Bob Dylan's "Blowin' in the Wind," tackle such themes as the plight of Vietnam veterans, poverty, and government corruption. One of his most popular songs, "Happy Birthday," was produced in 1980 as part of an initiative in which Wonder was involved to obtain federal approval for a national Martin Luther King Jr. holiday. Implemented as a federal holiday in 1986, the first Martin Luther King Day was commemorated with a concert at which Wonder performed. During the 1980s, Wonder also produced songs dealing with apartheid in South Africa, was active in the "We Are the World" initiative to focus global attention on the AIDS epidemic in Africa, and used his music to address themes of gang and domestic violence. In 2005, he was involved in a Live Aid concert to focus attention on debt relief and humanitarian aid to African countries.

See also: Black Folk Culture

Chishamiso Rowley

Bibliography

Davis, Sharon. *Stevie Wonder: Rhythms of Wonder.* London: Robson, 2006.

Perone, James E. *The Sound of Stevie Wonder: His Words and Music.* Santa Barbara, CA: Greenwood Publishing Group, 2006.

Work Songs

The work song was a secular African American form that accompanied work. Work songs can be traced to parts of West Africa, where functional music accompanied a variety of activities, such as domestic chores and fieldwork. Similar to spirituals, work songs were sung by a group that typically consisted of a leader and group. The typical work song was sung a cappella and either in unison or in a call-and-response pattern. In the call-and-response structure, the lead singer sung the call or melody, and the group added the response or refrain.

The leader had the freedom to embellish the melody, and the group could respond by interpolating vocal inflections, for example, moans and shouts. Improvisation and vocal inflections allowed workers to interpret the music and text in their own personal way.

During slavery, singing was an essential part of black culture because it addressed the emotional needs of slaves and created a sense of community. Work songs accompanied a variety of work, such as picking cotton and sweet potatoes, loading and unloading ships, and wielding axes and hoes. For slaves and laborers, singing relieved the monotony of work, alleviated tension, eased the enormity of their problems, and created a communal environment. Work songs that were sung on plantations, and subsequently on levees and prison farms, depicted the oppressed lives of slaves, stevedores, and inmates. The texts of work songs often provided an escape from the harsh realities of life as an African American. Because of their oppressed lives as African Americans, these songs, like the spirituals and blues, created a shared experience. Black slaves and laborers often commented on the transgressions of the boss, provided vivid descriptions of the work, or reminisced about a woman. "Rosie," a song about a woman and possibly sung in prison camps and on levees, allowed workers to transcend their presence to reminiscence about the past and contemplate the future. From the end of slavery and throughout most of the 20th century, work songs were an important part of prison culture. For example, in the convict lease system, a brutal system where men and women were subjected to oppressive conditions, work songs coordinated work, expressed the misery of the conditions, and depicted the oppressive life of the black inmate. Other common work songs included "Diamond Joe," "Look Down That Long Lonesome Road," "Lost John," and "Jumping Judy." Subsequently, by the mid-20th century, work songs had become obsolete and lost their significance, as popular genres became a reflection of progressive generations. Work songs were undeniably one of the most expressive secular folk forms that reflected the African American experience.

See also: Blues Music; Field Hands; Field Hollers; Slave Culture; Slave Plantation

Ralph A. Russell

Bibliography

Barlow, William. *Looking Up at Down: The Emergence of Blues Culture.* Philadelphia: Temple University Press, 1989.

Epstein, Dena. *Sinful Tunes and Spirituals: Black Folk Music to the Civil War.* Urbana: University of Illinois Press, 1977.

Levine, Lawrence. *Black Culture and Black Consciousness: Afro-American Folk Thought from Slavery to Freedom.* Oxford: Oxford University Press, 1977.

Southern, Eileen. *The Music of Black Americans: A History.* 3rd ed. New York: Norton, 1997.

Wright, Richard

Richard Wright (1908–1960) a novelist, short story writer, political journalist, and essayist, was most famous for the novel *Native Son*. Wright was born on a plantation in Mississippi. His father, Nathaniel Wright, was an illiterate sharecropper, and his mother, Ella Wilson Wright, was a schoolteacher. His birth name was Nathaniel Wright.

Richard Wright experienced many hardships before becoming a writer. His father abandoned his family when he was five years old, and his mother supported her family as a cook. When his mother became ill, his family went to live with several relatives in Mississippi, Arkansas, and Tennessee. He and his brother spent a period of time in an orphanage. Consequently, Wright was not able to complete a full year of school before the age of 12. However, in 1925, he graduated as the valedictorian from Smith Robertson Junior High School in Jackson, Mississippi, and the *Jackson Southern Register* published his first story, consisting of three parts, "The Voodoo of Hell's Half-Acre." Although Wright was excited about the publication, his family and friends felt it was unrealistic to believe that African Americans could overcome racial prejudices and barriers. Wright quit high school after only a few weeks to earn money.

In 1925, Wright discovered the *Atlantic Monthly, Harper's Magazine,* and naturalist writer H. L. Mencken. In 1927, Wright moved to Chicago and worked as a dishwasher and delivery boy until he gained employment with the postal service. In 1930, after the stock market crash, Wright lost his postal job and started to work on a novel *Cesspool*—published posthumously in the 1970s as *Lawd Today!*—that reflected his postal service experiences. In 1931, Wright published the short story "Superstition" in the short-lived *Abbott's Monthly Magazine.* He also wrote through the Federal Writers' Project.

Wright was a witness and participant in the Communist and the Pan Africanist political and philosophical movements. While living in Chicago, Wright was involved in the John Reed Club, a Communist literary organization, and he became an official member in 1933. He then published revolutionary poetry and short stories in *Left Front, New Masses,* and *Anvil.* By 1935, he found work with the Federal Negro Theater, under the Federal Writers' Project. He wrote some short stories and a novel during this time, but they were not published until after his death. Wright moved to New York, in 1937, and became Harlem editor of a Communist paper, *Daily Worker,* and coeditor of *Left Front.* He also helped establish the magazine *New Challenge.* In 1938, he published *Uncle Tom's Children,* which won him first prize for best book-length manuscript from *Story* magazine. He published "Bright and Morning Star" in *New Masses* and soon after became part of the magazine's editorial board. Wright eventually faulted the Communist party for not understanding that it relied on African Americans for support. He left the party in 1942 and in 1944 published a related essay in the *Atlantic Monthly:* "I Tried to Be a Communist." In 1949, it was printed again as *The God That Failed,* as a collection of essays by ex-Communists. In 1953, he also published *The Outsider.*

Richard Wright (photographed in 1939) is best known for his first published novel, Native Son. *(Library of Congress)*

In 1939, he married Dhimah Rose Meadman, a Russian-Jewish dance teacher, with author Ralph Ellison as his best man. Wright started to work on the novel *Little Sister,* but it was never published. He spent a short time with his wife in Mexico, but the marriage dissolved after a few months. He returned to New York and divorced in 1940. While returning to New York, Wright paid a visit to his father, whom he had not seen in 25 years. In his 1945 autobiography, *Black Boy,* which sold over 400,000 copies, he describes this visit in great detail. The novel also describes his determination to borrow books from an all-white library, by forging permission notes.

He finished *Native Son* in 1940, and it became an immediate international success, although it was banned in Birmingham, Alabama, libraries. The novel gained Wright both popularity and fortune in its first weeks of publication, selling 215,000 copies. It was also selected as a Book of the Month best seller. *Native Son* encouraged African Americans to reveal their discontent with the prejudices that they faced in American society. A stage adaptation of *Native Son* was written from 1940 to 1941, in collaboration with Paul Green. Wright was discontent with Paul Green's production, so Wright and John Houseman revised it, Orson Welles staged it, and it ran on Broadway successfully in the spring of 1941. Wright won a prestigious Spingarn Medal, in 1941, from the National Association for the Advancement of Colored People.

Wright married his second wife, Ellen Poplar, in 1941, and the couple had two daughters. In 1947, he and his family moved to Paris and stayed there for the rest of his life. While in Paris, Wright continued to enjoy reading and took to existentialism. He produced three novels during this period, but none were as well received as his earlier works. In 1960, Wright suffered a heart attack and died on November 28, at the age of 52. He is buried in Paris.

See also: Ellison, Ralph; Hughes, Langston; McKay, Claude

Nicole Joy DeCarlo

Bibliography
Fabre, Michel. *The Unfinished Quest of Richard Wright.* 2nd ed. Champaign: University of Illinois Press, 1993.
Rampersad, Arnold, ed. *Richard Wright: A Collection of Critical Essays.* Englewood Cliffs, NJ: Prentice Hall, 1995.
Rowley, Hazel. *Richard Wright: The Life and Times.* New York: Henry Holt, 2001.
Walker, Margaret. *Richard Wright: Daemonic Genius.* New York: Amistad, 1988.

Index